Diving the World

A guide to the world's coral seas

Beth and Shaun Tierney

Twenty years from now, you will be more disappointed by the things you didn't do than by the ones you did do. So throw off the bow lines. Sail away from the safe harbour. Catch the tradewinds in your sails. Explore. Dream. Discover.

Attributed to Mark Twain

Introduction

It starts long before we step onto the plane: the sense of anticipation; the gnawing expectancy that disturbs our sleep; the knowledge that we are heading somewhere new, where we will awake at dawn and stare down at the sea, conscious that we will soon be beneath the surface but never quite knowing what we will find there.

That's the thing about diving, you just never do know. You can't possibly predict that on Friday lunchtime you will be gazing up at a juvenile whaleshark, a fish that's over three times your own body length. Or that, as dusk gathers on Tuesday, you'll be eyeing a murderous pair of harlequin shrimp, amongst the smallest creatures in the sea, as they eat a starfish alive.

We have memories that are as vivid as the day they happened: mental polaroids of awesome moments in time. Like nearly touching a deadly blue ringed octopus while pointing out a nudibranch, or lying flat on the sand eyeball to eyeball with a pregnant male seahorse, or instinctively holding out a hand to a cuttlefish which then swam onto the upturned palm and squeezed gently, or the day we finally, finally got to play with a pod of spinner dolphins. Although we think they probably played with us.

It's not hard to understand why we fell so deeply for this lark. It's an excuse to explore some of the planet's least discovered places, far away from the normal tourist routes, where the only other people you see are those you came with. Diving is in our blood, like an addictive drug. No sooner has one journey ended than another must be planned.

Contents

Introduction

Essentials

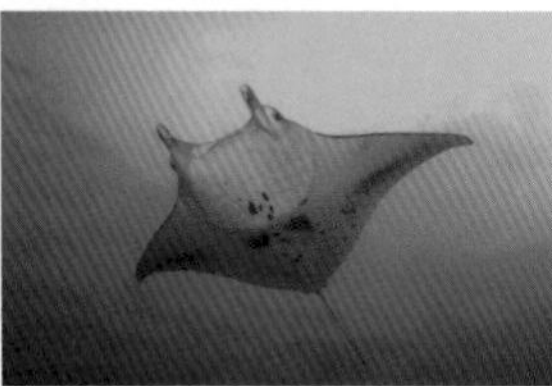

Australia

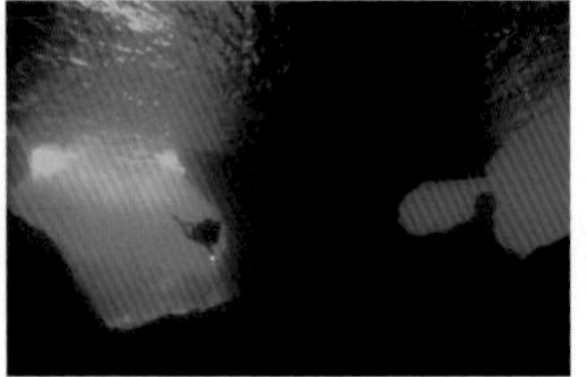

Papua New Guinea

Solomon Islands

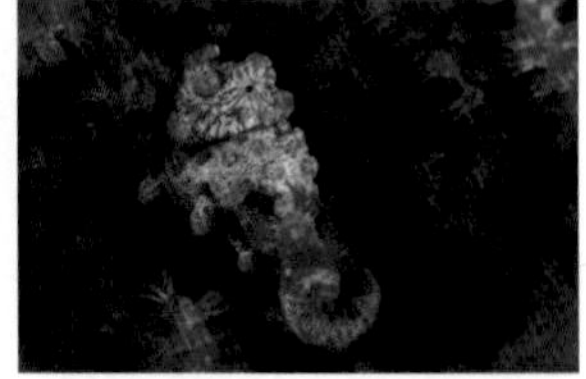

Fiji

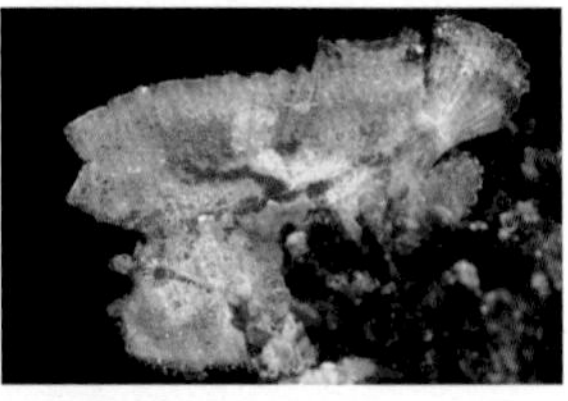

Galápagos

Belize

Mexico

Honduras

Egypt

East Africa

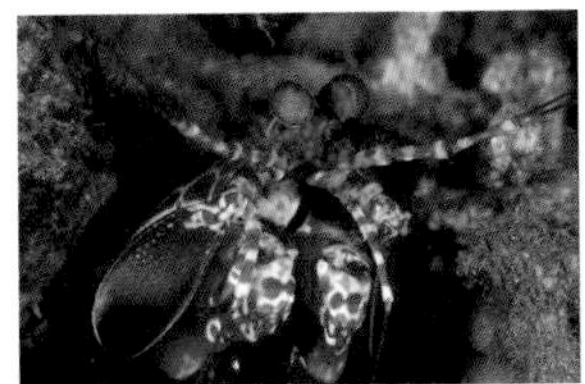

Maldives

Thailand

Indonesia

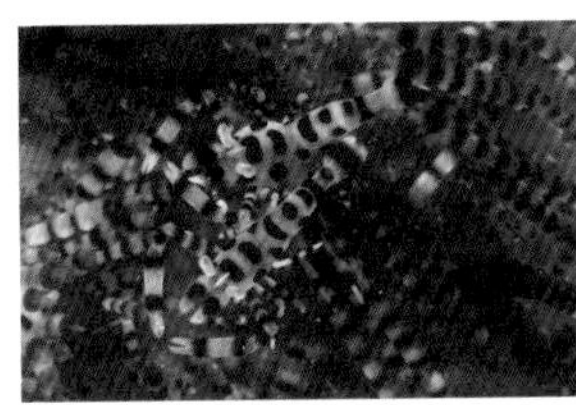

Malaysia

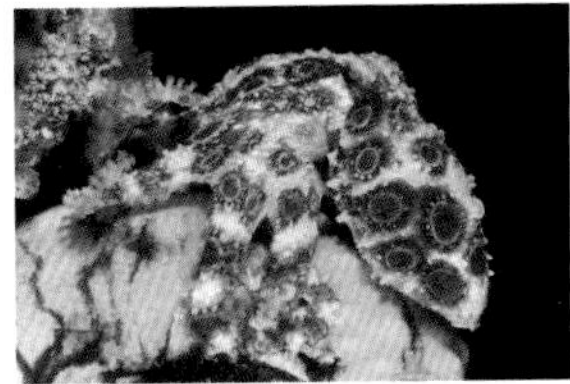

Philippines

Micronesia

About this book

Now before you say "Diving the World – that's not the world! Why have you left out my favourite dive in Scapa Flow, or Ginnie Springs or even Venezuela?" please read on. There was a strategy. Honestly. We have spent much of our misspent years travelling the world, testing the waters, watching the fish, finding our way from one country to another – always with that elusive goal of chancing upon the best ever dive. The one that we could look back on and know it would be as breathtaking today as it was then.

Dive travel is getting easier and dive destinations so much more accessible. Getting around the Mediterranean or the Caribbean is simple. Getting to destinations that are just that bit further takes research and planning and not everyone is confident doing that. If your two week holiday is going to max out your credit card, you want to be fairly sure that you'll like it when you get there. So when we were asked to do this book, we checked with our dive buddies, emailed almost every diver we've ever met and found that most people have a hit list of places they want to dive.

This book covers nearly every dive on those hit lists. It was surprising how similar they were and how almost every destination was within the belt between the two tropics. A few other countries kept popping up, including some of the world's most extreme destinations but for practical reasons they were left out. And, if you really wanted to know about the English Channel, we didn't do it. It wasn't on anyone's list.

However, every dive that is inside these pages, we have done. It's not our intention to claim this is the 'absolute' in dive guides, more that we will have given divers and divers-to-be enough information to feel secure about booking that all-important trip. We have tried to keep our comparisons as honest as possible and not be swayed by our personal loves and preferences. Where we could, we asked dive professionals for their opinions. We bounced ideas off ordinary divers and listened to their often emotional responses. We've mentioned up-and-coming destinations for those who like to be more adventurous and noted where a place should be avoided for one reason or another. But always remember that in all things to do with travel, change happens quickly.

Our hope is that you find inspiration here rather than definitive answers. The world is a small place these days, and the seas cover most of it. Explore, dream, discover.

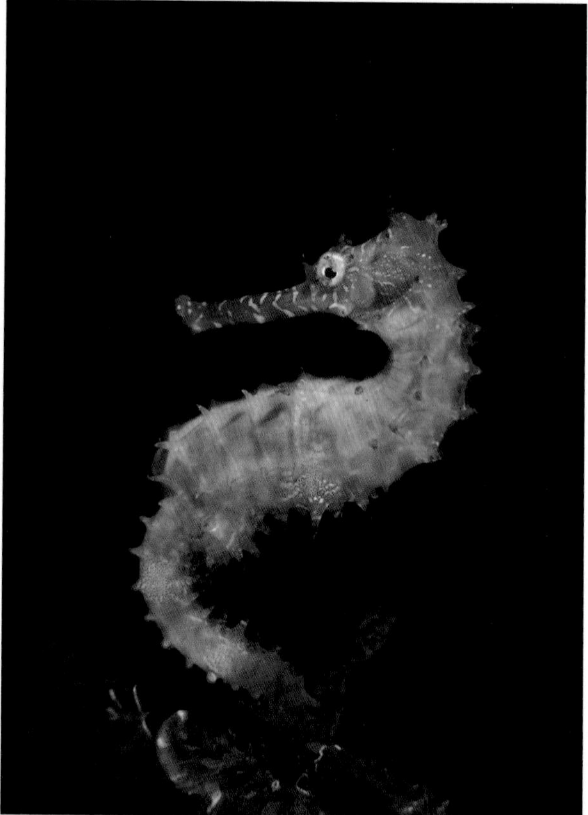

Using this book

This guide covers over 220 dive sites across 19 countries. We did our best to ensure that all information was up to date and, more importantly, first hand. However, things change in a heartbeat and you should regard what is written in these pages as reference rather than gospel.

Everything here has been based on our personal experiences. If you go at a different time of year, chances are your experiences will be different to ours. And that of course is the fun of dive travel. In trying to make sense of it for others we have created some loose grading systems. Please refer to the explanations that are on the inside back flap.

We spent long hours poring over books and websites trying to ensure that names for marine species, dive sites and locations were both correct and consistent. There are many and often conflicting terms so in general we have used what seems to be most frequent. This applies particularly to the spelling of common names for fish and marine animals. We chose to set a standard based on some well trusted sources which are listed on page 348.

Regarding photography, we would like everyone to know that the photos used in each chapter were taken only in the countries where they are shown and are a good indication of what you might see in each destination. Hopefully! The vast majority of images were taken by Shaun, plus a few by Beth (the price of being a camera slave) with the exception of John Rumney's very brave image of a tiger shark and Sean Keen's telling image of us at dawn (right).

About the authors

Our love of all things underwater first developed whilst snorkelling in Mexico during a round the world trip in the late 80s. We returned to London, gained our BSAC qualifications and headed off to do our first open water dives.

It was on that first dive in the Maldives that we came face to face with a whitetip reef shark. It was a heart-stoppping moment and the start of a love affair that has influenced our lives ever since.

We were working as a photo-journalist team in 1992 when we headed off around the world again, this time specifically to dive. During this incredible year we dived in many of the exotic locations featured in the book for the first time.

Over the past 15 years we have become increasingly involved in the dive world, and as photo-journalists have been lucky enough to have revisited, photographed and written about some of the best diving destinations in the world.

Our other editorial work covers both land and dive travel, marine biology and conservation and includes publication in many dive magazines worldwide as well as newspapers, books, travel guides and the Internet.

Essentials

Beauty in motion: just one of Yap's intensely graceful, eternally agile manta rays, *Manta birostris*

Diving the World

When you consider that seven tenths of the planet is covered in water, it may seem curious that most divers' hit lists were confined to the equatorial belt. But there is good reason. This is where the majority of accessible marine life resides. Of course, all oceans are teeming with life, but many seas are too deep and too cold to encourage the development of all but the most specialized species. These conditions also make many areas off-limits to sport diving.

The waters that surround the Equator are known to have remained tropical for millions of years. High light levels and sun-warmed waters encourage reef growth and provide time for marine species to diversify. This simple equation ensures that tropical waters are just that much richer than temperate waters.

However, nothing is ever really that simple, as the world's oceans – and diving zones – are also influenced by deep water plates, ridges, submerged volcanoes and currents. It has been known for many years that the waters in the Indo-Pacific region, stretching from Madagascar in the west to the Galápagos in the east, are far richer than those of the Atlantic.

Southeast Asia displays the highest levels of biodiversity due to the geological structure of the Pacific Ocean. A deep water string of submerged volcanoes that encircle the Pacific, known as the Ring of Fire, were a key element in the formation of the Earth's crust. Recent research has pinpointed the area around the top of Indonesian Sulawesi as the ring's epicentre with extremely high diversity figures in Borneo, the Philippines, Papua New Guinea and the Solomons. This area is now known as the Coral Triangle.

The other reason for higher species diversity in the Asia-Pacific basin is the way in which ocean currents transport cold waters around the planet. The Indo-Pacific is partly protected from arctic waters by the Russian and Alaskan land masses. As far back as the ice age, melting ice water flooded into the Atlantic, reducing its temperature enough to decimate the animal population, leaving just a small refuge in the area we know as the Caribbean.

Currents also distribute fish away from the Asian epicentre. The further you move away, the fewer species are found. In Indonesia, for instance, there are 123 species of damselfish, Papua New Guinea has 100. By the time you reach Fiji there are just 60 and way over in the Galápagos only 18. The Caribbean has a mere 16 across its entire sea. Australia, an exception to the rule, has the highest numbers of damsels at 132 as the continent covers tropical, temperate and cold waters.

This information is by no means a reason to ignore one country or another. The Galápagos may not have a large quantity of fish species but its isolated development means it has animals you will see nowhere else. Likewise, Indonesia supports many prolific and varied environments but if you want to see big animals you need to head for the more open waters of nearby Thailand. But wherever you go, remember that this is not a zoo. Nothing is guaranteed. Ever.

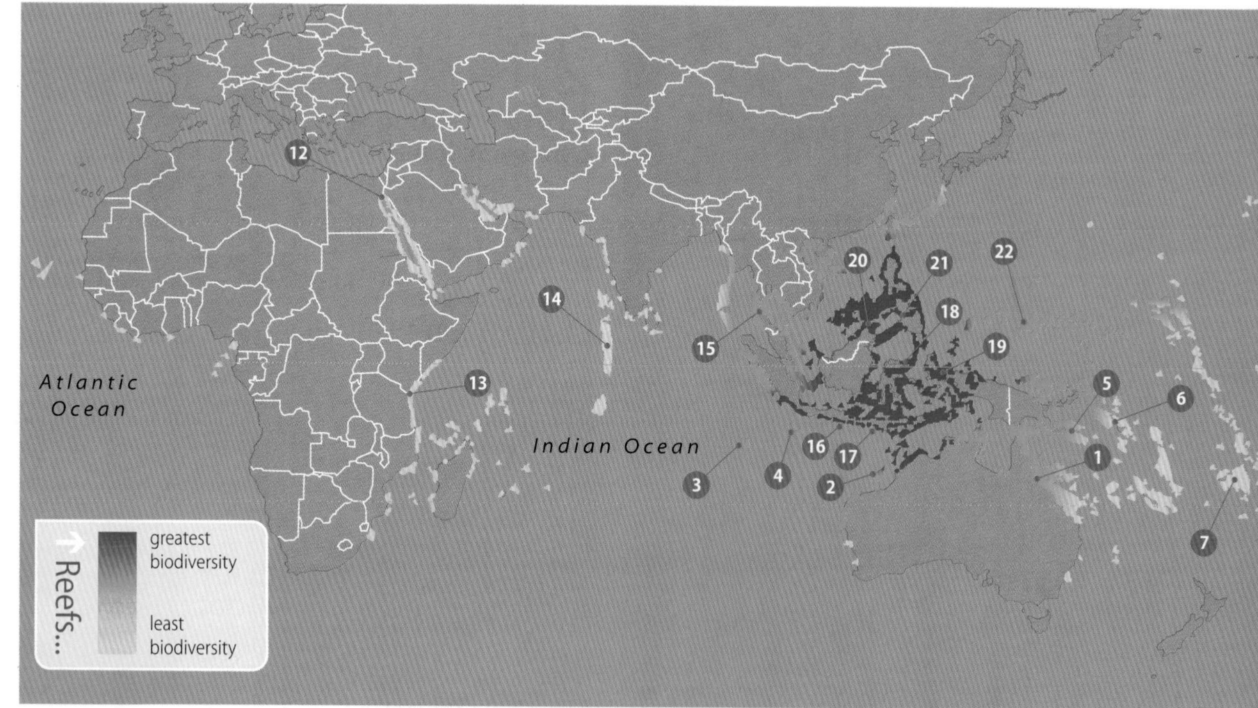

Marine species by numbers by region

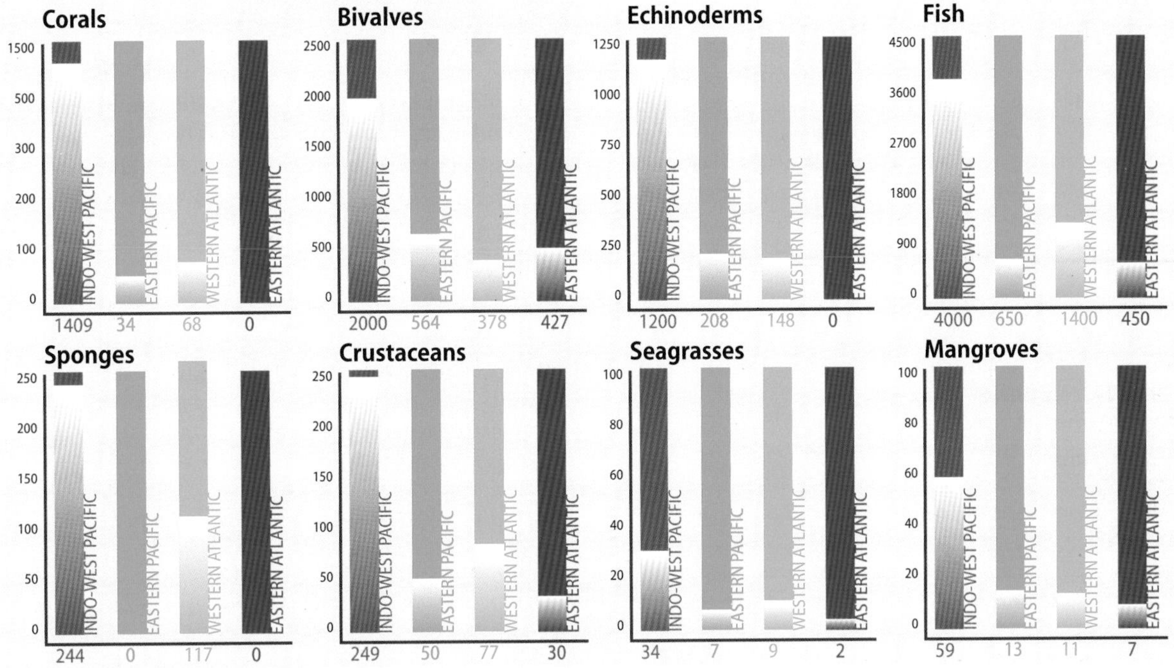

	Indo-West Pacific	Eastern Pacific	Western Atlantic	Eastern Atlantic
Corals	1409	34	68	0
Bivalves	2000	564	378	427
Echinoderms	1200	208	148	0
Fish	4000	650	1400	450
Sponges	244	0	117	0
Crustaceans	249	50	77	30
Seagrasses	34	7	9	2
Mangroves	59	13	11	7

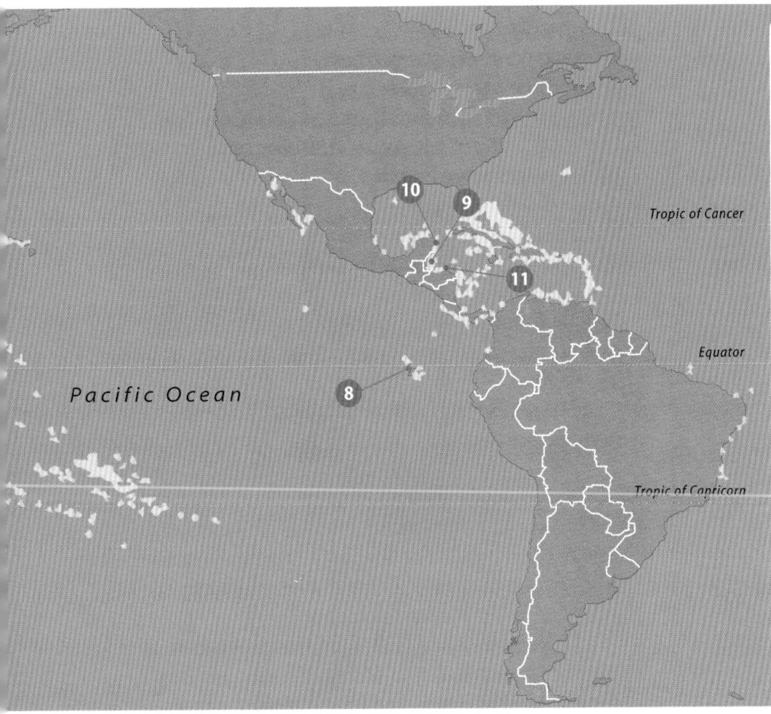

Pacific Ocean
Tropic of Cancer
Equator
Tropic of Capricorn

Dive regions...

N
1000 km
1000 miles

Planning a trip

Inspiration for the ultimate dive trip can come from this book, from magazine articles or tales from friends. Wherever you plan to go, specific details of getting there, and what to do once you're there, are covered in the respective chapters. But, before you start booking, take a look at the bigger picture. Does your dive destination have all the elements that you're looking for? It's not enough to know that someone else had fun – if you don't get what you personally want, you'll be disappointed. The way to solve this is to define your requirements before you start the booking process. First off, ask yourself, do you want to be on land or on a liveaboard?

Land-based diving

Being on land is perfect for people who are happy with fewer dives, have a non-diver or family with them or want to enjoy the local culture. There's more flexibility in a shore-based dive trip – you can go where you want, when you want, but there is usually a limit to the number of dives you can do. Unless you are in a dedicated dive resort, most run to a two dive per day plan. You will need to consider:

- Hotel standard: luxury versus rustic, large and lively or small and quiet
- Hotel location: near a beach, restaurants, bars and shops
- Other activities for the kids or a non-diving partner
- Is the dive centre on site or will you need to travel?
- Is the dive centre PADI, NAUI or BSAC regulated (see page 20)?

Buddy line

Signing your life away

There you are, just settling in to your room or cabin, full of excitement for your first dive day and along comes a whole raft of paperwork. First thing, acknowledge that your operator is in no way liable for any harm that might come your way. Second, promise that if anything does go wrong, and it was someone else's fault, you won't take action against them. Third, accept that even if there is a complete blunder, you will only ever blame yourself. But you sign the bits of paper regardless, knowing that deep down there is no choice. And in reality there isn't. If you question a disclaimer, or refuse to sign it, it's likely you won't be able to dive. Where disclaimers may once have been a declaration of fitness and training levels, they have since become a reflection of a society inclined to sue at the drop of a hat. There is nothing the average diver can do about this, except ensure that you choose reputable dive operations that you are confident will take all the necessary precautions to guarantee guests' safety.

Diving holidays are not like other holidays. They are not about lazing around in the blistering sun, waving at a passing cocktail waiter and spending hours over a three-course lunch. They are instead a series of all-action, adrenaline-rush days interspersed with balmy nights, waiting for dawn. Just so you can go and do it all again.

- Check for specific needs like nitrox or course availability
- Distance to the dive sites – is it shore or day boat diving?
- How many divers and guides will be on the boat?
- Are you expected to dive as a group or in buddy pairs?
- Are there other options for bad weather days?
- Camera facilities on the boat

Liveaboard diving

This is perfect for serious divers who like to do as many dives as possible, or those who just like floating about an idyllic location with no need to do more than eat, sleep and dive. On a liveaboard you will have access to remote areas with fewer divers and often better reefs. You will need to consider:

- Boat standard: luxury versus budget
- Maximum number of passengers
- Cabins: en suite or shared bathrooms, air-con or fan?
- Meals are included but ask if special diets can be catered for and what drinks are included
- How many dives in a day?
- Is nitrox available if you want it?
- Boat policy on buddy pairs, solo or group diving
- Are land visits scheduled?
- Are sites suitable for snorkelling?
- Camera and computer facilities, battery charging stations, rinse tanks
- On bad weather days can the boat shelter or be re-routed?
- Few boats accept young children but you may want to check

Weather

For any dive holiday, the weather is perhaps the single most important consideration. Are you going at the best time of year or the cheapest? If you go in low season and save some money don't be surprised if it rains or the seas are choppy.

Marine life tends to be seasonal too and full details are given in the following chapters. Be aware, however, that although some destinations are promoted as year round, their most famous attraction may not be. Pelagic species in particular move great distances and can often only be seen for a few months of the year. Also consider if you want to combine diving with land-based attractions. A cultural experience or wildlife safari may be ruined by rain while offshore it's not such an issue.

Wetsuits

Most countries covered by this book have similar, tropical climates with water temperatures averaging 27-28°C. Exceptions are noted in each country chapter. For these conditions you will need a 3 mm full wetsuit. A hood and a rash vest or fleecy lined skin is worth poking into a corner of your bag and will allow some layering up. You may appreciate this on the fourth dive of the day, where there are known thermoclines or if you stay still like many photographers do. However, some will shiver in 3 mm while others will open their zips to let in refreshing cool water. It's a personal issue that only time and experience will resolve.

Costs

There is no doubt that diving is an expensive sport. As a rule of thumb, a dive day worldwide will cost around US$100, including transport, two dives with tanks, weights and lunch, though this will vary depending on local staff costs and expenses. Training and course rates average in a similar way with a PADI open water course costing around US$375. See page 20.

When you are budgeting for your trip look at all the angles to see if you are getting good value for money. Many people reject liveaboards as the overall price can seem prohibitive. However, as many also include unlimited diving and extras like soft drinks, the cost in real terms may not be higher. To work out a value-for-money comparison, rather than looking at the package cost, try looking at the cost per dive. Add flights, accommodation, dive packs and extras (marine park fees or visas) together and divide by the number of dives you expect to have. Use this as a benchmark to see if your trip will be good value.

Using Thailand as an example, the overall cost of a deluxe 10 day liveaboard with four dives per day might be US$3900 (US$3900÷40 = US$97.50 per dive). Ten days at a 3-star resort with a 10 day dive pack (two dives a day) is US$2018 (US$2018÷20 = US$100.90 per dive). Both packages are available for October, both include flights and transfers, however the liveaboard includes three meals a day and all soft drinks while the hotel package only includes breakfast.

Lembeh Resort, North Sulawesi

Fees, taxes and surcharges

When you are planning and budgeting for your trip, allow a 'slush fund' for all those little extras you never quite know about until you arrive. These can be marine park fees, diver taxes that are ostensibly intended to support rescue services, or local recompression chambers and fuel surcharges, which are becoming ever more common. Individually, these costs are quite low but can add up. For example the marine park fee in Manado is US$15 but does last a whole year while Cozumel operations add US$2 a day.

Sunset from *MV Bilikiki*

Kapalai Resort in Borneo

Tips for trouble-free travel

- Make sure your passport has at least one free page and six months to run after your departure date
- Check visa requirements
- Take out travel insurance that specifically covers diving and dive equipment
- Take a copy or record of your passport numbers, travel insurance, qualification card, credit cards and any other documents and pack separately to the originals
- Tell someone at home where you are going to be.
- Check health requirements for your destination
- Take the right type of plug. Check out http://users.pandora.be/worldstandards/electricity.htm#plugs
- Take copies of booking forms and correspondence from your agent, hotel or dive centre
- Ensure your dive gear is working and you have the appropriate kit for your intended location
- Research your chosen destination; check government advisories and so on
- When you arrive you obey the law and respect local customs

Insurance

Travel insurance is an absolute necessity. Don't ever consider trying to save a few bucks by not covering yourself properly. You need a policy that will cover cancellation and delays, baggage and dive equipment, cameras and other valuables, money and, most importantly, medical emergencies. Ensure that any policy you take out has a clause covering repatriation home or to the closest recompression chamber. DAN – The Divers Alert Network – has thorough dive accident insurance but they do not automatically cover travel related issues (www.diversalertnetwork.org). Other insurers around the world offer policies that may suit personal needs just as well. Check out www.diveassure.com, www.divinginsuranceuk.com or www.scubasure.com.

Currency

It has become a worldwide standard for US dollars to be the currency of choice with dive operators although a few will quote and accept Euros. Consequently, all rates in this book are US$ unless otherwise stated.

Travelling with currency is much the same – US dollars are easy to exchange no matter where you go. Depending on current world politics, you may find it advantageous to have some cash in a second currency with you as well. Traveller's cheques are very secure but can be difficult to exchange. Another option is to take your bank cash card with you. There are few countries without cash machines these days. Most banks charge a commission but it's not going to be far different from the fee for a foreign exchange purchase.

Tipping

It's hard to be definitive about such a sensitive subject. Individual attitudes to tipping depend very much on where you grew up. In America it's an accepted way of life to tip generously for every service. In Europe, the attitude is more likely to be a considered sum for good service while in Australia and Singapore people don't tip as these countries have higher minimum wage structures.

When it comes to tipping your dive crew, consider whether their actions improved your trip and what their likely wage is. Many staff in Third World countries work very long hours for meagre wages. Liveaboard crews, in particular, are often on call 24 hours a day to ensure your safety and comfort.

There is no magic formula but a starting point could be US$5 per day. If you did three days shore based diving and had a guide and driver looking after you, US$10-15 would be generous. If you are a couple, US$20 might suffice. However, if you are on a liveaboard where a crew of 15 saw to your every need for 10 days, US$50 might be a little low. There is a trend among higher-end liveaboard operations suggesting that 10% of your trip cost is appropriate. At US$3000 a trip that would be US$300 – many divers find this offensive, regarding it as an extra charge. In the end, only you can decide what you thought the service was worth.

Kitting up!

Divers' code of conduct

- Be properly trained and always be ready to learn – no one ever knows it all.
- Pay attention to dive briefs as dive leaders understand local conditions.
- Always stick to the dive plan you are given – there are good reasons for it.
- Do not push your computer to the point of no return.
- Have an audible and visual emergency signalling device with you at all times.
- Dive with a buddy and respect the buddy system wherever you can.
- Be courteous, helpful and tolerant of other divers whether you like them or not.
- Respect other people's dive equipment and photographic kit.
- Respect the environment and ensure your buoyancy is correct.
- If you see someone doing something wrong, discuss it with them – sometimes people just don't realise.

Dive packs on sale

Booking

When it comes to making arangements, you can either contact an agent or book the trip yourself.

Agents have access to information and systems not available to the public and can be a mine of information. Book through a dedicated dive travel specialist and they will not only understand divers' needs but also be incredibly knowledgeable of the regions they promote. They'll have suggestions, up-to-date information on local situations and often first-hand experience. They will also take the flack if things go wrong, rearrange flights if schedules change or re-book you to another destination if there is a political or natural disaster.

The DIY option is becoming more popular as the Internet spreads its web. You can often find different or cheaper products but bear in mind that if you book direct you then assume complete responsibility for your own trip. You have to ask all the right questions, ensure you have the right papers and co-ordinate every aspect involved – flights, transfers, accommodation, diving, meals, sightseeing. It can be a hefty job but if you like a sense of adventure it can give you the flexibility to make on-the-spot changes.

The dive deck on *Sun Dancer II*

Kitting up and brief area

Airlines

Delays, overbooking, stray luggage – airlines can be a law unto themselves. Some treat their passengers as honoured guests while others bring a new meaning to the term 'cattle class'. Some airlines are so much better that paying a little extra can make the difference between a miserable long haul flight and a pleasant one. Ask yourself if you really want to save US$75 on a 12-hour flight and not fly with the airline that has seat-back TVs and on-tap entertainment?

Weigh up the pros and cons. An example involves transatlantic travel. If you fly with a European airline, alcoholic drinks are included while most American carriers charge as much as US$5 per drink. However, the latter have the best luggage allowances. Refer to the table on facing page for recommendations then visit seatguru.com so you can request your favourite seat.

Packing tips

- Reduce the weight of your kit by buying travel BCD's, lightweight regulators and a safety sausage rather than a reeled SMB. Invest in small, lightweight torches.
- Do not take scuba toys – or other toys – away with you.
- Don't take doubles of major items. Any dive centre that's worth diving with will have a spare if yours breaks down.
- Take a small repair kit with gaffer (duck) tape, superglue, a multi-tool, strong cord, plastic cable ties and a spare mask strap.
- If you are only diving for a few days consider hiring your equipment.
- Get out what clothes you think you need and halve them. Then halve it all again. No one cares what you look like underwater.
- Reduce toiletries by getting mini-bottles, take medicines out of packets and write instructions down.

Baggage

All divers bemoan their lot when it comes to baggage allowances. It can be very hard to pack your dive kit plus the usual holiday necessities *and* remain under the limit. The good news is that most scheduled airlines will waive a couple of kilos. However, that does mean 22 or 23 kg, not 28! It is now internationally accepted that all bags must weigh under 32 kg for health and safety reasons. In general, European airlines give 20 kg in economy, while American airlines use a bag size system. In late 2005, this became two bags of up to 23 kg each. Airlines flying to and from America, even if they are based elsewhere, will mostly allow the higher limit . Charter airlines allow 20 kg and are quite strict but many have introduced clearer and more affordable excess rates per kilo.

Whoever you fly with, if you exceed the limit be prepared to be charged. If you are faced with having to pay at check-in keep cool and try to negotiate based on being a sports person. Bear in mind that the standard complaint that 'golfers can take their clubs for free' is rarely true. Nor can surfers take their boards. Instead they both get a dispensation to take oddly shaped items. The few airlines that do allow free golf clubs also allow free dive kit.

Another item of note, always lock your bags. There is a trend of not doing so because "if security want to check, they'll break the lock". This is true but it's better than having a stranger sneak a look at the contents. There have been high profile cases of people being arrested for drugs offences after leaving unlocked bags in hotel foyers and airports. Carry spare miniature padlocks or use cable ties to secure your luggage.

Is your bag being loaded?

Checking in at Manila airport

Best airlines

Airline	Contact	Free baggage	Excess policy	Comfort*	Ranking**
AeroMexico	www.aeromexico.com	SP2	Dive bag US$50	31	✔✔✔
American	www.aa.com	SP2		33	✔✔✔
British Airways	www.ba.com	WP+SP1	Up to £30 per kg	31	✔✔✔✔
Cathay	www.cathaypacific.com	WP+SP1	On application	31	✔✔✔✔✔
Continental	www.continental.com	SP2		31	✔✔✔
Emirates	www.emirates.com	WP+SP2	Dive bag10 kg free	33	✔✔✔✔
Eva	www.evaair.com	WP+SP2	On application	33	✔✔✔✔
Garuda	www.garuda-indonesia.com	WP	1.5%	33	✔✔✔
Gulf	www.gulfairco.com	WP	On application	33	✔✔✔✔
Iberia	www.iberia.com	WP	1.5%	32	✔✔✔
JAL	www.japanair.com	WP+SP1	On application	33	✔✔✔✔
KLM	www.klm.com	WP+SP2	€20 per kg	31	✔✔✔✔
Malaysian	www.malaysiaairlines.com	WP	1.5% of full economy fare	34	✔✔✔✔
Monarch	www.flymonarch.com	WP	€6.50 per kg	29	
Philippine	www.philippineairlines.com	SP1	Up to US$200	32	✔✔✔
Qantas	www.qantas.com.au	WP+SP2	Sliding scale	31	✔✔✔✔
Qatar	www.qatarairways.com	WP+SP1	Extra 10 kg free	32	✔✔✔✔✔
Singapore	www.singaporeair.com.cg	WP+SP1	Extra 10 kg free (local policies vary)	32	✔✔✔✔✔
TACA	www.taca.com	SP2	Over 2 bags +US$100		
Thai	www.thaiair.com	WP+SP1	On application	34	✔✔✔✔
Thomson Fly	www.thomsonfly.com	WP	€7.50 per kg	31	✔✔✔
United	www.unted.com	WP+SP2	Dive bag US$80	31	✔✔✔
Virgin	ww.vigin-atlantic.com	AP+SP1	On application	31	✔✔✔✔

At time of publication: WP = weight policy, 1 bag, max 20 kg; **SP1** = old size policy, 2 bags, up to 70 lb /32 kg each – linear dimensions (length plus width plus height) not to exceed 62 inches/158 cm each; **SP2** = new size policy, 2 bags, up to 50 lb /23 kg each – linear dimensions as above. Additional weight 24-32 kg add US$25 per bag; **WP+SP1/2** = routes to and from the USA use SP, other routes use WP.

* The seat pitch in inches, i.e. the distance between rows in economy class.

** Source = *Skytrax Airline of the Year 2004*, based on passenger opinions.

Diver training

Learning to dive

For many, the underwater experience starts with watching someone else underwater and wanting to join in. So it's over to the hotel pool for a try dive session followed by a quick resort course. For those who then discover that their blood no longer circulates without nitrogen in it, it's time to take things seriously and get yourself qualified.

Training organizations

By far the largest and best known is **PADI** (Professional Association of Diving Instructors, www.padi.com) and although you will see PADI signs right around the world, they are by no means the only training organization. Well respected international ones include the **British Sub Aqua Club** (BSAC), **National Association of Underwater Instructors** (NAUI, www.naui.com) and **Scuba Schools International** (SSI, www.divessi.com).

Each organization has courses that work in varying ways including weekly club style meetings or resort and residential courses. Quality of training, however, depends very much on the person who is teaching you rather than the course itself. Many organizations are also money-making concerns so do your research, get some recommendations and go with what you feel is most suitable for you.

The all-important safety stop

Well, you know what the divers' motto is don't you? Early to bed, early to rise, dive all day, tell lots of lies. Anyway, this turtle, Bubba, is really – that – big.

Elvis Leslie, divemaster, Sun Dancer II

Courses

Learning to dive should include the following stages.

Basic training: often called Open Water, this first stage will give you the essential skills to get safely in the water but limits your depth and does not teach any rescue skills.

Next step: an advanced Open Water course will expand your dive knowledge and further in-water practice ensures competence in deeper water under differing conditions.

Last step: a Rescue Diver course is vital for learning how to save your own life or someone else's. It may be included in one of the stages above but if not ensure you do it. Once you have done these you can consider yourself qualified.

Continued training

At this point many people stop training, and that's fine, but consider doing either some speciality or higher level courses as they will help refine your skills. If you want to teach there are several stages that progress to an instructor's qualification. These courses should be augmented by plenty of in-water experience.

Speciality courses

If you don't want to instruct but do enjoy learning about the many subjects related to scuba, try a few of the great speciality courses that are around. There are ones that cover subjects like marine biology, photography and first aid. There are courses tailored for chidren as young as 8-9 or for people with very specific interests like wreck exploration or manta ray identification.

Where to learn

One option would be to go on holiday to somewhere lovely and, hopefully, qualify in warm waters under sunny skies. The downside of this is that you are giving up precious holiday time to sit in a classroom. Alternatively, you could book into a weekend school in your home country or join a club with weekly training sessions.

An open water qualification will cost in the region of US$450

depending on where you choose to train. Utila in Honduras is regarded as the cheapest place in the world with PADI Open Water courses at around US$200. With a bit of research you may well be able to match this in other countries but bear in mind that a very cheap course indicates that your operator may be forced to cut corners somewhere. Many rock-bottom courses do not include manuals and fees.

Tales from the deep

Learning with blacktips

Years ago, I did a few try dives while on holiday in Malta, but shortly after I got home, I found out I was pregnant and it was eight years before I had the chance to even think about diving again. When I did, I knew that the cool waters in the UK – or even Malta – just wouldn't be right for me so we decided on a holiday to the Maldives. The conditions were fantastic. The dive centre had formed a shallow pool just off the beach so the warm water and fish life just drew me right in. There were even baby blacktips swimming around as we did our training exercises. I was so comfortable in the water and so amazed by everything I was seeing that I never even thought about all the scary bits. I just loved doing the course and am really glad I choose to do it somewhere with such great conditions!

Sue Perkins, Telford, UK

Conservation

How big is your footprint?

A couple of years ago, Jean-Michel Cousteau spoke on Capitol Hill: "The ocean holds 97% of earth's water, drives climate and weather, generates more than 70% of the oxygen we breathe, absorbs carbon dioxide, supplies our fresh water through rain, provides food, and is a deep source of inspiration to our spirits." Yet our seas are heavily endangered and coral reefs are one of the most threatened ecosystems on the planet. Destruction is principally man-made and if it continues at its present rate, 70% of the world's coral reefs will disappear in a generation. And where will that leave us?

A diver's role may be a comparatively small one but always remember one of the first rules of diving – look, don't touch. Sadly, there are people who genuinely don't care and you have to wonder what it is they are doing if they have only gone down to destroy. There are a few things that you can do to help ensure the reefs and seas are still available in future years for other people to enjoy. Do not touch corals or any living organism as your hands can leave harmful oils. Pressure can damage a protective coating which allows harmful bacteria to penetrate. Don't wear gloves, unless absolutely necessary, as you will be too tempted to put hands down without thinking. Don't bring anything up from the seabed, not even a shell. It may seem to be dead, but you just don't know what tiny creature has crawled inside. Be careful to stay above the reef, good buoyancy is vital. Ensure all your gauges and equipment are either hooked to your BC or tucked in a pocket. And finally, watch what you do with your fins; it's easy to misjudge what is behind you.

There are many organizations and bodies dedicated to looking after our seas and the animals that live within them. For more information look at the **Marine Conservation Society** (www.mcsuk.org), the **International Fund for Animal Welfare** (www.ifaw.org), **WWF** (www.panda.org), the **Shark Research Institute** (www.sharks.org) and the **International Coral Reef Action Network** (www.icran.org).

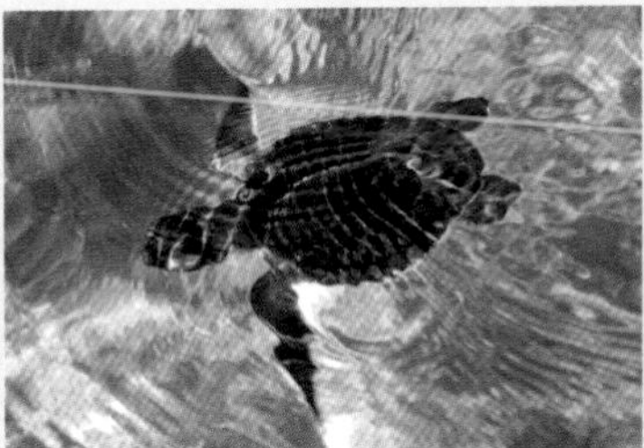

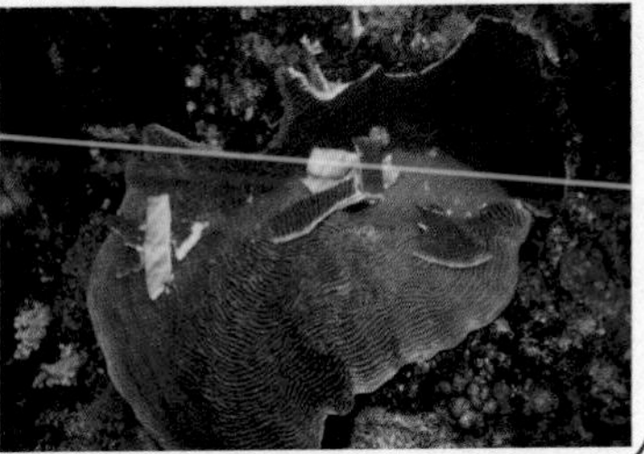

Underwater photography

"There's that saying that a boat is a hole in the water you throw money into. And underwater photographers would probably say something similar about their chosen occupation."

At some point in time almost every diver is tempted to leap in with a camera and try to capture the excitement and emotion of their dive. However, most are disappointed with their results. Taking a good photo at 30 metres is a completely different ball game to land photography – for two reasons. To start, you need special equipment, either a dedicated underwater camera or a housing to keep your usual one dry. Once this was a very expensive matter but developments in digital technology have made it all much more affordable.

Next, and perhaps most importantly, you also need to have at least a basic understanding of how light changes underwater. At its simplest, light is filtered by water, so the deeper you go the darker it gets. Colours are reduced because the deeper you go the less red light you – and your camera – will see. The result is blue, washed out pictures. To return light and colour to your images you will need a light source. Built-in flashes are unlikely to help much as they aren't very strong and, being mounted close to the lens, are likely to produce backscatter – reflections from particles suspended in the water. To resolve these issues add an external flash, or two, mounted a little way from your camera.

You also need to decide if you want to go with film or digital. If you already have a film camera then you could simply buy a housing and flashes for it. This way you will already understand your camera and feel confident in how to use it. You willl be saving something on the initial investment by using equipment you already have. Likewise, if you have a digital camera, there are many housings available now. However, if you are starting from scratch, think mostly about what it is you want to achieve. Do you just want some nice little prints to show the folks back home? Then get a small digital camera that is easy to use and easier to maintain. However, if you are hoping to blow your best ever picture up to poster size, you will need to invest in much higher calibre equipment and that will set you back a considerable sum of money.

At this point you do need to think about the differences between film and digital. Many in the professional market are sticking with film as the quality is not limited by pixel dimensions. But debate rages as to how long this will remain true. There are other pros and cons. With a digital card you are less likely to run out of shots; you can experiment a little underwater and see your results on the spot. However, unless you buy a top-end digital camera, you will get shutter lag, trouble with contrasting light situations and some very strangely coloured images when the camera just can't recognize what it's looking at. Also, you will spend more time uploading and adjusting your images before you can print them out.

Film, on the other hand, will handle strong and contrasting light conditions, doesn't try to adjust colours and fires in a millisecond. But

Film versus digital
The battle rages, the pros and cons are many and widespread and no short discussion will ever resolve which is better. As above, it all depends on what you want to do with your images.

Leaffish on film
The image on the left at the top was shot in the Solomons. Shaun used a housed Nikon F90 with two strobes and Fuji Velvia Film. Being able to direct the flashes and control exposure has given a crisp photo with the fish as focal point. The lack of light reaching the background creates a dramatic effect.

Leaffish on digital
The image beneath it was taken at exactly the same time and place but with a Nikon 5200 compact digital using just the camera's built in flash. The software has taken a reading for both the back- and fore- grounds as well as attempting to focus right across the image. The digital gives a surprisingly good result for such a small piece of equipment. The cost of that camera with its housing was about £400/$700, compared to the cost of the housed set-up which is worth perhaps £3000/$5000. However, a housed digital SLR camera, of similar level, would cost almost the same.

you only get 36 shots and you do have to learn how to make the camera work as you won't see results until you get home. In the end, your decision should be be based on the end result you want.

All underwater cameras require care and attention. An all-singing all-dancing SLR housing obviously requires more attention than a small digi-housing but if you don't take care of any equipment you'll soon find it has taken a salt water bath. In all things to do with underwater photography, there' s no substitute for practice and patience. Finally, there one more thing to contemplate if you decide to take up underwater photography and that's etiquette. Photographers should remember that having a camera doesn't automatically give them more rights to the marine realm: don't spoil someone's view of a fantastic marine find nor push in front of another diver. Likewise, non-camera sorts should consider how much they like seeing other people's pictures and respect all that photo equipment. It isn't nice to use the camera rinse tanks for your smelly suit. Always remember that you are in an alien environment: respect that environment as well as your buddies and yourself.

For more information, go to www.camerasunderwater.co.uk, www.oceanoptics.co.uk, www.backscatter.com, www.marinecamera.com

Top tips

- Buy the best underwater camera you can afford. Small, throwaway cameras will give you throwaway photos. Underwater, you are more reliant on the quality of your equipment.
- As there is water between your lens and your subject, the better the quality of lens, the better the picture.
- Use a flash – or two – to return colour to the image.
- Get as close as possible to your subject as things appear bigger than they really are and the strength of your flash is limited.
- Research the marine environment; learn what is dangerous and what is fragile.
- Approach marine creatures slowly, so as not to scare them off, and with respect. Some will retaliate if they think you are a threat.
- Don't exceed your capabilities as a diver.
- Ensure that you have good buoyancy control.
- Always put personal safety above getting a good picture.
- Finally, be courteous to other photographers and divers *and* instigate the six frame rule. If you are in a group with more than one photographer, suggest that if a particularly interesting subject is found, each person takes turns to shoot six frames then moves off, giving someone else a go. Once everyone has done so, you can always return. Never be that person who hogs a spot and ruins someone else's dive. This is particularly important on liveaboards or when the on board photo-pro is hoping to sell you their video.

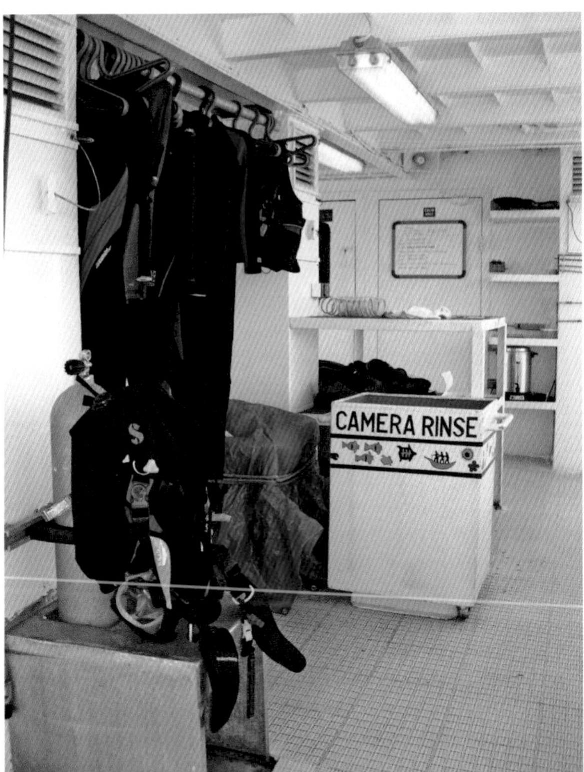

The dive deck and camera facilities

Perfect buoyancy control is essential

Health and first aid

There are many healthcare issues involved in being a diver and most of the "can I, can't I?" stuff will be covered by your training. The following information is for guidance only. If you are unsure about anything at all to do with how a medical condition may affect your ability to dive safely, make sure you contact a doctor with dive knowledge before you go away.

Before you go

There are several things you should take care of before you depart for any trip.

Insurance Never underestimate the necessity of good, diver-specific medical insurance.

Checkup If you do have any pre-existing conditions, take a quick trip down to your doctor and ensure you have both sufficient medications and information to handle your own healthcare. It may be a good idea to get a certificate clearing you to dive in order to show operators. Remember to have your teeth checked every now and then as trapped air in a cavity is a very painful thing.

Vaccinations for the tropics

With most divers heading off to at least one distant destination every year it's worth getting a full set of vaccinations then having boosters as and when necessary. Ensure you allow plenty of time to get this done in advance of your trip. For the countries listed in this guide you will require some or all of the following vaccinations:

- polio
- tetanus
- typhoid
- hepatitis A & B
- yellow fever
- rabies

There are other vaccines that may potentially be needed and individual requirements should be discussed with your GP/practice nurse or travel clinic

Anti-malarials

The best way to avoid getting malaria is not to get bitten. Yes, easier said than done, but the usual advice of a repellent lotion plus covered arms and legs after dusk will help enormously. However, because you can't avoid mosquitoes in damp environments such as kitting-up areas, you will need to take anti-malarial tablets. Which one to take is where it gets more complicated and the best advice is to research via your doctor/nurse or a travel clinic. Many have side effects such as nausea, diarrhoea and sun sensitivity so get as much advice as possible. Some anti-malarials are specifically not good for divers as they are reported to cause side effects like panic or anxiety. A very good website for current recommendations is www.fitfortravel.scot.nhs.uk. Also www.cdc.gov/travel.

Some malaria drugs need to be taken a week before entering an at-risk area and for four weeks afterwards so plan well in advance.

What to take

First aid kit These days it's easy to nip to the chemist or pharmacy and buy travel oriented medicines for your first aid and medical kit. In fact most of the medicines you need can be bought without prescription and the pharmacist can help you put together a suitable kit. Consider including these items:

- hydrocortisone cream for rashes and skin inflammation
- a really good analgesic, such as paracetamol or ibuprofen
- antihistamine tablets for mild allergic reactions
- an 'anti-itch' or steroid cream for use on insect bites
- a small tube of antiseptic cream or antiseptic wipes
- lots of band-aids and a small pack of sterile bandages
- seasickness remedy
- rehydration sachets
- an ear drying aid (eg Swim-Ear)
- small scissors
- a good Swiss Army type knife
- sinus decongestant tablets
- an anti-diarrhoea drug
- tweezers
- latex condoms

It is also worth considering some antibiotic preparations that need to be prescribed:

- a broad spectrum antibiotic for general infections. Discuss ciprofloxacin with your doctor as it is particularly good for marine infections.
- antibiotic drops for ear and eye infections
- an antibiotic ointment for skin infections

Most doctors are sympathetic to prescribing in advance if you explain why. Don't forget to get – and take – sufficient quantities of any medicines that you require on a daily basis, for instance if you are diabetic or use the contraceptive pill.

While you're there

The tropics are beautiful but they do throw up some health issues for travellers, especially those who arrive from colder climes. Here are some tips on ways to ensure your holiday isn't ruined but if in doubt always visit a local doctor. You may be reluctant to do this in some out-of-the-way village, but many doctors, even in the most remote countries, are highly trained. If you're unsure, ask a divemaster or hotel receptionist to find you a Western-trained doctor.

Dehydration One of the most common ailments for divers. No one ever drinks enough water and being dehydrated can lead to many other problems, not least of which is the bends. Drink at least two litres of water a day. Sugary soft drinks do not aid rehydration, nor, sadly, does beer. Cramps in your feet at night is a classic indication and you can use a sachet of rehydration salts to top up your levels quickly. Alternatively, add 8 level teaspoons of sugar and 1 level teaspoon of salt to 1 litre of water. Tastes foul though.

Sunburn and heat-stroke Perhaps the second most common ailment. Use factor 30 sunscreen to prevent sunburn and wear a hat while you are out on the water where there are lots of reflected rays.

Heat stroke arrives disguised as the flu (headaches, muscle aches and pains, fatigue) but with some stomach problems thrown in. If you suspect that's what you have, stay cool, drink lots of fluid and get some advice if you don't return to normal very quickly.

Mosquito bites Try not to scratch because if you do they may get infected by all the mini-nasties in seawater. Use an anti-itch cream and keep your hands in your pockets.

Seasickness Some people suffer, the rest are oblivious. If you suffer just a little, stay out in the fresh air and keep your eyes on the horizon until you get accustomed to the boat's movement. If you suffer badly, there is no doubt about it, drugs work the best. You will need to find a brand that doesn't make you drowsy and that may be a matter of trial and error. Some people swear by pressure bands, others by ginger as a natural remedy.

Ear problems Being immersed in salt water for hours at a time can cause a lot of trouble for ears. Always, always remember to clear your ears *before* you feel pressure, which will alleviate a lot of potential problems. However, do this gently as over-vigorous, repeated clearing can cause inflammation. People with recurring problems may want to use a steroid nasal spray several days before the trip and continue once diving. This will cut down on the inflammation caused by the normal barotrauma of diving. If your ears get sore, it may be best to rest them for a day. If you suspect you have an infection a good on the spot test is to press the hollow behind your ear lobe. If this is really painful start the antibiotic drops.

Sinus problems Coming from cooler climates to the tropics can bring on a cold or flu-like symptoms. Many people swear by nasal decongestants as these often make equalizing easier. However, they can also wear off halfway through a dive and cause a reverse ear block, so be careful. Nothing clears sinuses as well as a good salt water sniff if it's just a case of clearing some city pollution but anything that is very painful may indicate an infection. Again, take a day out, then start antibiotics if necessary.

Colds and flu A change in climate or the change from a busy life at home to a relaxed one somewhere nice and – wallop – you get a cold. Antibiotics will not help unless you have a specific infection so don't go swallowing the pills hoping for a miracle cure. Instead go back to mother's remedies – lots of fluid, plenty of rest, vitamin C (oranges and lemons) keep warm and take a mild painkiller.

Allergies More than anything else it seems that these are on the increase. Ensure you are carrying any necessary drugs with you but, more importantly, make sure that someone else knows where they are and what to do. Either your dive buddy or the divemaster should be fully informed. Specific food allergies such as seafood or nuts are extremely dangerous if you are miles offshore so carry an epi-pen with you at all times. Food intolerances to items like wheat or tomatoes can be treated with an oral antihistamine and skin reactions like those to neoprene or plankton can be treated with a steroid ointment.

Women's issues There are few women who would choose to go diving when they have their period. You can delay them by continuing the cycle of your contraceptive pill but ensure you get good advice on how long you can safely do this. If you don't take the pill but suspect that your period will come in the last few days of a trip, you can delay it by using a progesterone-only pill. This will stop it from coming for as long as you are taking it. Pregnancy is a little more of an issue. There is no definitive research on how a foetus might be affected by diving. Many women have dived before realizing they were pregnant with no ill effects, but is it worth the risk?

Accidents

The Bends We are all taught about decompression sickness when training and then most of us promptly forget what we were taught. Few divers would be confident enough to cope with a fellow diver with a suspected bend. That's why it's imperative to dive with a recognized and trustworthy dive operation who will ensure your divemaster is able to cope. All the same, it's as well to have basic knowledge of what is going on.

Symptoms can include joint or muscle pain, dizziness, difficulty breathing, extreme fatigue, skin rashes, paralysis and unconsciousness. Treatment will depend on how severe these symptoms are so first of all ensure that the person is in no immediate danger, is warm, can breathe and has a pulse. Then get help. If symptoms are mild (eg, fatigue, skin rash and itching) you will probably be advised to administer 100% oxygen and a litre of fluid. If symptoms are more severe, call for assistance. You will be advised if you should administer CPR,100% oxygen or fluids until you can reach a hyperbaric facility. Note that CPR is designed to keep someone going until they reach a tertiary care facility and will only be of use if you can reach one in 50-60 minutes. If there is no pulse within that time, stop.

Something to note here is that skin bends are becoming more common. Many divemasters suspect this may be because people are stretching their bottom time by spending extended periods at shallow depths then failing to do a safety stop as their computers are still well within limits. Research is on-going in this area, but always exercise as much caution as possible. You don't have to go deep to get bent!

Bruises, sprains and broken ribs It would be an amazing dive trip where someone doesn't drop a tank on their foot, slip on a wet deck or trip en route to the RIB. If you can get to a doctor do, otherwise apply the **RICE** principle… **R**est, use **I**ce on the injured area, use a **C**ompression dressing, and **E**levate it.

Nitrogen Narcosis Not an accident as such, except that narked divers often do silly things and can have one. The only treatment is to ascend to shallower depths and allow enough time on slow, controlled safety stops for the diver to recover. It may be as well to take a day off.

Severe headaches Again not an accident but may lead to one if ignored. Many people suffer from extreme headaches underwater. There are many contributing factors to this but one way to control them is to ensure you breathe constantly and gently. Try not to hold your breath – ever.

Marine creatures

No matter how careful we all are in the water there are times when the marine world takes exception to us being there:

Fish bites It may not happen often but there is the potential for an unimpressed fish to dash out and bite a diver. Triggerfish are the best known aggressors but even cute little Nemos are known to take a nip. More frequent perhaps is when poor-sighted morays emerge from a hole and chew on a finger that's too close. In all cases, clean out the wound thoroughly with clean water or vinegar then apply an antibiotic ointment. Large bites may become infected and need antibiotics and anti-tetanus treatment. So you should keep your jabs up to date.

Venomous animals Not that you would intentionally touch anything dangerous but should you happen to get too close, use one of these basic first aid treatments then seek professional advice.

The venom of some marine animals is broken down by heat and the following treatment can be used for sea urchins, crown of thorns starfish and stingrays. It will also aid, but is less effective on, stone, scorpion and lionfish, cone shells and seasnakes.

- clean the wound
- immerse in hot water (50°C) until pain stops (up to two hours)
- apply pressure immobilization: wrap a broad, firm bandage over the bite quite tightly and extend as high as possible over the limb. Keep still, apply a splint and bind so that the limb cannot be moved.
- seek advice on whether the person needs an antivenom or injection of long acting local anaesthetic.

Snorkellers should be very careful and wear swim shoes as many toxic animals bury themselves in the sand. If you step on a ray or urchins remove obvious spines or barbs, use the hot water treatment and antiseptic creams as necessary.

More commonly, fire corals, stinging hydroids and stinging plankton can be treated with acetic acid – vinegar or lemon juice – or an anaesthetic cream. Jellyfish stings can be treated this way but ensure you remove the tentacles using rubber gloves. Coral cuts are easily infected so wash the cut well with clean, soapy water or vinegar then apply an antibiotic ointment frequently. These will take a long time to heal unless you stay out of the water so you will need to repeat the treatment after each dive.

Spot the stonefish

Every time we dive, we descend into a realm where hidden dangers lurk in the form of unrecognized or misunderstood living creatures. We are all familiar with the more obvious nasties such as much-maligned sharks, seldom-aggressive barracuda and mildly stinging anemones. However, it pays to be aware of the creatures you may encounter underwater that can be a less obvious threat.

1 Cephalopod

Blue ringed octopus Rarely aggressive, hardly seen, this octopus spends most if its life hiding from predators. Take heed when those blue rings are flashing a warning – this fellow harbours tetrodotoxin, one of the most deadly poisons known to man. There are two species, ones found in southern Australian waters and those in the tropical Coral Triangle.

2 Crustacea

Mantis shrimp As cute as a puppy scampering around the reef floor, the mantis is deceptively dangerous. Two types are fondly described as thumbcrackers and spearchuckers depending on the shape of their modified front claws. When hunting or attacked these claws shoot out with enough power to crack a thumb or spear a hand.

3 Fish

3.1 Jellyfish There are many forms of jellies ranging from the deadly Australian box jellyfish to ones that have evolved to be completely harmless. However, most will have some capacity to sting as this is their only form of defence. Long trailing tentacles need to be avoided, especially by sensitive parts of the body.

3.2 Triggerfish Where most non-divers think scuba addicts are mad for jumping in with the sharks, perhaps the most dangerous fish encountered are the titan and yellowmargined triggerfish. When nesting they are incredibly aggressive and will chase off sea creatures and landlubbers alike. They also think nothing of nipping at a fin or an ear.

3.3 Lined catfish Spotting a ball of lined catfish rolling across the seabed is a highly entertaining moment, much loved by photographers. However, highly venomous, razor-sharp spines in

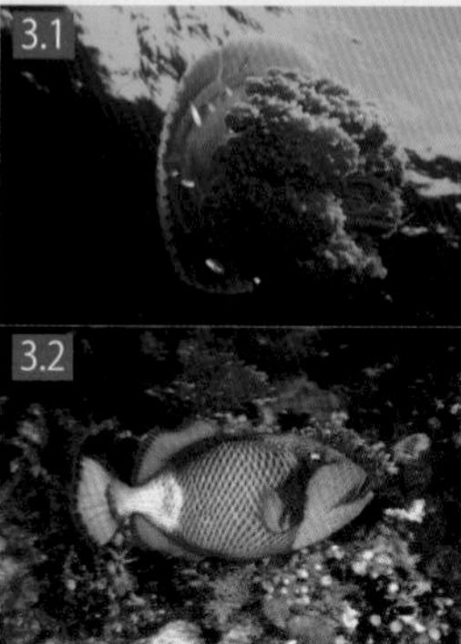

their fins are capable of inflicting a serious wound. The venom also causes vomiting, swelling, weakness and has been known to cause death.

3.4 Surgeonfish Named for the razor sharp caudal blade that sits in a groove in front of their tail fin. The blade slips in and out as the tail flexes. Be careful not to raise a hand to one of these fish, not even the ones that seem friendly and play in exhaust bubbles. Other fish with similar blades also include some unicornfish and tangs.

3.5 The Scorpionfish family This extended family is one of the reef's most contrasting, with some very beautiful species and some really ugly ones. Some contain a poison that is easily treatable while others are deadly. They all employ the same method of defence – a ridge of venomous spines runs along their bodies which, when depressed, can inject varying strengths of venom into the attacker. Generally, lionfish (page 104) stings are less serious than those of scorpionfish (page 234). Next are false stonefish, then the devilfish (3.5 below) whose venom is almost as potent as the potentially deadly stonefish (page 269). Many divers mistake scorpionfish for stonefish so compare the images on page 234 and 269.

4 Snakes and eels

4.1 Sea snakes Sea snakes suffer from a reputation they don't really deserve. Many are venomous but they are mostly curious and will not attack a diver who is not a tasty fish meal. If one appears to be taking too much interest, offer it your fin to 'taste' and it will soon leave. A snake will only bite if it is harassed.

4.2 Moray eels Most morays are usually gentle creatures. Their reputation for aggression is due to their poor eyesight and the way they search for food – head poking out of a hole, mouth gaping, teeth bared. If your hand is too close they will snap, thinking it's a fish. Their needle-like teeth are very sharp and can cut deeply.

5 Shells

5.1 Shells With over 100,000 species, it's a good thing that only a handful of shells are dangerous. These are mostly within the cone shell group which have a venom filled, harpoon-like radula dart or tooth. Injected into prey, its venom will paralyse and is toxic enough to kill humans. Never touch a cone shell and avoid other shells as some can sting.

5.2 Sea urchins Anyone who has ever put an unwary foot down on a sea urchin is unlikely to forget it. The brittle, needle-sharp spines easily penetrate skin, neoprene and rubber. The common, long-spined urchin is not toxic but others have potentially fatal poisons. Take extra special care over those that have swollen tips on the spines – these are poison sacs.

5.3 Crown of Thorns Starfish Part of the same group as sea urchins, the Crown of Thorns are better known for their ability to destroy large swathes of coral. At up to half a metre across, their thick rigid spines are tipped by sharp points. A sting from one will have similar effects to those of sea urchins but severe cases can cause paralysis.

6 Worms

Fire or Bristle Worms This caterpillar-like critter may seem innocuous and uninteresting but touch one and you will be sorry. Ultra-fine spines made of calcium carbonate easily penetrate gloves and wetsuits. Once embedded in the skin, the spines break and cause a burning sensation, swelling or rashes. Scrubbing with pumice may help remove them.

7 Corals

7.1 Corals Not only are corals fragile marine organisms that should not be touched so as to avoid damage, they should also be avoided as some will retaliate. All hard coral skeletons are made of calcium carbonate so can be hard and sharp and will cut or scratch soft skin. Some, like fire coral, also have stinging nematocysts (a microscopic cell containing a poisoned barb) which can penetrate skin and then burn or itch for some time.

7.2 Hydroids The swaying, fern-like clusters seen all over tropical reefs are often mistaken for harmless plants. However, hydroids (or seaferns) are animals with a sting in their 'fronds'. They contain hundreds of stinging cells in their tentacles. They are very unpleasant for divers but good resting places for decorator crabs, as below.

8 Rays

Stingrays The tail spines of stingrays harbour a sharp tapering barb with serrations along the edge. Stingrays will only attack in defence and injuries mostly occur when they are unwittingly stepped on. If that happens they will retaliate by whipping up their tail. The stinger leaves a puncture wound or cut. Some rays will also inject a venom.

Australia

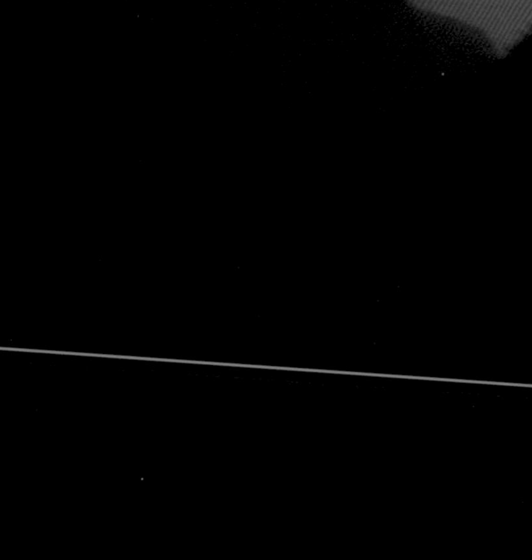

Geological oddities: undersea caverns lead to subterranean rivers and mythical grottoes on Christmas Island

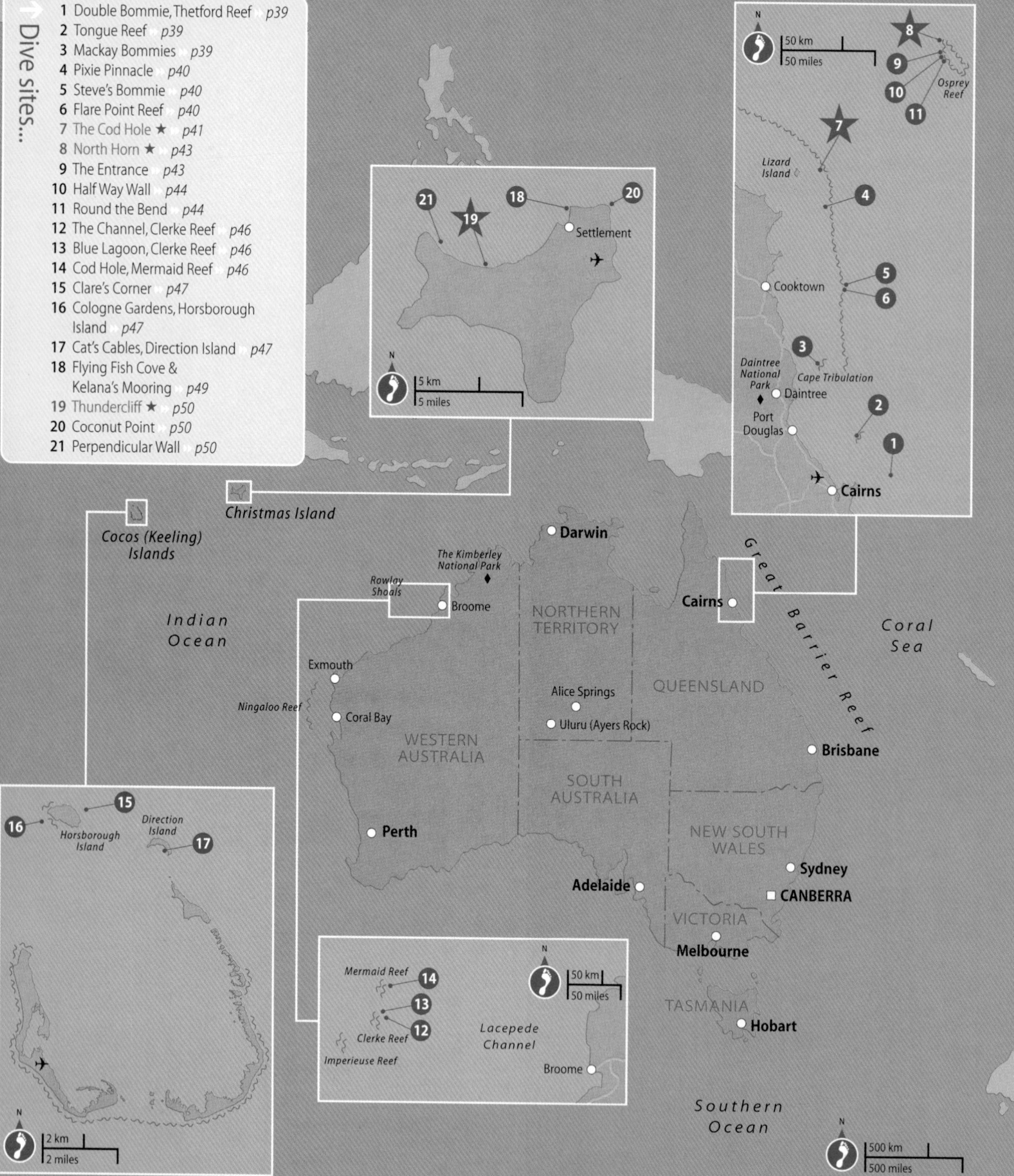
Dive sites...
1 Double Bommie, Thetford Reef p39
2 Tongue Reef p39
3 Mackay Bommies p39
4 Pixie Pinnacle p40
5 Steve's Bommie p40
6 Flare Point Reef p40
7 The Cod Hole ★ p41
8 North Horn ★ p43
9 The Entrance p43
10 Half Way Wall p44
11 Round the Bend p44
12 The Channel, Clerke Reef p46
13 Blue Lagoon, Clerke Reef p46
14 Cod Hole, Mermaid Reef p46
15 Clare's Corner p47
16 Cologne Gardens, Horsborough Island p47
17 Cat's Cables, Direction Island p47
18 Flying Fish Cove & Kelana's Mooring p49
19 Thundercliff ★ p50
20 Coconut Point p50
21 Perpendicular Wall p50
Settlement
5 km
5 miles
50 km
50 miles
Osprey Reef
Lizard Island
Cooktown
Daintree National Park
Cape Tribulation
Daintree
Port Douglas
Cairns
Christmas Island
Cocos (Keeling) Islands
Darwin
The Kimberley National Park
Rowley Shoals
Broome
NORTHERN TERRITORY
Cairns
Great Barrier Reef
Coral Sea
Indian Ocean
Exmouth
Ningaloo Reef
Coral Bay
WESTERN AUSTRALIA
Alice Springs
Uluru (Ayers Rock)
QUEENSLAND
Brisbane
SOUTH AUSTRALIA
Perth
NEW SOUTH WALES
Sydney
Adelaide
CANBERRA
VICTORIA
Melbourne
TASMANIA
Hobart
Horsborough Island
Direction Island
Mermaid Reef
Clerke Reef
Imperieuse Reef
Lacepede Channel
Broome
Southern Ocean
2 km
2 miles
500 km
500 miles

Introduction

The continent of Australia is a place of timeless beauty: from sun-warmed landscapes to dense tropical rainforests; chilly southern beaches to roasting barren deserts. The mind-boggling list of natural attractions is, for many, the biggest drawcard of them all.

'Big' is an adjective often used in conjunction with Australia. Its sheer size can be overwhelming and visitors rarely realize just how enormous the place is. The state of Queensland alone is about the same size as Mexico.

For divers, there's the biggest reef system on the planet – the Great Barrier Reef – that stretches across vast tracts of sea and encompasses several distinct climatic and geographical zones. Marine diversity is equally remarkable: you can even snorkel with one of the ocean's biggest animals, the dwarf minke whale. The Reef isn't the only diving in Australia's tropical waters, however: those continually searching for the next frontier will find unspoiled, undiscovered islands and atolls off the west coast.

On land, there are more attractions than you could ever hope to see. Major cities share a love of art and culture, sport and the great outdoors; you can sail past the Sydney Opera House and climb the Harbour Bridge; fly over Ayers Rock; tour wineries; camp beside kangaroos or trek in the Kimberley. Just don't hope to do it all in one trip.

“” *We recently discovered Christmas Island and were bowled over. We had no preconceived ideas and found some of the best diving we have ever done. Anywhere.*

Australia rating

Diving
★★★★

Dive facilities
★★★★

Accommodation
★★★★

Down time
★★★★

Value for money
★★★★

Essentials

Australia

Location	27°00′ S, 133°00′ E
Neighbours	Indonesia, New Zealand, Papua New Guinea
Population	20,090,437
Land area in km²	7,617,930
Marine area in km²	68,920
Coastline in km	25,760

Getting there and around

Most major airlines fly to Australia so there are no problems getting there. Contact your national carrier – even if they don't have a direct flight they'll probably have an agreement with an airline that does. Consider taking a stop en route as flying halfway round the globe in one go is guaranteed to get you nicely jet-lagged.

For divers, reaching the Great Barrier Reef (GBR) means getting to Cairns. Unfortunately, fewer major airlines land there now than did 10 years ago. Brisbane, a two hour flight away, is the closest alternative though you are more likely to get a decent price flying via Sydney. The latter is a more interesting place so try to build in a stopover there (see page 53). To fly direct to Cairns from Bali, Hong Kong, Singapore and Japan, try **Australian Airlines** (www.australianairlines.com). Tickets are issued by Qantas offices but you need to specify what you want or agents will route you on a **Qantas** flight (www.qantas.com.au).

For Western Australia, head to Perth. Nearly as many airlines land there as on the east coast. Or if you are routing via Singapore there's a weekly flight from there to Christmas Island with **AustAsia** (www.austasiaairlines.com) at about US$625.

Once you reach Australia, transport needs a little more thought. Because this is one enormous island, moving between any two points will take time. If you intend to see more than one state, flying is the only way to go. The two main internal carriers are **Qantas** and **Virgin Blue** (www.virginblue.com.au). However, to reach Western Australia's offshore destinations you will need to hop onto **National Jet Systems'** twice weekly flights (www.nationaljet.com.au) which cost around US$1300.

Australia has good bus and train networks, but as the trip from Sydney to Cairns takes up to 48 hours, that's not a sensible option. Car rental is easy and relatively cheap but again the distances involved make this less attractive. The best option is to fly over the long hauls and drive through the scenic areas. Although airport transfers are rarely included within Australia, any hotel or dive operator will advise how best to make the connection. There are minibus shuttles and taxis, both reasonably priced, but most people will hire a car for at least part of their time. Aussies are generally friendly and gregarious so you will always be offered help, advice and directions.

Language

English, though certainly not the Queen's variety, is the national tongue. The local dialect has been nicknamed 'Strine' in honour of the Aussie capacity to shorten every word and lengthen every vowel. Don't expect a local to pronounce a three syllable word when they can shorten it to two. Hence relatives becomes 'rellos', chardonnay becomes 'chardy'. And then you have a whole plethora of non-words that have almost become a parody of themselves. Here are a few to get you started:

hello	*g'day*
goodbye	*hooroo*
you're welcome	*no worries*
thank you	*good on ya, mate*
go away	*rack off*
gosh	*strewth (god's truth)*
good	*bonza, ripper*
beer	*amber nectar*

… and some really curious ones:

true	*fair dinkum*
condom	*franger*
crazy	*kangaroo loose in the top paddock*
poor	*hasn't got a brass razoo*

And if you see 'flake' in a fish & chip shop, it's shark meat.

Local laws and customs

Australia and etiquette? The average Aussie would be the first to laugh at that concept. Things are informal here. People generally live an outdoor life with an easy-going attitude. The national motto has got to be 'no worries, mate'. There are few pretensions, though some places such as Sydney and Port Douglas have their trendy establishments, so smart clothes for evenings out are a good idea. Beyond that it would be hard to insult an Australian – unless you pinch their drink!

Safety

Australia is a fairly isolated place. Its sheer size coupled with the small population means that even the biggest cities can feel like small towns to travellers from London, New York, Paris or Tokyo. The upside is that the crime rate is relatively low.

Personal safety, even in the state capitals, is no serious cause for concern. Although there are incidents, they're not common. However, when something awful does happen, it will get more press than you'd expect to hear about back home. Be careful if you're out for a late-night walk, especially lone female travellers. And if you visit one of the rowdier nightlife areas, such as Sydney's Kings Cross, keep your wits about you.

Dive regions are immensely traveller friendly but anywhere can attract a small-time thief. Dive and cameras bags are best safely stowed in the boot of a car.

Health

When it comes to medicine and health care, Australia is a world leader. Should you be unfortunate enough to get ill, you will be extremely well looked after. The chances of being unwell, however, are low. There are mosquitoes, but non-malarial, and other tropical diseases such as dengue are rare. The sun is very strong so a high-factor sunscreen is a must. The Aussie saying is 'slip, slap, slop': slip on a shirt, slop on sunscreen, slap on a hat. It's good advice.

Costs

Compared to other Western countries Australia is reasonably priced, but less so in tourist regions. Petrol is cheap compared to the UK (currently around AU$1.30/litre) making car hire affordable. There are restaurants to suit every budget; the major cities boast world-class eateries and little Port Douglas is home to three of the country's top seven restaurants. Very much based on the concept of fusion food, a three course meal here can cost well over AU$50 per head without wine, but it will be some of the most interesting food you will ever eat. At the other end of the scale, you can eat very cheaply in a tavern or pub where basic steak and chips will be around AU$20. Similarly with alcohol, a bottle of wine in a store can be just a few dollars while the same bottle in a restaurant will require a credit card.

Australia is very much a destination where you get what you pay for. Hotels work along much the same lines; cheap will mean basic or a little run down but usually clean; higher rates bring corresponding standards. Tipping is not the norm: Aussies rarely do as the minimum wage is comparatively high and strictly adhered to. You should only feel obliged to tip if someone has given excellent service and then it's mostly 10% or less.

Embassies → UK T+61 (0)52 6270 6666, USA T+61 (0)52 6214 5600, NZ+61 (0)52 8256 2000, Canada T+61 (0)52 6270 4000, Singapore T+61 (0)52 6273 3944. **Australia country code** → +61. **IDD code** → 0011. **Police/emergencies** → 000.

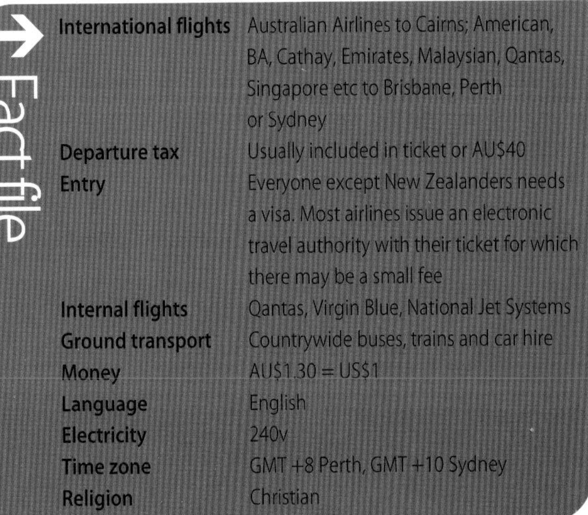

→ Fact file

International flights	Australian Airlines to Cairns; American, BA, Cathay, Emirates, Malaysian, Qantas, Singapore etc to Brisbane, Perth or Sydney
Departure tax	Usually included in ticket or AU$40
Entry	Everyone except New Zealanders needs a visa. Most airlines issue an electronic travel authority with their ticket for which there may be a small fee
Internal flights	Qantas, Virgin Blue, National Jet Systems
Ground transport	Countrywide buses, trains and car hire
Money	AU$1.30 = US$1
Language	English
Electricity	240v
Time zone	GMT +8 Perth, GMT +10 Sydney
Religion	Christian

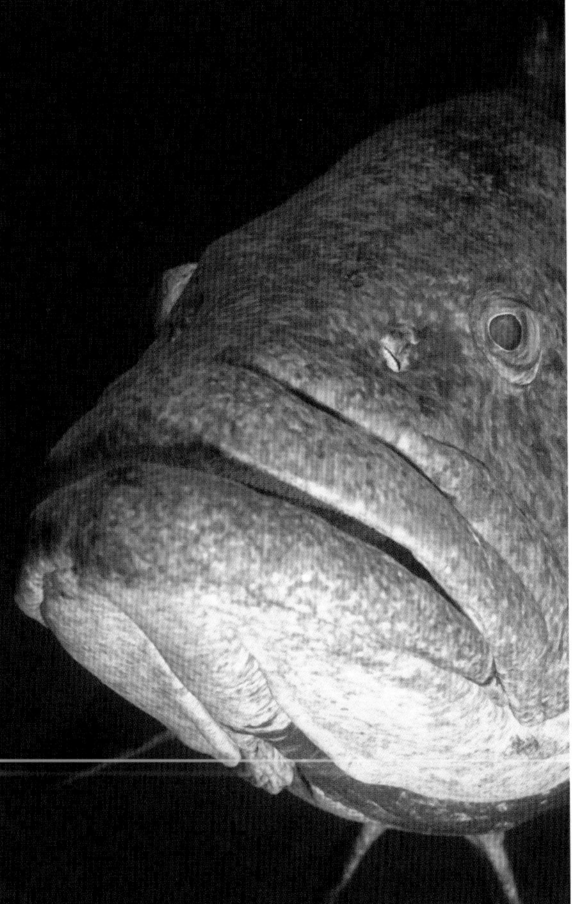

The ever-curious giant potato cod

Supported by
Christmas Island Tourism Association
Indian Ocean Diving Academy
Christmas Island Wet 'n' Dry Adventures
National Jet Systems
Christmas Island Travel
Sunset Resort
Shire of Christmas Island
www.christmas.net.au

Dive brief

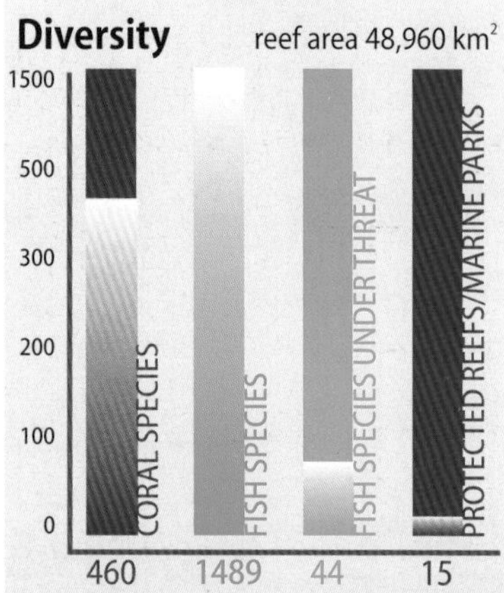

What makes Australia fascinating for divers is that it has over 25,000 km of coastline and spans several distinctive climate zones. The very tip of northern Queensland is just 10 degrees short of the Equator while Tasmania in the far south has a climate not unlike northern England.

This vast expanse has some of the most varied diving on the planet with cold water wrecks, bathtub temperature reefs and isolated atolls in the middle of nowhere. Commonly seen marine creatures range from the very biggest – such as the blue whales that slide down the eastern seaboard – to the very smallest seahorses (which you can spot in the middle of Sydney).

Although you could pick up a tank and dive almost anywhere, there are two main areas. The destination that lures most divers and non-divers alike is Queensland's Great Barrier Reef. It was even recently voted second in a major travel survey of 'top things to do before you die'. Directly across the continent, Western Australia is also on the hot-list, not because it, too, has a single major dive attraction but, in contrast, because it has several small, isolated destinations that are perfect for adventurers or those who might feel they've done everything else.

Bottom time

- **Great Barrier Reef** Colour and variety winding along the planet's largest reef » *p38*
- **Coral Sea** Pristine visibility over deep, open-water atolls » *p43*
- **Rowley Shoals** A remote dive adventure, accessible for only three months a year. » *p46*
- **Cocos (Keeling) Islands** Australia relocated to an almost unknown, isolated Indian Ocean atoll » *p47*
- **Christmas Island** Known as Australia's 'Galápagos' for its amazing environments » *p49*

Snorkelling

Snorkellers are well catered for, but not necessarily in the same places as divers. Much of the better diving is a long way offshore, while easy snorkelling is nearer the beach. Special day trips are run on the Barrier Reef which will ensure fun for both parties, but these tend to be on on large cruise-style boats to designated zones. Ask a dive centre for advice on smaller, more personal trips.

Young green turtle

Skunk clownfish on Great Barrier Reef

Australia is my birthplace, and if only I had a dollar for every time I was asked why I left. Well, apart from marrying a Brit, the answers would fill a whole book! What I would say though is that Oz is, without doubt, one of the world's most beautiful countries; an incredible, fascinating natural phenomenon. Unique wildlife, remarkable landscapes, seas so varied and colours so rich you can't possibly believe they are real. Even if it's a once-in-a-lifetime experience, it's one you must have.

The big decision

As this is the single longest haul you are ever likely to make there is absolutely no point in travelling so far to do just one thing. On the other hand Australia is so vast it's also impossible to do it all. Choose the one dive destination you fancy most and build a trip around that. It won't be difficult as tourism is set up to work in short, sharp bursts. In a three week trip you can dive, visit a rainforest or desert, see a major city and return home feeling rested and not needing another holiday.

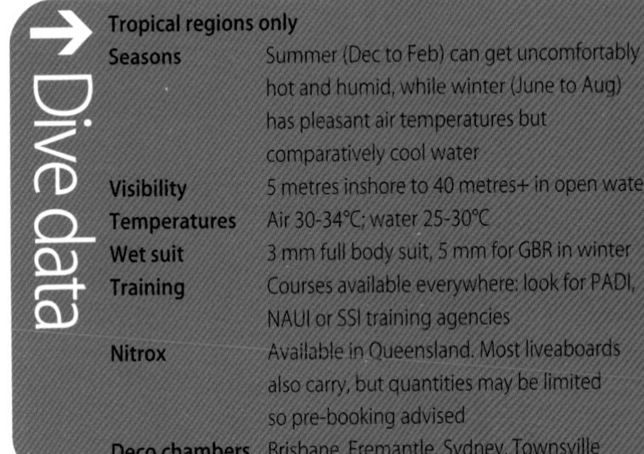

Dive data

Tropical regions only

Seasons	Summer (Dec to Feb) can get uncomfortably hot and humid, while winter (June to Aug) has pleasant air temperatures but comparatively cool water
Visibility	5 metres inshore to 40 metres+ in open water
Temperatures	Air 30-34°C; water 25-30°C
Wet suit	3 mm full body suit, 5 mm for GBR in winter
Training	Courses available everywhere: look for PADI, NAUI or SSI training agencies
Nitrox	Available in Queensland. Most liveaboards also carry, but quantities may be limited so pre-booking advised
Deco chambers	Brisbane, Fremantle, Sydney, Townsville

Conservation

It's a major issue

Australia is very protective of its natural resources and rightly so. Much of what you will see is unique in terms of both geological formation and position. You will be constantly reminded to respect this. What is a bit bizarre though is that at times you have to wonder who makes the policies and why. This is the home to the world's largest coral reef system yet the authorities not only allow people to walk on it, they encourage it. This activity is highly restricted, but still appears counterproductive. There are designated usage zones right down the length of the GBR – some are for recreation and sports, some for research, but most are for fishing. There is no way for these zones to be effectively policed. All that, along with the natural effects of weather and tides, means that you will not see the best of the Great Barrier Reef unless you take an extended trek away from the coast.

Sleek and graceful, a bronze whaler

The Napoleon wrasse, or Maori wrasse as it is sometimes known

Great Barrier Reef

The planet's longest coral reef system starts in Papua New Guinea and shadows the coast of Queensland before petering out just above the Tropic of Capricorn. This natural phenomenon stretches for 2300 km, has nearly 3000 individual reefs, 1500 species of fish, 400 corals and 4000 molluscs. It is a World Heritage Site, but that's not to say it's pristine along its entire length. This is an active, working, continually changing resource where divers have to co-exist with fishermen, tropical cyclones and exotic marine fauna such as the crown of thorns starfish.

This tiny chap is a bobtail, or bottletail squid

Pristine hard corals

It's easy to get the impression that accessing the GBR is relatively straightforward. However, it's a substantial sail offshore for most of its length, only nearing the coast in the far north. There are three sectors to the reef. The **Inner Reefs** sit on the lagoon created by the reef edge and the Queensland coast. These are within easy striking distance and are good day trips for novice divers and snorkellers but are shallow and often quite murky. Next come the **Ribbon Reefs**, the barrier reefs that create the outer edge of the lagoon just before it drops to the deeper continental shelf. Here, the waters are much clearer and the diving more exciting. Walls and pinnacles were formed by centuries of wave and tide action and the open waters attract pelagic species. Finally, there are the **Outer Reefs**, which sit a good 12 hours sail offshore in the Coral Sea. Actually outside the Great Barrier Reef, these are separated from Australia's continental shelf by a deep-water trough. This is open ocean, with virtually no land, and by far the most challenging diving you can do in this area. There are plenty of big animals and the corals are in good condition.

It doesn't matter where you base yourself in this region as diving is a well developed industry with its heart in the city of Cairns. Once a slightly seedy, down-at-heel outpost that only attracted vacationing miners and crews from the outback, Cairns cleaned up its act and is now a major heavyweight on the Australian tourist scene.

Cairns has lost ground over the last decade or so to the coastal resorts further north (including ultra-trendy Port Douglas which realised the value of turning its small river basin into a thriving marina), but it remains the best-serviced hub for divers, with the airport just minutes outside town and masses of dive shops, training facilities and organized tours. Port Douglas, an hour's drive north, is more user friendly, with a Mediterranean feel to it and enough operators to ensure that anyone who wants to dive or snorkel can do so. As well as Cairns and Port Douglas, you can also arrange to dive from other towns along the Queensland coast.

Inner Reefs

Within a couple of hours' sail from shore, these sites are usually under 20 metres deep and season dependent. Visibility is okay in the summer but in winter the water becomes murky. However, the sea remains calm while more distant reefs are exposed to incoming winds. Small coral outcrops are awash with tropical fish and some interesting critters lurk on the sand. These dives are often used for snorkelling and training novice divers. The restrictions this imposes (time and depth) may be frustrating for more experienced divers.

1 Double Bommie, Thetford Reef

- **Depth**: 12 m
- **Visibility**: poor to good
- **Currents**: mild
- **Dive type**: day boat
- **Snorkelling**: yes

Head due east from Cairns for an hour to find Thetford Reef which consists of a complex of coral outcrops with several different dive sites dotted around it. Double Bommie is a nice, easy dive. The coral species are not all that colourful or prolific but the reef's character is built on lots of small cut-throughs and tunnels. The outer edge attracts a bit more fish life; moorish idols and sea perch are quite common. Thetford also makes a great night dive as all the tunnel walls are covered in shrimp and small crabs.

The outrageous harlequin tuskfish

2 Tongue Reef

- **Depth**: 15 m
- **Visibility**: poor to good
- **Currents**: slight to medium
- **Dive type**: day boat
- **Snorkelling**: yes

This oval shaped reef is a short sail from Port Douglas and is a favourite for trainees and novices. Although the dive isn't challenging there are a lot of bigger animals including a resident turtle and Napoleon – or Maori – wrasse. The reef scenery is principally made up of staghorn corals which guard lots of smaller reef fish like butterflies and wrasse, sweetlips and coral trout. At certain times you can spot barramundi cod and even their spectacular juveniles which flutter about like hyperactive butterflies.

A chromodoris nudibranch

3 Mackay Bommies

- **Depth**: 18 m
- **Visibility**: poor to good
- **Currents**: slight to medium
- **Dive type**: day boat
- **Snorkelling**: yes

An hour or so from Cape Tribulation are these pretty, patch bommies. They sit on the inner lagoon and are calm and sheltered. Entry is over a sandy expanse of seabed where you find small coral outcrops interspersed with lots of huge clams in different hues. The reef is in good condition with some nice soft corals adding colour. There are crab-eyed gobies, pregnant shrimp in mushroom corals, clown and anemone partnerships and occasional jacks dart by. This is a good reef to spot the indigenous harlequin tuskfish.

Barramundi cod on Tongue Reef

Hard coral gardens

Ribbon Reefs

The fringing reefs that flow down Queensland's northeastern coast define the outer edge of the continental shelf before it drops off into the deep-water Queensland trench. These are the edge of the 'barrier'. There are two styles of dive: dramatic pinnacle dives and sloping reef walls that eventually drop to great depths. Visibility here is much better than on the inner reefs as the tides flow in and out between the ribbon formations. Currents can be a bit stiffer too but, of course, these attract larger pelagic species. You can dive the famous Cod Hole and, in winter, snorkel with pods of migrating dwarf minke whales.

4 Pixie Pinnacle

- **Depth**: 28 m
- **Visibility**: good
- **Currents**: mild to strong
- **Dive type**: liveaboard
- **Snorkelling**: yes

A good 10 hours north of Port Douglas, this small pinnacle rises from the seabed at around 30 metres to just below the surface. A slope near the bottom has nice soft corals and fans but hard corals are less prolific. Around the pinnacle there is good macro life, with nudibranchs like the *Notodoris minor*. Lots of red and purple anthias dart around a small cave with tiny pipefish keeping them company. The flame fire shell, which has an electric current lighting up its bright red tentacles, nestles in tight crevices and white leaffish hide amongst the plate corals. Out in the blue are small schools of chevron barracuda, trevally and midnight snappers.

5 Steve's Bommie

- **Depth**: 40 m
- **Visibility**: good
- **Currents**: can be strong
- **Dive type**: liveaboard
- **Snorkelling**: yes

A typical pinnacle dive but with a flat, sloping base. The coral at the bottom on the lee side is damaged but fin around into the current and the pace picks up. Schooling jacks hover in small groups and surgeonfish display courtship protocol by performing a male/female colour change dance. Tuna pass by out in the blue surrounded by rainbow runners while anthias dart in and out from the wall which has a good cover of tubastrea trees. If you are lucky you can spot the tasselled wobbegong – a very pretty, native shark.

6 Flare Point Reef

- **Depth**: 17 m
- **Visibility**: good
- **Currents**: medium to strong
- **Dive type**: liveaboard
- **Snorkelling**: yes

A gentle fringing reef with lots of small outcrops over a sandy bottom where you can find odd creatures like mantis shrimp and the world's largest nudibranch, *Notodoris minor*. There is a variety of unusual small fish that nest amongst the bommies. Female cuttlefish are frequently spotted here, laying their eggs in staghorn coral outcrops while being guarded by the male. Other males hover nearby and large schools of snappers hang out with rabbit fish.

Buddy line

Emergency signal devices are becoming an increasingly vital part of diver equipment as we travel to more remote regions where there is little boat traffic. It's easy to assume that because operators have become more sophisticated, someone will always be there, hovering over your head in the tender, waiting to pick you up. But people do go missing, as was the case with the unfortunate couple who were last seen on the GBR.

Reduce the chances of it happening to you by carrying at least one signalling device in case the tender driver can't see you. A bright orange safety sausage, an air horn connected to your direct feed, even an old CD in your jacket pocket could be the one small item that saves your life.

Soft coral feeding

Bubble coral shrimp

7 The Cod Hole

- **Depth**: 25 m
- **Visibility**: good
- **Currents**: none to strong
- **Dive type**: liveaboard
- **Snorkelling**: yes

In the early 1970s, famous biologists and adventurers, Ron and Valerie Taylor discovered a patch of reef consisting of three parallel coral ridges and gullies with a depression, or hole, to one end. The nature of the topography created a protected haven for several species of large marine animal, in particular giant potato cod and whitetip sharks. The word got out and not long afterwards, dive operators started feeding the fish to ensure their continual presence for divers. Ecologically this practice was unsound and is now discouraged.

However, the cod have remained and as you enter the water, they come to greet divers just as they always did. The giant potato cod is a curious chap and will hover close by as long as divers are in the water. Likewise, small Napoleon wrasse and large schools of red snapper will do the same. Leaving the hole, you'll see that the hard corals along the ridge are beautiful and in extremely good condition. In fact, the entire site is very pretty. As you work your way up and down the gullies you are likely to meet other cod being cleaned in a crevice or a small turtle resting on a bommie. Whitetip reef sharks often sit resting on the sandy seabed but take off as divers approach, no doubt feeling that the narrow gullies are just not big enough for everyone. There is one enormous clam – about 4 feet long – nestling in the top of one of the ridges.

For many people, the main attraction on the Great Barrier Reef is bound to be that most famous of dive sites, the Cod Hole. In all truth, we weren't looking forward to revisiting it. We had dived there ten years previously and it had been trashed. Too many divers, too many feeding sessions. Eco-tourism has kicked in and operators are much more responsible. Although some still feed the cod (no names mentioned), the practice is fading away. The corals have regenerated yet all the animals remain.

Meeting a giant potato cod at the Cod Hole

Close encounter

A deep guttural grunt vibrated through my body, and I spun around in the water trying to locate the source of the noise. There were four, possibly five minke whales surrounding me, gliding lazily through the water. A second grunt echoed and I repositioned my body on the line. My cousin, Nikki, lifted her head. "Did you hear that?" she said. I suspended my body upside-down, holding my head underneath the surface, listening carefully. The sounds were incredible, almost mechanical, and unlike anything I have ever heard.

I was on my uncle's dive boat, *Undersea Explorer*, and we were travelling between dive sites looking for the whales. The first was spotted roughly a kilometre away, the engines shut off and we started to drift. It was a bright, sunny day, yet there was a harsh wind and whitecaps littered the surface. After fifteen minutes, more whales began to appear. They came closer and closer to the boat, making passes by the bow. The crew threw out the drag lines and minutes later I was in the water hanging onto one, the whales approaching slowly. Their sleek, submarine-like bodies glided through the water effortlessly. When they were within ten to fifteen feet, they stopped dead, hovering in the water. Their large, squinted eyes swivelled, checking me out. I spotted one accelerating vertically from below. It was coming straight towards me but at the last moment it veered away. I could have reached out and touched it. I could see every detail on its shiny skin. Wispy patterns in shades of grey resembled cloud formations. Every dull scar stood out on its smooth, glinting back.

Being in the water with the whales seemed like such a personal encounter, as if I were important enough to get the attention of these amazing creatures. That evening on the boat some people talked about their experiences with tears in their eyes.

Stephen Soule, Boston, Massachusetts

Minke whale magic

Every winter, between June and August, a very special event takes place along the Ribbon Reefs. Pods of dwarf minke whales appear and, curiously, come to play with the dive boats. This strange behaviour was first noted a decade ago, when scientists realised that these minkes were different from 'true' minkes, which are only seen in the northern hemisphere, or Antarctic minkes. The GBR visitors have different skin colours and patterns and adults are some 2 metres shorter than their Antarctic cousins. At up to 8 metres long and weighing around 5 or 6 tonnes, these creatures will be one of the biggest things you'll ever get close to while in the water.

When a pod comes across a dive boat they often circle it before gradually coming closer and closer. It's possible to snorkel with them, though the rules for this are very strict.

Drag lines are attached to the bow or stern, with old tyre inner tubes tied at intervals along them. Snorkellers attach themselves to the line but are 'under pain of death' should they let go. This is to prevent the whales being frightened and disappearing. Scientists have been studying the dwarf minke behaviour and are aiming to understand their migration, lifestyle patterns and – most interestingly for divers – why they hang around boats.

Coral Sea

Heading away from the GBR, a group of isolated atolls were first discovered in 1803, the only inhabitants both then and now being a large population of seabirds. There are no land masses; the reefs are completely exposed but in pristine condition as they are visited only by dive boats. Getting there requires an overnight sail so a liveaboard is a must. There are several reef systems but the one that attracts the most visitors is Osprey, 160 km east northeast of Lizard Island. This 21 km-long oval drops to over 700 metres below sea level. It is ringed by sharp fringing reefs that protect an inner lagoon.

8 North Horn

- **Depth**: 40+ m
- **Visibility**: good to excellent
- **Currents**: slight to strong
- **Dive type**: liveaboard
- **Snorkelling**: for confident swimmers

North Horn is on the northwestern tip of Osprey and is subject to just enough in the way of current to attract schooling sharks. From the second you drop in, the clear visibility ensures a good view of the resident grey whaler sharks. Large barracuda often hang off the wall which drops to a ridge of enormous soft coral trees and fan corals. A horn shaped coral head juts upwards from about 20 metres and the resident whitetips circle it constantly. Smaller animals include coral trout, gobies and a variety of hawkfish. Doing a safety stop back on the shot line is always entertaining as the whalers perform belly rolls just below. This dive is quite a rush.

9 The Entrance

- **Depth**: 25+ m
- **Visibility**: good to excellent
- **Currents**: slight to strong
- **Dive type**: liveaboard
- **Snorkelling**: for confident swimmers

A group of hard coral bommies surround a narrow channel which leads to the inner lagoon. The sandy seabed harbours tiny critters like imperial shrimp on cucumbers and masses of commensal shrimp and goby pairs. The dive plan takes you around the bommies where there are colourful schooling fish, clownfish living in carpet anemones, hawkfish and blennies. Between two of the pinnacles, and just under the mooring line, there is a small double-ended cave. You can swim through carefully and, midway, see an anchor embedded in the coral. No one knows where it came from but it's thought to be late 19th or early 20th century.

Whip corals extending from a wall

A rare soapfish

Patrolling whitetip shark

Second World War communication cable

Tales from the deep

To catch a tiger by the tail

There we were, degassing at 5 metres while drifting along a remote coral wall, 30 metres visibility at least and over 100 turtles seen in the previous 40 minutes. A large shape came into focus. I thought, "That's a weird looking turtle gliding over there." Then the brain registered that this was not another turtle. "Holy ****, it's a tiger!" The other divers are transfixed as all 3.5 metres of her glides past, checking us out with her big, black, unblinking eye. A half circle around us and down she goes into the depths we had just come from. And we thought swimming with 100 turtles was cool!

A 12 foot inflatable is anchored in the blistering tropical sun while Richard Fitzpatrick, the head of the tiger research programme, wonders "where have all the tiger sharks gone?"

Action! A fin breaks the surface… and Richard leaps up, clutching a pole with a weird contraption on the end. He lunges and "the Claw" locks around the peduncle, the pole comes free and we have a tiger by the tail. A 3.5 metre female is now roped by her tail but within minutes, she relaxes. No hooks, low stress for the shark (and researcher) and much, much safer than the old days when baited hooks and jumping in to secure a rope around the thrashing shark were the go.

We were visiting Raine Island, the world's largest turtle rookery. This is no secret to marine predators like the tiger shark. As the turtles come in to nest, the tigers come in to feed and we come to study. Our shark research has been evolving since 1996. The focus was on whitetip and grey reef sharks until we set ourselves a new challenge - working with the mighty tiger. Almost nothing is known of these apex predators but with Fitzpatrick's "Shark Claw" we are able to place a satellite tag on their dorsal fin. These are activated every time a fin breaks the surface, allowing us to track tiger movements from space for months to come.

The biggest tiger shark we have tagged so far was a 3.5 metre female named "Lola". In November 2002, "Nicole" travelled along the outer barrier reef, north to Eastern fields and then around the tip of Cape York where she died in a fishing net .

John Rumney, Manager of Undersea Explorer

JOHN RUMNEY

10 Half Way Wall

- **Depth**: 25+ m
- **Visibility**: good to excellent
- **Currents**: slight to strong
- **Dive type**: liveaboard
- **Snorkelling**: for confident swimmers

This steep wall has sharp cut backs along its face. The mooring line drops to a rounded hump and an overhang full of whip corals that grow both up and down. At the base of the wall, a sandy area is home to blue flagtails and plenty of damselfish. There is a patch of lacy fire coral that protects pufferfish and well camouflaged stonefish. There are some lesser known small fish like bluestreaked gobies and midas blennies along with longsnout butterflies, whip coral gobies, and ever present whitetips.

11 Round the Bend

- **Depth**: 33+ m
- **Visibility**: good
- **Currents**: slight to strong
- **Dive type**: liveaboard
- **Snorkelling**: unlikely

This long wall is covered with large crusting plate corals, mostly montipora species, and interspersed with very interesting algae: sea grapes, turtle weed, coralline algae and sailor's eyeballs. The top 3 metres is very pretty with lots of pale lemon, blue and pink corals and sponges while at depth there are huge dendronephthya trees. Small gobies and blennies pepper the wall and critter life includes shrimp in mushroom coral. Out in the blue, whitetips, an occasional manta ray and starry puffers pass by.

Half spotted hawkfish

Western Australia

The biggest of Australia's five states and covering almost half her land mass, Western Australia is an empty yet immensely impressive wilderness. With so much coastline you'd be forgiven for thinking WA would be a magnet for dive centres but strangely it's not. There's some localized, cool water diving near Perth, but the only tropical diving on the mainland centres around Ningaloo Reef. And the reason why? Well, distances are enormous, the local population is small and all diving tends to be seasonal.

That's not to say that you can't dive Ningaloo all year round. You can, and some diving is said to be first rate, but the big attraction is the annual whaleshark migration. Between March and May these gentle giants slip up and down the reef then disappear again. Special day trips are set up: spotter planes fly over the reef then radio directions to the boats below. If a whaleshark is spotted all the boats head for it. You can't dive though, it's snorkelling only and even that is limited by time and numbers.

There are a handful of dive centres in Exmouth, a small town built to service the local military base, and tiny Coral Bay, 150 km to the south. Both have reasonable tourist facilities but, given the limitations, it's hard to see the value in travelling to Ningaloo from overseas. Some people go, see loads of whalesharks, love the dives and have a great time. But just as many are frustrated.

All the same, there is fabulous, and reliable, diving to be had; it's just that you have to travel some way from Western Australia's coast, out into the Indian Ocean. Three offshore destinations are a huge surprise: idyllic and isolated, yet incredibly impressive, are the Rowley Shoals, Cocos (Keeling) Islands and Christmas Island. Each has its own distinct geography and personality. **Rowley** consists of three pear-shaped atolls surrounding shallow lagoons. Similar in dimension and shape, each is north-south orientated, with the narrow end towards the north. They have near-vertical sides rising from very deep water and are smothered in vast swathes of hard coral. **Cocos (Keeling)** spans two small oceanic atolls that are 24 km apart, though only the southern atoll is occupied. Some 52 km of fringing reef surrounds a horseshoe-shaped lagoon. As the atoll is quite exposed, pelagic species are attracted here from the open ocean. **Christmas Island** is perhaps the most impressive of these offshore islands. Located 2600 km northwest of Perth, her closest neighbour is Indonesian Java, just 360 km away. There are almost as many endemic species here as in the Galápagos Islands (see page 116). This is the location of the famed annual red crab migration. The diving is an incredible mix of steep walls, pristine corals, huge schools of fish and pelagics. There is even accessible cave diving.

A cannon on the Cocos (Keeling) sea floor

Runners over reef

Surface interval

Creature discomforts

Australia is famed for its large number of incredibly interesting but also rather dangerous animals. Funnel web spiders can be deadly although there is now an antidote. Redback and black widow spiders give a bite that'll knock you sideways for several days. Blue ringed octopus are also extremely toxic and can be lethal for a child (so be wary in rock pools). The Queensland box jellyfish is another highly dangerous creature, as are saltwater and freshwater crocodiles – known locally as 'salties' and 'freshies'. The chances of seeing any of these creatures in the wild are fairly remote. Warning signs are everywhere alerting you to potential dangers and risk areas are also netted. But you still need to take precautions and get local advice before setting out.

Rowley Shoals

On the northwestern coast of Western Australia is the town of Broome; a strange and very multicultural little place. Its history is based around the pearl industry in the early 1900s and Chinese and Indonesian populations were here long before white Australians moved in. The pearl industry has declined somewhat and Broome now has the eerie atmosphere of a post-boom wild west frontier town. You can almost see the tumbleweed rolling down the streets after lunch on a Saturday.

Broome is the closest access point to the Rowley Shoals. This group of atolls is 260 km offshore and reaching it involves a very rough 12-hour crossing, which can only be made from September to November as conditions are too difficult at other times . However, once there, you will find some outstanding diving. Clerke and Mermaid Reefs have an unusually large tidal range of over 3 metres. Consequently there is some powerful but fun current diving. The water here is always clear, at least in dive season, so there's no risk of missing whatever pelagic life passes by.

A wary cuttlefish

12 The Channel, Clerke Reef

- **Depth**: 20 m
- **Visibility**: good to excellent
- **Currents**: mild to ripping
- **Dive type**: liveaboard
- **Snorkelling**: for confident swimmers

Between the outer edge of this circular reef and the inner lagoon is a sharp and narrow channel created by natural erosion. It transports water in and out during the extreme tidal changes and makes for a thrilling drift dive no matter whether you do it on the incoming or outgoing current. It takes a little nerve, too, as the water propels you faster through the confined space than you could ever do on your own. It's a roller coaster ride between the bommies and outcrops, past reef fish and corals. In contrast, the current is almost non-existent on the outer wall where large schools of jacks hang out, as do bronze whalers and occasional tiger sharks. This also makes an excellent snorkel especially on the outgoing current.

13 Blue Lagoon, Clerke Reef

- **Depth**: 30 m
- **Visibility**: fair to good
- **Currents**: mild
- **Dive type**: liveaboard
- **Snorkelling**: for confident swimmers

This fantastic turquoise lagoon is surrounded by sandy patches and small coral bommies. There are lots of pretty soft corals and good hard corals, interspersed with channels and swim throughs. Sailfin snapper, surgeonfish and trevally hover over the wall. Descending beyond the edge of the lagoon, a large sandy amphitheatre is occupied by a gang of inquisitive whitetips sharks. These school around the divers until they get bored. Back on the reef wall, Napoleon wrasse swim by with friendly pufferfish and batfish.

14 Cod Hole, Mermaid Reef

- **Depth**: 18 m
- **Visibility**: good to excellent
- **Currents**: mild
- **Dive type**: liveaboard
- **Snorkelling**: for confident swimmers

Not unlike its more famous Queensland counterpart, this Cod Hole is a maze of small bommies, crevices and cut throughs in the reef. There are a lot of very pretty soft corals, some small fans and masses of immaculate hard corals. There are three resident potato cod. One is around 1.5 metres long and very curious and is accompanied by another about 1 metre long. A third is a loner and has a distinctive paler skin. They all come very close, even nudging for attention. The rest of the dive consists of a lot schooling fish, including trevally, jacks and red snappers. This is also a site for seeing occasional bigger predators, including tiger sharks.

Fish soup: groupers, snappers and butterflies

Cocos (Keeling) Islands

This horseshoe-shaped atoll is much closer to Java than it is to Australia but a couple of decades back the local Malay population was given the choice to throw its fortunes in with Australia or turn to Asia for political and economic support. They chose Australia, which had had military placements there during both world wars, and more recently an animal quarantine station which is scheduled to re-open with the arrival of some Thai elephants destined for Sydney's Taronga Zoo.

Today, the islands' international airport has only two flights a week and with a population of just 630, this is probably one of the quietest places you will ever visit in your life – until you get under the water. The geographic location of these isolated atolls means that many pelagics are attracted to hunt around the lagoon's coral coated, steep outer walls. There are sharks on every dive, something you see in very few places these days. Inside the shallow lagoon the life is less prolific but that is made up for by a few small but interesting wrecks.

15 Clare's Corner

- **Depth**: 25 m
- **Visibility**: good
- **Currents**: mild
- **Dive type**: day boat
- **Snorkelling**: for confident swimmers

Along the top of the reef wall is a pattern of ridges and gullies. Napoleon wrasse patrol this area, especially over the reef flat where there is the most enormous flat table coral. Down on the wall, grey sharks stand off in the blue while the Napoleons follow divers from above. Small groups of barracuda and large groups of jacks hover over the deeper water. The gullies turn into a dog-leg shape and masses of fish shelter inside from larger predators. There are pyramid and several other butterflies, angels, snapper and rabbitfish. Returning to the mooring line, you pass the flat table coral which extends to over 3 metres wide and is completely pristine.

16 Cologne Gardens, Horsborough Island

- **Depth**: 35 m
- **Visibility**: fair to great
- **Currents**: mild to strong
- **Dive type**: day boat
- **Snorkelling**: for confident swimmers

The outer reef edge off Horsborough Island is completely smothered in hard corals, all in excellent condition. The variety of leather coral is particularly impressive. Dropping down to 38 metres there are some peach- coloured gorgonians that are patrolled by young whitetip sharks. These are very inquisitive and will follow along on a dive. At the top of the wall, where it returns to a gentle slope, are several different types of trevally swimming in mixed schools, clownfish in anemones and masses of pyramid butterflyfish. The channel beside this island is also the haunt of a pod of bottlenose dolphins. These absolutely delightful animals are attracted by the sound of the motor as the dive boat approaches. They wait for playmates to drop into the water with mask and snorkel then instigate a quick game of chase.

17 Cat's Cables, Direction Island

- **Depth**: 22 m
- **Visibility**: fair to good
- **Currents**: mild to strong
- **Dive type**: day boat
- **Snorkelling**: for confident swimmers

Inside the lagoon, the seabed is affectionately known as 'diving the desert'. Far from being a wasteland, however, the flat rocky surface is peppered with ridges and small corals where you find giant green morays, tiny pipefish and flounder. Giant triggerfish mate in this area and whitetip sharks, blacktips and grey reefs are all present. The occasional manta makes a fly-by. There is a small wreck, the remains of a fibreglass refugee boat; the engines and some of the structure is still intact but the hull is slowly disintegrating. Second World War telecommunications cables stretch across the seabed. A decaying cylinder houses lionfish and coral banded shrimp. If you're lucky you may see Cat, the resident dugong. You can often hear her calling but she has to be in the mood to make an appearance.

Friendly and playful spinner dolphins

For me, diving the 'Galápagos of Australasia' was all about seeing what dive sites my guests were prepared to sacrifice and how many I could possibly pack into their stay only to find, at the end of their holiday, yet another "postively-not-to-be-missed" list anyway...

Marcus Cathrein, Indian Ocean Dive Academy, Christmas Island

Christmas Island

Even closer to Java than Cocos, this is another Australian territory that occasionally hits the headlines for the wrong reasons due to its refugee station. Though covered in dense jungle, the island's economic mainstay was its enormous phosphate mine. Its days are numbered as the raw material runs out and the natural realm is given precedence; nearly two thirds of the island is now protected as national park. Native birdlife includes red-footed, brown and Abbot's boobies and several endemic species such as the Christmas Island frigatebird. There's also a unique fruit bat that is seen during the day soaring on the thermals. However, Christmas's biggest claim to fame is the red crab migration which occurs in latter part of the year. When the weather patterns are just right, millions of these brightly coloured crustaceans scuttle out of the rainforest and head straight for the coast where they throw themselves into the water to spawn. A few months later all the new-born crabs make their way back onshore and return to the rainforest.

“ This Christmas we have been averaging around 11 whalesharks a day, with 23 spotted in one day on 30 December. It's the best season of whalesharks we have ever, ever, ever had.... ”

Linda Cash, Christmas Island Tourism

Underwater is also very special. The reefs are smothered in the most unbelievable amount of pristine hard coral. The island is at the tip of a volcanic mountain that rises from the edge of the Java trench at 3000 metres. Visibility is outstanding, as much as 50 metres. Large pelagics patrol the outer edges of the reef. There's tuna, trevally, barracuda and reef sharks and, late in the year, whalesharks. Huge pods of spinner dolphins sometimes come to play with the dive boats. Critter life is less evident but there are some outstanding animals such as the rare dragon moray. Several coastal caves have formed and these can be safely explored. There is some excellent snorkelling here too. Typically, the reef shoulder is at 10 metres and diving is 'live boat' with a skipper always on board so snorkellers can spend time on the reef top with the boat close at hand.

18 Flying Fish Cove and Kelana's Mooring

- **Depth**: 35 m
- **Visibility**: excellent
- **Currents**: none
- **Dive type**: day boat
- **Snorkelling**: absolutely

This small, pretty bay is the island's only year-round mooring point but is also awash with marine life. There are two dives here. You can start by being dropped at Kelana's Mooring then swimming back to shore, or from shore for a fabulous night dive under the main jetty. The mooring is a favoured site for finding the spectacular, indigenous dragon moray. At about 25 metres a substantial stand of corals is filled with morays (at least five different ones are tucked down inside along with some debelius shrimp). It takes some searching but a shy dragon will be spotted tucked down deep. Further up in the shallows, there is some amazing marine life; an octopus, mating pufferfish, huge hawkfish and some nudibranchs. At night, and closer to shore, there is less coral but it harbours some interesting critters such as pink leaffish, lionfish, some crustaceans and sleeping parrotfish.

A 60-cm long robber crab

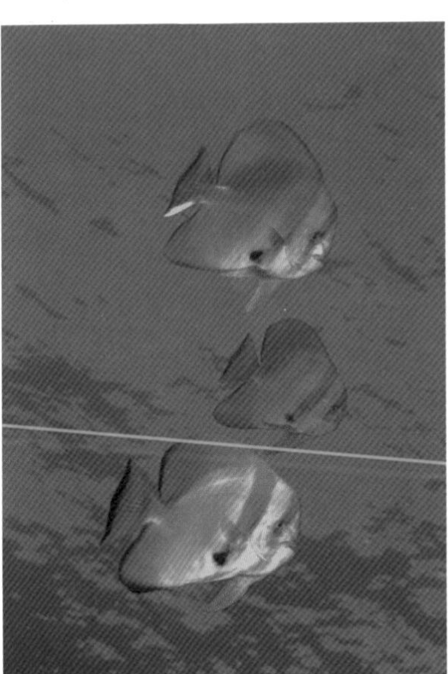

Elegant trio of batfish

Moray having his teeth cleaned

19 Thundercliff

- **Depth**: 8 m
- **Visibility**: fair to stunning
- **Currents**: none to mild
- **Dive type**: day boat
- **Snorkelling**: yes

A dive, a swim and a walk; this is probably one of the strangest dives you will ever do. Entering the water over a shallow section of reef you swim down into a sandy channel, under an overhang and into a wide-mouthed cave. Fin past a rock that juts almost to the surface with several hundred silver snapper swarming it, and continue on until you reach a dark cavern. You can surface to admire the stalagmites before descending into a narrow passage that leads to a much bigger cave, which is also full of impressive limestone structures. Next, you swim up to a beach and exit onto the rocks, before dekitting for a walk through the cave to a small pool of brackish water. Inside the pool is a rare red shrimp (as yet unnamed) that is attracted to torch beams, plus a surprise that no one knows about until they've been.

20 Coconut Point

- **Depth**: 38 m
- **Visibility**: excellent
- **Currents**: none to mild
- **Dive type**: day boat
- **Snorkelling**: yes

Three dives in one, this starts at a small sand gully under the cliff surrounded by a flat reef completely covered in small hard corals. Pyramid butterflies and Indian triggers mob you as you descend and there are dory, hawkfish, angels and rare gold spot scorpions. Beyond this, a sheer wall drops past 60 metres, and you can see all the way to the bottom. At 40 metres there are huge gorgonians, grey reef sharks, dogtooth tuna and trevally. Returning to the gully, it leads into a huge cavern with openings to the cliff face on two sides. The light inside has an eerie glow. At the back of the cave you can crab crawl over beautifully rounded rocks until the light fades. If you turn on your torch, you will discover a huge number of enormous lobsters nestled into virtually every crevice.

21 Perpendicular Wall

- **Depth**: 35 m
- **Visibility**: excellent
- **Currents**: none
- **Dive type**: day boat
- **Snorkelling**: yes

Before arriving at the dive site you will probably have already encountered some bronze whalers which are attracted by the engine noise. You can snorkel with them as they are inquisitive and have never been known to be aggressive in this situation. A pod of spinner dolphins visit here as well and, if you're lucky, they'll come right up to your mask to say hello. When you do reach the dive, you'll find an overhang full of parallel fans growing to catch the light like solar panels. You then fin around the bend in the wall where the view is breathtaking. Masses of gigantic gorgonians hang off the wall and there are some even bigger ones in a cave. Out in the blue there are grey reefs, a school of jacks and a school of midnight snapper. Up in the shallows are small cluster bommies of fabulous hard corals, many hosting colourful christmas tree worms.

How impressive is the dragon moray?

Thundercliff cave system

Drying out

Visiting Australia should be as much about what to do on land as it is to do with diving – well, almost – but limit yourself to one or two states or you'll need a holiday once you get home.

Great Barrier Reef

Cairns

Dive centres

Pro Dive, 116 Spence St, T+61 (0)7 4031 5255, www.prodive-cairns.com.au.
Tusa Dive, Shield St, T+61 (0)7 4031 1028, www.tusadive.com.

Sleeping

Cairns has loads of choice; everything from backpacker hostels to 5-star resorts.
$$$ **Tradewinds Esplanade**, 137 The Esplanade, T+61 (0)7 4053 0300, www.tradewinds-esplanade.com.au. Very nice 4-star hotel.
$$ **Coral Tree Inn**, 166-172 Grafton St, T+61 (0)7 4031 3744, www.coraltreeinn.com.au. Good quality 3-star hotel in town centre.

Liveaboards

Nimrod Explorer, PO Box 6905, T+61 (0)7 4031 5566, www.explorerventures.com. Nice boat but most cabins are for 4 people.
Spirit of Freedom, PO Box 1276, T+61 (0)7 4040 6450, www.spiritoffreedom.com.au. Luxury liveaboard with outstanding service.

Eating

Restaurants tend to be al fresco and informal.
$$$ **Mondo Cafe Bar & Grill**, 34 The Esplanade, T+61 (0)7 4052 6780. In the Hilton Hotel, great food served with superb views.
$$ **Rattle 'n' Hum**, 67-69 The Esplanade, T+61 (0)7 4031 3011. Casual with enormous portions of straightforward food.

Car hire

All the usual major rental agencies are at Cairns Airport. Small cars start at AU$55 per day, 4WDs from AU$100 per day. Better rates are available if you book online.

Port Douglas

Dive centres

Discover Dive School, Grant St, T+61 (0)7 4099 5544, www.discoverdiveschool.com.
Tech Dive Academy, 1/18 Macrossan St, T+61 (0)7 4099 6880, www.tech-dive-academy .com.

Sleeping

$$$ **Peninsula Boutique**, 9-13 The Esplanade, Port Douglas, T+61 (0)7 4099 9100, www.peninsulahotel.com.au. Stylish apart-hotel with the biggest bathrooms and a classy in-house restaurant.
$$ **Hibiscus Gardens Spa Resort**, 22 Owens St, Port Douglas, T+61 (0)7 4099 5315, www.hibiscusportdouglas.com.au. Nice and central, multi-storey resort with kitchenettes.

Liveaboards

Undersea Explorer, PO Box 615, Port Douglas, T+61 (0)7 4099 5911, www.undersea.com.au. Unique trips with the focus on conservation, education and scientific exploration.

Nightlife in Port Douglas

Cairns waterfront

Eating

$$$ Salsa Bar & Grill, 26 Wharf St, T+61 (0)7 4099 4922, www.salsa-port-douglas.com.au. Famous 'in' place for fabulous fusion food.
$$$ Sassi Cucina, corner Macrossan St and Wharf St, T+61 (0)7 4099 6100, www.sassi.com.au. Modern Italian creations with a mega-reputation.

The Daintree

Dive centres

Odyssey H20, T+61 (0)7 4098 0033, www.coconutbeach.com.au /odyssey-h2o. The dive centre for **Coconut Beach Rainforest Lodge** (below) but also work with all hotels in the area.

Sleeping

$$$-$$ Coconut Beach Rainforest Lodge and **Ferntree Rainforest Lodge**, Cape Tribulation Rd, T+61 (0)2 8296 8010, www.coconutbeach.com.au and www.ferntreelodge.com.au. Both situated in amazing rainforest settings.

Eating

$$$ Dragonfly Gallery Café, about 10 mins drive north of Coconut Beach, T+61 (0)7 4098 0121. It has a nice setting but the restaurants in both **Coconut Beach** and **Ferntree** are better value.

Sights

In the tropical north this is usually a DIY affair. Organized tours are expensive and inflexible so it's best to hire a 4WD and explore.
Cairns The centre of town is just a few square blocks of shops and restaurants, interspersed with tourist facilities like travel agents, dive shops and car hire agencies. The waterfront has been regenerated and there is a water park with giant fish sculptures. It's easy to arrange reef trips whether snorkelling, diving or sailing.
Port Douglas Life centres on Macrossan St, a row of stylish shops and restaurants that links the small town beach and jetty with the beautiful Four Mile Beach. This beach does get box jellyfish but areas are netted. The new marina is worth a daydream or two and there is a bird park just outside town.
Daintree Rainforest Regarded as the world's most important lowland rainforest, the Daintree is a World Heritage Site. You can drive through it but will need a 4WD vehicle to negotiate river crossings. Along the road that winds through the forest are nature trails, aerial walkways and guided tour facilities. Sections of the forest are designated working regions so you can visit tropical fruit farms and small cottage industries.
Cape Tribulation About two thirds of the way through the forest is Cape Tribulation, named by Captain Cook as the *Endeavour* went aground near here. It's the point where the Great Barrier Reef comes closest to the rainforest and is a beautiful spot. You need to take care though as saltwater crocodiles inhabit nearby creeks.

Koala up a gum tree

Western Australia

Perth

Sleeping

It's a good idea to stopover for at least a night before heading to an offshore dive zone.
$$ Saville Park Suites, 201 Hay St, T+61 (0)8 9267 4888, www.savillesuites .com. Classy apart-hotel in the business district. Discounted rates at www.wotif.com.
$ Comfort Inn, 285 Great Eastern Highway, Belmont, T+61 (0)8 9277 2733, www.choicehotels.com. The closest accommodation to the airport. Basic budget motel with courtesy transfers.

Eating

Most hotels have their own restaurant.
$$$ Vivace, 71 Bennett St, T+61 (0)8 9325 1788. Just around the corner from the **Saville Suites** is this reasonably priced Italian bistro.

Broome

Sleeping

$$ Cable Beach Club, Cable Beach Rd, T+61 (0)8 9192 0400, www.cablebeachclub.com. The closest hotel to the beach. Good views.
$$ Sea Shells Resort, 4-6 Challenor Drive, Broome, T+61 (0)8 9192 6111, www.broome.seashells.com.au. Right opposite the exquisite pink **Cable Beach**.

Liveaboards

Kimberley Escape and **Great Escape**, The Great Escape Charter Company, PO Box 1133, T+61 (0)8 9193 5983, www.kimberleyescape.com. The most experienced operator sailing to Rowley plus inland adventure cruises (no diving).

Eating

$$ The Old Zoo Café, Challenor Drive, Broome, T+61 (0)8 9193 6200. Beside **Sea Shells**, modern home-style cooking.
$$ Sunset Bar and Café, part of the **Cable Beach Club**, for seafood and salads and sunsets.

Sights

Distances are immense in this state so you either need lots of time and a car to get around on your own or enough money to pay for an air-based tour.
Perth Visit the botanical gardens where the view over the city skyline is superb. The Swan Bell Tower is home to the original 14th-century bells from Saint Martin-in-the-Fields in London. Just to the north is the Aquarium of Western Australia and just south is the port of Fremantle, one of the oldest cities in the country.
Margaret River The newest of Australia's award-winning wine regions. Take a couple of days to tour the vineyards, explore the towns and wander the forests. There's even an underwater observatory – and cool water diving – at Bussleton Jetty. At least 4 hours' drive from Perth.

Monkey Mia This small beach resort attracts visitors to see the resident pod of bottlenose dolphins. Every day they come in to knee-deep water to be fed but interaction is highly controlled. The resort is 800 km north of Perth. A 2-day mini package holiday (flights, hotel and entrance fees) costs about AU$550 per person.

The Kimberley North and west of Broome, this national park is spectacular. The landscapes are carved by ancient forces: there are caves, rivers and rock formations to rival Ayers Rock. Distances are huge but you can get to the town of Derby and on to Tunnel Creek relatively easily. Tours cost around AU$300 per day.

Ayers Rock In the middle of Australia – and the middle of nowhere – this enormous stone monolith, more properly known as Uluru, is a sacred aboriginal site. Getting there requires a flight from Perth (2½ hours) or Cairns (3 hours). You will need to stay at least one night to see how the rock changes over the day as the light moves across it.

Surface interval

A stopover in Sydney

Not exactly on the diver trail, Sydney is the biggest and most cosmopolitan city in the country. Yet it is also a compact city where a stopover for say, two nights and a day, will give you a taste of life. Head down to Circular Quay, where the Harbour Bridge sits to the west and the Opera House to the east. Walk towards the Bridge and explore The Rocks, the oldest part of Sydney. The area is full of small museums, galleries and shops. Wander across to the Opera House, marvel at its bizarre architecture then head behind it to the peaceful Botanic Gardens. Back at the Quay take a public ferry across the harbour for a waterfront view. A trip to the seaside suburb of Manly takes 40 minutes each way or you could head just 15 minutes across to Taronga Park Zoo. Sydney's nightlife is centred on wild and raucous King's Cross but for a more peaceful evening try the Darling Harbour complex, the next bay east of the bridge.

Transport: Ferries are a fun way to sail the harbour. Circular Quay to Darling harbour is 25 minutes and AU$4.80. The city centre monorail system links many of Sydney's attractions, but not the harbour, and is AU$9 for a day pass.

Cocos (Keeling) Islands

Dive centres

Cocos Dive, PO Box 1015, Cocos (Keeling) Islands, T+61 (0)8 9162 6515, www.cocosdive.com. AU$180 per day. Packs including accommodation and flight from Perth cost AU$2299.

Sleeping

$$ **Cocos Castaway**, Cocos (Keeling) Islands. Well located Balinese- style rooms with kitchenettes and sea views.

$$ **Cocos Seaview**, Cocos (Keeling) Islands. A little outside the centre but pretty rooms with large verandas. Contact this and **Cocos Castaway** through **Cocos Solutions** www.cocos-solutions.com.

Eating

Accommodation is plentiful but there is a lack of eating places. However, all rooms have cooking facilities.

$$ **Tropika Restaurant**, opposite the pub, Cocos (Keeling) Islands. Decent cafeteria-style cooking, open daily unless the owner gets 'diverted'.

$ **Mutiara Café**, located in the airport complex, Cocos (Keeling) Islands. Opens for breakfast and lunch (Mon-Fri), with dinner on Wednesday night for fabulous Malay food.

Christmas Island

Dive centres

Indian Ocean Diving Academy, Rocky Point Complex, Gaze Rd Settlement. T+61 (0)8 9164 8090, www.ioda.cx. Great service and divemasters. AU$140 per day, 6 days/12 dives AU$815.

Sleeping

$$ **Captain's Last Resort**, Gaze Rd Settlement, Christmas Island, just along from the dive centre. T+ 61 (0)8 9298 8314. A stunningly located, couples-only cottage right on the cliff face.

Christmas has plenty of good eateries but accommodation is limited and booked up by short-term contract workers. Try **Mango Tree Lodge**, a B&B style guesthouse, **Christmas Cottages**, 2-bed bungalows with gardens, or **Indian Ocean Lodge**, a modern 4-bed house. The **Sunset** is close to the dive centre. Divers are often placed there but businessmen are given priority. Only book if they guarantee an upstairs front room. Contact **Christmas Island Tourism**, www.christmas.net.au.

Eating

$$ **Golden Bosun Tavern**, Rocky Point Complex, Gaze Rd Settlement. T+61 (0)8 9164 7152. Serves sunset with drinks and straightforward cooking.

$$ **Rumah Tinggi**, Gaze Rd Settlement. T+61 (0)8 9164 7667. Modern fusion food with a view over the sea.

Sights

This is nature at its most accessible: stand under **Hugh's Waterfall**, see the magnificent views from **Margaret Knoll** or watch the blowholes on the prehistoric south coast. Wander the rainforest and look for endangered endemic birds or dodge the millions of crabs. If you can be there during the red crab migration, you'll never see anything like it again. A 4WD is a must.

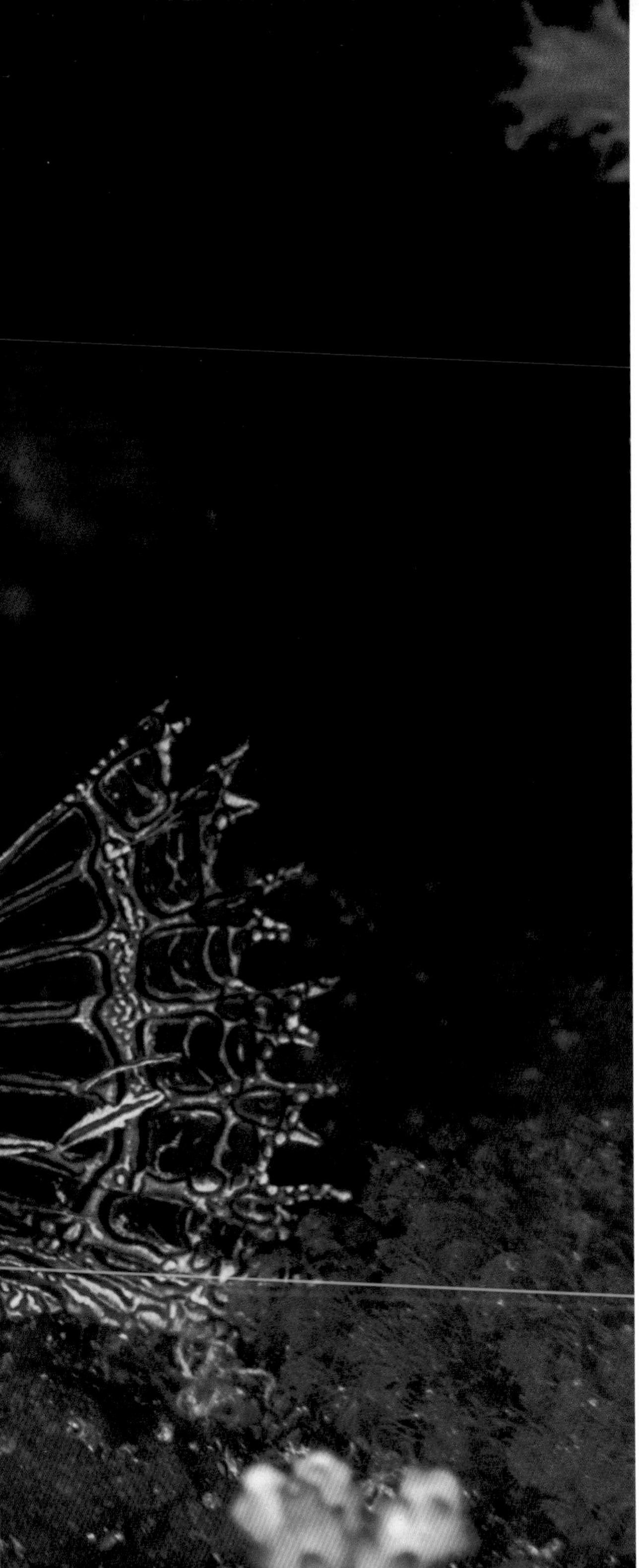

Papua New Guinea

Marine fashion victim: thoroughly eccentric and bizarrely dressed, the lacy scorpionfish, *Rhinopias aphanes*

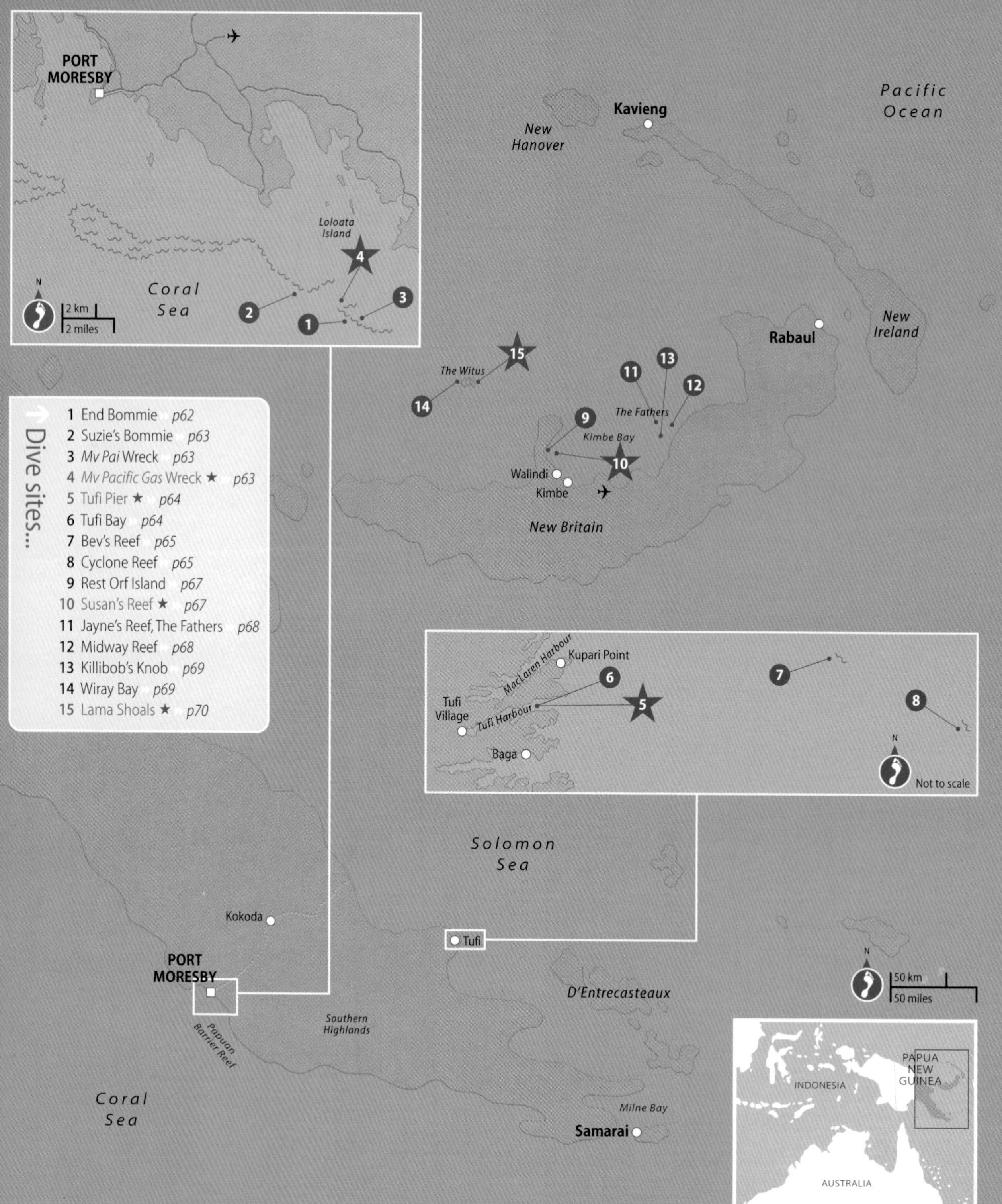

PORT MORESBY
Loloata Island
Coral Sea
2 km
2 miles
Kavieng
New Hanover
Pacific Ocean
Rabaul
New Ireland
The Witus
The Fathers
Kimbe Bay
Walindi
Kimbe
New Britain
Dive sites...
1 End Bommie p62
2 Suzie's Bommie p63
3 Mv Pai Wreck p63
4 Mv Pacific Gas Wreck ★ p63
5 Tufi Pier ★ p64
6 Tufi Bay p64
7 Bev's Reef p65
8 Cyclone Reef p65
9 Rest Orf Island p67
10 Susan's Reef ★ p67
11 Jayne's Reef, The Fathers p68
12 Midway Reef p68
13 Killibob's Knob p69
14 Wiray Bay p69
15 Lama Shoals ★ p70
Kupari Point
MacLaren Harbour
Tufi Village
Tufi Harbour
Baga
Not to scale
Solomon Sea
Kokoda
Tufi
PORT MORESBY
D'Entrecasteaux
Southern Highlands
Papuan Barrier Reef
50 km
50 miles
Coral Sea
Milne Bay
Samarai
PAPUA NEW GUINEA
INDONESIA
AUSTRALIA

Introduction

A remarkable landscape of towering mountain ranges where roads don't exist, where chilly highland forests plummet to lush, tropical coasts and idyllic tiny islands and sheer-sided fjords lead to some of the world's least explored and most impressive coral reefs. This is Papua New Guinea: high drama both above and below the water line.

Marine bio-diversity is just about the highest on the planet with some of the richest, most extensive and most pristine reefs in the world. You can enter the water anywhere in the country and it's likely that the only damage you'll find will be natural. There is no substantial fishing industry nor any illegal activities that affect the reefs.

There is instead just about every marine creature you could hope to see, from the tiniest seagrass pipefish to a pod of spinner dolphins. Wherever you choose to go, you will find an outstanding dive experience with consistent year-round conditions.

Back on land, it is said that there are still places where visitors have failed to tread and indigenous tribes still live traditional lives: shells and feathers are used as currency, men isolate themselves from women, wear gourds on their penises and spend years in special huts growing ceremonial wigs. You're unlikely to see a lot of this tribal culture as it's all so remote, though villages close to dive resorts are friendly and welcoming.

“” *PNG is perhaps the Last Frontier. It's not the easiest of places to get to but it is a destination for divers who want undiluted adventure.*

Papua New Guinea rating

Diving
★★★★★

Dive facilities
★★★★

Accommodation
★★★★

Down time
★★★

Value for money
★★★★★

Essentials

Papua New Guinea

Location	6°00′ S, 147°00′ E
Neighbours	Australia, Indonesia, Solomon Islands
Population	5,545,268
Land area in km²	467,498
Marine area in km²	2,366
Coastline in km	5,152

Getting there and around

Small nations like PNG have little in the way of mass tourism – such a bonus these days – but consequently getting into the country will cost. There's simply not enough competition to bring flight prices down. **Air Niugini** (www.airniugini.com.pg), the national carrier, has inbound flights from Singapore, Manila, Tokyo, Cairns, Brisbane, Sydney and even the Solomons. The flights up from Australia to Port Moresby are often **Qantas** codeshares (www.qantas.com.au) so you may end up on one of their planes. From Asia, flight times run at around six hours and are often overnight. The route from Singapore is convenient for divers originating in both Europe and America as it connects with many of **Singapore Airlines'** (www.singaporeair.com.sg) inbound flight schedules.

The cheapest route is Cairns to Port Moresby at around US$500 plus taxes. Singapore to Moresby return is around USD$1000 plus tax. Internal flights run in the region of US$200. However, bear in mind that these rates are held by very few international agents and can be hard to find. The good news is that the airline does allow divers an extra 10 kg of baggage.

There are frequent internal flights connecting the outer islands and sections of the mainland. These are run by **Air Niugini** or **Airlines of PNG** (www.apng.com). Dive resorts arrange airport transfers; just hop off the plane and look for the person who is looking for you. There are so few tourists, it will all be terribly obvious.

Local laws and customs

With its strong colonial influences, daily life in PNG has a tendency to feel quite westernised. Even if you get out into a local village, you won't feel too out of place. Missionary groups have had so much impact that many people regard themselves as Christian although traces of original culture still shine through. Life in the resorts is a casual affair with few pretensions. In Port Moresby the way to dress would be smart casual.

Traditional dancer

Language

No one really knows how many indigenous tribes live in PNG but there are over 750 languages so there is no way you could ever hope to learn even a few words of each! Thankfully, there is one that links all the tribal groups you are likely to encounter – Tok Pisin, an age-old mix of Melanesian and English. Of course, everyone in the diver orientated business will speak English.

hello	*halo*
see you later	*lukim iu behain*
yes	*ya, yes*
no	*no/nating*
please	*plis*
thank you	*tenkyu*
sorry!	*sori*
how much ...?	*hamas ...?*
good	*gut*
great!	*em nau!*
one beer	*wan bia*

and a computer mouse is **lik lik rat!**

Safety

Port Moresby has a reputation for not being the safest place in the world. You are warned not to take valuables out with you at any time and to keep out of the city centre at night. This area attracts a lot of poorer, unemployed people. Alcohol problems lead to petty crimes and occasional muggings. However, as divers you are unlikely to even see the centre of Moresby except on a day trip, which would be escorted by someone from your hotel. If you venture into the highlands take an organized tour with a guide who will ensure you stick to tourist-friendly areas. Around the coastal resorts, local villagers are welcoming and divers are often invited to events and festivals.

Health

Standards are high in resorts and hotels, so health concerns only include all the usual tropical warnings on water, sun, mosquitoes and so on. There is one thing to note though – the only decompression chamber in the country is in Port Moresby. As much of the diving here is deep, and because the water is warm enough to keep you under for long periods in a day, you do need to be very aware of what your dive computer is telling you. Be safe rather than sorry.

Costs

PNG is regarded as one of the world's more expensive destinations, mostly because the flight prices are so high. Although Port Moresby is a stone's throw from Australia, importing goods is costly and getting those goods to where they are needed can be a slow and expensive affair. There is little road transport across the mountainous main island so everything has to come by ship or plane. This can be amusing when Chef says, sorry no eggs, the plane is late! The knock-on effect is high rates in the resorts which are mostly run by ex-pat Aussies, so at least they never run out of beer.

As tourism numbers are comparatively low, there are few choices for either general tourism or diving. Most of it is high end. Resorts and liveaboards do, however, include meals and diving in their rates so although the initial cost may seem high, it's generally good value. A daily rate for a land resort averages US$200 per person per day with two boat dives while the liveaboards are over US$300. Some include alcoholic drinks in their rates. Value for money is a better way to judge this unique location, see page 13.

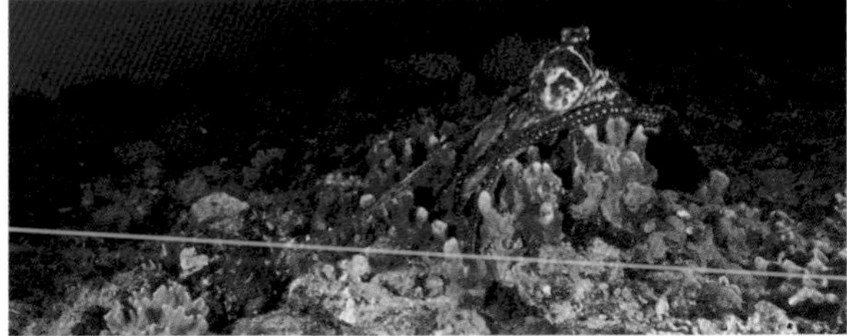
Mating octopus

Airlines → Air Niugini T0845 8387901 (UK), T1300 3611380 (Aus), T949 7525440 (US). **Embassies** → UK T+675 3251677, USA T+675 3211455, Australia T+675 3259333, Canada T+675 3224800. **Papua New Guinea country code** → +675. **IDD code** → 05. **Police** → 000.

Fact file

International flights	Singapore Airlines via Singapore, Qantas via Sydney or Brisbane Air Niugini from above hubs
Departure tax	Included in ticket but there is an extra 30 kina airport tax
Entry	Visa issued on arrival at Jackson Airport (25 kina) or obtain one from your closest Embassy
Internal flights	Air Niugini, Airlines of PNG
Ground transport	Provided by all dive operations
Money	3 kina = US$1
Language	English and Tok Pisin
Electricity	240v
Time zone	GMT +10
Religion	Christianity mixed with indigenous

Meeting a cuttlefish

Dive brief

Diving

The string of islands that make up PNG sit inside what is now being termed the Coral Triangle. This refers to the islands and reefs that stretch from above northern Australia through Indonesia to Borneo and the Philippines. Sitting on the edge of the Pacific Ring of Fire, this region is the most bio-diverse on the planet. There is, simply put, more of everything – 70% of all coral species found in the Indo/Pacific region, nearly 900 fish species and 500 corals. The figures sound impressive because it is impressive.

What's more, PNG also boasts every significant marine ecosystem and island type – from reef systems to sea beds, mangrove deltas and deep ocean trenches. There are over 40,000 square km of coral reef found along PNG's coastline, so no matter what your personal marine interest is, you are bound to find it somewhere in the country.

In such a hugely diverse environment what attracts many, especially underwater photographers, is the smaller reef building life, the nursery areas full of weird and wacky creatures. There is also a substantial amount of Second World War paraphernalia littered around as parts of the country were occupied by Japanese forces.

Bottom time

Loloata Island
A haven for many rare creatures and some spectacular wrecks » p62

Tufi
Where reefs get into recycling, and they win » p64

Kimbe Bay
Famous for its many iridescent colours on as many pristine coral reefs » p66

The Fathers
Picture-postcard images, above and below the water line » p68

The Witus
Dramatic diving around the remains of a submerged volcanic crater » p66

Another of the country's big bonuses is that there is no particular dive season. It matters little what time of year you choose to go as conditions are fairly consistent. A final consideration is that diving in this country is as close to unlimited as you can get. All

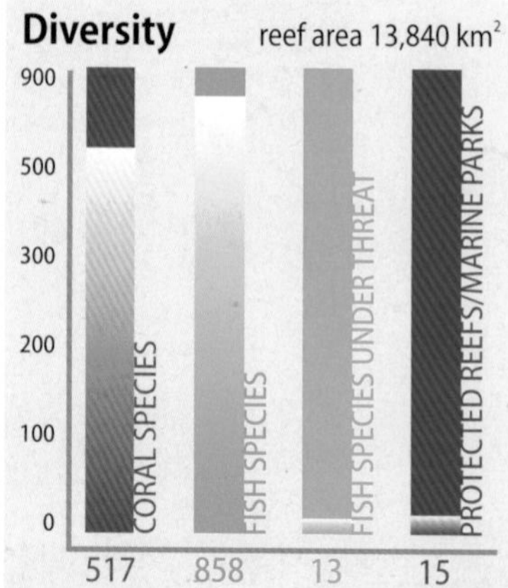

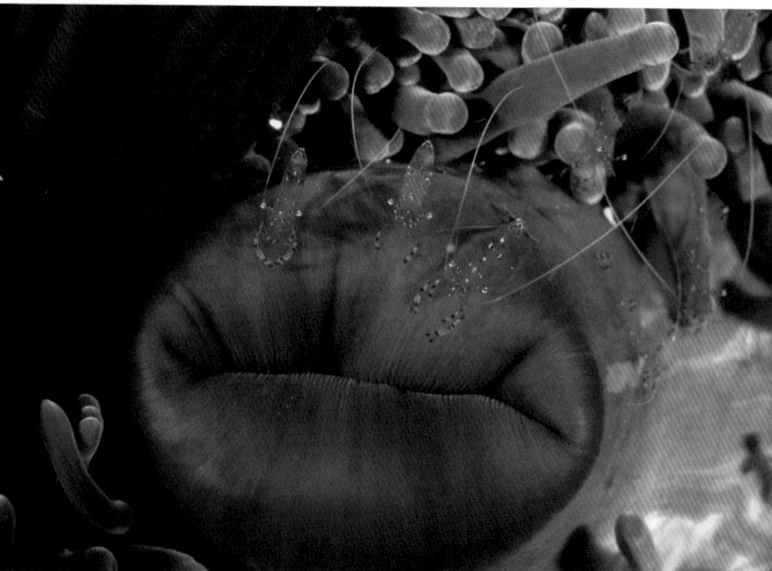

Pregnant commensal shrimp on the mouth of an anemone

Like many people it took us a long time to commit to going to PNG. Until we'd been we just couldn't see the value in upping our travel budget enough to cover the extra costs of the travelling involved. Of course, once we had done it, we realized there was no reason to think up excuses again. Now we try to find excuses to go and see another part of the country. This is a superlative destination for serious divers.

liveaboards schedule five dives a day, most resorts have three boat dives and you are welcome to shore dive whenever you like. Initial costs may seem high but this is a great value-for-money destination.

Snorkelling

Many offshore reefs tend to be very deep affairs with dives starting at around 15 metres and dropping off to unfathomable depths. However, as the visibility is nearly always fabulous, floating over these reefs would be quite a blast. There are exceptions to this; some of the reefs closer to Port Moresby, for example, have reduced visibility so may be less appropriate. On the other hand there are masses of coastal reefs that are just a few metres deep.

Buddy line

Surface marker buoys

Surface marker buoys should be an essential part of every diver's kit, yet the bulky nature of many reel types mean they are often the first item a travelling diver ditches. In some countries, dive centres have very stringent rules about carrying a safety device and some really don't give much of a damn. There are places that insist on bulky dive flags being strapped to a diver's tank – curious as they are very hard to use from this position. Others want you to carry extremely non-eco-friendly cylume sticks on night dives. Instead try a simple safety sausage on a long string which weighs nothing and rolls into pocket. And you can buy tiny night lights that operate with a battery. While it's important to respect dive centres who are looking after your best interests, make a point of taking your own safety devices and discuss your preferred equipment with them. You'll be glad you did this the first time you have to take a fin off in three-foot swells and wave it at a retreating RIB.

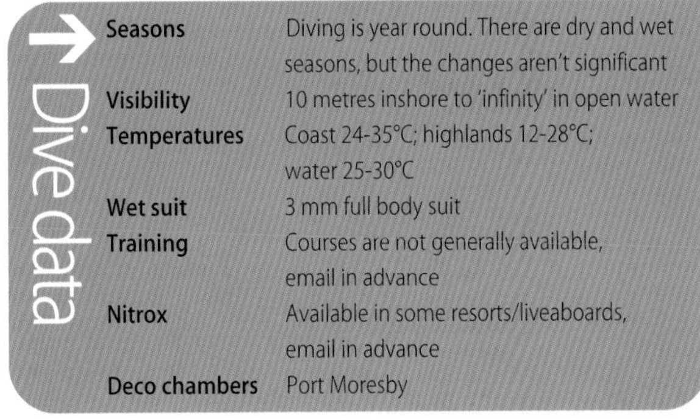

Dive data

Seasons	Diving is year round. There are dry and wet seasons, but the changes aren't significant
Visibility	10 metres inshore to 'infinity' in open water
Temperatures	Coast 24-35°C; highlands 12-28°C; water 25-30°C
Wet suit	3 mm full body suit
Training	Courses are not generally available, email in advance
Nitrox	Available in some resorts/liveaboards, email in advance
Deco chambers	Port Moresby

The big decision

When it comes to PNG as a destination, once you get your head around the comparative costs and distances, selecting a specific place to go to can be difficult. To go so far and only do a small part of the country would be a shame. To get the most out of your time, do more than one dive region. No one resort or boat is better than the other. All have their own style, whether it's romantic views from colonial bungalows or dive-your-brains-out liveaboards targeted at photographers. The diving is fabulous right across the country.

Colour and clear water

Loloata Island

Just south of Port Moresby, the nation's capital, is a little haven of marine splendour. Loloata Island Resort is under half an hour from the airport, just 15 minutes from shore and on the edge of the Papuan Barrier Reef. The resort gets a good through flow of diver and non-diver traffic which adds to its charm. One night you might dine with some fellow divers, the next with an Australian politician.

The island itself is a long oval shape with a steep central hill and a flat strip around its edge. There is nothing on the island apart from the resort which has become an unofficial wildlife reserve with rescued native animals and beautiful gardens. Bungalows line the water's edge and face the day's entertainment – also known as the sunset.

The dive reputation is one of a serious muck diver's haven with magnificent critters in every shape, size and colour, including almost guaranteed sightings of the splendid lacy scorpionfish. The reefs themselves are impressive. Hard coral growth is substantial, soft corals pretty and colourful. They host plenty of schooling fish like jacks, groupers and snapper as well leaffish and morays. Then there's the wrecks. Local waters are littered with them although they've mostly been scuttled over the years for the benefit of divers.

Unlike the rest of PNG, seasons here are notable. There are two doldrums – April to May and October to December – when the sea is calm and the visibility is better. December to April is wetter and June to October is dryer. Water temperatures range from 25°C in August and September up to 30°C in March and April. Diving is year round regardless of conditions as it is easy to find protected sites.

1 End Bommie

- **Depth**: 22 m
- **Visibility**: fair to good
- **Currents**: mild
- **Dive type**: day boat
- **Snorkelling**: yes

This site is a well known haunt for the *Rhinopias frondosa* or lacy scorpionfish. The main reef has a saddle that connects it to a smaller circular outcrop with lots of soft corals and pristine hard corals along the outside wall. One section is smothered in tubastrea, purple and white soft corals and vast numbers of anthias all darting in and out. There are fish everywhere you look. The flat reef top is where the divemaster will point

Magenta-coloured slender anthias

out the rhinopias – no chance of seeing one of these perfectly camouflaged creatures on your own. The resident one is mostly black with yellow and white patterns on his skin making him very hard to distinguish from the surrounding corals and crinoids.

2 Suzie's Bommie

- **Depth**: 27 m
- **Visibility**: fair to good
- **Currents**: can be strong
- **Dive type**: day boat
- **Snorkelling**: yes

A cone-shaped pinnacle rises up from about 30 metres to 10 at the top. Around the base are some good fans and plenty of fish but the further up you rise the thicker the fish life becomes. Giant sweetlips shelter against the tubastrea along with pairs of barramundi cod. Above are masses of anthias then, as you reach around 12 metres, you encounter huge numbers of oriental sweetlips, jacks, snappers, surgeonfish and batfish. These are all schooling together in a massive ball. A lone Napoleon wrasse hangs around with the other species. Down in the corals, there are leaffish in varying colours – olive, lime and silver – and marbled dragonets. Small longnose hawkfish free swim around whip corals and mantis shrimp run in and out of their burrows.

3 *MV Pai* Wreck

- **Depth**: 26 m
- **Visibility**: fair to good
- **Currents**: slight
- **Dive type**: day boat
- **Snorkelling**: no

This wreck of a small prawn trawler is 25 metres long. The mast rises up from the deck at about 20 metres to around 12 and is completely encrusted by tubastrea corals, soft corals – dendronephthya and gorgonia – in all sorts of colours. They all support a mass of anthias and glassfish. A surprising number of longnose hawkfish sit in amongst it all as well as some pipefish and gobies in crevices. The cabin is intact with fans and corals filling in the old window holes and some really big silver groupers hanging around inside.

4 *MV Pacific Gas* Wreck

- **Depth**: 39 m
- **Visibility**: fair to good
- **Currents**: can be strong
- **Dive type**: day boat
- **Snorkelling**: no

Originally owned by Pacific Gas, this cargo vessel was sunk in 1986 specifically to create a dive site. The currents that wash over her can be quite strong so she has filled up with lots of corals, mostly tubastrea but there are plenty of small soft corals doted around. The propellors are sitting at 45 metres and the main cabin at the stern rises up to over 20 metres. There is less coral cover at depth but plenty of jacks, snappers and a couple of really big groupers. Back up at the bow some gear wheels are exposed on the deck and there are two leaffish (pink and khaki) and a moray sitting below with a cleaner shrimp in his mouth. Travelling up the mast for a safety stop there are masses of anthias, sweepers and crinoids. There's even a resident dendronephthya crab hiding in some soft coral.

MV Pacific Gas

Sweetlips on Suzie's Bommie

Tufi

Of all PNG's coastal landscapes, Tufi is possibly the most impressive. As you fly in to the landing strip (aka playground and football field) you see a series of deep fjords that cut sharply back into the mainland. If there was snow sitting on them, you would think you were flying over northern Norway. Instead, the landscape is painted in shades of rich green; tropical forests leading down steep cliffs to deep, dark seas. Sitting right on the top of one fjord is tiny Tufi village.

Diving, and staying here, is a very special experience. Built as a Second World War base, romantic wooden bungalows surround the original structure. The views are to die for. The walk down to the dive jetty involves a daily greeting ceremony with local villagers. When you reach the jetty you get that first taster of the critter life that lives there. Baby batfish float just inches beneath the surface while just below is perhaps one of the best muck dives of your life. You name it, you'll see it here.

Not far from shore there are also some fantastic reef systems between Tufi and the D'Entrecasteaux islands. They are in gin-clear water, lush with corals and massive schools of fish that seek shelter amongst them. A long way offshore are several wrecks that are worth a visit if the weather allows. They are deep (over 50 metres) and trips are infrequent. If you miss them, it hardly matters as Tufi Bay has its own wrecks, reminders of the days when US forces were stationed here.

5 Tufi Pier

- **Depth**: 12 m
- **Visibility**: fair to good
- **Currents**: none
- **Dive type**: shore
- **Snorkelling**: yes

For muck diving aficionados, there is nothing quite like this dive. It is classic muck. Just below the wooden jetty are decades of detritus, from soft drink crates to old beer bottles and tyres. Bits of plastic net jostle with rotting 40 gallon drums but, no matter what ugly old bit of rubbish you look at, it will be a thriving marine colony. Kitting up on the wooden jetty, you can admire all the juvenile batfish floating right up near the surface. Descend to less than three metres to find handfuls of ornate ghostpipefish, pairs of robust ghostpipefish and pairs of hairy ghostpipefish. Inspect a soft drink crate to find nudibranchs crawling over it or an old beer bottle for a blenny or two. Seahorses and frogfish reside around the pylons. Hiding in amongst the algae are scorpions, lionfish and cowries. If you do this dive at dusk you may spot a pair of harlequin shrimp preparing their supper by killing a starfish or one of the resident mandarin fish that also come out to feed under cover of darkness.

6 Tufi Bay

- **Depth**: 42 m
- **Visibility**: fair to good
- **Currents**: no
- **Dive type** : shore
- **Snorkelling**: no

Heading downwards from the jetty past all the magnificent macro life, you first pass a rock where a pinnate batfish lives. Eventually you reach 40 metres and discover the detritus of the Second World War base. When the American forces shipped out, they dumped a lot of unwanted items into the bay. You can see interesting bits of broken metal, engines, chains and the remains of a patrol boat. There is a nearly intact Land Rover, it's screen encrusted with muck and small flat corals and just a few feet away is a torpedo tube, with the torpedo still in it. Nearby is a 50 mm gun and the hull of the PT boat which still has its engine. The inside is completely covered in cleaner shrimp and small cardinals.

Allied cowrie

Spinecheek anemonefish

Chromodoris coi nudibranch

7 Bev's Reef

- **Depth**: 32 m
- **Visibility**: fair to good
- **Currents**: none
- **Dive type**: day boat
- **Snorkelling**: yes

This is one of the best reefs in the area, although there is some damage on the top caused by wave and storm action. Around the edge are some good soft corals and as you circumnavigate it, you encounter several schools of mating surgeonfish. The walls harbour small critters like flabellina – and other – nudibranchs. Eagle-eyed spotters might see a crocodilefish or ghost pipefish. Some have seen white grouper with yellow and black markings. As you ascend back to the flat plateau, you are surrounded by a huge number of schooling fish: chevron barracuda, masses of spanish mackerel, schooling jacks, yellow tailed snappers, damsels, angels and fairy basslets.

8 Cyclone Reef

- **Depth**: 50 m
- **Visibility**: good to stunning
- **Currents**: slight
- **Dive type**: day boat
- **Snorkelling**: no

This large reef was formed in 1975 when a cyclone blew through and rearranged the existing terrain. The storm even created a small island that is now used by birds. There are actually two dives here: one on the pinnacle which is connected to the main reef via a deep saddle at 26 metres; the other on the wall which drops to 60 metres. There are a lot of black coral bushes all full of fish that sit on the branches like nesting birds. There are schools of yellow tailed snappers, rainbow runners and tangs, plus grey reef sharks at about 40 metres or so. At the same depth are a lot of very long whip corals. Coming back up to the main part of the reef there are a lot of good hard corals, which is surprising considering the cyclone.

An olive sea snake

Squid laying eggs

Harlequin shrimp feasting on a starfish leg

Kimbe Bay and the Bismark Sea

New Britain Island is just a 50 minute flight from Port Moresby and forms the northern barrier with the Bismark Sea. This is one of PNG's best known and most spectacular dive regions. Although it's not such an emotive way to do so, the best way to describe this area is with figures – over 400 species of reef building corals have been recorded in Kimbe Bay. This is more than half the total number of known coral species in the world. Plus there's around 900 species of fish. And that's just a taster of what it's like.

There are two options for diving here: you can choose between land based and liveaboard. Walindi Plantation Resort is located in an old coconut plantation that was established in the 1930's but became a pioneer dive resort in 1969. Besides the heavy focus on the marine realm, nature conservation is paramount. Bungalows huddle beneath a tamed tropical jungle, rich with rare orchids and facing into Kimbe Bay. The Walindi Nature Centre is next door and home to the Mahonia na Dari (Guardian of the Sea) Project which focusses on marine education and conservation.

Kimbe Bay is ringed by dramatic volcanic landscapes and it is beneath these that some of the more adrenaline pumping diving can be found. Heading off on one of the two liveaboards based here will take you northeast to the Fathers Islands or northwest to the Witus.

The **Witu Islands** are volcanic and rise from very deep water. Garove, the main island is horseshoe shaped with the harbour inside the sunken caldera. The waters here are incredibly nutrient rich and schools of pelagic fish are attracted to the currents. As interesting are the many small flat bays just off the coast, whose black sand seabeds are a haven to some weird and wacky small animals. Across in the **Fathers group** a series of volcanic cones protrude from the horizon. The Father is flanked by his two sons and beneath are dramatic, sloping walls . When the currents are running schools of barracuda, scalloped hammerhead sharks and even dolphins can be seen – and swum with.

Some say that the best visibility is from January to April but that seems an unnecessary statement as the comparison would be between excellent and really excellent. Currents can be strong though, a benefit to the marine life, but as there are so many dive sites avoiding strong currents is not a major issue.

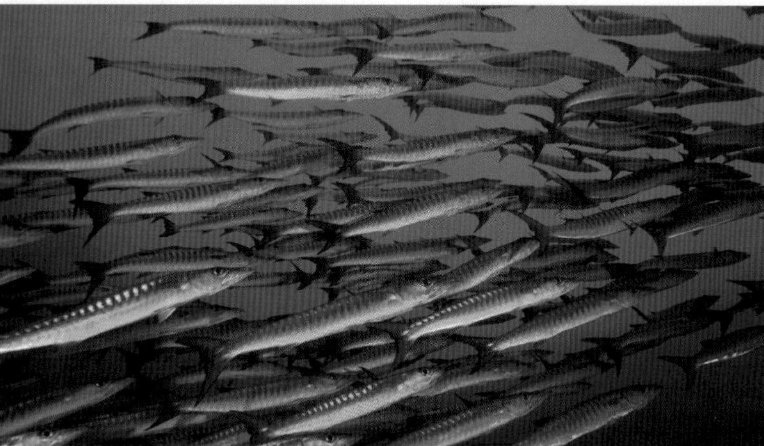

Barracuda by the score

Bright pink fans clashing with deep blue water

Conservation

Paradise found
Nature has taken an interesting turn here. This is the world's third largest rainforest: the jungles host as many bird and plant species as nearby Australia with endemic species like tiny tree kangaroos, enormous Queen Alexandra Birdwing butterflies and the world's largest pigeon. Perhaps most importantly, the islands are home to 38 of the world's 43 birds of paradise.

9 Rest Orf Island

- **Depth**: 18 m
- **Visibility**: fair to good
- **Currents**: slight
- **Dive type**: day boat/liveaboard
- **Snorkelling**: yes

Just 30 minutes from Walindi, this is a true picture-postcard island with a tiny, white sand beach. The beach dips down in a semicircle to a small reef wall which extends on either side. The sandy sea bed has patchy outcrops that support some brightly coloured soft corals and creates homes for critters such as dendronephthya crabs. Around the base of these outcrops you can spot crabeye gobies and other tiny sand fish like flounders. Titan triggerfish nest here as well so you need to keep an eye out for them. As you descend to depth there are some really good whips and fans and different shades of black coral that flourish in the currents. The entire reef is decorated with plenty of schooling tropical fish and clownfish in their host anemones.

10 Susan's Reef

- **Depth**: 50 m
- **Visibility**: fair to good
- **Currents**: slight
- **Dive type**: day boat/liveaboard
- **Snorkelling**: no

Just a little way from Rest Orf Island, this incredibly pretty site consists of a submerged ridge that connects a small reef to a much larger one. The channel between the two is what makes it such an outstanding dive. The currents that funnel through encourage the growth of an incredible number of bright red whip corals which coat almost every surface. One stand of whips is alive and dancing with razorfish who mirror the sun's rays as they turn their bodies this way and that, trying to remain hidden. Brightly coloured crinoids sit on the gorgonians and sponges and masses of fish hang off the walls. Longnose and pixie hawkfish are common residents as are angel and parrotfish.

Tales from the deep

While the Northern Hemisphere is choking on snow …

I'm on my back, foot slung up on my bookshelf with a stomach full of codeine. I'd just done a double back flip with a half-pike onto the bottom deck. Right on the side of my left foot. Right in front of the crew. Now, Nelson the Impregnator is in charge; the infamous Digger is fixing regulators with a six-pound hammer and Elsie, the divemaster, is trying to throttle him.

It is not a good time for this to happen. Our sole purpose for the next few weeks is to locate the best dive sites on the south coast of New Britain. We head off into the night to rediscover Lindenhaven, an island-studded lagoon close to the mainland. It lies straight off the Solomon Trench in the Solomon Sea, the third deepest part of the world's oceans. I already knew a couple of wide-angle dive sites there where purple leaffish were spotted, as well as Halameda ghost pipefish, winged pipefish, flying gurnards – everything seemed to be going off. Perfect. But I could only sit there on my backside and listen to everyone rave "did you see this…" "did you see that…"

Lindenhaven had also been home to a Japanese floatplane base station and there is plenty of war wreckage. We found one plane intact, upside down and in 60 ft of water. Digger had to open the bomb bay doors and was attacked by an exotic blue ribbon eel (pity it didn't get him) who had been guarding two bombs which, unbelievably, were still sitting in their racks.

Feeling very pleased with ourselves, we headed to Waterfall Bay, 75 miles back towards Rabaul. There we dived the Blue Hole, a magnificent place which can be found up a freshwater river. In the hole, the depth and clarity of the blue is almost impossible to describe. As the sun comes up you can look towards the surface from about 100 ft and see the dense jungle as if it was just above you.

We're starting trips to this region now. So while the Northern Hemisphere is choking on snow if you're looking for a destination in the South Pacific that is warm and dry, I'll be there. With an operational ankle.

Alan Raabe, Captain & Owner, MV Febrina

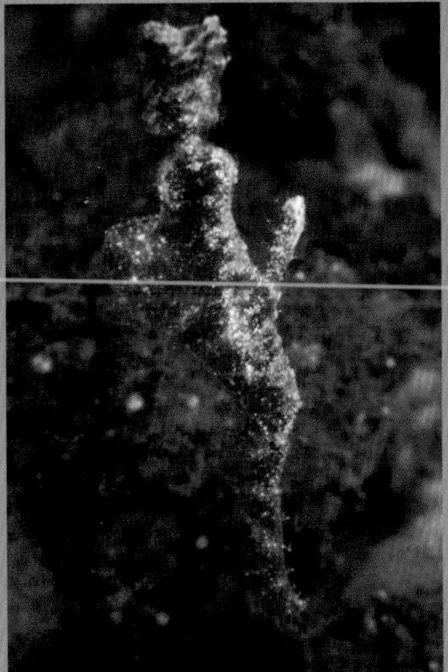
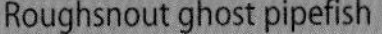

Roughsnout ghost pipefish

Ridged leather coral

Temperatures rising

Diving in other parts of PNG
Although this is an unexplored country, there are dive operations almost everywhere. Some are famous for one thing, some for another. **Milne Bay**, furthest east on the Papuan mainland, is credited with being the place that turned 'muck' diving into an art form. **Rabaul**, on the northern tip of New Britain, has a harbour awash with shipwrecks. Some were toppled by volcanic eruptions while others went down during the war. **Madang**, on the northern shore of the mainland, has highly varied reefs and is known for a great variety of fish life. **Kavieng** is on New Ireland but directly opposite New Hanover island. These two islands create a barrier to the open ocean and are swept with deep water tidal currents, consequently earning Kavieng the nickname of PNG's pelagic capital. Simply choose a dive style and go for it.

11 Jayne's Reef, The Fathers

- **Depth**: 36 m
- **Visibility**: good to stunning
- **Currents**: can be strong
- **Dive type**: liveaboard
- **Snorkelling**: for strong swimmers

This steep-sided circular pinnacle has strong currents running along on one side. There are whip corals and fans and swarms of jacks passing by. Despite the currents, it's easy to spot some minute creatures even at depth – a huge barrel sponge has sangian crabs on it and pygmy seahorses reside on a gorgonian known to the divemasters. These are as small as 4 mm so you need that divemaster to spot them for you! The reef top is quite rubbly due to the effects of tide and currents but this is a prime area for octopus. At the right time you can even see them mating, one extending a tentacle to attract another. Eventually you will see the male inserting his specially modified arm into the female to transfer his sperm packet to her. There are small hawksbill turtles who are very friendly, swimming right up to divers. In amongst the small corals are orang-utan crabs and tiny commensal crabs living in the algae.

12 Midway Reef

- **Depth**: 30 m
- **Visibility**: infinity
- **Currents**: slight
- **Dive type**: liveaboard
- **Snorkelling**: yes

Looking down over the top of this reef is like looking through air. The visibility seems endless. The reef is circular with a small saddle and secondary pinnacle to one side. On the main section the wall drops off pretty steeply all the way around and the hard corals are pristine. At the saddle a handful of grey whalers patrol between the two sections of reef with schools of big-eye trevally and surgeonfish circling above. Napoleon wrasse hover in the shallower areas where there are incredible beds of staghorn coral with anthias, fusiliers and damsels darting in and out. Schooling snappers dance around and you'll also see several pretty anemones beneath the boat. Macro life here is very good with squat lobsters in crinoids, dendronephthya crabs, popcorn shrimp on carpet anemones and several spinecheek anemonefish. Lucky divers might even spot a boxer crab!

Grey reef shark at Killibob's knob

Anemone and friends, skunk clownfish

13 Killibob's Knob

- **Depth**: 18 m
- **Visibility**: good
- **Currents**: medium
- **Dive type**: liveaboard
- **Snorkelling**: no

The tops of two coral pinnacles sit at 10 and 15 metres below the surface and between them is a cut through that drops to about 25 metres. This geography often attracts sharks who patrol the channel looking for supper. Now, though, they patrol because the site is used as a shark dive. A bait bucket is attached to a mooring which attracts both greys and whitetips. The sharks whizz between the pinnacles, ever hopeful that something will drop out of the bucket. (For those who don't approve, note that the bait bucket is sealed and the sharks are not fed). Once you've had your fill of shark theatricals, the side of the reef is also very interesting. There are some nice corals, with moray eels and porcelain crabs hiding out. Small rubble patches reveal minute boxer crabs but all the while the big action continues with tuna, barracuda and trevally passing by.

This tiny squat lobster is also known as a sangian crab

14 Wiray Bay

- **Depth**: 22m
- **Visibility**: good
- **Currents**: no
- **Dive type**: liveaboard
- **Snorkelling**: yes

This dive is in a tiny bay off Wiray Island which looks like something very primeval. The black sand bottom has the odd log, palm leaves and coconut husks, but little coral. The divemasters hop from spot to spot to show off the critters: halameda crabs, sangian crabs on a sponge, sand divers as they puff up their necks, panda clowns, mantis shrimp, popcorn shrimp in those cauliflower-shaped anemones and masses more. It is also an outstanding night dive with masses of cone shells – literally hundreds, wandering around. There are tiny dwarf scorpionfish and decorator crabs including one that covers itself with bright green algae balls, a school of flashlight fish and several wine-red sea hares. The biggest surprise though are massive platydoris nudibranchs, possibly the largest there is. These join together head to tail then travel at speed across the sand.

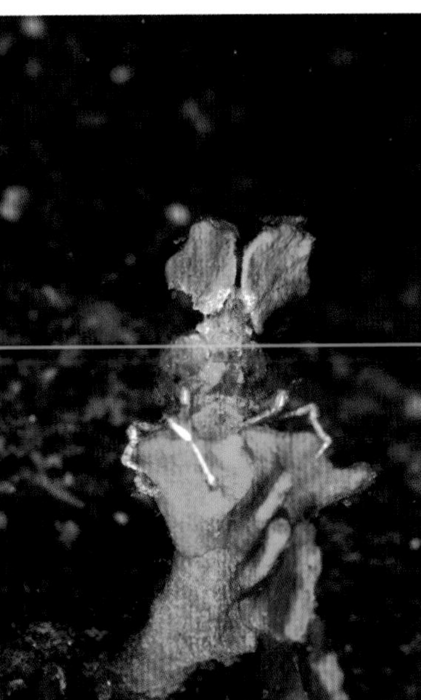

Halameda crab on halameda algae

Undercurrents

For a country that doesn't hit the average person's radar, PNG has had a highly eventful history. First inhabited by Asian settlers, the first European contact was by a Portuguese explorer who named the island *Ilhas dos Papuas* – Island of the Fuzzy Hairs – in 1526. Shortly after a Spaniard called it New Guinea because he thought the people looked like those from Guinea in Africa. Other explorers followed, their legacy showing in names like Hoskins, Bougainville and Moresby.

Several centuries passed before the Dutch claimed authority over the west of the island. Germany followed, taking the north while Britain declared a protectorate over the south. In 1906, administration was handed to newly independent Australia. During the Second World War parts of the country fell to the Japanese who retained much of it until they surrendered. Post-war, the eastern half of New Guinea reverted to Australia and Indonesia took control of the west. PNG was granted self-government in 1973, and full independence in 1975.

Nowadays most of PNG's concerns are either internal or with Indonesia. Troubles occur between mainlanders and islanders who regard each other racially and culturally distinct. At present the situation is calm and PNG's problems are more in line with global ones – catastrophic drought caused by El Niño and volcanic eruptions. In July 1998, three giant tsunamis hit PNG's northwest coast. Tourism is still in its infancy but you have to wonder if it will ever grow up.

It's always non-stop action on Lama, you can dive it at any time of day and there always seems to be something going on. But what really captivates is the clarity of the water – when we were there it seemed we were diving in air. You can just hang in the blue and watch the dramas of this prolific reef unfold.

15 Lama Shoals

- **Depth**: 45 m
- **Visibility**: stunning
- **Currents**: yes
- **Dive type**: liveaboard
- **Snorkelling**: possibly

Lama Shoals sums up the very best of diving in this area. The reef is a long oval and drops off to extreme depths. And when the currents lift the reef is revealed in all its glory. As you descend below the mooring, the black coral bushes are really showing off, tones of gold and silver flicker in the sun. Midnight snappers, sweetlips and longnose hawkfish nestle in the bushes and a few bigeye trevally hang around them. They are obviously stragglers because, as you descend further, you meet the most enormous school of them. This is just the start of the action. Further along the wall, another shoal appears up above then a third way below. A school of a barracuda stand off in the blue, possibly due to the large dogtooth tuna cruising along the wall, or maybe it's the arrival of some spanish mackerel.

The top of the reef is at around 15 metres and there are plenty of smaller creatures to balance out the dive. Dwarf scorpionfish nestle in the small corals and lionfish hover beside fans. Crinoids decorate the sponges, while schools of unicornfish and pyramid butterflies add to the colour. Good spotters may see small morays living in crevices behind schools of tiny anthias. Up above the reef top a school of batfish resides near the safety stop rope, good entertainment for the deco-stop you are bound to have after this dive.

Dolphins below *Febrina*

Whip corals are synonymous with PNG diving

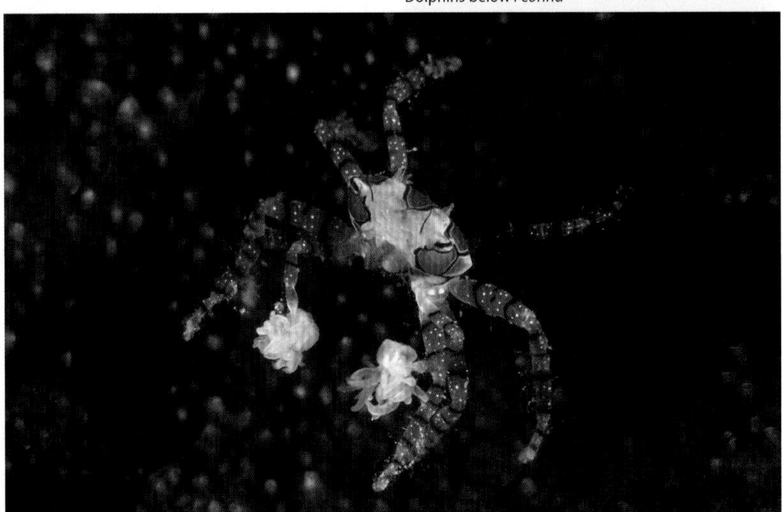

The utterly beautiful, oriental-eyed boxer crab

Crinoids on tubastrea coral

Although Papua New Guinea is an extraordinary natural environment, access to very remote areas is difficult and not recommended. Not surprisingly, most tourism is based around areas where diving is popular so from any resort you can access organized tours that will give a taste of the real country. For a complete listing of all PNG's dive operators go to www.pngtourism.org.pg/png/cms/diving /diving.htm

Loloata Island (and Port Moresby)

The capital is about 6 hrs from Singapore and 1½ hrs from Cairns.

Sleeping and diving

$$$ **Loloata Island Resort**, PO Box 5290, Boroko, NCD, T+675 3258590, www.Loloata.com. Straightforward rooms on a private island cum nature reserve just 30 mins from the airport. Rates include diving and all meals.

$$ **Airport Hotel**, Jacksons Parade, PO Box 1942, Boroko 111, NCD, T+ 675 3245200. Less than 5 mins from the airport. Popular and decent overnight accommodation, including courtesy transfers. The hotel's restaurant is very good.

Sights

While the city centre may be best avoided, there are a few small attractions worth seeing in Moresby. If you haven't time to explore the highlands or rivers, take a trip to the **National Museum and Art Gallery** on Independence Hill. The building is based on traditional architecture and the displays will give you a feel for art and cultural artefacts. The **National Capital Botanical Gardens** (8 kina) are even more worthy of a couple of hours as they have an extraordinary collection of tropical plants including palms, heliconias, cordyline, pandanus and native trees. Most impressive though is the display of orchids unique to Papua New Guinea. There is also a section with native birds including a few birds of paradise and the world's largest pigeon. Any driver will be keen to take you past the **National Parliament House**; this building blends modern architecture with traditional design.

The view from below

Tufi

Tufi is about an hour's scenic flight east of Port Moresby on New Guinea Island and right in the heart of fjord country.

Sleeping and diving

$$$ **Tufi Dive Resort**, PO Box 1845, Port Moresby, T+675 3296000, www.tufidive.com. Romantic, colonial style bungalows sitting on the edge of the fjord and beside a tiny village. Packages include all meals and diving.

Sights

If you were heavily into trekking you could walk the 96 km **Kokoda Trail** from Port Moresby to Kokoda, then on to Tufi. This Second World War trail was the supply route used by Australian Forces (ably helped by Papuans) in 1942 to stop the Japanese advance on Port Moresby, a key target as an air assault on bases in northern Australia could be launched from here. This would have seriously effected the Allied counter-offensive against the Japanese. Conditions on the trail were very bad and many troops on both sides were killed in the fierce fighting.

However, somewhat easier would be one of the half-day walks the resort organizes. You can head up the eastern ridge towards Mount Trafalgar, stopping at one of the local villages on the way to talk with the women and children (who just adore digital cameras!) until you reach the end of the fjord and can see MacLaren Harbour. On the way are hornbills, parrots and cockatoos and spectacular scenery. **Mount Trafalgar** itself would take another 3 hrs and need an overnight stop. Alternatively, you can reach Baga village by walking for 2 hrs along the fjord's western ridge. There are many other villages on the way and the one that's closest to Tufi, Kupari Point Village, often invites guests to join in traditional events.

Kimbe Bay and the Bismark Sea

Hoskins airport on New Britian is about an hour's flight from Port Moresby. Onwards to Walindi resort is 45 mins transfer by car.

Sleeping and diving

$$$ **Walindi Plantation Resort**, Kimbe Bay, T+675 9835441, www.walindi.com. Orchid strewn bungalows under tropical trees overlooking a beautiful bay. Resort packages include meals and diving. This is also the home port for liveaboards *Febrina* and *Star Dancer*.

Liveaboards

MV Febrina, T+675 9835441, www.febrina.com. Based at Walindi Resort, *Febrina* is a legend amongst liveaboards. 10-11 day schedules include Kimbe and the Witus and Rabaul to the south coast. Rates from US$350 per day.

MV Star Dancer, T+675 9835441, www.peterhughes.com. Part of the Peter Hughes Group and part managed by the Walindi operation. A large, luxury vessel that does 6-7 day charters. From US$300 per day.

International agencies

Dive Discovery, 7 Mark Dr, Suite 18, San Rafael, California, 94903, T+1800 8867321/ 415 4445100, www.divediscovery.com. Dive travel specialists based in San Francisco, with close links to all PNG operators and can issue and send Air Niugini tickets to anywhere in the world. They will also tailor-make a personalized itinerary.

The jetty at Loloata

Villagers visit *Febrina* to trade

Surface interval

In the highlands …

As most of PNG is smothered in steep mountains, almost half of her population live in the highlands. The incredibly lush vegetation and lack of roads has ensured that much of this region has remained well protected from prying eyes. Conditions are simple, with some tribes still virtually unknown to westerners and white people regarded with curiousity or suspicion. Villagers still conduct their lives far removed from first-world concerns. Some areas are considered unsafe due to tribal warfare though this is mostly a cultural event and rarely affects tourism. The **Southern Highlands** are easily accessible and are home to the Huli Wigmen, amongst the most photographed people in PNG.

… and up a river

Often referred to as the Amazon of PNG, the mighty **Sepik River** is 1100 km long and up to 1.5 km wide. It is a natural highway for the Sepik people and is flanked by mangrove swamps and flat lowlands. The Alexander Mountains and Hustein Ranges on either side create a unique ecosystem for plant, bird and animal life. What attracts tourists though, is the intensely spiritual nature of the Sepik people. The *Haus Tambaran* (spirit house) is integral to daily life: men hide sacred objects from the women and congregate to discuss village business. Canoes are carved with crocodile totems and legends recorded on cooking implements. The Sepik's unique handicrafts are a huge draw for the many who sail – or canoe – up the river to visit the tribes that live along its banks.

I have some very wild tales about travelling through Papua New Guinea to see her primitive and mesmerising cultures. I've been up the highlands to see the Huli Wigmen and the Mudmen of the Waghi Valley. But my favourite trip was by canoe to visit the remote villages on the Sepik River in northern PNG. This was after 12 days of diving and an unreal contrast. The only person who would dare to come with me was my brave friend Sandy. We slept in rural villages on the river (hotter than hell and humid to match, mozzies and no breeze) and had to get really creative with the non-toilet situation. Our guide was from one of the villages and all the people knew him – but they hadn't seen white people for ages. It was fun to see how they reacted to two white girls pulling up in dug-out canoes. My aim was to search out some old and unusual handicrafts, not the copies that you can buy down in Port Moresby, beautiful though they are. Our guide got the gist of what I was after and well after we went to sleep, people would appear from all over to show him their old pieces. Some I would not take as they were very important and ancient, regarded as spirits from their ancestors. I was amazed by my meetings with these very special people and I am so grateful that they wanted to share their past with me. I have a story from each villager about the items I bought from them so they will all be catalogued and maintain their ancestral story. Papua New Guinea is just an incredible place.

Cindi La Raia, President, Dive Discovery, California

Fjord-like vista of Tufi Bay

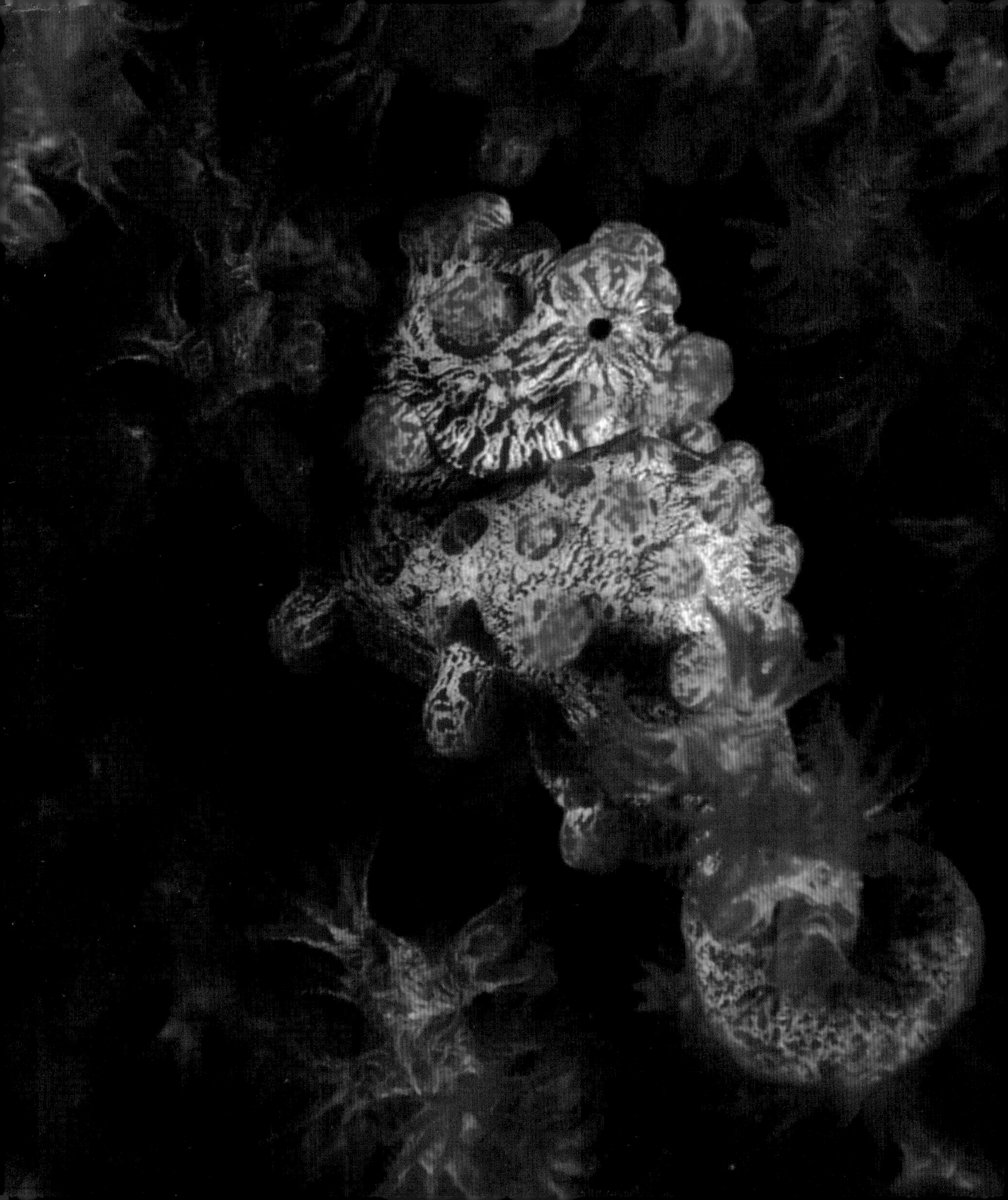

Solomon Islands

Small but perfectly formed: one of the diminutive pygmy seahorse family, *Hippocampus barbiganti*

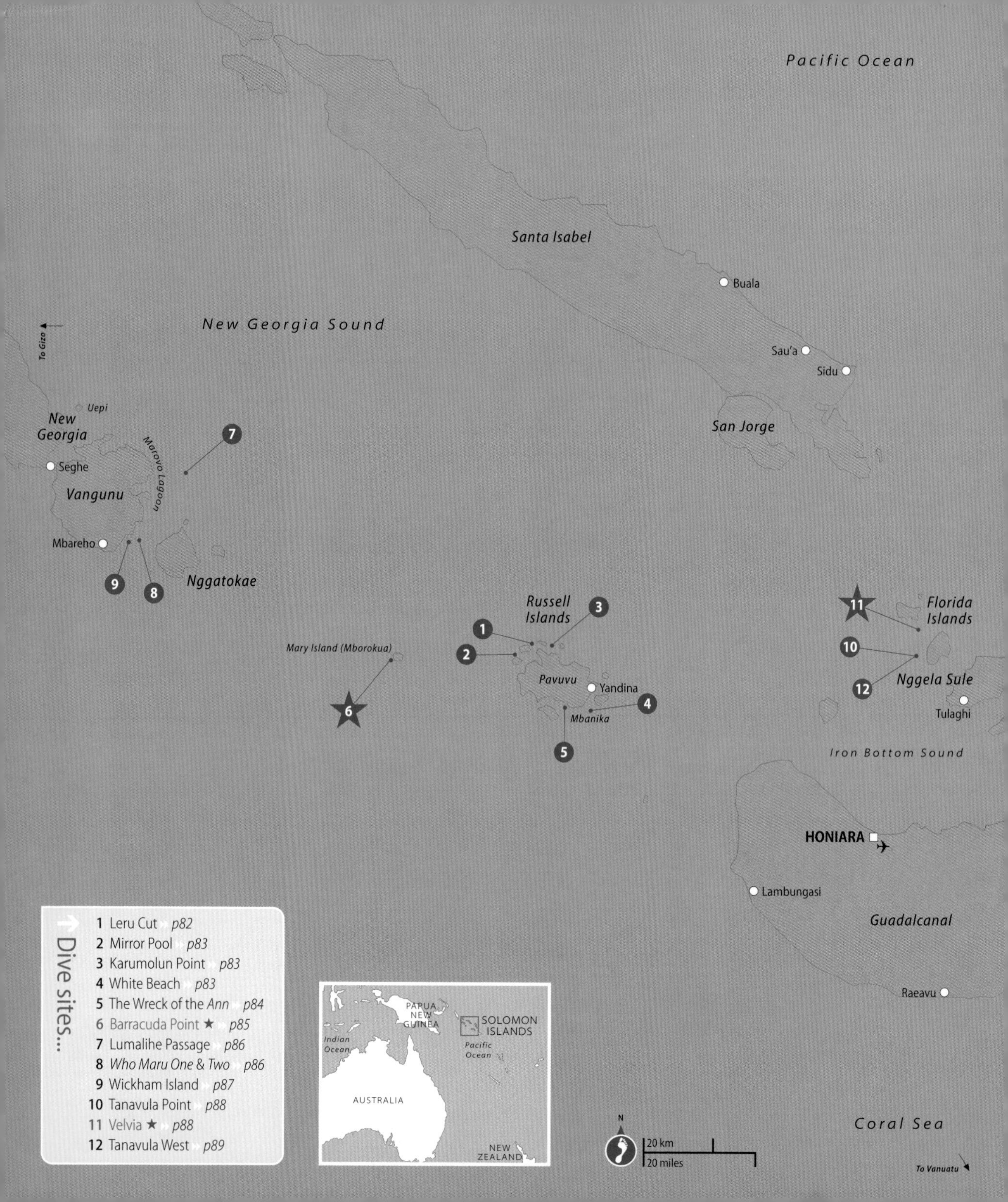

Pacific Ocean

Santa Isabel

Buala

New Georgia Sound

To Gizo

Sau'a

Sidu

Uepi

New Georgia

San Jorge

Seghe

Marovo Lagoon

Vangunu

Mbareho

Nggatokae

Russell Islands

Florida Islands

Mary Island (Mborokua)

Pavuvu

Yandina

Nggela Sule

Mbanika

Tulaghi

Iron Bottom Sound

HONIARA

Lambungasi

Guadalcanal

Raeavu

PAPUA NEW GUINEA

SOLOMON ISLANDS

Indian Ocean

Pacific Ocean

AUSTRALIA

NEW ZEALAND

Coral Sea

N

20 km

20 miles

To Vanuatu

Dive sites...

1 Leru Cut » p82
2 Mirror Pool » p83
3 Karumolun Point » p83
4 White Beach » p83
5 The Wreck of the *Ann* » p84
6 Barracuda Point ★ » p85
7 Lumalihe Passage » p86
8 *Who Maru One & Two* » p86
9 Wickham Island » p87
10 Tanavula Point » p88
11 Velvia ★ » p88
12 Tanavula West » p89

Introduction

Sail away from dusty, busy Honiara while the sun is setting and watch the sky turn to the colour of blood. Pass over Iron Bottom Sound, the scene of many a bloody battle just a few short decades ago, its history reflected in the day's end. Overnight, the scenery will change to a more soothing affair, shades of deep green and darkest blue.

The little known Solomon Islands are a rare treat for those who commit to discovering one of the few dive destinations in the world where there is a little bit of everything. No matter what your preferred dive style, be it reefs or wrecks, caves or walls, you will find it.

The waters around this string of islands saw some of the longest battles of the Second World War and the evidence is littered across the sea bed. However, the marine realm has engulfed the man-made detritus and reclaimed it as its own. Its presence is accepted by the animals, and there are certainly plenty of them: from the smallest critters to enormous schools of pelagic fish, you will find almost every marine species group.

Life in the Solomons today reflects little of its history. Gone are the headhunters of ancient times, the European colonists and the zealous missionaries, leaving behind the laid-back and friendly islanders.

“” We probably appreciate our time in the Solomons more since we came away. Looking back, it's hard to quantify the sheer variety and scope of everything we saw.

Solomon Islands rating

Diving
★★★★

Dive facilities
★★★★

Accommodation
★★★

Down time
★★

Value for money
★★★★

Essentials

Getting there and around

There really is only one way to get to the Solomon Islands and that's from Brisbane in Australia. There are other international flights but they tend to be from places even more remote such as Fiji, Papua New Guinea and Vanuatu. **Solomon Airlines** (www.solomonairlines.com.au) fly three or four times weekly from Brisbane. Whatever they may tell you, bear in mind that their schedules change frequently. Their website has no online booking facility so you will need to use a travel agent or **Qantas** (www.qantas.com.au) to book flights.

Once you have arrived in the capital, Honiara, internal transport is a little more straightforward. Solomon Airlines internal flights are frequent and connect all the smaller destinations. Costs are reasonable – Honiara to Seghe (for Uepi) is around US$70.

There is also a network of large passenger ferries and small motor boats, known as canoes. These are small fibreglass cruisers with an outboard and no shelter. They go almost anywhere but can take a very long time. For diving resorts like Gizo in the north west and Uepi Resort in Marovo Lagoon flights are far more practical. However, to get better coverage of the whole of the country's diving, you can make it so much easier by hopping on a liveaboard. That way all your transfers are sorted.

Language

English is the universal language though each village has it's own local tongue (there are around 70 in all). The one that links them all together is Pijin English, an age-old amalgamation of Melanesian and English. If you can string together a few words, normally shy villagers will open up.

hello	*halo*
see you later	*lukim iu*
yes	*ya*
no	*no/nating*
please	*plis*
thank you	*tanggio*
sorry!	*sorie*
how much is...	*haomas nao ...*
good	*nice tumas*
great dive!	*good fella dive*

Local laws and customs

The people of the Solomons are now mostly Christian, with variations from Anglican to Seventh Day Adventist. No matter where you are, the people are devout and you will be better regarded if you claim some form of Christian belief. Outside Honiara, the Solomons' way of life is based on a system of clans or families in which the headman rules. If you go exploring independently, it is best to contact him. Just ask the first person you meet if it's "Ok to be here" and if he's not the landowner, he'll take you to meet the chief.

Village traders

Solomon Islands

Location	8°00′ S, 159°00′ E
Neighbours	Australia, Papua New Guinea, Vanuatu
Population	538,032
Land area in km²	27,540
Marine area in km²	910
Coastline in km	5,313

The government put this overpass over a really busy road near the hospital to make it safe for people to cross. But, of course, no one will use it, especially the women as they can't risk being higher than the men on the road below. Then they decided to put a tunnel under the road, but of course the men won't use that in case there's a woman above! You'd think they would have learnt the first time.

Craig 'Monty' Sheppard, Manager, MV Bilikiki

Local villagers are open and friendly but women should always cover their thighs and shoulders. Some other curiosities are that shaking hands is thought unnatural, as is looking directly into someone's eyes. Tabu (taboo) is an important part of life and means both sacred and forbidden. There are lots of taboos that relate to male/female relationships, for instance, couples won't touch each other in public, so Western couples are better not doing so. Also, a woman mustn't stand taller than a man. If you are unsure of anything, just ask the closest villager whether it's an ok thing to do.

Safety

Like many small nations that are undergoing constant change, crime against travellers is rare, but increasing. You will only ever encounter the usual sort of petty crime and, generally, only in Honiara, if at all. There is a little bit of bag-snatching and isolated reports of hotel rooms being broken into, so ensure your valuables are not left on display. Personal safety is not an issue, but note that it isn't regarded as acceptable for women to be out wandering around at night.

Health

Health care in the Solomons exists but facilities are highly variable. The bigger issue is that there are few chemist shops in the country so it's important to have a good first aid kit with you. Obviously better resorts and the liveaboards will be able to assist if anything should happen but it's best to be prepared. Having said all that, there isn't much to guard against, with the notable exception of malarial mosquitoes. Use a repellent on land.

Airlines → Solomon Airlines in Honiara T+677 20031; in Gizo T+677 60173; in Brisbane T+617 (0)3407 7266. **Embassies** → UK T+677 21705; USA T+677 23426; Australia T+677 21561; NZ T+677 21502. **Solomon Islands country code** → +677. **IDD code** → 00. **Police** → 911.

→ Fact file

International flights	Solomon Airlines from Brisbane
Departure tax	SBD$40
Entry	EU, US and Commonwealth – valid passport required for stays of up to 30 days, return ticket required
Internal flights	Solomon Airlines
Ground transport	Internal flights by small planes and motorized 'canoes'
Money	SBD$7 = US$1
Language	English and Pijin English
Electricity	240v
Time zone	GMT +11
Religion	Various Christian denominations

Costs

The Solomons economy is not exactly buoyant. Both the post-colonial legacy and past political instabilities mean that tourism comes at a price. This is one of the reasons for going on a liveaboard – everything is included in the cost except alcohol, which is charged at US rates. Meals in Honiara are a hit and miss affair. There are a few Chinese restaurants where a meal can cost SBD$100 a head without drinks. In the hotels, a burger and chips with a beer will be SBD$55 and the quality is not all that high. Speaking of quality, the hotels themselves are nothing to get excited about. The top one in Honiara charges 4-star prices for 2-star quality and that theme runs throughout the city.

A steering wheel embedded in the reef

Dive brief

Diving

Presented with a nation that consists of 992 islands, all lush green and all ringed by coral reefs, you may feel a little overwhelmed by the prospect of choosing which will best suit your dive requirements. But the decision is easy simply because there's not much choice. The Solomons only get something like 5,000 visitors a year so tourist facilities haven't taken over the place and there are just a handful of options for divers. Honiara, Uepi Island and Gizo are the main ones but the most expedient option would be to combine a few of the above by hopping onto one of the country's two first-class liveaboards.

This is a dive destination that holds the rather impressive accolade of a little bit of everything. There are walls, reefs, caves and wrecks. There's big stuff (sharks and turtles) and schooling stuff (jacks and barracuda). There's a bit of history (Second World War wrecks) and, at the far end of the scale, there's even some muck diving (seahorses and inimicus) plus you'll find animals that have become famous drawcards elsewhere such as pygmy seahorses. What you won't get is huge numbers of each of these things. As the locals are first to admit, they have variety rather than quantity. In 2004 a scientific survey found that the Solomons also have far higher biodiversity numbers than was once thought, promoting the area to inclusion in the Coral Triangle.

They also have year-round diving. Like anywhere, there is a wet season, which runs from December to April, but the rain is intermittent and the water temperature is uniformly warm regardless of the season.

Bottom time

Russell Islands
Shallow caves, fertile reefs and a choice of Second World War wrecks » p82

Mary Island
Pelagic hyperaction around an inactive volcano » p85

Marovo Lagoon
The world's largest lagoon with a double barrier reef » p86

Florida Islands
Prolific and diverse reefs with exciting dives just a short trip from the capital » p88

Diversity

reef area 5,750 km²

Coral species	Fish species	Fish species under threat	Protected reefs/marine parks
494	1019	2	8

An unknown Second World War wreck

Roughhead blenny peering at the camera

We asked our cruise directors, Michelle and Monty, what had kept them in the Solomons for six years... that's six full years living in a tiny boat cabin, working 24/7 and showing demanding diver guests around. Their answer was pretty much what we expected: a little bit of this, a bit of that. Every dive has something a little different to the one before. By the end of the cruise, we couldn't have agreed with them more.

Dive data

Seasons	December to April – wetter, May to November – dryer
Visibility	5 metres inshore to 40 metres in open water.
Temperatures	Air 30-34°C; water 27-29°C
Wet suit	3 mm full body suit
Training	Courses available in Honiara, Uepi, Gizo
Nitrox	Available on liveaboards
Deco chambers	Honiara and Townsville, Australia

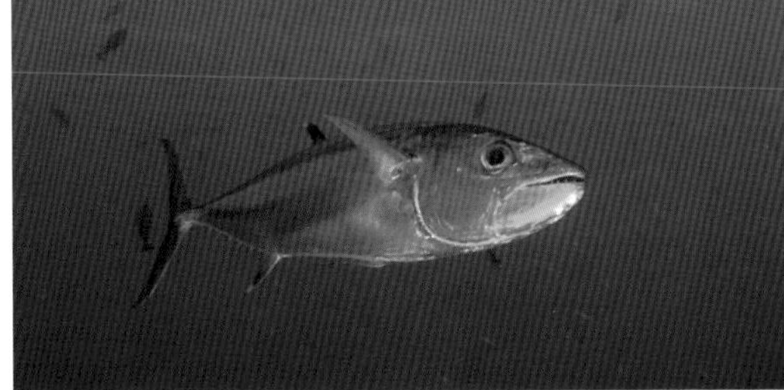

Dogtooth tuna at Barracuda Point

Snorkelling

Many reefs start just below the water line but are often murky in the shallows. The resorts have easy access to shallower reefs but these are not as impressive as deeper clear-water dive sites visited by the liveaboards. Strong currents are rare so you can snorkel almost everywhere, just check conditions first.

The big decision

Divers are attracted to the Solomons despite knowing little about it. It's one of those places that has a certain mystique. Others may have been and passed on the word or the reputation of one of her two liveaboards has filtered through. No matter what has attracted you, you won't be disappointed. Australians, who are on the doorstep, tend to go to the island resorts but to get the most out of this distant island chain being escorted around by boat is the best way to go. Either way the variety of diving is what keeps divers happy.

Buddy line

Buddy diving
One of the fundamentals of learning to dive is safety in numbers. Never go off on your own in case you get lost, your equipment fails or you run out of air. Any number of small problems could escalate into a bigger one and there you are, completely on your own with no one to help. One-Ocean-Buddies has become a popular euphemism for keeping another diver in your line of sight but remember that being able to see another person 50 metres away isn't going to help if he's not looking when you get caught in a fishing net. A 50-metre swim will seem interminable if you're out of air. The flip side of this argument, especially for solo travellers, is that you can't rely on a less experienced diver or complete stranger anyway, so you may as well be on your own. It's your choice but better to be safe than sorry.

White bonnet anemonefish at Mirror Pool

Dive log

Russell Islands

Heading northeast from Guadalcanal, the first island group encountered is the Russells. Regarded as having 'a thousand and one islands' the largest is Pavuvu, a steep-sided island covered in coconut palms. In fact, many of these islands are coconut plantations. The land is leased from the custom owners and planted with palms. The islanders then collect the fallen coconuts and take them to the main town of Yandina to sell.

The rest of the time the islanders live a traditional seabound life. Long days are spent in dugout canoes over the coral reefs that completely ring these tiny islands. Where there isn't a section of reef it's usually because there is a small cave complex. The geography of coastal Pavuvu is riddled with small underwater caves that open into tree-lined pools. The diving here is easy with little in the way of currents and the boat can avoid any strong winds simply by sheltering on another side of an island. This is also the location of romantically titled Sunlight Channel, a haven for the US forces in the Second World War and now a fantastic dive site.

1 Leru Cut

- **Depth**: 20 m
- **Visibility**: fair
- **Currents**: no
- **Dive type**: liveaboard
- **Snorkelling**: yes

Tucked into the tree-lined coast, this dive is a little murky due to sediment and run-off but at the same time is quite a spectacle. A deep cut in the reef wall leads back under the island about 75 metres and bends in the middle. When you get to the end you ascend inside a tiny pool surrounded by deep green jungle. The filtered rays of light are very moody and the inside of the cavern has pretty rock formations. Outside, there are lots of fish hanging off the reef wall, with large schools of rainbow runners, midnight snapper and bumphead wrasse. On the wall itself there are lots of smaller creatures, even small ornate ghostpipefish hiding in crinoids.

Bloodspot nudibranch

Undercurrents

The Solomons' Second World War wrecks

The country's capital, Honiara, sits on the little-known island of Guadalcanal. Little known except that is, to those who know their Pacific war history. The Battles of Midway and the Coral Sea may be better known but the battles fought here were regarded as pivotal in the Second World War.

The Japanese had been advancing through Micronesia and across the north of New Guinea. Unopposed, they made for the Solomons with the intention of building an airfield. When America became aware of this threat to the vital communications link to Australia, they decided an offensive was imperative. Guadalcanal was the first American amphibious counter-offensive of the war and highly risky as they were at the farthest extreme of their supply chain. It was also one of the longest battles in the Pacific, running for six months. Eventually the Japanese were driven off, with Imperial Headquarters privately admitting defeat and ordering an evacuation. They had already been gone for some time before US operations realised what had happened.

Naval losses off the north coast of Guadacanal were so great that the area became known as Iron Bottom Sound. There are a variety of ships and planes sitting at the bottom of the sound but the largest warships are beyond safe sport diving limits. Visibility is rarely good in this area. Elsewhere, the Solomons are riddled with Second World War era wrecks, some of which are more accessible.

2 Mirror Pool

Depth: 18 m
Visibility: fair
Currents: no
Dive type: liveaboard
Snorkelling: yes

Almost two dives in one, this dive starts at a small cave that has a shallow opening in the reef edge. When you swim back into it, being careful not to disturb the water too much, you see that the pool above has a mirror finish reflecting the surrounding trees and plants. Outside the cave is a maze of large coral bommies. One patch of hard coral is smothered in Paguritta hermit crabs – tiny crabs with an extended mitten on their claws that hide in old Christmas tree worm holes. A little further along is a bonnet anemonefish, thought to be indigenous to this region. It has white lines down its face and a spot for its hat. Whitetip sharks patrol along the wall, which has quite a steep drop, and part way along is a sloping rubble bed where cuttlefish hang out.

The cave at Leru Cut

3 Karumolun Point

Depth: 33 m
Visibility: medium
Currents: mild
Dive type: liveaboard
Snorkelling: yes

This small patchy reef runs around a tongue-shaped peninsula. In the shallows, the corals are not in pristine condition and neither is the visibility until you drop below 15 metres. However, there are many soft corals and a lot of fans that seem to do well in the currents that split at the point. Dropping right down to around 30 metres there are often huge schools of jacks that are mingling with a small school of barracuda. The fish life is very impressive with clownfish, gobies and plenty of adult damsels that are either guarding their egg patches or newly hatched juveniles. Hunting around on the seabed back up in the shallows, you will find numerous nudibranchs and many pairs of Randalls shrimp goby and their partner shrimp.

Japanese bow gun

4 White Beach

Depth: 45 m+
Visibility: fair to excellent
Currents: mild
Dive type: liveaboard
Snorkelling: yes

This absolutely stunning site sits in Sunlight Channel on Mbanika Island. The dives centre around a munitions dump from a US supply base that was hidden behind the mangrove ringed coast. When the troops shipped out they dropped everything from their base into the sea. In the shallows there are three flat topped barges. Originally lined up along the shore and tied to wooden pylons, they are now partially below sea level and smothered in small corals and critters. Under the nearby mangroves are schools of archerfish and you can sit quietly watching them shoot jets of water at the flies in the trees above. At the deepest point of the dive there is a tractor and a crane, and loads of mechanical litter – even steering wheels that are so encrusted in coral you almost don't recognize their shape. Slowly finning around you can spot old bombs, torpedos and masses of bullets. There is healthy crusting coral covering everything left from the dump plus small fish colonies, several mantis shrimp, some great gobies, weird opistobranchs, nudibranchs and pyjama cardinals.

Archerfish hunt in the mangroves

5 The Wreck of the *Ann*

- **Depth**: 36 m
- **Visibility**: fair to excellent
- **Currents**: mild
- **Dive type**: liveaboard
- **Snorkelling**: no

This wreck of a cargo boat was deliberately sunk just over 15 years ago. She is completely intact and sits virtually upright on a sandy slope quite close to the shore. In fact, you could do this as a shore dive. The visibility here is often very good so you can see right from the bow to the stern. The decks are covered in enormous elephant's ear sponges in several different colours. The wheelhouse is full of glassy sweepers and there are several lionfish prowling around them. There is just one gaping hold which appears to be completely empty but, if you take some time, you may spot both pipefish and nudibranchs. Back on deck, there are still some mechanical winches, all covered in crusting corals. Although there are few fish around the wreck is very impressive. When it's time to ascend for a safety stop, you can gas-off on the surrounding reef. It's a little patchy but there are several different types of clownfish and anemones. Some have cleaner shrimp and some porcelain crabs.

The wreck of the *Ann*

Tiny gobies reside on corals

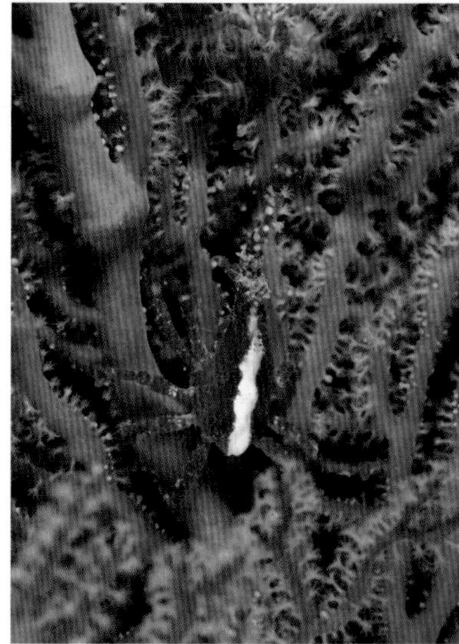

Spider crab on matching gorgonian

Mary Island

6 Barracuda Point

- **Depth**: 40 m+
- **Visibility**: excellent
- **Currents**: mild to strong
- **Dive type**: liveaboard
- **Snorkelling**: for confident swimmers

Due west of the Russell Islands is tiny, isolated Mary Island. More correctly known as Mborokua, this completely inactive volcano sits part way between the Russell Islands and Marovo Lagoon. Mary is ringed by coral reefs but her star attraction lies in an underwater tongue-shaped promontory that juts out from the coast and has sloping walls on either side. As you enter the water you are met by a huge ball of jacks that circle ceaselessly over the top of the tongue, then as you descend towards the point, you find another smaller ball. Continuing downwards there are small gangs of chevron barracuda then countless numbers of needlenose barracuda. Amongst it all, grey reef sharks patrol to and fro across the reef and in the evenings, hunt amongst the balls of jacks. Down at 30 metres plus, on the tip of the tongue, there are a lot of whip corals, fans and different coloured elephant ear sponges, and plenty of whitetip sharks. On the top of the reef, the hard corals are pristine and swarming with smaller, colourful fish as well as several Napoleon wrasse that follow divers curiously.

It was on our third dive here that we noticed the grey reef shark moving closer and closer to the ball of jacks. Suddenly, he whipped his tail and zoomed right into the middle of the ball. The jacks split into a million directions, like some fantasy firework, the predator accelerated away with his catch, and the jacks slid quickly back into formation. Just like it had never happened.

Tales from the deep

A treasure hunt

One thing that impressed us about diving the Solomon Islands was the diversity of dive sites. It seems that we encounter a 'Barracuda Point' dive site at nearly all the destinations we visit, but Barracuda Point at Mary Island in the Solomons was one of the most spectacular. When we slipped into the water, we were immediately in the presence of sharks, huge schools of jacks, bumphead parrotfish, other large pelagics and yes, even some barracuda. At one point, after looking up from video-taping a large school of jacks, we found we had become part of their school, being circled by hundreds of fish. While we love to see the large things, we are equally thrilled by small critters as well. Our favorite critter dive was White Beach. This site was used to distribute supplies during the Second World War to the US marines on Guadalcanal. All the equipment left behind by the United States was pushed into the ocean, creating an artificial reef inhabited by weird and wonderful animals. This site reminded us of a treasure hunt of sorts, with the treasure being scads of beautiful nudibranchs, pipefish, lionfish and several species of clownfish. A bonus for us was finding these weird and beautiful critters hiding among the abandoned jeeps, mortar shells, barges and other artifacts.

Steve and Suzanne Turek, Redding, California

Jacks away

Young humphead wrasse

Lionfish displaying

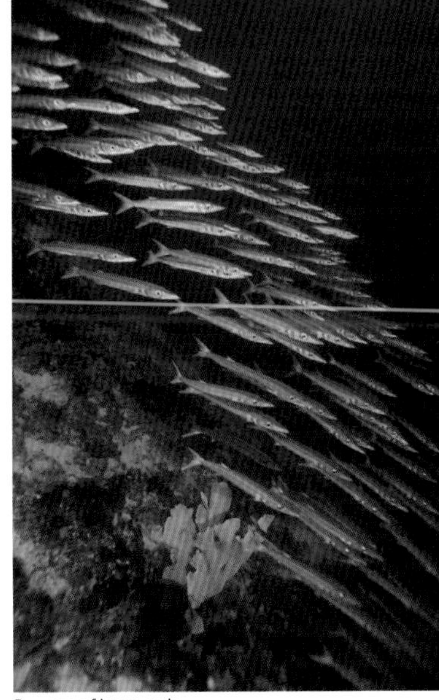

Swarms of barracuda

Marovo Lagoon

One of the largest lagoon systems in the world, Marovo is unusual in that it has a clearly defined double barrier reef. This complex reef system, running about 100 km from one end to the other, is bordered by several substantial volcanic islands – New Georgia, Vangunu and Nggatokae – and on the other by a barrier reef made up of several hundred islands.

Inside the lagoon there are mangrove islets and sand cays, raised reefs with extensive mangrove forests and freshwater swamp forests. Rivers and streams carry sediments off the volcanic slopes of all three islands and create a coastal plain with estuaries and deltas along the southwestern edge. The north and eastern edges of the lagoon have a string of narrow barrier islands which form a series of elevated reefs. In the south, the islands form the double barrier with the two chains of islands separated by waters up to 80 metres deep.

Much of the diving is inside the lagoon or in the channels that lead in and out. The water is shallow and nutrient rich so visibility is rarely fantastic, certainly not much over 20 metres. Some of the barrier islands, like Uepi, which are long, narrow islets, sit between the ocean-facing fringing reefs and lagoon-side fringing reefs. Only about 20 islands are inhabited, with coconut farming and fishing being the main cash earners. The lagoon has been promoted as a potential World Heritage Site due to its incredible environmental diversity.

Corals, sponges and crinoids

7 Lumalihe Passage

- **Depth**: 36 m
- **Visibility**: fair
- **Currents**: mild to medium
- **Dive type**: liveaboard
- **Snorkelling**: yes

This channel between two of the uninhabited islands that edge Marovo has several dive options as you can travel along both sides and the outer walls on either incoming or outgoing tides. The channel walls are steep sided and eventually drop to 50 metres or so on the outside of the lagoon. There are plenty of fans and soft corals making the site really colourful although the visibility can be low due to run-off from the lagoon during tide changes. Several fans have the Denise pygmy seahorse on them and there is a resident black leaffish. Travelling along the wall, small fish include longnose hawkfish and decorated dartfish. On the top of the wall is a sandy channel coated in garden eels and surrounded by small coral outcrops. Amongst them are bloodspot nudibranchs, moray eels, small bumphead parrotfish and crocodilefish.

Elephant ear sponge in deep water

8 *Who Maru One* and *Two*

- **Depth**: 40 m
- **Visibility**: poor to fair
- **Currents**: slight
- **Dive type**: liveaboard
- **Snorkelling**: no

All Japanese warships were named after a place and tagged *Maru*, meaning return. The theory was that the boat would then return home safely but these two cargo boats didn't and no one knows what they were called originally. They sit a few hundred metres apart from each other in a section of the lagoon where the Japanese moored their supply ships. The first sits on the sand at 40 metres. On the bow there is an anti-aircraft gun and, just below, the anchor is still in its hawser. At the stern, there is a huge gash in the side where it was torpedoed and you can see signs of the ship's original purpose such as cable reels and winches. The wreck is covered with a lot of black coral, longnose hawkfish and small yellow damsels. On the mast, there is a circular depression with a coral trout and Debelius shrimp. The second vessel is similar but in shallower water. The Japanese version of a 50 mm Howitzer sits on the bow. You can see the gash where a torpedo went through one side of the hull and then bent the other side out of shape. The structure is also smothered in lots of yellow and white black coral bushes and plenty of fish.

9 Wickham Island

- **Depth**: 28 m
- **Visibility**: poor to good
- **Currents**: medium
- **Dive type**: liveaboard
- **Snorkelling**: unlikely

Wickham is an incredibly pretty island, a classic tropical speck of white beach backed by greenery. The dive is just the opposite, a little murky and definitely 'mucky'. It starts at a small promontory that leads away from the beach and drops quite sharply to over 30 metres. The wall is covered in good fans and soft corals, crinoids and whips. It's all very colourful and pretty but the real action starts once you rise back up to the sand slope that extends from the beach. At depths of around 12-15 metres the whole seabed turns into a fantastic muck dive. There are more varieties of shrimp than you would care to name, similarly gobies in the sand and then there are harlequin crabs, seahorse, inimicus – or devilfish – and mantis shrimps. You can even spot some curious commensal relationships such as a black cucumber with two tiny fish living on it.

Brightly coloured reef

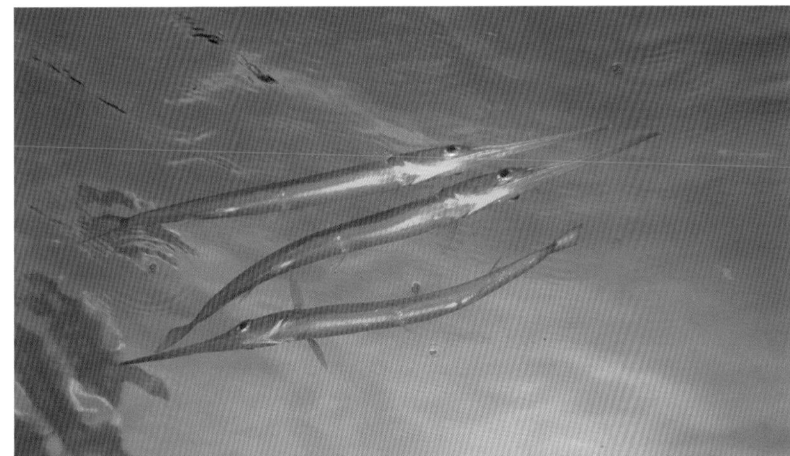

Needlefish hover just below the surface

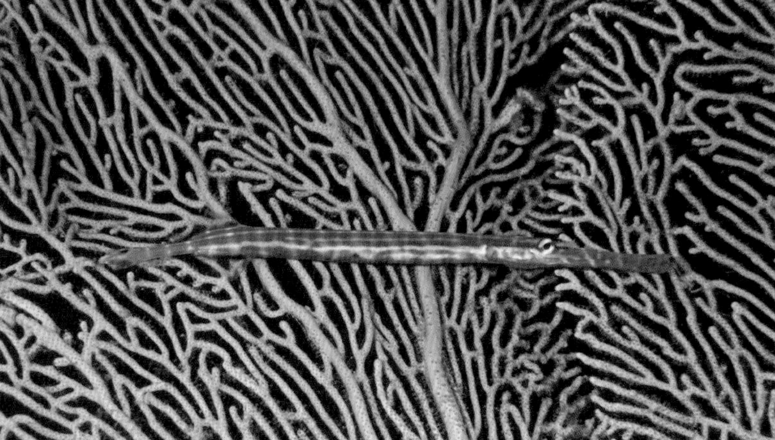

Trumpetfish hovering over fans

Second World War bullets create a home for a blenny

Florida Islands

The closest group of islands to Honiara, the Floridas border the opposite side of Iron Bottom Sound. Just 90 minutes or so by motor canoe from the capital, this group is less well known as a dive destination. The main island of Nggela Sule was garrisoned by the Japanese as they hoped to build a seaplane base nearby. The Americans liberated the area and it became a base for the US war effort in the Pacific. Once the seat of the British administration, Tulagi was destroyed in the heavy fighting.

The impact of the war was great with almost all of the pre-war plantations destroyed. These had been the mainstay of the local economy and little was done to re-establish them or introduce other forms of employment for the islanders. The islands are now very quiet places with little happening other than a bit of dive tourism. The diving, however, is far from quiet, for here are some of the country's most exciting and diverse reefs.

Parrotfish in cool shades

10 Tanavula Point

- **Depth**: 28 m+
- **Visibility**: good
- **Currents**: mild to strong
- **Dive type**: liveaboard
- **Snorkelling**: unlikely

This long sloping reef is dog-legged and drops from about 12 metres down to 40 metres. At the start it's covered in fans and patchy coral. There are some huge pink gorgonians that are known homes for the barbiganti pygmy seahorse and it's possible to spot both juvenile and adult barramundi cod. As you travel around the crook in the reef, the currents pick up. You may get caught in a pressure point where the currents merge but this attracts some pelagic life – sharks are often spotted out in the blue and occasionally eagle rays fly past. There are also some very large schools of fish that take advantage of the currents. These include rainbow runners, jacks, bumphead parrots, surgeon fish, snappers and more whitetip sharks.

Whip corals in rosy tones

11 Velvia

- **Depth**: 35 m+
- **Visibility**: good
- **Currents**: generally strong
- **Dive type** : liveaboard
- **Snorkelling**: unlikely

Named after the photographers' favourite film, this open sea mound has a flat top with isolated coral mounds but is mostly sand and coral rubble. However, the sides drop all around to walls rich with life and fans. The deeper you go, the more lush it becomes. Nestling in the cracks and crevices are large green morays and several lobsters. There are sharks off in the blue but the focus is more on small creatures – lots of nembrotha nudibranchs, octopus and mantis shrimp plus masses of nesting fish. Damselfish are particularly active and you can see them herding newly born babes just millimetres long right up to youngsters of an inch or so. Aggressive sergeant majors also guard their eggs while clownfish couples can be spotted aerating the next generation.

Baby batfish with orange rim

12 Tanavula West

- **Depth**: 30 m
- **Visibility**: good
- **Currents**: generally strong
- **Dive type**: liveaboard
- **Snorkelling**: unlikely

A wide, gently sloping plateau starts at about 12 metres and then drops off to a sharper slope and wall. On the slope there are coral bommies interspersed with soft corals, fans and whips. The edge of the plateau then leads towards a corner in the reef where two bommies sit beside each other. There is a small overhang in the larger one where a turtle tucks itself in to avoid the current that takes off as soon as you pass this point. The dive then becomes a rapid drift over a section of flat reef to a broad rubble patch where there is often a school of blacktip sharks milling round.

MV Bilikiki

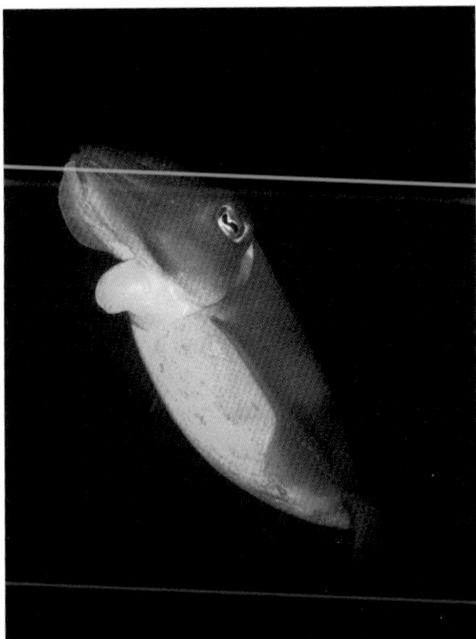
Cuttlefish at night

Tales from the deep

Seven year itch?

We have a dive site that is consistently good for macro subjects. It's called Velvia which will strike a chord with all the photographers out there. Nudibranchs, stonefish, octopus, cuttlefish, anemones, mantis shrimp, caledonian stingers, scorpionfish, crocodilefish, moray eels, crabs, shrimps – I could go on and on, but the things I have mentioned are generally seen by at least one diver on every dive, not to mention the more unusual things that frequently inhabit the dive site. We constantly witness unusual events but with fairly ordinary creatures which continually increases my appreciation and admiration for nature.

It was octopus mating time and within about 30 minutes I had seen around 10 pairs of octopus. They were as bold as brass and had no fear of divers or bubbles. I settled in on the sandy bottom to watch a female play with two males. She was perched on a rocky coral head luring the boys to her, but when they approached she would slither into a crevice and just leave out a tentacle. When one male approached her, the other would chase him away. This went on for 20 minutes, until she tired of it and darted off.

One male followed her, but the other looked a little shell-shocked and just perched up high with his legs straight less than a metre away from me. I slowly moved closer – expecting him at any moment to take cover or propel away – until I got face to face with him. This is not how Solomon octopii normally act. They are supposed to be shy and retiring. This made me curious, so slowly – and apprehensively I might add – I reached out and gave him a little rub between the eyes with my finger. Lo and behold, the cheeky little thing seemed to actually like it. He leaned into my finger and kind of moved his head around like a dog getting a good scratch behind the ears. My dive was soon over, but that is one encounter I will never forget.

Michelle Gaut,
Manager, MV Bilikiki

Drying out

To be honest, these islands are not packed full of things to do apart from admire the delightful scenery. The most you will find in the way of history or culture is in the capital, Honiara.

Honiara

Dive centres

If you are stuck in Honiara for a couple of days and want to dive one of the accessible wrecks in Iron Bottom Sound, ask at your hotel for information on up-to-date facilities as there currently does not appear to be a dive operator in the city. You can, however, stay in the Florida Islands at **Tulagi Dive Centre** (www.tulagidive.com.sb), which has simple accommodation and can access both local wrecks and the ones in Iron Bottom Sound.

Sleeping

$$ Kitano Mendana, Mendana Av, Honiara, T+67720071. Opposite the museum and on the only stretch of town beach, this '4-star' hotel is of a surprisingly low standard and overpriced. Booking a beach view will get you a better room but ending up with what you book is a game of chance.

$ King Solomon, Hibiscus Av, Honiara T+67721205. Up the hill behind town – also rundown but cheaper. Top floor rooms have a nice view.

Liveaboards

Bilikiki Cruises, office on Mendana Av, T+705 3632049, www.bilikiki.com. Canadian-owned Bilikiki Cruises run 2 first-class liveaboards, *Bilikiki* and *Spirit of the Solomons*. The boats run different itineraries. *Bilikiki* has all en suite cabins, while *Spirit* has a mixture of en suite and shared. Both have unparalleled service and fabulous food.

Eating

Both the above hotels have restaurants and snack bars where a burger and chips meal costs from SBD$55. There are several small Chinese restaurants along the main strip and the **Lime Lounge** café opposite the main pier does a nice line in coffee, cakes and sandwiches.

> ## Temperatures rising
>
> 
>
> **Vanuatu**
>
> A couple of hours from Honiara is another not-so-well-known island group, Vanuatu. Like the Solomons, it's familiar to those who know their Second World War history and to divers who have read about the *President Coolidge*. This American luxury liner was co-opted into service then sunk accidentally as she attempted to approach Espirito Santo with reinforcements for the battles at Guadalcanal. Now, she is the largest, most intact diveable wreck in the world and said to make the trip to Vanuatu worthwhile despite the reefs there not being in their Vanuatu is just 2-3 hours from Australia and New Zealand, www.vanuatutourism.com.

Sights

The capital of the Solomons is **Honiara**, a small, hot and dusty city, with (as one of our American buddies says) few redeeming features. With apologies to the local people, who are very friendly, Honiara is worth little more than a night. Chances are you will be forced to stay a night due to the flight schedule. While you are there, drop into the tiny museum and see the miniscule displays, then wander the shops along the main road. If you are interested in Second World War history, visit the US Memorial at Skyline Ridge, with its description of the Guadalcanal Campaign. The Japanese Peace Memorial on Mt Austin has panoramic views over the capital, Iron Bottom Sound and the Florida Islands. There is also a casino 10 mins from the harbour back towards the airport. Everything of note in town is within walking distance. For everything else a taxi would probably be easiest. They are not metered so negotiate a price for a tour.

Island visits From your liveaboard, several visits to local villages are scheduled. These stops of an hour or two are perfect for a glimpse of village life. Homes are still built traditionally with thatching and local timbers and the islanders are very proud of the way their villages look. Every house has a tended garden with orchids displayed much like the average English garden would have roses. You are usually met by children carrying flowers and the giving of small gifts such as pens and toothbrushes is appreciated. Wander the daily fruit and vegetable market, where the women sell the surplus from their own gardens, and then the fantastic displays of handicrafts brought in by local craftsmen. Carved wooden bowls and masks are superlative but the prices are far higher than you would expect in similar countries. Bartering is expected and you can also take things like old snorkelling gear to part exchange for handicrafts. As these people rely on fishing for their diet an old snorkel and mask is a useful swap. It's also likely that you will experience one of those traditional song and dance afternoons as the local people are striving to keep their traditions alive by performing age-old dances for the passing tourists. It is amusing to see lengths of plumbing pipe substituted for bamboo canes to create musical instruments.

Visits from the islanders One of the charms of being on a liveaboard in the Solomons is the frequent visits from the Islanders. No matter what region you are in, local people come out to visit the big ship. Especially for the children, this is quite an event. They paddle out in their wooden dugouts to trade vegetables and flowers, watch the divers or simply have a chat. The crew of *Bilikiki* take an active role in the lives of these people both commercially and personally.

Marovo Lagoon

Sleeping and diving

$$ **Uepi Island Resort**, www.uepi.com. Sitting on the edge of the Marovo Lagoon, it has simple wooden bungalows. There is an onsite dive centre, which is SSI accredited for courses. Rooms start at US$160 and a dive is US$50. Bookings through **Dive Discovery** (see below).

Gizo

Sleeping and diving

$$ **The Gizo Explorer Hotel** and **Dive Gizo**, T+67760199, www.divegizo.com. On the waterfront in the centre of town. Seven night packages including accommodation and diving start at US$900. Contact **Dive Discovery** (below).

International agents

Dive Discovery, 7 Mark Dr, Suite 18, San Rafael, California, 94903, T+1 (1)800 8867321/ 415 444 5100, www.divediscovery.com. Dive Travel specialists based in San Francisco who have close links with *Bilikiki* and can issue and send Air Solomons tickets to anywhere in the world. They will also tailor make any itinerary.

MV Bilikiki

Iron Bottom Sound at sunset

Cruising around Marovo

Market day

No worries!

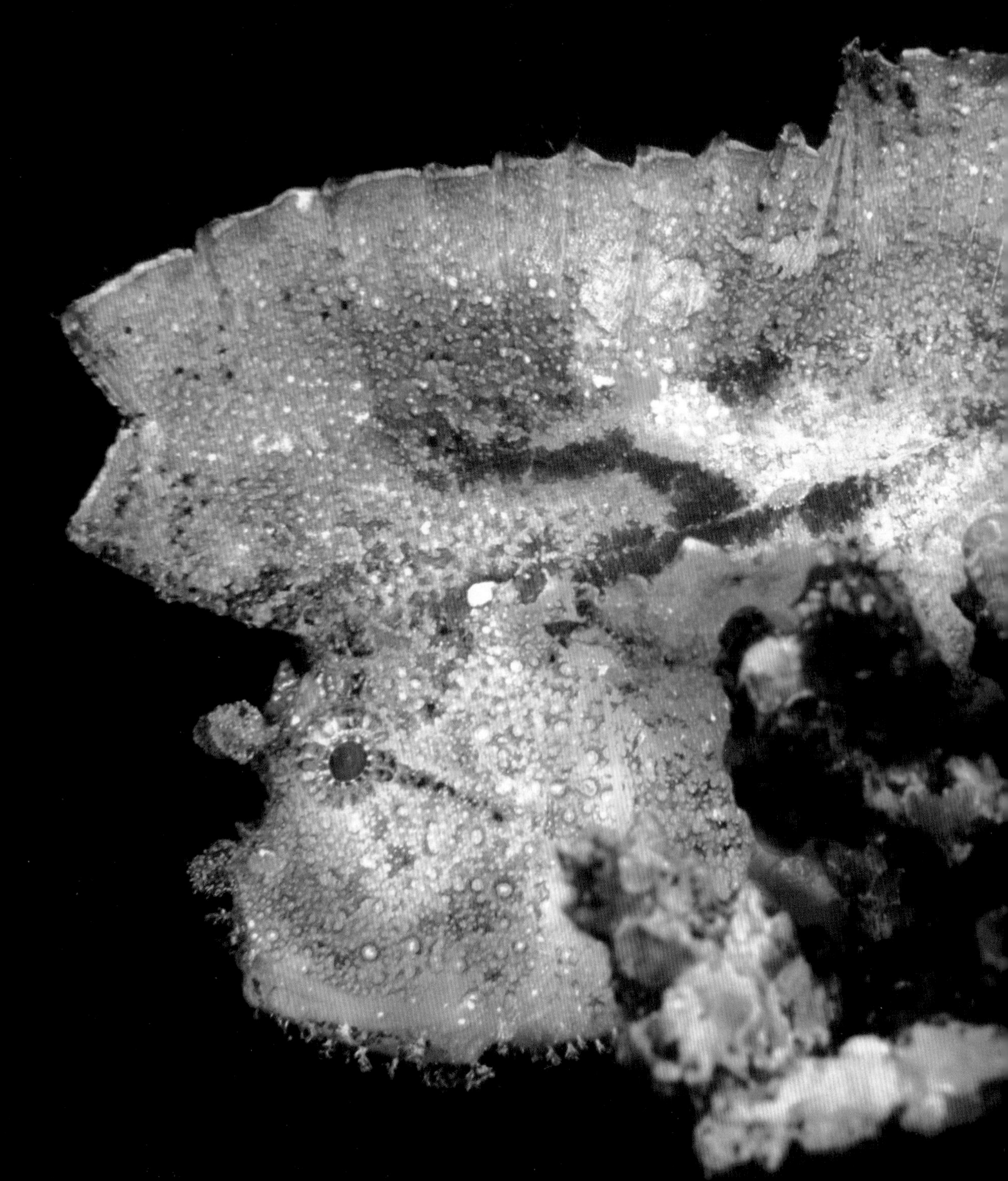

Master of deception: camouflaged and motionless, the ever-patient, leaffish, *Taenianotus triacanthus*

PAPUA NEW GUINEA
Coral Sea
FIJI
AUSTRALIA
Pacific Ocean
Labasa
Vanua Levu
Savusavu Bay
Savusavu
Somosomo
Straits
Bouma National Heritage Park
Wairiki Mission
Lavena
Somosomo
Taveuni
Yasawa
Yadua
Nabowalu
Koru
Rakiraki
Tavua
Ba
Makogai
Mamanuca
Koroyanitu National Park
Lautoka
Mt Victoria
Wakaya
Ovalau
Koro Sea
Namotu
Tavarua
Nadi
Viti Levu
Korovou
Baliki
Nairai
Nausori
Gau
Sigatoka
SUVA
Navua
Pacific Ocean
Beqa
Vatulele
Moala
Ono
Totoya
Kadavu
Maluku
N
20 km
20 miles
Dive sites...
1 Magic Reef, Magic (Namotu) Island p100
2 Wilke's Passage, Mamanuca p101
3 Plantation Pinnacles, Mamanuca p101
4 Alice in Wonderland p102
5 Mystery Reef p103
6 Nuggets p103
7 Goldilocks p103
8 The Corner, Rainbow Reef p104
9 The Great White Wall, Rainbow Reef ★ p104
10 Blue Ribbon Eel Reef p105
11 The Ledge p105

Introduction

The truly exotic mixed with a taste of the past, a pinch of embarrassing history and a mass of multicultural intrigue; these are the alluring Fijian islands, the epitome of the South Pacific.

Lying across the 180 degree meridian, this is where the dawn of each new day occurs, the rays of the rising sun lighting up Fiji's picturesque spits of land, all ringed by coral reefs.

What sets these seas apart from other nearby island groups is their colour. There is a whole world of rainbows below the waterline that has caused many a diver to wax lyrical over what they have seen in the crystal clear waters. Intensity of colour is only outdone by the profuse marine life. No matter where else you have been, you won't have seen anything quite like this.

On land, the peace of the islands belies an eventful and shadowy past. However, though it was once known to wary outsiders as the 'Cannibal Islands', Fiji is now one of the friendliest nations you could ever visit. Days here are full of soft, warm air and clean, blue waters.

“” *Our memories of diving these far-flung islands are as vivid as the colours we saw. Light might fade underwater but the mental polaroids never will.*

Fiji rating

Diving
★★★★

Dive facilities
★★★

Accommodation
★★★★

Down time
★★

Value for money
★★★★

Essentials

Fiji

Location	18°00′ S, 175°00′ E
Neighbours	New Caledonia, Samoa and Tonga
Population	893,354
Land area in km²	18,270
Marine area in km²	1,217
Coastline in km	1,129

Getting there and around

While the Americans and Aussies get it easy, there is nowhere that is quite so far away from Europe as Fiji, sitting right on the international date line. Fiji's main international airport is Nadi and all scheduled flights land there rather than at Suva, the capital. The shortest route is to head west via the US, taking a flight to Vancouver or Los Angeles then connecting across the Pacific. The total trip time is in the region of 25 hours but if you go via Asia it will be closer to 30 hours. **Air New Zealand** (www.airnewzealand.com) can take you all the way or you can combine **British Airways**, **Virgin** or **United** with a **Qantas** (www.qantas.com) or **Air Pacific** flight (www.airpacific.com). Air Pacific is Fiji's national carrier and the flight from Los Angeles takes 11 hours. They also fly from Tokyo which is around 9 hours.

For Australians it's a much shorter trip. From Sydney or Brisbane you can also use low-cost carrier **Virgin Blue** (www.virginblue.com.au) if you fancy a stopover in Australia though you'll spend longer in the air using this route.

Once you have arrived, travelling between the islands is a breeze. **Air Fiji** is the main internal carrier. Hop onto one of their small aircraft for a scenic ride to all the best diving areas. They also do a fantastic value air pass at around US$300 for four flights. **Sun Air** (www.fiji.to) also connects many islands.

Around the islands themselves, there are plenty of transport options. Buses run virtually everywhere, although schedules are best described as 'loose'. Taxis are inexpensive and metered plus there are ferries, though these are time consuming. There is car rental (Avis, Hertz and so on) but unless you are on Viti Levu you are unlikely to need one.

Language

Although almost everyone in Fiji speaks English, many Fijian terms are included in everyday use. Pronunciation is similar to English but with a few changes to the phonetic alphabet. Not that anyone will care if you get it wrong but it will help to get you to the right place if you pronounce the name correctly. Some common changes include:

Looking over the Somosomo Straits

'b' becomes 'mb', 'c' is 'th' ,'d' is 'nd', 'g' is 'ng' and 'q' is 'ngg'. So Nadi is actually pronounced 'Nandi', and Beqa is 'Mbengga'.

hello	*bula (mbula)*
goodbye	*ni sa moce (ni sa mothey)*
yes	*io (ee-o)*
no	*seqa (senga)*
please	*yalo vinaka (yalo vee naka)*
thank you	*vinaka (vee naka)*
sorry	*lomana*
one beer	*dua (ndua) bia*
good	*vinaka*

Local laws and customs

Fiji's population consists of around 50% indigenous people, who are Christians, and 45% who are descendants from indentured Indian workers; a mix of Hindu, Muslim and Sikh. All Fijians are incredibly friendly and the usual courtesies will go a long way. However, there are a few specific rules to remember if you visit a local village: hats and sunglasses are thought to indicate disrespect for the chief; shoes should not be worn indoors and both sexes should cover knees and shoulders; avoid touching a Fijian person's head and, in very traditional villages, women may be expected to wear their hair loose.

When visiting a village, it is customary to take a gift of kava root and you may be asked to drink kava with the villagers on arrival (see page 107). Remember to be cautious with praise – if you admire something too much, the owner will feel obliged to give it to you. Finally, bear in mind that homosexuality is illegal here and drugs offences carry severe penalties.

Safety

Like anywhere, a dose of common sense will keep you and your possessions safe. The Fijian islands are generally crime free but in the city centres there is some small-time petty theft and occasional muggings. In a country which virtually shuts down on a Sunday – the day of rest – this upsets the older generation who are saddened by the rise in crime and what they see as a lack of respect amongst Fijian youth. Compared to western countries, crime is still minimal, but as many people live close to the bread line so opportunistic theft is becoming more common. As ever, don't leave dive gear, cameras or anything of value on display, not even on a hotel balcony.

Health

Fiji carries few health risks for visitors other than the usual issues of too much sun and not enough water leading to dehydration. However, there is a problem with mosquitos during the day and occasional outbreaks of dengue fever. If you are in an urban area use plenty of repellent. You won't encounter them in coastal regions. Medical facilities are of a reasonable standard but most, including the recompression chamber, are on Viti Levu. Make sure you have a basic medical kit with you.

Costs

Value for money is a given in Fiji. There is a wide selection of hotels, from dirt cheap to expensive. Diving and accommodation packages in smaller resorts can start from as little as US$150 per day, add food and it might be US$200. Some of the more sophisticated resorts can be several hundred dollars a day, but you can sleep comfortably for much less. If you don't want to be limited to staying, diving and eating in only one place, you can always use the closest resort's dive centre. Small, local restaurants are simple and cheap and you'd be hard pressed to spend F$20 a head on a meal. A local Fiji Bitter will be around F$3. Chinese food is common on the smaller islands, Indian food on Viti Levu. Getting traditional Fijian food is more difficult but resorts will do a 'lovo night' when a meal is cooked over hot stones. Apart from Nadi and Suva, there won't be a huge selection of restaurants or shops. Tipping isn't customary in Fiji, although you may find it's expected in the more expensive resorts and some will have a special staff fund.

Airlines → Air Fiji T+679 3313666, Air Pacific T+679 6737421, Qantas T+679 6722880. **Embassies** → UK T+679 3229100, USA T+679 3314466, Australia, T+679 3382211, New Zealand T+679 3306090. **Fiji country code** → +679. **IDD code** → 00. **Police** → 911.

Fact file

International flights	Air New Zealand, Air Pacific, Qantas
Departure tax	F$30
Entry	EU, US and Commonwealth – valid passport required for stays of up to 4 months
Internal flights	Air Fiji and Sun Air
Ground transport	Taxis, buses and ferries
Money	F$1.70 = US$1
Language	English
Electricity	220v
Time zone	GMT +7
Religion	Christian, Hindu, Muslim, Sikh

Schooling jacks in crystal clear water

Dive brief

Diving

Fiji's reefs have earned more elaborate, flowery descriptions than appears logical – until you get there. Terms like underwater rainbows, technicolour wonderlands and kaleidoscopic colours are used to exhaustion. However, this country, nicknamed the 'soft coral capital of the world', deserves every fancy description that comes its way. Yes, divers and writers do tend to over-enthuse but just one dive amongst this most incredible array of rainbow-hued soft corals and you will understand. It's not just that the colours seem extraordinarily bright in amongst the clear waters, it's the sheer range of colours that clash with each other. Sometimes gaudy might be a better tag.

But it's not just about colour. Like much of the South Pacific, Fiji diving is varied and exciting. There are shallow reefs and sheer walls, narrow tunnels leading past caverns with overhangs and small caves to explore. Pelagic life is plentiful and small schooling fish continue to paint the reefs with colour. The corals can be found all over, from huge fans close to the surface to fragile black corals found well below normal diving limits.

All this is possible thanks to the 30 metres-plus visibility that keeps the depths well lit. Plankton blooms during April and May or November and December can reduce the visibility a little but they bring in filter-feeders and pelagics. Conditions are fairly easy, drift diving is straightforward and the water temperatures are consistent.

Bottom time

Viti Levu
Fiji's main island is ringed by many others – exotic names and exotic locations » p100

Vanua Levu
Sheltered sites in Savusavu Bay with an intense variety of marine life » p102

Taveuni
The dramatic Somosomo Straits inspired the country's title, 'soft coral capital of the world' » p104

Snorkelling

Protected lagoons around many of the smaller islands means that snorkelling in Fiji can be very rewarding. However, these spots are not always in the same places as the best diving. Taveuni would be one of the better exceptions to that as would the tiny, sandy islands of the Yasawa Group, off Nadi. Viti

Diversity reef area 10,020 km²

Coral species	Fish species	Fish species under threat	Protected reefs/marine parks
398	355	1	12*

* not all parks are internationally recognized

Coral outcrop plastered in soft corals

There are few places in the world these days that manage to live in the 21st century yet remain "unspoilt". Of course everyone's description of unspoilt varies, but there is little in Fiji to taint the experience. It's calm, it's quiet, and it has amazing diving. And yes, we would go back.

Dive data

Seasons	Summer (wet season) November to April, subject to occasional cyclones. Winter (dry season) May to October
Visibility	20 metres (summer) to 50 metres (winter)
Temperatures	Air 20-31°C; water 25-30° C
Wet suit	3 mm full body suit. 5 mm in cooler months
Training	Generally available, look for PADI or NAUI affiliated schools
Nitrox	Generally available
Deco chambers	Suva

Levu has very few easily accessible snorkelling areas but resorts arrange trips to offshore reefs where snorkelling is much better.

The big decision

The biggest issue for many divers is the distance to Fiji and it cannot be denied that it's a little out of the way for most. Furthermore those flights are not so cheap that they are too tempting to ignore. What is tempting though is the quality of what you will see and do underwater. This area seems removed from many of the problems facing our planet's seas. There is tourism, and marine tourism, but it doesn't engulf the country or its personality. There is fishing but the industry isn't overwhelming. Because of the sea conditions, events like El Niño have little detrimental effect. You may only go once but it will be a once in a lifetime experience.

Buddy line

Reverse profiles
Way back in the days before dive computers, you learnt to dive on tables. The rule was always to do your deepest dive first. Always. Then computers came along which recorded all your dive data as you dived so that it didn't matter if you did 'accidentally' go deeper on the second dive than the first as that clever software made appropriate adjustments. Shortly after, dive centres started to make a fuss about this and the No Reverse Profile rule was born. Some operators take this to the limit – there's even one ridiculous operation in the Red Sea that will give you a yellow card for doing it. Second offence, it's a red card and you're off the field and banned from diving. Anyway, while there is a lot of logic in lessening your risk factor as the day goes on, there is absolutely no evidence that reverse profiles are more likely to cause a bend. If you choose to query that, check out the findings of the international workshop held at Washington's renowned Smithsonian Institute; www.si.edu/dive/ds-research.htm.

Whitetip in hiding

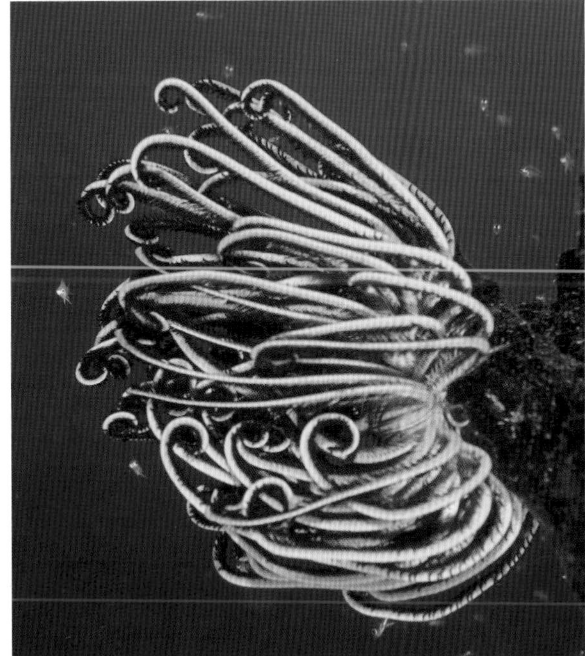

Crinoid in buttercup yellow

Viti Levu

This is Fiji's main island and location of the political capital, Suva. However, as international flights tend to land at Nadi on the west of the island most tourism is based there. Both cities are tiny by European or American standards but can be interesting for a day or two.

Many divers head straight out to one of the more distant island groups where the diving is definitely better. However, there is pleasant diving around Viti Levu. Just off Nadi's shoreline are two chains of islands that are classically pretty cays. The Mamanucas are the nearest group, the Yasawas a little further north. The Mamanuca Islands are riddled with small resorts and dive centres and some of the sites along the outer barrier reef can be quite exciting. Quite a few of the island resorts are targeted at budget travellers so courses are good value.

The southern coast of Viti Levu has been nicknamed the Coral Coast and Beqa Lagoon on the southeast coast is popular. Hundreds of divers come to this area as access is easy and facilities are good. Over 10 miles across, the lagoon is actually the crater of an extinct volcano. There is a very popular shark feed dive at Shark Reef, where you have a good chance of coming face to face with reef, bull and tiger sharks.

Conditions around Viti Levu are good but less so than the outlying islands as this area is more prone to cyclones. Visibility can be about 30 metres, at best, but all that lovely, white sand does muddy the water when the winds are up. At the same time, surface conditions can be rocky and while reef conditions are good, they are nowhere near as impressive as other parts of the country.

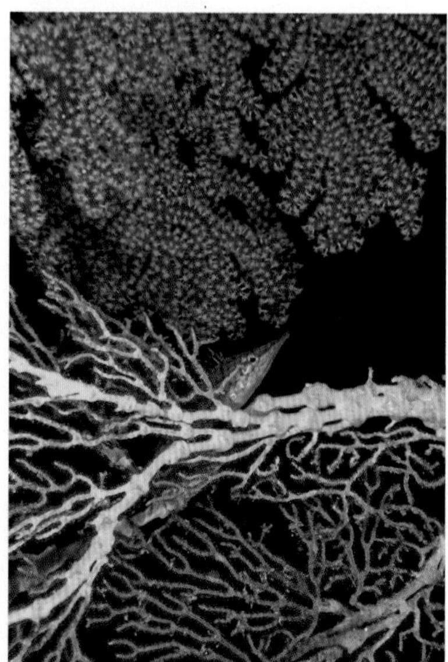

Longnose hawkfish peaking through a fan

1 Magic Reef, Magic (Namotu) Island

- **Depth**: 20 m
- **Visibility**: fair to great
- **Currents**: usually mild
- **Dive type**: day boat
- **Snorkelling**: yes

Magic Island is little more than a small cay ringed by beautiful white sand that sits on the edge of the barrier reef. The reefs around her perimeter can be dived either from Nadi or from one of the many local island resorts. Diving in the passage between this island and nearby Tavarua can be quite exhilarating. The coral life takes second place to the incredible numbers of fish. As you near the wall, you will encounter some schooling barracuda, turtles and perhaps a shark or two. Back in shallower waters, it's small colourful fish like lions or butterflies and black and white banded seasnakes feeding in the corals.

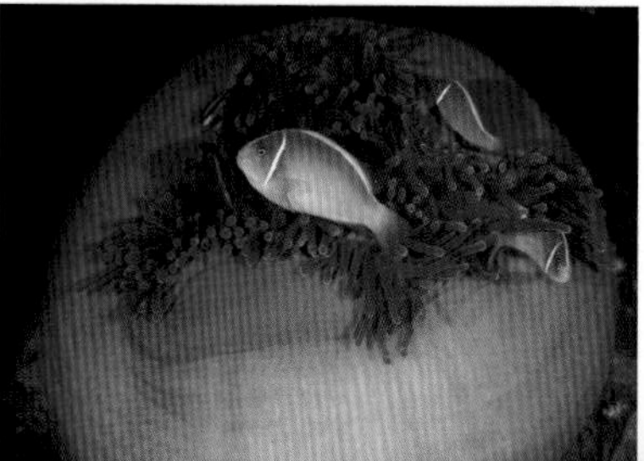

Pink anemonefish and matching anemone

2 Wilke's Passage, Mamanuca

- **Depth**: 22 m
- **Visibility**: very good
- **Currents**: mild to strong
- **Dive type**: day boat
- **Snorkelling**: yes

It's unusual for an open water dive site to also be good for snorkelling. This one is, and it's also a great place for dolphin spotting as well as being a favourite for surfers. The passage, to the northwest of Magic Island, cuts through the outer edge of the barrier reef. The flow of water creates decent waves on the outside (for the surfers and the dolphins), while the lagoon on the inside is good for snorkelling. There's an interesting drift dive below and though currents in the passage can be strong they are not so fierce as to make it difficult. Schools of barracuda and trevally are attracted by the movement, the corals flourish in the nutrient-rich waters and it's fingers crossed for a dolphin.

3 Plantation Pinnacles, Mamanuca

- **Depth**: 22 m
- **Visibility**: very good
- **Currents**: usually mild
- **Dive type**: day boat
- **Snorkelling**: yes

Head a little further north than Namotu and you are inside the Mamanuca lagoon. This is one of the better known sites in the area. A group of three pinnacles protrude from the seabed and as conditions here are usually easy, you can do several circuits around them and some swim-throughs before slowly ascending up the sides of the main one. At the base there are some black coral trees with their resident longnose hawkfish, while there are small fans and plenty of other corals along the sides. At the top, the macro life is particularly interesting with nudibranchs and starfish, masses of anemones and clowns, leaffish and morays.

Tales from the deep

Shark feeding at Beqa lagoon

In Beqa Lagoon there's an innocuous site where shark feeding takes place. Every diver that visits Shark Reef must pay F$10 which goes to two local villages to compensate them for not fishing the reef and for protecting it from other fishing and diving boats.

After an extremely thorough brief, our four dive guides, together with two huge sealed bins full of dead fish, dropped into the water. The guests followed, taking up positions behind a constructed one-foot-high coral wall. With metal mesh gloves covering his hands, one guide began hand feeding. Soon a huge ball of snapper and trevally was joined by half a dozen grey reef sharks. Shy at first, they slowly circled ever-closer before taking food from the guide's hand. Behind us, white and blacktip reef sharks buzzed back and forth, excitedly waiting their turn. After about ten minutes I got my first sight of a bull shark, a full size pregnant female. Then as we started our ascent, a very swift-moving and impressive silvertip shark passed by overhead in search of food.

During the briefing for our second dive, one of the guides commented that this is normally when the tiger sharks make their appearance. "Yeah right, I've heard that one before" thinks I, quite immune to exaggerated marketing speak. Within minutes, I saw several large bull sharks, then I thought it was another in the distance. But the stripes were plainly visible… just a few metres above was the legendary tiger. I saw her circle five times, then she passed straight over my head, easily within arm's reach. At this stage I was doing my best to melt into the boulder behind me. It was so close I could have smelt her breath! What a truly awesome moment!

There is lots of heated debate about the merits of shark feeding and diving. Many argue that the feeding is unnatural and breaks regular behavioural patterns. They also claim that most attacks on humans take place during a feeding activity. Whilst I cannot deny that it does alter the sharks' behaviour, it must be noted that no serious accidents have ever taken place at this shark feed. Indeed, sports such as spearfishing have a much worse safety record, and there are no calls to ban that activity. One thing is for sure, if this shark feeding concession was not operating, these sharks would have been killed a long time ago by fisherman.

Sheldon Hey, General Manager, Dive the World

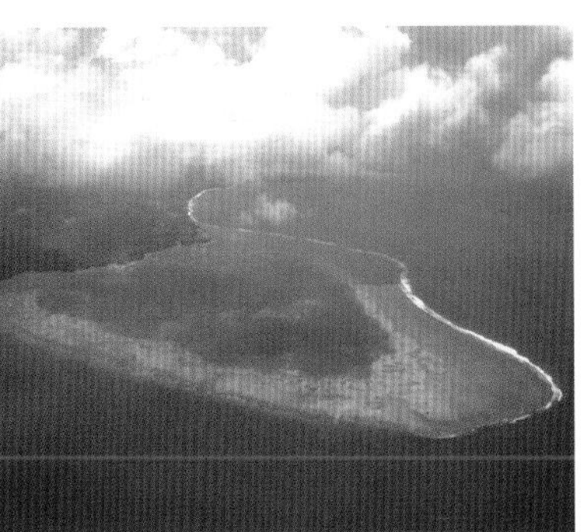

Islands from the air

Blue ribbon eels are common

Vanua Levu

This is the second largest island in Fiji yet it is incredibly undeveloped, except around the capital, Savusavu. While there is limited infrastructure and services, you can get an insight into multi-cultural Fijian daily life. There's not a lot of sightseeing to be done but who needs that when you have some of the country's best diving just moments from shore.

There are sheer walls for drifting over and caves to explore. Fish life is varied and prolific and sightings of pelagic species are reasonably common. One of this area's best features though is her ability to provide dives for everyone. There are plenty of sheltered dives inside Savusavu Bay while the more exhilarating Somosomo Straits are still close enough to enjoy in a day.

Likewise, the island has a good mix of accommodation, from upmarket to small and independent. The diving season is year round but from April to October it's dryer, with visibility best from July to September when the surface can get quite choppy. During the summer months of November to April water temperatures reach 30°C and it's calm.

"" Diving here is the stuff that legends are made of and many consider this region to be the home of the world's most prolific soft corals.

4 Alice in Wonderland

- **Depth**: 22 m
- **Visibility**: good to stunning
- **Currents**: usually mild
- **Dive type**: day boat
- **Snorkelling**: no

This site is located towards the outer reaches of Savusavu Bay. The story goes that it was named after the huge mushroom-shaped coral heads that cover the wide, open patch reef. The area is exposed to currents flowing from the south and east so there are lots of schooling fish. Small whitetips cruise in to feed and even lurk about underneath the 'mushrooms' which are in impeccable condition. There is some interesting macro

Leopard shark resting on seabed

life with plenty of cleaner shrimp hopping around tube anemones and coral banded shrimp under sponges. An unusual sighting is the juvenile rockmover wrasse whose spiky decorations make it hard to spot while it flits about in the surface rubble.

5 Mystery Reef

- **Depth**: 20 m
- **Visibility**: good
- **Currents**: medium
- **Dive type**: day boat
- **Snorkelling**: no

This isolated reef is half an hour or so from shore at the edge of Savusavu Bay and just a little past Alice. The sea floor here is also scattered with hard coral heads but these are painted with a huge number of multi-coloured soft corals. There are plenty of fish too as the whole reef seems to be a breeding ground. There are clownfish with their babies, moorish idols chasing each other in mating games while newborn damselfish hide behind their parents, and even tiny scorpionfish sitting on the seabed. Spanish mackerel, coral trout, angels and parrotfish are also in residence.

Juvenile anemonefish

6 Nuggets

- **Depth**: 18 m
- **Visibility**: excellent
- **Currents**: medium
- **Dive type**: day boat
- **Snorkelling**: unlikely

On the southern edge of Savusavu Bay, the Nuggets are two coral heads. The main pinnacle has a base about 50 metres around, at 18 metres deep, and rises to just below the surface. It's a tiny area but a whole coral world resides there. There are myriad soft corals surrounded by schools of fairy basslets, from the tiniest babes to adults. Masked bannerfish and damsels flutter about the steep walls and young angels seem to pop out of tiny caves every few seconds. Leaffish are spotted nestling in crevices and occasional jacks circle above. On the surrounding sandy seafloor titan triggers nest. They can be very aggressive while guarding their eggs so it's best to watch from the safety of the pinnacle. The second, smaller bommie is covered in golden soft corals with lionfish, scorpions and moray eels poking about while giant pufferfish hover nearby.

A cave full of colourful soft corals

7 Goldilocks

- **Depth**: 20 m
- **Visibility**: good to stunning
- **Currents**: can be strong
- **Dive type**: day boat
- **Snorkelling**: no

Heading south and around the outer edge of Vanua Levu, but still only half an hour or so from town, you reach the Koro Sea. Away from the protection of the bay, currents here are much stronger and consequently coral growth is thicker and more lush. As you descend over the reef you encounter a vast carpet of hard corals. There seems to be a huge variety in a very small area. You swim around the edge of the reef until you reach a large bommie that is thronged by tropical fish while beneath are several small rays. A little further on, a second bommie stands out from a distance. It is completely smothered in bright yellow soft corals, hence the name of the dive site. Bright yellow plumes seem to drip from every crack and crevice. Of course, there are plenty of other corals plus nudibranchs, unicornfish and damselfish guarding their eggs.

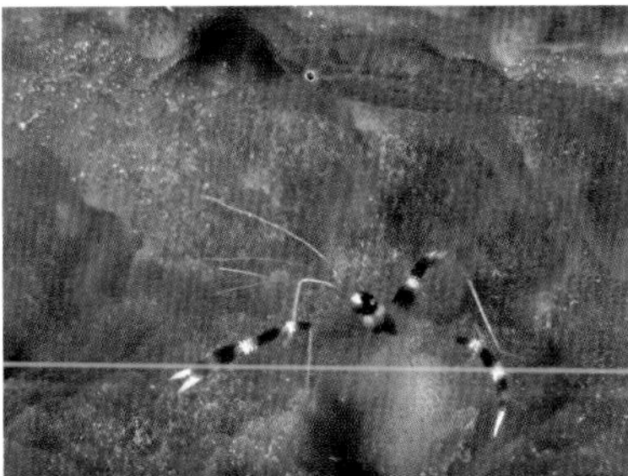

Banded boxer shrimp

Clown triggerfish with wacky skin patterns

Taveuni

This 'small but perfectly formed' island is opposite Vanua Levu. Its steep hills are shrouded in riotous flora which earned it the title of 'Garden Island' and although the scenery is simply awe-inspiring it pales in comparison to the beauty of the diving in the Somosomo Straits.

This stretch of water separating Taveuni from Vanua Levu almost single-handedly earned Fiji the title of soft coral capital of the world. The narrow channel funnels water from south to north and back again, supplying nutrients, stimulating growth and ensuring the health of reef-building animals. The currents are constant, not always strong but ever-present. In the continual flow the corals are always out feeding, revealing the multiple tones for which it was christened 'Rainbow Reef'. All this attracts plenty of fish, too, and pelagics hover over the deep blue channels. Diving is best from April to October, when the water is clearest with visibility up to 50 metres, but it can be chilly. In the wet season, the water is warmer but visibility is around 30 metres.

Dripping soft corals

Anthias under hard coral

On land, Taveuni is a rural sort of place. There are some small villages, the biggest being Somosomo, but her real attractions are the lakes and waterfalls, rare birds and indigenous flowers of inland Bouma National Heritage Park

8 The Corner, Rainbow Reef

- **Depth**: 18 m
- **Visibility**: good
- **Currents**: medium to strong
- **Dive type**: day boat
- **Snorkelling**: for strong swimmers

Rainbow Reef was named after the immense profusion of multi-coloured soft corals that envelope the entire reef. The topography is highly varied with walls, caves and many swim-throughs. The Corner is an area of shallow coral gardens on the inner edge of the reef interspersed with sandy channels. There are young whitetip sharks hiding under table corals and groups of giant clams. The bommies that struggle towards the surface are covered in anemones, with anthias dancing amongst the soft and hard corals. This a great site for spotting nudibranchs.

Lionfish prowling

9 The Great White Wall, Rainbow Reef

- **Depth**: 31 m
- **Visibility**: great
- **Currents**: medium to strong
- **Dive type**: day boat
- **Snorkelling**: for strong swimmers

Diving the Great White Wall means diving with a current and if, for some reason, it has dropped off completely, there is no point in going. The start of this dive involves descending over the reef edge then a swim downwards through a tunnel which has two exits. The first exit is at 10 metres and you might encounter a moray near here but the more exciting exit is at 30 metres. You emerge onto a sheer wall that plunges to unfathomable depths to find yourself surrounded by a fantastic swathe of pure white. The water running over the wall has encouraged all the soft corals tentacles out to feed. The effect is luminescent, almost like snow on a hill which glows when the sun's rays bounce off it. There are huge quantities of these small soft corals which are actually a pale pink or mauve though you can only see that if you shine a torch on them. A few whip corals and fans sprout from the wall, so you may spot longnose hawkfish or gobies sheltering. Meanwhile, off the wall large humphead wrasse swim along in tandem with the divers, and reef sharks are seen hanging around in the shallows, but their attraction pales in comparison to the overall effect of the landscape.

The vision of these same-coloured corals, after several days of gaudy, multi-toned reefs, is really quite breathtaking. The light they reflect back from the reef is a little ghostly, definitely a bit other-world.

10 Blue Ribbon Eel Reef

- **Depth**: 20 m
- **Visibility**: fair to good
- **Currents**: slight to strong
- **Dive type**: day boat
- **Snorkelling**: not really

This drift dive is just a few minutes boat ride from shore. As you drop over the reef you are met by patches of purple soft corals that make it easy to bypass the main attraction – the blue ribbon eel. This is one of those sites where they are almost guaranteed though few people spot them first time round. These elusive creatures retreat rapidly into their holes in the sand as soon as they feel threatened. However, the dive guides know where they are and wait for a few minutes nearby until they pop out again. Although they are a couple of feet long you usually only see about a hand's length. This is enough to admire the vivid bands of blue and yellow on an adult male. All yellow ribbon eels are thought to be female and black and yellow ones are juveniles. There are plenty of fish here, too, swarming around the corals.

11 The Ledge

- **Depth**: 25 m+
- **Visibility**: fair to good
- **Currents**: mild
- **Dive type**: day boat
- **Snorkelling**: not really

Located only 10 minutes from shore this pinnacle rises from the seabed at about 80 metres to about 5 metres below the surface. While the current can be quite strong in the shallows, as you descend it drops right off. The pinnacle is isolated from nearby reefs so many fish are attracted to it and pelagics shelter in its overhangs and crevices. There are plenty of lionfish, moorish idols, butterflies and damsels. Trevally school around the edges and there are plenty of beautiful soft corals. As this site is so close to shore it also makes a great night dive.

Fantastic Fijian visibility

Drying out

Kava ceremony on Taveuni

Fiji's main island, Viti Levu, has the highest levels of sports, activities, some colonial history and a few museums while the more distant islands are peaceful havens for relaxing and for nature lovers.

Viti Levu

The coastal and offshore island resorts on the west are less than an hour away from Nadi airport. Accommodation is wide ranging, a little something for every budget. Beqa Lagoon and the Coral Coast are around 2½ hrs away from Nadi and, again, there is a variety of resorts.

Dive centres

Subsurface Fiji, PO Box 3002, Nadi, Fiji Islands, T+679 6666738, www.fijidiving.com. This large, efficient dive company works with almost all resorts in the Mamanucas, from backpacker to top class.

Sleeping

$$$-$ **Lagoon Resort**, Fairway Place, Pacific Harbour, T+679 3450100, www.lagoonresort.com. At the end of the Coral Coast and close to Beqa Lagoon, this lovely resort works with Beqa Adventure Divers (www.fiji-sharks.com).

$$$-$$ **Malolo Island Resort**, PO Box 10044, Nadi Airport, T+679 6669192, www.maloloisland.com. A beautiful resort on a beautiful island. Subsurface Fiji packages are good value (above).

$$ **First Landing Resort**, PO Box 348, Lautoka, T+679 6666171, www.firstlandingfiji.com. Just15 mins north of the airport and a great stopover or chill-out spot.

Liveaboards

MY Nai'A, PO Box 332, Pacific Harbour, Fiji, T+679 3450382, www.naia.com.fj. Nai'A sails around the central Fijian area. It may be expensive but this is the boat with 'the' reputation.

Eating

All resorts have onsite restaurants. In Nadi town there are international, Indian and Chinese restaurants but for the biggest pizza you will ever see head for **Mama's Pizza** on Queen's Rd.

Sights

Nadi Not a very pretty place but there is some decent shopping. Day tours that include the centre also head to the Vatukoula Gold Mines near the market town of Tavua and Viseisei Village, which is regarded as the 'foundation village' of Fijian heritage and culture.

Koroyanitu National Park Located 10 km east of Lautoka, the park has beautiful bush walks, waterfalls, archaeological sites and lush native rainforest.

Ba and Rakiraki Ba is an Indian town known for its mosque and colourful bazaar. Rakiraki is the home of Ratu Udre, Fiji's last known cannibal. His tomb at the town junction is surrounded by 999 stones, which represents the number of people he ate.

Sigatoka Archaeological digs on these south coast sand dunes have uncovered skeletons and artefacts dating back to 15 BC.

Suva The political capital has markets, shopping and nightlife, a few museums and the governmental buildings. Like Nadi, there is little to hold you here for more than a day.

Ovalau Island Northeast of Suva, this tiny island is home to Levuka, Fiji's first capital, and most historic location. A national heritage site, it's well worth a visit to see its gloriously faded main street.

Vanua Levu

Fly for 45 mins from Nadi, 40 mins from Suva or 15 mins from Taveuni to Fiji's second largest island, Vanua Levu.

Sleeping and diving

$$$ **L'Aventure Divers and Jean Michel Cousteau Fiji Islands Resort**, Private Mail Bag, Savusavu, Fiji Islands, T+679 8850694, www.fijiresort.com. Upscale dive resort with large traditional bungalows and pretty landscaped gardens.

$$$ **Koro Sun Resort**, Hibiscus Highway, Savusavu, T+679 8850262, www.

korosunresort.com. A large resort complex, where you can even buy your own slice of paradise should you feel so inclined. On site dive centre and all the usual facilities.

$$ **Hot Springs Hotel**, PO Box 208, Savusavu, T+679 8850195, www.hotspringsfiji.com. Comfortable hotel with views of the bay and town.

Eating

Captain's Café Restaurant, Copra Shed Marina, PO Box 262, Savusavu, T+679 8850457. Great steak, fish and pizzas served on the deck by the marina. Fabulous views.

Sights

Downtown Savusavu With the feel of a Wild West staging post, there's just one road with banks, ATMs, a post office and an internet outlet. There are two marinas: the **Copra Shed** is an old warehouse that has some tourist shops and a café. A bit farther along is **Waitui Marina**, where you can chill out on the decks over the bay.

Salt Lake Kayaking Drive up the Hibiscus Highway to a salt water river that leads to a salty lake, the island's largest.

Waisali Rainforest Reserve A gentle walk through dense rainforest with the cooling spray of the waterfall at the end.

Tunuloa Peninsula Said to be the island's best birdwatching spot, including the rare and fabulous silk-tail.

Waivunia Village Take an organized excursion to see the the village, homes, meeting hall and church. The villagers display arts and crafts and hold *kava* ceremonies for the uninitiated.

Taveuni

Just 80 mins from Nadi, 45 mins from Suva and a mere 15 mins from Savusavu, the peaceful Garden Island is a magnet for divers, walkers and nature lovers.

Sleeping and diving

$$$-$$ **Maravu Plantation Resort and Swiss Divers**, c/- P.A Matei, Taveuni, T+679 8880555, www.maravu.net, www.swissfijidivers.com. Lovely, colonial-style resort overlooking the sea. Just 10 mins from the airstrip and with the dive centre right next door.

$$-$ **Garden Island Resort and AquaTrek**, PO Box 1, Waiyevo, Taveuni, T+679 8880286, www.aquatrek.com. This comfortable resort is near the village of Somosomo, about 20 mins from the airstrip and minutes from the Meridian line.

Eating

There are restaurants on Taveuni but most are linked to one resort or another. Unless you have transport getting around at night is difficult. Consequently, most divers book meal packages at their resort.

Sights

Bouma Falls In the National Park, these 3 waterfalls are in a remote area but are fairly easy walks. And you can swim beneath them to cool off once you arrive.

Lavena Village A picturesque and traditional village where you can meet some of the villagers. The spectacular beach is a great snorkelling spot.

Lake Tagimoucia This old crater lake, which is filled with floating plant life, is just below Des Voeux Peak, the second highest spot on Taveuni. The hike is strenuous, about 3-4 hrs each way, but the views are amazing. You may spot Fiji's most famous flower, the tagimoucia, subject of local legend. Bird watching is said to be excellent.

Vuniuto Village Cultural Tour If time is short take this organized village tour. You can see demonstrations of Fijian crafts such as basket making and mat weaving, traditional cooking displays and preparation of the traditional drink *yaqona* – more widely known as *kava*.

***Kava* Ceremonies** It's a great honour to be invited to join a *kava* ceremony, the ritualized drinking of a bowl of muddy brown water, with the village elders. *Kava* is a root from the pepper family and when ground and soaked in water, has a very faint narcotic effect. Expect numb lips at least. Ceremonies are held constantly to celebrate all sorts of events, even a local sports day. It's generally a male preserve but female tourists will be tolerated.

Wairiki Mission This old Catholic mission overlooks the site where local warriors once defeated thousands of Tongans then celebrated their victory by cooking them in a lovo oven and eating them with breadfruit! The priest who advised the warriors was 'rewarded' for his help by the building of the large mission.

International Agents

Dive Worldwide, 28 Winchester Rd, Romsey, Hampshire SO51 8AA, UK, T+44 (0)845 1306980, www.diveworldwide.com. Knowledgeable agent based in the UK. Tailor-made holidays to everywhere but the owner has a particular penchant for Fiji.

Dive the World – Fiji An informative and useful website (www.divetheworldfiji.com) and booking service for Fiji liveaboards, dive centres and accommodation.

Landing at Taveuni

Old town Levuka

Galápagos

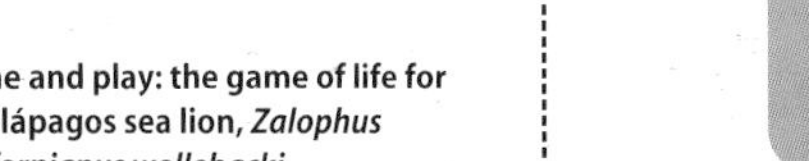

Come and play: the game of life for a Galápagos sea lion, *Zalophus californianus wollebacki*

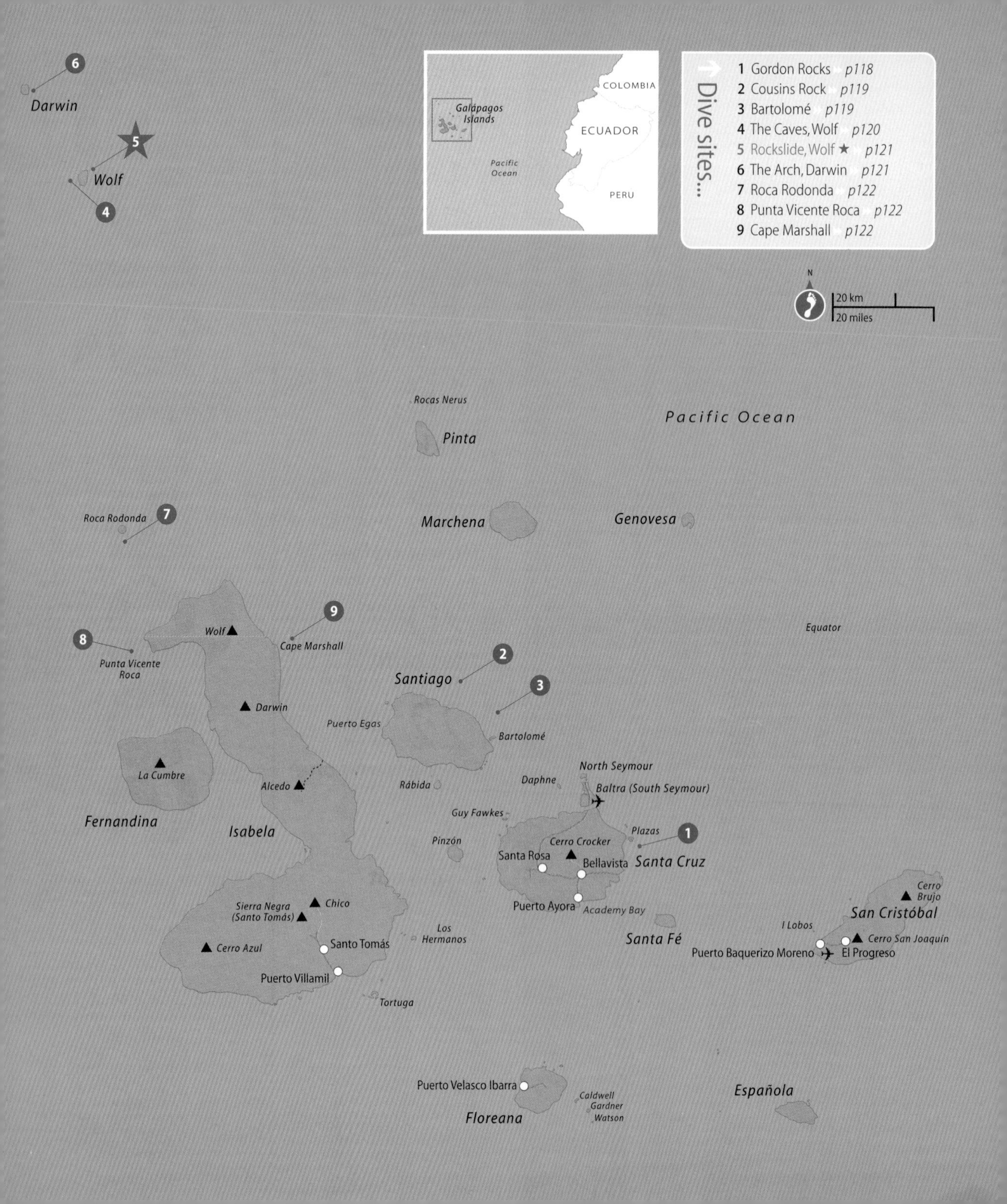

Darwin
Wolf
Galápagos Islands
Pacific Ocean
COLOMBIA
ECUADOR
PERU
Dive sites...
1 Gordon Rocks p118
2 Cousins Rock p119
3 Bartolomé p119
4 The Caves, Wolf p120
5 Rockslide, Wolf ★ p121
6 The Arch, Darwin p121
7 Roca Rodonda p122
8 Punta Vicente Roca p122
9 Cape Marshall p122
N
20 km
20 miles
Rocas Nerus
Pacific Ocean
Pinta
Roca Rodonda
Marchena
Genovesa
Equator
Wolf
Cape Marshall
Punta Vicente Roca
Santiago
Darwin
Puerto Egas
Bartolomé
La Cumbre
North Seymour
Daphne
Baltra (South Seymour)
Alcedo
Rábida
Guy Fawkes
Fernandina
Isabela
Plazas
Pinzón
Cerro Crocker
Santa Rosa
Bellavista
Santa Cruz
Cerro Brujo
Sierra Negra (Santo Tomás)
Chico
Puerto Ayora
Academy Bay
San Cristóbal
Los Hermanos
I Lobos
Cerro Azul
Santo Tomás
Santa Fé
Cerro San Joaquín
Puerto Baquerizo Moreno
El Progreso
Puerto Villamil
Tortuga
Puerto Velasco Ibarra
Caldwell
Gardner
Watson
Española
Floreana

Introduction

Lying on the Equator, nearly a thousand kilometres west of mainland Ecuador, the Galápagos Islands are home to some of the most fascinating and unique wildlife on earth; both above and below the water. On this ancient archipelago of harsh volcanic landscapes, animals rule and human visitors are reduced to the role of voyeur. Here you keep your distance and allow the animals to come to you and, given their legendary fearlessness, they usually do.

While biodiversity figures may not be as high as in some other countries, the number of endemic species is unparalleled. On land you can approach newborn sea lion pups. Their parents simply lift their heads and give you a cursory glance while marine iguanas bask by your toes. Beneath the incessant waves nearby, the main attraction is the vast numbers of sharks, especially schooling hammerheads that block out the sun in vast numbers. On other occasions, they appear solo sitting by your shoulder.

Despite their relative isolation and the costs of getting there, the Galápagos Islands are a popular destination. A steady stream of people flies in daily, passing along well trodden routes to witness the spectacular wildlife show.

“” *We saw things here that we may never see again simply because they are nowhere else.*

Galápagos rating

Diving
★★★

Dive facilities
★★★

Accommodation
★★★★

Down time
★★★★

Value for money
★★★

Essentials

Ecuador

Location	0°00′ N, 90°00′ W
Neighbours	Colombia, Peru
Population	13,363,593
Land area in km²	283,560
Marine area in km²	6,720
Coastline in km	2,237

Getting there and around

While finding a flight to Ecuador isn't difficult, finding one that will take you in a modicum of comfort is less easy. The most obvious route is via major American hub cities, Houston and Miami. Both have daily connections to the capital, Quito, and port city of Guayaquil. Avoid stopping in Guayaquil as it has little to recommend it.

Continental (www.continental.com) fly from London via Houston, **KLM** fly from Amsterdam and **Iberia** from Madrid. However, all these routes have a serious downside. By all accounts Iberia are notorious for delays and refusing divers excess baggage. Continental let you take extra weight but in-flight service leaves a lot to be desired while KLM stops en route. Better options include **Virgin** (www.virginatlantic.com) or **British Airways** (www.ba.com) flights to Miami. From there connect to **American Airlines** (www.aa.com), who have the most economy legroom but charge you for alcoholic drinks.

Many flights arrive in Quito either early in the day or very late at night. If you don't have a hotel courtesy transfer, head straight for a bright yellow cab, which will cost US$5 to the 'New City'. Avoid unlicensed "taxi amigos" which will cost extra. From Quito you then connect to either San Cristóbal or Baltra for the Galápagos. Baltra is closest to Puerto Ayora, the largest town on the islands, but San Cristóbal is where all liveaboards are based. Flights with **AeroGal** (www.aerogal.com.ec) and **TAME** (www.tame.com.ec) cost around US$500. There are also flights between the two islands, or you can fly in to one and depart from the other. Internal bookings are handled by your Ecuadorean agent.

Getting around in Quito is easy. The city is divided into the New City, where most of the upmarket hotels, bars and restaurants are located, and the colonial Old City. There are plenty of taxis and they mostly charge US$2-3 for trips within the city. There is also a good network of trams and buses but if time is short stick to taxis. When you arrive in the Galápagos, everything will be handled by your dive operator.

A very old giant tortoise

Language

Spanish is the universal language though some indigenous languages are still used in remote highland areas. English is only spoken in upmarket hotels and restaurants and tour agencies. Away from the capital there's not much point in asking for directions, unless you have some Spanish. Taxi drivers speak just enough to understand where you are going while pointing and smiling in restaurants works wonders. It's easy to learn a few words of basic Spanish (see also page 146):

how are you?	*¿cómo está?*
I'm fine	*muy bien gracias*
see you later	*hasta luego*
excuse me	*perdón*
where is …?	*¿donde está …?*
I don't speak Spanish	*no hablo castellano*
a coffee	*un café*
black coffee	*café negra*
white coffee	*café con leche*
black coffee with milk added	*café cortada*
fresh orange juice	*jugo de naranja*
when does the bus/boat leave?	*¿cuando sale el bus/barco?*
more slowly, please	*mas despacio, por favor*
I don't like…	*no me gusta…*

Local laws and customs

Ecuador is an overwhelmingly Catholic country with just a small minority following alternative forms of Christianity. Some indigenous Ecuadoreans have adapted their Catholicism to incorporate traditional beliefs. Behaving with courtesy and respect, especially inside churches, is advised at all times, and try not to lose your temper in public.

Safety

Most Ecuadoreans are very friendly and helpful but, as in any large city, care should be taken in Quito and common sense should prevail. Avoid walking in dark areas at night, don't display expensive cameras or flashy jewellery and take only what cash you need. The Old City is virtually dead at night and best avoided, especially around the bus terminal, but stepping out in the New City is generally OK. Guayaquil, on the other hand, has a reputation for petty crime and is subject to frequent civil disturbances.

Health

If you are going to get sick it's only likely to be a bit of altitude sickness in Quito. The city is 2800 metres up and the air is thin. It's usual to feel a little more tired than you would normally and perhaps a bit breathless. Quito doesn't seem to have any vehicle emission laws, which exacerbates things a little. Some people also report stomach upsets and sinus problems. And take care when eating in seafood restaurants; try to get a recommendation.

Down at sea level, in the Galápagos, mosquitoes can be a problem at dusk and, depending on the time of year you visit, the sun can be very strong (remember you're sitting on the Equator). There is no malaria in or around Quito or in the Galápagos but there is said to be some risk in Guayaquil and the Pacific Lowlands.

Costs

As an expensive liveaboard is the best option for diving the Galápagos this may seem like a costly trip. There is also a hefty US$100 per person National Park tax, which is collected at the airport on arrival. That aside, there is little extra to pay for except the odd souvenir or drinks. If you want to spend a few days on land, there are plenty of hotels and restaurants at all budget levels. See page 124 for some recommendations.

Mainland Ecuador, however, is particularly good value. There are masses of hotels at all levels, though standards are variable. Hotels rated 5 star can be more like a 3 star back home, while a 3 star may actually be perfectly adequate. Eating out in Quito is a pleasure. There are trendy fusion restaurants where a fabulous two-course meal with a bottle of wine costs just US$15 a head. If that's too much, snack bars are cheap and ubiquitos. There is a 10% service charge on bills but adding a bit extra is usual. Add a little for cab drivers and a dollar for porters. Dive boat crews will expect a tip, see page 14.

Airlines → Aerogal T+593 (0)2 2257202; American Airlines T+593 (0)2 2260900; British Airways T+593 (0)2 2540000; Continental T+593 (0)2 2557170; Iberia T+593 (0)2 2566009; KLM T+593 (0)2 2986820. **Embassies** → UK T+593 (0)2 2970800, USA T+593 (0)2 2562890, Australia T+593 (0)4 2680700. **Ecuador country code** → +593. **IDD code** → 00. **Police in Quito** → 911. **Police elsewhere** → 101.

Fact file

International flights	Virgin or British Airways to Miami American or Continental to Quito
Departure tax	US$25
Entry	EU, US and Commonwealth – valid passport required for stays of up to 90 days
Internal flights	AeroGal or TAME for the Galápagos
Ground transport	Countrywide bus and train routes
Money	The US dollar is the official currency
Language	Spanish
Electricity	110/220v
Time zone	GMT -5
Religion	Catholic

A Mexican hogfish a long way from home

Dive brief

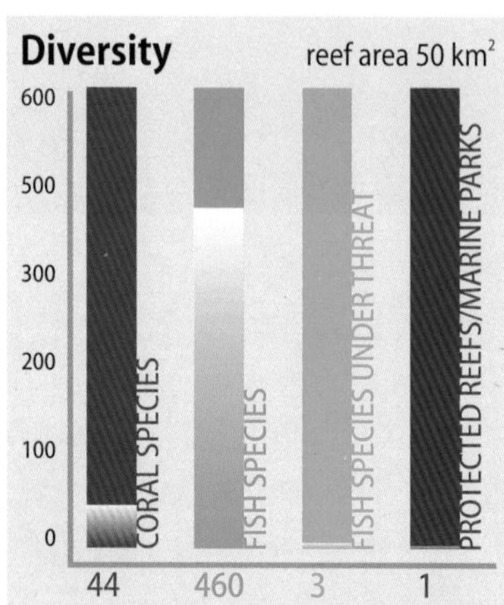

Diving

More than almost any other dive destination, planning a trip to the Galápagos requires a high level of understanding of local conditions. This is not diving for the faint-hearted: the water can be icy, it's rarely dead calm and currents and surges are an every-dive occurrence.

There are wide seasonal differences from summer to winter. The warmest months are December to May when the weather could be regarded as sub-tropical, or almost tropical in the north. June to December is the cold season, which sees some unusual anomalies such as huge banks of mist around Roca Rodonda. However, it's all confused by global climate changes, the less than reliable effects of varying sea currents and the fact that each island has its own microclimate.

The attraction of the Galápagos is the likelihood of seeing large pelagics and there certainly are plenty. The marine life is big with a capital B. You can swim with a hundred hammerheads or do your safety stop surrounded by 20 silky sharks, so if that's your thing you won't leave disappointed. The best time for the biggest and most prolific animals is the winter when they are attracted by cooler waters. Whalesharks start appearing at the end of May, when the water temperature starts dropping down to around 15°C. When the water warms up again, rising to 28°C, the chance of seeing mantas improves. But no matter what time of year you come thermoclines are a serious issue. One minute you can be swimming in water at 25°C then, within seconds, it will drop to 14°C. No joke! This also plays havoc with visibility so it's hard to predict when the best time to visit would be. Generally speaking, though, the most favourable periods are those around the change of seasons; ie, November-December and April-June.

The Galápagos sheephead wrasse

Bottom time

The central zone
Calmer, warmer and prettier diving, this area is protected from the harshest currents and conditions by Isabella, the largest island » *p118*

The north
Rock-your-dive-boots off with countless hammerheads and eagle rays at two extremely isolated outposts, Wolf and Darwin Islands » *p120*

The western zone
Open to the Pacific and influenced by all the equatorial currents; an area of wildly varying conditions and incredibly diverse marine life » *p122*

As for marine life, hammerheads are seen all year round and on almost every dive. Galápagos, whitetip and silky sharks are common companions. Eagle rays and marble rays are everywhere as, of course, are curious and playful sea lions. There are smaller creatures as well – seahorses, morays and even nudibranchs – so it's worth looking down for some of the dive, not just out into the blue. There is, however, very little in the way of coral so the reefs are not classically pretty.

Snorkelling

Although there are shallow bays around some of the islands that are quite good for snorkellers, liveaboard dive trips head out for the better dive sites around submerged pinnacles where the surge is rough. There are some nice snorkel sites but if that's all you want to do book onto a naturalist trip instead.

A dive trip to the Galápagos is one full of expectations which are, in our experience, unlikely to be met. It's not that they aren't fascinating and incredibly special, but neither we nor anyone we met there had a clear idea of what they would find. You think you are going to see whalesharks and you get hammerheads; you think you're going in the warm season and you get ice-cold thermoclines. Darwin said: "It is not the strongest of the species that survive, nor the most intelligent, but the one most responsive to change". That hits the nail right on the head for divers. Be prepared to go with an open mind, adapt to the conditions and you will enjoy it.

Dive data

Seasons	Roughly, December to May – warm June to November – cold
Visibility	10-40 metres
Temperatures	Air 30-34°C ; water 13-28°C
Wet suit	5 mm full body suit summer minimum, 7 mm semi-dry winter minimum
Training	On land
Nitrox	Can be pre-booked
Deco chambers	Puerto Ayora There are no airlift facilities

Diver safety

It should be noted once again that this is not easy diving. Entries can be in huge swells and getting back on the RIB then onto your boat is no fun. Currents can be so strong you have grab hold of the nearest rock with two hands (bring gloves!) and washing machine conditions occur regularly. Most dives are within normal depth limits but some are very deep and neither solo nor decompression diving is allowed. Only do what you know you are capable of and obey your computer. All this might seem a little over the top, especially when the sun is shining and the sky is blue, but this is not a place to underestimate the power of nature.

Buddy line

The right equipment

Having the right equipment for the job is more important in the Galápagos than almost anywhere else although the principal applies all over the world. Before you head off on any dive trip find out what the currents will be like, the likely water temperature and what safety devices you need. One thing we are all taught is how to minimize our effect on the environment and gloves are banned for fear that divers will touch everything in sight. In the Galápagos, however, you need to wear gloves when diving. If not you may well slice your hands open on the enormous barnacles that smother the rocks. Be reassured that there is no reef building coral in this region to damage! Take a thicker wetsuit than you think you will need – or extra layers.

The big decision

The Galápagos islands are on almost every diver's hit-list but before rushing out to book, there are a couple of things to consider. Are you experienced – and adaptable – enough to cope with rough and unpredictable surface water conditions and equally unusual ones below? Are you picking the right boat? Some are 100% diver focussed and some have more flexible schedules that include plenty of land visits. Bear in mind that, although this is an extraordinary experience, it is not an easy one.

Feeding amongst the rocks, a Galápagos sea lion

Dive log

The central zone

Most divers fly from the mainland to San Cristóbal on the eastern side of the archipelago as this is the departure point for all main liveaboards and cruises. From the airport to the small port is just a five minute drive and it's here that you get your first taste of Galápagos wildlife. The dock is surrounded by tiny boats and masses of sea lions; sitting on the boats, the steps, the sand and on every available rock.

Thirty minutes flight away is the Galápagos' second entry point, Puerto Ayora on Santa Cruz. This rather pretty little port town is also the economic hub of the islands. If you are going on a liveaboard this will probably be your last stop – and well worth it. It also makes a great base for those who prefer to day dive. There are several good dive centres that have small, fast boats to take you to local reefs.

Either way, both islands sit in the centre of the Galápagos and are the best places to start, allowing you to acclimatise to local dive conditions. The waters here are some of the easiest, a little shallower and a little warmer than elsewhere plus dive sites tend to be in protected coastal bays. The best aspect of this region though is that, post diving, you can take trips ashore to see the landscape and wildlife as the islands have "pedestrian access".

1 Gordon Rocks

- **Depth**: 27 m
- **Visibility**: fair
- **Currents**: slight to ripping
- **Dive type**: day boat/liveaboard
- **Snorkelling**: no

Not far from Santa Cruz island, two large rocks about 100 metres apart protrude above the water line and indicate the remains of an ancient volcano. The sunken caldera is marked by half-moon-shaped rocky masses on each side, the top is open to the currents and the bottom has three large pinnacles dividing the space. In the centre another pinnacle is thought to be the point of eruption. You can dive right around the site, inside and out, but beware – the dive is also

A solitary Galápagos penguin

A green turtle in 'La Lavadora'

known as 'La Lavadora' (the washing machine) and currents at certain points are fearsome. Large schools of eagle rays fly past, along with a green turtle or two. Around the sunken walls are some special macro animals such as barnacle blennies and giant hawkfish. If you head out through one of the channels between the pinnacles you encounter strong currents which attract large schools of king angelfish and, on the outside edge, several hammerheads. The outer walls are absolutely sheer and full of bubble-shaped holes – erosion evidently – and each is inhabited by a pencil urchin or fish while gangs of young sea lions race up and down the walls playing with each other.

2 Cousins Rock

- **Depth**: 32 m
- **Visibility**: fair
- **Currents**: strong
- **Dive type**: day boat/liveaboard
- **Snorkelling**: no

A little north of Bartolomé, this rock rises about 10 metres above the water and is home to passing birds and sea lions. These slide down the rocky walls to meet divers as they enter the water and then swim away over a series of terraces carved into the rock. The stepped wall is smothered in black coral bushes displaying tones of gold and yellow, with lots of longnose hawkfish flitting about. The giant Galápagos seahorse can be spotted amongst their branches and the unusual blue-eyed damsel. Sandy bottomed ledges house impressive starfish and gangs of whitetips. As you descend to the bottom of the wall, a tongue of land pokes out into the current and there are several types of ray surfing out in the blue. However, the main attractions are the sea lions which dart around divers and schools of tiny snapper, and a large school of small pelican barracuda.

3 Bartolomé

- **Depth**: 5 m
- **Visibility**: poor to fair
- **Currents**: slight
- **Dive type**: day boat/liveaboard
- **Snorkelling**: yes

No, it's not a dive, it's a snorkel. But this is well worth it – even for hardened tank-suckers – as Bartolomé is home to one of the few remaining colonies of Galápagos penguins, though sadly, their numbers are in decline. These birds, only about a foot tall, zip past underwater at the speed of light. You're more likely to see them sunning themselves on the rocks, where they stand proudly over inferior snorkellers, though quite a distance apart from each other as they have a strong sense of personal space. Other marine life includes massive starfish, blennies flitting about the rocks and small schools of butterfly fish. Snorkellers slip into the water just beside the huge, pointed rocky pinnacle that soars into the sky and neatly divides the island. Sea lions romp about on the beach nearby, so this is probably not the best place to go on land. Afterwards, take a walk up the nearby volcano to admire the view over a lunar landscape formed by ancient volcanic activity.

Undercurrents

The Galápagos currents
Some 5 million years ago a series of volcanic eruptions created the chain of islands we now call the Galápagos. This is still one of the world's most active volcanic regions and that, along with the isolated position of the islands, creates a unique environment. What makes the marine life so unusual though, is that the Galápagos are at the crossroads of seven major ocean currents. The most influential are the Equatorial (Cromwell) current which sweeps in cold water from due west, the warm Panama current from the northeast and the cold Peru (Humboldt) from the south. Each of these currents brings its own particular species, resulting in a rare mix of tropical, subtropical and temperate marine life.

The Mexican hogfish as a teenager

The giant hawkfish, largest of its kind

Sea lion ballet

Tales from the deep

Nothing but animals ...

The first time I saw the Galápagos Islands was way back in 1969. My friend and I had heard about a navy ship going down there to do some research and that they were willing to take a few passengers. So we signed up. The trip across was awful, terrible weather and very rough, so we spent most of the crossing outside staring at the horizon. We finally arrived and, of course, back then, there was nothing there except the animals. Tourism visits had not yet been organized, so we had no guides nor anybody to look after us. The crew would drop us off on an island during the day with some water and mandarins. We were free to spend the day just wandering around, getting as close to the wildlife as we wanted. At dusk the ship would come back and collect us. We had no idea what they were doing all day but it was quite an experience for us. I never forgot it and when my husband and I decided to start a business together, it seemed the obvious thing to do, to work with these unique islands.

Dolores Diez, Vice President, Quasar Nautica Expeditions

A Pacific spotted scorpionfish

The north

There's very little point in going all the way to the Galápagos and not seeing the two northernmost islands – Wolf and Darwin. They are regarded as the ultimate in diving on this archipelago as well as being the most isolated islands.

Only reached by liveaboard, Wolf is an overnight sail north of the central islands, with Darwin at least another four hours on. These sheer-sided, rocky land masses are home to birds – red-footed boobies settle in every nook and cranny while frigates circle above – but little else. You cannot make landfall on the islands and, for that matter, neither can the other animals. Even the sea lions struggle to find resting spots.

Because both islands are a long way north and protected by others to the south, the Humboldt current has a lesser effect here and the water is a little warmer. Note – a little, for even when the surface temperature is 28°C, the thermoclines at depth can still be icy. Despite this there is one big attraction – hammerhead sharks. No matter what time of year you come, these two outposts are famous for attracting enormous schools of them. At certain times of year there are whalesharks too but most divers come here to immerse themselves amongst these strange, prehistoric-looking creatures.

4 The Caves, Wolf

- **Depth**: 28 m
- **Visibility**: poor to good
- **Currents**: slight to ripping
- **Dive type**: liveaboard
- **Snorkelling**: no

Sitting at the base of Wolf's sheer cliffs beside a protruding pinnacle, you look down at the water and know that the currents are absolutely fearsome. The clue is in the surface movement. The site, however, is marvellous: a wall of very large boulders interspersed with several caves. You drift along to the first which has a swim through (although it would be better described as a suck through). The second is protected by some big boulders that create a break in front. Snappers and butterflyfish take advantage of the calmer water and hover around the boulders while whitetip sharks rest inside. There are a lot of morays on the wall and a lot of Galápagos sharks off it. Some are over two metres long and swim with the hammerheads. Marble rays flit along the sea bed. Near the end of the wall you can divert to a nearby underwater pinnacle but you are more likely to get swept off the end the wall and into a strong upcurrent.

5 Rockslide, Wolf

- **Depth**: 35 m
- **Visibility** : fair to good
- **Currents**: slight to ripping
- **Dive type**: liveaboard
- **Snorkelling**: no

On the other side of Wolf an ancient rockslide has formed a gentle slope that descends to about 200 metres. Traversing the enormous boulders in a surge often requires a crab walk, hand-over-hand, to take you down to the open channel. Stopping at about 20 metres, you can watch the schooling hammerheads come in. There are at least thirty in the blue, often very many more. It's worth descending a little further to watch them hover above your head but beware – the deeper water can be like ice. Glancing back up the slope, the resident school of eagle rays passes by for a look at the divers, letting the exhaust bubbles caress their tummies. Behind, and up in the shallows, Galápagos sharks cruise by and enormous green turtles hide in the crevices. Ascent takes you through a school of pompano which block out the suns rays. As you glance back downwards on your safety stop, you realise that there are rather a lot of silky sharks approaching. They stay to admire your fins as long as you stay to gas off.

6 The Arch, Darwin

- **Depth**: 35 m
- **Visibility** : poor to fair
- **Currents**: ripping
- **Dive type**: liveaboard
- **Snorkelling**: no

One of the archipelago's most impressive landmarks is Darwin's Arch. The eroded remains of a forgotten eruption mark the site of an oval- shaped reef that drops away to great depths. The gradual slope is covered in huge boulders and currents sweep up from who knows where to hit the rocky reef broad side and then veer off in all directions. No matter where you enter the water, you seem to catch both the surge and current so it's a case of dragging yourself down over the boulders – admiring some morays and lobsters as you go – then making your way to the sandy channel to the east. As you move forward you slowly become aware of the silent wave of hammerheads above you. Some are curious and move in closer, while others watch from a distance. Visibility over the channel is not always all that good as the currents lift the sand but your reward for peering into the blue may be a bottlenose dolphin – a frequent visitor – and, it is said, whalesharks in the winter months.

Eagle ray on a fly-by

I was a little scared sometimes. We would be going up and down in the surge so often. I am not experienced enough to feel completely secure. But I never thought I would see the hammerheads so close. It was amazing.

Inés Yturbe, Mexico City

Darwin's Arch

Soft corals on rocky scenery

The western zone

Isabela is the largest island in the group and creates a barrier between the open Pacific Ocean and the rest of the Galápagos archipelago. She is shaped rather like a seahorse, which seems appropriate as the islands have their very own indigenous version.

Isabela's other claim to fame is that her position divides the current patterns in such a way that stepping off her western coast can be like stepping into a tub of ice water. The cold Cromwell current sweeps in from the west, hits Isabela and Fernandina and then is directed north to Cape Marshall and on to Roca Rodonda. This, along with the fact that the region's volcanoes are still highly active, creates yet another mini-ecosystem.

7 Roca Rodonda

Depth: 35 m
Visibility: poor to fair
Currents: slight to strong
Dive type: liveaboard
Snorkelling: no

Heading south from Wolf, the first real land mass you come across is the isolated Roca Rodonda, or Round Island. This is the tip of a still active, submerged volcano with lots of volcanic gases fizzing up through the sea bed. Descending over the familiar landscape of barnacle covered boulders, you notice gangs of small fish hunkering down in the cracks and crevices. Actually, they're basking in water which has been warmed by streams of hot gas. You would almost think they were bubbles in a glass of champagne except for the hint of sulphur. Cold water thermoclines here are extremely uncomfortable, probably due to the contrast with the naturally warmed water. You also need to be aware of some serious down currents on this site. Dives can be called off or aborted, which is a shame as the life is impressive and includes hammerheads, king angels and schooling surgeonfish.

8 Punta Vicente Roca

Depth: 35 m
Visibility: fair to good
Currents: medium to strong
Dive type: liveaboard
Snorkelling: no

South and slightly west of Rodonda lies the northwestern tip of Isabela. This dive site lies beneath a pretty cove which is itself beneath the eroded remains of a volcanic cone. The geography of the dive mirrors the landscape above with hills and deep crevices, walls and lots of tumbled boulders. The walls and gullies are covered with lots of little corals.The mola-mola, or oceanic sunfish, makes the odd appearance and green turtles are common. One particularly unusual fish is the harlequin wrasse. It is consistently inconsistent in appearance and comes in various shades of orange white or black. It's all quite colourful but the water can be breathtakingly cold. At the end of the dive you surface into warmer water and huge schools of native salema, a smaller member of the grunt family and the favourite diet of fur seals and sea lions.

Pufferfish taking a break

9 Cape Marshall

Depth: 35 m
Visibility: poor to fair
Currents: ripping
Dive type: liveaboard
Snorkelling: no

This long sharp wall sits almost exactly on the Equator. It's covered in tiny yellow gorgonian corals, which are rarely more than about 20-25 centimetres long, their growth stunted by the surge and currents, and looking like heather on the rocks. As you enter the water you see quite a lot of life out in the blue – a small school of hammerheads, maybe a couple of turtles and even golden cow rays. There are some unusual puffers like the yellow spotted burrfish and guinea fowl puffer. Thermoclines can lower the temperature down to 15°C and the visibility drops as you pass through them. If you make it around the point and into the nearby bay, there is a bit more protection for the animals and some interesting smaller fish are seen, especially at night.

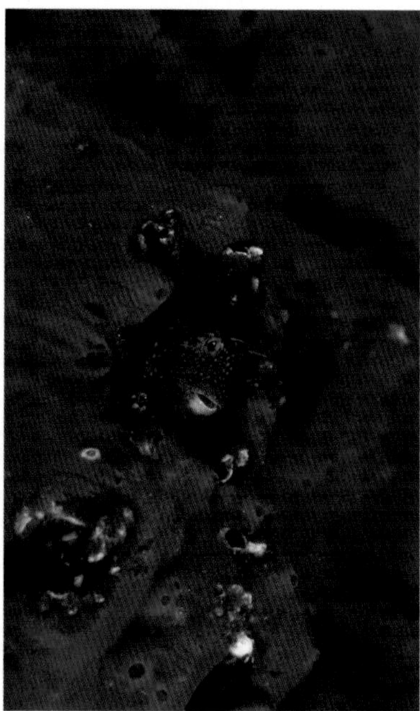

Barnaclebill blenny living in a barnacle shell

Drying out

Lammer Law

The Galápagos Islands

Puerto Ayora, capital of Santa Cruz, is a lively town with quite a cosmopolitan feel. There are lots of hotels with restaurants on site, restaurants with dive centres attached and a healthy selection of cafés, bars and dive facilities. Puerto Baquerizo Moreno, the capital of San Cristóbal, is pretty enough but very small and little more than a departure point for your liveaboard or cruise.

Dive centres

Nauti Diving, Av Charles Darwin, Puerto Ayora, Santa Cruz, T+593 (0)525 27004, www.nautidiving.com. Friendly and lively with a wide variety of diving. Prices as above or packs including 4 nights' accommodation from US$599.

Scuba Iguana, Av Charles Darwin, Puerto Ayora, Santa Cruz, T+593 (0)525 26497, www.scubaiguana.com. Very professional with thorough programmes from courses and day trips to cruises. Two local dives US$80, day trips from US$110.

Sleeping

$$$ **Finch Bay Eco-hotel**, Barrio Punta Estrada, Puerto Ayora, Santa Cruz, T+593 (0)525 26297, www.finchbayhotel.com. In a quiet location a few minutes' water taxi ride across the bay from Puerto Ayora, price includes breakfast and transfers. They also have an on-site dive centre.

The blue-footed booby

$$ **Silberstein**, Darwin y Piqueros, Puerto Ayora, Santa Cruz, T+593 (0)525 26277, www.hotelsilberstein.com. Close to the Darwin Research station. Modern but with character, has a pool, pretty gardens and a very nice restaurant. Price includes breakfast and transfers.

$ **Orca**, on the coast by the Playa de Oro beach just a mile from the airport on San Cristóbal, Puerto Baquerizo Moreno, T+593 (0)525 20233. The best hotel in town, small and charming with a restaurant and dive centre attached.

Liveaboards

Lammer Law is one of the most respected dive boats in the region. She is a trimaran with large, luxury cabins, fabulous meals and flexible schedules both for diving and land excursions. Contact via **Galápagos Classic Cruises** or **Quasar Nautica** (see below) or www.lammerlaw.com.

Sky Dancer is part of the Peter Hughes Fleet and is regarded as a more diver-specific boat with 4 dives a day scheduled regardless of conditions. Contact **Galápagos Classic Cruises** (www.galapagoscruises.co.uk) or www.peterhughes.com.

Eating

$$$ **Angermeyer Point**, across the bay from Puerto Ayora, T+593 (0)525 26452. Open Tue-Sat 1900-2200, Sun brunch 1100-1600. Take a water-taxi from the port to get to this former home of Galápagos pioneer and artist Carl Angermeyer. Gorgeous setting over the water but make sure you take insect repellent. Excellent, innovative and varied menu, attentive service.

Sights

All cruise boats, whether nature or dive orientated, ensure that you will see a good variety of wildlife on the islands.

Isla Lobos Just a short sail from San Cristóbal, this island makes a fantastic late afternoon stroll. Cross the sandy beach to walk to within inches of blue-footed boobies, get an evil look from the marine iguana who is definitely not moving from your path and

Inés and a marine iguana

Undercurrents

Politics and the Galápagos
Politics and diving shouldn't be mixed but too often they are. A political stance by the government may change the way dive, cruise and fishing operations work in, for example, national parks or World Heritage sites. In some countries, fishermen are encouraged to swap their permits for dive ones. The concept is to help protect an already fragile eco-system and depleted fishing stocks by re-employing them inside the tourist industry. However, dive companies become concerned that without proper investment and retraining, there will be issues with dive safety and practices. For divers it's important to check that whoever they dive with, the company has the correct permits to operate. Always ensure you dive with a company with a good reputation.

admire a whole herd of sea lions snoozing under a tree. You will be advised to be quiet and not disturb the mums with new pups but you would find it hard to compete with the noise of babes suckling.

Puerto Egas on Santiago is another well trodden nature trail and perhaps the highlight of any trip. The large natural bay requires a wet landing (jumping into the surf from your tender or RIB) but after that the walk around the coast is easy. Fur seals and sea lions live in rocky, lava-ringed pools and are curious enough about their human visitors to approach them. Marine iguanas bring their body temperatures back up to normal after a hard day's fishing by wiggling into sun-warmed crevices and, if you are lucky, you might spot the endemic Galápagos Hawk guarding a kill. Bright red Sally Lightfoot crabs skitter about in the rock pools and indigenous mockingbirds peck at berries on scrappy Palo Santo trees. Herons stalk along the rocks beside the tourists while lava lizards run away at the slightest footfall.

Quito

All listings for Quito are in the New City unless indicated otherwise.

Sleeping

$$$ **Swisshotel**, Av 12 de Octubre, 1820 y Luis-Cordero, T+593 (0)225 67600, www.quito.swissotel.com/. First-class international chain with all mod-cons including the **Amrita Spa**.

$$ **Grand Hotel Mercure Alameda**, Roca 653 and Av Amazonas, T+593 (0)225 62345, www.accorhotels.com. International standards and free internet access.

$ **La Cartuja**, Plaza 170 and 18 de Septiembre, T+593 (0)225 23577, www.hotelacartuja.com. In the former British Embassy, includes breakfast, good restaurant, spacious comfortable rooms, lovely garden, very helpful and hospitable.

Eating

$$$ **Cafe de la Roca**, Roca E4-183 and Juan Leon Mera, T+593 (0)225 65659. Open Mon-Fri only. Stylish with great staff, modern Ecuadorean food.

$$$ **La Sala**, Reina Victoria 1137, T+593 (0)225 46086. A few minutes' walk from the main hotels, has a superb, eclectic mix of Ecuadorean and modern international food.

$$$ **Tianguez**, on Plaza de San Francisco in the Old City, T+593 (0)229 54326, www.sinchisacha.org. Mon-Fri, lunch, Thu-Sun, lunch and dinner. Great location and serves local specialities.

Shopping

The **Artisans' market**, at Jorge Washington and Juan Leon Mera, in the New City, has a selection of traditional handicrafts, t-shirts and a lot of modern jewellery stalls. Open daily. **Artesanía Latino Americana**, at Av Amazonas 300 and Jorge Washington, has a good range of crafts at reasonable prices.

Local agents

Quasar Nautica, Brasil 293 and Granda Centeno, T+593 (0)224 46996, www.quasarnautica.com. One of the biggest dive tour organizers in Ecuador. They are responsible for several specialist dive boats including *Lammer Law* and *Mistral* as well as several naturalist cruise boats.

Safari Tours, Foch E5-39 y JL Mera, T+593 (0)225 52505, USA/Canada toll free T1-800-4348182, www.safari.com.ec. Excellent source of diverse travel information, day trips and activity tours – mountain climbing, cycling, rafting, trekking and jungle trips.

International agents

Galápagos Classic Cruises, 6 Keyes Rd, London NW2 3XA, T+44 (0)20 8933 0613, www.galapagoscruises.co.uk. Customized bookings for all land and dive trips, sailing and cultural tours throughout the continent. The owner, Ania Mudrewicz, lived in Latin America and is very knowledgeable.

Dive Worldwide, Sutton Manor Farm, Bishop's Sutton, Alresford, SO24 0AA, T+44 0845 1306980, www.diveworldwide.com. Tailor-made diving holidays around the world. Pacific islands, African hideaways, liveaboards, ice diving and much more.

48 hours in Quito

Although the Galápagos Islands themselves offer plenty to do when you're not diving, the best way to dry out after a trip is to spend some time on mainland Ecuador. **Quito**, the capital, was declared a World Heritage site in 1978 and is worthy of the title. Much of the colonial Old City dates from the early 1500's although there were settlements here long before. Sadly, the colonists wiped all traces of the Inca past.

On your first day, take a taxi to the **Plaza Grande** – also known as the Plaza de la Independencia – in the Old City and admire the four sides of the square. On each is a building that represents the varying governing bodies. The Cathedral on the west was consecrated in 1572, the Archbishop's Palace is opposite, the 18th century Government Palace is on the north and the modern Municipal Palace is on the south side. The Cathedral will sell you a walking tour map which will take you down the Street of the Seven Crosses, where every other building houses something of interest. There are churches, galleries and lifestyle museums and even a small museum that explains the history of currency in the region, from Inca times to the present. Many of the attractions are free while a few want a dollar or two.

After the morning walk, divert to the **Plaza San Francisco**, a few minutes away. This colourful square was built over an indigenous trading market. There is a wonderful restaurant, *Tianguez*, right on the square that is a perfect spot for people watching. While away a couple of hours with an icy beer and some lunch. There is a good handicrafts store attached to the restaurant. Once you are refreshed you can view the overwhelming interior of the Franciscan church, convent and museum and then continue exploring more of the Old City's cobbled streets.

If you have a second day to sightsee, and it's a Saturday, book a day trip to the markets at **Otavalo**. This town is a haven for all sorts of artisans, plus a day tour will also give you a taste of the Ecuadorean countryside. Tours start by departing the city to the north then drive up through the Andes past several points of natural beauty. Stops are made at the **San Pablo lake** and **Imbabura volcano**, and in the valley of **Guallabamba** where the major industry is flower growing. Stops are also made at several local cottage industries that are hidden away in towns you wouldn't know existed. There is no pressure to purchase anything, this is just about displaying local talent and traditions. By late morning you arrive in Otavalo where the market is both a shopoholic's and photographer's dream. Indigenous handicrafts jostle for space with fresh fruit, vegetables and local spices. Modern artists sell their work at very reasonable prices. It is amazingly colourful and lively. The return route to Quito goes via the nature reserve at **Cotacachi-Cayapas**, which surrounds a sunken caldera and is backed by the volcano itself – though it's often hidden in the cloud layer.

Shoeshine boy in Plaza San Francisco

Handicrafts in Otavalo

Gardens in the sea: season by season, a ceaseless display of marine tranquillity at Lighthouse Reef

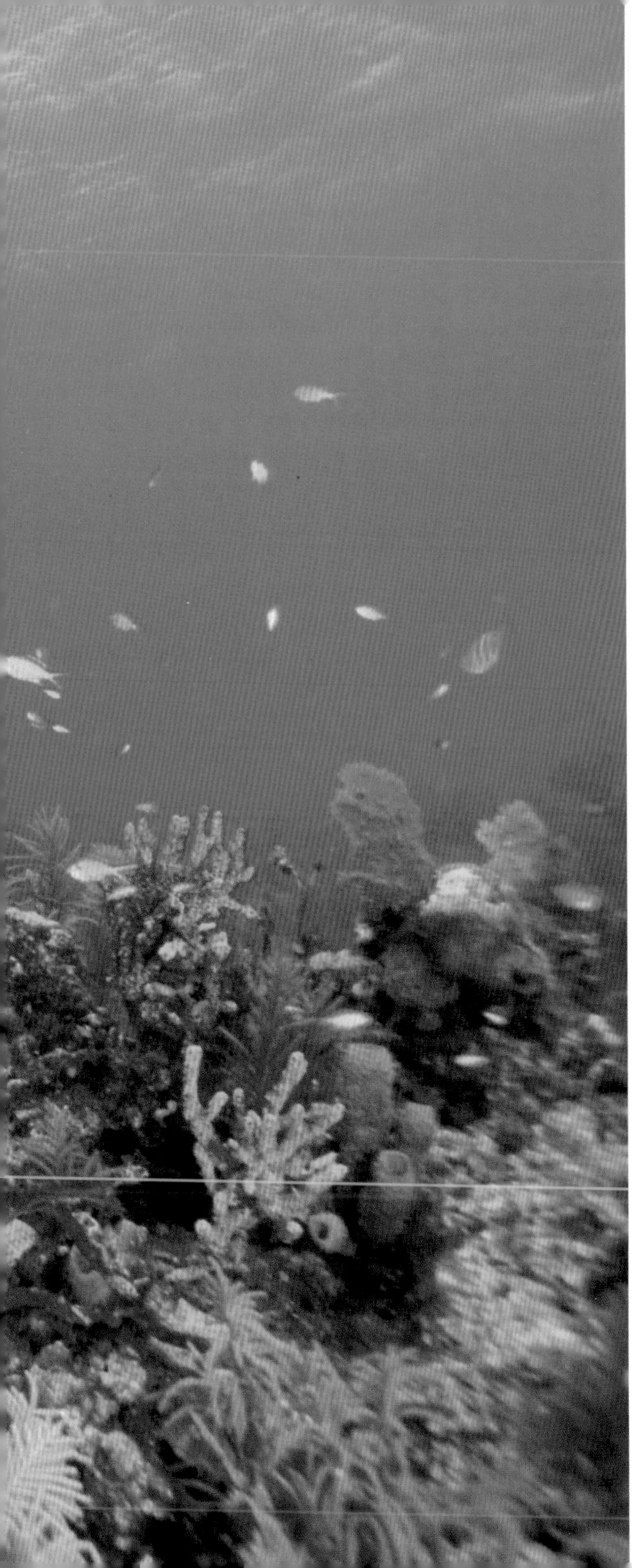

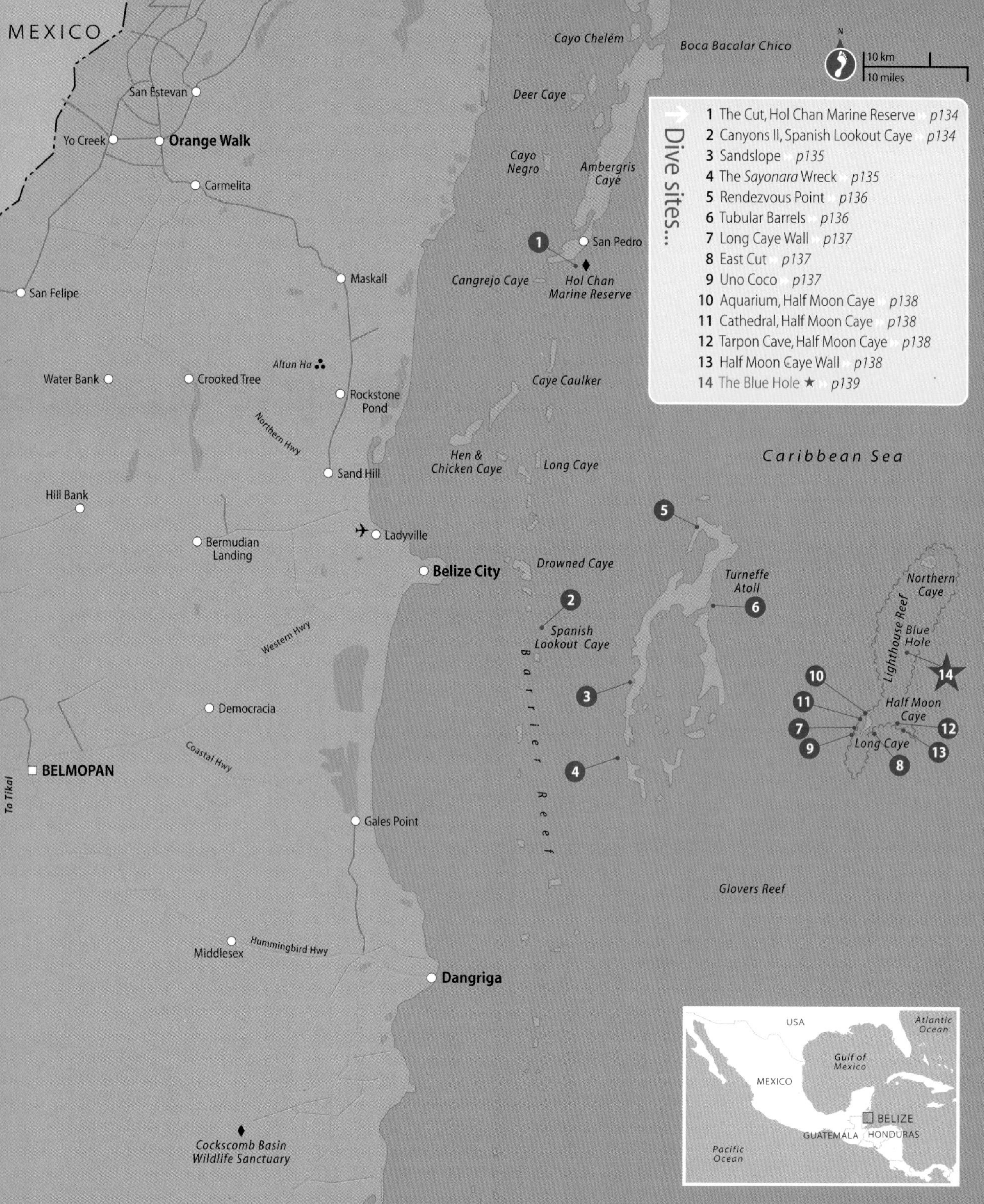

MEXICO
San Estevan
Yo Creek
Orange Walk
Carmelita
San Felipe
Maskall
Water Bank
Crooked Tree
Altun Ha
Rockstone Pond
Northern Hwy
Sand Hill
Hill Bank
Ladyville
Bermudian Landing
Belize City
Western Hwy
Democracia
Coastal Hwy
BELMOPAN
To Tikal
Gales Point
Middlesex
Hummingbird Hwy
Dangriga
Cockscomb Basin Wildlife Sanctuary
Cayo Chelém
Boca Bacalar Chico
Deer Caye
Cayo Negro
Ambergris Caye
San Pedro
Cangrejo Caye
Hol Chan Marine Reserve
Caye Caulker
Hen & Chicken Caye
Long Caye
Caribbean Sea
Drowned Caye
Spanish Lookout Caye
Barrier Reef
Turneffe Atoll
Northern Caye
Lighthouse Reef
Blue Hole
Half Moon Caye
Long Caye
Glovers Reef
N
10 km
10 miles
Dive sites...
1 The Cut, Hol Chan Marine Reserve p134
2 Canyons II, Spanish Lookout Caye p134
3 Sandslope p135
4 The Sayonara Wreck p135
5 Rendezvous Point p136
6 Tubular Barrels p136
7 Long Caye Wall p137
8 East Cut p137
9 Uno Coco p137
10 Aquarium, Half Moon Caye p138
11 Cathedral, Half Moon Caye p138
12 Tarpon Cave, Half Moon Caye p138
13 Half Moon Caye Wall p138
14 The Blue Hole ★ p139
USA
Atlantic Ocean
Gulf of Mexico
MEXICO
BELIZE
GUATEMALA
HONDURAS
Pacific Ocean

Introduction

Shaped by the ice age, the Caribbean Sea developed in isolation from the world's other oceans. It's almost as if she was at the back of the queue and missed out on her fair share of marine species. However, she did inherit the world's second largest barrier reef, of which Belize has its fair share.

Diving here isn't a mind-numbing assault on the senses. This is a more subtle underwater experience. Pastel-coloured soft corals and neutral-toned hard corals create a delicate backdrop for marine life that prefers not to demand attention but instead waits for more patient and observant divers to notice the small but satisfying differences. Much of Belize is a surprise.

Although the country edges the western side of the Caribbean, her personality is more Latin American. With a history shaped first by the Maya and then by colonial invaders, you would be forgiven for assuming more in the way of cultural diversions. In reality, however, the country's landside charms lie in its many gifts from nature. The Maya Mountains, clad in deepest emerald green, roll down to coastal plains that seem to hover over the heat haze. Off the coast, azure waters are punctuated by tiny spits of sand with sparse coconut palms and mangrove glades, and beneath the sea, like a gentle sunset, the radiant colours fade to the soft and muted tones of the reefs.

“” *What makes this such an interesting dive destination is that the more you know, the more you will enjoy it.*

Belize rating

Diving
★★★

Dive facilities
★★★

Accommodation
★★★

Down time
★★★

Value for money
★★★

Essentials

Getting there and around

At a time when air travel couldn't be easier, it seems bizarre to find a country that's a little difficult to get to. Belize is one of those rare places, simply because it doesn't have a national carrier. Several airlines land at Belize City (**American**, **Delta** and **US Airways**) but the one that flies most frequently is **Continental** (www.continental.com) with several daily flights from Houston and Newark. Although Continental have a comprehensive network of routes, their comfort factor is not so good. Like most US carriers, in-flight entertainment is minimal, they charge for alcoholic drinks and service is not always the friendliest. The good news, especially for Europeans, is that they have a generous luggage allowance.

Alternatively, fly as far as the US with any other carrier (say **BA**, **Virgin**, **Qantas** or **Air New Zealand**) and then connect to a shorter Continental flight or one with Central American airline **TACA** (www.taca.com) who also fly out of Houston. TACA also have flights from Los Angeles, Miami or San Francisco but these may entail flying via another Central American city. Yet another option would be to fly into Cancún, on Mexico's Yucatán Peninsula, and travel overland from there. This would allow you to dive both countries. There are buses from Cancún to Chetumal, on the Mexican side of the border, every few hours, and then a more regular service from there to Belize City. Total journey time, including border crossing, is around 12 hours. Sadly, this is very hard to pre-book but see page 141 for advice.

Once you have arrived in Belize, dive liveaboards depart from the dock at Fort George in the city or, if you choose to visit one of the islands, there are two local airlines, **Tropic Air** (www.tropicair.com) and **Maya Island Air** (www.mayaairways.com), that shuttle people around the country in fleets of small aircraft. Wherever you are going, your dive operator will advise on transfers.

If you want to take a day tour, an inland tour or even head to nearby Guatemala to see one of the major Maya sites, there is plenty of transport. Water taxis head to the various cayes and on land there's a good public bus system. The network covers the whole of the country and fares are cheap, although the buses are somewhat rickety. The two airlines listed above also have schedules that allow for day tours by air.

Half Moon Caye

Language

The official language is English. There are others in use, including two versions of Mayan, but the only other language you'll come across is Spanish. Here are a few basic words and phrases (see also page 112):

hello	*hola*
goodbye	*adiós*
see you later	*hasta luego*
yes	*sí*
no	*no*
I don't know	*no se*
okay	*vale (like ballet)*
please	*por favor*
thank you	*gracias*
I'm sorry	*lo siento*
how much is ...?	*¿cuánto es ...?*
a beer/water	*una cerveza/agua mineral*
good	*bueno*
great dive	*una buceada fantástica*

Belize

Location	17°15′ N, 88°45′ W
Neighbours	Guatemala, Honduras, Mexico
Population	281,084
Land area in km²	22,806
Marine area in km²	31,000
Coastline in km	386

Local laws and customs

Belize is an informal country with a very casual lifestyle and feels more Caribbean than neighbouring Mexico and Honduras. About half the population is Catholic and the remainder a mixture of other Christian religions. It's important to be courteous and polite here but there are no specific customs that need to be observed. As always, just use your common sense.

Safety

Belize City is not a particularly pretty place. Much of it has an air of faded grandeur. For visitors, the biggest threat is from pickpockets and while the tourist police patrol Fort George – where the Radisson Hotel and dock are located – it is best to avoid walking around the rest of the city at night, especially around bus stations. If you're heading out, ask hotel reception to get you a taxi. This will be cheap and is particularly recommended for female travellers. Outside of Belize City, the country is relatively safe. People are mostly friendly and welcoming in the main tourist centres. The main offshore islands of Ambergris and Caye Caulker get very busy, so it's a good idea to leave your valuables in the hotel safe. Drug use is illegal so be careful not to get drawn in too far to that laid-back Caribbean lifestyle.

Health

While the appearance of things in Belize might make you think that standards would be low, the country actually has a good health record with trained health workers and a clinic in most villages as well as good hospitals in Belize City. Bottled water is easy to find in all the larger towns but if you are heading off the beaten track for the day, take some with you.

Costs

In terms of costs, Belize can be as expensive or as cheap as you want it to be. In Belize City, Caye Caulker and Ambergris you can easily find a decent guesthouse for around US$40 a night and eat in one of the local restaurants for less than US$10. Seafood is good, unless you go in conch season when it's conch curry, conch burgers and conch and chips. Of course, you could spend much more in upmarket eco-lodges owned by the rich and famous (Francis Ford Coppola runs a group of very upmarket and expensive hotels) and private island resorts on the outer reefs. A beer in a local bar will be around US$1.25, or up to US$2.50 in a resort. Service charges of 10% are added to some bills but if not tipping is at your discretion. Small change on a small bill or around 10% is acceptable. For dive crews see page 14.

Airlines → American Airlines T+501 (0)223 2522; Continental T+501 (0)227 8309; Delta T+501 (0)225 3429; Grupo TACA T+501 (0)227 7363; US Airways T+501 (0)225 3589; Maya Island Air T+501 (0)226 2435; Tropic Air T+501 (0)226 2012. **Embassies** → UK T+501 (0)822 2146, US T+501 (0)227 7161, Mexico T+501 (0)223 0193. **Belize country code** → +501. **IDD code** → 00. **Police** → T911.

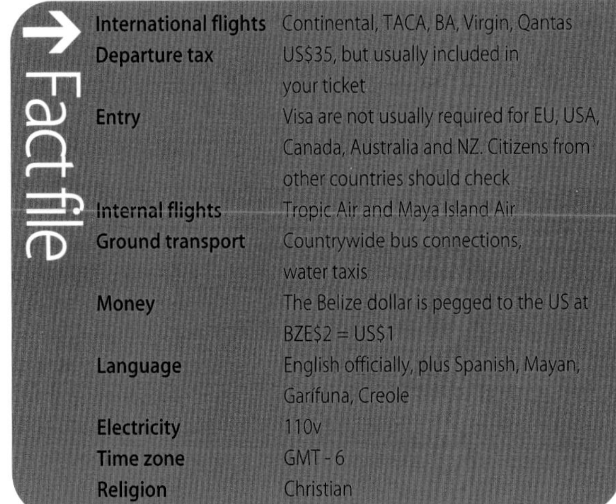

→ Fact file

International flights	Continental, TACA, BA, Virgin, Qantas
Departure tax	US$35, but usually included in your ticket
Entry	Visa are not usually required for EU, USA, Canada, Australia and NZ. Citizens from other countries should check
Internal flights	Tropic Air and Maya Island Air
Ground transport	Countrywide bus connections, water taxis
Money	The Belize dollar is pegged to the US at BZE$2 = US$1
Language	English officially, plus Spanish, Mayan, Garifuna, Creole
Electricity	110v
Time zone	GMT -6
Religion	Christian

Squirrelfish sheltering in a pipe

Dive brief

Diving

The countries that form a bridge between North and South America are fringed by the world's second largest barrier reef (Australia's Great Barrier Reef is the largest). The Great Western Barrier Reef runs for 300 km down Mexico's Yucatán Peninsula, south through Belize then on to Honduras.

The Great Western Barrier Reef offers the best diving in the Caribbean but as this is an isolated sea it has far lower biodiversity rankings than Asia or the Pacific. You only have to look at the relatively low figures for corals to see why this region isn't as colourful. Nevertheless, the fish life is fascinating. Of the 430 species in the Caribbean, 195 are in Belize.

There is diving from just off the coast to the more distant atolls outside the reef barrier. The areas closest to shore suffer a little from run off. So, the further out you go, the better the visibility. The small cayes which sit between the mainland and the barrier reef are interesting for their distinct marine habitats. There are three main atoll groups: Turneffe, east from Belize City, and Lighthouse Reef, a little further out, are the two most impressive, while Glovers Reef to the southeast, though regarded by many locals as inconsistent diving, is also less explored.

Dive sites are, in the main, a mix of gentle, open mounds and steeper drop-offs. These are characterized by sharp channels that cut through the reef rim. Conditions are generally easy. Currents are generated by tides but as the tidal range is seldom greater than half a metre more challenging conditions only occur in the numerous cuts through the barrier reef. This is, of course, where you find the best habitats for large fish and rich coral growth.

Bottom time

The inner barrier reef
The central section of the world's second largest continuous reef system » *p134*

Turneffe Atoll
A gently shelving, oval-shaped reef with varying conditions right around its rim » *p135*

Lighthouse Reef
Location of one of the planet's most famous underwater caverns, the Blue Hole, but with much more to discover » *p137*

Diversity

reef area 1,330 km²

Coral species	Fish species	Fish species under threat	Protected reefs/marine parks
57	195	6	9

The red hind grouper

Diver and fish at Tarpon Cave

Our first trip to Belize was way back in 1992. At the time we didn't much like the diving. Sure it was pleasant but seemed a bit colourless, a bit bland. We returned last year to discover that there is a far more interesting world down there than we first realized. It takes a bit of time to recognize that you get out of it what you put in. Do some research into the localized species, then slow down, relax and you will see so much more than you thought you would. It's all a bit like a spring day: calm, gentle and refreshing.

Snorkelling

For those who prefer not to submerge, Belize is a great snorkelling destination. There's the Hol Chan Marine Reserve near Ambergris Caye and another at Caye Caulker. Many of the reefs around the outer atolls come in close enough to shore to offer good snorkelling as well and you can see pelagics in just a few feet of water. There is little coral but a lot of seagrass which attracts bottom feeders like rays and nurse sharks.

The big decision

The big attraction for Belize is the Blue Hole, famously lauded by Jacques Cousteau as one of the world's 'must-dives'. As it's way out on Lighthouse Reef the best way to get there is on a liveaboard, especially as Lighthouse Reef Resort is currently closed for rebuilding (see page 140). Sailing out is also more comfortable and gives the chance to tour the best of the atolls on the way. There are plenty of resorts across all the islands for those who prefer to be land based. Depending on your outlook, you may prefer a liveaboard as some resorts target other marine sports such as fishing.

Buddy line

Non-stop diving

This has become quite a debate – is it safe to dive for 10 days non-stop? If you are on a liveaboard boat that sets sail for that long, you may feel you have no choice – unless you are willing to take a day out and sunbathe. Current thinking is that you should take one day off in seven but there is no definitive evidence that this reduces your risk of DCS. Be sure to obey your computer and don't push it to the limit. If your decompression countdown is up to 18 hours, spend a couple of dives at shallower depths.

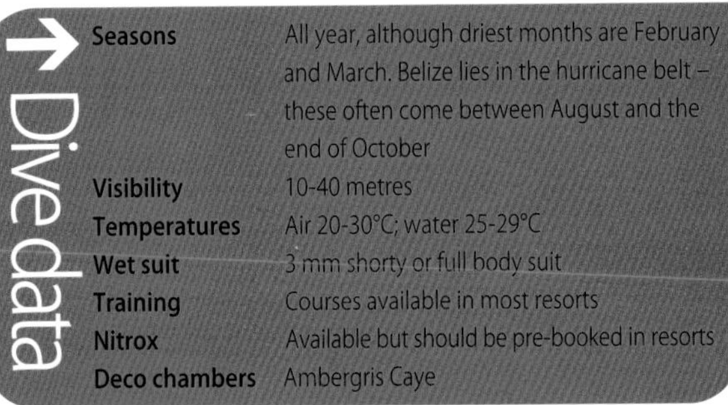

Dive data

Seasons	All year, although driest months are February and March. Belize lies in the hurricane belt – these often come between August and the end of October
Visibility	10-40 metres
Temperatures	Air 20-30°C; water 25-29°C
Wet suit	3 mm shorty or full body suit
Training	Courses available in most resorts
Nitrox	Available but should be pre-booked in resorts
Deco chambers	Ambergris Caye

Half Moon Caye National Monument

A 2.4 metre-long tarpon

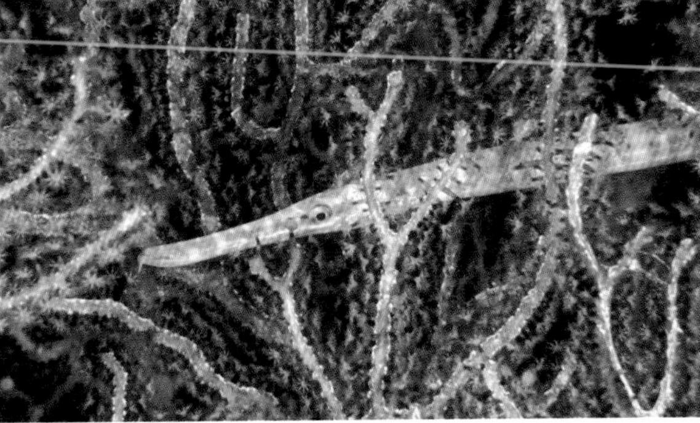

Trumpetfish sheltering in a fan

Dive log

The inner barrier reef

Belize's barrier reef is less than an hour from Belize City and only a mile off the shores of Caye Caulker and Ambergris Caye. To the south of these two popular islands is a series of small cayes and reefs, many with evocative names like Drowned Caye, Hen and Chicken Caye and Spanish Lookout Caye, all a reflection of their illustrious pasts.

East of these small islands, a deep marine trench separates the inner reef from the deeper atolls of Turneffe and Lighthouse Reef. The area inside the reef is shallow and well protected with some good diving within the small marine parks where there are also restrictions on fishing. Because there are several different eco-systems, there's a wider diversity of species.

There are mangrove islands, seagrass beds and coral reefs all within 10 miles of the coast. The mangrove cayes are habitats for seabirds while fish, shellfish and marine organisms begin their lives within the protection of the mangrove roots. The coral cayes, recognized by their palm trees, are ringed by reefs, lagoons and seagrass beds. Each of these are havens for a variety of marine species.

Pastel-hued soft corals

1 The Cut, Hol Chan Marine Reserve

- **Depth**: 12 m
- **Visibility**: fair
- **Currents**: unlikely
- **Dive type**: day boat
- **Snorkelling**: yes

This small marine reserve is a favourite for both divers and snorkellers. It's not particularly challenging diving, and can be crowded, but it's a good example of a really pleasant inner Belizean reef. The structure runs east-west creating a long winding ridge with cuts, fan corals and hard coral outcrops. The outer side gently slopes down to about 12 metres then heads off to the distant reef edge. There are a lot of large pelagic fish as this is a no fishing zone. You can see grouper and barracuda plus angelfish and masses of bluestriped grunts. Up in the shallow seagrass beds, snorkellers can meet nurse sharks, rays and morays, often in waist-deep water.

2 Canyons II, Spanish Lookout Caye

- **Depth**: 25 m
- **Visibility**: fair
- **Currents**: can be strong
- **Dive type**: day boat
- **Snorkelling**: possibly

This reef, at the southern end of Drowned Caye, is a short distance from Belize City yet has to be one of the more interesting dives in the inner reef area. Within seconds of hitting the water you are likely to encounter spotted eagle rays, large crabs, lobsters and grouper. Smaller animals nestle into the reef's cracks and crevices and include arrow crabs, tiny cleaner shrimp, coral banded shrimp and morays. Off over the wall there are great barracuda and tuna watching curiously. An area of mangrove swamp is a fantastic nursery ground for lobster and molluscs and, if you are lucky, you may even see manatees feeding on the seagrass beds.

Turneffe Atoll

As you sail east from Belize City, passing over the barrier reef, you meet a series of atolls divided by deepwater marine trenches. Turneffe Atoll sits on the first, and shallower, of two submarine ridges. Lighthouse Reef is on a separate ridge farther to east.

The Turneffe Islands are about 20 miles east of Belize. This is the largest of the country's atolls and the closest to the mainland. It's different from Lighthouse (further east) and Glovers (which is due south) in that many of the islands here are covered in mangroves. There are 200 or so cayes dotted around, all providing shelter for a range of small marine animals as well as nursery grounds for all sorts of creatures. Tides and winds distribute nutrients around the atoll and consequently, fish populations are substantial.

Each side of Turneffe has differing conditions. The north and west can be choppy while the eastern side drops off to greater depths. There are dive sites right around the atoll although the shallow lagoon waters and numerous islands make navigating through it a risky business.

Two morays keeping company

3 Sandslope

Depth: 36 m
Visibility: fair to good
Currents: none to medium
Dive type: day boat/liveaboard
Snorkelling: yes

This oval shaped reef has lots of small bommies and coral patches around it. There is good coverage of corals such as seaplumes, rods and whips and even some fan corals that are several feet high. These all thrive in the currents created by the atoll's tidal flow. The very pretty indigo hamlet is resident here as is his cousin, the shy hamlet. These small skittish fish are easy to miss, unlike the huge lobsters that settle anywhere they find comfortable, such as the inside of a really tall vase sponge. As the site is away from the coast you will see some of the more unusual Caribbean fish such as sargassam triggerfish and diamond blennies. There are also shrimp in corkscrew anemones, spinyhead blennies in sponges, spotted morays and arrow crabs, plus lots of jawfish and angelfish.

4 The *Sayonara* Wreck

Depth: 33 m
Visibility: good
Currents: none to mild
Dive type: day boat/liveaboard
Snorkelling: yes

This long sloping wall off the southwest of Turneffe drops to over 40 metres and has a pure white sandy seabed with seaplumes and large barrel sponges scattered across it. Diving along the ridge there are a lot of cuts and gullies which create nice swim-throughs for divers and shelters for the fish. Large mackerel pass overhead and are followed by the solitary ocean triggerfish. Heading back towards the mooring you come to the wreck of the *Sayonara*, a cargo boat deliberately sunk in 1985. There's nothing much left of its wooden hull save for a lot of mechanical detritus but there are an incredible number of indigo hamlets and just as many spotted trunkfish. The rare toadfish is known to live on this reef. If you want to see this elusive creature stick closely to your dive guide!

Lobster in a sponge on sandslope

Tales from the deep

Images of Belize
The smell of a street corner BBQ; the gritty road that leads away from this noisy, clogged city; reassuring reminders that dreams are usually not this real.

The elegant form and colour composition of the skittish sargassum triggerfish with its blue hue, patch of white above the eyes and small, dark, choco-like sprinkles.

Playing hide and seek at Turneffe with the elusive waving beard of the endemic white-spotted toadfish. The contrast between the been-there-done-that diver's disdain for the Blue Hole and the face of a new and hesitant diver, at 115 feet, as the imposing stalactite formations the size of a 15-diver-carrying-dive-boat come into sight.

Learning to appreciate every site for what it kindly offers and being rewarded, when accepting such offers, with the capacity to see something I was once blind to, like the many neck and decorator crabs, diamond, quillfin, and spinyhead blennies, amongst others, that became beloved and popular stars in my videos. All of these things are what keep me here, smiling, after having worked as an instructor and video pro with a liveaboard cruising Turneffe and Lighthouse Reefs, almost exclusively, for close to a year.

Vladimir Soto, Padi IDC Staff Instructor, was born in Mexico City and works in Belize, Monterrey Bay and Sri Lanka

5 Rendezvous Point

- **Depth**: 21 m
- **Visibility**: good
- **Currents**: mild to strong
- **Dive type**: day boat/liveaboard
- **Snorkelling**: yes

Sitting on the northwestern side of Turneffe atoll, this dive site is located on the edge of one of the few entries to the inner lagoon. The wall begins at 15 metres and gradually slopes down with a series of grooves and canyon formations. The topography is quite gentle with fewer tunnels than in the south of the attol. However, even these shallow grooves through the reef are full of life with swarms of glassfish, small neon gobies and arrow crabs sheltering inside. The sloping wall has a variety of sponges and plenty of schooling fish, plus you may glimpse a blacktip shark, eagle rays or turtles.

6 Tubular Barrels

- **Depth**: 22 m
- **Visibility**: good
- **Currents**: mild to medium
- **Dive type**: day boat/liveaboard
- **Snorkelling**: yes

This rather gentle site is in the middle of the eastern side of the atoll. The wall is quite shallow but covered in an amazing array of sponges – long, yellow tube sponges, azure vase sponges and huge barrel sponges that stand proud of the surrounding pastel-toned soft corals. All this is ringed by small shoals of fish, plenty of flamingo tongue shells and arrow crabs. There are cleaning stations and a surprising number of boxfish. A pod of bottlenose dolphins are regular visitors here and can also be seen at Wonderland. This dive is quite similar but a little way north on the east of the atoll.

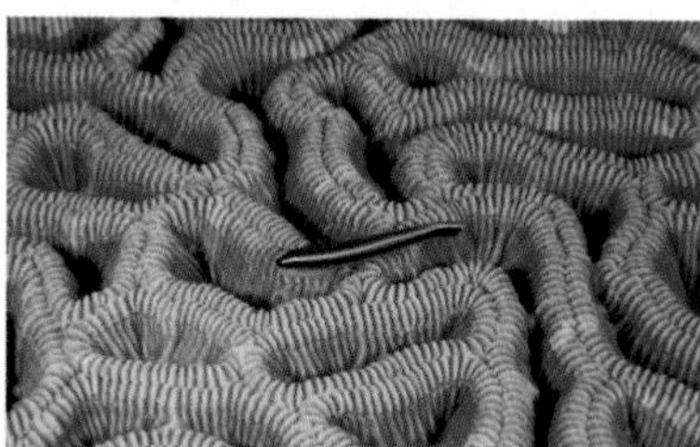
Neon goby

Outstanding reef sponges

The indigo hamlet, which is just 13 cm long

Lighthouse Reef

The most quoted reason people come to dive Belize is to witness the geological spectacle made famous over 30 years ago by one Jacques-Yves Cousteau: the Blue Hole at Lighthouse Reef.

Just 50 miles southeast of Belize City yet the most distant of her atolls, Lighthouse Reef is only 30 miles long and eight miles wide but, despite its limited size, this is where you'll find the best diving in Belize. Apart from the Blue Hole National Monument, there is plenty of excellent diving, most of it at Half Moon and Long Cayes, both of which are some distance away from the Blue Hole.

Both cayes are ringed by impressive sites with walls cut by deep grooves and channels, caves and caverns. Each of the sites has a similar profile although some are backed by flat shelves with seagreass beds which are perfect for stingray hunting.

The diving at Lighthouse is subject to weather conditions but even if the the winds pick up from one direction, then you simply move to the opposite coast. There are so many sites so close together that conditions will always be good somewhere. Moreover, The Blue Hole is smack-bang in the middle of it all so you'll never miss out.

7 Long Caye Wall

- **Depth**: 33 m
- **Visibility**: good to excellent
- **Currents**: slight
- **Dive type**: liveaboard/day boat
- **Snorkelling**: yes

This reef is covered in very pretty corals, in many subtle shades of beige, peach and lavender. Entry is over a sandy bed with some small patchy outcrops that you swim around until you reach a series of bommies that direct you over the wall. A promontory juts outwards from here and is covered in really impressive, five-feet-high tube sponges, with finger sponges, whips and sea fans across the terrain. A bevy of bright blue basslets dance around, competing with the damselfish for space. Swimming back from the outer edge through the gullies you find filefish and Nassau grouper, lots of brightly-coloured creole wrasse, angels and boxfish. Back under the boat, schools of jacks, chubbs and permit fish hang out.

8 East Cut

- **Depth**: 25 m
- **Visibility**: good to great
- **Currents**: slight to medium
- **Dive type**: liveaboard/day boat
- **Snorkelling**: yes

On this similar wall dive, entry is over a flat-topped section of the reef which you swim across then over some bommies until you reach a sharp drop. The wall goes down to 40 metres or so but stopping at the rim you can find juvenile drums flitting about. Along the wall are some of the biggest barrel sponges you will ever see, one in particular is almost 2 metres in diameter. Sitting on the top are tiny yellow arrow crabs, as well as dramatic black and grey fans. Back up on the top are the usual suspects in terms of fish life as well as a couple of small tuna patrolling back and forth along with a small turtle.

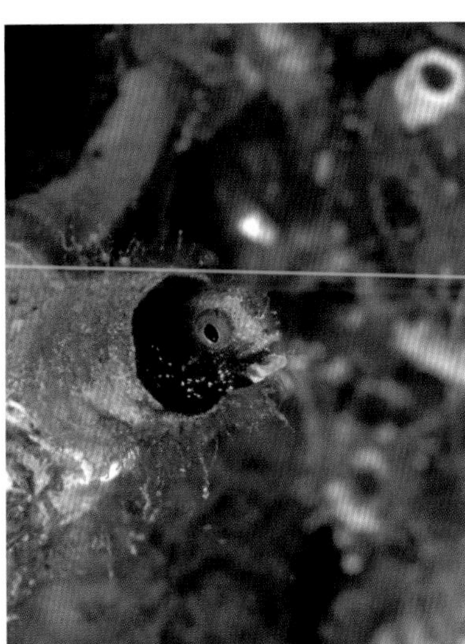

The comical roughhead blenny

9 Uno Coco

- **Depth**: 22 m
- **Visibility**: good to excellent
- **Currents**: slight
- **Dive type**: liveaboard/day boat
- **Snorkelling**: yes

This dive goes under a variety of names from Uno Coco to Tres Cocos depending on how many coconut palms are growing on the shore at the time. A sharp wall drops from 10 metres to 40 metres and is smothered in life and dense with all sorts of corals, large sponges and crusting algaes. It is perhaps the best covered reef in the area. There are enormous green morays co-habiting in one hole and crevices are thick with gangs of lobster. In fact, almost every cranny you poke your nose into has something in it – like condos for marine life. Under the boat a load of massive tarpon hover over the plateau and just above them are schools of jacks and chubbs forming big waves of silver. Up on top of the wall a ridge of coral is backed by a sandy section. This is a great night dive, when it's easy to spot scampering lobster and furtive octopus.

Face to face with a giant barracuda

10 Aquarium, Half Moon Caye

- **Depth**: 20 m
- **Visibility**: great
- **Currents**: slight to medium
- **Dive type**: liveaboard
- **Snorkelling**: possibly

Not dissimilar to the rest of the dives along the west of the atoll, this is another very pretty wall. It's dog-leg shaped with lots of twists and turns and goes all the way down to about 60 metres. Running along the wall are large fans, soft corals and some very big sponges which are surrounded by clusters of fish. Just over the edge a very friendly giant barracuda hovers, keeping completely still, to watch the divers. Also on the wall are two very large midnight parrotfish – these guys are the largest parrots and grow to 75 cm! Angels, boxfish, porkfish, butterflies and damsels flit amongst the prolific corals and sponges and there are even some tunicates. If you're watching the blue, you may spot eagle rays below and, heading back to the boat, you'll see swarms of jacks, snapper and chubb, shadowing its hull.

Adult spotted drum at Half Moon Caye

Three jacks in a channel

11 Cathedral, Half Moon Caye

- **Depth**: 35 m
- **Visibility**: excellent
- **Currents**: slight
- **Dive type**: liveaboard
- **Snorkelling**: possibly

Although this wall is nowhere near as pretty as some of the others at Lighthouse, the topography is far more interesting with lots of cut backs and gullies in the reef to swim through. At the bottom of the wall are large lobsters hiding in the crevices (at certain times you'll notice that the females are pregnant). Coming back up the wall and into the cuts you are often met head on by large mackerel trying to get out. Swimming back over the upper section of the reef are lots of little roughhead blennies in holes, flamingo tongue shells and banded coral shrimp. The bigger pelagic fish always seem to be hanging out under the boat – chubbs, jacks, snapper, creole wrasse and a very inquisitive great barracuda.

12 Tarpon Cave, Half Moon Caye

- **Depth**: 40 m
- **Visibility**: excellent
- **Currents**: slight
- **Dive type**: liveaboard
- **Snorkelling**: possibly

This dive, on the east of Lighthouse, has fabulous topography. Entry is over a seagrass bed at about 8 metres which leads across an area of sand covered in conch. At about 20 metres you are then faced with a barrier formation that rises up again to 15 metres. There are tunnels that cut through the barrier to the reef rim, leading to the outer wall and depths of well over 60 metres. Swimming into one tunnel, you'll meet a five-foot tarpon, his scales metallic silver and highly reflective, virtually waiting to have his photo taken. A small cave further along is dark with silversides and you can watch a barracuda swoop in to feed on them. As you exit, another great barracuda is hanging around waiting his turn. Swimming along the outer wall an eagle ray passes by below then, a few seconds later, you might see a turtle. Back up on the reef top schools of black and blue tangs go crazy in the algae. Doing a safety stop over seagrass is a good time for spotting stingrays as they fluff up the sand, looking for food.

13 Half Moon Caye Wall

- **Depth**: 18 m
- **Visibility**: excellent
- **Currents**: mild
- **Dive type**: liveaboard
- **Snorkelling**: yes

This is similar to Tarpon Cave with a grassy bed, a sandy bed, then a raised rim of coral outcrops that separates the lagoon from the sea before dropping back down to a steep wall. This makes a good end-of-day dive as you can spend time over the seagrass bed where bright silver tarpon and tiger groupers hang about. There are also quite a few small grey rays, always harassed by jacks, and a large southern stingray. A baby French angelfish lives around a few discarded pipes, keeping a squirrelfish company. A bed of manatee grass protects newborn juveniles like filefish and bandtail puffers. Baby surgeons shelter in coconuts shells and spotted eagle rays swoop over the sand.

Queen angelfish

14 The Blue Hole

- **Depth**: 45 m
- **Visibility**: fair to good
- **Currents**: none
- **Dive type**: liveaboard/day boat
- **Snorkelling**: only around the reef rim

The Blue Hole gained overnight celebrity status following Jacques Cousteau's 1970 *Calypso* expedition. Sitting at the midpoint of Lighthouse Reef, it was believed to have been a cave whose roof fell in at the end of the Ice Age. The circular opening is over 300 metres across and drops to around 150 metres deep. At around 40 metres there is a shelf with ancient stalagtites. As limestone can't form underwater, this is evidence that the cave was once above sea level. The dive is approached by dropping straight down in a vertical line to see the stalagmites. The water temperature drops substantially by the time you reach 45 metres. You only get a few moments to admire the stalagtites and an occasional grouper that has descended with you then it's time to ascend again. Apart from the few fish, the dive is surprisingly lifeless but operators have picked up on the fact that the area was visited by grey reef sharks and now use bait to attract them. As you ascend for a safety stop they circle, hoping for further handouts.

As a dive, this is a completely unique and exhilarating experience, especially for beginners who have rarely, if ever, been so deep. However, the hole does look far more impressive from the air, when its dark blue circle is surrounded by intense turquoise water. The operators say that novice divers are highly disoriented by the depth; also that there are more cameras lying on the bottom than in your average camera store. A decent carabiner (or d-clip) may be a good idea, no matter how seasoned you are.

There is no doubt about it – this dive is quite an adrenaline rush.

Tales from the deep

Into the Blue

As a relatively new diver I had heard stories about the Blue Hole. I got the opportunity to dive the site this past June. The mystery, the obscurity, the unknown that surrounds this gigantic former cave that sits off the coast of Belize had aroused my curiosity. Then came the day of the dive. The excitement built as I donned my tank and rolled backwards off the tender into the depths. Then the enigma became a reality when all 16 of us had to descend in a large circle in unison, the DM clanging on his tank constantly to keep everyone together. "What is this?" I asked myself "an exercise in descending to 130 feet and ascending slowly?" Where were the sea monsters? Where were the flashing lights, or the massive surge that would carry me to unknown depths, never to be seen again? No corals, no fish, no reef creatures. Only a few overfed, lethargic sharks and groupers waiting for the next batch of divers to descend into its depths.

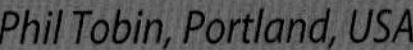

Phil Tobin, Portland, USA

Grey reef sharks attracted by boats chumming the water

Drying out

Belize is slightly overshadowed by neighbouring countries when it comes to land-based attractions. Hers are more subtle and sit quietly in the background. That said, there are some interesting places to see and things to do.

Belize City

Dive centres

Hugh Parkey's Belize Dive Connection, PO Box 1818, Belize City, T+501 (0)223 4526, www.belizediving.com. Working from the marina at Fort George, this professional outfit will arrange day trip diving to all major sites.

Sleeping

$$ **Radisson Fort George Hotel and Marina**, 2 Marine Parade, Belize City, T+501 (0)223 3333. Lovely hotel with all the facilities. Conveniently located right on the waterfront. Their jetty is the departure point for Peter Hughes' **Star Dancer II** and also used by Hugh Parkey's **Dive Connection**.

$ **Villa Boscardi**, 6043 Manatee Drive, off Northern Highway, T+501 (0)223 1691, www.villaboscardi.com. Small guesthouse just north of the city. In a quiet residential area and run by a Belgian/Italian couple.

Liveaboards

Peter Hughes Star Dancer II, 5723 NW 158th Street, Miami Lakes, FL, 33014, T+1 (1)305 6699391, www.PeterHughes.com. Luxurious vessel with good service, great cabins, spacious dive deck, nitrox, cordon bleu meals and drinks included.

Haulover Creek in Belize City

Belize Aggressor III, PO Box 1470, Morgan City, LA 70381, T+1 (1)985 3852628, www.aggressor.com.

Eating

Most restaurants in Belize City are linked to hotels, although there are lots of small cafés, mostly Chinese-run. Ask your hotel reception for recommendations for eating out.

Turneffe Atoll

Sleeping and diving

$$ **Blackbird Caye Resort**, PO Box 13099 Burton, WA 98013, T+1 (1)206 4630833, www.blackbirdresort.com. Very nice 3-star resort with good facilities and plenty of activities for non-divers. Restaurant and dive centre on site.

$ **Turneffe Flats Lodge**, PO Box 10670, Bozeman, MT 59719, T+1 (1)623 2982783, www.tflats.com. The second resort on this atoll with pretty rooms and plenty of marine based activities.

Lighthouse Reef

Sleeping and diving

$$$ **Lighthouse Reef Resort**. This was the premier – and only – resort at Lighthouse Reef. At the time of publication it is closed until 2008 when it will reopen as a 5-star resort. Check www.scubabelize.com for latest information.

Spanish Lookout Caye

Sleeping and diving

$$ **Spanish Bay Conservation & Research Center**, Spanish Lookout Caye, T+501 (0)223 4526, www.spanishbayresort.com. Small resort with a strong focus on marine research.

Sights

Because Belize is such a small country, getting to the various sites is fairly easy, even ones that are some way inland.

Belize City The former capital is divided in two by Haulover Creek: to the south is the commercial centre and to the north Fort George. The two halves are connected by the Swing Bridge, the only manually swung bridge in the world still in operation. The Fort George area includes the City Museum, (US$5 entry) the National Handicrafts centre, Post Office, City Hall, Memorial Park and the Lighthouse. Cross over the Swing Bridge to the commercial centre and wander along the front to St Johns Cathedral, the oldest Anglican Cathedral Church in Central America, and the Baron Bliss institute (the cultural centre). A walk around the city, popping in and out of a few shops and an internet café, will take about half a day.

Caye Caulker Even if you're not staying here, the island is worth a visit. It's extremely laid-back with just one main road and lots of sandy lanes. The town occupies the south of the island with cafés, shops and restaurants in pretty clapboard houses. The north of the island is mostly mangroves and forests, with walking trails and good birdwatching. This is a good place to chill out if you have a few spare days. Water taxis from the Swing Bridge take 45 mins and cost US$17.50 return.

Ambergris Caye Bigger and brasher than Caye Caulker, this island is much more developed with a museum and cultural centre and lots of restaurants and bars. There are Maya remains dotted around but these can be hard to find. You can arrange a tour or visit Little Iguana and Rosario Cayes just offshore for some birdwatching, while San Pedro Lagoon is a good place to spot crocodiles, racoons and countless bird species. For nightowls, or those who don't like liveaboards, this is a good place to be based. Water taxis from the Swing Bridge take 75 mins and cost US$27.50 return.

Cockscomb Basin Wildlife Sanctuary About 2 hrs south of Belize City, in the shadow of the Maya Mountains, this sanctuary covers 100,000 acres of tropical forest rising from sea level to the summit of Victoria Peak. It was originally established in 1984 as a reserve to protect a large jaguar population, as well as other resident wildlife. There are plenty of of birds and beautiful flora but the chance of seeing a jaguar or one of the other wildcats is slim. Expect to pay around US$60 for a day tour.

Surface interval

Across the borderline

If you've never dived the Great Western Barrier reef, a two-centre trip to Belize and Mexico would seem like the logical thing to do. But it's not that easy. Getting from Mexico to Belize by air is just not possible, even though it would take less than an hour. There were flights in the past but not any more. So how to do it? Well, providing you have a day to spare, it's fairly straightforward. Hop onto one of Mexico's ADO buses anywhere along the Yucatán coast. These first-class buses depart almost every hour and will drive you in comfort to the border city of Chetumal. The scenery is nothing to get excited about but it's only 5-6 hours from Cancún and they run a film or two on the way. At Chetumal's modern bus station change to a Novelo bus for Belize. These are nowhere near as fancy as ADO but it's only another two hours. To make the trip in a single day, you need to leave from Cancún or Playa del Carmen around 0600-0700. There is a Novelo connection around 1300-1400, or after 1800. Times are vague as Belize observes different time zones to Mexico. Alternatively, stay in Chetumal for the night, where there's a Holiday Inn, and catch the morning bus. The ADO fare is about USD$15 and the Novelo fare is US$14.

Altún Ha Just 1 hr north of Belize City, this Maya city (Altún Ha means 'Rockstone Pond') dates from around 250 BC and was a major ceremonial and trading centre linking coastal villages with the interior. An impressive carved jade head representing the sun god, Kinich Ahau was discovered here. Day trips from Belize city from US$50.

Half Moon Caye National Monument As part of the Lighthouse Reef system, you are guaranteed to visit this reserve on your liveaboard. Half Moon Caye is protected as one of only two Caribbean nesting areas for the red-footed booby. There are said to be 4,000 of them, along with frigates and around 90 other bird species plus iguanas, lizards, and loggerhead turtles. You can wander the beaches or head along the narrow nature trail to a bird viewing platform.

Belize City street

Tikal Regarded as the most important of all the Maya archaeological sites, Tikal is just over the border in neighbouring Guatemala and deep in the Petén jungle. There are dozens of stone temples and palaces, some dating from 300 BC, though the main buildings were built between AD 500 and AD 900. You can arrange a tour from Belize City or fly to Santa Elena and stay stay overnight in the twin town of Flores, perched on a tiny island in Lake Petén Itzá. Check out the **Tropic Air** website (www.tropicair.com) for day and overnight tours.

International agent

Roatan Charter, PO Box 877, 12251 Curley St, San Antonio, FL 33576, T+1 (1)352 5884131, www.roatan.com. Based in America but with strong family links to the region – very knowledgable.

Peter Hughes' *Sun Dancer II*

Mexico

Homes of the gods: shrouded in mystery, the Maya underworld lies beneath Mexico's Yucatán Peninsula

Península Río Lagartos
Las Coloradas
San Felipe
Holbox
Povenir
Boca Iglesia
Chiquilá
Loché
Panabá
Colonia Yucatán
Cancún
Caribbean Sea
Sucila
Tizimín
Espita
San Andrés
Cristóbal Colón
Puerto Morelos
Nuevo Xcan
Dzitas
Valladolid
Chichén Itzá
Playa del Carmen
Xcaret
Tixcacalcupul
Cobá
San Miguel de Cozumel
Chankanaab National Park
Cozumel
Xelhá
Tulum
Yucatán Peninsula
Tepich
Tihosuco
San Ramón
Melchor Ocampo
Laguna San Felipe
Cenote Azul
José María Morelos
Polyuc
Felipe Carrillo Puerto
Sian Ka'an Biosphere Reserve
N
10 km
10 miles
USA
Gulf of Mexico
MEXICO
Caribbean Sea
Pacific Ocean
COLOMBIA
Dive sites...
1 Tortugas p150
2 Moc-che p151
3 Chun-zumbel p151
4 Barracuda Caves p151
5 Dos Ojos p152
6 Bat Cave, Dos Ojos ★ p152
7 Chac-Mool Cenote p153
8 Taj Mahal p153
9 Palancar Caves p154
10 La Ceiba Reef p154
11 Punta Tunich/Yucab/Tormentos p155
12 The Devil's Throat, Punta Sur ★ p155

Introduction

Mexico is a contradiction in terms: both a natural paradise and a burgeoning commercial nation. Here, cartoon-like landscapes of cactus bushes on scrubby soil ring industrial cities; ancient architectural monuments constructed with holy reverence contrast with mile upon mile of modern tourist development.

The country's rich history is often neglected in the rush to compete with (or serve) her mighty neighbour. Yet the inhabitants of this vast land were once a superpower in their own right. Back then, it was a world where men were sacrificed in gruesome rituals or left to drown in deep water sinkholes with no hope of escape.

These sinkholes (or *cenotes*) are now modern-day dive sites and one of the most captivating underwater experiences to be had anywhere on the planet.

The country's coastal waters meanwhile reveal unexpected marine life and curious underwater geography. Here, for example, are some of the fastest drift dives you will ever encounter. Of course, there are reefs and fish and walls, but their attractions pale in comparison. In Mexico, you need to scratch beneath the surface to find a more rounded marine world.

“” *One day it's a swim through the dark history of a Maya murder mystery, the next it's a speed-demon ride at five knots along a wall.*

Mexico rating

Diving
★★★

Dive facilities
★★★

Accommodation
★★★

Down time
★★★★

Value for money
★★★

Essentials

Getting there and around

Choosing how to reach Mexico is all about options – and there are plenty. Wherever you commence your trip, reaching this vast nation is just too easy for words. Check out a reputable flight website like Expedia or Travelocity for ideas as almost any airline you can think of will get you there using a codeshare partner. Base your flight plan on whichever route is the shortest or if you fancy a stopover in one of the various hub cities you will transit through.

One way to narrow the field is to choose your destination first. This guide covers the Mexican Caribbean – or Yucatán Peninsula – and there are two major airports in this area, Cancún and Cozumel. There are even charter flights to these if you're willing to give up the comfort of a scheduled carrier. This is an important consideration. Scheduled flights cost a little extra but you get more comfortable seating and better in-flight facilities. On that note bear in mind that most US carriers have poorer on-board services than their European, Asian or Antipodean counterparts although their luggage allowance is far more generous.

You could also travel via neighbouring Belize, Honduras or Guatemala if you want to dive a second country or do some sightseeing. TACA (www.taca.com) flies between all the Central American countries but their routes often require an extra transit point. There is also a good, regular bus service that links Belize City to the Yucatán coast, though this is hard to pre-book. See page 141 for advice.

Once you have arrived in either Cancún or Cozumel, transfers and transport options are as numerous as flights. Either your hotel or dive operator will collect you, or arrange for someone to do so. Or go to an online service to prearrange a taxi. Touring the Yucatán is also relatively straightforward. Car hire is reasonably cheap (from US$40 per day), buses go everywhere, ferries link the offshore islands and there are masses of organized tours.

Chichén Itzá

Language

Although there are regional indigenous languages in Mexico, like Mayan and Nahuatl, you are unlikely to encounter anything except Spanish. In busy Cancún or Cozumel, almost everyone will speak English. In smaller resorts towns like Playa del Carmen you might find a shop assistant who prefers to use Spanish but that will be the exception. A few words go a long way (see also page 112):

hello	*hola*
goodbye	*adiós*
yes	*sí*
no	*no*
I don't know	*no se*
okay	*vale (like ballet)*
please	*por favor*
thank you	*gracias*
I'm sorry	*lo siento*
how much is ...?	*¿cuánto es ...?*
a beer/water	*una cerveza/agua mineral*
good	*bueno*
great dive	*una buceada fantastica*

Local laws and customs

Mexico is a land full of rich history and vibrant customs. Her influences range from ancient Toltec, Aztec and Maya through Spanish colonialization and Catholicism right up to the present day trade agreement with the US. The Yucatán coast has become incredibly Americanized in recent years and feels rather like an extension of Florida. It's unlikely that you will upset anyone providing you apply the usual rules of courtesy and politeness.

Safety

The Yucatán is a fairly safe place to be, whether you are in raucous Cancún, casual Playa del Carmen or over on busy Cozumel. Like anywhere, walking about at night showing off your expensive jewellery or with a wallet in

Mexico

Location	23°00′ N, 102°00′ W
Neighbours	Belize, Guatemala, United States of America
Population	106,202,903
Land area in km²	1,923,040
Marine area in km²	49,510
Coastline in km	9,330

your back pocket is an invitation for trouble, as would be leaving dive bags unattended in a bus station. However, one of the more reassuring aspects of travelling here is that the police presence is strong with special Tourist Police booths dotted about most resorts. They are manned by a multilingual force and will help with maps, directions and advice and, of course, you can go to them if you have a problem.

Health

Healthcare facilities in the Yucatán are best described as being in a state of flux. As the area has expanded, medical facilities have struggled to keep up. The best are said to be on Cozumel while in Cancún they are regarded as questionable. Playa del Carmen sits somewhere in the middle. If there was a real medical emergency, Mérida, the capital of Quintana Roo state, has superlative medical services. Providing you have all the right inoculations and stay hydrated chances are that little will go wrong beyond a case of Montezuma's Revenge. What is interesting about this area though is that you can buy almost any prescription drug your heart desires... even the infamous little blue pill. If you are a frequent traveller, you may find malaria tablets or antibiotic ear-drops are cheaper here than at home. However, be sensible and only buy what you know your doctor has prescribed in the past.

Costs

Mexico is not the cheap destination it once was. As the economy becomes more and more closely aligned with the US, so prices rise. The Yucatán was once principally rural until Cancún was built as a tourist city. Its development has now spread right along the coast with many large resort complexes. Accommodation elsewhere ranges from simple B&Bs to 5 star hotels. As there is a lot of competition you can get some great deals. This is also reflected in food and drink costs – you can go trendy or traditional and there is never any reason to pay full price for a beer (40 pesos) when you can almost always get two-for-one. The US dollar is interchangeable with pesos and often a restaurant will give you a better exchange rate than the banks. One thing to be aware of though is that you may find your budget takes a hammering in high season, when costs are often doubled. There are also a lot of scams that involve being served with a dish or wine you didn't order and then being charged substantially extra. Always check your bill before paying. Another scam involves transport. For example, if you buy a return ferry ticket between Playa del Carmen and Cozumel, ensure it is a return and not just one way. That said, this area does provide a good value trip as long as you keep an eye on things.

Airlines → Aeromexico T+52 (01)998 884 3571, American T+52 (01)998 8860086, Continental T+52 (01)998 8860006, KLM/Northwest T+52 (01)998 8860044, Mexicana T+52 (01)998 8819090, United T+01 800 003 0777. **Embassies** → UK T+52 (01)998 8810100, USA T+52 (01)998 8830272, Canada T+52 (01)998 8833360, Australia T+52 (01)5531 5225. **Mexico country code** → +52. **IDD code** → 00. **Police** → 066.

→ Fact file

International flights	Mexicana, United, Continental, BA, Virgin, KLM, TACA
Departure tax	Mostly included in your ticket, otherwise US$46
Entry	Visas not required for most nationals for Stays of up to 180 days
Internal flights	Aeromexico and subsidiaries
Ground transport	Countrywide bus connections, ferries, car hire
Money	10 Mexican pesos = US$1
Language	Spanish but English is common.
Electricity	110v
Time zone	GMT -5
Religion	Catholic

Meeting a turtle on Playa's Tortugas dive site

Dive brief

Diving

Mexico, of course, has two coastlines; the Pacific Ocean and the Caribbean Sea. While there is diving off the west (Pacific) coast, it's the Caribbean side that grabs most attention. Like neighbours, Belize and Honduras, the Yucatán Peninsula sits along the edge of the the Great Western Barrier Reef. You would think that conditions would be fairly similar in this whole region but, while you might see similar things, this northern end of the reef has its own distinctive dive personality.

It's all to do with currents. The Caribbean is a shallow basin into which water floods from the Atlantic. The Caribbean Current moves across the top of the South American continent and travels counter clockwise, and northwest, towards the Yucatán coast, where it becomes the Yucatán Current. The water then has little choice but to force its way through the comparatively narrow Yucatán Channel between Mexico and Cuba. From there it eddies around the Gulf of Mexico before heading off around Florida and up the US east coast. This is what gives the Yucatán its dive character. The currents created can be fierce. It's rare to be able to stay still on a dive when the water regularly rips along at over 2 knots.

Bottom time

Yucatán Peninsula
Calmer conditions and gentler reefs along the top end of the Great Western Barrier Reef » p150

The Cenotes
Strange and eerie diving in underground freshwater rivers and limestone caves » p152

Cozumel
Clear water and lightning-speed drift diving over tortuous marine topography » p154

It also means that the reef animals here are only the ones capable of living in this environment. Some people may be disappointed by the lack of animal encounters. There are plenty of pelagics and lots of schooling fish but as there is a dearth of lush corals, smaller creatures are less prolific. However, the underwater terrain is fabulous, with plenty to explore both at sea and inland in the underground, freshwater caverns and rivers.

Diversity* reef area 1,780 km²

Coral species	Fish species	Fish species under threat	Protected reefs/marine parks
81	225	8	9

*Includes information for the Pacific

Trumpetfish hovering on Chun-zumbel

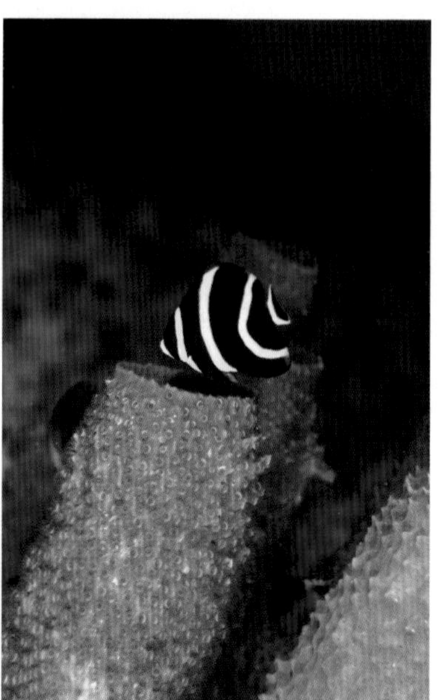
Grey angelfish juvenile

Mexico is one of the countries that we spent a lot of our trekking time in. The diving is consistent, and lots of fun. The marine life is not hugely diverse but what makes the area well worth the trip are the differing styles of diving, from wild drifts, to shallow reefs to the bizarre world of the cenotes. Mix it all up and you will get to do something special. The ultra-modern coastal resorts are absolutely no reflection of the country as a whole which is far more complex and varied. You could do yourself a favour and head inland to see some of her fascinating culture or just spend your time being completely hedonistic.

Snorkelling

Cozumel is a great snorkelling destination. In fact much of its marine reputation was based on its shallow-water marine reserves, many of which are now theme parks. The mainland is more exposed and subject to some surf which stirs up the sand on the patchy reefs that are closer to shore, so visibility can be poor. It should be noted that there are many motorized watersports in this area and snorkellers should get advice on safe areas. You can also snorkel in the *cenotes*, some of which have special parts. At certain times of year, you can also travel to Holbox, off the peninsula's northern tip, to see the migrating whalesharks.

The big decision

The Yucatán is more about what type of holiday you want rather than what type of diving. Its entire being is devoted to the pleasures of a two week sojourn in the sun. There are endless activities, organized tours, theme parks, great nightlife, places to go and things to see as well as a dash of history and a lot of colour. There is something for everyone and that makes it a great destination for families – especially those with teenagers – or for couples – though in high season, some people may find it all a bit too hyperactive. Underwater there's some unusual diving to be had, the different styles adding a certain novelty to the experience.

Playa del Carmen's ferry terminal

→ Dive data

Seasons	All year, although April to October has the best visibility. Chances of hurricanes in August and September
Visibility	20-60 metres
Temperatures	Air 20-30°C; water 24-29°C
Wet suit	3 mm shorty or full body suit, 5 mm+ for the cenotes
Training	Courses available everywhere, standards vary
Nitrox	Limited availability, check in advance
Deco chambers	Cozumel, Playa del Carmen

Spotted cyphoma on a sea whip

Porkfish and grunts schooling together

Arrow crab inside a vase sponge

Dive log

Yucatán Peninsula

The Yucatán is a diverse region with colonial Spanish cities, incredible Maya ruins, fabulous natural resources and miles of perfect white sand stretching along the coast. It's no surprise then that a couple of decades ago some bright spark decided to turn it into a tourist region. Cancún was chosen as its centre.

Today, the Yucatán Peninsula is the country's top tourist region and a major dollar earner. The area is recovering quickly after Hurricane Stan hit in 2005. Facilities include two major airports, an efficient transport infrastructure and mega-hotel after mega-hotel marching down the coast. Those who visited before the boom might wince at such rampant development, but head down to Playa del Carmen just an hour south and you'll find some of the old Mexico – mixed with enough modern amenities to keep everyone happy.

Though the Great Western Barrier Reef has almost petered out by the time it reaches this northern point, there are some pleasant diving experiences to be had. Head a little away from shore to find reef top plateaux swept by strong currents. These attract a fair number of pelagic species. Shallow reefs, moments from the beach, are more protected than those off Cozumel (see page 154), and conditions are usually easy.

1 Tortugas

- **Depth**: 19 m
- **Visibility**: good
- **Currents**: medium to strong
- **Dive type**: day boat
- **Snorkelling**: no

At first glance, this site appears to be an incredibly flat reef plateau with very little life on it. The current is strong and the corals grow to just a few centimetres. Even the seaplumes are only 30 cm high. As you

Playa del Carmen

Gigantic tarpon

descend, you encounter a current that whips you across the reef. There's little time to do more than focus on the number of blue vase and other small sponges. Then you start to notice the masses of turtles (tortugas) that are feeding on them, many of which are quite old and studded with barnacles. As you come to the end of the plateau, you run into the big surprise, a resident school of tarpon. These are BIG fish, nearly two metres long, with metallic silver scales and a very grumpy expression. There seems to be hundreds of them hovering effortlessly while a small nurse shark often sits below them.

2 Moc-che

Depth: 14 m
Visibility: fair
Currents: mild to strong
Dive type: day boat
Snorkelling: possibly

Descending to this small reef, you find a patchy outcrop just a metre or two high and covered in typical Caribbean corals. This is a classic example of the dives here. Seaplumes and small fans are all in shades of brown and beige with some pale purple interspersed. Although at first glance it seems a bit uninteresting, the fish life is quite a surprise. There are lots of schooling snappers, grunts and porkfish hanging about the fans. Nestling in tiny overhangs you find soapfish, lobster and huge green morays plus small, black and white blotched morays, masses of arrow crabs and periclimines shrimp in corkscrew anemones. There are often conch, small stingrays and electric rays buried in the sand.

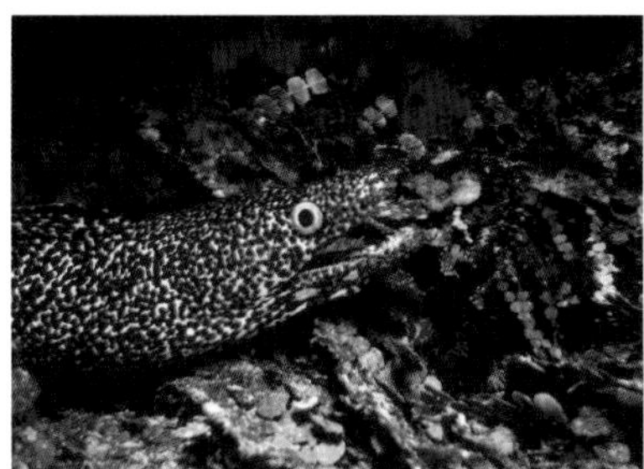

A spotted moray in halameda algae

3 Chun-zumbel

Depth: 10 m
Visibility: fair
Currents: slight to medium
Dive type: day boat
Snorkelling: possibly

Just a few minutes off Playa's beach, this site is relatively shallow and visibility can be low, as it is ringed by so much sand. The reef is enclosed by low walls, just a few feet high, with a flat and patchy reef top. The surface is covered in a fair number of pastel-coloured fans and sponges add splashes of colour. They are often surrounded by schools of grunts – including the cutely named Sailor's Choice. There are a variety of angelfish with their tiny offspring: blacklipped, french and grey. The reef edges are marked by small overhangs where you find porcupine puffers, lots of flamingo tongue shells, arrow crabs and shrimp in every nook. There aren't a lot of anemones in this region but if you spot one it's likely to house a porcelain crab or two. An occasional great barracuda hovers over the sand.

Lone barracuda at Barracuda Caves

Solitary nurse shark on Tortugas

4 Barracuda Caves

Depth: 14 m
Visibility: fair
Currents: mild to strong
Dive type: day boat
Snorkelling: sometimes

To the south of Playa del Carmen and just beyond the Xcaret eco-park, this comparatively shallow reef is surrounded by low walls with overhangs and mini caves. The upper surface of the reef is covered in a gentle garden of soft corals and a substantial variety of sponges. Around the edge of the reef, there are a few small caverns that you can enter. One is particularly good for spotting lobster and in late summer you are likely to see adults that have reached quite a size. There are plenty of little critters such as arrow crabs and coral banded shrimp on the walls. Another cave, a little further along, has a resident green moray who is quite tame as morays go. The great barracuda is resident (hence the name) and though normally a solitary chap, he can be seen in small groups.

Queen angelfish amongst sponges

The Cenotes

The Yucatán Peninsula is a limestone platform several million years old. Over the centuries, changes in both geology and weather patterns resulted in the creation of a vast system of underground caverns and sinkholes (*cenotes*). After the last ice age, when ocean levels rose, these caverns filled with seawater, creating a network of subterranean rivers that extended miles inland. These inland cenotes were flooded by rainwater and used by the ancient Maya as a source of fresh water. Thus, the *cenotes* played an important role in the Maya religion and mythology. They believed the underworld gods lived in their depths and people were sacrificed to appease them.

Nowadays, these ancient geological peculiarities – many of which are full of stalactites and stalagmites – form a series of unique dive sites, less than an hour from Playa del Carmen. They vary in difficulty from those that are only for experienced cave divers to some that are extremely shallow and easy. There are guide ropes and daylight floods in from fissures in the earth above or secondary *cenotes* along the river. Most fascinating is when you pass through a halocline – where salt water sits over fresh. Conditions are not difficult although the water is pretty chilly compared to the sea. You will be briefed by your divemaster on being especially careful with buoyancy and to use a special finning technique. Some *cenotes* also involve a lot of multilevel movement so be careful with your ears.

Looking down on a cenote

5 Dos Ojos

- **Depth**: 8 m
- **Visibility**: crystal clear, but dark
- **Currents**: none
- **Dive type**: shore
- **Snorkelling**: yes

Dos Ojos means two eyes and refers to two circular cenotes that are quite close together. Entry is via a small cave in between, which has a wooden platform built under an overhang. The water feels icy as you jump in, especially as the surrounding jungle is so humid. And it is mosquito heaven! The system is well roped with guidelines to follow but entry without a guide is not allowed. The first descent into an enormous yawning cave is breathtaking then you are quickly led into a dark and gloomy passage past fragile rock formations. The first part of the system leads off towards one of the 'eyes' and is quite open, with several areas where shafts of daylight shine through. You'll even see snorkellers swimming above you in some parts. The experience becomes more surreal once you enter the tunnels that are completely black, lit only by your torch beam. You round corners to discover weird and wonderful formations, swim past rocky towers that glitter with minerals then into vast cathedral-like chambers.

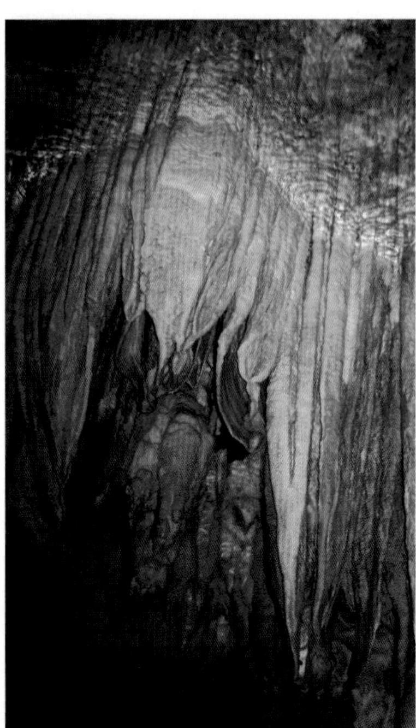

Stalagtite formations in Dos Ojos

6 Bat Cave, Dos Ojos

- **Depth**: 11 m
- **Visibility**: crystal clear, but dark
- **Currents**: none
- **Dive type**: shore
- **Snorkelling**: yes

The second 'eye' in Dos Ojos is in the opposite direction from the system entrance, away from the busier areas. Once past the gaping opening, the cave drops into a mass of narrow tunnels. Exploration of these is restricted to professionals while the sport diver route passes more beautiful limestone formations with doorways and arches, leading to huge, cavernous rooms. Stalactites hang from every available space on the ceiling, sometimes converging to form thick columns. The depth is shallow all the way and there is very little daylight. At the furthest point from the entry, you reach the Bat Cave where you can surface and see the colours in the limestone sparkling like jewels, and tiny bats hanging from crevices. As you return to the cave entrance, you will be instructed to turn off your torch. It's an eerie experience!

7 Chac-Mool Cenote

- **Depth**: 13 m
- **Visibility**: good
- **Currents**: none
- **Dive type**: shore
- **Snorkelling**: yes

Hidden further into the Yucatán jungle, this *cenote* feels less touristy than popular Dos Ojos – providing you arrive early. Later in the day, busloads of day trippers arrive from Cancún. The entry here is through a natural rock pool and the whole scene is quite exotic with plenty of colourful birds flitting to and fro, perching on tree roots that reach down to the water and diving for bugs. The entry point at Chac-Mool is via Little Brother *Cenote*, where you descend through a school of black catfish into a large cavern. This *cenote* has several haloclines – salt water at the bottom with a layer of fresh on the top. Where the two meet you can see a distinct line and, as you descend through it, the visibility decreases and the water seems to be like jelly. Below the halocline, it's also a few degrees warmer. Again, there are two directions in this system, one of which leads to the air dome where you can ascend inside to see the dome edges covered in stalactites that extend down into the water.

Tales from the deep

The special holes

The very first time we stepped into that cool water it felt like we were entering into the secrets of the Earth. Every moment was a surprise: we passed from brightness to obscurity, catching the light's effects dropping through the jungle right onto a fossil, seeing the sun's rays expose ancient mysteries, slaloming stalactites and stalagmites, tracing roots sneaking out of earth from the Maya's sacred underworld.

We decided this was the place to settle for a while and absorb the atmosphere. The water visibility was infinite and gave us the feeling we were flying in another galaxy. We moved on, then suddenly, reaching a halocline, where salt water mixes with fresh, appearing as an incredible fantastic cloud. Magic.

Sophie and Patricio Durante run Go Cenotes *in Playa del Carmen*

8 Taj Mahal

- **Depth**: 14.5 m
- **Visibility**: good
- **Currents**: none
- **Dive type**: shore
- **Snorkelling**: no

This is a much less busy site, probably because there are no facilities at all, just lots of welcoming mosquitoes. However, Taj is one of the most interesting cenotes as it has a variety of features but fewer limestone formations. The river system runs in a straight line away from the entry point which is accessed down some steep steps. The opening cavern drops to over 10 metres and you pass through the jelly-like layers of 'Halocline Tunnel'. This leads through a cavern full of giant rocks, past the impressive limestone formations of 'Close Encounter' and then to 'Cenote Sugarbowl'. Rays of light illuminate massive tumbled boulders (the sugar cubes) and an old tree stump dripping in detritus from the jungle above. This bowl drops to down 14 metres where the water is much warmer – a good spot to pause a while – then leads on to the end of the system. A small U-turn brings you to 'Bill's Hole', another tiny *cenote* full of leaves and bits of decaying plant matter. Good buoyancy is imperative here. The route back is past more stalagmite formations, such as 'The Candlestick', until you reach 'Points of Light', a tiny fissure in the ceiling above which shines a sharp beam onto a pile of rocks.

An ancient fossil embedded in rock

Cozumel

Mexico's largest island, Cozumel is just 12 miles off the Yucatán Peninsula. At 28 miles long and 10 miles wide, the island is separated from the coast by an extremely deep oceanic trench. This, along with the island's location, creates a funnel for the strong currents that flow up from the south and are then squeezed out into the Gulf of Mexico.

Cozumel was a sleepy place until Jacques Cousteau visited in the 1960's. Since then diving has become a huge part of the island's life. Cozumel is an incredibly popular dive destination. There are something like 180 dive centres on the island, catering for Americans taking a quick weekend break or the passengers from the many cruise ships that dock daily. You are rarely on a reef on your own, sometimes there can be as many as four boat loads of divers all jostling for space. It has been said that the cruise ship activity has damaged the reefs but in reality it's not the ships, just the sheer numbers, that may spoil your diving days here.

The west coast is bordered by a double row of parallel reefs and, unless you are in a very protected cove, the waters are never still. Move just a short way into the ocean and you will meet currents that often hit five knots – even as much as eight at times! You can descend on one dive site and ascend on a completely different one. It may sound a bit scary but can be a highly exhilarating experience.

This aggressive water movement has sculpted these long reefs by eating away at softer core materials, leaving a wildly varied and complicated terrain. The area is riddled with so many tunnels, channels and grooves that the reefs feel like a giant maze. Inside all the caverns and overhangs, smaller marine creatures take a break from the activity, while the rushing waters attract some bigger pelagics. Of course, corals here are not prolific as their delicate structure doesn't cope well with these conditions.

Spur and groove dives

Open reef plateau and soft corals

9 Palancar Caves

- **Depth**: 31 m
- **Visibility**: can be breathtaking
- **Currents**: slight to ripping
- **Dive type**: day boat
- **Snorkelling**: no

This dive starts quite deep with a quick descent down over the reef edge to 30 metres. From there, and rising up to about 18 metres, the wall becomes a tortuous maze of tunnels. There are architectural spires and buttresses, gullies and canyons all winding to and fro between the outer wall and the inner reef. At the base of the wall, a sandy slope plummets into the depths. There are countless caves and canyons along this stretch but not as much marine life as you might expect. There are schooling grunts and snapper, and undoubtedly lots of small fish, morays and crustaceans in the tunnels but you are far too busy having fun swimming through the labyrinth to really notice them.

10 La Ceiba Reef

- **Depth**: 12 m
- **Visibility**: good to great
- **Currents**: slight to medium
- **Dive type**: shore
- **Snorkelling**: yes

Just offshore from the **La Ceiba Hotel** and beside one of the cruise liner piers, this small beach and cove makes a great dive for novices, critter-hunters and night dives. The wreck of a DC3 passenger aeroplane sits to the south of the bay. The plane, sunk deliberately as a film prop, is now fairly broken up but the scrap metal provides shelter for a range of fish. A current often sweeps the bay – not too strong – and pushes divers along towards the next pier. You pass over small coral heads that are smothered in Christmas tree and featherduster worms. At night there are parrotfish hiding in their mucous bubbles and morays nestled in the rocks. Small octopus are quite common as are hermit crabs, shrimps and blennies.

11 Punta Tunich/Yucab/ Tormentos

- **Depth**: 28 m
- **Visibility**: good to excellent
- **Currents**: unbelievable
- **Dive type**: day boat
- **Snorkelling**: no

While each of these dives is individually quite satisfying, what defines this stretch – and Cozumel diving – is what happens when the currents pick up. And they often do, extending an invitation to a triple-value dive. Dropping over the wall at Punta Tunich, it's not unusual to hit the water and find the current is moving faster than three knots. At that level you can drift along, stopping every now and then to admire something. However, if it's over five knots, there is no option but to move away from the wall and enjoy the passing show as you are swept over Tunich, past Yucab Reef and onto Tormentos. You're not likely to see anything much in detail but riding the stream is quite a rush. The ever-present schools of grunts will accompany you and there are sometimes creole wrasse. As you fly along you can also spot angelfish or lobster on the wall.

12 The Devil's Throat, Punta Sur

- **Depth**: 38 m
- **Visibility**: breathtaking
- **Currents**: strong to ripping
- **Dive type** : day boat
- **Snorkelling**: no

Although this dive is one of the most popular on the island, it can only be done when conditions are just right and is restricted to advanced divers (though the definition of 'advanced' is often loose). Punta Sur is at the very southern tip of Cozumel and is washed by currents, surge and some surf. The top of the reef is at 26 metres and you can always see this even from just below the surface. The first stage of the dive is to fin into a cave system which turns quickly into a descending tunnel. Lobster often lurk here in the dark. You continue the swim through the tunnel until you emerge on the reef wall, before quickly re-entering another cave that leads to a second complex of coral tunnels. About four metres in, the tunnel narrows considerably as you enter the 'Devil's Throat'. There are several passageways including one that exits on a sheer section of wall at 37 metres. Another leads to the 'Cathedral', a vast cavern lit by beams of sun filtering through fissures in the reef. There aren't that many fish as the point is so exposed but you still see angels and butterflyfish swimming along the reef edge. At depth there are some whip and black corals and large rays surfing in the current.

Conservation

Playing with Flipper

In more commercial resort areas, organized animal encounters are becoming quite commonplace. Settle on the bottom and watch a chainmail-clad divemaster feed some overexcited whitetips that are only there as they know they will be fed. Join an organized dolphin experience where 'rescued' animals are trained to entertain divers who pay humungous rates for the privilege of seeing creatures they think they will never see in the wild. There are two sides to this argument. Do you encourage an animal that should be in the wild to do something outside its remit? Do you save some of these creatures for future generations by ensuring their survival, even if that means hemming them in? Remember that pandas may have been saved by zoo breeding programmes, while the Tasmanian Devil is no more. Recently an American aquarium announced the purchase of two young whalesharks. Their response to outraged conservationists was that they had saved the whalesharks' lives. Whilst that may be true in the short term, no one can predict the effect of captivity on these gentle giants. Is it even possible to provide a suitable, contained habitat? Few zoos live up to the ideals we would like them to have and even fewer truly understand the impact on marine species. Only you can decide if you think that this type of diving is a good thing and whether you want to support it.

Lobster inside the Devil's Throat

Drying out

Mexico is a vast and fascinating country with more to do than you could possibly cover in a two week holiday. Unless you have time and are willing to include some internal flights, it would be best to restrict sightseeing to around the Yucatán Peninsula.

Playa del Carmen

Dive centres

GoCenotes, Av 1 between Calle 24 y 26 Nte, T+52 (01)984 8033924, www.gocenotes.com. Well structured, pre-organized daily dive programme right across the area. Modern equipment and multi-lingual guides.

SeaLife Divers, Mamitas Beach/Playa Tucan at Calle 28, T+52 (01)984 8030809, www.sealifedivers.com. Right on the white sand beach, flexible and friendly dive centre with various good value dive packs that include local reefs, Cozumel trips and fully escorted cenote diving.

Sleeping

$$$-$$ **Condo Ali**, Nueva Quinta Building, Av 5 y Calle 28. Luxury 2-bed villa with a rooftop jacuzzi and view of the sea. On the lively main road with good access to both the beach and all nightlife. Bookings through SeaMonkey Business, below.

Serenaded at *La Choza*

$$ **Villa Amanecer**, 286, Av 1 y Calle 26 Nte, T+52 (01)984 8732716, www.villa-amanecer.com. Small, friendly hotel in quiet location just back from the beach and opposite **GoCenotes**.

Eating

There are masses of restaurants in Playa del Carmen with virtually every cuisine known to man. For decent, straightforward Mexican food try **La Vagabunda** on Av 5 between Calle 24 y 26, or, for a slightly more upmarket style of Mexican, try **El Sazón** next door.

Local agents

SeaMonkey Business, T+52 (01)984 8030809, www.seamonkeybusiness.com, partners to **SeaLife Divers** and running a full service agency for hotels, villas, diving, tours and airport transfers.

Cozumel

Dive centres

Deep Blue – Extended Range Divers, Av Rosida Salas 200, T+52 (01)987 8725653, www.deepbluecozumel.com. Custom dive packages that cater for more experienced divers, plus fast, modern boats.

Del Mar Aquatics, Carretera a Chankanaab Km 4, T+52 (01)987 8725949, www.delmaraquatics.net. Linked to the *Casa del Mar Hotel* and with good dive and accommodation packages.

Sleeping

$$$-$$ **Casa Mexicana**, Av Rafael E Melgar. T+52 (01)987 8729090, www.casamexicanacozumel.com. New and very modern hotel right in the centre of town. Rooms at the front have views over the channel, port and cruise liner dock.

$$ **Casa del Mar**, Carretera a Chankanaab Km 4, T+52 (01)987 8721900, www.casadelmarcozumel.com. Resort-style hotel a little north of town and on a quieter section of the coast.

Eating

Like everywhere in the Yucatán there's every

style of restaurant imaginable.
$$$ **Pepe's Grill**, Av Rafael E Melgar and Rosado Salas. Upmarket local and international fare.
$$ **La Choza**, Calle Adolfo Rosado Salas 198, at Av 10, T+52 (01)987 8720958, www.lachozarestaurant.com. Genuine Mexican home cooking.

Sights

No matter where you are based, all the following sights are easily accessible. The ferries that link Cozumel to Playa del Carmen only take 45 minutes and leave hourly. Apart from what is listed here, there are numerous traditional holiday activities like golf, skydiving, kayaking and jungle treks. **Cancún** is a purpose-built tourist city where you can see staged bullfights, dolphin shows and shop-till-you-drop. It's a very commercialized place, which may not suit everyone. Details are not included here. Prices quoted are generally for tours starting on the coast; allow an extra US$20 if you are on Cozumel.

Chankanaab National Park, Cozumel The original marine park in this area. The shallow lagoon is a great place to get your toes wet if you're not a diver, although you can dive here as well. There are snorkelling facilities and shallow marine pools for children. The botanical garden has hundreds of tropical plant species and many iguanas. There is also the opportunity to join in a man-made "dolphin experience". Only you can decide if that's a good thing. Entrance is US$10.

Chichén Itzá West of Cancún, this sacred Maya city is the best known in the region and its pyramid is something of an icon. It has 91 very steep steps to the top and if you climb it, your calves will be sorry. There are many other buildings around the complex, including an ancient observatory and a ball court. Here the ancient Olmec ball game was played, which gave a whole new meaning to the term 'sudden death' – the winners (or losers, no one knows which) were decapitated after the game. Tours from US$60.

Tulum An hour's drive south from Playa, this ancient site was both a Maya seaport and an astronomical centre. It's not as impressive as many others in Mexico but it does have the most breathtaking location facing the rising sun and looking over the sea. As it's very easy to reach, the site gets busy in the late morning when tour buses arrive. You can take one of these (US$60) or go independently but get there early.

Xelhá A little further north from Tulum, this once natural complex of waterways and mangroves is now a themed aquarium and park. There are swimming lagoons, *cenotes'*, ancient caves and organized activities like swimming with dolphins and jungle walks. A good day out for those with young kids and non-divers. Entrance fees with limited access range from US$15 (children) to US$29 (adult) up to an all-inclusive day pass at US$28/56 respectively.

Xcaret Just south of Playa and a little like Xelhá, this is sold as an eco-archaeological park. Inside the complex are marine based activities plus a Museum of Culture and Archaeology, a replica Maya Village and special evening events like recreations of ball games and dance extravaganzas. You can even get married here! At US$80 (adult) and US $60 for children it's quite pricey, but with lots to do.

Sian Ka'an Biosphere reserve This is a UNESCO World Heritage Site and covers an area of rare coastal wetlands with over 20 archaeological sites, 100 or so mammal species and 300 bird species. It is also a nesting site for two endangered sea turtles. The management of this site is far more heavily biased towards eco-tourism and the natural world. Day tours are US$68 or you could join conservation group, **Global Vision International** (www.gvi.co.uk) and assist their coral, fish and crocodile surveys.

Holbox On the very northeastern tip of the Yucatán, tiny Holbox sits just off the coast. This island still reflects life in the region before mass tourism hit and for that alone it's worth a trip. However, it won't last as it's also a whaleshark highway. Between late June and August, it is said that you can snorkel with more whalesharks than you can count on all your digits at once. In reality, you are more likely to spend a long, hot day on the water and then see one or two, if you're lucky. Day trips by bus run from US$100 or you could go by private Cessna for US$280, www.aerosaab.com.

SeaLife Divers at Playa del Carmen

Traditions live on in Playa del Carmen

Chichén Itzá

Honduras

Baubles and beads: ruby hued marine jewellery adorning the cryptic teardrop crab, *Pelia mutica*

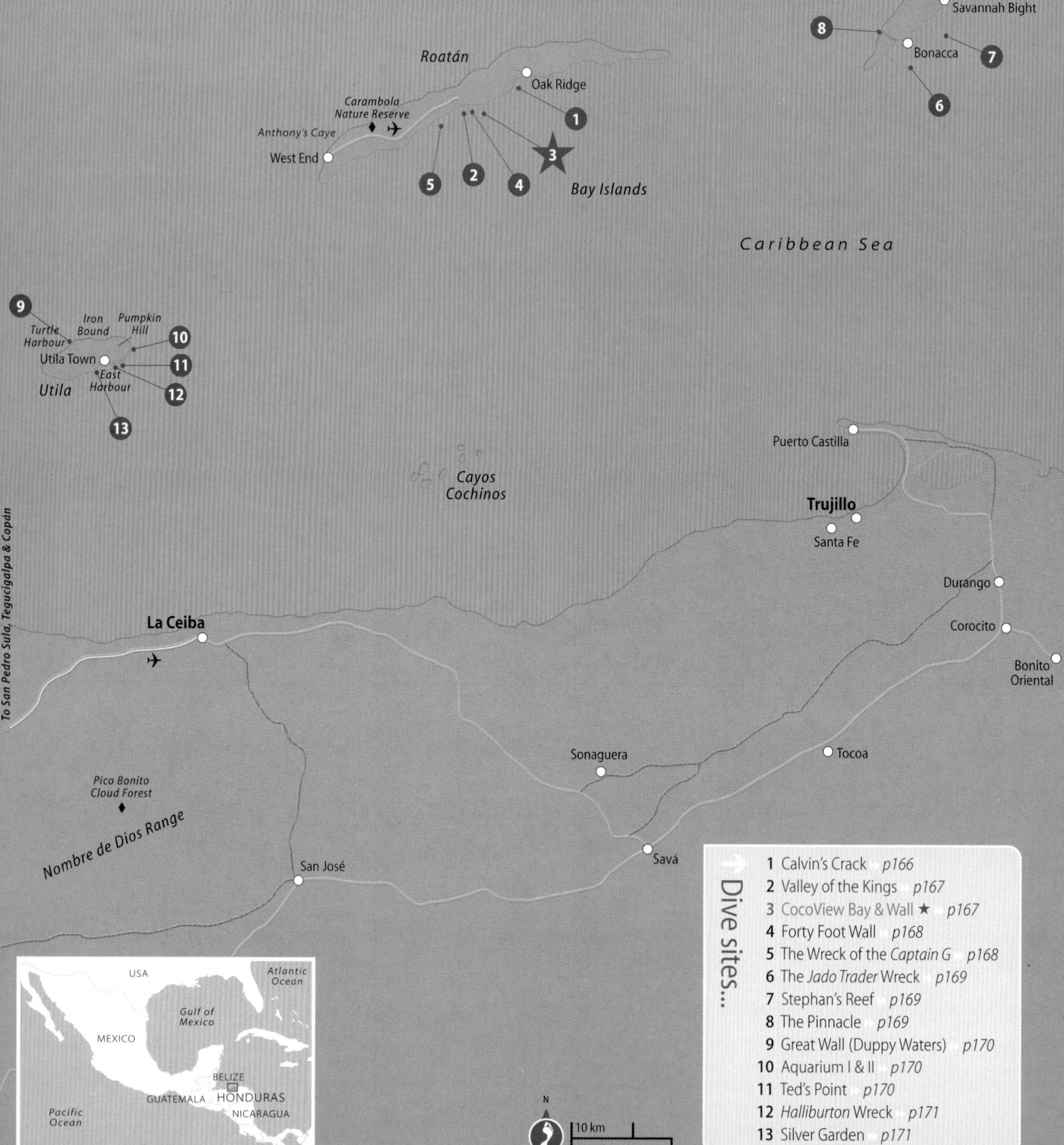

Guanaja
Savannah Bight
Bonacca
Roatán
Oak Ridge
Carambola
Nature Reserve
Anthony's Caye
West End
Bay Islands
Caribbean Sea
Iron
Bound
Pumpkin
Hill
Turtle
Harbour
Utila Town
East
Harbour
Utila
Puerto Castilla
Cayos
Cochinos
Trujillo
Santa Fe
Durango
La Ceiba
Corocito
Bonito
Oriental
To San Pedro Sula, Tegucigalpa & Copán
Sonaguera
Tocoa
Pico Bonito
Cloud Forest
Nombre de Dios Range
San José
Savá
USA
Atlantic
Ocean
Gulf of
Mexico
MEXICO
BELIZE
GUATEMALA
HONDURAS
NICARAGUA
Pacific
Ocean
N
10 km
10 miles
Dive sites...
1 Calvin's Crack p166
2 Valley of the Kings p167
3 CocoView Bay & Wall ★ p167
4 Forty Foot Wall p168
5 The Wreck of the Captain G p168
6 The Jado Trader Wreck p169
7 Stephan's Reef p169
8 The Pinnacle p169
9 Great Wall (Duppy Waters) p170
10 Aquarium I & II p170
11 Ted's Point p170
12 Halliburton Wreck p171
13 Silver Garden p171

Introduction

A string of jungle-clad islands lies off the northern coast of Honduras. These are the beautiful Bay Islands. Surrounded by warm Caribbean waters and gentle coral reefs, their image is one of a simple, more peaceful lifestyle. Yet these islands have a secret. The surrounding reefs are home to the highest marine diversity in the entire Caribbean Sea. Some 96% of all marine species found there reside in these waters.

Like the other countries that sit on the Great Western Barrier Reef, the style of diving is very laid-back. To discover the hidden treasures underwater you just need to look beyond the subtle tones of her coral reefs.

Landside, you would never know that these islands were fought over so ferociously as evidence of past pirate exploits has faded into oblivion. Once Spanish galleons sailed these waters, searching for new lands, riches and, above all, glory. Dutch and English schooners soon joined them in clandestine missions, plundering their gold and their rum – and a share of the glory – before retreating to the hidden coves of the Bay Islands to covet their booty.

These days, it's all about enjoying the spoils of nature. The colourful islands have abandoned their pirate history to become a diver's haven. Jungle-covered hills still watch over boats nestling in hidden coves but nowadays the islands' riches are found beneath the waterline rather than above.

“” *Peer at what seems to be a really ordinary bit of reef and realize you have just found a treasure of your own – the cryptic teardrop crab that looks just like it was sprinkled with rubies.*

Honduras rating

Diving
★★★
Dive facilities
★★★★
Accommodation
★★★
Down time
★★
Value for money
★★★

Essentials

Honduras

Location	15°00′ N, 86°30′ W
Neighbours	Belize, El Salvador, Guatemala, Nicaragua
Population	7,167,902
Land area in km²	111,890
Marine area in km²	200
Coastline in km	820

Getting there and around

There are several airports in Honduras. Each of the Bay Islands has its own: from the charmingly rustic open-air strip on Utila to the modern, international terminal on Roatán. There are also international airports in the capital, Tegucigalpa, second city, San Pedro Sula and coastal La Ceiba. So it's something of a surprise that it's not all that easy to get there – at least, not without several transit stops on the way. To keep these to a minimum, fly to either Houston or Miami and then take a direct flight to Roatán with Central American group, TACA (www.taca.com). They fly from Miami on Sundays and Houston on Saturdays, leaving mid afternoon. If you're coming from Europe, the connection should be relatively quick and painless but allow at least three hours for US immigration and transit. If you can't travel on a weekend, TACA has daily flights via San Pedro Sula but you may get stuck overnight. Continental (www.continental.com) currently also fly to Roatán from Houston.

Once in Roatán, getting to Utila or Guanaja is cheap and easy. There are several small airlines that link the islands via La Ceiba on the coast. These include: Atlantic (www.atlanticairlines.com.ni), Isleña (www.flyislena.com) and SOSA (www.aerolineassosa.com). Most inter-island connections via La Ceiba are only 20 minutes or so and are generally quick and efficient. There are also ferries between Roatán, Utila and La Ceiba but not to Guanaja.

On arrival in Roatán, hotels normally collect their guests but, if you are advised to get a taxi from the airport, they are reasonably priced and plenty meet arriving flights. On Utila and Guanaja you will be met at the airport.

Once you are in the Bay Islands you may not feel the need to go anywhere else but it is easy to reach the mainland and spend a few days in the cloud forest coastal region or head across to the Maya ruins at Copán, near the border with Guatemala. Information on organizing tours is on page 173.

Maya head at Copán

Language

Spanish is the official language and is spoken across the country though English remains the main language on the islands. While Spanish is mostly only used by government officials on the islands, it's still worth trying out a little. See also page 112.

hello	*hola*
goodbye	*adiós*
see you later	*hasta luego*
yes	*sí*
no	*no*
I don't know	*no se*
okay	*vale (like ballet)*
please	*por favor*
thank you	*gracias*
I'm sorry	*lo siento*
how much is ...?	*¿cuánto es ...?*
a beer/water	*una cerveza/agua mineral*
good	*bueno*
great dive	*una buceada fantastica*

Local laws and customs

Honduras is principally a Catholic country although a few ancient indigenous religions are still practised. Compared to Belize and Mexico to the north, Hondurans are somewhat more reserved. You may not notice this so much in the Bay Islands; more so if you head inland. As ever, dress conservatively, be courteous and polite and make a point of greeting people – in Spanish preferably.

Safety

Honduras used to have a reputation as not being the safest place to visit. This was not helped by the massive disruption to travel caused by Hurricane Mitch in 1998. Today though, the infrastructure has been repaired and, for divers, there should be few problems. Meaning, that if you have pre-booked and stick to the main tourist routes, you will be fine. Sadly, backpackers and those who head well off the beaten track become targets for muggings and petty crime. The large mainland cities are not places to wander about at night on your own. The coastal area around Tela is regarded as particularly worth avoiding – the beaches are lovely but there's no diving there anyway. Remember that this is a poor country and, wherever you are, take all the usual precautions: don't be ostentatious with your valuables and dive kit, leave jewellery behind when you go out, stay with a friend after dark and don't, under any circumstances, get involved in anything to do with drugs.

Health

Medical facilities are a mixed bag. On the islands you will find an English speaking doctor easily but not on the mainland where pharmacists are seen as a first line of 'defence'. For any minor ailment head there first; they are well trained and basic drugs are easy to obtain. Generally health risks are low and apart from sun block and insect repellant you aren't likely to need much. However, on the insect front there is one noteworthy nuisance: the no see-um. These biting midges live in the sand and are a real problem. Although they don't spread disease they do cause plenty of discomfort for their victims. Protect yourself as you would for mosquitoes or simply stay off the sand. They'll still get you but perhaps a bit less often.

Costs

Honduras is not an expensive country. In fact, Utila is regarded as one of the cheapest places on the planet to learn to dive. However, costs in most hotels on the islands don't necessarily reflect the cost of living of the country. Many are US-run with US or European staff. Nonetheless, Honduras represents better value than many of her neighbours. Most resorts are completely focussed on dive tourism and offer great packages that include everything except your nightly cocktails. A beer in a local bar will be around $1.50, but up to $5 in a resort. Service charges are added to some bills and where it isn't tipping is the done thing – between 10% and 15%. For dive crews see page 14.

Airlines → Grupo TACA/Isleña T+504 4451387, Aero Lineas SOSA T+504 4451154, Atlantic Airlines T+504 4451179. **Embassies** → UK T+504 5502337, USA T+504 2369320, Canada T+504 2324551. **Honduras country code** → +504. **IDD code** → 00. **Police** → 119.

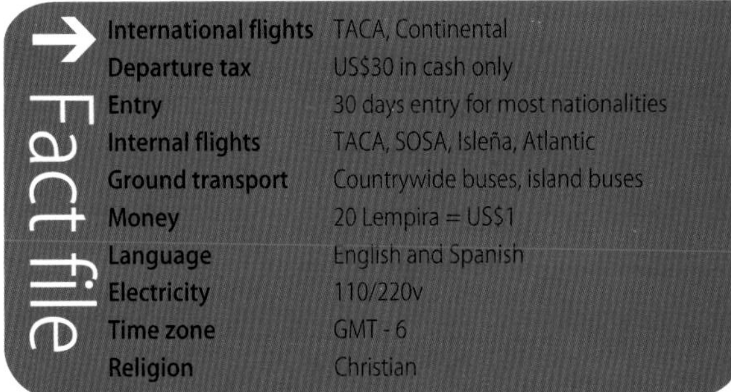

Fact file

International flights	TACA, Continental
Departure tax	US$30 in cash only
Entry	30 days entry for most nationalities
Internal flights	TACA, SOSA, Isleña, Atlantic
Ground transport	Countrywide buses, island buses
Money	20 Lempira = US$1
Language	English and Spanish
Electricity	110/220v
Time zone	GMT - 6
Religion	Christian

Purple spotted sea goddess nudibranch

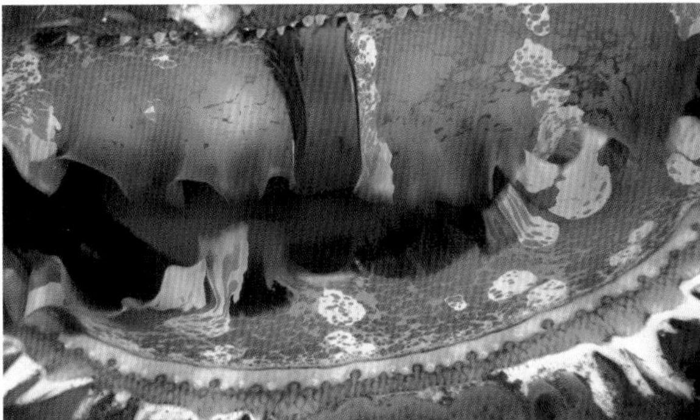

Atlantic thorny oyster

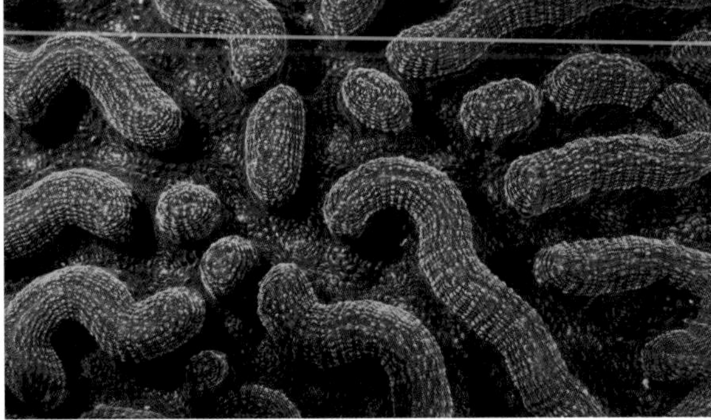

Cactus coral

Dive brief

Diving

Although the Caribbean Sea doesn't have the quantity of marine species found in some areas of the world, there are more species around the Bay Islands than in any other part. This diversity is due to their location at the very bottom of the Great Western Barrier Reef and the geography of Central America. The region is volcanic in origin and sits on an isthmus of land connecting two major continents; the meeting point for many species from north and south.

There are a couple of dozen islands in the Bay group, all sitting 30 or more miles offshore, but the islands which most attract divers are Roatán and Utila. Guanaja and the Hog Islands (Cayos Cochinos) also have some good diving but are less visited as they have restricted accommodation options. Each island has a distinct landside personality but the underwater environment is similar. The reefs have a basic structure of hard corals with a top layer of soft corals, mostly referred to as sea plumes. These look like twiggy tree branches until the currents bring the polyps out to feed and they turn into soft and furry feathers. Sea rods are also abundant, as are numerous smaller corals like cactus and disc corals in iridescent colours.

Fish species range from typical angels and butterflyfish to greater soapfish (which lie flat on the sand unless disturbed) and diamondhead and quillfin blennies. Pelagic sightings sometimes include nurse and reef sharks, as well as eagle rays and turtles. Seahorses are another regular feature of diving this region, although hard to spot. Rare bluebell tunicates are one of the most colourful features of these reefs. Hundreds of these tiny blue creatures cluster together in a dazzling display. Conditions are fairly easy with consistent water temperatures and not too much in the way of currents.

Bottom time

Roatán
Great shore diving inside the lagoon and exciting wall diving outside on the fringing reef » p166

Guanaja
Pleasant diving for those who want to get away from the crowds » p168

Utila
Gentle slopes and craggy shores in the south contrast with steep walls and deeper water in the north » p170

Clusters of Bluebell Tunicates

French Harbour on Roatán

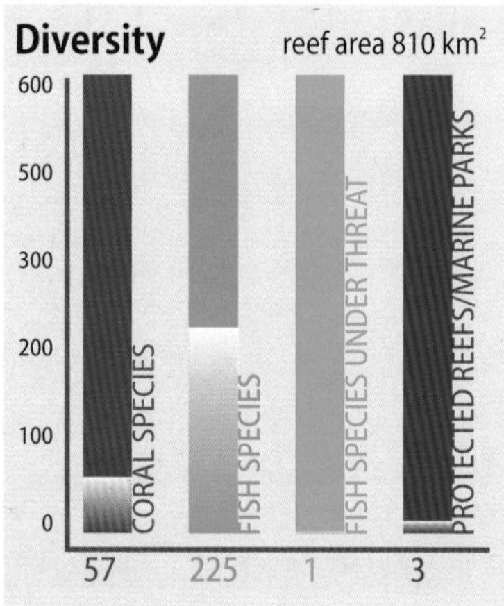

Snorkelling

Gently shelving beaches, protected bays and calm water add up to some great snorkelling no matter which of the Bay Islands you are on. As there is such a strong commercial focus on the dive industry you will even find that resorts have created artificial reefs close to shore (including small boat wrecks on shallow beaches). The areas around jetties can be great for critter hunting but watch out for passing boats.

The Bay Islands are incredibly laid-back. No matter where you go, you feel completely immersed in that distinctive style of island life: hammocks under palms, rum cocktail in hand, the sun setting fiery red over cool turquoise. But perhaps the very best thing is the remarkable value for money. Diving is the lifeblood of these islands and there is just enough competition to ensure that that costs are kept to realistic levels.

The big decision

The Caribbean will always be an alluring destination but for really serious divers the lack of variety can sometimes be disappointing, especially if you have travelled a long way to get there. Honduras, however, has the advantage of being the most diverse marine region within the Caribbean Sea. The hardest decision will be where to go. Each island has its own personality but at least they are all close enough together to organize a multi-centre trip.

Buddy line

Decompression

The risks of decompression diving are drummed into us from day one: "this is dangerous, so don't do it."

So how do you handle being in a region where the dives are constantly deep and constantly long? Well, all training agencies now recommend additional safety stops whether you hit deco-time on your computer or not. This sensible policy should become second nature to all divers. Always be aware that no computer is infallible. The first ever dive tables were based on navy research using masses of ultra-fit young men. As more research has become available, dive computer manufacturers have adjusted their algorithms, making them more and more conservative for fear of being wrong or (worse) sued. There is simply no definitive evidence available to prove if you go into deco you'll get bent, nor that if you stay at 15 metres you won't. There are simply too many variables.

Dive data

Seasons	All year, but can be wet between October and January
Visibility	10-30 metres
Temperatures	Air 20-29°C; water 25-28°C
Wet suit	3 mm full body suit
Training	Very cheap training facilities, especially on Utila
Nitrox	Available but should be pre-booked in resorts
Deco chambers	Roatán, Utila

The *Prince Albert* wreck

Roatán

The largest of the Bay Islands at 58 km long but less than 8 km wide, Roatán is the busiest and most famous due to her international airport. It's also a great place to start a two-centre trip. The island has a highly developed infrastructure, with several towns and villages, many hotels and dive resorts plus a strong US influence.

The centre of the island is jungle-bound and lush, with hills falling steeply to the sea. The coast is ringed by sandy beaches, riddled with tiny keys and mangroves and studded by deep water inlets called blights. It was these that gave the island her history. A safe haven for boats, they were used by huge numbers of pirate ships. Several colonial powers had a presence in these waters during the 16th century, fighting for possession of huge tracts of valuable hardwoods. Eventually, these traders departed for more lucrative shores and Roatán was taken over by the pirates of the Caribbean and the infamous Henry Morgan. The pirates were well organized, built sophisticated fortifications to defend the island and it wasn't until the 1740's that a combined Spanish army and navy offensive removed them. The British legacy remains in place, however, in the names and language of the island's inhabitants,

Roatán has a quite a variety of diving. A barrier reef, sitting just below the surface, rings the island a short way offshore. Inside this reef a gentle lagoon has calm and protected diving, while outside, especially in the south, there are steep walls, fissures, ledges and overhangs. Northern sites tend to be more gentle with sloping walls and reefs but right around the island conditions are similar and never very difficult.

Cracks run through reef walls

1 Calvin's Crack

- **Depth**: 30 m
- **Visibility**: good
- **Currents**: mild
- **Dive type** : day boat
- **Snorkelling**: yes

Rather like a game of follow the leader , this dive involves a drop down to the reef top plateau at about 15 metres before descending into a sharp crack in the reef. The divemaster waves to an enormous green moray who is watching the morning's divers and then he drops out of sight. The dive group files through after him and everyone exits from the tunnel at 27 metres. A slight current runs on the wall so you drift with it and admire all the huge fan corals which are displaying their fluffy feeding tentacles. Gigantic, metre-wide mithrax crabs huddle into the cracks and lobsters wave a claw.

The giant mithrax crab

2 Valley of the Kings

- **Depth**: 32 m
- **Visibility**: good
- **Currents**: mild
- **Dive type** : day boat
- **Snorkelling**: yes

This is one of the more impressive walls along the south coast as it seems to have some of the biggest corals and sponges in the area. Fan corals wave over the top of overhangs, competing for attention with azure vase sponges and amazingly long red and pink rope sponges. Winding through them are black and white spotted morays and a lot of reef fish. French angelfish are common and tend to follow divers. Relatively rare sargassam triggers can be spotted, too.

3 CocoView Bay and Wall

- **Depth**: 32 m
- **Visibility**: poor to good
- **Currents**: none to slight
- **Dive type** : day boat
- **Snorkelling**: absolutely

CocoView Resort is on on a tiny private key and nestles in a shallow part of the lagoon with a channel leading to the outer reef. The lagoon has virtually been turned into a diving theme park but don't be put off by that. This is a great dive and snorkel. Just off the beach is a partly submerged kitting up table, where you haul on your fins and then drop to your knees. A heavy chain leads away from the table, past jawfish, shrimp and upside-down jellyfish to the wreck of the *Prince Albert*. This 47-metre-long island freighter is pretty much intact with lots of coral growing on the structure. You can swim through the open holds and around the decks. When visibility is good you can see her entire length and, as one end is just seven metres deep, snorkellers can too. Heading off to one side, another chain leads from the bow to the fuselage of a DC3 aeroplane with pufferfish and octopus huddling in its remains. There are two diveable walls on either side of the channel. These attract some schools of fish and colourful rabbitfish, parrots and rock beauties. Divers need to be a little careful near the walls due to dive boat traffic. As you head back to shallow waters keep your eyes on the seagrass beds for flounder. Visibility in the lagoon can be poor, especially in the rainy season, due to run-off and tides.

Tales from the deep

Underwater, everyone hears you scream!

Early in our diving days we headed to Anthony's Key Resort, on Roatán. In the briefing for our daytime dive on Overheat Reef, Divemaster Emilio informed us that he would be doing a controlled feeding of the two resident green morays, and that the eels might swim up to us in search of food. Don't be afraid, just put your hands in your armpits, OK? A novice diver named Juanita from Toronto appeared to take it all in her stride. Sure enough, when we reached the bottom at 55 feet, two big, free-swimming eels were already patrolling for a handout. We settled to our knees on the sandy bottom, hands safely tucked away as instructed. Emilio pulled fish scraps from a plastic bag he carried in his pocket and the morays circled him and snapped up the pieces. Emilio quickly ran out of fish and showed the eels two open palms (the international signal for 'all gone'). But the eels were still looking hungry. And looking for more food: in BC pockets, between our legs, sniffing around our heads. It was comical (in retrospect), the sight of big, toothy eels tangled in the fins of divers wriggling out of their way with armpit-holstered hands, trying to appear calm. This happy mayhem was interrupted for everyone at the same instant, heads turning in unison toward the direction of a gurgly scream. Juanita was bolting for the surface, a big moray having invaded her personal space. Her husband, SriPrikash, gave a powerful kick and, releasing one (and only one) hand from its under-arm shelter, stretched out and snared her ankle at the last possible moment. Having puffed all of our air, we headed for the surface as a group in an orderly fashion.

You can have your thoughts about the wisdom of feeding underwater animals but don't let anybody call it 'controlled'.

David Barr, Chicago, USA and Mandura, Australia

We sat on our balcony which hovered over one-metre-deep water. It was so clear we could count the blades of seagrass. Then along came an eagle ray. And its mate. They flapped gently to and fro through the grass, watching and waiting, sniffing for dinner. Just there, right in front of us.

An unusual pufferfish

Octopus watching divers

4 Forty Foot Wall

- **Depth**: 22 m
- **Visibility**: good
- **Currents**: mild
- **Dive type** : day boat
- **Snorkelling**: possibly

Not very imaginatively named, this wall drops from about 25 feet to – you guessed it – 40 feet. The outer wall has some good sponges and soft corals with lots of schooling snapper and spadefish. However, the big attraction here is the coralline algae covering the top level of the reef. Hidden in amongst the bright green carpet are quite a few longsnout seahorses. Of course there are jacks, lobster, crabs and goodness knows what else, but who cares when you have just discovered one of these most beautiful and endangered creatures.

5 The Wreck of the *Captain G*

- **Depth**: 22 m
- **Visibility**: good
- **Currents**: mild
- **Dive type** : day boat
- **Snorkelling**: yes

Not far from French Harbour, this dive has a slightly different profile from much of the coast. The bay is shallow and slopes gently down from a few metres deep until it reaches a steeper wall. Just off the edge are the remains of a shrimping boat. She is quite broken up but the mast and rigging give the general shape. Lots of little animals hide in amongst the remains. There is a lot of coral and sponges in the surrounding area with large groupers, tuna, giant barracuda and plenty of schooling fish and turtles are also known to swing through.

Delicate arrow crab on the reef

Guanaja

East from Roatán is the island of Guanaja. Christened by Christopher Columbus the 'Island of Pines', she is more mountainous than Roatán and relatively undeveloped. There are no roads, although the airport does have a tarmac runway, and very little of anything else.

Most residents live in the capital, Bonacca, which is spread across two tiny keys just offshore and completely covered by houses. When someone wants to build a new house, they erect it on stilts over the water – in front of a neighbour – and the island grows further out to sea, almost by the day.

Guanaja survives in a sense of splendid isolation which has been furthered by the effects of 1998's Hurricane Mitch. Although this humdinger of a storm took its toll right across the Bay Islands, it was Guanaja that bore the full brunt. Most of its famous pine trees were swept away and the reefs on the southern side of the island took a battering. Despite the damage, the marine world has picked itself up and is regenerating nicely. The corals may be less impressive than around the rest of the Bay Islands but in a week here you could easily spot over 100 different species of fish.

However, despite the reef's will to live, it seems that business never quite recovered and the nice resort that was here eventually closed down. There are two other resorts, both are somewhat rustic but if you are looking for a real getaway they may well be for you.

The male quillfin blenny

6 The *Jado Trader* Wreck

- **Depth**: 34 m
- **Visibility**: good
- **Currents**: mild to medium
- **Dive type** : day boat
- **Snorkelling**: yes

Lying on her side, the *Jado Trader* is a 240 foot freighter that was deliberately sunk to form an artificial reef in the 1980's. The hull rests at 36 metres on the sand between two reefs. As you descend you are met by a gang of heavyweight groupers and lots of schooling snappers. Sprouting all over the structure of the hull are small colonies of hard and soft corals. Down on the sand, you can sit with the deck towering above you and meet the enormous resident green morays. These guys are incredibly friendly and will wind themselves around you.

7 Stephan's Reef

- **Depth**: 20 m
- **Visibility**: good
- **Currents**: mild
- **Dive type** : day boat
- **Snorkelling**: yes

A gentle slope leads down from just a few metres to around twenty. This area was affected by Mitch and there is a lot of coral rubble but not so much that it isn't still an interesting dive. A sandy-bedded channel harbours some small soft corals with slender filefish hiding amongst their flat blades. Slipper lobsters huddle under tiny crevices and the rubbly area is great for hunting out small creatures like nudibranchs, arrow crabs and shrimp. You can also spot both male and female diamond and quillfin blennies as well as delicate juvenile spotted drums.

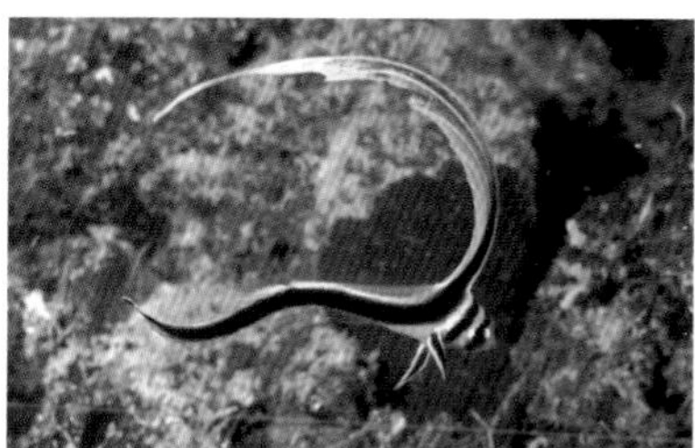

Juvenile spotted drum

8 The Pinnacle

- **Depth**: 30 m
- **Visibility**: poor to good
- **Currents**: mild
- **Dive type** : day boat
- **Snorkelling**: yes

The leeward or northern side of Guanaja can be reached by motoring through a canal that bisects the island just beside capital Bonacca then runs past the airport. There is a cluster of dives around the mouth of the canal, including this sharp pinnacle stretching up from the seabed to sit between two walls. Getting around it can be a bit of a tight squeeze but the narrow tunnels are fun to swim through. As you drop down towards the bottom there are some really good black coral bushes but they often get covered by the silt that washes through the canal. The walls are covered in large barrel sponges, azure vase sponges and gorgonians.

Giant barracuda in stealth mode

Temperatures rising

Going up or down?
When it comes to Cayos Cochinos – the Hog Islands – it's hard to tell. The two islands and 13 cayes, 17 km from the mainland, are protected as a marine reserve. The shallow barrier reef is regarded as the macro capital of the Bay Islands and is a haven for some of the rarer sea creatures in this region. In the past, Cochinos attracted the backpacker set who could stay very cheaply in the one local village – but always complained bitterly about the no-seeum population. There is now just one resort, which is highly eco-orientated, but that's about it. There is no doubt that the islands are idyllic, completely remote and unspoilt and those who love them, do so with a passion. Everyone else heads for livelier Roatán and Utila.

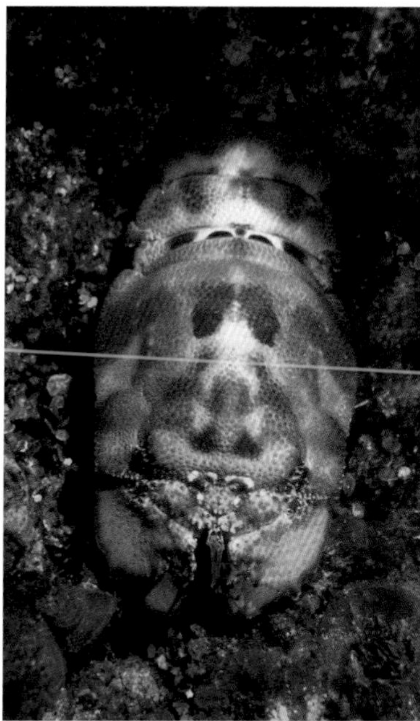

The oddly shaped slipper lobster

Utila

Heading 30 nautical miles southwest from Roatán you'll reach Utila, an island completely different in character to her bigger neighbour. The island is as flat as Roatán is hilly and while Roatán has attained a certain level of sophistication, with its influx of tourism and development, Utila retains an air of casual chaos.

From the moment you set foot on the airstrip (no terminal, no check-in desks, no luggage handler) you realise that this is one chilled-out little place. A favourite with travellers and hikers, the small town has just one main road that connects the small hotels, shops, restaurants and more dive centres than you can wave your kit bag at.

As Utila sits right on the edge of the continental shelf, the style of the diving is slightly different to Roatán. On the southern coast the dives are shallow, maximum depths rarely reaching over 25 metres, but with lots of interesting cracks and crevices along the reef walls. This makes for some great swim throughs, with overhangs and sand channels to investigate. While the marine species are naturally similar to Roatán, there seems to be more variety in the fish life and more critters.

On the north side of the island, the diving becomes more dramatic, with steep walls and drop-offs. This side of the island is affected by prevailing weather conditions, so you may not get up there as much as you would like. It is also recognized as a whaleshark highway, with regular sightings in the dry season.

Utila town at sunset

9 Great Wall (Duppy Waters)

Depth: 36 m
Visibility: very good
Currents: none to medium
Dive type : day boat
Snorkelling: yes

Just outside Turtle Harbour is one of the most spectacular dives on the north of the island. A sharp slope descends quickly to a wall that seems to drop off into infinity. The slope is covered in sponges and corals and many leopard morays reside amongst them. As you go over the lip there are huge fan corals and giant barrel sponges pushing out into the sea. Fish hovering off the edge include great barracuda, jacks, creole wrasse and occasional turtles. Back up on the top of the reef there are plenty of juvenile fish plus grey angels, Townsend angels and damsels, and scorpionfish hide under the soft corals. As the dive boats head back to the south coast they are often accompanied by a pod of dolphins.

10 Aquarium I & II

Depth: 16 m
Visibility: fair to good
Currents: mild
Dive type : day boat
Snorkelling: yes

The eastern end of Utila is made up of jagged volcanic rock formations. The Aquarium sites are quite shallow and great for exploring the unusual formations under the shoreline. Caves and overhangs have been shaped by crashing waves, leaving chimneys and blowholes. You can sit in relatively calm water and watch the powerful action above you. Inside the caves, if you look down, are some interesting fish, such as the greater soapfish, mantis shrimp and trunkfish. A little deeper are large garden beds of swaying soft corals, whip and rope corals. In amongst them are flutemouths and parrotfish, banded jawfish and peacock flounders.

A school of bluestriped grunts

11 Ted's Point

Depth: 23 m
Visibility: good
Currents: mild
Dive type : day boat
Snorkelling: yes

Just outside East Harbour on the south coast, this is a favourite night dive. A sloping sandy patch leads down to the remains of a small sailboat that is covered in tunicates and sponges. If you know what you're looking for you may find the nocturnal cryptic teardrop crab sitting on a sponge. There are beds of garden eels between small outcrops of brain coral. Flamingo tongue shells feed on the soft corals and neon gobies rest on sponges. There are Pederson cleaner shrimps on corkscrew anemones and lots of other night crustaceans. Another curious find is the swollen claw mantis, a tiny chap just 5-6 centimetres long.

Friendly grey angelfish

12 *Halliburton* Wreck

- **Depth**: 30 m
- **Visibility**: poor to good
- **Currents**: mild to medium
- **Dive type** : day boat
- **Snorkelling**: no

This 30-metre-long cargo ship was sunk in May 1998 to create an artificial reef. She sits just off the lighthouse at the edge of East Harbour so visibility isn't great. The wreck catches the tides and murk from the bay but the flow of nutrients is aiding coral growth. She rests in an upright position in a sandy patch of the seabed and is marked by two buoys. One is attached to the bow at about 20 metres and this is a good place to start. As you descend you can see some corals decorating the hold and large grouper usually hang around below the bow. You can then swim around the hull or through a few openings until you reach the wheelhouse. There is a bicycle locked to the rail outside and large snappers and groupers hover inside unless disturbed. A giant green moray often slithers around. Finally, ascend up the second mooring line for a safety stop.

Cleaner shrimp on finger sponge

Juvenile slender filefish

13 Silver Garden

- **Depth**: 26 m
- **Visibility**: good
- **Currents**: mild to medium
- **Dive type** : day boat
- **Snorkelling**: yes

The garden is actually a shallow sandy shelf with outcrops and small channels to explore. At their edge is a steeper drop-off where hard corals are in good condition. A large school of horse eye jacks seems to continually hang off the wall, interspersed with another school of creole wrasse – the males chasing after the females. Giant green morays lurk in the cracks and crevices in the reef and slender filefish try to camouflage themselves against seawhips. Up in the shallows – which is a good snorkelling area – are lots of juvenile fish, blennies sitting on sponges and harlequin pipefish.

The long-snout seahorse is endemic to the Caribbean

Drying out

These three islands are not places with masses of culture or history. Although their past was rather colourful, there are few established remains to visit. However, if history is your thing, one of the most spectacular Maya sites lies at Copán, near the border with Guatemala.

Roatán

The largest of the Bay Islands and with the most facilities for sleeping, diving and sightseeing, this is the best place to start – if only because it's where the airport is.

Sleeping and diving

$$$ **Anthony's Key Resort**, on the northwest coast, www.anthonyskey.com. One of the founding resorts with masses of activities including a marine research facility, dolphin encounter programme and many other organized activities. Good for families. Meals and diving included in weekly package rates of around US$150 per day.

$$ **CocoView Resort**, sitting on a small private key half way along the south coast, T+504 4557500, www.cocoviewresort.com. Club-style resort which attracts a lot of US groups. All meals and diving are included in weekly package rates of around US$130 per day. Plus the bay is definitely the best shore dive on the island.

$$ **Inn of Last Resort**, 5 minutes from the town of West End, T+504 4454108, www.innoflastresort.com. Nice wooden bungalows on the beach and a fabulous seafood restaurant. Has a dive centre but feels more orientated to short stays.

Sights

As Roatán gets busier – mostly because cruise ships dock here now – more organized activities have sprung up. You can go horseriding or white-water rafting, visit an iguana or butterfly farm or go sailing for a day. Be aware that all tours may get booked up when one of the visiting cruise liners disgorges its passengers.

West End For a bit of retail therapy head down to West End for a few hours. The town is under a mile from end to end but has plenty of restaurants and gift shops.

Carambola Nature Reserve Walk up Carambola Peak for fabulous views over the island then hike the nature trails to see palm trees, ferns, orchids, growing spices and mahogany. Iguana Wall on the cliff is a protected zone for iguanas and parrots.

Oak Ridge A true Caribbean fishing village, where you can imagine what life might have been like back in the pirate days. Most buildings are built over the water and the locals get about by boat.

Guanaja

Sleeping and diving

$$ **End of the World Resort**,T+504 991 1257, www.guanaja.com. Very simple wooden bungalows in an impressive hillside setting. Package rates of around US$120 per day with a dive centre on site.

Also watch out for the 3-star **Posada del Sol**, a very nice hotel, currently shut but rumour has it due to reopen.

Sights

There's not much in the way of organized sightseeing on this island. You can go hiking in the hills, where the birdwatching can be impressive and there are several waterfalls. At

Jetty on Roatán

Dive boats on Guanaja

either **Bonacca** or **Savannah Blight** you can see a little of local life. At the time of writing a new artificial reef was being created to celebrate the discovery of the island by Columbus. Called **Mestizo Reef**, it includes statues of him, plus Honduran hero, Lempira, and Spanish cannons and bells.

Utila

Sleeping and diving

$$$ **Laguna Beach Resort**, www.utila.com. 5 mins by boat from the town of Utila, this secluded and romantic resort has great packages, including diving and all meals, at around US$130 per night.

$$ **Mango Inn**, Utila Town, T+504 4253326, www.mangoinn.com. Small Caribbean style inn set in a pleasant garden. Works with Utila Dive Centre.

$$ **Utila Lodge**, www.utilalodge.com. Right in town but built on a series of jetties over the bay. Nice rooms and great views at sunset. Good dive operation with an onsite school. The Shark Research Institute, also based here, run seasonal whaleshark field trips (whaleshark spotting is never guaranteed). General packages including diving and all meals at around US$130 per night.

Sights

There's not a huge amount to do on Utila although there are organized hikes to see the rock formations at **Iron Bound** or up through the small patch of forest at **Pumpkin Hill**. There's an iguana breeding station, some horseback riding and, of course, whaleshark spotting. Apart from that, wander along the main road for a few drinks at a sunset bar or investigate the excellent handicraft shops.

International agents

Roatán Charter, PO Box 877, 12251 Curley St, San Antonio, Florida, T+1 (1)352 5884131, www.Roatán.com. Based in America but with strong family links to the region, this very knowledgeable agent has full details of all resorts and can issue flights tickets from US hubs onwards.

Surface interval

There are two sidelines to any dive trip to Honduras that are absolute musts but both require a little time spent on the mainland. Many island operators can organize these trips for you.

Up in the clouds

Just across from the islands on the mainland is the spectacular **Pico Bonito Cloud Forest**. The mountains here rise to 2700 metres and are nearly always swathed in clouds, created when the cool mountain air meets warmer temperatures at the coast. Against a backdrop of the towering Nombre de Dios mountain range, you can explore the forests and spot one of the 325 known bird species. You can hike through the park and, if you are lucky, see jaguar or puma, tapir, deer or white-faced and spider monkeys. On the hillside is a splendid lodge converted from an old chocolate plantation – the pods hang over your door – and they say that the big cats have been known to sit on guest's terraces. The Lodge at Pico Bonito: AP 710, La Ceiba, Atlantida T+504 4400388, www.picobonito.com. Rooms start at US$155 and packages are great value.

Down and out in the ruins

Possibly one of the least known of the Maya sites, yet one of the best to visit, the extensive **Copán Ruinas** are a World Heritage Site and regarded as strategically important to the region. There are many exquisitely carved 'stelae', which tell tales from Maya history, and some extremely well-preserved temples. Archaeologists are constantly discovering new sections, one of the latest being some hidden tombs. You can walk through tunnels beneath the impressive ruins and visit the new museum where some of the more fragile finds have been placed. Copán town is a rather pretty place with cobbled streets and plenty of restaurants and shops. Tours from the Bay Islands run at around US$250 for two days and one night.

Stela at Copán

Copán

Pico Bonito

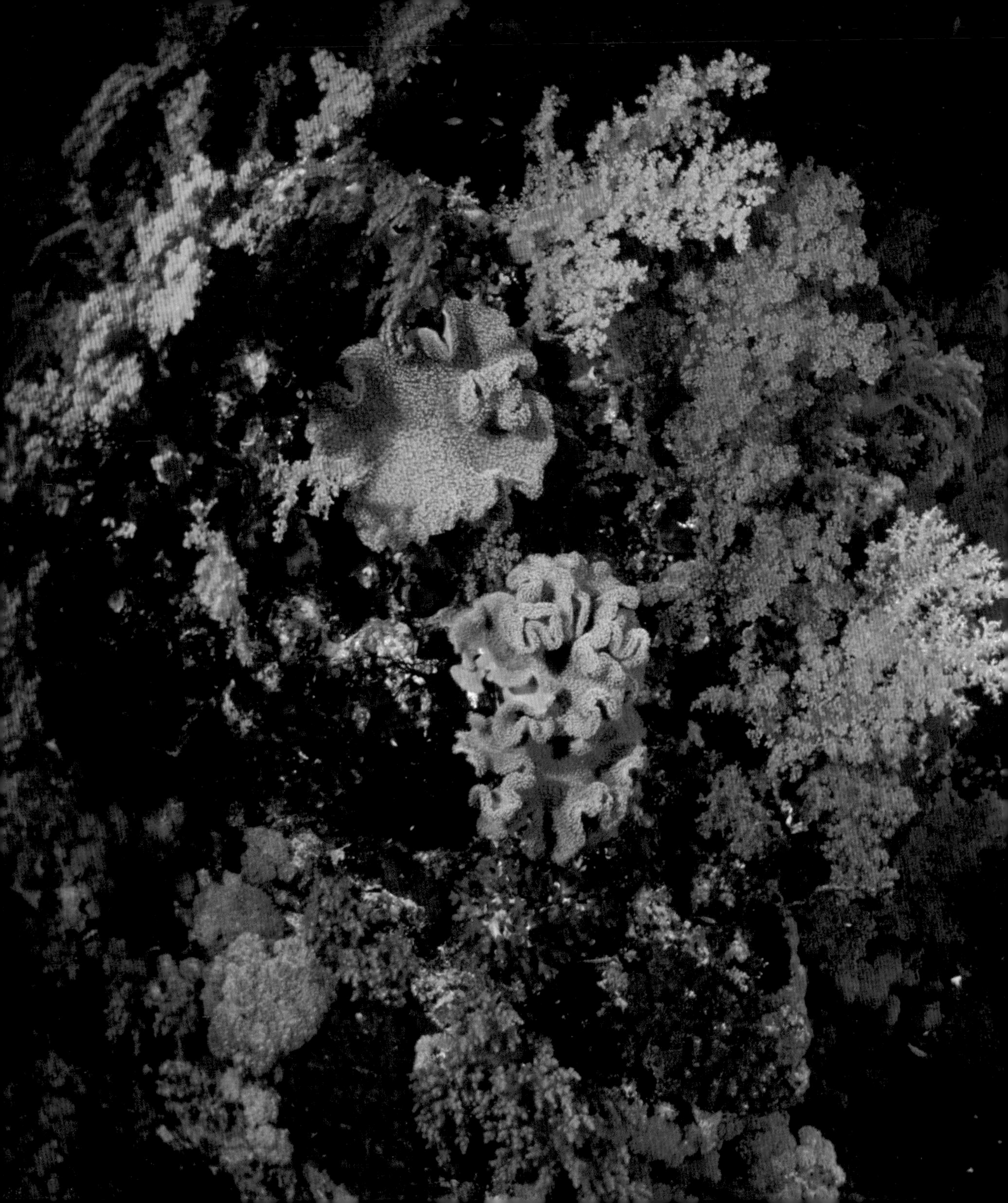

Egypt

Candid camera: plummeting walls painted in riotous colour, committed to film on Little Brother

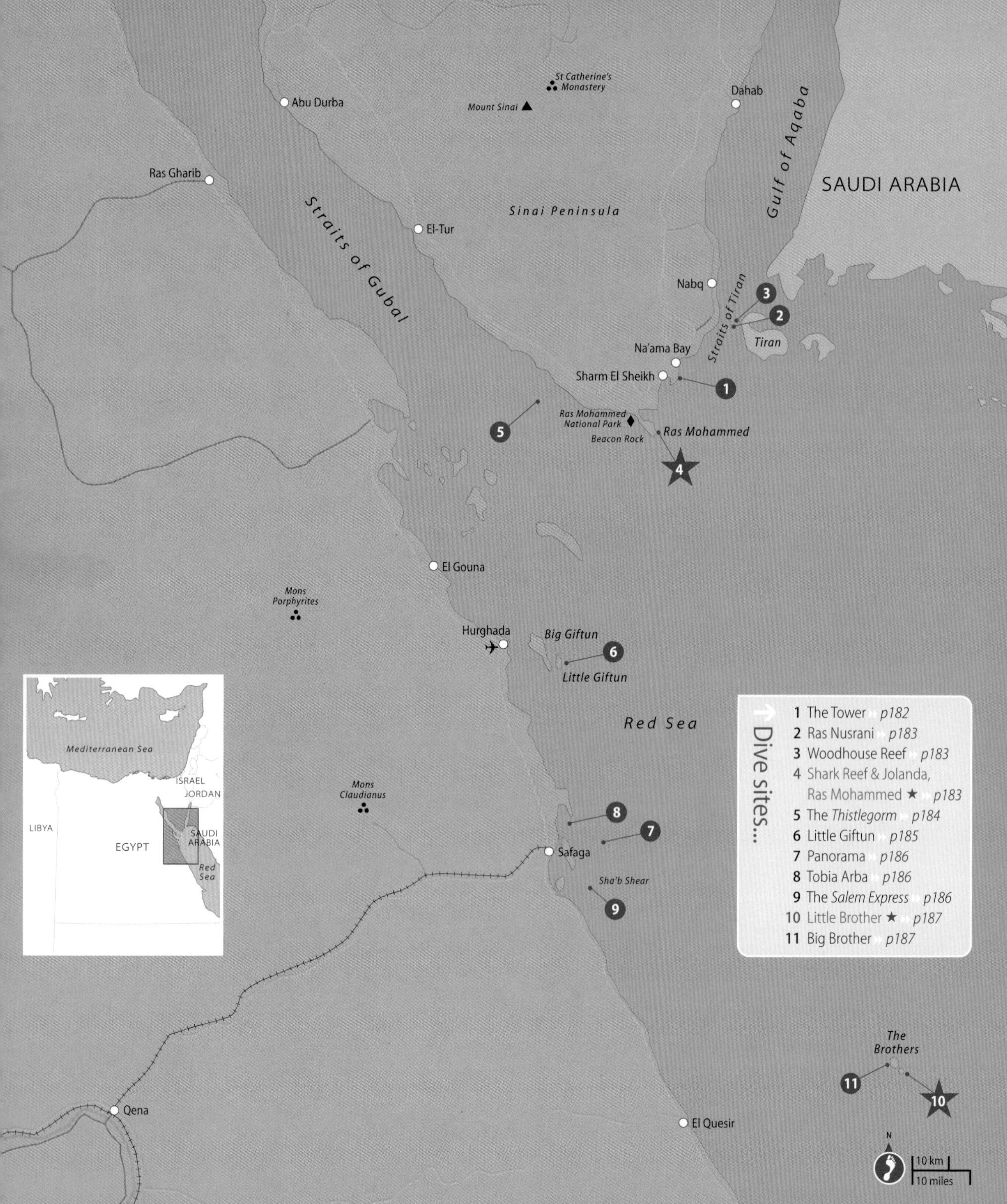

St Catherine's Monastery
Mount Sinai
Abu Durba
Dahab
Gulf of Aqaba
SAUDI ARABIA
Ras Gharib
Straits of Gubal
Sinai Peninsula
El-Tur
Nabq
Straits of Tiran
Tiran
Na'ama Bay
Sharm El Sheikh
Ras Mohammed National Park
Beacon Rock
Ras Mohammed
El Gouna
Mons Porphyrites
Hurghada
Big Giftun
Little Giftun
Red Sea
Mons Claudianus
Safaga
Sha'b Shear
The Brothers
Qena
El Quesir
Mediterranean Sea
ISRAEL
JORDAN
LIBYA
EGYPT
SAUDI ARABIA
Red Sea
Dive sites...
1 The Tower p182
2 Ras Nusrani p183
3 Woodhouse Reef p183
4 Shark Reef & Jolanda, Ras Mohammed ★ p183
5 The Thistlegorm p184
6 Little Giftun p185
7 Panorama p186
8 Tobia Arba p186
9 The Salem Express p186
10 Little Brother ★ p187
11 Big Brother p187
N
10 km
10 miles

Introduction

The lands surrounding the Red Sea are steeped in legend and ancient history. Here it was, according to the story from Exodus, that the waters parted to save the Israelites from the Egyptian army. Here was the cradle of civilization, where great races built unrivalled monuments and developed technologies we still rely on thousands of years later.

The name itself is something of an enigma. One explanation is that the Red Sea is so called because it periodically turns a faint red, from seasonal blooms of red algae that live near the surface, while local folklore suggests that the reflection of the fiery sunrises and sunsets were the inspiration. Whatever the reason, the Red Sea is, in reality, far from red. The intense variety of blues mask the riches of her hidden coral reefs. Being the world's most northern reef system, the marine life stakes out a special place in the diving world. You can expect the corals, the pelagics, the critter life, to all be just that little bit different from elsewhere on the planet. And they are.

Seven nations border this narrow ribbon of sea but Egypt grabs most attention. The lands of the Pharaohs may not be what you expected. Coastal resorts are highly developed and ancient monuments are a long way away. Not that this appears to matter to the million or more divers who descend continually throughout the year.

“” There's no doubt there's some fantastic diving here, it's just that you need to be willing to share the experience with many others.

Egypt Rating

Diving
★★★

Dive facilities
★★★

Accommodation
★★★★

Down time
★★★

Value for money
★★★★

Essentials

Egypt

Location	27°00' N, 30°00' E
Neighbours	Israel, Jordan, Libya, Saudi Arabia, Sudan
Population	77,505,756
Land area in km²	995,450
Marine area in km²	6,000
Coastline in km	386

Getting there and around

If you live anywhere in Europe, you'll already know that getting a charter flight to any Egyptian coastal resort is as easy as grabbing a dive magazine and booking a package. You could make your life a little more complex and try to fly scheduled – and you would be more comfortable – but as it's only few hours on the plane, you may as well take the cheaper charter option.

However, if you're coming from anywhere further afield you'll need to do some research. Most major airlines have connections to Cairo, with European carriers routing you through their home base. Choose a flight based on where you would like a stopover: for London try **British Airways**, **Alitalia** for Rome, **KLM** for Amsterdam, to name just a few. **Singapore Airlines** and many Middle Eastern airlines such as **Emirates**, connect Australasia to Cairo, where you can swap to an **Egypt Air** (www.egyptair.com) internal flight. You could also go **Egypt Air** all the way as their network is extensive and a stopover in Cairo is quite an experience.

Once you have arrived at the Red Sea coast, you will be collected by your dive operator, assuming you have booked a package, or at least a night, in advance. As these resorts can get horribly busy, arriving without a booking isn't recommended.

Getting around during the day is easy enough. There are taxis but a price should be agreed in advance. Mini-buses provide shuttles between hotels and restaurants for a nominal sum and there are public buses and ferries that cover longer distances.

Language

From the ancient days of hieroglyphics through to the modern day, language in Egypt has changed many times. However, once Islam took hold, Arabic became official. Local dialects are spoken across the region with Egyptian differing even between the north and south. God's Will, *inshaalha*, and never mind, *maalish*, are two phrases you will hear constantly. Dive crews seem to enjoy teaching a few words here and there. Phonetic translations as follows:

Camels at the Pyramids

hello	*salam alekom*
goodbye	*maasalaama*
yes	*naam*
no	*la*
ok	*taieb*
please	*men fadlak*
thank you	*shukran*
excuse me	*ismahlee*
how much is this?	*kum hada?*
water	*moya*
good	*kowiees*

Local laws and customs

Egypt is principally Muslim and there are a few things to be aware of, though only if you travel inland from the coast. The Red Sea resorts are highly Westernized and tourist savvy but what you can get away with on the coast may be frowned on in Cairo. Both sexes should dress modestly and avoid displays of affection in public. If you are with local people remember to eat with your right hand only and try to never show the soles of your feet (obviously a little difficult while you're diving). Women should be prepared to cover all bare skin and accept that you will be spoken to through your male partner or dive buddies.

Safety

In Cairo, as in any other city, be aware of what is going on around you. Personal safety is no more of an issue here than any major capital but be sensible about where you go and at what time of day. Women, especially those who are fair or redheaded may feel uncomfortable due to the amount of attention they receive.

The Red Sea coast is a whole different kettle of fish. But though resorts are modern and feel perfectly safe, recent terrorist activity will discourage some potential visitors. Be assured that the security services are highly vigilant in all dive areas.

Health

Tutankhamen's Two-step, Pharaoh's Revenge, the Nile Quickstep... you guessed it, euphemisms for a classic case of Egyptian stomach upset. Food in Egypt is often specifically targeted at tourist tastebuds and it is this that appears to cause problems. Local-style cooking is often fresher. If a place looks clean and well patronized, especially by Egyptians, it's a good sign. Be sure to keep up your fluid levels; it's a great way to combat tummy troubles. For other health issues chemists or pharmacists are well trained. If you need assistance, hotels hold details of English speaking doctors. And beware of the sun – in midsummer temperatures can reach over 50°C. Factor 8 sunscreen is close to useless in this environment. Get 30 plus.

Costs

As most people pre-book a package it can be hard to judge the value of a room. For instance, any one of the Hilton Hotels are around US$80-100 per night, but a week-long package from London that includes flights, accommodation and diving might be as little as US$800. Meanwhile, eating out is something you can quantify and is great value. There are many restaurants in many styles. A burger and chips will be as little as EG£15 while a steak may push the cost up to EG£35. Local food is harder to find but is always great value. A large beer in a local bar will be around EGP£6. Tipping – or baksheesh – is a way of life in Egypt. Salaries are low, especially for those who work in the service industries, so 'donate' an Egyptian pound or two to everyone, from cab drivers to room boys to the chap who watches your shoes when you a visit a mosque. On restaurant bills, consider 10%. For dive crews see page 14.

Airlines → Air Canada T+20 (0)2 758402, British Airways T+20 (0)2 5780743, Egypt Air T+20 (0)2 5915200, Qantas T+20 (0)2 769529, TWA T+20 (0)2 5749913. **Embassies** → UK T+20 (0)2 7940852, USA T+20 (0)2 7973300, Canada T+20 (0)2 7943110, Singapore T+20 (0)2 7495045. **Egypt country code** → +20. **IDD** → 00. **Police** → 0.

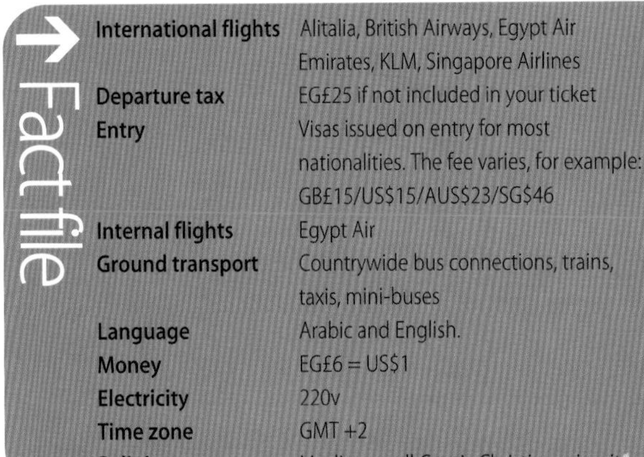

Fact file

International flights	Alitalia, British Airways, Egypt Air Emirates, KLM, Singapore Airlines
Departure tax	EG£25 if not included in your ticket
Entry	Visas issued on entry for most nationalities. The fee varies, for example: GB£15/US$15/AUS$23/SG$46
Internal flights	Egypt Air
Ground transport	Countrywide bus connections, trains, taxis, mini-buses
Language	Arabic and English.
Money	EG£6 = US$1
Electricity	220v
Time zone	GMT +2
Religion	Muslim, small Coptic Christian minority

Cuttlefish playing at disguise …

… Starfish don't need to!

Dive brief

Diving

At 2240 km long, 380 km wide and up to 2150 metres deep the Red Sea is a lifeline for her neighbouring countries. The northern end is enclosed – or was until the building of the Suez Canal – while the southern opening into the Indian Ocean is extremely shallow, preventing deep ocean currents entering the gulf. The surrounding deserts and extreme temperatures create the highest salinity in any open sea yet it still sustains one of the world's most impressive marine systems.

Being isolated from the both the Indian Ocean and the Mediterranean Sea (originally) means this most northern coral reef system has an unrivalled biological set-up. Almost 10 percent of her species are endemic: they might look like something you've seen somewhere else but chances are they're a unique form. Crustaceans, cephalopods, molluscs – they're all there along with schools of reef fish and pelagic fish. Sharks swoop past in the current and dolphins play in the bow wave on an almost daily basis.

Whether you've headed for the Sinai or the south or somewhere on a boat out in the middle, the dives will be similar. Seasonal variations can be marked though. When it's windy you will know all about it as surface conditions can be very choppy. Summers are exceptionally hot and plankton blooms are linked to temperature changes and can occur at any time, as can a change in the currents.

Bottom time

The Sinai Peninsula
Famed reefs littered with even more famous wrecks » p182

The south coast
Popular Red Sea reefs with the potential to surprise » p185

The Brothers
Potentially breathtaking diving in a pristine environment » p187

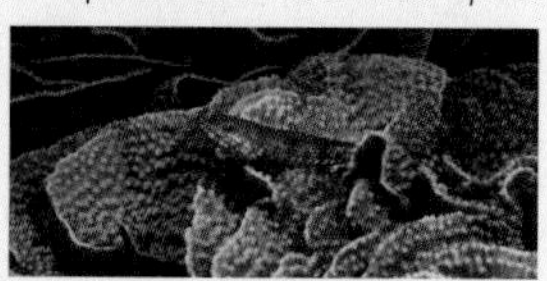

Snorkelling

There are beach-side reefs to investigate but even if you don't dive it's worth heading out on a boat with the divers as many of Egypt's offshore reefs can be snorkelled. The only issue for snorkellers will be the weather. Be very aware of how harsh the sun can be in summer. As the water here is cool, you may not realize that you are burning. Conversely, when it's winter you may need a wetsuit as the water temperature drops sharply.

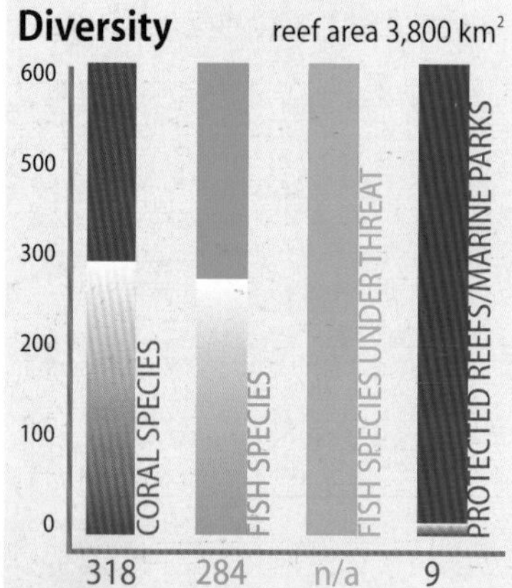

A leopard flounder pretending to be sand

When we learnt to dive, the swimming pool in central London made our training dives in Cyprus look exotic. In turn, those dives meant that our first trip to the Red Sea took on the status of a pilgrimage. After several trips there we got a hankering to go further. We spread our wings and spent the '90s traversing one continent after another. We've been back to Egypt since and it's good to be reminded that this is one of the world's better coral reef systems. Catch it at the right time of year in the right part of the sea, with the right boat, and you will get diving as good as almost anywhere. However, you have to remember that because this is such an easily accessible destination, it's also one of the busiest and most crowded places you will ever dive.

Dive data

Seasons	All year, July-August is extremely hot, December-January can be very cool
Visibility	10-40 metres
Temperatures	Air 20-30°C; water 20-28°C
Wet suit	Summer: 3 mm full body suit; winter: 5 mm+
Training	Courses available in most resorts, standards vary
Nitrox	Available
Deco chambers	Sharm El Sheikh, Hurghada, El Gouna

The big decision

The Red Sea is only a stone's throw from southern Europe and though you can dive much of it, Egypt is the easiest country to reach. It's cheap and perhaps the least politically sensitive country. Choosing a specific destination inside the country is only difficult in that there is little difference between the resort areas; a little bigger or smaller, a little busier or quieter, there's not much in it.

Conservation

This is not a souvenir shop
We all like to bring a little something home. But why is it that some divers think it's clever to take items they find underwater? Once in Thailand, we discovered an anchor embedded in the reef. It was thick with corals and small fish. We showed it to another diver in our group and off we went. He then used his dive knife to prise it from the reef, causing damage to both. Everyone else was mortified but he just couldn't see the problem. Likewise, when we first dived the Thistlegorm – not long after it was discovered – it was thick with remnants of her past. Now, souvenir hunters have removed trophies such as steering wheels or badges and her cargo of vehicles is no longer pristine. Before being tempted to take something, remember that not only is this the future of diving but many wrecks are also graves. You wouldn't go stealing from a cemetery, would you?

Dancing anthias are synonymous with Egypt diving

Crocodilefish can be hard to spot

Countless yellowfin goatfish

Sinai Peninsula

Diving in the Sinai is legendary. This area is one of those 'must do' places: home to Egypt's first marine park – Ras Mohammed; the Straits of Tiran and the Straits of Gubal; entrance to the Suez Canal; and where many a wreck is found. Despite the numbers of boats, operators and divers, this is an area of distinctive beauty.

Dive tourism was born in a tiny fishing village which grew out of all recognition to become the upscale resort of Sharm El Sheikh. There are hotels, dive centres, restaurants and more hotels, but at its heart is Na'ama Bay, a crescent shaped cove that somehow helps to retain the town's charm. It's a lively place, with lots to do. There's golf and camel riding, you can arrange a trip out into the desert with a Bedouin guide or head off on a tour to a medieval site but the focus is pretty much dive, dive, dive – and party.

On either side of Na'ama, the resorts in Shark Bay and Old Sharm (Sharm El Maya) are good for those who like it a little less frenetic. Facilities are just as good and you are only a short taxi ride away from the centre. Development continues to spread right up the coast towards Israel. In Dahab, a small number of hotels and dive centres have set up and are good for those who like a quieter life. Numbers of visitors, both on land and in the water, are fewer here, yet the diving is still impressive. Nearby are St Catherine's Monastery and Mount Sinai, said to be where Moses received the Ten Commandments.

If you are a novice and want to gain experience there are plenty of dives to practise on: shallow wrecks, pretty reefs, drifts and caves – it's all there. For more experienced divers, there's all of that plus some deeper wrecks and more exposed conditions. The only downside is the numbers. You will never be the only boat moored over the Thistlegorm. Sometimes there are so many you need both hands to count them.

Bannerfish in formation

1 The Tower

- **Depth**: 20 m
- **Visibility**: good
- **Currents**: slight to medium
- **Dive type**: shore
- **Snorkelling**: yes

This shore dive is popular both day and night. The entry over the reef can be a little tricky at low tide so most divers take a spectacular short-cut through a small cave. The mouth is part way across the reef top and as you swim down it opens into a wider passage then exits on the reef wall. You could drop as deep as 40 metres, and may encounter a whitetip or two, but the most interesting parts of the dive are under 20 metres. The marine life is a microcosm of all things Red Sea – masses of anthias flitting in and out of soft corals, moray eels, butterflies, lionfish and plenty of crustaceans. At night every surface is alive with shrimp and decorator crabs which are attracted by the moonlight shining through the opening.

2 Ras Nusrani

Depth: 24 m
Visibility: good
Currents: can be strong
Dive type: day boat/liveaboard
Snorkelling: yes

This name means Christian Headland and, like everywhere in the Sinai, the location leads to more than one dive. The wall below the tip of the point is quite steep and at its base there is a good covering of soft corals and gorgonians. In the shallows is a background of hard corals which harbour scorpionfish and anemones with clownfish. Glassfish shoals hover in small caves while in open water there are fusiliers, jacks and surgeons. Moving south from the point you come to another dive site called White Knights. It's an equally good dive but more interesting is that mantas sometimes flap lazily to and fro between these sites.

3 Woodhouse Reef

Depth: 24 m
Visibility: good
Currents: can be strong
Dive type: day boat/liveaboard
Snorkelling: yes

Heading east from Sharm are the Straits of Tiran where a series of reefs are great dives yet troublesome for boat navigation. As you approach, you will see a couple of partially submerged, wrecked hulls. Woodhouse is a long narrow reef where the top is quite shallow but it drops steeply on both sides. Divers get dropped on the east and drift along the wall. Coral cover is good all the way along and you can spot many animals such as morays sheltering in amongst them. Because of the current, there is more action in the blue – turtles whizz by occasionally and there are jacks, tuna and snapper. Up in the shallows are creatures such as pipefish and blue-spotted rays.

4 Shark Reef & Jolanda, Ras Mohammed

Depth: 20 m
Visibility: good
Currents: can be very strong
Dive type: day boat/liveaboard
Snorkelling: current dependant

Off the very southern tip of Ras Mohammed are several dives loosely known as 'Ras'. The actual sites mostly referred to are the twin peaks of Shark Reef and Jolanda. Their joint status derives from dives starting on one and finishing on the other. A submerged sea mound is separated from the mainland by a shallow channel and rising from it are the two peaks, themselves linked by a saddle. The dive starts off as a drift at Shark Reef where a dramatic wall drops into the blue. You float past a reef wall swarming with orange and blue anthias and over colourful soft corals feeding in the current. Reef sharks (black and whitetips) are often seen here and the lucky may spot a hammerhead. Next, you pass over the saddle, then it's on to the coral gardens at Jolanda. You may spot a few cargo remains from the freighter of the same name but the wreck itself dropped into the deep during a storm in the 80's. The dive finally ends in the shallows beyond Jolanda. Giant Napoleon wrasse are sometimes seen here and approach divers inquisitively.

Nosy!

Sweetlips sheltering

Clown carpet

5 The *Thistlegorm*

- **Depth**: 25 m
- **Visibility**: fair
- **Currents**: can be strong
- **Dive type**: day boat/liveaboard
- **Snorkelling**: no

The Straits of Gubal, the stretch of water that leads to the Suez Canal, are a shipping graveyard. One of the most renowned dives here is the *HMS Thistlegorm*, a British cargo vessel bombed during the Second World War en route to resupply troops. Now she is like a deserted shop, with holds full of motorbikes, engines and even toilets that never reached their destination. Conditions here are highly variable – when it's calm it's an easy dive but if the wind and waves pick up, it 's not a place for novices. The hull is lying almost upright at 30 metres and is pretty much intact. Descent is down a line tied to the forward section from where you can swim into a few of the holds then down towards the stern. This took the brunt of the bomb blast but you can see the propellor, crew quarters and some anti-aircraft guns. The wreck is well colonized with corals and fish life and just off to one side, if you can tear yourself away, is a locomotive engine.

Descending to the *Thistlegorm*

Tales from the deep

The *Dunraven*

In the Northern Red sea, on a point called Beacon Rock, lies the wreck of the *Dunraven*. Built in 1873, she was a sail and steam hybrid, utilizing sail when conditions permitted.

This ship came to an untimely end on the 25th April, 1876. According to records she ran aground due to a navigation error. However, our dive guide told a different tale. The Captain caught the Master of the ship below decks with his wife. The two men fought a great battle and in the heat of the fight, the distracted crew did not notice the approaching rocks. Whether this has any truth, or is an apocryphal tale, only goes to make this a more interesting dive.

Descending the buoy line to the stern of the ship, we found the wreck lying upside down at 30 metres. A large intact propeller was encrusted in coral and below that was an opening. We entered into relative darkness but soon became accustomed to the gloom. Rows of portholes let light through to create a mysterious atmosphere. Slowly, working single file forwards, we came across two large boilers surrounded by glassy sweepers and the odd overfed lionfish. Then, leaving the interior, we explored the bow. There were Napoleon wrasse and giant morays amongst the ever-present anthias. Finally, we headed over to explore the adjacent reef which was a nice end to the dive.

It was here that my buddy and I were joined by a lone dolphin. Both of us are photographers, so we were way behind the main group. I turned to see 'our' dolphin close by. With the camera stuck in front of my face and a smile so wide that my reg nearly fell out, I was amazed to watch this inquisitive fellow almost touch noses with my buddy. We spent some 20 minutes with him until my air was so low I had to come up.

I have dived this wreck a few times and, to be honest, it is far from the best in this region. However, that experience made the *Dunraven* a memory to be cherished forever.

Sean Keen, Polegate, UK

The south coast

Opposite Sharm, but on the other side of the Straits of Gubal, are a series of small towns. Like their northern neighbours, these have grown up to become sophisticated resorts. Fly into Hurghada and you can easily reach any of them.

Hurghada

Once a small Bedouin encampment, this is now Egypt's biggest beach resort. From downtown Dahar, the beach stretches for many kilometres north and south. The whole coastline is connected by the Corniche, a single road that is lined with resorts, shops, restaurants, dive centres and facilities for a range of sports, from golf to windsurfing. Dahar is a working Egyptian town, busy and unattractive. Offshore, the reef once suffered from misuse and over-diving. However, in 1992 a group of operators formed a conservation group, organizing mooring buoys and protective schemes. The reefs are now safeguarded under the same rules as Ras Mohammed and regenerating well, although ones closer to shore are not as profuse as you might hope. Day boats head out to better reefs and you can book special fast boats to reach the wrecks in Gubal. Hurghada is also the starting point for many liveaboards which travel all over the southern Red Sea, including the isolated Brothers Islands.

El Gouna

Just a short drive north of Hurghada, this town is actually a custom-built resort. Fancy landscaping has turned the original desert into a maze of palm tree- and hotel-studded islands surrounded by turquoise lagoons. There's a small, insignificant 'downtown' section, a full complement of diver and non-diver activities and a certain sense of seclusion not found in busy Hurghada. As El Gouna is a little closer to Gubal, day trips head up there as well as to the offshore reefs.

Safaga

The shipping port of Safaga, an hour south of Hurghada, has lent its name to another resort. Few tourists see the small port town as it lies away from the tourist zone which is located in a bay a few kilometres north. There are just a handful of hotels with on-site dive centres. Quieter than Hurghada, the reefs here are generally in good condition but surface conditions can be a little rougher. Safaga is a highly favoured destination for windsurfers and has hosted world championship competitions.

6 Little Giftun

- **Depth**: 28 m
- **Visibility**: fair to good
- **Currents**: slight to medium
- **Dive type**: day boat/liveaboard
- **Snorkelling**: yes

A short sail offshore from Hurghada are Big and Little Giftun islands. These are popular sites for novices and trainees so the corals are not at their best, especially in the shallower areas. However, the wall on Little Giftun is an exception. Entering the water opposite the lighthouse, you drop in to find a current that will carry you on a drift through a forest of pink and yellow fans. Longnose hawkfish hide in these and scrawled filefish try to do the same. There are a lot of schooling fish and giant morays that free swim along the wall.

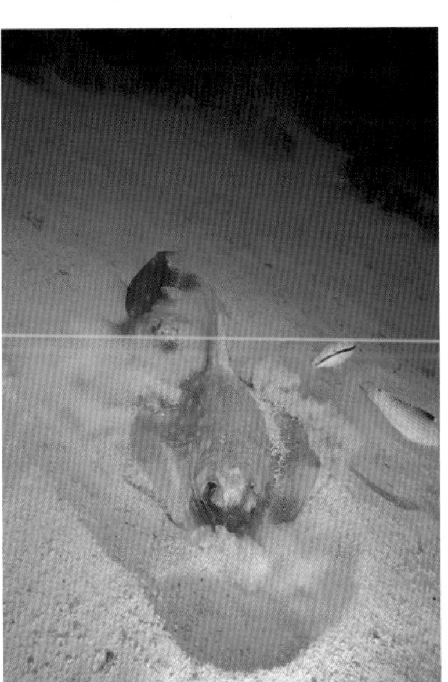

A blue spotted ray hunting in the sand

Masked butterflyfish

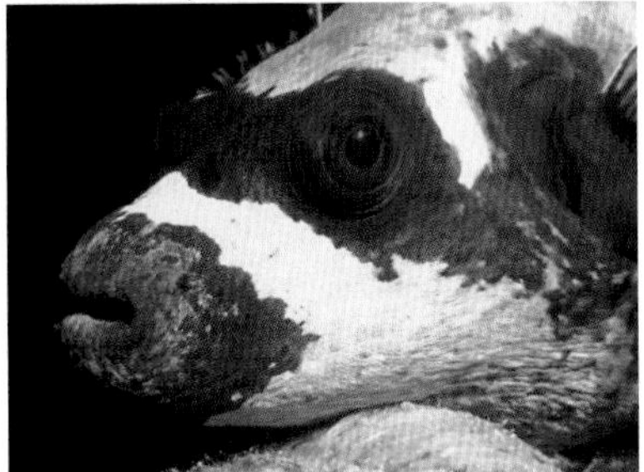

Masked pufferfish

Sardine ball

Temperatures rising

The Deep South

Beyond Safaga, there are several destinations that are expanding rapidly due to the new international airport at Marsa Alam. Once only reached by boat, Daedelus and Zabargad reefs can now be accessed from the hotels and dive centres at El Quesir and Marsa Alam. Day boat diving from either town is reliable and a growing access point for St John's Reef, Zabargad and Rocky Island. Operators also hope that they will be able to sail from here to enter Sudanese waters. This would bypass the obstacles involved in travelling direct to the Sudan. By all accounts diving there is exceptional but due to the unsettled political situation, bureaucratic regulations change almost daily and liveaboards are frequently cancelled.

7 Panorama

- **Depth**: 33 m
- **Visibility**: good
- **Currents**: none to mild
- **Dive type**: day boat/liveaboard
- **Snorkelling**: yes

Regarded as one of the south's most impressive reefs, this long coral mound can be dived from several points. On all sides, gentle slopes lead to about 25 metres, then drop suddenly to unreachable depths. There are plenty of overhangs along the walls. The northwest corner is lacking in soft coral growth but turtles and morays hide amongst the craggy rocks formed by hard corals. On the opposite corner, it's a little more colourful; whitetips are regular visitors and there are a surprising number of bottom dwellers like crocodilefish and blue spotted rays. Masked puffers huddle down inside sponges and stonefish blend perfectly into the background.

8 Tobia Arba

- **Depth**: 19 m
- **Visibility**: good
- **Currents**: mild
- **Dive type**: day boat/liveaboard
- **Snorkelling**: yes

Although this is named Seven Pillars there only seem to be five – well at least that's all you have time to find in an average dive. The pillars rise from a flat, sandy seabed and are marked by their interesting formations. Small caves are full of glassy sweepers, overhangs protect butterflyfish couples and corals and anthias cover curved walls. You can swim through small tunnels and find moorish idols nosing around. On the sand are seagreass ghost pipefish and, at night, Spanish Dancers.

9 The *Salem Express*

- **Depth**: 22 m
- **Visibility**: good
- **Currents**: mild to medium
- **Dive type**: day boat/liveaboard
- **Snorkelling**: yes

A recent and controversial addition to the dive list is the wreck of the *Salem Express*. In 1991, this passenger ferry was heavily overloaded with pilgrims returning from Mecca. She was only a few hours short of Safaga when she hit the reef at Sha'b Shear and sank with a huge loss of life. Many operators feel that she should be left in peace and will not dive here. However, others will and you will be briefed on treating the wreck with the respect it deserves. Suffice to say that trophy hunting would be exceptionally bad form. The *Salem* is majestic in her demise, lying on her side at just 32 metres. There are many signs of the people who were on board at the time, such as suitcases and liferafts rotting quietly on the sea floor. She appears peaceful and is succumbing to the elements which are taking her back in the usual cycle of life. Small corals are forming on the hull, pipefish and octopus hide in crevices and puffers hover like silent sentinels.

A turtle on Panorama Reef

The *Salem Express*

The Brothers

El-Akhawein, better known as the Brothers Islands, have staked their place in diver folklore as the surrounding marine park was closed for many years. The islands consist of two harsh rocks that rise steeply from the sea bed. Big and Little Brother are a six hour sail from Hurghada and the crossing can be rough but once you are there you will find a flawless reef system, reminiscent of the Red Sea of past decades. Corals here are still pristine – get your buoyancy right – and as the only reefs for miles, they attract a large number of fish and pelagics. It is said that you can see amazing shark numbers here, including oceanic whitetips, hammerheads and threshers. These only appear when the currents are running so night diving is banned. Less experienced divers may find the going tough. Moorings are limited and tucked away on the calmer sides of these tiny islands. The authorities are supposed to restrict the number of permits given to liveaboards but appear to over-supply them. Don't be surprised if your promised four days at the Brothers ends up being less than two because your captain can't find a vacant spot.

Coral wall on Little Brother

Tales from the deep

Sardines and tins

So I get this phone call from my buddy who says, "How would you like to dive the Red Sea?" My only question was, "Are we going to dive the Brothers?" "Four days" was a reply that I wanted to hear. The Brothers is reported to be one of those magical places in the dive world – best-on-the-planet gorgonians, two wrecks, every kind of shark, schools of fish in every camera shot. "I'm in. When do we go?"

We had a day to do our checkout dives, cross the sea and let the anticipation build. We dove Little Brother first and the scenery was wonderful. Picture-perfect giant sea fans, the expected schools of fish everywhere and an assortment of critters that sat and watched as the current took me around the island. Finally, I took my nose out of the reef and noticed a shark so odd I had to swim after it. There was nothing wrong with that shark – it was a hammerhead, duh! My first hammerhead sighting.

And there the dream ended. Sadly, the most abundant species on The Brothers during my visit were the liveaboards. The only unexposed mooring spot is on Big Brother, where the boats were packed like sardines in a tin. Inside boats dive Big Brother, outside boats cross over to Little Brother, as we did. We could not return, however, because of the new boats that arrived and took our place. The tin ran out of room for more sardines and we were forced to return to the mainland, losing half of our scheduled time. Our captain substituted some new dive sites but they were not the Brothers; not what I really came for.

Bruce Brownstein, Los Angeles, USA

10 Little Brother

- **Depth**: 38 m
- **Visibility**: gin clear
- **Currents**: mild to strong
- **Dive type**: liveaboard
- **Snorkelling**: no

Opinions on currents are relative to what you have done but a truly strong current will threaten to rip the mask from your face. Fortunately, at Little Brother the pace can be fairly easy going, depending where you start the dive. Entering at the northern point of the island a tongue leads seawards. This section is a faster, drift dive where thresher sharks, greys or hammerheads pass by. What you see will depend on the season. Amazing soft corals carpet the south, across a steep wall that looks like a manic Gaugin painting. At its base, there is a forest of huge fans. Small caves and overhangs are thick with surgeonfish, butterflies, moorish idols and anthias flitting and flashing across the reef wall.

11 Big Brother

- **Depth**: 36 m
- **Visibility**: gin clear
- **Currents**: mild to strong
- **Dive type**: liveaboard
- **Snorkelling**: no

This northern island is marked by a stone lighthouse, manned by the military, that dominates the otherwise pancake-flat vista. There are two diveable wrecks, a large freighter named the *Namibia* and a supply boat, the *Aida II*. Both are splendid, if very short dives. The *Aida* lies on an extremely steep slope with her bow resting at 25 metres or so. Her propeller isn't reachable in normal sport diving limitations so all you will manage is a quick peep unless you go into deco, which is frowned upon due to the remoteness of the islands. Along the southern side of the island the reef catches strong currents so there is plenty of fabulous coral and a huge variety of marine life.

Drying out

While Egypt is a fascinating country, the Red Sea coast has less than its fair share of ancient sights or cultural attractions. Drying out time is focussed on other sports or daytime relaxation and night time partying.

Sinai Peninsula

Dive centres

If you have pre-booked a package, you probably won't get a choice of dive centre. There are many run by many nationalities. Few are less than professional.

Red Sea College, Sultana Building, Na'ama Bay, T+20 (0)69 3600145, www.redseacollege.com. One of the original operators. Well run programmes, plus, for experienced divers, the new Diamond Service which buys an upgraded service, with a little seclusion and luxury.

Sinai Divers, Hotel Ghazala, Na'ama Bay, T+20 (0)69 3600697, www.sinaidivers.com. Also in Dahab and Hurghada with a wide variety of courses.

Emperor Divers, Rosetta Hotel, Na'ama Bay, T+20 (0)122340995, www.emperordivers.com. Full service dive centre with branches in Hurghada, Nuweiba and Marsa Alam.

Sleeping

There are a huge number of hotels but the majority are in Na'ama Bay and tend to be large complexes. It's worth choosing a higher level of hotel as 3-star in Egypt is less impressive than elsewhere.

$$$-$$ **Hilton Hotels**, www.hilton.com. There are Hiltons in Sharm El Maya, Na'ama Bay and Shark Bay. All are modern hotels with good facilities in convenient locations.

$$$ **Jolie Ville Moevenpick Resort**, Naama Bay, T+20 (0)69 3600100, www.moevenpick-hotels.com. Similar to the Hiltons and close to all the nightlife.

$ **Camel Dive Club and Hotel**, Na'ama Bay, T+20 (0)69 3600700, www.cameldive.com. Small, diver-orientated hotel with onsite restaurants. The *Camel Bar*, on top, is good for relaxed sunset views and light meals. This is a popular divers' haunt.

Eating

$$ **Dananeer** Opposite the *Movenpick Hotel*. International style with steaks and seafood.

$ **Sinai Star** A proper Egyptian restaurant. No menus, just fabulous catch-of-the-day seafood served with rice, salad and dips. Located in Old Sharm in the market, don't be put off by the lack of fancy decoration.

Sights

Ras Mohammed National Park Contrary to popular belief, at least in diver brains, Ras isn't just about diving. Landside there are some fantastic, 'other world' landscapes to admire plus rare mammals, thousands of birds and some unusual flora species. About US$50 for a guided day trip.

Undercurrents

Liveaboards

One of the big issues with the Red Sea is the number of dive centres and liveaboard operators flooding the market. Mix this with divers wanting ever cheaper holidays and operators undercutting each other and you will get a drop in standards. Nowhere is this more evident than in the number of complaints about Egyptian liveaboards: the air-conditioning doesn't work, the food is poor or not enough of it, the dives were limited, safety standards were low. These are heard along with high-profile tales of boats hitting reefs at night or leaving divers behind. (Heaven help us all). There is just one thing to say about this, you get what you pay for. Go cheap, ask for a deal, but don't expect a full service boat if you do. *"As authors, we are sad to say that we have never been on a liveaboard in the Red Sea that we would recommend to our friends. There are good ones out there but you'll have to ask around for recommendations."*

Fishing boat transformed for diving

St Catherine's Monastery Dating back to AD 300, this religious site is worth a visit for its varied history. Now owned by the Greek Orthodox Church, there is a collection of illuminated manuscripts, works of art and of course, the site of Moses' Burning Bush. About US$50 for a guided day trip.

Mount Sinai This is where Moses is said to have received the Ten Commandments. To reach the top it's either 4000 steps or a 3-hr walk along a winding path, but many make the pilgrimage. About US$50 for a guided day trip.

Surface interval

24 hours in Cairo

Egypt's capital is a shock to the system. Hot, dirty, completely manic, it's a non-stop pulsating, gyrating, merry-go-round of people. There are close on 16 million in the capital and mostly you will feel that they are right in your face. But to go to Egypt and not see the pyramids? A day in the city will give you a chance to sample her incredible history. Head out to the pyramids, admire the Sphinx, then, unless you are horribly claustrophobic, stretch your calf muscles by walking down the 45 degree ladders inside the great pyramid of Cheops at Giza. Afterwards head back into the centre and visit the Egyptian Museum. Gaze on the face of god-king Tutankhamen, before heading to one of the city's many bazaars for a little retail therapy. At sunset take a Nile dinner cruise, terribly touristy but at least you can say you've done it. Day Tours run from US$30-100 depending on content and distance covered.

$$ **Intercontinental Citystars,** Omar Ibn El Khattab St, Cairo, T+20 (0)2 4800100, www.ichotelsgroup.com. Classy city centre hotel, only a few minutes from the airport.

$$ **Sophitel Le Sphinx,** 1 Alexandria Rd, Giza, T+20 (0)2 3837444, www.sofitel.com. Lovely, modern hotel right beside the pyramids.

The south coast

Dive centres

In Hurghada, as in Sharm, you may not get a choice of dive centre but as this area is rather sprawling you are best going with the dive centre in your hotel or the one next door.

Diver Lodge, Hurghada, T+20 (0)65 465100, www.divers-lodge.com. Located between the *Intercontinental* and *Hilton Hurghada Resort*. Used by divers in both hotels, well run outfit with friendly divemasters and crews.

Euro Divers, Hurghada, T+20 (0)65 447485, www.euro-divers.com. In the *Grand Hotel Hurghada*, Swiss owned, well run dive centre, also in El Gouna.

Dive Tribe, El Gouna, T+20 (0)65 3580120, www.divetribe.com. On site at the *El Gouna Mövenpick Resort*. Multilingual dive centre accepts divers from any El Gouna hotel.

Sleeping

Hilton Hurghada Resort, Safaga Rd, Hurghada, T+20 (0)65 3465036, www.hilton.com. Big complex that feels small, with a nice beach out the front.

Hotel Shams Safaga and Diving Centre, Safaga Rd, Safaga, T+20 (0)65 251781, www.shams-dive.com. Peaceful resort set back from the beach. Onsite restaurant, dive centre and a decent house reef.

$$ **Sultan Bey**, Kafr El Gouna, El Gouna, T+20 (0)65 3545600, www.optima-hotels.com. Bedouin-style hotel in nice gardens. Rooms have balconies.

Cairo women cooking bread

Eating

$ **Felfela**, Sheraton Rd, Hurghada, T+20 (0)65 442410. This Egyptian restaurant is justifiably famous. Amazingly good food served on terraces that catch a cool breeze from the Red Sea. No booze though.

Sights

There isn't a huge amount to do heading out from either Hurghada, Safaga or El Gouna but you could arrange to visit a couple of ruined, ancient Roman sites. There's **Mons Porphyrites**, where the Romans mined a stone called Imperial Porphyry (a purple and white crystalline rock) and left behind temples, shrines and fortresses. **Mons Claudianus** was a Roman settlement in the 1st and 2nd centuries AD and the base for mining a grey granite that was sent to Rome. The ruins include a Pantheon, Hadrian's Villa and an unfinished temple. Day trips are around US$50.

Tomb pictures inside a pyramid

East Africa

Speed demon: with the fastest marine attack mechanism, the mantis shrimp, *Odontodactylus scyllarus*

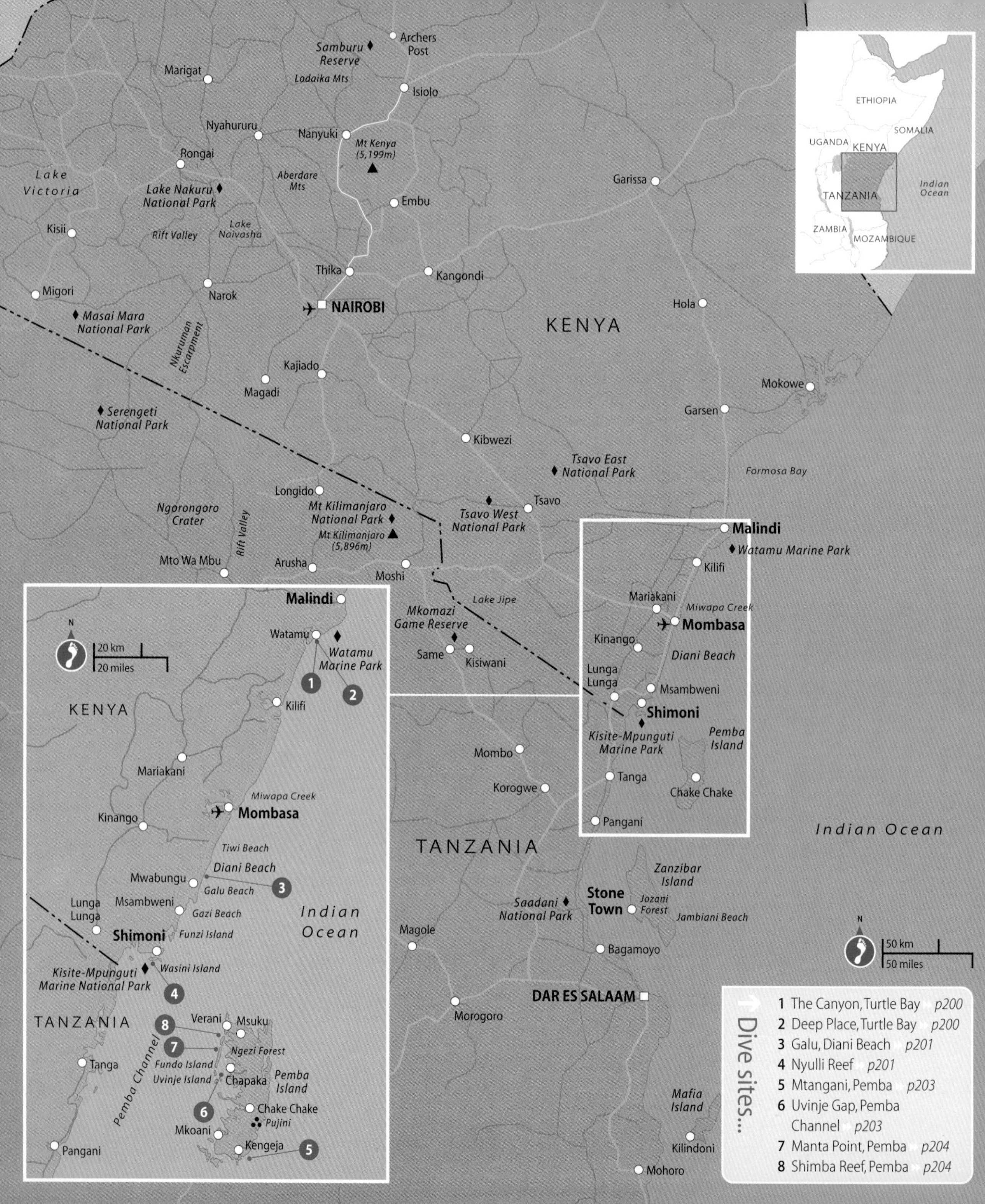

Dive sites...
1 The Canyon, Turtle Bay p200
2 Deep Place, Turtle Bay p200
3 Galu, Diani Beach p201
4 Nyulli Reef p201
5 Mtangani, Pemba p203
6 Uvinje Gap, Pemba Channel p203
7 Manta Point, Pemba p204
8 Shimba Reef, Pemba p204
KENYA
TANZANIA
Indian Ocean
NAIROBI
DAR ES SALAAM
Malindi
Mombasa
Shimoni
Stone Town
Watamu
Watamu Marine Park
Kilifi
Mariakani
Miwapa Creek
Kinango
Tiwi Beach
Diani Beach
Galu Beach
Mwabungu
Lunga Lunga
Msambweni
Gazi Beach
Funzi Island
Wasini Island
Kisite-Mpunguti Marine National Park
Verani
Msuku
Ngezi Forest
Fundo Island
Uvinje Island
Chapaka
Pemba Island
Pemba Channel
Tanga
Chake Chake
Pujini
Mkoani
Kengeja
Pangani
20 km
20 miles
Samburu Reserve
Archers Post
Marigat
Lodaika Mts
Isiolo
Nyahururu
Nanyuki
Mt Kenya (5,199m)
Rongai
Lake Victoria
Lake Nakuru National Park
Aberdare Mts
Embu
Garissa
Kisii
Rift Valley
Lake Naivasha
Thika
Kangondi
Migori
Narok
Hola
Masai Mara National Park
Nkuruman Escarpment
Kajiado
Magadi
Mokowe
Garsen
Serengeti National Park
Kibwezi
Tsavo East National Park
Formosa Bay
Longido
Ngorongoro Crater
Mt Kilimanjaro National Park
Mt Kilimanjaro (5,896m)
Tsavo
Tsavo West National Park
Mto Wa Mbu
Arusha
Moshi
Lake Jipe
Mkomazi Game Reserve
Same
Kisiwani
Kisite-Mpunguti Marine Park
Mombo
Korogwe
Zanzibar Island
Jozani Forest
Jambiani Beach
Saadani National Park
Magole
Bagamoyo
Morogoro
Mafia Island
Kilindoni
Mohoro
50 km
50 miles
ETHIOPIA
SOMALIA
UGANDA
ZAMBIA
MOZAMBIQUE
Indian Ocean

Introduction

Wide open plains baking in the African sun, ancient tribes facing up to the reality and challenges of modern life, herds of exotic animals roaming wild and free.

At least once in your life you have to come face to face with the big five. It's a heart-stopping, spine-tingling moment when a male lion walks straight up to you – inches from your open Land Rover – and looks deep into your eyes. If you're a diver, however, it might seem awfully hard to give up peaceful days spent floating in warm waters for a close encounter with nature on dry land. But you don't have to. East Africa is one of the most alluring diving destinations simply because you can do it all.

While inland the landscape is baked to exquisite shades of gold and terracotta, Kenya and Tanzania's coastal waters are cool indigo and deep turquoise. Islands are lush with coconuts and mangroves and, under perfect blue skies, tiny dhows float over little-known fringing reefs. These reefs meander gently along the shoreline, protecting the coasts and creating nursery grounds for a range of rainbow-hued reef fish. And although larger animals are mostly to be found on land, the marine life is still exciting enough to justify a visit.

“” The big surprise underwater is the critter life – we have seen things here we would once have only expected in Asian waters.

East Africa rating

Diving
★★

Dive facilities
★★

Accommodation
★★★★

Down time
★★★★

Value for money
★★★

Essentials

East Africa	Kenya	Tanzania

Location	00°00' N, 39°12' E
Neighbours	Somalia, Ethiopa, Sudan, Uganda, Rwanda, Burundi, Zambia, RD Congo, Malawi, Mozambique
Population*	70,595,946
Land area in km^2 *	1,455,287
Reef area in km^2*	4,210
Coastline km*	1,960

* combined figures

Getting there and around

If you live anywhere in Europe, getting to East Africa is a cinch. But if you're coming from any other continent you'll probably need to route through either a main European hub or the Middle East. Nairobi is the best place to head for as there are easy onward connections. **Emirates** (www.emirates.com), **British Airways** (www.ba.com) and **KLM** (www.klm.com) all fly to Nairobi.

From Nairobi there is a substantial network of small airlines that link safari parks, islands and the coast. **Kenya Airlines** (www.kenya-airways.com), **Precision Air** (www.precisionairtz.com) and **ZanAir** (www.zanair.com) connect anywhere that counts across the two countries.

Other options include **KLM's** route to Kilimanjaro – should you want to climb a mountain before submerging – or charter flights to Mombasa if you only want to stay on the coast. There are a huge number of European charters but this may not be the best way to get there as luggage allowances for divers are an issue. Finally, you can always take a **shuttle bus** (www.riverside-shuttle.com) from Nairobi to Kilimanjaro via Arusha for a mere US$35, but it is a five-hour bus ride.

All of this may seem complex, but you can make it easy by choosing your ideal safari (see page 207) or dive centre, then turning over the arrangements to a dive or safari company. They will advise on current schedules, make the relevant bookings and organise transfers from your arrival airport.

For days out rely on your dive centre or hotel for advice and assistance. Although some areas are tourist friendly, and local transport is available, in cities and bigger towns independent travel is not recommended.

Hippos wallowing in the Mara River

The sign for the equator on top of the Rift Valley

Language

With a couple of hundred tribal groups across the region, the local language that links most people – apart from English – is Swahili. It's a language that has influenced many others – safari, meaning journey, is now a universal term. Here are some basic words:

hello	*jambo*
goodbye	*kwaheri*
yes	*ndiyo*
no	*hapana*
thank you	*asante sana*
sorry!	*pole!*
how much is ...	*ngapi ...*
good	*mzuri*
great dive!	*adhimu mbizi!*
no problem	*hakuna matata*
one beer	*mojo bia*

Local laws and customs

The people of both Kenya and Tanzania are an almost equal mix of Christian, Muslim and tribal religions. Be sensitive to local practices. Common sense goes a long way – don't walk around half dressed in a Muslim coastal town, for instance – but generally the people in both countries are fun-loving and outgoing.

Safety

Neither of these countries is regarded as the safest place in the world to travel to. Government advisories recommend travellers are cautious, avoid political rallies and stay out of city centres at night. If you are out and about after dark, catch a cab, carry as little as possible and nothing of value. The people are poor and good at spotting an opportunity. Nairobi's nickname is 'Nai-robbery' but much of the crime is petty. Lone female travellers should be extra cautious if only because you will appear vulnerable.

Now that the bad news is over, here's the good news. Dive regions tend to be well away from hubs of political sensitivity and your dive centre will collect you (and all that expensive equipment) from wherever you are. Safari parks are well policed, hotels employ security guards and locals just love tourists, who they see as generous and friendly. So keep smiling.

If you want to go anywhere outside of what you have pre-arranged, ask your hotel reception or a divemaster. An escort will be found for just a few dollars and that will buy a lot of peace of mind.

Fact file

International flights	British Airways and KLM via Europe, Emirates via Dubai. European charters to Mombasa mostly require you to book a package holiday
Departure tax	US$20, if not included in your ticket
Entry	Visas are required for all (except Irish), US$50 for 90 days in each country
Internal flights	Precision Air, ZanAir, Kenya Airlines
Ground transport	Countrywide bus connections
Language	Swahili is the official language, but English is common
Money	Kenyan shillings Ksh78 = US$1 Tanzania shillings Tsh1150 = US$1
Electricity	220-240v
Time zone	GMT +3
Religion	Christians, Muslims, animists and tribal variations

Health

East Africa requires most of the standard jabs (see page 24) and malaria is also a risk but all these potential dangers are easy to protect against. HIV is a problem right across Africa and it is known that approaches are made along the Kenyan beach strip. Not only do you risk AIDS but, if caught, the local will be jailed. Be smart. Don't do it.

Costs

Value for money almost becomes irrelevant once you've spent your day sitting beside a new-born zebra or snorkelling some of the bluest waters you have ever seen. It's unlikely that you will have to pay for much outside your package and it's simply not all that practical to go to East Africa as a diver for less than two weeks unless you pre-book. Most hotels are complexes, with an on-site dive centre, and will include breakfast and dinner. If you venture outside for a special-occasion meal it won't be cheap in local terms, but it won't break the bank. Think in the vicinity of US$30-40 dollars a head. There are occasional snack bars on the Kenyan beaches and a lunch there may be as cheap as US$5. Local drinks are priced according to the standard of your hotel so are much cheaper outside the hotel complex. Tipping is the norm, 5-10% for meals and cabs; for a drivers, guides and divemasters, see page 14.

Airlines → British Airways T+254 (0)20 334362, KLM T+254 (0)20 332674, Kenya Airways T+254 (0)20 210771, Emirates T+254 (0)20 215994. **Embassies** → in Nairobi: UK T+254 (0)20 2844000, USA T+254 (0)20 3636000, Australia, T+254 (0)20 4445034, New Zealand T+254 (0)20 2720295. **Embassies** → in Dar es Salaam: UK T+255 (0)22 211010, USA T+255 (0)22 2666010, New Zealand T+255 (0)22 2668001. **Kenya country code** → +254. **Tanzania country code** → +255. **IDD** → 000. **Police** → 999.

Schooling bluelined snapper

Zanzibar - Pemba - Tanzania

Dive brief

Diving

While big animals are a given in East Africa, the marine realm is less well known. The two most diver-friendly countries are Kenya and Tanzania. This stretch of African coast is protected by a long barrier reef that is completely exposed at low tide. This gives protection to the shoreline but takes a pounding from the constant wave action and the effects of the sun when the tide is out.

Every day at low tide, the reef top is exposed and the lagoons behind become so shallow that snorkelling or even swimming is often out of the question. Diving is restricted to the times of day when there is enough water for the boats to navigate over the reef. This is usually the morning. Visibility can be reduced by the constant movement of water over the shallow, sandy seabed. The water is consistently warm and the El Niño phenomena took its toll a few years back (see page 204), but fortunately only on the shallower sections.

However, once you are out over the reef edge, or off one of the nearby islands, and get below 10 metres or so, the marine realm comes alive. There are some small pretty coral gardens and the gentle coastal reefs are havens for smaller fish and critters. Napoleon wrasse, moray eels, ghost pipefish, snappers and butterflyfish are all in evidence; turtles are frequently seen and the migratory patterns of mantas and whalesharks traverse this stretch of coast. They are occasionally spotted by divers, but less often than the operators would care to have you think. If you get out in the blue, there are plenty of pelagic fish.

Bottom time

- **Watamu Marine Park** Kenya's most protected coastal marine park » *p200*
- **Diani Beach** A gently shelving reef system that parallels the coast » *p201*
- **Kisite-Mpunguti Marine Park** Uninhabited islands sitting on the Tanzanian border » *p201*
- **Pemba Island** Exciting deep-water diving in the Indian Ocean » *p203*
- **Pemba Channel** Calmer waters around a multitude of tiny islands and bays » *p203*

Snorkelling

Conditions for snorkellers are probably better than the above comments would lead you to believe. Floating over a shallow reef at low tide is less of an issue with no tank on your back. Most hotels run snorkelling trips to just outside the reef, but watch the time – at extreme low tide you may have to walk back over a fragile exposed reef, which won't do it any good at all.

Diversity

reef area 4,120 km^2

Coral species	Fish species	Fish species under threat	Protected reefs/marine parks
277	322	18	17

Kenya and Tanzania figures combined

Juvenile regal angelfish off Pemba

When we first started travelling, a safari was right at the top of our hit list and we were not disappointed. The Masai Mara, Ngorongoro Crater, the Serengeti... these places are burnt into our memories, and every now and then remind us that there is more to life than diving. While the warm waters and iridescent colours of the African marine realm are delightful, the quality and variety of diving isn't quite enough. But put it together with a safari and this is a trip that can't be rivalled.

The big decision

Choosing a dive destination in East Africa will be dictated by where else you want to go, if anywhere. If you just want a relaxing break with a few morning dives and a few afternoons out, the Kenya coast is for you. There are masses of hotels and most have dive centres. The diving will be pleasant and you will have access to day trips into the coastal game parks. If you want to get off the beaten track and sample an Africa of a bygone era, Tanzania's islands are the place to head for. Their waters also have more prolific marine life and the open ocean on the outside of Pemba can supply some exciting adrenaline rush dives. Tanzania's safari regions are also bigger and wilder.

Firedart goby emerging from his hole

Dive data

Seasons	All year, although March to May is rainy and visibility can be disappointing
Visibility	10-40 metres
Temperatures	Air 25°-34° C Water 25°-29° C
Wet suit	3 mm shorty or full body suit
Training	Courses available in most hotels, standards vary; look for PADI/SSI schools
Nitrox	Not easily available
Deco chambers	Mombasa

Temperatures rising

Just a hop, skip and a jump southwards from Tanzania is less well-known Mozambique. Sitting inside the tropical belt, this former Portuguese province is slowly hitting the dive radar. Due to a lack of infrastructure and facilities, it has been slow to stake a claim as an international dive destination, but the reef system holds promise. South African operators are now opening up the region to adventurous divers. Check it out at www.divethebig5.co.za. Likewise Madagascar, sitting opposite, is opening up its shores. This is the fourth largest island in the world and recent surveys indicate there are some previously unknown species of coral and fish. www.bluedive-madagascar.com.

Spinner dolphins in the bow wave

Dive log

Kenya

The coast that stretches north and south from Mombasa is paralleled by low-lying coral reefs. Its basic structure is of hard corals which form small drop offs and gentle sloping banks. The corals tend to be slower-growing, hardier varieties that can survive pounding Indian Ocean swells. There are plenty of colourful fish and if you are really lucky you may get the chance to see a whaleshark or manta ray as it meanders up the coast.

This whole stretch of coastline is subject to a substantial tidal range that exposes the reef – making diving possible for only part of the day. This means that currents can be strong, although rarely unbearable, at certain times and visibility is never crystal clear. Below the waves, the reef scenery is consistent, so choosing a specific location will probably be easiest if you exclude a couple of less-appropriate ones. The beach resorts directly around Mombasa town suffer from its industrialised nature so can easily be ruled out. Likewise Malindi, the other main centre on the coast, is affected by the run-off from the Sabiki River. Despite being designated a national marine park, diving around Malindi is limited to between May and December.

For those who want the best available diving, three small regions promise better all-round conditions. **Watamu Marine Park** is about 90 minutes north of Mombasa, and is the location of the very pretty **Turtle Bay**. The area holds marine park status and, although it is heavily tidal, the formation of the bay means that it is possible to swim and dive for longer periods of the day. This is some of the best diving in the country.

Heading south from Mombasa, the section of white-sand coast known as **Diani Beach** is very highly developed with hotels and dive centres marching towards the Tanzanian border. The good news is that they are well spaced out with decent landscaping, so you are unlikely to notice the extent of the development.

Traditional dhow sailing past Pemba

Just a few kilometres from the Tanzanian border is the **Kisite-Mpunguti Marine National Park**. The only access to this area, apart from the day trips Diani hotels offer, is via the town of Shimoni where there is a lone dive-orientated hotel. The park borders onto the deeper waters of the Pemba Channel so the diving is a little more adventurous and slightly less limited by tidal changes.

1 The Canyon, Turtle Bay

- **Depth**: 20 m
- **Visibility**: fair
- **Currents**: can be strong
- **Dive type**: day boat
- **Snorkelling**: for strong swimmers

This classic Kenyan dive is just a short boat ride to outside the main reef then a descent to the reef top at about 10 metres. The reef structure is hard coral with some small soft corals for colour. Over the edge is an archway where you can sometimes find resting turtles. If the current is running, and it often is, whitetips will spin past in the blue. The divemasters say this is one of the best places to spot passing whalesharks, but you are more likely to spot lobsters, lionfish, butterflies and nudibranchs.

2 Deep Place, Turtle Bay

- **Depth**: 25 m
- **Visibility**: fair
- **Currents**: can be strong
- **Dive type**: day boat
- **Snorkelling**: possibly

Just along the outer reef from The Canyon, this is a rather nice wall that can sometimes be a drift dive. It's not all that deep and you can investigate the sandy bottom where some interesting smaller creatures like lionfish hang out. Moray eels poke their noses out of the wall at passing divers and plenty of colourful fish hang around, such as anthias, butterflies, angels and so on. There are often sightings of turtles and large Napoleon wrasse around here.

3 Galu, Diani Beach

- **Depth**: 20 m
- **Visibility**: fair to good
- **Currents**: none to strong
- **Dive type**: day boat
- **Snorkelling**: yes

At the right time of day – morning – this can be a very pretty dive and is often used for training up new divers. There are plenty of fish to see with butterflies and wrasse all over the reef. Lobsters, octopus and small rays hang around in the cracks and crevices of the hard corals and turtles are frequent visitors. Later in the day the current can lift, which makes the dive a bit of a challenge for the inexperienced.

4 Nyulli Reef

- **Depth**: 20 m
- **Visibility**: good
- **Currents**: mild to strong
- **Dive type**: day boat
- **Snorkelling**: yes

Head out from Shimoni to the reefs that encircle the small islands of the Kisite-Mpunguti Marine Park to find a reasonable variety of dive sites. Some have suffered damage in the past, both from natural and man-made causes, but a few reefs are very impressive and the deeper waters attract bigger schools of fish. Nyulli Reef starts at about 20 metres then drops sharply to over 40. Shoals of pelagics like barracuda have been seen and reef sharks are common visitors although you are unlikely to get close.

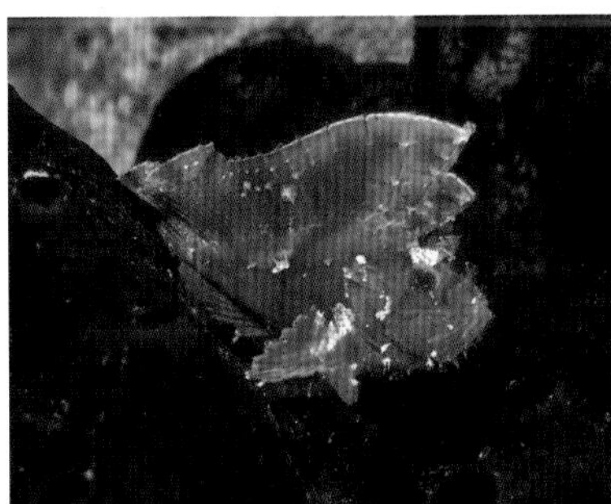

Distinctly in the pink, a leaf scorpionfish

Tales from the deep

What could be better?

It was 8 o'clock, the sky was nice and blue, the sea calm and it was already getting hot. I was about to dive Verena, a site just a few minutes' boat ride from Turtle Bay Beach Club.

As we descended towards the bottom of a shallow canyon a large Napoleon wrasse watched our approach. We explored nooks and crannies until our dive leader pointed out a honeycomb moray – it was about as long as I'm tall and as thick as my thigh, with those distinctive honeycomb markings. We swam over the sandy bottom and disturbed a stingray about five feet across. A whitetip reef shark swam lazily towards a small coral outcrop just where the canyon narrows. As we approached the outcrop, a manta ray, as large as my living room (3.5 metres), appeared from behind us. We dropped to the bottom so we didn't scare it off and it looped up towards the surface and back down, its left wing passing right over my head. So majestic, so serene and with a deceptive turn of speed for something so graceful. It swam off, turning back the way it came and was gone.

We finished the dive and climbed back on the boat, thinking to ourselves "what could be better?" when our dive leader shouted "whaleshark". We grabbed masks and fins and jumped back in. It was passing right by us and we saw its profile with those distinctive white spots and the ridges along its side. We all tried to follow but the whaleshark just carried on its way probably not even noticing the four irrelevant objects, trying unsuccessfully to keep up.

Two years later, I returned with my girlfriend. We went on a safari that covered most of Kenya. We saw loads of wildlife including all the big five and have stories to tell about those adventures! Then we went to Watamu for a week. However, this time no mantas, no sharks - all the big animals had been and gone. It was disappointing but life can be like that. The only creature worth mentioning this time was a honeycomb moray. I wonder if it was the same one?

Roy Calverley, Redhill, UK

Napoleon wrasse on the reef

Tanzania

Unlike Kenya, Tanzania's diving is based around the small islands which lie off her coastline rather than off the coast itself. Pemba and Zanzibar are the best known. Both have good facilities but, while Pemba is more dive focussed, Zanzibar is more of an all-round holiday destination.

Pemba is so close to the Kenyan coast that it's actually easiest to get to there from Shimoni, a 30-minute boat ride away. There are two distinct styles of diving: the east side is exposed to the open ocean so the diving is mostly big blue. Rough seas and strong currents can sometimes bring in schools of sharks. Hammerhead sightings are said to be common, but they are generally deeper than sport-diving limits will allow. To the south of the island, the channel that separates Pemba from Zanzibar is similar and best accessed by liveaboard.

For more classic reef diving the western side hosts shallow walls, sloping reefs and a surprising amount of unusual critters such as ghost pipefish. The geography is similar to Kenya and liable to the vagaries of time and tide. The reefs are a little way offshore and the inner lagoons extremely shallow. Currents are an every-dive occurrence, although they are nowhere near as strong as on the eastern side. And as there are so many small islands it's always easy to find a sheltered location.

Zanzibar is just south of Pemba and 40 km from the mainland. It has a unique mix of history, culture and natural beauty. Although the diving here is not so different from Pemba, it tends to be less exciting. This is due to an even shallower reef system and water that is rarely gin clear. Diving on the western coast is, again, subject to tidal changes. There's a good variety of reef fish, plus turtles, barracuda, blue spotted rays and so on, and the gentle, shallow reefs are popular with less experienced divers.

Ornate ghost pipefish in a crinoid

Porcelain crab on a sea pen

5 Mtangani, Pemba

- **Depth**: 35 m
- **Visibility**: excellent
- **Currents**: ripping at times
- **Dive type**: liveaboard
- **Snorkelling**: no

When they say that the currents that run off Pemba's east coast can be strong, it's no exaggeration. This water races, and less experienced divers may find the challenge hardly worthwhile, unless of course, a school of hammerheads comes past. The issue here is that when they do, they are often deeper than you can sensibly go to look at them. The dive will be spent pretending to fly through unbelievably clear blue water watching them, or some whitetips, below you. It's still quite an adrenaline rush.

6 Uvinje Gap, Pemba Channel

- **Depth**: 30 m
- **Visibility**: good
- **Currents**: slight to medium
- **Dive type**: liveaboard/day boat
- **Snorkelling**: yes

There is a series of dives in the Gap that include a small wall and a section of sandy bottom. In daylight hours you can explore the small caverns that dot the wall and harbour glassfish and crocodilefish. At night though, the sandy bottom turns to pure excitement with the critter life reminiscent of far distant countries. Octopus, cowries and mantis shrimp appear from nowhere, rare seagrass ghost pipefish are easy to spot and morays are out feeding.

Swimming crab on a sea cucumber

Tales from the deep

From snow-covered Kilimanjaro to the deep blue

I'd just climbed Kilimanjaro and like most people in my group had suffered with the altitude. So the thought of heading to Zanzibar and getting well below sea level was pretty appealing.

The place we stayed at was on the east coast, on Jambiani Beach, a gorgeous stretch of sand lapped by Bombay Sapphire-blue water. Our hotel, the Sau Inn, was conveniently attached to a PADI dive centre and also had a pool, great for first-time divers to practise in.

The first dive was Stingray Alley and with my (extremely attentive!) instructor close by I descended through fairly clear water to 19 metres. Almost immediately I was rewarded with the sight of a blue-spotted stingray gliding along the ocean floor. There were plenty of colourful fish including trigger, clown, parrot, butterfly and unicorn fish flitting about amongst the brain and fire coral, along with an unidentified sea snake.

The next site, Lagoon Mounding, was just 15 metres deep, and featured more or less the same fish, at least to my untrained eye! Overall the diving was good, if unspectacular, although as a relatively inexperienced diver it's hard to know how it compares to other places. The best bit? The almost psychedelic colour of the water and the amazingly friendly people.

Sue Starkie, Portsmouth, UK

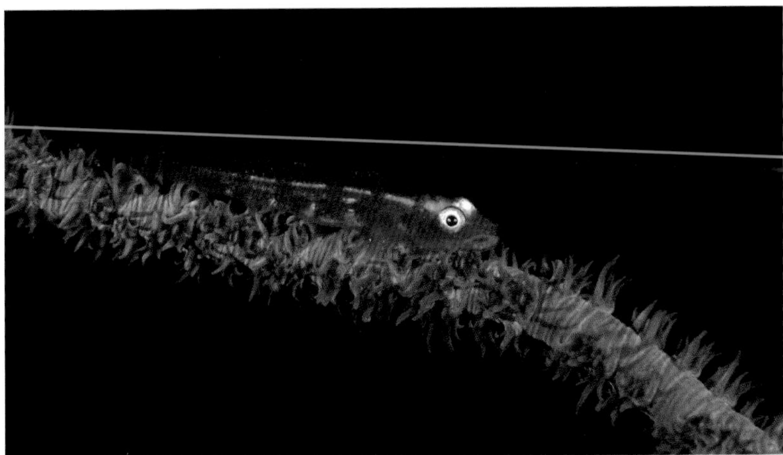

Wire coral goby, just 30 mm long

7 Manta Point, Pemba

- **Depth**: 22 m
- **Visibility**: fair
- **Currents**: slight to medium
- **Dive type**: day boat
- **Snorkelling**: yes

As soon as someone sees a manta on a dive site, it gets named in honour of the event. So what are the chances of seeing a manta at Manta Point? Well, opinion varies but that doesn't spoil the dive. As this site is tucked in amongst the protective islands off the west coast, currents are less aggressive and the pace is easy. Visibility isn't that impressive but there are plenty of animals. Schools of snapper hang about on the round reef that leads to a small pinnacle. Turtles often pass by, as do mantas, barracuda and jacks when the current is running. Otherwise, its angels, triggerfish and Napoleon wrasse.

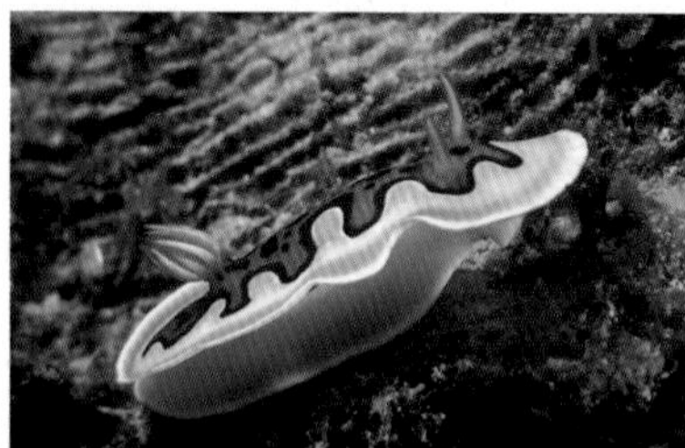

Chromodoris nudibranchs are common

8 Shimba Reef, Pemba

- **Depth**: 20 m
- **Visibility**: fair
- **Currents**: slight to medium
- **Dive type**: day boat
- **Snorkelling**: yes

Many of the shallower reefs in this region are affected by their position. The warm, shallow waters mean that hard corals struggle to survive especially as they are exposed at low tide. This reef shows a lot of damage because of this and constant wave action, yet somehow manages to be an interesting dive anyway. Taking the time to inspect the rubble-strewn crevices will reveal all sorts of interesting animals. These include several different coloured leaffish, all sorts of shrimp and even small lobster. Swimming about in the bigger caverns and overhangs are angelfish, snappers and coral grouper.

Delicate skin patterns on a geometric moray

Coral grouper dodging the camera

Conservation

El Niño

The big news in the late 1990s was the advent of El Niño. This climatic phenomenon occurs every four years or so off the western coast of South America when expected upwellings of cold, nutrient-rich water simply don't occur. It often becomes evident during the Christmas season (El Niño means Christ Child) when the surface waters of the eastern tropical Pacific Ocean warm to levels that are regarded as particularly abnormal. The almost instant effect is the severe depletion of plankton and fish.

In the bigger picture El Niño also affects Pacific jet stream winds, altering storm tracks and creating unusual weather patterns in various parts of the world. The changes are most intense in the Pacific, but in 1997-8 became the subject of worldwide attention when the impact went global.

Many shallow coral reef systems were badly damaged, even as far away as the East African coast. In regions like this, where the waters are naturally warm and shallow anyway, the repercussions were devastating. Hard corals bleached to pure white as there were insufficient nutrients to support their life cycle. The good news, however, is that corals, especially soft corals, do regenerate faster than you might think. Recent research has even noted that some hard corals are starting to re-establish themselves, with new colonies growing over old.

Drying out

It would be madness to travel to East Africa and not see her greatest resources – the vast wilderness of the Serengeti plains, the fascinating culture of the Masai tribes and the mass migrations of hundreds and thousands of wild animals. All are waiting to be discovered.

Kenya

Sleeping and diving

$$$ **Hemingways Resort**, PO Box 267, Watamu, T+254 (0)42 32624. Just along the bay and much quieter but more expensive. Rates reflect the higher standards. Dive with Turtle Bay (see below).

$$$ **Turtle Bay Beach Club**, PO Box 10, Watamu, T+254 (0)42 32622, www.turtlebay.co.ke. Lively resort hotel sitting right on the bay. All-inclusive rates (room, food, drinks, land activities). **Turtle Bay Divers** are at the Turtle Bay Beach Club.10 dive pack US$400.

$$$-$$ **Papillon Lagoon Reef**, PO Box 5292, Diani 80401, T+254 (0)40 3202627. Quite a way down the Diani strip, nice rooms with pretty gardens. All inclusive. **Baracuda Diving Team** are on site. www.baracudadiving.com. One dive is US$50, 10 dive pack US$400.

$$$-$$ **Southern Palms Beach Resort**, PO Box 363, Diani, T+254 (0)40 3203721, www.southernpalmskenya.com. Swahili-style rooms, closer to Mombasa. **Dive the Crab** are on site, www.divingthecrab.com. 10 dive pack US$450.

$$$ **Norfolk Hotel**, Harry Thuku Rd, Nairobi, T+254 (0)2 250900, www.lonrhohotels.com. With its original foundations steeped in colonial history, this resort-style hotel is pricey but means there is no need to face Nairobi's hustle unless you choose to.

$$ **Stanley Hotel**, Kimathi St & Kenyatta Av, Nairobi, T+254 (0)2 228830, www.sarovahotels.com. Also a part of local colonial legend and once the haunt of the likes of Ernest Hemingway.

Eating

$$$ **Ali Barbour's Cave** is located right on Diani Beach about 30 km south of

Elephants in the Masai Mara

MY Jambo sails Pemba

 Mombasa. This rather unique restaurant is inside a series of naturally formed coral caves and although you sit underground, the roof is open to the stars. The menu is a curious mix of African spicing and modern international style. A three course meal can cost upwards of US$40 per head.

$$ **Thorn Tree Café**, located in the **Stanley Hotel** (see above), and a Nairobi tradition. Pizza, pasta and coffee from US$20.

Curry houses in Nairobi are good and cheap but stay close to your hotel.

Sights

Malindi An hour or so north of Mombasa and quite near Watamu, this small town is the biggest tourist attraction on the north coast. It looks rather frayed but gives an insight into life on the coast. A tour costs around US$30.

Mombasa One of the oldest cities in East Africa, the original town dates back some 700 years. It is a curious combination of old and new, with plenty to see, do and buy, however it is a manic place, noisy and bustling. Tours costs US$30.

Wasini Island In the Kisite-Mpunguti Marine Park and only accessible by boat. Tours run via the town of Shimoni. The island is steeped in history and a day tour (US$95) includes a visit to the village, lunch at the incredible **Charlie's Claw** restaurant and snorkelling in the marine park. Contact www.wasini-island.com.

Lioness eyeing up the tourists

Tanzania

Sleeping and diving

$$$ **Fundu Lagoon and Dive 710**, on the southwestern side of Pemba and only accessible by boat, T+255 (0)24 2232926, fundu@africaonline.co.tz. This upmarket resort has tented rooms that are bungalows in disguise. Rates include three meals, drinks and some excursions at US$260 per person per day. US$60 per dive, six dive pack US$300.

$$$-$$ **Manta Reef Lodge and One Earth Diving**, T+254 (0)41 471771, www.mantareeflodge.com. A dive-orientated resort on the northwest tip of Pemba. Charming, rustic rooms with meals included. Two tank dive US$80, 10 dive pack US$350.

Liveaboards

Two liveaboards ply the channel between Pemba and Tanzania. **MY Kisiwani** is a modern steel-hulled vessel and costs around US$1500 per person per week. **MY Jambo** is a small wooden yacht, rates around US$1600 per person per week. Bookings through the agents listed below.

Sightseeing on Pemba

Chake Chake The largest town on Pemba is also the administrative capital. There are shops, banks, ruins of an 18th century fort, a small dhow port and a fish market along the water's edge.

Pujini About 10 km southeast of Chake Chake are the ruins of a 15th-century fortified palace. It was the seat of the infamous Mohammed bin Abdul Rahman whose name is synonymous with cruelty and hard labour. Archaeologists have found an underground shrine and there's some interesting architecture. A day tour including both of these will be around US$60 per couple.

Ngezi Forest On the northern tip of Pemba, this is the last remains of a huge tract of indigenous forest, home to the Pemba flying fox, a bat endemic to the island. The flora is impressive and the nature trail can be good for bird life. Walking tours cost around US$25.

Sightseeing on Zanzibar

Stone Town The old city and cultural heart is now a World Heritage site. Built in the 19th century, the town consists of winding alleys, bustling bazaars, mosques and grand Arab houses. You can spend a lot of time wandering and admiring bygone splendours.

Spice Tours The history of Zanzibar is spices. Cloves, nutmeg, cinnamon and pepper brought the Sultans of Oman and the beginnings of the infamous slave trade. Plantation tours are very educational and demonstrate the use of spices in cooking, cosmetics and for many ailments. Plus you can shop!

Jozani Forest In the east central region of Zanzibar, this is home to the rare red colobus monkey. These monkeys are indigenous, full of character, and roam freely beside Syke's monkeys, small bucks and bushpigs. The elusive Zanzibar leopard is said to feed here at night but has not been seen for several years. Return flight from Pemba US$110, day tours around US$75.

International agents

Africa Discovery, 77 Mark Dr, Suite 18, San Rafael, CA 94903, T+1 (1)415 444 5100, www.africa-discovery.com. Experienced dive and safari specialists that will tailor-make any itinerary.

Aquatours, 29A High Street, Thames Ditton, Surrey, KT7 0SD, T+44 (0)20 8398 0505, www.aquatours.com. Established agent with broad range of programmes.

Catfish Dive & Safari, 2 Homefield Road, London, SW19 4QE, T+44 (0)7870 588514, www.catfishdive.co.uk. New and enthusiastic agent for both diving and tours right across the region.

Masai giraffe

On safari in Tanzania

Surface interval

A week on safari

There are more safari operators across these two countries than you can shake a camera at. Every hotel, dive centre, travel agent or taxi driver will have their favourite. Mostly, they are very good and are regulated by the government.

... in Kenya

Start from the coast and finish in **Nairobi**, or start from Nairobi and finish on the coast. Whichever way you go, the possibilities are endless. The most remote parks and best animal populations are inland. Head north to **Samburu**, where landscapes are classic Africa: deep-red soil lush with acacia trees. Unusual animals here include the long-necked gerunuk, Grevy's zebra and the reticulated giraffe. A change of pace will take you to endless - and pink - **Lake Nakuru**. The population of flamingos is so enormous that from a distance the water looks rose tinted, especially at dusk when the sun sets across millions of pink feathers. Finally, in the **Masai Mara National Park** you can stop and visit ancient tribes who still adhere to their traditional way of life. No TVs out in the mud huts although old film canisters are regarded as one of the better earlobe stretching devices. Meanwhile, the baboons eat wild figs, which ferment in their tummies and they tend to fall out of the trees rather inebriated! Quite amusing when it's around your luxury tented campsite! **Tsavo East** is close enough to the coast to allow a day trip. You might see elephant herds and lions, but buffalo, giraffe and various deer species are more likely. This park also has some very interesting bird life. Day trips cost from US$140. One week budget safari from US$950, luxury from US$2100. Contact www.pollmans.com.

... in Tanzania

There are countless pre-organized options, but start by flying to **Arusha**, not far from Mount Kilimanjaro. Flying over her is quite a sight and if you fancy the climb, there are several different routes – some are regarded as quite gentle at five days up and one day to get back down. Expect to pay around US$1800 for the pleasure. Alternatively, enjoy some cool mounatin air at a lodge before setting off for the **Ngorongoro Crater**. This ancient gorge is just beautiful, and is occupied by elephants, giraffe, rhino, lions, cheetahs and zebra. It is a very intense experience as the animals are concentrated in a small space. At sunset you can sip icy beer on the rim of the crater while admiring the baboons and giraffe just feet away. Next explore the wide open Serengeti. Days are long, hot and grubby but the rewards are high. All the big cats live here and hippos wallow in ponds. The great wildebeest migration is beyond spectacular as is watching a pride of cheetahs making a kill. Evenings are spent around a campfire after cleaning up in a hot bush shower. Sleep under canvas listening to the sounds of nocturnal animals on the prowl. No need to panic, there are armed guards. Budget safaris US$1500 – to luxury US$3200. Contact **Ranger Safaris** at www.rangersafaris.com and **Africa Discovery** at www.africa-discovery.com.

When booking a safari check the following:

- Small groups so that every passenger has a window sea!
- 4WD rather than a mini bus; this gives better access in the parks
- Lift-off roofs provide better views and photo opportunities
- Company policy on taking children – it varies
- Campsite standard – 'luxury' may mean a private hole-in-the-ground toilet with a bucket and heated water shower hanging from a tree; or it could be permanent rooms but with canvas walls

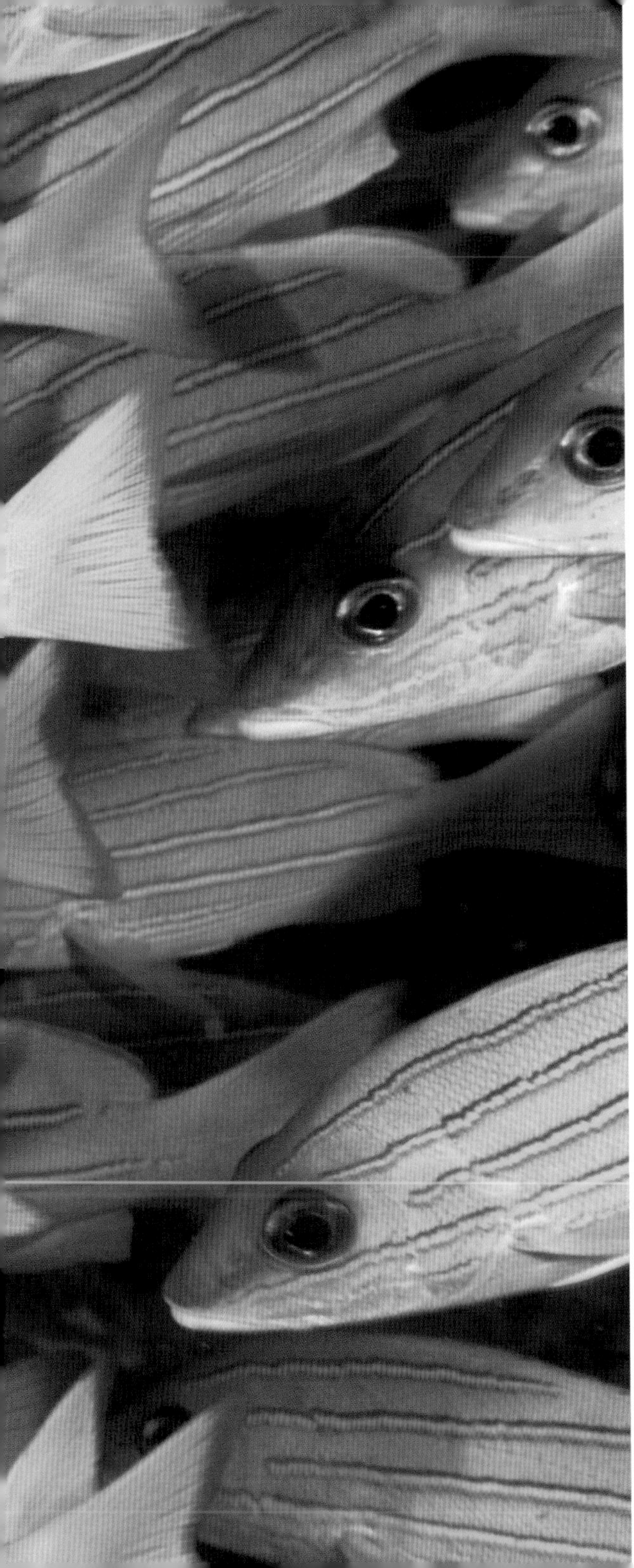

Fish soup: masses upon masses of Ari Atoll's often countless numbers of bluestripe snappers, *Lutjanus kasmira*

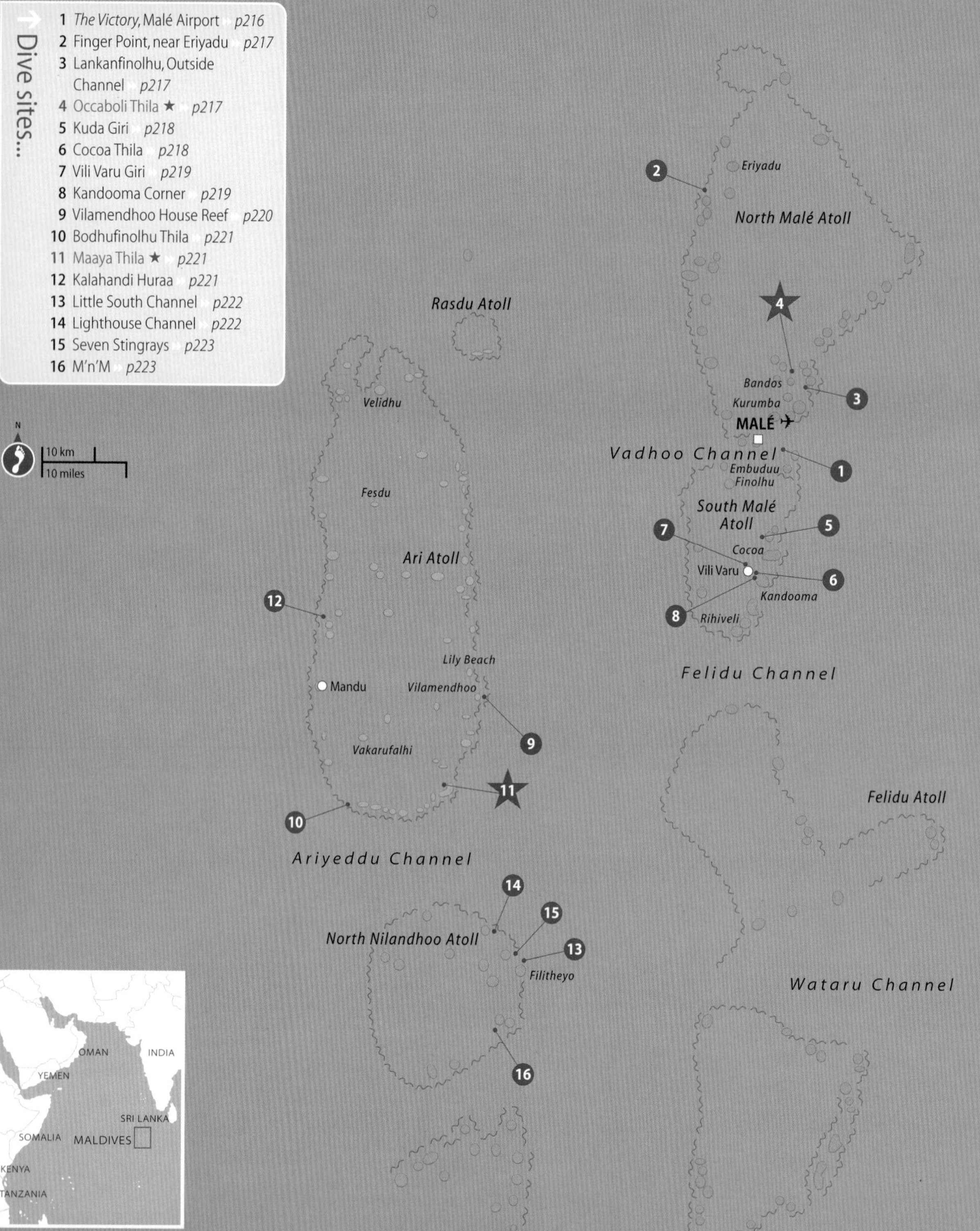

Dive sites…
1 The Victory, Malé Airport p216
2 Finger Point, near Eriyadu p217
3 Lankanfinolhu, Outside Channel p217
4 Occaboli Thila ★ p217
5 Kuda Giri p218
6 Cocoa Thila p218
7 Vili Varu Giri p219
8 Kandooma Corner p219
9 Vilamendhoo House Reef p220
10 Bodhufinolhu Thila p221
11 Maaya Thila ★ p221
12 Kalahandi Huraa p221
13 Little South Channel p222
14 Lighthouse Channel p222
15 Seven Stingrays p223
16 M'n'M p223
N
10 km
10 miles
Eriyadu
North Malé Atoll
Rasdu Atoll
Bandos
Kurumba
MALÉ
Vadhoo Channel
Embuduu
Finolhu
South Malé Atoll
Cocoa
Vili Varu
Kandooma
Rihiveli
Velidhu
Fesdu
Ari Atoll
Lily Beach
Mandu
Vilamendhoo
Vakarufalhi
Felidu Channel
Felidu Atoll
Ariyeddu Channel
North Nilandhoo Atoll
Filitheyo
Wataru Channel
OMAN
INDIA
YEMEN
SRI LANKA
SOMALIA
MALDIVES
KENYA
TANZANIA

Introduction

All those dreams of playing Robinson Crusoe – being cast away on your own private island and getting back to nature – can all come true in the Maldives. What's more, you can do all that with hot and cold running water, someone to wait on you hand and foot and go diving at the same time.

Your first glimpse of the Maldives will be the spectacular aerial view of her diminutive islands as you fly in to the capital, Malé. As you try to work out which one is yours, rest assured that they are all equally beautiful and all have fabulous diving.

This tiny, waterborne country has been bypassed and overlooked over the centuries due to the hazardous fringing reefs that have also been its saving. Their untarnished natural beauty, both above and below the waterline, is now their prime appeal. There are fish, fish and yet more fish. There's other marine life too, but there is nowhere else quite like this for swimming amongst pretty tropical fish.

Drying out time isn't exactly a succession of cultural diversions. In the Maldives you make your own entertainment. For here, watching the stars in the sky can be far more rewarding than watching them on screen.

“” Our first ever dives, way back when, were off tiny Bandos. On Christmas Day, we came face to face with a whitetip shark and were completely, utterly, hooked.

Maldives rating

Diving
★★★★

Dive facilities
★★★★

Accommodation
★★★★★

Down time
★

Value for money
★★★★

Essentials

Getting there and around

Getting a flight to the Maldives used to be fairly challenging but the country is now so popular that flying to the capital, Malé, is simplicity itself. There are dozens of charter flights that arrive on a daily basis, mostly from European cities. To access them you need to book a flight and accommodation package via a travel agent in your home country.

If you're coming from Asia, Australia, North America – or Europe but want to travel in substantially more comfort – there are several scheduled airlines that fly in regularly. These include **Singapore Airlines** (www.singaporeair.com), **Emirates** (www.emirates.com), **Sri Lankan Airlines** (www.srilankan.lk) and **Qatar Airways** (www.qatarairways.com).

Once you arrive at the airport, you will be collected by your hotel, dive centre or liveaboard. (In the Maldives, these are one and the same thing.) There is very little in the way of independent travel; it does exist but arriving without pre-booking is not advised. Most transfers from the airport are by seaplane. This is a great experience – sitting in a 20-seater seaplane then flying over fantastic seascapes until you reach your own little paradise isle. A few resorts, mainly those in the North Malé atoll, will collect by speedboat as the trip is less than an hour. These journeys can be bumpy so be prepared with seasickness tablets if your stomach is senstive.

Once you are on your island, you're not going very far – maybe to the next island on an organized day trip – so getting around is just not an issue.

Language

When the country was first opened to tourism, as mentioned below, many workers were imported from elsewhere and English became the most commonly used language. Now, many of these migrant workers can speak almost any language you care to throw at them. The native language is Dhivehi, which has many influences from right across the region. It is also the root of one of the most used words in this book – atoll. Anyone who has tried to learn a little Arabic may

An island in North Malé Atoll

notice some similarities.

hello/goodbye	*salaam alekum*
yes	*aan*
no	*noon*
thank you	*shukriyaa*
sorry!	*ma-aafu kurey!*
how much is ...	*agu kihaavareh ...*
good	*rangalu*
great dive!	*barabaru feenume*

And what about impressing the boat boys with 'what is the name of this reef?' which is *mi farah kiyanee kon nameh.*

Local laws and customs

The Maldives is a Muslim nation but you won't come across much in the way of religious customs. Many staff – such as waiters and receptionists – are from Sri Lanka or India. Originally this was an attempt to ensure that the locals were not unduly influenced by western ways. Now, more and more native Maldivians are working within the tourist industry. The resorts are tolerant of other cultures but do ask that you respect the private compounds where staff live, and especially the small mosque that is on every island. Women are also asked not to sunbathe topless and it is regrettable that some visitors ignore this request. The Maldivians are such nice people that you do have to wonder why. If you go to a non-touristy island, or into Malé, dress conservatively.

Maldives

Location	3°15′ N, 73°00′ E
Neighbours	India, Sri Lanka
Population	349,106
Land area in km²	210
Marine area in km²	996
Coastline in km	644

Safety

You 're on holiday in what looks like paradise and it's hard to imagine anything going wrong. Personal safety has, until very recently, been an almost insignificant concern. If there was to be any petty crime or theft it would probably be at the hands of a fellow tourist, certainly not a local, but don't tempt fate and leave valuables on show.

Of course, things do go wrong, as the tsunami of Christmas 2004 demonstrates. However, this freak disaster indicates that the biggest risk you run on the Maldives will be nature taking revenge. Kick some hard coral and you will get cut. Put your hands down on fire coral and you'll get stung. It's important to read up on the marine life and learn what you can and can't do safely.

Health

There are medical facilities in Malé and many resorts have a nurse or doctor on call. They may not be on your island but close by. However, there is little in the way of risks here. Food standards are high, though you should drink bottled or purified water. Mosquitos are more prolific on lush islands than ones with less natural vegetation. The sun, however, can be fearsome, though you may not realize due to those cooling sea breezes. Use lots of sunscreen and drink plenty of water to avoid dehydration.

Costs

As everything is imported into the Maldives, costs can be high. By 'everything' we mean everything – from staff to drinking water, lettuces to t-shirts. There is virtually no agriculture, no food or drink industry, no manufacturing. Hotel rates run from a reasonable US$50 per night to an astonomical US$1000. Meals are also expensive but almost all resorts include breakfast and most give room rates that include dinner. There is currently a trend to rebuild many of the original island hotels as upper-class resorts. These are beautiful but expensive and not aimed at serious divers anyway. The best way to keep your costs down to a reasonable level is to book on a liveaboard or into an all-inclusive resort as there will be fewer hidden extras. Otherwise, everything is signed for and charges tallied at the end of a stay. It's easy to run up larger than expected bills though and tipping is expected. At the end of your holiday leave a 'gift' for your waiter or room boy, who will have taken care of you consistently during your stay as the system allots specific staff members to each room. Around US$10 per week is often suggested. For dive staff see page 14.

Airlines → Singapore Airlines T+960 (0)3320777, Emirates T+960 (0)3314945, Sri Lankan T+960 (0)3323459, Qatar Airways T+960 (0)3334777. **Embassies** → All these are in Sri Lanka: UK T+94 (3)11 2437336, USA T+94 (3)11 2332725, Australia T+94 (3)11 2698767. **Maldives country code** → +960. **IDD code** → 00. **Police** → 119.

→ Fact file

International flights	Singapore Airlines via Singapore, Emirates via Dubai, Sri Lankan via Colombo, Qatar via Doha
Departure tax	Mostly included in ticket or US$12
Entry	EU, US and Commonwealth – visa for 30 days issued on arrival
Internal flights	Maldives Air Taxis and Sun Express
Ground transport	Water taxis
Money	The US dollar is the accepted currency
Language	All European languages are widely spoken
Electricity	230v
Time zone	GMT +5
Religion	Muslim

Oriental sweetlips being cleaned

Dive brief

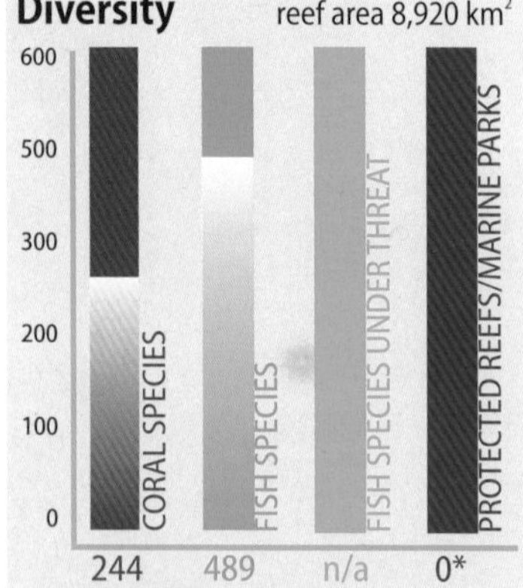

Diving

Fish, fish and yet more fish. There is no doubt about it, this is the place to go for them. Like no other tropical destination, the reefs and atolls here host some of the most amazing quantities of colourful schooling fish that you will ever see. Right across the country, diving feels just like being immersed inside a great, big aquarium.

On the other hand, this is not the place for prolific corals. The 1998 El Niño took its toll in these shallow waters but get down a little deeper and you'll hardly know it had happened. Even before that event, the corals were never the main attraction so if you don't go expecting to see them, you won't be disappointed. There are patches of colourful soft coral and hard corals live and regenerate in the deeper, cooler waters providing a backdrop to the myriad fish life.

Pelagic species can be an absolute treat. While large schools of fish like jacks are less common, some big animals are well known. Nothing is ever guaranteed but there are feeding stations for mantas, specific reefs that whalesharks are known to haunt and a good supply of sharks, especially in areas that get strong currents.

Currents are one of the defining features of Maldivian dives and vary with the seasons. Before you choose a resort check what direction the prevailing winds will be coming from. Currents run in line with the winds and bring in clearer waters from the open ocean. From May to November is the southwest monsoon. Winds transport clearer water from that direction so you will get better visibility if you go to the west of an atoll. December to April is the northeast monsoon, so at that time it's better on the east of an atoll.

Bottom time

North Malé Atoll
The most explored, the most dived but possibly still the best especially for fish numbers » *p216*

South Malé Atoll
More adventurous channel dives with strong currents and a lone wreck » *p218*

Ari Atoll
Wide open spaces with the biggest variety of dive styles – reefs, wrecks and walls » *p220*

Nilandhoo Atoll
Remote and quiet diving in barely investigated waters » *p222*

The blue blanquillo

The Maldivian islands have become pretty busy these days. Which is not to say that they have lost that Robinson Crusoe atmosphere. No matter how much development there is, the castaway style is cultivated and exploited. However, if you are the sort of diver who's looking for true isolation, with no other people and no other dive boats in sight, you may find it just a bit too crowded.

Dive data

Seasons	The southwest monsoon is May to November: go to the west of an atoll The northeast monsoon is December to April: go to the east of an atoll
Visibility	Varies according to location and season, from 10-30 metres
Temperatures	Air 25-30°C; water 25-29°C
Wet suit	3 mm full body suit
Training	Courses available on all resort islands but pre-booking is essential
Nitrox	Becoming more common but not everywhere yet
Deco chambers	Bandos and Malé

Snorkelling

There are some who claim that you can see as much while snorkelling as diving and this is one place where that might just about be true. The small fringing or house reefs that encircle nearly every island are full of life. During the day, you can spend hours floating along the reef watching all sorts of pretty creatures like the ubiquitous powder-blue surgeonfish. At night you can just sit dangling your feet off the jetty and watch baby sharks congregate, attracted by the lights.

The big decision

The Maldives tends to be where most European divers graduate to after they've done the Red Sea. It's a bit further but a lot more exotic. The tiny islands are romantic and standards are generally high. Although the greatest draw is still the marine life, it has also become highly attractive for those who want to windsurf, sail, be pampered in a spa or bake in the sun. There are around 100 designated resorts and choosing the perfect one can be confusing. Most are perfect for couples while others tend to cater for families. Some are managed by a particular nationality and attract the same nationality. You need to do your research and decide what's right for you.

Serious divers should opt for an island with a good house reef, where shore and night diving is available. Families may want to look for islands with bigger beaches and more facilities. Location is another consideration – the closer to the airport, the shorter the transfer time but the remote islands will be less busy. Finally, if you can abandon the island castaway dream, try a liveaboard and dive more than one atoll.

Buddy line

Diving and flying

There isn't a single diver amongst us who doesn't want to dive right till the very last. But the risk of flying too close to diving is well publicized. The general rule has always been to wait 24 hours before flying. DAN however, issued new guidelines based on work and research presented at a DCS workshop. These apply to air dives followed by flights in commercial airliners. They say that for a single no-decompression dive, a minimum interval of 12 hours is required and for multiple dives per day or multiple days of diving, a minimum interval of 18 hours. However, for dives requiring decompression stops, there is little evidence on which to base a recommendation so allow a pre-flight surface interval substantially longer than 18 hours. Always remember, it's better to lengthen these times and be safe, rather than sorry!

Hawksbill on the reef

North Malé (Kaafu) Atoll

Home to both the capital, Malé – which you're unlikely to see before you get whisked to a waiting transfer – and the international airport, the resorts here were the first to be developed. Islands vary in size from those that require only a 10-minute walk around the rim to those that take as much as 40 minutes. In general resorts here tend to be smaller but more sophisticated than ones further afield as the original ones have been rebuilt to higher standards. Where once it was brackish, cold water showers, now it's jacuzzis and spas, fancy eco-resorts with international style restaurants, gyms and sports facilities. A few are still as rustic and charming as when they were first built, a little on the rundown side but more in tune with the feel of the islands.

The diving in this atoll is regarded by some as the best in the country. There is a mixture of channel and thila (small submerged reef) diving and this creates very exciting conditions. For some divers, the strong currents can be off putting which in terms of conserving the reefs is not such a bad thing as fewer people are there to damage them. However, with so many resorts, many divers regard both the region and the diving as just too crowded.

1 *The Victory*, Malé Airport

- **Depth**: 30 m
- **Visibility**: fair to good
- **Currents**: can be very strong
- **Dive type**: day boat/liveaboard
- **Snorkelling**: no

The Victory sank on Friday, February 13th, 1981, although no one is clear what happened. The most touted theory is a navigational error. All the crew escaped. The wreck is a 110-metre steel cargo ship that you descend to along a rope attached to the midship mast. Surface currents can be strong so the rope is a necessity but once you reach the deck, you are sheltered. From here you can investigate the holds which are teeming with fish or head around the outside of the hull. There are often some big pelagics like turtles and grouper around the seabed near the anchor. Part of the accommodation area and the bridge is also open for investigation but space is tight. Most dive centres limit this site to experienced divers.

The wreck at Kuda Giri

Bannerfish are nosy!

2 Finger Point, near Eriyadu

- **Depth**: 27 m
- **Visibility**: good
- **Currents**: slight to ripping
- **Dive type**: day boat/liveaboard
- **Snorkelling**: no

Entry is over a small thila that is attached to the main reef by a sandy saddle. The current here can be extremely strong which attracts big animals. Napoleon wrasse hover over the sand as do whitetip sharks, then, as you descend to the point of the thila, you can spot eagle rays on a fly past, whitetips circling just off the reef edge and even grey sharks standing off in the blue. The thermoclines can be severe here too. Back on the main reef where the coral is mostly rubble (natural effects taking their toll), you are likely to see octopus, a lot of small schooling fish and small turtles.

3 Lankanfinolhu, outside channel

- **Depth**: 15 m
- **Visibility**: fair to good
- **Currents**: slight to strong
- **Dive type**: day boat/liveaboard
- **Snorkelling**: only for experienced

This is a well known manta ray cleaning station. The dive starts with a drift along the channel, passing an occasional shark and some schooling fish until you reach a depression in the rocks behind a small outcrop covered in cleaner wrasse. This is where the mantas come to get spruced up and diver groups sit and wait for them to appear. Of course, nothing is guaranteed so you may only see them further along the channel. Sometimes it's juveniles circling closer and closer, swooping between all the divers bubbles, at other times adult mantas swoop past divers then head out into the blue. The coral here has sadly been turned to rubble by the diver activity and there is little other life on the cleaning station.

4 Occaboli Thila

- **Depth**: 32 m
- **Visibility**: fair to good
- **Currents**: slight to strong
- **Dive type**: day boat/liveaboard
- **Snorkelling**: strong swimmers only

While perhaps not the most exhilarating dive in the Maldives, this site sums up the best of being in a real-world aquarium. Just an hour or so north of Malé the site consists of a circular main reef, a small narrow thila lying off its southeastern corner and a coral rock which creates a canyon between the thila and the main reef. The canyon is a real magnet for fish that are attracted by the currents that pass through. There is a resident family of Napoleon wrasse, several tuna and many small schools of jacks all whizzing about. At depth there are bluelined snapper and oriental sweetlips. Fish life is prolific with parrotfish, surgeonfish, bannerfish, butterflies and so many other species you can't absorb it all. An overhang is thick with glassfish and as you approach them they part in silent waves to reveal a giant grey moray behind. Back on the top, the reef slope is covered in small table corals just inches across, lots of little soft corals and colourful tunicates in between. There are more small tropical fish and some bottom feeders such as blennies.

Descending into Occaboli's canyon feels like being a kid with your nose pressed against the glass wall of an aquarium. There is that peculiar sense of complete disbelief – you are looking at so many fish at once you just can't absorb what they all are. After being nudged by a two-metre-long Napoleon you just give up and start grinning instead.

Smiler, the fang blenny

Grey reef shark prowling

South Malé (Kaafu) Atoll

With the upper rim of South Malé Atoll just about touching the bottom of North Malé, you could almost consider these two regions to be the one and the same. The style of the resort islands are much as they are elsewhere in the country – each is ringed by rooms tucked under trees with views out over the reefs or lagoon. However, this atoll is slightly less developed with fewer hotels as it's that bit further from the airport.

The southern part of Kaafu is separated from the north by the deep Vadhoo channel and, being smaller and due south, is protected by its bigger neighbour from the more severe wind and sea conditions. Diving is mostly on the east side in the narrow channels that carve through the rim of the fringing reef. There are only six of these so the tides sweep in and out at a great rate and the currents can really rip! At certain times of year the visibility will be flawless, at others it can drop down but this attracts the bigger animals to feeding stations.

There's a decorator crab in there!

5 Kuda Giri

Depth: 37 m
Visibility: fair to good
Currents: mild
Dive type: day boat/liveaboard
Snorkelling: yes

This small cargo boat supposedly sank elsewhere and was moved across to the side of the *giri* (a small submerged coral reef) to create a dive feature. And it certainly has done that, attracting a lot of marine life. It is about 30 metres long with one cargo hold at the back which you can enter though it is too confined to penetrate very far. The outside of the hull is in perfect condition and the rear deck has some scaffolding which is being coated by small crusting corals. The propellor sits at 27 metres and is covered in black coral branches. Up at the midships section an old cage has a resident grey frogfish inside it. After diving the wreck you can gas off over on the *giri* where there is some good critter life including leaffish, filefish and the Maldivian clownfish.

6 Cocoa Thila

Depth: 26 m
Visibility: fair to good
Currents: mild to ripping
Dive type: day boat/liveaboard
Snorkelling: possibly

This large flat-topped reef is surrounded by a sloping wall running most of the way around. At one end it becomes quite steep and is interspersed with small overhangs covered in pastel-hued soft corals – pink, lemon and mauve. On the reef top, if the current is running, you encounter huge schools of collared butterflyfish hovering beside groups of oriental sweetlips. The site is also known for green turtles which you need to approach very carefully as they take off if spooked. There is one enormous green adult, at least two metres from head to tail, which sleeps under the ledges. There are several others of varying sizes that reside on the plateau but mostly you see them as they take off to the surface for a gulp of air.

Investigating the wreck at Kuda Giri

7 Vili Varu Giri

- **Depth**: 18 m
- **Visibility**: fair to good
- **Currents**: mild
- **Dive type**: day boat/liveaboard
- **Snorkelling**: yes

This small flat thila makes a perfect night dive. The top level is exposed at low tide so there are a lot of boulders and rubble but under cover of darkness all the nocturnal animals emerge to hunt. As you descend onto the plateau, you can spot decorator crabs that are incredibly well camouflaged, some spider crabs, lots of sleepy fish nestling into the cracks and crevices and scorpionfish in the rubble area. A sandy slope then drops to a low wall on one side which is encrusted with dendrophyllia corals and lots of small pastel tunicates. Amongst these are more nocturnal shrimp and crabs, ornate ghostpipefish hiding in black coral branches and there are a couple of shallow caverns where green turtles rest.

8 Kandooma Corner

- **Depth**: 23 m
- **Visibility**: good
- **Currents**: strong
- **Dive type**: day boat/liveaboard
- **Snorkelling**: no

This long thin reef extends out to a point or corner where there are often fierce currents that attract big pelagic action. More often than not, though, it won't be possible to dive here as the currents are simply too strong. Fortunately, the other, calmer side can be equally interesting. From the flat top there is a small ridge and overhang that slopes down to 30 metres or so. There are lots of tubastrea corals and quite a bit of dendronephthya soft coral surrounded by masses of fish. In the overhangs you can often find small green turtles munching on some lunch, or a resting whitetip shark. On the top of the reef there are a huge schools of parrotfish, black surgeonfish and rainbow runners. These appear in massive waves to feed on algae-covered rocks.

You looking at me?

Temperatures rising

Keep your distance

As time goes by and island development continues, the government opens more and more atolls for tourism. Baa and Raa in the far north, once regarded as the frontier, now have six resorts between them. In the south, Meemu Atoll has just opened its first resort. It has even been suggested that a second international airport is built near Gan, the 1940's British naval station that became a resort in 1996. This atoll, Addu, is 450 km from Malé and a real outpost to explore.

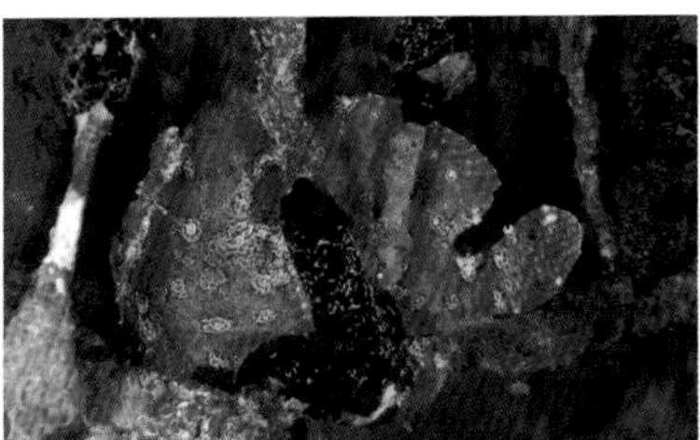
Frogfish in residence

White collar butterflyfish schooling

The male redfin basslet

Ari (Alifu) Atoll

The largest atoll in the country, and some way south and west of the Malé atolls, Ari is still comparatively close to the airport as seaplane transfers generally take less than an hour. This atoll has resorts dotted right around its rim and there are also a few on islands in the central lagoon which have easy access to all the dive sites.

This is a huge atoll with potentially the most varied diving in the country. There are many more thilas – submerged reefs – which are less prone to strong currents than channel and outer rim dives, which is a big bonus for less experienced divers. There are lots of caverns and overhangs to explore and there's one more thing that gives Ari an edge at certain times of year – the southeastern corner is a whaleshark haunt and you might be lucky enough to see several in a day. Visibility is low, however, as they come here to feed when the plankton blooms.

Cave exploration on Vilamendhoo

9 Vilamendhoo House Reef

- **Depth**: 28 m
- **Visibility**: good
- **Currents**: usually mild
- **Dive type**: shore dive
- **Snorkelling**: yes

This is one of the most diver friendly islands in the country and shore dives are marked by exit numbers from the beach. Exit 10 is on the northern side of the island. The wall here is almost completely vertical, dropping to about 28 metres, then slopes to the seabed. It isn't all that pretty, with lots of scrappy coral and rocks interspersed with dark green tubastrea, but quite dramatic all the same. Fish life is good and there are some unusual nudibranchs and tiny morays with yellow and black spots. There is a small cave at about 15 metres deep that is bursting with glassy sweepers. At its entry there are pretty pipefish, flatworms, lots of different types of shrimp and a large grey moray just inside.

Free swimming leopard shark

10 Bodhufinolhu Thila

Depth: 32 m
Visibility: poor to good
Currents: medium
Dive type: day boat/liveaboard
Snorkelling: yes

As well as having several good dive sites running along its edge, the southwestern rim of Ari is a known whaleshark highway. The divemasters watch for tell-tale shadows en route to a dive and often spy one or two in the depths before coming across one shallow enough to snorkel with. Then it's a mad leap into the water for a few minutes before the magnificent beast drops down and heads away. On a good day, this pattern will be repeated several times. The whalesharks can be extremely nosy and will come right up to the boat providing no one is in the water splashing about. They even lift their heads out to see what's there. At this dive site, the visibility is low – the whalesharks come to feed on the plankton – but you drop down onto a small thila where there are passing squads of mobula rays, whitetips circling and a small school of barracuda above.

Batfish family

11 Maaya Thila

Depth: 20 m
Visibility: low to fair
Currents: medium to strong
Dive type: day boat/liveaboard
Snorkelling: unlikely

One of Ari's better known dive sites, Maaya Thila is also a protected zone. The thila is a typical submerged oval that you can easily swim right around in a single dive. There are some outcrops just off one end that have plenty of feeding corals and it's worth swimming across to them as grey sharks often patrol the sandy channel. Back on the main reef, the activity is most exciting when you hit the point of oncoming currents so dives here are always best when these are strongest. You can see all sorts of marine life and the variety is impressive: there are resident batfish, oriental sweetlips, clown and titan triggers, octopus and morays.

12 Kalahandi Huraa

Depth: 32 m
Visibility: fair to good
Currents: medium to strong
Dive type: day boat/liveaboard
Snorkelling: unlikely

This steep, sloping wall is covered in crusting corals. The current can be quite strong but the wall is interspersed with a series of swim throughs where jacks and sweetlips shelter. There are some big overhangs with fans and soft corals. Back up on the wall you encounter small whitetips or Napoleon wrasse. Part of the way along the wall is a coral outcrop connected to the main part of the reef by a saddle where you might find a lurking leopard shark. They are usually docile creatures and the ones here seem unperturbed by divers, swoop around nosily before settling on the sand. Up on the top of the reef there are wrasse, more whitetips and plenty of schooling fish.

Tales from the deep

Eye to eye contact!
We had only been up from our dive a few minutes when another whaleshark appeared. Another – the fifth of the day – but this one was the biggest and the closest. We could tell this because she parked her entire seven metres down the length of the dhoni, raised her head and peered at us. I wasn't even close to ready so Beth jumped in with the camera then the crew swung the boat around and told me to jump. When the bubbles cleared, I discovered I was just inches away from the whaleshark's face. She made eye contact with me for several very long seconds then, gliding away, gave me a gentle whack with her tail as if to say goodbye. The next day I found a nice little bruise on my arm as a reminder! As if I needed one.

Shaun Tierney, Photographer, London

Nilandhoo (Faafu) Atoll

Due south of Ari, North and South Nilandhoo Atolls were only opened for development in 1999 and so far there are just three resorts. This area is comparatively isolated so there is a stronger presence of local Maldivian people. The developed islands are bigger and require more staff who come from other parts to work in the resorts.

The diving here is a little different to North and South Malé and more like South Ari's slightly flatter topography. Thilas that sit inside the atoll are protected from stronger tidal currents, making them easier sites. However, there are still plenty of channel dives and steep walls on the outer rim. And as there are so few resorts, the dive sites are never crowded. Even if several boats leave the dive centre at the same time, they scatter to different points. It must be said that the marine life is more wary of divers here. There *are* plenty of pelagics but they soon scatter.

The ubiquitous powder blue surgeonfish

Walls covered in white corals

13 Little South Channel

- **Depth**: 36 m
- **Visibility**: poor to good
- **Currents**: mild to medium
- **Dive type**: day boat
- **Snorkelling**: unlikely

The terrain drops into a deep channel where you are told you will see some very deep water outcrops. However, if the visibility is poor you can't see them. Large tuna cruise through in the current but there is more life back on the reef wall. Here, a few small caves and ridges are full of very pretty soft corals in pinks and lemons. One cavern has a ridge running inside it which is a haunt for lobsters, often as many as six at a time. Small turtles head up to the surface for a breather then swim back down to the rocks where they chew on some sponges.

Octopus or rock?

14 Lighthouse Channel

- **Depth**: 33 m
- **Visibility**: good
- **Currents**: generally strong
- **Dive type**: day boat
- **Snorkelling**: unlikely

This dive involves dropping down into an open channel to look for big animals. An occasional manta ray will swing up from great depths, peer about, then swim away again. A little further along, a group of young whitetips patrol the ridge over the drop off. Ascending back up to the reef, there is a broad slope, from 30 metres to 10, where patches of hard coral are surrounded by anthias, sweetlips and butterflyfish. Amongst the corals are green leaffish and different coloured nudibranch egg rings, one being laid by a funeral jorunna nudi.

Suddenly we saw another really unusual nudibranch. It had a white skirt with orange and black central pattern. We'd never seen it before and neither had our divemaster. Much later we discovered it was a *chromodoris glenei*, rarely seen outside the Maldives.

Schooling bluestripe snappers

15 Seven Stingrays

- **Depth**: 28 m
- **Visibility**: good
- **Currents**: generally strong
- **Dive type**: day boat
- **Snorkelling**: unlikely

This site is indicative of the atoll's diving. A long, flat reef has seven gentle mounds rising from its contours. Entry to the side drops you right into the current so you drift into the blue to search out large animals. These are mostly tuna and there seems to be little other activity. Back over the reef, you can count the 'stingrays' or mounds passing beneath you as the current grows stronger. By the time you reached the sixth, it can be pretty stiff and you are unlikely to stay still. There are substantial schools of yellow snapper and rainbow runners and on the seventh mound there are plenty of carpet anemones with clownfish, porcelain crabs and white-eyed morays underneath.

16 M'n'M

- **Depth**: 19 m
- **Visibility**: good
- **Currents**: generally strong
- **Dive type**: day boat
- **Snorkelling**: unlikely

This circular thila has a distinct structure, dropping from just below the surface to 35 metres in a perfectly straight wall. There are quite a few little caverns and a couple of very nice caves that you can swim through. All of these have a healthy covering of small white fan corals which are extremely delicate. There is a lot of colour here too, with the wall covered in multi-hued sponges, tunicates and small soft corals. Nudibranchs crawl amongst the sponges and mantis shrimp can be spotted on the cavern floors. The very unusual comet can be found here. This fish's skin patterns mimic the whitespotted moray, especially if threatened. They (and occasional lobster) are resident on the wall near the entry and exit point.

Tales from the deep

Secret Manta Spot

We had received a hot tip. Lots of mantas had been seen in the area and we knew the place was a hotspot for mantas surface feeding. There had to be something to attract the animals beyond a food source. It was likely there was an undiscovered 'cleaning station'.

We cruised to the area where the reef met the channel and marked the point with the GPS. It takes many years of experience to read the water and reef beneath the boat with any accuracy and the patience and skill of our skipper was called upon to hit the right spot. We gathered the divers and briefed them for an exploration dive – we just asked them to stick with us and hopefully we would see some mantas.

We felt a little nervous as they suited up. We didn't know what to expect and could just find a lot of sand. We jumped in exactly on the GPS point, down a shallow slope of hard coral reef towards a sandy area. We saw lots of lovely hard corals but no sign of a manta. We decided to swim slowly into the current and take a look inside the channel. There was a wide expanse of snowy white coral sand beyond the reef heaped into drifts.

Suddenly we saw a large shape out across the sand. We slowly made our way towards it and beckoned the divers to follow us. As we got closer we made out a group of three mantas slowly circling on the far side of the channel. We stayed very low and continued to swim across the channel until we were kneeling watching the mantas circling above our heads and being tended by cleaner fish. The longer we stayed the more mantas appeared and we all became mesmerized by the spectacle.

Over the past three years we have dived this site many times and it continues to amaze. We have regularly seen over 40 mantas visiting the cleaning station and it remains our special site as very few other dive guides have learnt of our secret spot.

Anne-Marie Kitchen-Wheeler and Matt Kitchen, Cruise Directors of MV Sea Queen*, have been diving in the Maldives since the early 1990's.*

Drying out

When asked what there is to do in the Maldives when you're not under the water, the answer is pretty much to get in the water. Apart from diving, there's swimming, snorkelling, windsurfing and sailing. Some resorts run night fishing trips and some run boat trips to other islands. Newer resorts are introducing spas and gyms. If you are near Malé, you can hop over for a visit, but there is little to see apart from the buildings that house local businesses. If your island is near a designated locals' island you can often go across for an hour or two, buy a soft drink and a t-shirt and head back. Almost all entertainment is centred in the resorts. Many will organize guest versus staff volleyball or even soccer matches. Some have a visiting band for a weekly disco but beyond that, you can read a book under a palm tree, watch the sunset and try to name the star constellations. All resorts listed have a resident dive centre.

When the devasting tsunami of Boxing Day 2004 hit the region, many Maldivian islands were flooded. Fortunately, the low lying atolls escaped some of the more aggressive tidal effects as the water simply rose over them then receded. Many resorts have used this as a reason to renovate and reopen a more sophisticated version. There are many more resorts than are listed here but many were still closed at the time of writing.

If you are having trouble choosing a resort, hop on what is endearingly called a 'safari boat' in the Maldives. After being met at the airport, a 10-min transfer will drop you onto a comfy floating hotel. Depending on the prevailing weather, you then sail around two or even three atolls. Evenings are spent moored near uninhabited islands, while days are filled by hopping onto the dive dhoni which shadows your home then takes you off to find the best dives around.

North and South Malé Atolls

Sleeping and diving

$$$ **Bandos Island Resort**, T+960 (0)6640088, www.bandos.com. 45 mins' boat ride north from the airport. Recently rebuilt into quite a sophisticated resort. It has 1 of only 2 decompression chambers in the country, a medical centre, shops, many sports facilities, both wet and dry, and a tiny deserted island just a few minutes away. Kuda Bandos is one of the country's most photographed islands.

$$$ **Kurumba**, T+960 (0)3323080, www.kurumba.com. 10 mins from the airport. Done up to ultra-trendy spa specifications. The decked bar looks across to the port area, there are several

Undercurrents

The cost of tourism

When travellers first discovered this tiny nation, tourism was highly restricted. Only so many islands were designated to accept foreign visitors and most were built, managed and operated by neighbouring countries. Local people were not allowed to have any contact with the outsiders. Of course, once the world discovered just how beautiful the Maldives were and started flocking in, the government saw the financial reward and tourism was allowed to grow. Year on year, more islands are earmarked as suitable for development. There are two downsides to this. Firstly the islands are literally shrinking. At a maximum of three feet above sea level, this type of growth won't be sustainable if global warming continues. Secondly, some resorts are mining coral and sand for use as building materials. It is said that this is 'only coral rubble' but this seems to ignore the fact that many reef building creatures live in the rubble. Some resorts are not exactly designed to be sympathetic to the environment. One is built on stilts and to get between your room and the restaurant you have to call a boat! If all this concerns you, look for a resort that promotes eco-tourism.

restaurants and masses of pampering facilities. Proximity to the capital's boat and shipping lanes makes this resort feel a little busy. However, it's a brilliant stopover pre or post liveaboards.
$$$ Rihiveli, T+960 (0)441994, www.rihiveli-maldives.com. Seaplane transfer in 45 mins. At the far end of the South Malé Atoll, surrounded by a lagoon with 2 uninhabited islands just a short walk – yes, walk – away, this is a great place for getting in touch with the Maldives before tourism hit. There's still plenty of comfort though, and great food.
$$ Eriyadu, T+960 (0)6644487, www.aaa.com.mv. At the top of North Malé, but only an hour by speedboat. More of an escapist's island, Eriyadu is still much as it was a couple of decades ago, a little frayed but no unnecessary frills. Simple bungalows hide under the palms. Strong focus on diving with a resident Werner Lau Dive Centre, www.wernerlau.com.

Ari Atoll

Sleeping and diving

$$$ Lily Beach, T+960 (0)6680013, www.lilybeachmaldives.com. About 45 mins by seaplane from Malé. This resort was built over the site of a small garden island. It is quite spacious and the large bungalows have their bathroom in the garden.
$$$-$$ Vilamendhoo, T+960 (0)6680637, www.aaa.com.mv. About 45 mins by plane from Malé, this is one of the country's older resorts and is a heavy focus on diver service and a great house reef. The accommodation comes in various grades and is all good. The gardens are well established and feel very tropical. Diving run by Werner Lau Centres.

Nilandhoo Atoll

Sleeping and diving

$$$ Filitheyo, T+960 (0)6740025, www.aaa.com.mv. An hour and 15 mins by seaplane from Malé. The lone resort in the north of the atoll sits on a comparatively large island. Its centre is full of natural vegetation and on one side is a perfect white sand beach. The rooms here are billed as Balinese style, meaning lots of timber, and mostly sit in pairs. This resort is sold as a 'romantic' destination as they have a few water bungalows sitting over the reef edge. In reality it is more a family style resort as the beach and a pool attract a lot of people with children. Diving run by Werner Lau Centres who have nitrox.

Other atolls

The resorts listed above are the ones that have been experienced – and enjoyed – by the authors. But that's not to say that there aren't many more excellent operations right across the country. Most resorts will have an on-site dive centre, some are independent and others part of larger groups. If you don't have a resort recommendation, look to dive centres run by well regarded operations like **Pro Divers** (www.prodivers.com) who can be found at Kuredu, Komandoo, and Vakarufalhi. **Euro Divers** (www.euro-divers.com) operate from seven islands across the country including Kurumba, Velidhu and Lohifushi. **Diverland** (www.diverland.com) have bases at Embudu, Summer Island and at far off Gan.

Filitheyo dive centre

Mooring in Ari

Liveaboards

Sea Queen and **Sea Spirit/Maldives Scuba Tours**, Finnigham Barns, Walsham Rd, Suffolk IP14 4JG, T+44 (0)1449 780220. Two British-owned and run liveaboards based on traditional Malidivian boats and although small are very comfortable. A dhoni runs in tandem with each main boat and all diving and equipment is kept on board.
Peter Hughes Ocean Dancer, 5723 NW 158th Street,Miami Lakes, FL, 33014, T+1 (1)305 6699391 www.PeterHughes.com. The newest vessel to join the Peter Hughes fleet with the same standards of luxury and service. Huge cabins, spacious dive deck, nitrox and cordon bleu meals. 7 nights cost around US$2195.

Boats

Relaxing on the beach

Eriyadu

Thailand

Size matters: diver overshadowed by five full metres of awe-inspiring, juvenile whaleshark, *Rhincodon typus*

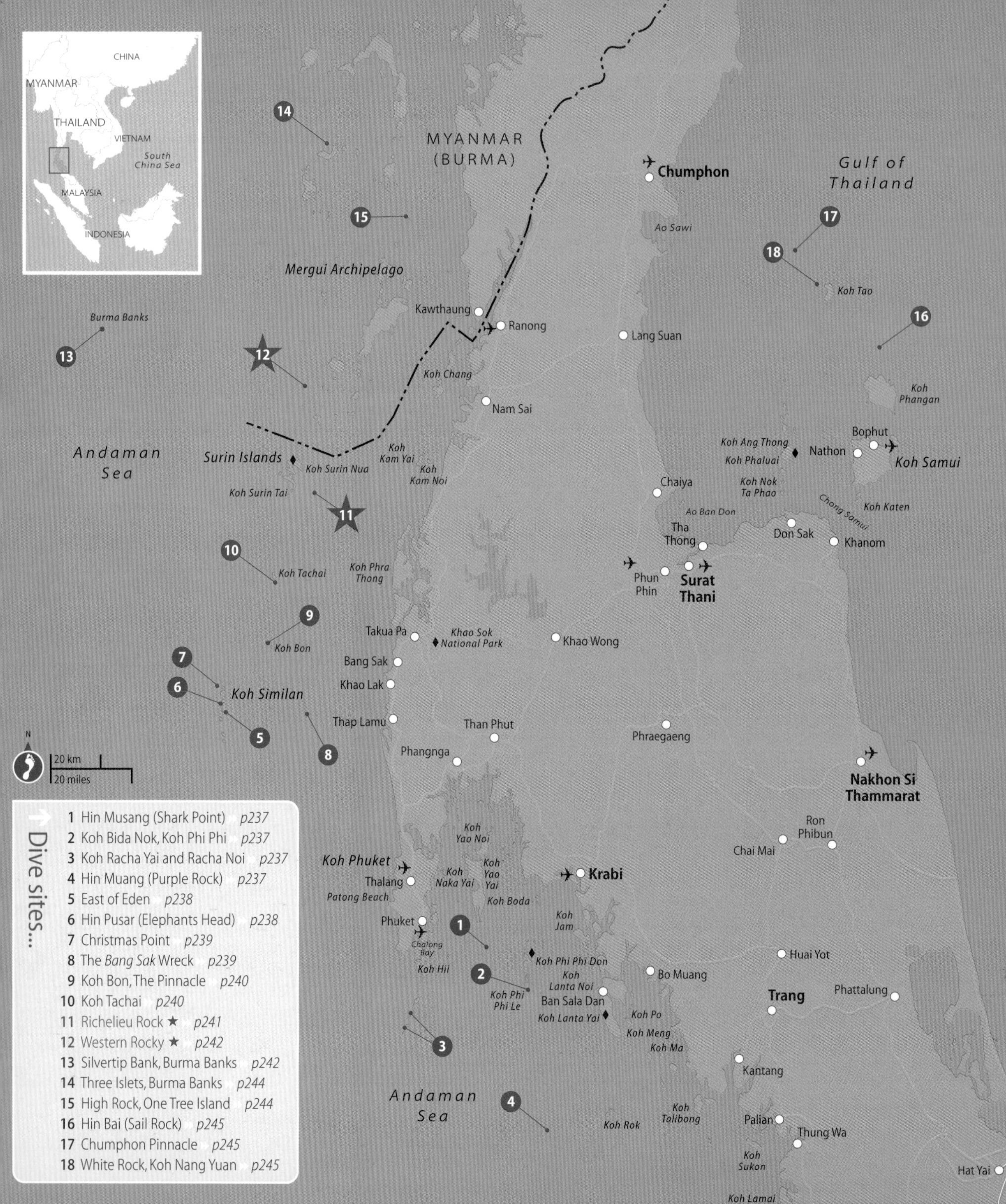

CHINA
MYANMAR
THAILAND
VIETNAM
South China Sea
MALAYSIA
INDONESIA
MYANMAR (BURMA)
Gulf of Thailand
Andaman Sea
Mergui Archipelago
Burma Banks
Chumphon
Ao Sawi
Koh Tao
Kawthaung
Ranong
Lang Suan
Koh Chang
Nam Sai
Koh Phangan
Surin Islands
Koh Surin Nua
Koh Kam Yai
Koh Kam Noi
Koh Surin Tai
Koh Ang Thong
Koh Phaluai
Nathon
Bophut
Koh Samui
Koh Nok Ta Phao
Chaiya
Ao Ban Don
Chong Samui
Koh Katen
Tha Thong
Don Sak
Khanom
Koh Tachai
Koh Phra Thong
Phun Phin
Surat Thani
Koh Bon
Takua Pa
Khao Sok National Park
Khao Wong
Bang Sak
Khao Lak
Koh Similan
Thap Lamu
Than Phut
Phraegaeng
Phangnga
20 km
20 miles
Nakhon Si Thammarat
Koh Yao Noi
Ron Phibun
Chai Mai
Koh Phuket
Thalang
Koh Naka Yai
Koh Yao Yai
Krabi
Patong Beach
Koh Boda
Phuket
Koh Jam
Chalong Bay
Koh Hii
Koh Phi Phi Don
Huai Yot
Bo Muang
Koh Lanta Noi
Ban Sala Dan
Koh Phi Phi Le
Trang
Phattalung
Koh Lanta Yai
Koh Po
Koh Meng
Koh Ma
Kantang
Andaman Sea
Koh Talibong
Koh Rok
Palian
Thung Wa
Koh Sukon
Koh Lamai
Hat Yai
Dive sites...
1 Hin Musang (Shark Point) p237
2 Koh Bida Nok, Koh Phi Phi p237
3 Koh Racha Yai and Racha Noi p237
4 Hin Muang (Purple Rock) p237
5 East of Eden p238
6 Hin Pusar (Elephants Head) p238
7 Christmas Point p239
8 The Bang Sak Wreck p239
9 Koh Bon, The Pinnacle p240
10 Koh Tachai p240
11 Richelieu Rock ★ p241
12 Western Rocky ★ p242
13 Silvertip Bank, Burma Banks p242
14 Three Islets, Burma Banks p244
15 High Rock, One Tree Island p244
16 Hin Bai (Sail Rock) p245
17 Chumphon Pinnacle p245
18 White Rock, Koh Nang Yuan p245

Introduction

Exotic pearls in the ocean, tiny white gems surrounded by iridescent turquoise. Swaying palms, gentle breezes, sunsets stained red like tropical cocktails. And deep, indigo seas that reveal rainbows beneath. The waters that surround Thailand are the stuff that divers' dreams are made of.

From the smaller, peaceful reefs south off Phuket to the high drama of the Burma Banks, the variety of diving is astonishing. Even the sometimes murky waters around the islands in the Gulf of Thailand are lush enough to keep divers smiling. Thailand's seas may not be as diverse as other parts of Asia – biodiversity rankings are lower by quite a way – but with more than its fair share of pelagic animals, you can forgive it almost anything. Especially as it is one of the most likely places to dive with that revered gentle giant, the whaleshark.

When it's time to let the nitrogen leach out, days on land are a treat. Thai culture is rich and heady, peppered with orange-clad monks, golden Buddhas and brassy nightlife. Thai cuisine is outstanding and her people are charming. This is, after all, the Land of Smiles.

“” *Every time we return to the Andaman Sea, we're reminded just how rewarding the diving there can be.*

Thailand rating

Diving
★★★★

Dive facilities
★★★★★

Accommodation
★★★★

Down time
★★★★

Value for money
★★★★

Essentials

Getting there and around

Thailand is one of Southeast Asia's easiest countries to travel in. There are international airports right around the country, a decent bus system, trains linking Bangkok with the south and ferries to all the islands.

As the best diving is based in the south of the country, international flights via Singapore are often the most practical option. The city makes a great stopover (see page 275) and as airports go, Singapore's Changi is one of the best. Indoor gardens, free internet, on-site hotels and pool all mean it's worth routing this way, rather than via Bangkok. **Singapore Airlines** (www.singaporeair.com) flight network is excellent, no matter where you start from. At Changi swap to their regional airline, **Silk Air** (www.silkair.com), which has twice daily flights to Phuket and Krabi. If you're heading to Koh Samui use **Bangkok Airways'** daily connection (www.bangkokair.com).

Of course, if you've never been to Bangkok, you may think it's worth a stopover (see page 249) in which case **Thai Airways** (www.thaiair.com) have plenty of flights with good connections to all dive regions.

Transfers from your arrival airport are no problem – just ask your hotel or dive centre to pick you, and all that heavy luggage, up. Depending on the package you have booked, this may cost a nominal sum, or be free.

For internal travel and land tours, rely on your dive centre or hotel for advice and assistance. It's perfectly OK to wander off on your own. Although traditions are still evident, westernised standards prevail. Thai nature means you will always find someone willing to help. Nearly everyone speaks English or another European language.

Local laws and customs

Thai etiquette is based around courtesy and calmness. Keep a cool head at all times and you won't go wrong. On the subject of heads, never touch a Thai there, not even an affectionate pat for a child. Never show the soles of your feet or use a foot to point. Feet are the lowest part of the body so it's considered an insult.

The Thai Royal Family are much revered, so no criticism is allowed, not even in jest. Buddhist monks should be treated with equal courtesy and women should never touch one. If you visit a temple or are away from the beach, sensible, modest clothing is preferable. On the beach, well anything goes!

Iridescent gold coral fan reflecting the sun

Language

Thai is a tonal language – two words may look and be spelt the same way but pronounced differently and mean different things. That makes it hard for your average westerner to learn and to make matters worse, it has a different alphabet. But like most countries, the Thais are honoured, and amused, if you try a few words. Here are a few basics to help you charm your divemaster or waiter.

hello, goodbye	*sa-wùt dee krúp (kâ)*
yes/no	*chái/mâi chái or: krúp (kâ)*
thank you	*kòrp-kOO/mâi ao*
no thank you	*kòrp-kOOn*
excuse me, sorry!	*kor-tôht krúp (kâ)*
how much is …	*tâo-rài …*
where's the …	*yòo têe-nai …*
great dive!	*Dam naam dee mak mak*

(Use *krúp* for males and *kâ* for females.)

Thailand	
Location	15°00′ N, 100°00′ E
Neighbours	Myanmar, Cambodia, Laos & Malaysia
Population	64,185,502
Land area in km²	515,139
Marine area in km²	252,000
Coastline in km	3,219

Safety

Thailand is a relatively stable country and personal safety isn't too much of an issue. Although there are sporadic incidents, these are rare and common sense should keep you safe. Women should be aware that although they may get hassled a little, this is still one of the safer Asian countries. Teaming up with a dive buddy may be a good idea. Petty crime is more of a problem, especially in tourist areas. In places where nightclubs are up-scale, drink spiking does occur. There are also tales of travellers on internal buses or trains being handed a coke by a friendly local then waking up hours later having been relieved of their wallets.

Dive centres tend to be in well populated and traveller friendly places. If you have made arrangements with a local operator they will collect you from the airport then deposit you safely at your accommodation or dive boat. Camera carriers should be aware that Pelican cases scream an invitation to a petty thief as do laptop bags and mobile phones. Don't leave dive equipment unattended, especially not swanky dive bags with big logos plastered all over them.

Note that penalties for possession of drugs are severe and can include the death penalty. Also note that there is a continued threat of terrorist attacks in the far south of the country, along the border with Malaysia.

Health

In tourism focussed areas, staying healthy is not an issue. Standards are high, hotels will have doctors on standby and decent medical facilities are available should you need help. Basics, like aspirin and insect repellant are easy to get. Beware of too much sun, mosquitos at dusk and drink bottled water. There is very little risk of malaria in the southern coastal regions and mosquitos don't make it out to sea. Also be smart when it comes it extra-curricular activities – Thailand has an epidemic of HIV infection and AIDS and HIV is common amongst prostitutes of both sexes. For recommended vaccinations, see page 24.

Costs

Thailand is good value for money for divers. Although everyone's version of value varies, you can get a decent three-course meal and a local beer or two, while sitting under a coconut palm watching the sunset. And all for less than ten dollars (sometimes a lot less). A beer is less good value though, with the excellant local brew, Singha, around a US$1.50 a bottle. Tipping isn't the norm although in touristy areas it's becoming more common. Room rates can be whatever you need them to be. In the dive areas, US$15 will buy a reasonably comfortable room, while a more upmarket hotel can cost anything up to US$100. Naturally rates are higher in Bangkok where it's worth paying for comfort.

Airlines → Silk Air T+66 (0)76 213891, Thai T+66 (0)76 211195, Bangkok T+66 (0)76 225033. **Embassies** → UK T+66 (0)2 305 8333, USA T+66 (0)2 205 4000, Australia T+66 (0)2 287 2680, NZ T+66 (0)2 254 2530. **Thailand country code** → +66. **IDD code** → 001. **Mobile Police** → 191. **Tourist Police** → 1699.

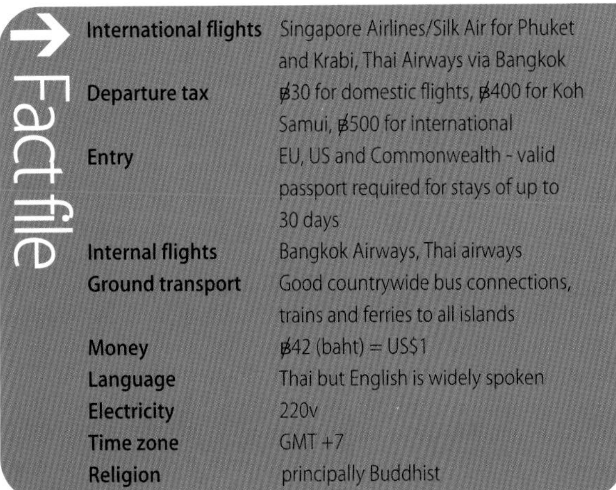

→ Fact file

International flights	Singapore Airlines/Silk Air for Phuket and Krabi, Thai Airways via Bangkok
Departure tax	฿30 for domestic flights, ฿400 for Koh Samui, ฿500 for international
Entry	EU, US and Commonwealth - valid passport required for stays of up to 30 days
Internal flights	Bangkok Airways, Thai airways
Ground transport	Good countrywide bus connections, trains and ferries to all islands
Money	฿42 (baht) = US$1
Language	Thai but English is widely spoken
Electricity	220v
Time zone	GMT +7
Religion	principally Buddhist

Diving Thailand's prolific reefs

Sea Bees Diving

Learn to dive with us!

You will be surprised to discover how easy it is to learn to dive. In just four days you can become a certified diver. Diving is one of the safest recreational activities with the proper instruction. Our course choices are comprehensive and extensive. That's because we're one of the few dive centres in Thailand that offers the complete range of PADI and CMAS certification courses from beginner to professional instructor.

Stay in one of our Dive Resorts!

The Sea Bees' own Palm Garden Resorts in Phuket and Khao Lak are both located in a lush, tropical environment. All bungalows enjoy a private terrace overlooking the large swimming pool and garden. Both pool have a Jacuzzi, a paddling pool and a waterfall. This is truly a tropical paradise. The bungalows offer all the amenities you would expect from a modern dive resort such as air conditioning, TV, minibar, safe, charging station and ensuite bathroom with hot water shower.

Adventure in good hands!

Dive brief

Diving

Thailand's diving is defined – or perhaps confused – by its position between two seas. The western coastline faces the Indian Ocean and is heavily affected by its deep water currents and contrasting monsoons. May to October sees driving, onshore winds pushing from the southwest. By November, calm seas return when the monsoon swaps over to the northeast. Over in the Gulf, the wind patterns have the opposite seasonal effect.

There are reef structures all the way along both coastlines but on the west these are far more extensive, particularly around the offshore islands. All the way from south of Phuket right up into Myanmar, there is fantastic diving. Colourful corals and sea fans are plentiful. There are huge granite boulders, spectacular swim throughs and swarms of colourful fish. Pinnacles rise from the deep and submerged reefs offer protection in isolated regions.

In contrast, the Gulf and her islands are subject to their position in a very shallow sea. At less than 60 metres deep, and with twice daily tides, they are susceptible to heavy sedimentation and river run off. These harsh conditions have restricted reef diversity and coral numbers. All the same, there is good diving to be had around a few of the southern islands but the further north you go, heading towards Bangkok, the more likely it is that visibility will disappoint.

Bottom time

- **Phuket and Krabi** Gentle diving around picture-postcard islands with pretty reefs » *p236*
- **The Similans** The ultimate Thai marine park where diversity is at its most impressive » *p238*
- **Surin Islands** Including Richelieu Rock – the 'do-not-miss' dive' of the country » *p240*
- **Mergui Archipelago** Unexplored reefs and submerged pinnacles to the north » *p242*
- **Koh Samui and the Gulf** Variable conditions in shallow waters, occasionally sensational » *p245*

Snorkelling

Thailand is a mixed bag: currents are unpredictable and often strong, and wind conditions can change rapidly making for rough surface conditions. Many of the better dive sites visited by liveaboards are exposed and submerged pinnacles may be off-putting for all but the strongest swimmers. However, there is decent snorkelling in the coastal areas – the Similans, south of Phuket and around some of the Gulf Islands.

Diversity*

reef area 4000 km²

Coral species	Fish species	Fish species under threat	Protected reefs/marine parks
705	308	22	16

*Thailand and Myanmar figures combined

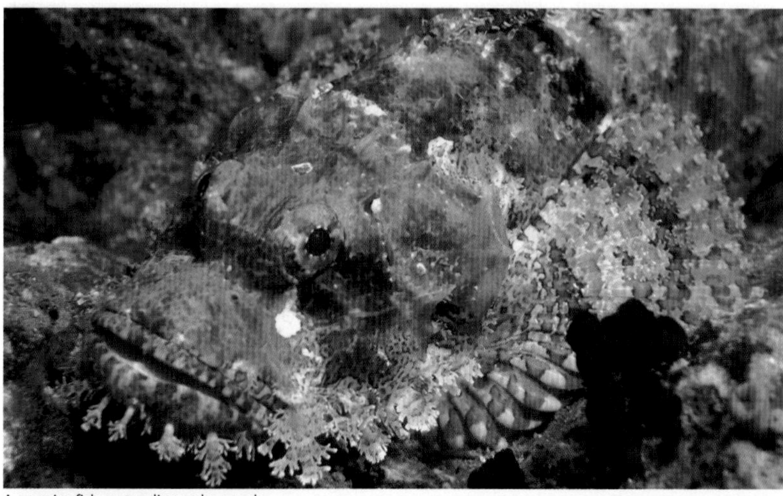

A scorpionfish pretending to be a rock

When we're asked why we keep returning to Thailand – or why we recommend it – we can only quote some of the special moments that have happened... floating over the crystal clear, turquoise waters of the Similans. Dawn on the Burma Banks watching whales breach. The moment the light went out at Richelieu Rock as a whaleshark swam over us and when we met another in the Mergui Archipelago a day later. Discovering a perfect pink ghost pipefish on a perfect pink coral. Exploring the inky depths of a wreck at night. And just simply knowing that below lies a marine adventure that's hard to rival. We have never been disappointed diving off Thailand's west coast.

→ Dive data

Seasons	November to May on the west coast June to October on the east coast
Visibility	5 metres near inshore to 'infinity' in open water in the Andaman Sea
Temperatures	Air 30-34°C; water 27-30°C
Wet suit	3 mm full body suit. Take a rash vest for the 4th dive of the day
Training	Courses available in Phuket, Krabi or the Gulf. Look for PADI 5 star (or equivalent) training agencies
Nitrox	Freely available on land. Most liveaboards also carry but quantities may be limited. Pre-booking advised
Deco chambers	Pattaya, Bangkok, Phuket and Koh Samui

The big decision

Once you have decided to dive Thailand, choosing a specific destination may seem daunting. However, Thailand is very seasonal, so your next choice is simply when to go. If it's between November and May, then you're heading to the west of the country. If you are limited to May through October, the Gulf of Thailand will make for a better holiday, although not necessarily the best diving. If you're a qualified diver, then there is no better way to explore the wonders of the Andaman Sea than being on a liveaboard.

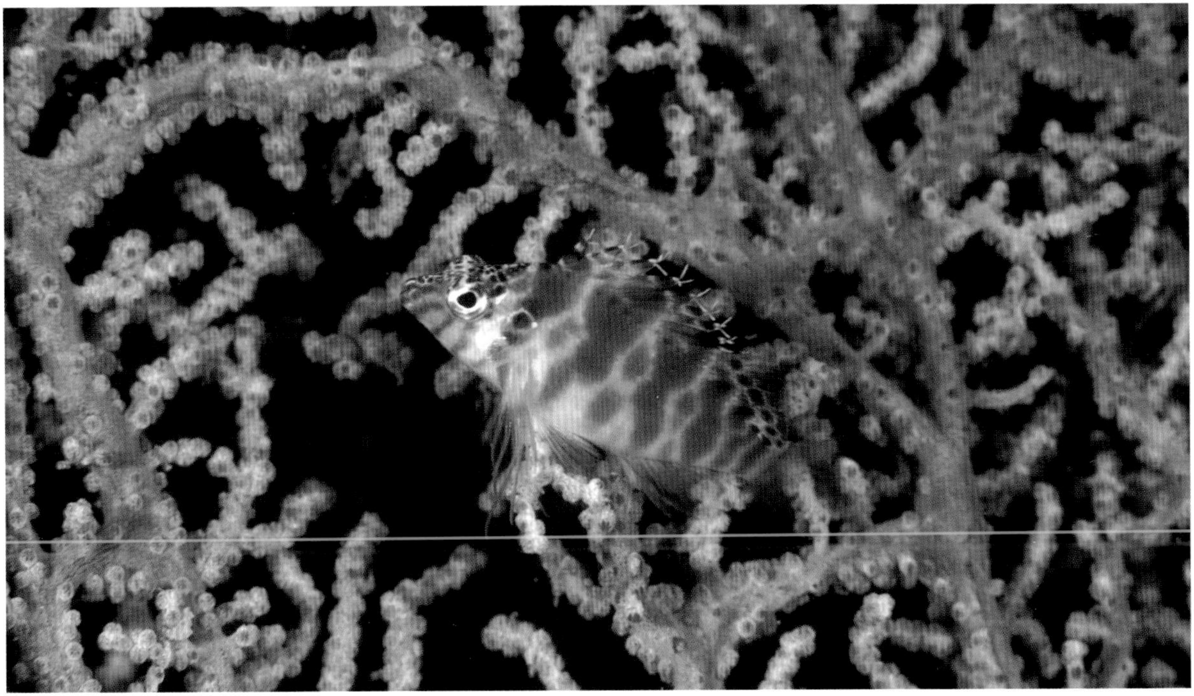

Threadfin hawkfish hiding on a fan coral

Phuket and Krabi

Just a one hour flight from Bangkok and 90 minutes from Singapore, the small area that includes both Phuket Island and the nearby town of Krabi is the starting point for diving in Thailand. These two places embrace some of Thailand's most idyllic scenery – The 'Man with the Golden Gun' was filmed on Koh Tapu and 'The Beach' on the Phi Phi Islands. Two international airports and masses of facilities, both for divers and non-divers, make this the perfect place to begin your dive journey. And most of the dive sites in this area can be reached from either town.

Phuket

Whether on land or below the waves, the island of Phuket has it all, from loud and raucous but picture-postcard pretty, Patong Beach to calm and quiet Chalong Bay where all the yachts anchor. You can take your pick of whatever resort style suits you best as almost everywhere has a dive shop. Phuket is also the main departure point for day boats and liveaboards to the treasured Similan Islands Marine Park as well as for cruises further north to the Burma Banks.

Arranging a training course, day trips or a liveaboard cruise is simplicity itself. Thousands of divers flock here to take advantage of the abundant facilities but be aware that dive sites close to the island tend to have reduced visibility, sometimes as low as 10 metres. The gentle west coast beaches are great for less experienced divers and trainees but the seabed may be stirred up by motorized watersports enthusiasts. There is fun diving for less demanding divers, but sail offshore for an hour or so and the difference can be surprising.

Krabi

Where Phuket is mostly brash and crowded the beaches and islands around Krabi are comparatively peaceful and laid-back. Surprising when you think that it's less than a two hour drive away and has its own airport. Originally a haunt of backpackers and long term travellers, the beaches and offshore islands near this compact and bustling town are idyllic and, despite becoming increasingly popular in recent years, Krabi has successfully managed to achieve a comfortable balance.

You could easily spend some substantial time here. The sunsets are amazing, the food superb and the diving first-class. An hour or so in a traditional longtail boat will drop you by untouched reefs, where the only other divers are the ones you arrived with.

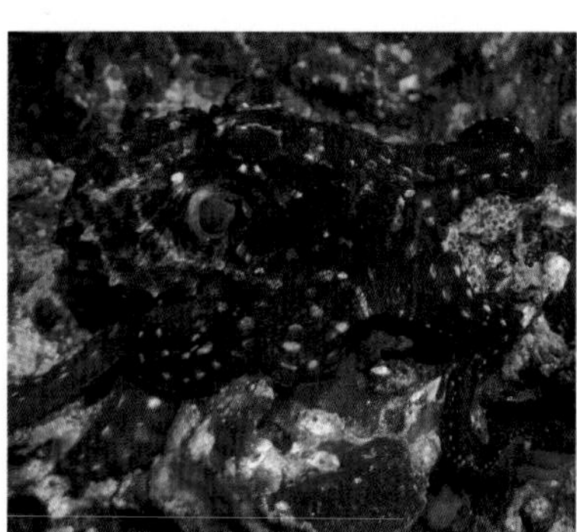

Andaman sea octopus

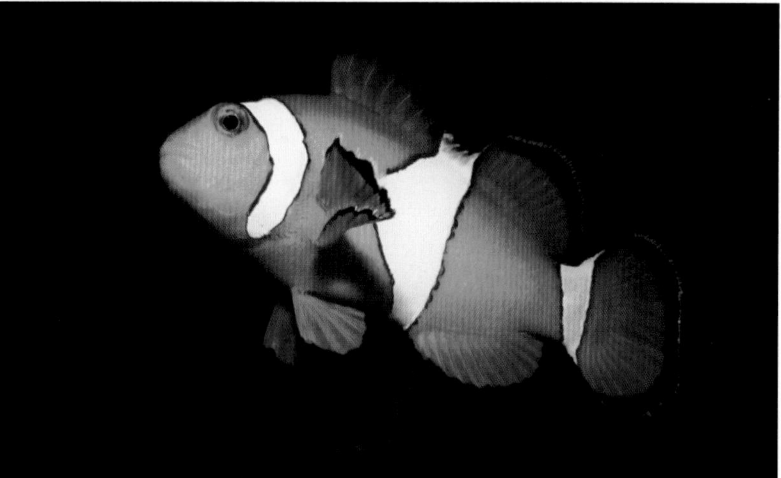

The clownfish emerging from its host anemone

1 Hin Musang (Shark Point)

Depth: 24 m
Visibility: fair to good
Currents: can be strong
Dive type: day boat
Snorkelling: for strong swimmers

Approaching a small craggy rock surrounded by deep blue water gives no indication of the abundance of colour below the surface. This limestone pinnacle is part of a marine reserve and coated in beautiful yellow and orange sea fans and plenty of soft corals. All this provides shelter for masses of tropical fish and crustaceans. Seeing a leopard shark is almost guaranteed as they are nearly always resting on the sea bed here. Currents can be strong at times so dives are often a drift.

2 Koh Bida Nok, Koh Phi Phi

Depth: 27 m
Visibility: fair, seldom great
Currents: slight to medium
Dive type: day boat
Snorkelling: yes

The Phi Phi Islands, made even more famous by Leonardo di Caprio and his co-stars, are really very beautiful, if a bit overdeveloped. The fabulous landside scenery extends down below the water line. Caves, overhangs and swim-throughs have been carved into the soft limestone rock leaving lots of nooks and crannies for the marine life. The southern tip of tiny Ko Bida Nok is a perfect example of the dives here: the shallow bay on the eastern side has huge gardens of staghorn corals and incredible numbers of colourful reef fish like triggers, surgeons and butterflies. The visibility can be limited but there always seems to be something interesting to discover here.

3 Ko Racha Yai and Racha Noi

Depth: 24 m
Visibility: fair to good
Currents: slight to strong
Dive type: day boat
Snorkelling: yes

These two sister islands (large rock and small rock) have some of the best year-round diving near Phuket. At the top of Racha Yai two delightful bays feel just like swimming pools. They gradually drop to the sandy seabed and the currents are mostly gentle. The nutrient rich coastal waters attract large schools of tropical fish. Perfect for novices! The reefs at Racha Noi on the other hand are a bit deeper and the currents stronger than at her sister island to the north. There are huge underwater boulders and a good chance to see manta rays, reef sharks and blue spotted stingrays.

4 Hin Muang (Purple Rock)

Depth: 25 m+
Visibility: 10-40 m
Currents: mild
Dive type: day boat
Snorkelling: yes

If you ask a divemaster what you'll see, the likely response will be anemones and clownfish. And what an understatement that would be. This completely submerged reef is shaped a bit like a loaf of bread that someone has chopped across the middle and is aptly named. Purple hued anemones form enormous carpets, more than you will ever seen in one place. Then there's the purple and pink soft corals that drip down the gully and, if you look closely, you'll see that the whole place has purple toned fish: scorpionfish, lionfish and even octopus display indigo hues hoping to stay hidden. There are some bigger animals hanging around, too, but it's hard not to focus on all the tiny critters hidden in the folds, branches and crevices. The macro life is wonderful. The gully provides shelter from the currents and clownfish dart out curiously to check out the interlopers. Tiny caves are full of purple cleaner shrimp and, occasionally, you'll find rarer creatures hiding along with them. Ornate ghost pipefish – in shades of purple – are often seen by those who take the time to look.

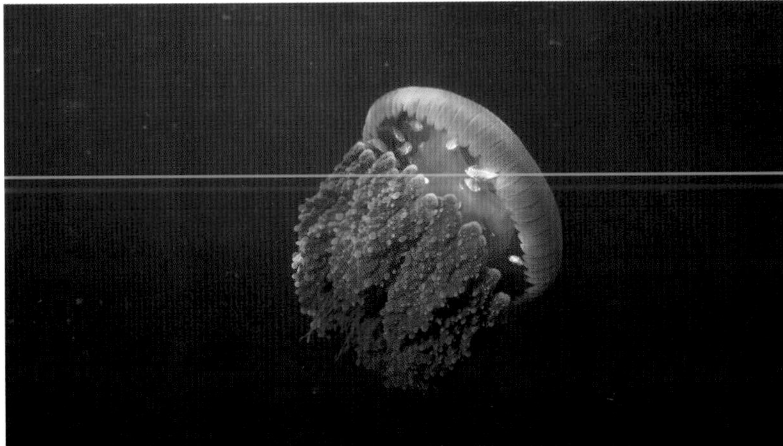

Juvenile cardinals sheltering in the bell of a jellyfish

A toxic flabellina nudibranch eating a hydroid

The Simillans

For many people a dive trip to Thailand means just one thing – the Koh Similans National Marine Park. This chain of nine tiny islands, 55 nautical miles northwest of Phuket, is ringed by perfect beaches and amazing coral reefs. Visibility rarely drops below 20 metres and can reach mythical proportions. Currents sometimes catch divers unawares but, from November to April, conditions are usually excellent with March and April the calmest.

What makes the Similans so attractive are their two completely different sides. To the east the islands have pure white sand and hard coral gardens that slope gently down to over 30 metres. Colourful soft corals and sea fans are plentiful, the diving is easy and the pace is calm. The west is much more dramatic, with currents that swirl around huge granite boulders creating spectacular swim-throughs. It's a bit like diving between skyscrapers that have been reclaimed by the sea.

It is possible to see and dive the Similans in a long day trip from Phuket, however, the Similans are so beautiful, do yourself a favour and book a liveaboard. It's unlikely you'll want a lot of down time but when you're not diving, you can admire the pristine views or walk on an idyllic, deserted beach.

5 East of Eden

Depth: 28 m
Visibility: good
Currents: usually mild
Dive type: liveaboard
Snorkelling: yes

A sloping reef wall drops to a secondary reef completely encrusted with big fans and rainbows of huge soft corals. Masses of glassy sweepers flit and dance in the light like sparkling stars. Schooling trevally and tuna swim overhead while the upper reef hides plenty of delicate small creatures like ornate ghost pipefish. You can even catch sight of the indigenous Similans sweetlips here. At night, the site re-ignites with all sorts of nocturnal activity. Nestling in almost every crevice you shine a beam onto are cleaner shrimp or tiny pink crabs. Hermit crabs scramble everywhere, arrow crabs poke their noses up from a gorgonian branch. Stay completely still, but divert your beams a little away from the wall, and you'll be rewarded with tiny, shy cuttlefish peeking out from matching crinoids. Heading back uphill to the sandy sea floor, decorator crabs are on the prowl, along with cowries and cone shells. A tiny cockatoo wasp fish may be playing dead in a sandy crevice or a stealthy octopus will wait for the right moment to nip out for a quick meal.

6 Hin Pusar (Elephants Head)

Depth: 40 m
Visibility: good to excellent
Currents: can be strong
Dive type: liveaboard
Snorkelling: yes

The series of unusually shaped granite boulders that reach up from invisible depths and emerge on the western side of the island gave this dive its name. Beneath the water they tumble over each other to form a complex of arches and tunnels. Small fans nestle into crevices for protection from the surge while critters crawl on the sheer rocky surfaces and slither in and out of burrows. Snappers, butterfly and surgeonfish appear in hundreds rather than handfuls. The site can get strong currents as water rushes between the boulders but the action attracts reef sharks, rays and schooling fish. Big guys wander past to check you out then slip away in the flow to see what's behind the next boulder. This is high drama diving at all times.

Similans beach and islands

The indigenous Similans sweetlips

7 Christmas Point

- **Depth**: 25 m
- **Visibility**: excellent
- **Currents**: medium
- **Dive type**: liveaboard
- **Snorkelling**: unlikely

This dive site is just off Koh Bangu, Island number 9. Its scenery is classic Similans – huge, square lumps of rock all tumbling over each other to create a really dramatic dive. The boulders form a series of arches and swim throughs, often washed with lively currents and surges. As you fin through the passageways you encounter an enormous variety of fish that are doing the same thing. There are groups of jacks, fusiliers and red tailed bannerfish. The Similans sweetlips is often caught hiding in a cave away from the surge and blue spotted rays nestle in crevices. The rock walls are coated with small soft corals and sponges and in some channels there are some large sea fans feeding in the currents. Puffers and angels hang around these for shelter. When you exit from the maze to some sand flats you can also spot the occasional whitetip shark, blue ribbon eels – both adult and juvenile – and spotted jawfish.

8 The *Bang Sak* Wreck

- **Depth**: 18 m
- **Visibility**: poor to good
- **Currents**: medium
- **Dive type**: liveaboard/day boat
- **Snorkelling**: unlikely

Like most wrecks, the *Bang Sak* is much more than she appears at first glance. The hull of an old tin dredging boat, she is now a solid square of metal resting on the seabed. She only sank in 1984 so the structure is very well preserved. You can even see some of the mechanical parts like the gear wheels and metal scoops. Visibility can be quite poor, due to the silty surrounds, but it really doesn't matter. Her real value is as a haven for a wealth of tiny critters. Circumnavigating the hull is like a nudibranch treasure hunt – there are more shapes, sizes and colours than you are likely to see elsewhere. While focussing on these diminutive creatures, you also start to notice a whole lot more – estuarine stonefish, tiny flounders on the sand and unusual miniature spindle cowries gripping baby whip coral branches. There are blotched morays in crevices, a honeycomb moray, lots of lionfish and tiny peacock flounders. Of course the wreck is also known for its resident leopard sharks who nestle on the sand and a school of porcupine puffers that hover constantly over the top deck.

Dive flag at sunset

Hans Tibboel and friend

Tales from the deep

Whalesharks at the *Bang Sak* Wreck

April Fool's Day 2004 – we were diving on the small *Bang Sak* Wreck, a favourite spot for critter-lovers. The wreck is literally studded with nudibranchs, lionfish, flounders, schooling porcupinefish (!) and tons of juvenile reef fishes. Because it's fairly shallow, the wreck is an excellent site for nice long and slow dives so both myself and Mark (the other dive guide) were already well over an hour underwater.

I was hovering just above the wreck when suddenly a bunch of large cobias showed up and disappeared again. My heart started beating a bit faster because cobias are often following large animals like mantas or whalesharks. I started to swim in the direction that they had disappeared. I found the cobias again and saw they were followed by a 6-metre whaleshark! I immediately started following the whaleshark and banging my tank to let the divers know that "something big" was happening. I soon heard somebody else banging too and found Mark following yet another whaleshark!

Two whalesharks with lots of cobias circling in very shallow water right above the wreck... but to our surprise none of our divers with them. Mark signalled to me that he would go up and look on the surface for our guests. After 5 minutes or so, still no other divers and no Mark either so I got worried and slowly surfaced as well. To my surprise all divers were already back on board and Mark was trying very hard to get them back in the water but to no avail. They all thought that we were making an April Fool's Day joke and just wouldn't believe it. Only after my surfacing and us both frantically trying to let them know that this was happening for real did our guests decide to get back in the water.

We were lucky enough to have two very relaxed whalesharks for another 90 minutes or so. It was one of those dives I will never ever forget and makes me realize again and again how fortunate I am living, working and diving in a country with such a great variety of marine life. Thailand's diving is always good but sometimes it can just be pretty amazing!

***Hans Tibboel** is Cruise Director on Phuket-based liveaboard,* Ocean Rover.

Surin Islands

Head north from the Similans and just before you hit Burmese waters are a chain of islands formed by a series of enormous underwater pinnacles. The jungle-covered granite outcrops of Koh Bon, Koh Tachai and Koh Surin are a designated national park and enveloped by excellent reefs and prolific marine life.

The islands of the Koh Surin National Park are exposed to deep ocean currents so there are frequent pelagic sightings. All sorts of sharks, manta rays and schooling barracuda are regular visitors. At the end of this string, and just 20 km from Surin, is the dive site that has it all – Richelieu Rock. In fact, if the gods are smiling on you and your dive buddies, this could be the one do-not-miss dive of your life. But, in diving, nothing is ever guaranteed.

9 Koh Bon, The Pinnacle

Depth: 35 m +
Visibility: poor to good
Current: generally strong
Dive type: liveaboard
Snorkelling: unlikely

The water around Koh Bon can be gloomy from suspended plankton. The sharp sided pinnacle rises up from who knows where to about 20 metres. All the rocky surfaces are smothered with yellow soft corals, clusters of golden toned fans and surrounded by yellow snappers. The effect of the sunny hues in amongst the deep, dark water is rather surreal. Leopard sharks often rest on a ledge while just off in the blue are mingled schools of batfish and jacks. There could be as many as two hundred; perhaps more. The water can be as thick with fish as it is with plankton. The soup attracts a mass of animals to feed and it is a marvellous sight. Unfortunately, hovering at such depth for too long isn't all that wise and a safety stop on a nearby shallow reef is required. Although it will be hard to drag yourself away, you may be rewarded with a manta. They often make appearances, swimming swiftly through the small channel between the pinnacle and the nearby reef, no doubt attracted by the seasonal smørgasbord.

10 Koh Tachai

Depth: 35m +
Visibility: good
Current: generally strong
Dive type: liveaboard
Snorkelling: unlikely

Southeast of the island lies a submerged reef made up of hard corals and scattered boulders. As the currents are swift here, a mooring rope leads down to where it's possible to shelter from the currents. At the bottom a resident school of batfish hover around a cleaning station. An unusual carpet anemone protects porcelain crabs and eggshell shrimp (these have white spots down the insides of their transparent bodies). On the boulders just below masses of swooping jacks, trevally and mackerel nip in and out to feed on glassy sweepers. And to complete the complement of pelagic fish, a massive shoal of chevron barracuda swirl constantly above the pinnacle.

Bluering angelfish

Temperatures rising

Diving in the Andamans
It may seem a long way from Thailand but inquisitive dive operators are now heading to the far side of the Andaman Sea – to the Andaman Islands. Actually part of India, sea access to this remote group is easiest from Phuket although sailings are not being scheduled regularly – yet. The latest news though is that the Barefoot Group (www.barefootindia.com) have opened two new eco-resorts and the owners have wisely arranged a weekly charter from Bangkok. This could be the start of something big.

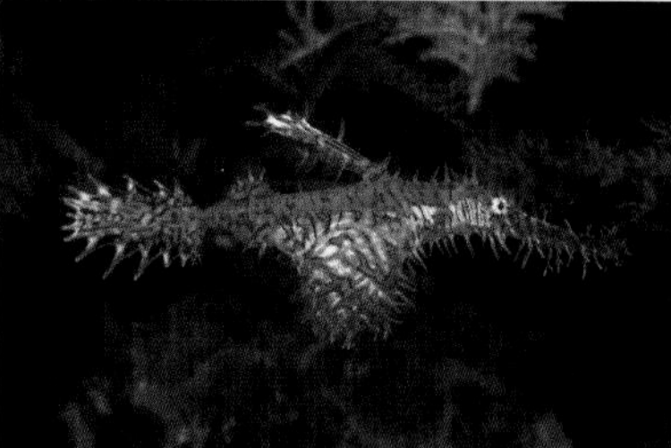

Ornate ghost pipefish on Richelieu

Hermit crab investigating some coral

Blue spotted ray on the sea floor

On a single dive we saw minute harlequin shrimp pairs and four enormous whalesharks, two curious turtles and several elegant seahorses. Not to mention masses of morays, giant groupers, nudibranchs, ghost pipefish, schooling snappers... the list could go on and on. Suffice it to say, you could spend days here and still not see everything the Rock has to offer.

Tales from the deep

A first for everything

There were so many firsts: our first time in Thailand, first time on a liveaboard and the first time I'd achieved a lifelong ambition. To set the scene, I'm half way through a glorious morning dive with my head down a crevice trying to position my camera for a shot of two delightful harlequin shrimp when I felt this hand grab my ankle. As I turn around, all my buddies are screaming, pointing and most of all grinning and I soon realise why. A most beautiful, seven-metre long whaleshark is gliding over our heads. I knew they were sometimes seen on The Rock, but never in my wildest dreams did I think it would happen for me. It was definitely a 'Dom Perignon' moment.

Andrew Perkins, Telford, UK

11 Richelieu Rock

- **Depth**: 32 m
- **Visibility**: medium to stunning
- **Current**: None to strong
- **Dive type**: liveaboard
- **Snorkelling**: on calm days only

The idea of describing the splendour that is Richelieu Rock in a paragraph or two is more than a challenge, it's nigh on impossible. This isolated, submerged hill is without doubt the dive site that has it all. From the tiniest of tiny critters to the ultimate in grace, size and beauty: the whaleshark. Entering over the top of the rock it's worth heading straight down to the base where there are masses of healthy, colourful soft corals and several enormous groupers. Back on the slopes there is a wealth of smaller creatures to admire: lionfish, seasnakes, cowries and trumpetfish, beautiful soft corals, angels and butterflies, seahorses, scorpionfish, white-eyed morays, clownfish, mantis shrimp, turtles, potato cod, reef sharks, barracuda, snappers and mantas. Every surface seems to house yet another fascinating resident.

But at all times, keep an ear out for the sounds of manic tank banging. This is the signal that a whaleshark has been seen and you should make a mad dash towards the sound. When the conditions are right, you may be really lucky and see several in a day. Both adults and juveniles are attracted to the Rock and this is one of the few places in the world where you can still dive with them. Pay them the respect they deserve.

The gentle leopard shark with remora and cobia mates

Mergui Archipelago

These days most liveaboard operators extend their itineraries to include some time amongst the spectacular reefs in the far south of Myanmar – and for good reason. The diving here is superlative. The reefs that abut the border with Thailand are impressive – there are several marine sanctuaries and a wide variety of habitats.

Just a short sail north of Richelieu Rock you cross the border to Kawthaung. A visa is not required but some convoluted formalities take place whilst on board. This includes paying a 'Port & Park fee' of US$150 in clean notes. A local interpreter/guide is installed on the boat, then should you wish to disembark, there is just time enough to admire the dazzling gold temples and local handicrafts, before heading for the Mergui Archipelago, passing some incredible scenery along the way. The reefs are mostly pristine although inshore sites suffer a little from silt run-off and boat traffic. Even so, there is plenty of exciting muck diving to be had just an hour or so from port, though the further out you head the better it gets.

12 Western Rocky

- **Depth**: 25 m
- **Visibility**: good to excellent
- **Current**: none to strong
- **Dive type**: liveaboard
- **Snorkelling**: possibly

How do you improve on diving Richelieu Rock? Simple, sail up to Burma's Western Rocky. This area was closed for quite some time to allow it regenerate. Now it is a site that rivals her nearby Thai neighbour. An enormous submerged pinnacle is ringed by sheer walls that plummet vertically from the surface. The sharp sides are covered in glistening cup corals, crinoids grip onto crevices and there is a splendid cathedral-like arch at the end of the wall. Swimming through it and onto the next segment of wall you are surrounded by masses of stripy snappers. Just beside the main rock is a series of smaller pinnacles that have more walls to explore and reaching them requires passing over the most fantastic fan corals smothered in glassy sweepers. Banded sea snakes investigate tiny caves while porcelain crabs and eggshell shrimp shelter in carpet anemones. Schools of squid take refuge in the lee of a wall and nurse sharks hide in the narrow cave that bisects the rock. You may even be fortunate enough to encounter a young whaleshark here.

Turtle fly-by

Organized shark feeding

Undercurrents

Myanmar: a message from the publishers
The diving in Burmese waters is superb but should divers visit a country with one of the worst human rights records in the world? While many contend that sport and politics should not mix, we feel it necessary to make an exception here. Human rights groups and campaigners, including Aung San Suu Kyi, the Nobel Peace Prize winning, democratically elected leader who is held under house arrest by the government, argue that tourists should not visit the country because this lends moral credence to the regime as well as giving it financial support. Those against a boycott argue that visiting the country gives tourists the chance to financially support the local communities who rely on money from visitors, that international visitors act as a defence against further human rights abuses and that isolating the regime provides no incentive for it to change. Ultimately the decision as to whether or not to visit the country is a personal one. Footprint would advise all potential visitors to make themselves aware of the arguments on both sides in order to make a fully informed decision. For more information visit the Footprint website at: www.footprintbooks.com.

13 Silvertip Bank, Burma Banks

- **Depth**: 35 m +
- **Visibility**: good to excellent
- **Current**: mild to strong
- **Dive type**: liveaboard
- **Snorkelling**: no

It's a great pity that when a site gets well known as the place to see sharks, it also gets a bit too well known to fisherman. A few years ago the Burma Banks were absolutely bereft – not a shark to be seen. However, recently they seemed to have returned. The Banks are a large area that encompass a few different dive sites. The entire plateau is carpeted with small fans and some pretty, soft corals. There's schooling snappers, trevally and several queen triggerfish. The reef edge drops dramatically and if you peer down into the depths you're likely to glimpse some whitetips passing by. Back up on the flat plateau, several species of shark will make irregular appearances – nurses, reef sharks and even large silvertips. They swoop around divers and seem quite curious but slide away just as easily. On occasion, dive crews set up a shark attraction dive. It may not be your thing, but the feed bucket always attracts a few wary young silvertips and the regular star of the show, Max, a resident nurse shark. She now appears to be almost tame but should naturally be treated with respect.

On occasion, dive crews set up a shark attraction dive. It may not be your thing, but the feed bucket always attracts a few wary young silver tips and the regular star of the show, Max, a resident nurse shark. She now appears to be almost tame but should naturally be treated with respect.

14 Three Islets, Burma Banks

- **Depth**: 25 m+
- **Visibility**: 10 to 40 m
- **Current**: medium to strong
- **Dive type**: liveaboard
- **Snorkelling**: unlikely

Also known as Shark Cave, this dive consists of three small islands. The middle one is the largest at 100 metres wide. On the northwest corner a channel is home to a group of grey reef sharks. The walls are covered in tubastrea and small corals while the swift currents entice them out to feed. Outside of the channel, at the base of the rock, is a treasure trove of small creatures like orang-utan crabs and tigertail seahorses. Aggressive mantis shrimp crack open shells on the reef wall while back on the reef slope are long snout pipefish and occasional, destructive crown-of-thorns starfish. Always a sad sight, these are also food for the boxer crabs which shelter beneath.

15 High Rock, One Tree Island

- **Depth**: 35 m
- **Visibility**: fair to good
- **Current**: mild to strong
- **Dive type**: liveaboard
- **Snorkelling**: possibly

There's this rather comical but very pretty rock sitting in the middle of nowhere with a lone tree crowning it. The sheer sides drop below the surface to form a wall on the northeast and a rocky slope on the south-west. Lively currents make it worth sticking close to the reef while hunting out some of the resident critters. For such an open water dive it's odd that small critters seem to grab most of the attention: 25-centimetre long nudibranchs, covered in fronds like a piece of seaweed, intricate ornate ghost pipefish and unusual long snout pipefish. Frogfish hide at the back of fan corals while a seahorse pair, one yellow, one dark brown and heavily pregnant, might be spotted on the finger sponges. Toxic sea urchins with their residents cardinalfish decorate the sea floor.

Swimming with a school of bigeye snapper

Conservation

Whalesharks

Their white spots glimmer at a distance. As they swim towards you, their massive forms take shape. It's a heart stopping moment – your first ever sighting of a whaleshark!

Neither whales nor sharks, these massive fish are the most gentle residents in the sea. They are also the largest, growing to as much as 12 metres long. Whalesharks have no natural predators except, of course, man.

Thailand is one of a few countries that has brought in legislation to protect them but, sadly, illegal hunting continues. The crew of *Ocean Rover* have been logging sightings for some time. After many years of frequent appearances, sometimes as many as 40-50 in a season, the 2000-2001 season only brought one or two sightings. In 2002 this increased to 14, however, by 2004 the count had dropped to just three.

Many people believe this beautiful creature should be protected by international law. Environmental activists are lobbying for the whaleshark to be placed on the CITES Endangered Species list, however, scientific information is patchy and they have not been successful so far.

Koh Samui and the Gulf Islands

There'll be many who feel the Gulf of Thailand deserves more attention, and credit where it's due, there are plenty of reasons to visit this side of the country. The main one being that when the weather is off on the west, it's just delightful here. However, as the east coast is not open to the rigours and influences of the Indian Ocean it has less in the way of prolific reefs.

Koh Samui

Koh Samui is the main tourist island. It's very pretty with an excellent infrastructure and plenty of accommodation on picture-postcard beaches. The reefs around the island tend to be murky but the gentle, shelving beaches are popular spots for taking a course. Once training is underway, most centres take divers to the nearby **Ang Thong National Marine Park** where hidden lagoons and sheer limestone cliffs reflect the beauty of the underwater scenery. Also a good trip for snorkellers, the diving is pleasant but not too challenging.

The Gulf Islands

Ko Tao (Turtle Island) and near neighbour, **Ko Nang Yuan**, have recently become the epicentre of diving in the Gulf of Thailand. The reason is simple. Unlike Samui, where you really need to travel for an hour or more to reach the best sites, these islands have good diving just seconds from the beach. It's an ideal area for beginners and there are many dive centres catering for them.

However, you have to always remember that conditions in the Gulf are highly variable which is why serious divers tend to stick to the west coast. Even in peak season visibility can be as low as 3 metres, but will clear to an incredible 40 metres in an instant.

16 Hin Bai (Sail Rock)

- **Depth**: 30 m
- **Visibility**: fair to good
- **Current**: mild to strong
- **Dive type**: day boat
- **Snorkelling**: for confident swimmers

The most famous dive trip from Samui is Hin Bai or Sail Rock. Jutting out of the water 18 km offshore, and rising from 30 metres to the surface, it is covered in beautiful green and yellow corals and frequented by large marine animals like reef sharks and rays. Most spectacular is the journey upwards through an underwater chimney that is flooded with beams of sunlight. It feels like ascending inside a cathedral spire. The entry point is at

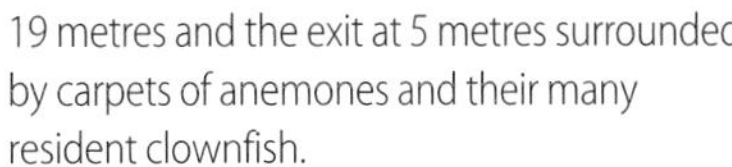

19 metres and the exit at 5 metres surrounded by carpets of anemones and their many resident clownfish.

17 Chumphon Pinnacle

- **Depth**: 36 m
- **Visibility**: fair to stunning
- **Currents**: can be strong
- **Dive type** : day boat
- **Snorkelling**: no

The best dive in this area is undoubtedly Chumphon Pinnacle, where tales of big marine mammals have hit legendary status. A massive granite pinnacle soars from 40 metres to about 16 metres below the surface and is surrounded by a group of smaller ones. Diving here is a bit like a wander through an underwater mountain range. There is a huge variety of life, giant groupers and batfish hover around while white-eyed morays reside amongst the colourful coral gardens. Not only are huge schools of jacks spotted regularly, occasionally sailfish, whalesharks and even whales are, too.

18 White Rock, Koh Nang Yuan

- **Depth**: 23 m
- **Visibility**: fair to good
- **Current**: mild to medium
- **Dive type**: day boat
- **Snorkelling**: yes

Ko Nang Yuan is the only place in the world where three islands are joined together by sandbars. The islands are ringed by a variety of shallow dive sites and there are some beautiful arches to swim through. The most exciting dive is White Rock, actually two submerged granite pinnacles. The site is a great place for finding all sorts of reef creatures, and being quite shallow, makes a good night dive. However, it's main claim to fame is local personality, Trevor, the terrible triggerfish. This giant trigger is a chap with an attitude problem and despite being a permanent resident on a fairly busy dive, has been known to nip unwary divers' fins.

A curious whitemouth moray eel

Drying out

Thailand is a country with lots to do when you're spending that last day gassing off, taking a break mid-trip or if you have a non-diver with you.

Phuket and Krabi

These two centres are an hour's flight south of Bangkok or 90 mins from Singapore. There are more dive centres, hotels and restaurants than you could possibly need, with a huge variety of standards and prices.

Dive centres

EuroDivers, Laguna Beach Resort, Bang Tao Bay, Phuket 83110, T+66 (0)76 324352. They have a central reservations office in Chalong, T+66 (0)76 280814, www.euro-divers.com.
Sea Bees Diving, 1/3 Moo 9 Viset Rd, Ao Chalong, Phuket 83130, T+66 (0)76 381765, www.sea-bees.com. This business has several very professional arms, including a dive centre and resort in Chalong on Phuket and two good value liveaboards, *MV Marco Polo* and *MY Genesis 1*. They also have another resort and dive centre at Khao Lak, an hour or so north of Phuket.
Southeast Asia Divers, PO Box 15, Patong Beach, Phuket 83150, T+66 (0)76 281299, www.phuketdive.net. They have offices in Chalong, Kata Noi Beach and near Patong. Courses up to instructor level.

The Buddha

Ao Nang Divers, Krabi Seaview Resort, 143 Moo 2, Ao Nang, Krabi 81000, T+66 (0)75 637242-45, www.aonang-divers.com.
Aqua Vision,137 Moo 2, Ao Nang, Krabi 81000, T+66 (0)75 637415, www.aqua-vision.net.

Sleeping

Phuket has more places to stay than you can imagine but, as standards change frequently, ask your dive operator for recommendations. Unless you are a serious party animal, avoid the central Patong area.
$$$-$$ **Amari Coral Beach**, Phuket 83150, T+66 (0)76 340106-14, www.amari.com /coralbeach. First-class resort on Patong Beach.
$ **Kata Minta**, 56-58 Moo 2, Patak Rd, Kata Beach, Ao Muang, Phuket 83100, T+66 (0)76 333283-5, www.kataminta.com. Boutique-style hotel just off Kata Beach.
$ **Sea Bees Palm Garden Resort**, 1/3 Moo 9 Viset Rd, Ao Chalong, 83130 Phuket, T+66 (0)76 381765, www.sea-bees.com. Part of Sea-Bees diving. Small and friendly resort near Chalong Bay.

The nicest place to stay in the **Krabi** area is on Ao Nang Beach.
$$-$ **Ao Nang Sea Front Thai Resort**, 273 Moo 2 Beach Rd, Ao Nang, Krabi 81000, T+66 (0)75 637591, www.aonang-thairesort .com. Fantastic location on beautiful Ao Nang.
$$-$ **Krabi Seaview Resort**, 143 Moo 2, Ao Nang, Krabi 81000, T+66 (0)75 637242, www.krabi-seaview.com. European-style hotel and service.
$ **Wannas Place/Andaman SunSet Resort**, 32/1 Moo 2, Ao Nang, 81000 Krabi, T+66 (0)75 637322, www.wannasplace.com. Small, friendly and with a seaside restaurant.

Liveaboards

Ocean Rover, 43/20 Moo 5, Viset Rd, Tambon Rawai, Amphur Muang, Phuket, 83130, T+66 (0)76 281388, www.ocean-rover.com. This luxury liveaboard is probably one of the world's best. Run by highly experienced **Fantasea Divers** the focus is on superb service both in and out of the water. The boat is particularly camera friendly.

MV Anggun, 18/17-18 Chaofa Rd, Moo 8, Chalong Muang, Phuket, T+66 (0)76 381221, www.genesis-liveaboards.com/anggun.htm. Another boat in the luxury class where service is excellent.

Mermaid Liveaboards, 3 Soi Sansabai, Patong Beach, Phuket 83150, T+66 (0)76 341595, www.mermaid-liveaboards.com. Mid-range vessels with a good reputation.

Jonathan Cruiser, Scuba Venture Co. Ltd. 283 Patak Rd, Karon Beach, Phuket 83100, T+66 (0)76 286185, www.jonathan-cruiser.com. Well regarded budget liveaboard.

Eating

Restaurants include stalls in night markets (Patong's is amazing) to 5-star cuisine in the top hotels. The turnover of restaurants is frequent and what was good on one trip may not be the same on the next. For the best, up-to-date recommendations ask your divemaster or, if you like Thai cuisine, just look for the places that have locals in them.

Local agent

Dive The World – Thailand, 210/26 Ratuthid Rd, Patong Beach, Phuket 83150, T+66 (0)76 344736, www.DiveTheWorldThailand.com. A helpful, thorough and extremely knowledgeable agent for all Thai dive centres, accommodation and liveaboards.

Festivals

If you're in Phuket in April you'll catch **Songkran**, the Thai New Year water festival. It is heralded by masses of Thais filling plastic bins with water and ice, driving the streets and ditching it over the unwary. And they do love dousing tourists! The tradition behind this energetic event lies in the cleaning of hands and with that washing away any bad thoughts or actions. Scented water is also poured over the shoulder and slowly down the back while saying good wishes and words of blessing for the coming New Year. Great fun and completely harmless so join in the spirit of the day.

Surface interval

An exotic cuisine ...

As most of your time is likely to be spent on board a floating hotel, chances are you won't get to sample a great variety of Thai restaurants. That's a great shame as this is one of the world's most interesting cuisines. The blends of herbs, spices and fresh produce are continually stimulating. Be adventurous and walk into anywhere that looks appealing - higher prices don't necessarily mean better food, usually just air-con. For some people the quantity of chilli may seem too much, so bear in mind that coconut based dishes will be milder. Seafood, cashews and peanuts figure heavily so allergy sufferers should carry adrenaline if necessary. It's unlikely that you will eat a meal in Thailand that isn't outstanding in some way.

... and great bargains

Retail therapy is a major attraction in all the towns across Southern Thailand. There are boutiques and local markets everywhere, hawkers will even approach you on the beach with T-shirts and sarongs. Generally the quality of textiles is high. Traditional handicrafts are less common in these areas than in other countries but a bit of searching will turn up hand-made umbrellas and wooden carvings from the northern Chang Mai region. Technically, you should not buy buddhas as their export is regarded as illegal. Jewellery is cheap and very pretty but the quality isn't always up to western standards. There are many scams when it comes to gemstones. Unless you know what you are looking at, that may be best avoided. Finally, you can get custom-made wetsuits in Phuket. These are good value and nice quality but ensure you allow enough time for the seamstresses to get the fit exactly right.

Traditional longtail boat returning to Ao Nang

Sights

These two main centres encompass both natural and man-made attractions. And it's all easily accessible – simply head out on your own or arrange a day trip through your hotel or dive centre. Either of these will advise on transport options.

Wat Chalong Temple On the south east outskirts of Phuket Town, this is just one of 29 Buddhist monasteries on the island. Free, but dress modestly.

Khao Sok National Park A few hours' drive north of Phuket this is a protected area of lowland rainforest complete with animal conservation projects and entertainment like canoeing and elephant treks. All inclusive safaris cost US$75 for 1 day or 3 days, US$250.

Koh Tapu Now known as James Bond Island, this is a 15-min boat ride from Krabi and is incredibly pretty but also highly touristy. It's a fun trip all the same. Day tours US$30-35.

Phi Phi If you don't stay on the Phi Phi islands you can always retread Leonardo's steps for a day. Ferry from Phuket is about US$10.

Thalang National Museum Just north of Phuket town, it contains ancient artefacts and exhibits on the famous Battle of Thalang. Entry US$0.70.

The Similans, Surin, Richelieu and Mergui Archipelago

The Similan Islands are 55 nautical miles northwest of Phuket, Surin 110 nm and the Burma Banks, 130 nm. Consequently, this is liveaboard territory with little options for diving this area as a land based trip. Although the Royal Family does have a rather lovely place on Similan No 4, the only public accommodation (also on No 4) is a campground with tents and a few simple bungalows – not really a place for divers toting loads of equipment with them. Likewise, there is limited accommodation on Koh Surin Nua.

Koh Samui and the Gulf Islands

Also an hour from Bangkok and 90 mins from Singapore but directly across the country on the east coast, Koh Samui is the tourist heartland of this region. The busier it gets, the more that tourism on smaller nearby islands grows.

Dive centres

Big Blue Diving Centre, 20/1 Moo 1, Koh Tao, Surat Thani 84280 and also on Samui, T+66 (0)77 456050, www.bigbluediving.com.

Pro Divers, 125/5 Moo 3 Maret, Lamai, Koh Samui, 84310, T+66 (0)77 233399, www.prodivers.nu.

Samui International Diving School, Beach Rd, Chaweng Beach, Chaweng, Koh Samui, 84140 and also on Ko Tao, T+66 (0)77 422386, www.planet-scuba.net.

Nangyuan Island Dive Resort, 46 Moo 1, Koh Tao (Koh Nangyuan), Suratthani, 84280, T+66 (0)77 456088-93, www.nangyuan.com.

Sleeping

$$$ **Poppies Samui Resort**, Chaweng Beach 28/1 Moo 3, T Bophut, Koh Samui, Suratthani 84320, www.poppies-samui.com. Part of the delightful group born in Bali.

$$-$ **Chaweng Cove Resotel**, 17/4 Moo 3 Bophut Chaweng Beach, Koh Samui, Suratthani 84320, T+66 (0)77 422509 www.chawengcove.com.

$ **Koh Tao Cabana**, Sairee Beach Koh Tao, Suratthani, T+66 (0)26 733322, www.koh-tao-palace.com. Great location on Paradise Cape.

$ **Nangyuan Island Dive Resort**, 46 Moo 1, Koh Nangyuan, Suratthani, 84280, T+66

Thai longtail boats moored in the Similans

Chaweng Beach

Water fight at Songkran

(0)77 456088-93, www.nangyuan.com. Idyllic and classy resort.

Eating

On Samui, restaurants litter every beach front and shopping centre. Everywhere is good so make a judgement on who you can see already eating there. On the smaller islands you will probably be limited to your hotel.

Sights

The main attractions of all the pretty Gulf islands tend to be nature orientated – walking, waterfalls, idyllic beaches and so on. However, Koh Samui, which is more heavily populated, has some interesting sites. If time is short, arrange a day tour through your hotel or dive centre.

Wat Phra Yai Nicknamed Big Buddha Temple, this very intricate structure boasts a 12-m high statue and has superb views over the island. At Big Buddha Beach, free.

Wat Khunaram temple A bit of an oddity, this contains a perfectly mummified monk. Near Lamai beach.

Nathon Samui's main town is full to bursting with shops and markets.

Surat Thani To see a working Thai town and the regional capital, catch a ferry from Don Sak (45 km from Samui town). The crossing takes 1½ hrs, US$1.30. This may seem a long day but is worth it in mid-Oct to see the Chak Phra Festival. This is literally 'the procession of hauling the Buddha image'. The lively festival marks the Buddha's return to Earth and local people organize land and waterborne processions including boat races on the Tapi River where traditional long boats are manned by up to 50 oarsmen.

If you fancy watching some Thai kick-boxing, head for the stadium at Chaweng. Ringside seats from US$12.

International agents

Dive Worldwide, 28 Winchester Road, Romsey, Hampshire, SO51 8AA, UK, T+44 (0)845 130 6980, www.diveworldwide.com. Knowledgeable agent based in the UK, will tailor-make Thai holidays.

Surface interval

24 hours in Bangkok

Completely manic, outrageously noisy and charming beyond belief, Thailand's capital is well worth a stopover. Although you could spend a week there, a single day's itinerary will give a taste of the city's best features. Start by taking a 3-wheeled tuk-tuk to the Grand Palace, a superlative example of traditional Thai architecture. Walk to the Chao Praya River, to Tha Chang Pier, and hop a Chao Phraya Express river boat to Wat Arun, the Temple of the Dawn. If you started early, re-embark for a short cruise upriver and back for a local's view of Thai river life then hop off at Thra Phra Arthit jetty. From here you can walk to 'the' place for cheap designer goods, Khao San Road. Restaurants here and along the river are a good lunch option. And finally for a touch of class, taxi to Jim Thompson's House. Credited for creating the silk industry, his home is now an interesting museum.

Sleeping

$$$ **The Peninsula Bangkok**, 333 Charoennakorn Rd, Klongsan, Bangkok 10600, T+66 (0)2 8612888, www.bangkok.peninsula.com. Right on the river for honeymooners and special events.

$$ **Holiday Inn**, 981 Silom Rd, Bangkok 10500, T+66 (0)2 2384300, www.ichotelsgroup.com. Central hotel, with easy airport access.

$ **New World Lodge Hotel**, 2 Samsen Rd, Soi Samsen 2, Banglampoo, Pranakorn, Bangkok 10200, www.newworldlodge.com. Not far from Khao San Road's shopping marvels is this comfy, budget hotel.

Eating

Everything from fast food to top-notch hotel cuisine. Walk into any small restaurant where you see locals eating something good. If the menu is Thai, point at your neighbour's meals.

Transport

Tuk-Tuks are open-air motor tricycles that offer big-thrill rides through the city – great fun but negotiate the price before getting in. Metered taxis are less fun but air-con. The Chao Phraya Express river boats are cheap and stop at all the above places of interest.

Wat Arun on the Chao Praya River, Bangkok

Indonesia

The hitchhiker's guide: riding on a toxic fire urchin, a mating pair of Coleman's shrimp, *Perclimenes colemani*

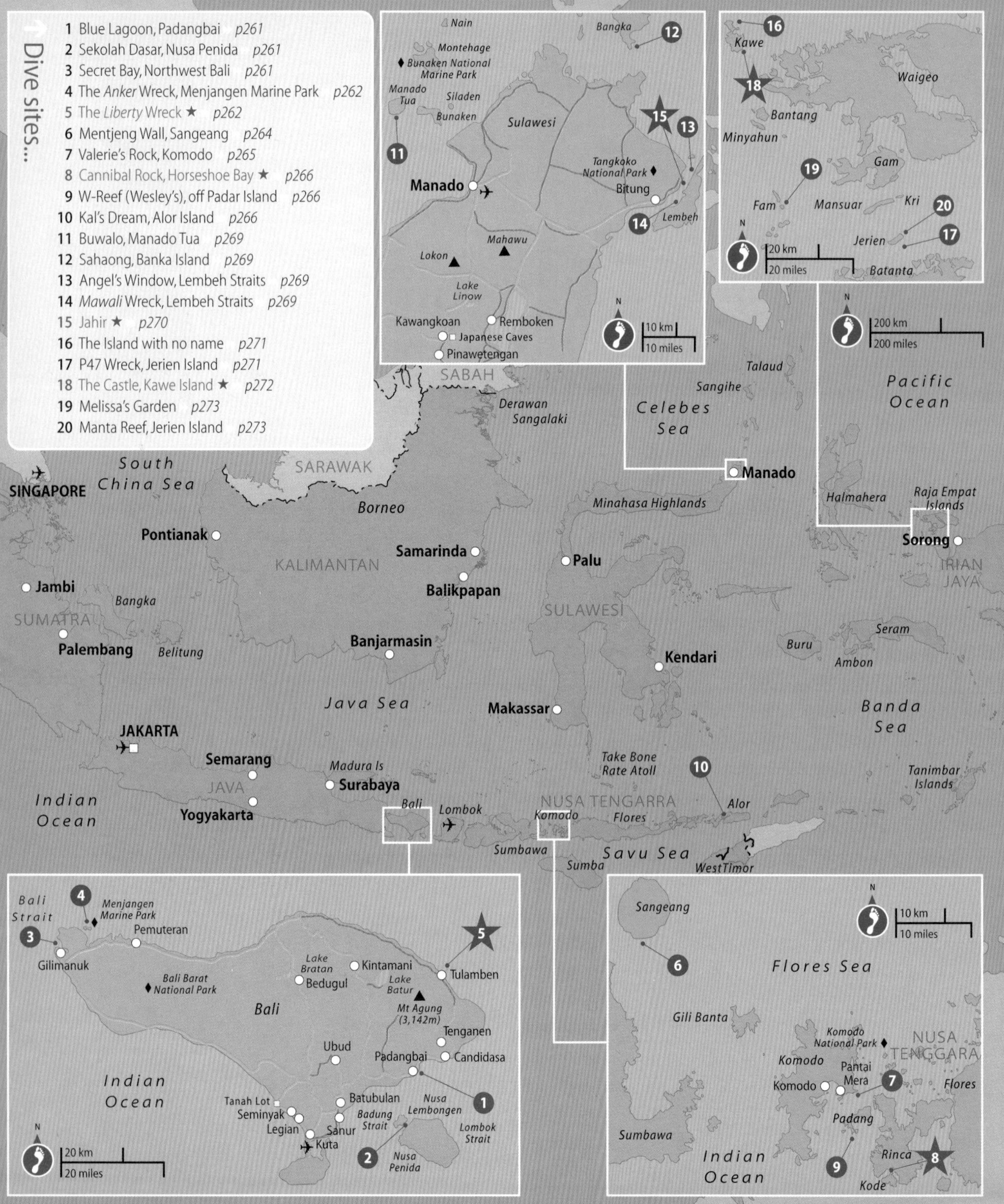
Dive sites...
1 Blue Lagoon, Padangbai p261
2 Sekolah Dasar, Nusa Penida p261
3 Secret Bay, Northwest Bali p261
4 The Anker Wreck, Menjangen Marine Park p262
5 The Liberty Wreck ★ p262
6 Mentjeng Wall, Sangeang p264
7 Valerie's Rock, Komodo p265
8 Cannibal Rock, Horseshoe Bay ★ p266
9 W-Reef (Wesley's), off Padar Island p266
10 Kal's Dream, Alor Island p266
11 Buwalo, Manado Tua p269
12 Sahaong, Banka Island p269
13 Angel's Window, Lembeh Straits p269
14 Mawali Wreck, Lembeh Straits p269
15 Jahir ★ p270
16 The Island with no name p271
17 P47 Wreck, Jerien Island p271
18 The Castle, Kawe Island ★ p272
19 Melissa's Garden p273
20 Manta Reef, Jerien Island p273
Nain
Bangka
Montehage
Bunaken National Marine Park
Manado Tua
Siladen
Bunaken
Sulawesi
Tangkoko National Park
Manado
Bitung
Lembeh
Mahawu
Lokon
Lake Linow
Kawangkoan
Remboken
Japanese Caves
Pinawetengan
10 km
10 miles
Kawe
Waigeo
Bantang
Minyahun
Gam
Fam
Mansuar
Kri
Jerien
Batanta
20 km
20 miles
200 km
200 miles
Pacific Ocean
SABAH
Derawan
Sangalaki
Celebes Sea
Talaud
Sangihe
Manado
SARAWAK
South China Sea
SINGAPORE
Borneo
Minahasa Highlands
Halmahera
Raja Empat Islands
Sorong
IRIAN JAYA
Pontianak
KALIMANTAN
Samarinda
Palu
Balikpapan
Jambi
Bangka
SUMATRA
SULAWESI
Palembang
Belitung
Banjarmasin
Kendari
Buru
Seram
Ambon
Java Sea
Makassar
Banda Sea
JAKARTA
Semarang
Madura Is
Surabaya
Take Bone Rate Atoll
Tanimbar Islands
JAVA
Yogyakarta
Indian Ocean
Bali
Lombok
NUSA TENGGARA
Komodo
Flores
Alor
Sumbawa
Savu Sea
Sumba
West Timor
Bali Strait
Menjangen Marine Park
Pemuteran
Gilimanuk
Bali Barat National Park
Lake Bratan
Bedugul
Kintamani
Lake Batur
Tulamben
Mt Agung (3,142m)
Bali
Tenganen
Ubud
Padangbai
Candidasa
Indian Ocean
Tanah Lot
Seminyak
Legian
Batubulan
Sanur
Kuta
Badung Strait
Nusa Lembongen
Lombok Strait
Nusa Penida
20 km
20 miles
Sangeang
Flores Sea
10 km
10 miles
Gili Banta
Komodo National Park
NUSA TENGGARA
Komodo
Komodo
Pantai Mera
Flores
Padang
Sumbawa
Indian Ocean
Rinca
Kode

Introduction

Sunrise over the mountains reflected in a deep blue bay. A Balinese woman, resplendent in traditional dress, presents her morning offering to the gods. A tiny basket of rice, fruit and flowers is left for the guardian that looks over the sea.

Despite the incredible changes the country has seen in recent years, Indonesia has completely retained her sense of tradition. From peace-loving Bali to the outer reaches of Irian Jaya, this water-bound land is one of the world's most fascinating.

There are countless islands; so many, in fact, that some haven't even been named. Indonesia is the world's largest archipelago, her broad arc forming the southern edge of the Coral Triangle, where the planet's biodiversity rankings are at their highest. Every inch of water has the potential for mesmerizing diving. Some is high powered and adventurous, some just as calm as you could wish for. Animals that are rare elsewhere are common here. No matter what it is you look for, chances are you will find it.

On land there are almost as many cultures, arts, religions and cuisines as there are islands. Diversity is not confined to Indonesia's world beneath the seas.

“” *This diving, this country, it gets in your blood. It becomes a drug that you need to keep taking.*

Indonesia rating

Diving
★★★★★

Dive facilities
★★★★

Accommodation
★★★★★

Down time
★★★★

Value for money
★★★★★

Essentials

Indonesia

Location	5°00' S, 120°00' E
Neighbours	Australia, Malaysia, Philippines, Papua New Guinea
Population	241,973,879
Land area in km^2	11,909,624
Marine area in km^2	3,100,000
Coastline in km	54,716

Getting there and around

Travelling to Indonesia is simplicity itself. International flights arrive from almost everywhere although European and American flights usually stop once on route. Carriers include **Singapore Airlines** (www.singaporeair.com.sg), **Qantas**, **United**, **Eva**, **Malaysian** and **Thai**. **Garuda**, the national carrier, is not such a good option as their flights stop more than once. Singapore is the closest transfer point for long-haul travellers. The city also makes a great stopover (see page 273) and, as airports go, Singapore's Changi is one of the best. There's free entertainment and internet, on-site hotels and even a swimming pool so routing this way adds that little extra to your trip. Along with their regional airline, **Silk Air** (www.silkair.com), Singapore Airlines can deposit divers almost anywhere they need to be. They fly to Manado, Jakarta, Bali and even tiny Lombok. There are also a couple of regional alternatives: **Australian Airlines** (www.australianairlines.com.au) connect all Australian state capitals with Bali and **Air Asia** (www.airasia.com) have recently put Bali and Jakarta on their network.

There are plenty of internal travel options: this country has a large population that requires cheap transport and lots of it. There are masses of ferries as well as smaller airlines covering domestic routes. The best are **Garuda** (www.garuda-indonesia.com) and **Merpati** (www.merpati.co.id), but don't be surprised if your operator books you onto a little-known airline that may only have a few specialized routes. As long as you have pre-booked a package, transfers from the airport will be included. If not, taxis are very reasonably priced and are usually metered.

If you fancy a day or two to explore, you can either ask your dive centre or hotel to arrange a driver and van or just wander up the road until someone asks if you would like transport. "Transport, mister?" is one of Indonesia's universal sayings. You'll hear it along every street, on the beach or in a restaurant. It's the way a lot of people earn a living and, providing you set a price first, you're unlikely to have any problems.

Language

There are many languages across Indonesia but education policies have ensured the national language, Bahasa Indonesia, is spoken everywhere. It's fairly easy to learn and grammar and pronunciation are straightforward. The only confusing issue is getting to grips with the variations within a simple saying – the way you say hello varies by the clock!

good morning (until 1100)	*selamat pagi*
good day (until 1500)	*selamat siang*
good afternoon (until dusk)	*selamat sore*
good evening	*selamat malam*
welcome	*selamat datang*
goodbye (if leaving ...)	*selamat tinggal*
... and if you are staying	*selamat jalan*
yes	*ya*
no	*tidak*
please	*tolong*
thank you	*terima kasih*
sorry	*ma'af*
how much is ...	*berapa harganya ...*
you're welcome	*kembali*
good	*bagus*
great dive!	*menyelam yang bagus!*
one beer/water	*satu bir/air*

Local laws and customs

There are many and varied religions across Indonesia, which makes it difficult to define a behavioural pattern for tourists. Anywhere divers are likely to go will be 'tourist tolerant' but take local advice if you are unsure. Indonesia is mainly Muslim but has strong Buddhist, Hindu, Christian and Animist communities. Indonesia's own version of Islam is strongly influenced by these others, which in turn influence each other. The religion most people encounter is Balinese Agama Hinduism which is not the same as Indian Hinduism. Its calming presence is strongly felt in day-to-day life.

Safety

Indonesia has experienced more than its fair share of trouble and strife over recent years. Terrorist actions, natural disasters and racial tensions in out-of-the-way regions have all hit the headlines and created a mood of concern. Before planning a trip take advice from those on the ground (your travel agent, dive centre or hotel) and check your government's travel advisory website.

That said, however, crimes against tourists are rare, except in highly populated towns which have been affected by an economic nosedive. Sadly, it is budget travellers who bear the brunt of this as they tend to use public transport and stay in cheaper, less secure accommodation. Divers travelling to a suitable resort and using private transport are unlikely to encounter trouble. If you are out at night take only what you need and keep valuables concealed. Lone women should be aware of the mixed message they are sending to a society that regards sexual openness as taboo, yet is inundated with Western culture that promotes sex as a selling tool.

Health

Divers are unlikely to fall ill, other than a case of traveller's tummy. Many hotels have purified tap water or supply bottled. There are plenty of medical facilities but these vary depending on the relative wealth of a particular locality. Medical consultations are costly for locals and many simply can't afford it. For a visitor, a trip to the doctor can be an interesting experience. Your hotel will supply a translator who, along with the doctor, giggles at the colour of your skin before handing over a bag of pills and inviting you in for a cup of tea with the family. Rest assured that most doctors are Singapore or Malay trained and know their stuff. It's just a communication problem. After all this entertainment, you might like to donate a little extra to help a local family.

Costs

Of all Southeast Asia's destinations Indonesia consistently provides the best value for money. You can spend a fortune on an all-singing all-dancing hotel room with private pool and maid, but it will still be only half of what it would cost elsewhere. There is a huge variety of accommodation, from modern to traditional; a small, simple bungalow will be as little as US$20, but spend around US$60 and you can have a palace. Food is much the same; you can enjoy a delightful meal in a small, local restaurant on Kuta Beach for under US$10 or visit an ultra-trendy affair a mile along the bay and pay up to US$100. Drinking is cheap too; a large bottle of the local brew, Bintang, will be a dollar or so, a bit more in the resorts. Tipping is the done thing and, when deciding how much, bear in mind that salaries are very low here. As costs are low by Western standards you can afford to be generous. For dive crews, see page 14.

Airlines (all in Bali) → Singapore/Silk Air T+62 (0)361 768388, Eva T+62 (0)361 756488, Qantas T+62 (0)361 289281, Garuda T+62 (0)361 254747, Malaysian T+62 (0)351 288716, Merpati T+62 (0)361 751374. **Embassies** (all in Bali) → UK T+62 (0)361 270601; USA T+62 (0)361 233605; AUS/NZ T+62 (0)361 235092. **Indonesia country code** → +62. **IDD code** → 001. **Police** → 110.

Fact file

International flights	Singapore Airlines/Silk Air
Departure tax	International 50,000 rupiah, domestic 11,000 rupiah
Entry	Visas required for most nationalities, US$25 on entry
Internal flights	Garuda or Merpati
Ground transport	Plenty but use private rather than public
Money	10,000 rupiah = US$1
Language	Bahasa Indonesia, English is widely spoken
Electricity	220v/110v
Time zone	GMT + 8 (Bali/Manado) GMT + 9 (Irian Jaya)
Religion	Muslim, Hindu, Christian, Animist

Giant frogfish in a sponge

Dive brief

Diving

The Indonesian archipelago consists of an estimated 17,000 islands stretching east to west over 5000 km. These sit ringed by five different seas and include around 18% of the world's coral reefs, so you can take it for granted that there is some pretty impressive diving here. The incredible variety of dive regions is only outdone by the number of dive sites at each.

A couple of decades ago there was little in the way of formal dive facilities but that is no longer the case. Areas that are easy to get to, like Bali and Manado, have plenty of professional dive operations, while some of the more distant areas require a liveaboard and an adventurous spirit.

Dive styles vary region by region and sea by sea. The islands of southern Nusa Tenggara, for example, are affected by cooler, deep water upwellings from the Indian Ocean while the northern Lembeh Straits are characterized by protected, nutrient-rich waters fed by ancient volcanic activity. Wherever you decide to go, it is most important to know that this country is regarded as the world's most biodiverse marine environment. A recent survey recorded the Raja Empat islands as having 950 species of fish, 450 corals and 600 molluscs. Four new fish species and seven new corals were discovered and the area is being proposed as another World Heritage Site.

Bottom time

- **Bali** A microcosm of Indonesian dive styles – wrecks and reefs, large and small creatures » *p260*
- **Komodo and Nusa Tenggara** High drama and challenging conditions surround this World Heritage Site » *p263*
- **Manado** The Bunaken Marine Park and neighbouring islands are relatively untouched » *p268*
- **Lembeh Straits** The ultimate marine nursery and a photographer's mecca » *p268*
- **Irian Jaya** An unexplored region with the planet's highest numbers of coral and fish » *p271*

Snorkelling

With so many coral reefs the options for snorkelling are endless. Balinese beaches have reefs that reach right into shallow protected bays. The tiny Gili Islands north of Lombok are a favoured haunt as is Bunaken Island off Manado. More adventurous dive regions will have fewer snorkel options as currents can be strong. That shouldn't put non-divers off though as all good liveaboards ensure tenders stay over dive sites whenever someone is in the water.

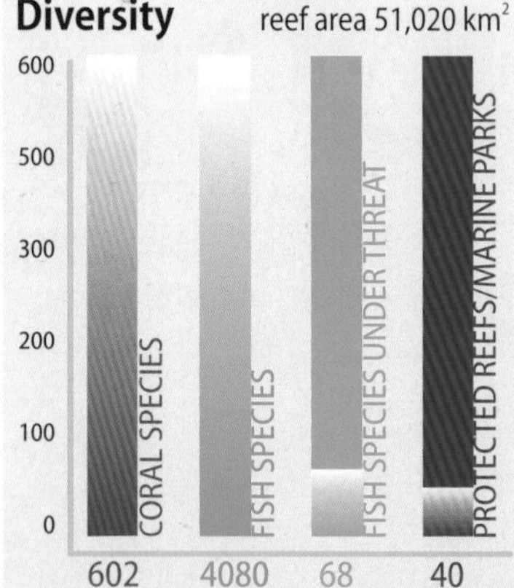

How many fish and corals?

> If there was only one country in the world we could go to, Indonesia would be it. We have seen it develop and change; we have been there in both peaceful and troubled times and we still love it the most. There is something about the people and their incredible integrity that keeps it at the centre of our affections. On the dive side, well, you just can't beat it. Every season there is something fresh – a new region opens, an old one goes out of favour only to bounce back a little later. This is an ever-changing, never static, marine environment.

The big decision

There are so many wonderful dive destinations in Indonesia that choosing between them can be a quite an effort. Geography doesn't help as, generally, the diving is year round. For those who haven't been to Indonesia before, it is probably worth considering what else you might do when out of the water. If you want nightlife and culture, Bali has it all. If you want to do nothing more than stare at the view then head for Manado or Lembeh. For non-stop diving try a Komodo or Irian Jaya liveaboard. The other pointer will be what you like to see. Descriptions of the unique features of just a few regions follow but there are many more in less accessible areas. It all depends on how adventurous you are.

Buddy line

Reef hooks rule

Everyone knows how delicate corals are, how the slightest touch can destroy years of growth, how even a tiny kick can break a brittle staghorn. And there's that terrible sinking feeling when you get caught in a current and hear that crack, knowing that you have accidentally broken something. However, there are times when the ocean has its own way; currents pull and push and just staying still becomes a safety issue. That's when a reef hook comes into its own. Many purists have criticized their inclusion in a diver's kit but it's a comparative issue. The small surface area of the hook tucked under a rock or some dead coral minimizes damage – it's a lot less than a hand – and allows divers to inflate their jackets and hang in the current safely.

Dive data

Seasons	May-September, SE monsoon (dryer); November-March, NW monsoon (wetter)
Visibility	5 metres inshore to infinity in open water
Temperatures	Air 19-36°C; water 23-32°C
Wet suit	3mm full body suit, add 2 mm extra for Komodo in spring/autumn
Training	Courses available in Bali, Manado and most resorts. Look for PADI 5-star (or equivalent) training agencies
Nitrox	Freely available on land. Most liveaboards also carry it but quantities may be limited. Pre-booking advised
Deco chambers	Bali, Manado, Jakarta, Singapore

It's all about disguise: a longnose hawkfish in hiding

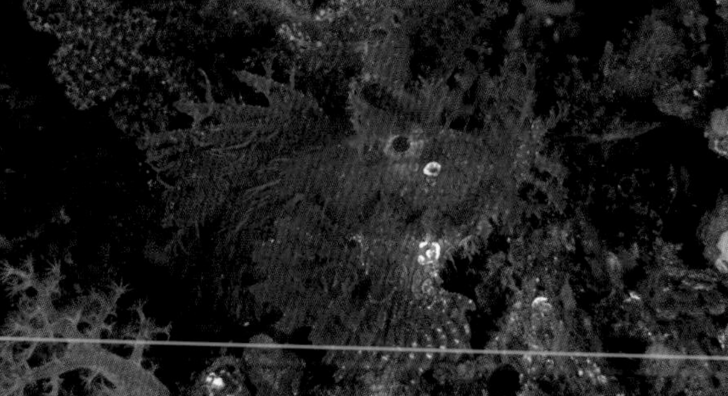

A rare *rhinopias frondosa* dressed up as soft coral

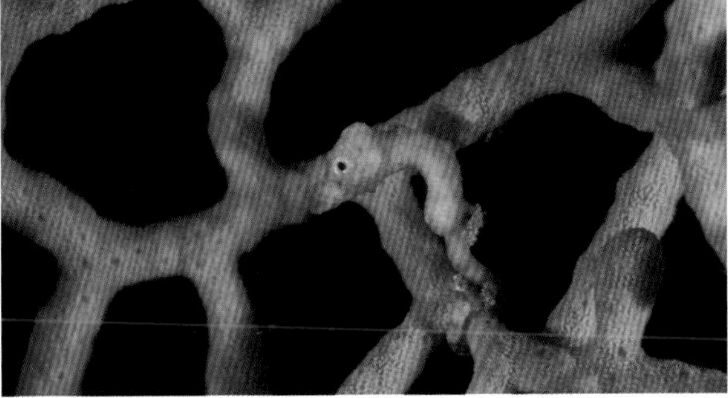

And the world's smallest seahorse (*hippocampus denise*) as a fan coral

Tulamben
Jemeluk
Padangbai
Candidasa
Nusa Penida
Secret Bay
Menjangan
Puri Jati

2 361 730107 · fax: +62 361 735368

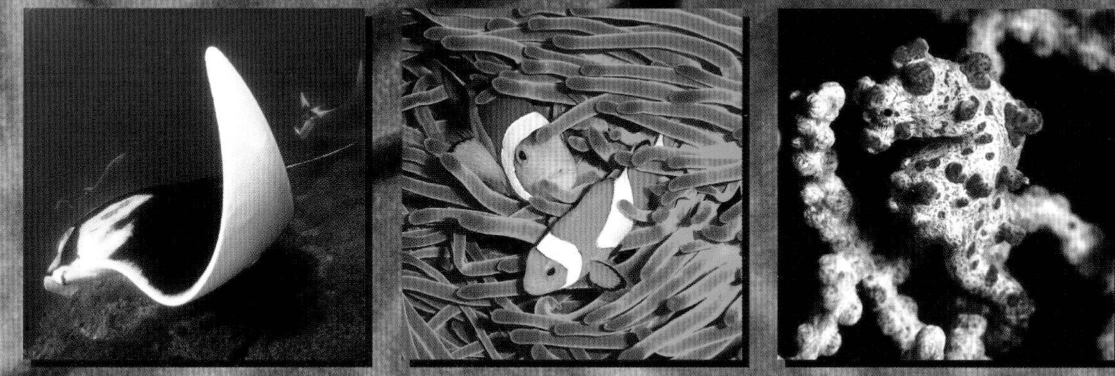

AquaMarine
Diving - BALI
dive the diversity of
BALI
PADI
INTERNATIONAL RESORT ASSOCIATION
GOLD PALM RESORT
R 6344
GO ECO
explore conserve observe
www.projectaware.org
Go ECO Operators - We are committed to environmentally responsible business practices and to providing our customers with dive experiences that enhance visitor awareness of our local aquatic environment.
Photographs courtesy of James Fatherree & Will Postlethwaite.

Bali

This tiny volcanic island is one of the world's most stunning. Even the Balinese call their home the 'Island of the Gods'. The combination of a balmy climate, unique culture, delightful people and great diving all adds up to one supremely good dive destination. Strangely, the island is often overlooked by divers who use it as a staging post to head to more distant marine parks, yet Bali's fringing reefs are too good to miss.

Bali is a vaguely triangular shape and has three different coastal environments. The southwestern shore leads straight into the Indian Ocean; the beaches are white sand and surfers arrive in droves to catch the best wave action. This is the most popular tourist area. The airport is nearby and lively Kuta and Legian beaches are riddled with shops, bars, restaurants and every type of hotel you could wish for. Although there's no diving right here, there are dive centres that organize courses and day trips across the island.

The southeastern coast is quieter with just one tourist centre, Sanur. There are plenty of facilities here too but it's not quite so manic. Offshore are fringing coral reefs and several islands but the far south is still affected by currents and surf. As you head north, the reefs improve and at the island's easternmost point – underneath mighty, active Mount Agung – they are flourishing. The rich nutrients supplied by volcanic soil ensure that all marine life thrives in these conditions. The peaceful little towns of Candidasa, northeast of Sanur, and Tulamben, due north from Candidasa on the northeast coast, both make an ideal base for divers. Tulamben is the location of Bali's most famous dive, the *Liberty*. From Candidasa too you can reach the wreck easily, as well as all the dive sites along this section of coast, or you can head across to do the drift dives off Nusa Penida island in the Lombok Channel.

Heading around the top edge of Bali, to the northern shore, the environment is a little mixed. The soil here is volcanic too, but less dark. The small and extremely shallow bays attract many fascinating, unusual creatures which are regarded as the ultimate by underwater photographers. The offshore islands of the Menjangen Marine Park are superlative with deep walls and clear water. The towns up here are much less touristy; a reminder of how the island was 20 years ago.

Imperial shrimp on a sea cucumber

The wreck of the *Liberty*

1 Blue Lagoon, Padangbai

- **Depth**: 22 m
- **Visibility**: fair to good
- **Currents**: slight
- **Dive type**: day boat
- **Snorkelling**: yes

Padangbai (Bay) is actually the ferry port for Lombok, the next island to the east. Here there is a group of dive sites across several bays and some offshore rocky outcrops. Blue Lagoon, just north of the main bay, has a pale, sandy seabed, interspersed with small patches of hard coral. These are havens for the animals living on or beneath them: they are always surrounded with small fish and one bommie usually has a whole gang of leaffish on it – pink, white, brown and green. There are plenty of nudibranchs on the sand along with black ribbon eels, tiny juvenile sweetlips, masses of blue spot rays and stonefish. This has also recently been noted as a residential area for the rare and unusual rhinopias. This, the least well known of the scorpionfish family, is currently getting a lot of attention as many new species are being discovered.

2 Sekolah Dasar, Nusa Penida

- **Depth**: 35 m
- **Visibility**: good
- **Currents**: can be ripping
- **Dive type**: day boat
- **Snorkelling**: possibly

Across the Badung Strait from Bali, the dives around Penida and her sister isles, Nusa Lembongen and Nusa Ceningan, are renowned for fierce currents and the big stuff they attract. These dives are always strong drifts and, as the current can pick up at any moment, they aren't suitable for novices. Much of the reef scenery is quite flat. The reef slopes gently down to a wall where there are some very large barrel sponges and few nice fans. Hard corals form a flat carpet across the topography although there is some damage – from the currents more than anything else. Tuna, jacks, mackerel and turtles are seen fairly often. One of the most popular sections of reef is at Sekolah Dasar (primary school) where the highlights are just as likely to be small: orang-utan crabs, porcelain crabs, clownfish on anemones and mantis shrimp.

3 Secret Bay, northwest Bali

- **Depth**: 10 m
- **Visibility**: poor
- **Currents**: mild
- **Dive type**: shore
- **Snorkelling**: yes, but poor visibility

Just beside Gilimanuk harbour, where enormous ferries depart for Java, is a shallow bay which has entered the realms of dive legend. The sand is pale and fine so it's easy to stir it up, the depth is under 12 metres and the seabed is protected by an offshore reef. The currents that sweep up the narrow Bali Strait are funnelled into the cove, bringing all sorts of animals. Some start life here as plankton then grow and breed in the protected environment. There is little in the way of corals – just old detritus: branches, cans and other rubbish interspersed with patches of seagrass and algae – a classic muck dive. There are iridescent gold seahorses living on a rotting tree branch, lots of filefish and puffers, juvenile batfish, many colourful and unusual nudibranchs and maybe an octopus squeezing its way into a can or coconut shell. Really lucky divers might spot the lime green Ambon scorpionfish, a very small and hairy member of this family with lacy wings.

Scrawled filefish are shy

Mating *hypselodoris bullockii* nudibranchs and egg ring

Yellow leaf scorpionfish stay motionless

Tigertail seahorses hide in rubble

4 *Anker* Wreck, Menjangen Marine Park

- **Depth**: 45 m
- **Visibility**: fair to stunning
- **Currents**: mild
- **Dive type**: day boat
- **Snorkelling**: yes, over the wall

Anker is the name of a local beer but this wreck has nothing to do with the brew: it's said to be an old slave boat. The wooden hull sits on a gentle, sandy slope at around 40 metres. There is little left to see as the timbers have decayed almost beyond recognition, but they are heavily encrusted with beautiful soft corals and small fans. The surrounds are thick with barrel sponges and flitting fish. On the gradual ascent back up and along the wall, more fans and whip corals grow from cracks and crevices in the reef until you reach shallow beds of hard corals with masses of swarming fish.

Tales from the deep

The Duck's Tail

While I would have preferred to have fallen in love with somewhere called The Island of the Sleeping Dragon, or similar, in fact, my absolute favourite Balinese dive site is the small crescent-shaped island of Gili Biaha on Bali's east coast. The Balinese call it Likuan, Duck's Tail, which is, I admit, quite cute. The surge can be less than cute, however.

Biaha is just north of Amuk Bay, an area with some of Bali's most stunning diving. I have encountered vast numbers and great diversity of fish, abundant sharks and frequent pelagic visitors, all set against a backdrop of chiselled black walls with beautiful, healthy corals and often superb visibility.

The island is surrounded by a remarkably healthy reef with a rocky slope on the north and a wall in the south. This rugged black wall, with breaking waves above, is utterly beautiful in places. At times it is almost as if the fish are superfluous – but not quite! I adore the schools of red-toothed triggerfish and it was here that I saw what must be the world's coolest fish, a bearded soapfish.

Where else can you see juvenile emperor angelfish, blue ringed octopus, rare nudibranchs and frogfish on the same dive as 3.5-metre mola-molas (oceanic sunfish)? There is also a cave in which whitetip reef sharks sleep. The protected area outside the cave is home to anglerfish, leaf scorpionfish, octopus and cuttlefish, and sometimes takes up my entire dive.

Annabel Thomas is British and owns AquaMarine Diving, Bali

5 The *Liberty* Wreck

- **Depth**: 30 m
- **Visibility**: fair to stunning
- **Currents**: slight to medium
- **Dive type**: shore
- **Snorkelling**: yes

The *Liberty* is part of diver folklore. Just 30 metres from shore is the broken hull of a Second World War US supply ship. Torpedoed in 1941 by a Japanese submarine, she lay beached for 20 years before Mount Agung erupted and pushed her down the sloping seabed where she broke up. Now, she is one of the best artificial reefs you will ever see. Divers come from all over the island to wander along the pebble-strewn beach then slide into the water. Visibility varies depending on the season and run-off from the nearby river mouth but, even when it's low, the dive is magnificent. As you fin towards the hull you pass the resident oriental sweetlips, then the wreck materializes from the blue. There are jacks swirling above, large Napoleon wrasse in amongst them and, on rare occasions, magnificent mola-mola are seen. The superstructure is thick with corals, sponges, fans and crinoids surrounded by lots of fish and although you can't penetrate the structure you can see guns, toilets, boilers and the anchor chain. Right at the bottom are some gorgonians that are known to have pygmy seahorses on them. There are also leaffish, dragonets and more nudibranchs than you thought possible in one dive. The bay to the side of the wreck is equally interesting. The black sand slope drops gently to 15 metres or so before heading into deeper waters. There are small patches of coral, sponges and anemones plus plenty of detritus. Ornate ghost pipefish shelter in crinoids and even blue ringed octopus can be caught prowling about. At the eastern end of the bay, the sand slope leads to a short wall that has basket sponges and gorgonians with longnose hawkfish in residence.

“ ” A trip to Bali with no dive on the wreck is simply not an option.

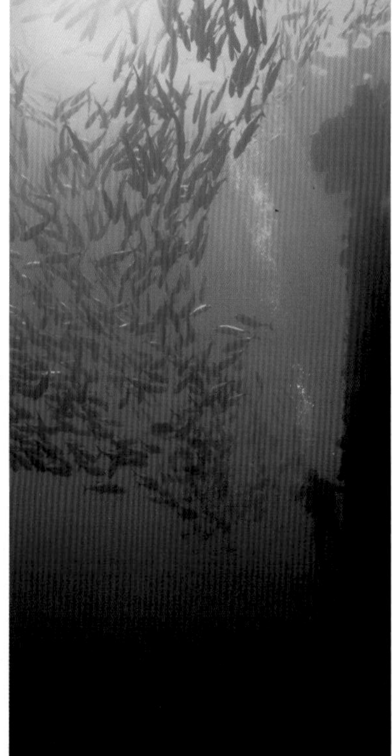

A school of spinning jacks resides over the *Liberty*

Komodo and Nusa Tenggara

A long chain of islands stretches east from Bali, ending eventually at Timor. The most famous of these is tiny Komodo, home of the world's largest – and most offensive – lizard and now a World Heritage Site and National Marine Park. Other islands are sometimes forgotten in the rush to reach Komodo, yet the entire chain encompasses one of the planet's most interesting geological features.

A century ago, British naturalist and explorer Alfred Russel Wallace travelled through these remote islands and recognised an invisible line that divides the region. This became scientifically acknowledged as the 'Wallace Line' and separates Bali from neighbouring Lombok. The Lombok Strait is the deepest channel in the region. To its west, the islands are tropical Asian; to the east they more closely resemble arid Australia.

The lushness of Bali's shorelines contrasts strongly with landscapes further east. By the time you reach Komodo you find brown hills and sparse foliage. Not a typical view of the tropics yet majestic all the same. Many visitors come only to see the famous Komodo dragon, a 4-metre-long monitor lizard and one of the ugliest creatures on the planet.

However, diving around these islands couldn't be more appealing. The reefs are spectacular, with a mixture of large and small animals on every dive. It must be noted though, that this is some of the most challenging diving in Indonesia. As the chain's position separates the Indian Ocean from the Java Sea, currents are unpredictable. At times they can be a rapid drift or toss you about like a washing machine. What's more, cold water upwellings can be breathtaking. It's not like that all year but the harder conditions often correlate with the best animal spotting seasons.

Further east is Flores, a Christian island that hosts another unique inland feature, the three coloured lakes of Keli Mutu. Back on the coast, the diving is less than pristine due to a tsunami and earthquake in the early 1990s but many liveaboards pass this way to reach Alor. This furthest outpost has steep walls, unexplored reefs and some famed adrenaline-rush dives.

This whole region is best travelled by liveaboard. Although there is some land-based diving, the best sites can only be reached by boat. It's unlikely that you will have some of the better sites completely to yourself as this area is big business with many liveaboards plying the route.

Banggai cardinalfish

A proliferation of fish, sponges and corals

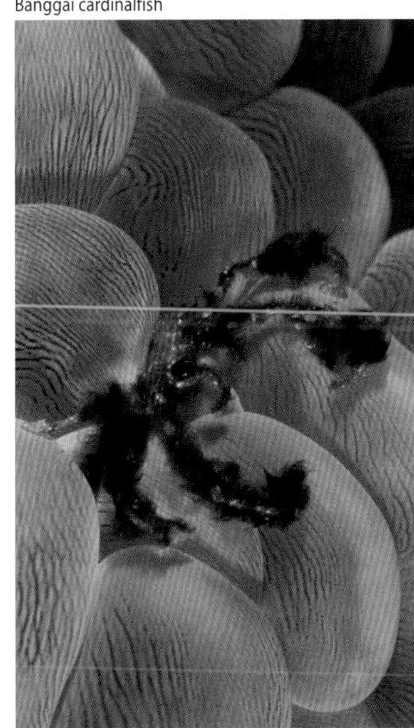

The hairy orang-utan crab

Tales from the deep

Kararu's fable

Kararu was named after the Indonesian word for minke whale. It was rumoured that a minke whale nursery existed within the borders of the Komodo National Park. So this seemed like a good name for our new company. In the seven years of diving the area the location of the nursery remains a mystery. But we have some stories. Recently, in the middle of July, we were hosting a group of very well-to-do English families with numerous children ranging in age from young to teen. They had very little experience of diving and we were conducting, a rarity for Kararu, some discovery courses onboard. Dawn is always dramatic in this area. With a warm croissant and hot mug of thick black Javanese coffee in hand I was gazing out to sea when I spotted what were undeniably whale spouts in the entrance to the bay where we were anchored. With the determination of a recently appointed scoutmaster I gathered up the guests and we hopped into the tenders to see if we could snorkel with the pod of what I believed to be the fabled Kararu. The Kararu remain a fable; for what we discovered were a pod of 12 sperm whales, mothers with calves. This I later discovered accounted for the forward angled spouts. They were extremely inquisitive. We spent most of the morning snorkelling with them and shooting video. With reluctance we returned to the vessel for refreshments and recuperation. When we looked out on the horizon we saw the last tail breach the water as the pod dived. Nevertheless, all who experienced the encounter agreed that Kararu might be named after the mystical minke whale but the sperm whale had our vote for now.

Tony Rhodes is the English owner of Kararu Dive Voyages, based in Bali

6 Mentjeng Wall, Sangeang

- **Depth**: 21 m
- **Visibility**: good
- **Currents**: none or strong
- **Dive type**: liveaboard
- **Snorkelling**: possibly

Liveaboards sail from Bali towards Komodo making a couple of stops en route. One is at tiny Sangeang Island. On her southern point is a small, nondescript beach that disguises a fantastic dive site. The shallow bay has good coverage of hard and soft corals and plenty of small fish. However, the real interest lies in the wall off to one side where there are curiosities like colonial anemones. The wall bottoms out at around 20 metres into a black sand seabed. Around the base of the wall are crinoids with ghost pipefish, sponges with crabs, sea whips with gobies and shrimp. There are frogfish, saron shrimp and, for the eagle-eyed, boxer crabs under small rocks, but the biggest attraction here are all the nudibranchs, nicknamed 'butterflies of the sea'. At the last count, nearly 40 different species had been logged on a single dive.

Razorfish disguised as sea grass

Weird slipper lobster

Whip corals sprouting towards the sun

7 Valerie's Rock, Komodo

- **Depth**: 28 m
- **Visibility**: good
- **Currents**: mild to ripping
- **Dive type**: liveaboard
- **Snorkelling**: possibly

This pinnacle is just off Pantai Mera – Pink Beach – and not far from the entrance to the Komodo National Park. It is rumoured to be named after Valerie Taylor. The shallow bay encloses a sloping reef and a tower of rock that rises from just under 30 metres to reach the surface at low tide. It seems like perfection from the dive boat but once in the water you will experience Komodo at its most temperamental. Temperatures can drop from the previous dive's comfortable 28°C to a brain-numbing 20°C. The currents can rip and if you're not careful you're over the site and out the other side before the rest of the group has even managed to enter. At other times, however, it can be the most impeccable dive in the world: calm, warm water and all sorts of weird and wonderful creatures such as leaffish, scorpionfish and sea hares. Bits of detritus turn out to be solar-powered nudibranchs and even the pretty stuff that makes an appearance is worth being careful over – you can see toxic sea urchins here. You might even see a dozen mobula rays sail over your head – provided you're looking up at the time, of course.

Bobtail squid

Temperatures rising

With such a broad spectrum of islands and seas in this one country there is always a new area gaining favour, even as another loses it. In addition to the sites reviewed here there is good diving off Kalimantan (Indonesian Borneo) from both Derawan and Sangalaki Islands. The very impressive Sangihe-Talaud group leads north from Manado to the Philippines, while from the south of Sulawesi there is access to the Take Bone Rate Atoll, Indonesia's largest. The best diving here is available from popular but pricey Wakatobi Resort. The Banda Sea is another magnificent area that was closed for much of the late 1990s due to localized civil and religious disturbances, but is now calm and reopening to dive tourism.

Kararu sailing through Raja Empat

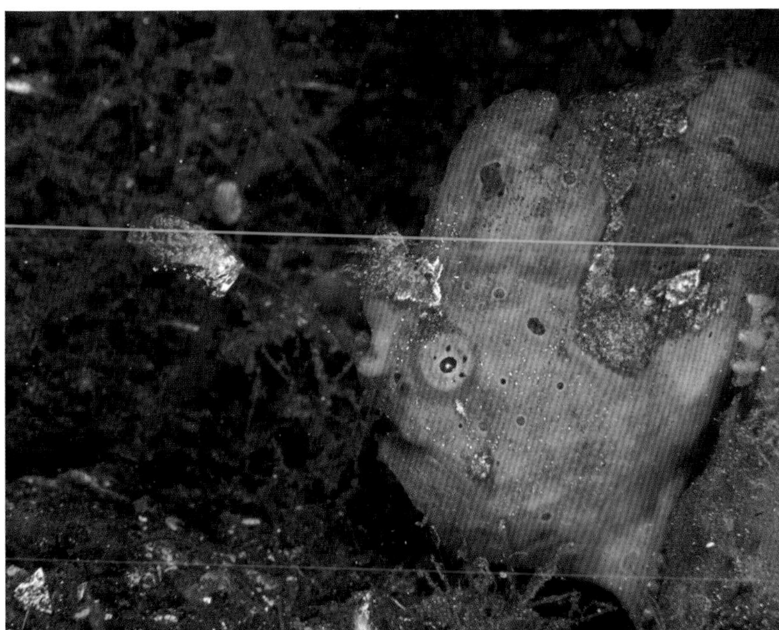

A frog (or angler) fish using his lure to fish

8 Cannibal Rock, Horseshoe Bay

Depth: 40 m
Visibility: poor to good
Currents: can be strong
Dive type: liveaboard
Snorkelling: yes

Horseshoe Bay is within the Komodo Marine Park, at its most southerly point. Nestled between Rinca Island and Nusa Kode, the bay is now world famous for its incredible diversity. You name any small critter and it's bound to have been seen here. There are several dive sites but Cannibal Rock is perhaps the most famous for its all-round variety. The site is a sloping, submerged mound smothered in soft corals, olive green tubastrea corals, many-coloured crinoids and iridescent sea apples. A member of the sea cucumber family, these round balls bear a vague resemblance to red apples until they poke their tentacles out to feed. They are extremely rare elsewhere. Amongst the corals you can see frogfish, mushroom coral pipefish, seasnakes and orang-utan crabs. A lot of the more bizarre life is at great depth so it's easy to go into deco if you're not careful. Pygmy seahorses are seen on pink fans at 32 metres and toxic sea urchins cluster on the slopes beyond 30 metres, harbouring both Colmans shrimp and zebra crabs. Night dives are another treat, where every tiny crustacean seems to come out and show itself. There is some pelagic life here too but visibility is variable so you may only see passing tuna. Minke whales are said to pass through the bay: you might only see a fin or fluke, but you'll certainly hear them calling.

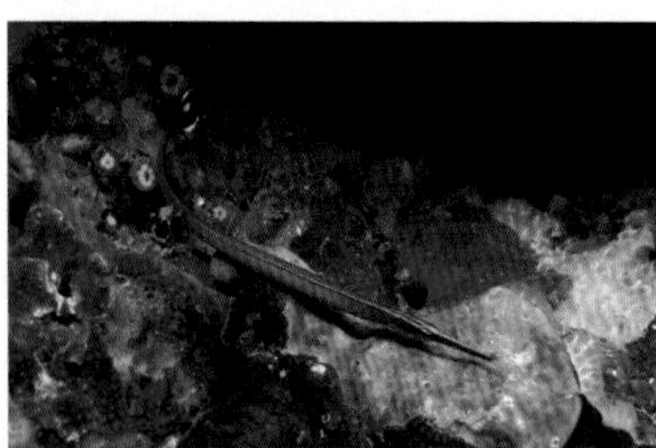
A *doryrhamphus janssi* pipefish

9 W-Reef (Wesley's), off Padar Island

Depth: 20 m
Visibility: poor to fair
Currents: medium
Dive type: liveaboard
Snorkelling: unlikely

Named after one of Indonesia's finest sea captains, W-Reef is a series of three long, oval shaped underwater pinnacles that run parallel to each other and almost break the surface. Their positioning makes for a fantastic zig-zag swim between each of the channels they create. Every surface is painted with colour and the life on the pinnacle walls is almost as diverse as at Cannibal Rock. There's a small cave jam-packed with lionfish, anthias dance in every crevice and moray eels poke about. Small creatures include orang-utan crabs, imperial shrimp on cucumbers, mating nudibranchs and clown frogfish, though it's hard to keep your eyes down and focussed on them with gangs of huge tuna passing overhead, giant barracuda watching from their safe haven in the surge just below the surface and manta rays flitting by.

Spot the crinoid shrimp in the crinoid

10 Kal's Dream, Alor Island

Depth: 26 m
Visibility: excellent
Currents: medium to rip-your-mask-off
Dive type: liveaboard
Snorkelling: definitely not

Because Alor is the chain's furthest destination, it goes in and out of favour with liveaboard operators. This is something of a pity as it's a great area: remote and unspoiled. If you make it that far you won't be jostling for space with several other dive boats. The variety of diving here is as impressive as Komodo, although diversity is perhaps a bit lower. The most famous dive is Kal's' Dream, a heart-thumping, jaw-dropping rush of big animals in fearsome currents. The site sits smack bang in the middle of the open water between Alor and Pura islands. The dive-masters mostly look down at the swirling eddies and say 'no way' but when the tides are just right, you can drop to the top of the pinnacle. Dives often start peacefully and you get the chance to spot mantis shrimp, moray eels, barramundi cod and some large groupers while siting in the lee of the pinnacle. When the currents start to lift you crawl up the side, hook on in the flow and wait for the action to start. Grey reef sharks move in to accompany the fusiliers, triggers and surgeonfish, as do whitetips, tuna and schooling snapper. Sometimes you might see barracuda, or even a hammerhead. After watching the show for a while, ascent is a slightly risky game of releasing your hook from the rocks and ensuring you don't fly to the surface.

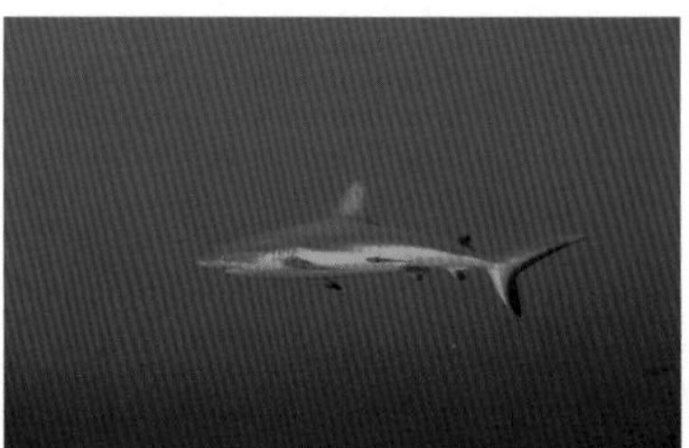
One of Kal's grey reef sharks

Dropping down further and further on this vertical wall, the water is beyond crystal-clear. Sunlight illuminates the reef's jewel-like colours, sparkling more brightly than you could ever imagine …

Northern Sulawesi – Manado and the Lembeh Straits

The bizarrely shaped island of Sulawesi sits centrally in the Indonesian archipelago but it's the far northern arm reaching towards the Philippines that has captured the hearts and minds of both scientists and divers. Way up on this narrow stretch of land are two destinations that offer the most incredible diving. Their styles are diametrically opposed and complement each other perfectly.

The entire island is ringed with reef systems so it may seem odd that most diving centres around northern Manado. However, there is good reason why Manado Bay, her small offshore islands and the coast that leads around to the Lembeh Straits have all become diving hotspots.

Scientists believe that this area probably contains the greatest degree of biodiversity in the world and is the heart of the Coral Triangle. Although research isn't conclusive, exceptionally high levels of certain species have been noted. There are communities of extremely rare animals and even evidence of living coelacanths which, until 1938, were thought to be extinct .

The Bunaken Marine Park encompasses four islands, Manado Tua, Montehage, Nain and Siladen. The reefs are relatively untouched despite the area being so busy. This is due partly to the steep wall formations that drop rapidly to deep water and partly to their protected status. The diving is varied with open plateaux, some muck diving and even a wreck. The coastal suburbs of Manado City have several good resorts where accommodation and dive operator standards are high. There are also resorts on the islands themselves which have a charming, castaway feel.

Outside the marine park, and in more open ocean currents, the diving at Bangka Island is particularly good and can still be accessed by day boat. However, the destination that draws most is the narrow and dark Lembeh Straits which have become a 'must' for marine biology enthusiasts and underwater photographers. With Sulawesi to the west and Lembeh Island on the east, the narrow channel between is riddled with dive sites fed by rich, volcanic nutrients. This is by no means pretty diving; visibility is always low, but it is one of the few places where you can be guaranteed sightings of some of the world's most unusual animals. You really can say 'seahorse' to a divemaster and they will ask "What type?" Although muck diving made the area's reputation there is also some nice wall diving and a couple of Second World War wrecks. For many years there was just one resort but, with the growing popularity of dive tourism, there are now several first-class resorts.

Undercurrents

Current patterns
Indonesian diving is marked by its incredibly complex sea conditions. In some countries currents are strong but straightforward; a dive becomes a drift and you drop in and go with the flow. Here it's not so simple. The archipelago sits on the Equator and is subject to weather and wind patterns from both hemispheres. It is also affected by deep oceanic currents from both the Indian and Pacific Oceans. Add several seas to the mix and you stand even less chance of predicting what will happen underwater. Tidal range is just the usual 1 to 3 metres, but the flow of these tides past so many islands adds to the unpredictability. Surprisingly though, the seas are not all that rough.

A decorative spider crab – really

11 Buwalo, Manado Tua

Depth: 35 m+
Visibility: fair to good
Currents: mild to strong
Dive type: day boat/liveaboard
Snorkelling: unlikely

Dormant volcano Manado Tua dominates the skyline as you look out from the shore. Its steeply sloping sides slip beneath the surface, then drop off to great depths. This site, on the southern edge, is typical of many of the marine park dives but, as it faces out to sea, it also attracts some bigger pelagic species. A narrow, flat segment of reef descends to a wall covered in hard and soft corals, fans and sponges. It's a riot of colour as these species compete for space with tunicates and crinoids. Every nook and cranny has a nudibranch, clownfish or coral banded shrimp; there are even leaffish and frogfish. If you can bear to look away from the wall there are turtles and seasnakes. Reef sharks patrol the deeper waters and eagle rays are seen in the distance. Back in the shallows, gas off while admiring blue ribbon eels, fire and dart gobies.

12 Sahaong, Bangka Island

Depth: 33 m
Visibility: good
Currents: generally strong
Dive type: day boat/liveaboard
Snorkelling: unlikely

As this site is in the open waters just north of Sulawesi the visibility is better. When you drop into the water you encounter a semicircular slope that leads to a set of pinnacles breaking the surface. There is a phenomenal number of schooling fish; barracuda, jacks, rainbow runners and fusiliers darken the water. Soft corals, in the most gorgeous orange tones, plaster every surface – really a delightful sight. The current dances a bit up and down the wall; midnight snappers sway in the blue as whitetip sharks buzz around them. A tiny fan coral houses a pygmy seahorse and there are plenty of morays hiding around the table corals.

13 Angel's Window, Lembeh Straits

Depth: 25 m
Visibility: fair
Currents: slight to strong
Dive type: day boat/liveaboard
Snorkelling: unlikely

The Lembeh Straits are mostly macro-orientated but there are several good wall dives at the northern end. This is one of the prettiest and is actually a pinnacle with a wall on one side. It is broken by a short swim through at 25 metres that leads around the base and back up a sandy slope. The cave is quite small with little inside but a few fin strokes brings you out beside some red fans that host both the barbiganti pygmy and denise pygmy seahorses. Coming back up the slope, there are leaffish, clusters of squid eggs on the sand, orang-utan crabs, imperial shrimp on cucumbers and some red whip corals. Around a bend, the reef drops back to a small wall and ends in a rocky section covered in sergeant majors defending their eggs against the onslaught of butterflyfish.

A commensal 'magnificent' shrimp on a snake eel

14 *Mawali* Wreck, Lembeh Straits

Depth: 35 m
Visibility: poor to fair
Currents: slight to strong
Dive type: day boat/liveaboard
Snorkelling: no

Just five minutes south from the dive resorts, this wreck is a sunken Second World War Japanese freighter. She lies on her side constantly washed by nutrient-rich tides and is beautifully encrusted with crinoids, black coral trees and soft corals. Some hard corals have grown on the structure, facing into the current, and around these hover an enormous number of fish – lionfish in particular. As you drop over the side, passing fans that thrive in the currents, you can peek inside the old holds. There is little inside apart from fish – but plenty of them – and it can get very murky when exhaust bubbles disturb the silt. Outside, a group of adult batfish will be nosing around, attracted by the activity. Moray eels hide in crevices and, as you ascend back over the hull, you'll spot everything from tiny pipefish and nudibranchs to scorpionfish and cuttlefish.

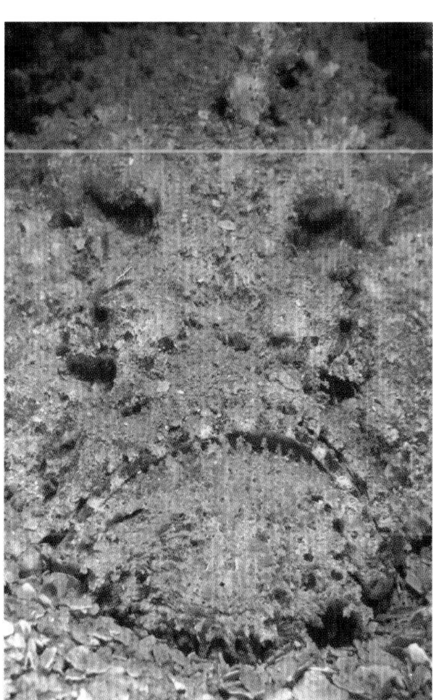

Practising being ugly, a stonefish

15 Jahir

- **Depth**: 15 m
- **Visibility**: poor to fair
- **Currents**: none to slight
- **Dive type**: day boat/liveaboard
- **Snorkelling**: yes

Much of what's great about Lembeh can be summed up by a muck dive such as this. This is one of the divemasters' favourites (the name is made up of the initials of those who found it) and is one amazing dive. It's a fabulous hop from one 'pet critter' to the next; so much so that sometimes Lembeh dive site logs look like a fish ID list. Here is the one from Jahir: cockatoo waspfish, juvenile cuttlefish, juvenile scorpionfish, dwarf scorpions, tiny stonefish, thorny seahorses, mating swimming crabs, hairy crabs, decorator crabs, flying gurnards, flounder, frogfish in several colours and varieties, *Inimicus* (devilfish), robust ghost pipefish and fingered dragonets. All these are seen regularly and most in a single dive. At night the site really come into its own as you see creatures you met earlier plus nocturnal ones that have emerged – free-swimming snake eels, moon snails and tiny shells trucking across the sand – plus there are a few special events. This is a known nursery site for flamboyant cuttlefish. They lay their eggs inside discarded coconut shells and you can see newly laid eggs: even sometimes a just-hatched baby. This is also a good spot for the mimic octopus. As you catch it in a torch beam it will go into party-trick mode and become a flounder, a crinoid or a snake eel.

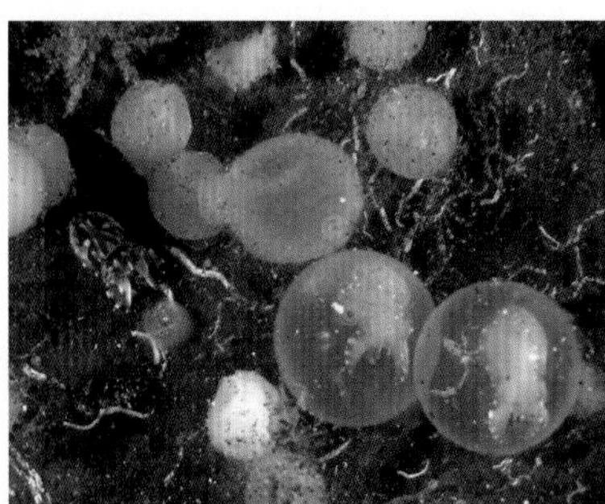

A just-born flamboyant beside egg cases

Entering the water you glance down at the barren black sand and wonder what you are doing there. Then a few seconds later you notice a creature trying to be something else. Then another. Then more and more, until it all turns into critter overload.

Mimic octopus in a not-quite-sure moment

Irian Jaya

The newest region to come under diving scrutiny is the western end of New Guinea. Also known as West Papua and Irian Jaya, the islands and waters here are as remote as anywhere can be, yet surprisingly easy to reach. The reefs were surveyed a couple of years back by a group of Australian scientists whose research registered the world's highest counts of corals, molluscs and crustaceans. Not long after their reports hit the press a whole new dive industry developed.

To get to Irian Jaya you fly into tiny Sorong, whose Jefman Airport could best be described as endearing. The long strip runway is just that. You pass through a few huts while the crew collect your bags then walk to the water's edge where your liveaboard awaits. The city itself is a boat ride away and, by all accounts, well worth missing.

Once you are out on the water you will see just how unpopulated the area is. Most islands are limestone and there is little natural water. The people who live here tend to be seafaring and remain fairly close to Sorong. All this is good news for divers. The corals are pristine and the quantity of tropical fish is outstanding. Most diving – so far – is in the Raja Empat Islands, where clouds of fish are so thick you can barely see through them. On some dives you can count 14 different corals in a patch just a metre square. Larger animals are less common: turtles and sharks are wary and stay away from noisy divers' bubbles, though there are several manta cleaning stations. The wrecks of two Second World War planes are found here and no doubt others will be discovered as more time is spent in the area. Conditions are generally easy with good visibility and consistent water temperatures. Strong currents are comparatively rare but they can pick up at short notice so it's sometimes necessary to slip into the lee of a site to avoid them. At present there are just two small resorts but several liveaboards visit in specific seasons.

16 The island with no name

Depth: 32 m
Visibility: good
Currents: mild
Dive type: liveaboard
Snorkelling: possibly

Just a few feet from the Equator is this incredibly beautiful island which, surprisingly, has no name. The dive site starts on a steep wall and at its base there is a deep cave to explore. At the rear are flame fire shells that reveal an electric current running through their tentacles. Back out on the wall a tiny fan houses the denise pygmy seahorse. The wall itself is smooth sided with sponges, some crusting algae and tiny corals. It flattens to a ridge beneath the limestone cliff where the rocky topography is fairly barren. Amongst the boulders are some unusual creatures like Paguritta hermit crabs and blue ringed octopus. This dive can be done at night, when the wall comes alive with nocturnal crustaceans and nudibranchs. Psychedelic bobtail squid nestle on the wall beside decorator crabs. It's easy to enter the cave accidentally so be careful! Back on the top, cuttlefish feed in the shallower waters.

Batfish on sentry duty

17 P47 Wreck, Jerien Island

Depth: 35 m+
Visibility: good to stunning
Currents: mild
Dive type: liveaboard/day boat
Snorkelling: no

On 2 October, 1944 two American fighter squadrons, 310 and 311, took off from their base at Noemfoor Island near the city of Biak. Their mission was to attack a Japanese fleet thought to be near Ambon Bay but, on arrival, they discovered that the reports had been misleading. After strafing a few enemy craft they decided to return to the closest base: 310 Squadron landed at Middleburg but 311 Squadron was caught in bad weather; they flew until they ran out of fuel and were forced to ditch near Jerien Island. All seven crew were rescued. There are now two plane wrecks sitting on the base of the reef; one belonged to flight leader, Steven O'Benner (P47D-21), the second was element leader Kenneth J Crepeau's (P47D-16) although no one is sure which is which. One is deeper and not easily accessible, while the other is upside down at 30 metres. It is virtually intact and covered in light coral growth.

One of the P47 wrecks

Tales from the deep

Passage of Time

Beads of sweat formed on my brow as I peered through the dense foliage. I glimpsed exotic birds as they unfurled brilliantly coloured wings; bird-sized spiders lay in wait on webs that sparkled in the noonday sun. I readied my camera, took my last breath of fresh air, and stepped off the boat into the swirling waters that marked the beginning of The Passage.

This must be one of the world's coolest dive sites, a 20-metre-wide passage, literally separating Gam and Waigeo islands. The Passage is best when the current is running. And on this day it was. Limited visibility made dodging the large boulders that lay scattered along the bottom tricky. But the shallow depths ensured enough light penetrated the murky water for me to navigate past schools of bumphead parrotfish and sergeant majors. Unfortunately, despite my best intentions, I'd become separated from the group. I finned steadily out from the centre of the narrow channel, and popped up to take my bearings.

Large branches spread out over the edge of the water, dropping leaves and flowers intermittently in the current. Spitting archerfish lurked near the surface, while nudibranchs proliferated amongst the ascidians that lined the bottom. The walls were festooned in gigantic orange sponges, and big sea fans grew to within inches of the waterline.

I continued along the edge, taking care to keep out of the eddies that threatened to carry me bodily back to the centre of the passage. I found a single cavern, dark stalactites hanging down, green vines draped on the ceiling like some party banners. Further exploration led to another cavern, where a single shaft of light penetrated the rock enclosure. I swam over to the light, gently kneeled down in the folds of silt and looked up into the sky.

David Espinosa, Editor, Scuba Diver Australasia

Wobbegong sharks have tasseled skin and blend in with their surroundings

18 The Castle, Kawe Island

- **Depth**: 32 m
- **Visibility**: good
- **Currents**: mild
- **Dive type**: liveaboard
- **Snorkelling**: possibly

This truly amazing site had not been named in 2004. The circular, perfectly straight-sided bommie is shaped by sharp, forbidding walls that rise above you like battlements. A deep gouge cuts through the outcrop from one side to the other and is filled with midnight snappers and surgeonfish. At the mouth of this tunnel is a bright pink fan with a whole family of pygmy seahorses on it. Descending to the base, a complete circuit reveals a cave with a tiny exit higher up the wall. Schooling batfish patrol on one side like sentries and masses of small fish cower in the black coral bushes. The sheer walls are tempered by pastel soft corals and colourful crinoids, nudibranchs, marbled dragonets and flatworms. Another sharp knife cut in the wall is packed full of red soldierfish and a lone barramundi cod. A saddle leads to a smaller satellite pinnacle off to the northwest side. This rises up to about 15 metres and has less soft coral cover but more and larger black coral bushes. Napoleon wrasse hover out in the blue with several titan triggers and schools of snapper.

There was no doubt in our minds that we were diving around an ancient castle, complete with a drawbridge and a dungeon, battlements and a keep.

19 Melissa's Garden

Depth: 25 m
Visibility: good
Currents: mild, strong patches
Dive type: liveaboard/day boat
Snorkelling: for confident swimmers

This long oval reef complex has a flat top and sloping sides. At one end are two submerged pinnacles that rise up almost to the surface. The entire reef is covered in hard coral outcrops interspersed with small soft corals, masses of crinoids and fish. This is one of those places where you feel you are in fish soup; there are so many schooling fish hanging around and the sandy bottom is smothered in garden eels. When you get closer to the two small pinnacles, the currents are stronger but the life is cracking: big snapper and sweetlips, masses of anthias, sergeant majors, damsels, butterflies and young batfish up in the blue. Their parents hover under a hard coral head nearby. As you swing back into the lee of the pinnacles there are octopus and several feeding seasnakes, imperial shrimp, mushroom coral pipefish and the juvenile rockmover wrasse. Peaceful, well-camouflaged wobbegong sharks lift up from the corals when disturbed, then resettle onto the reef. Tuna pass by out in the blue with whitetips, a turtle and a school of small barracuda.

20 Manta Reef, Jerien Island

Depth: 8 m
Visibility: good to stunning
Currents: medium to strong
Dive type: liveaboard/day boat
Snorkelling: no

As the boat approaches this reef the crew watch for wing flaps and the race is on to see if there are mantas, frequently seen around this submerged plateau. As you drop into the water the smaller ones are flying right beneath the dive tender. The current here rips across the plateau, pulling divers away from the entry point in the same direction as the mantas. There is little coral so the strategy is to find some dead rock and use a reef hook to stay still. Waiting for just a few minutes is usually enough for them to come back. Larger ones will sit still, feeding in the current (no hooks required by them). You can creep closer but need to be cautious as these animals are still wary of visitors. At certain times of year you can even spot pregnant mothers.

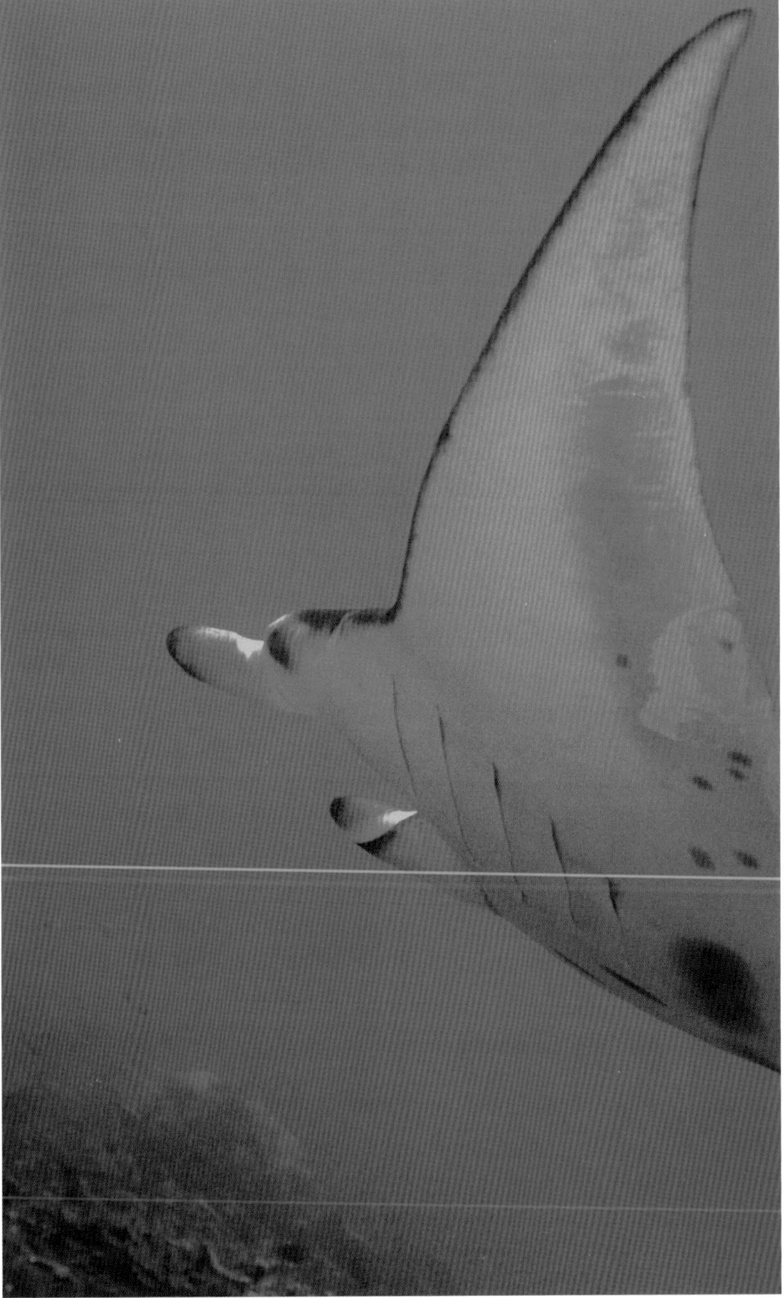

Manta swooping in to a cleaning station

Drying out

Bali

Dive centres

There are many dive centres across Bali. Each targets specific nationalities, particularly the Japanese. Others are general watersports companies. Standards vary so make enquiries with other divers if you are unsure.

AquaMarine Diving – Bali, Jl Raya Seminyak 2A, Kuta, T+62 (0)361 730107, www.aquamarinediving.com. Bali's only British owned and managed dive shop with first-class service, great dive guides and full client insurance. Organizes accommodation and dive packages plus tailor-made land excursions.

Crystal Divers, Jl Duyung No 25, Sanur, T+62 (0)361 286737, www.crystal-divers.com. Run by two Danish ex-pat women, friendly outfit located in the heart of Sanur.

Skubaskool, Jl Dyanapura/Abimanyu No 9, Seminyak, T+62 (0)361 733845, www.skubaskool.com. Small, charming dive centre with courses in French and English plus island-wide diving trips.

Sleeping

There is accommodation at every level right across the island. Many resorts have several grades of room to choose from. Those below are listed clockwise around the island, starting at Kuta.

$$$$–$$ **Patra Bali Resort and Villas**, Jl Ir H Juanda, South Kuta Beach, 80361, T+62 (0)361 751161, www.patra-jasa.com. A fabulous, international-standard resort just a few minutes from the airport but not at all noisy. Luxury garden villas with private pools or spacious 2-roomed suites.

$ **Poppies Cottages**, Poppies Gang 1, Kuta, T+62 (0)361 751059, www.poppiesbali.com. The original Balinese resort right in the heart of lively Kuta. Charming, traditional bungalows sit in even prettier gardens. Great value.

$$$ **The Elysian**, Jl Sari Dewi N18, Seminyak, 80361, T+62 (0)361 730999, www.theelysian.com. At the far end of the Kuta-Seminyak beach strip, 20 minutes from the airport. Quiet location just back from the beach but near many higher-end facilities. Modern Balinese-style villa complex. Each house has a private pool.

$$$–$ **Taman Sari Bali Cottages**, Pemuteran Bay, northwest Bali, T+62 (0)362 94755, www.balitamansari.com. A garden hotel with simple budget bungalows to high-end villas with Balinese antique furniture. Really great restaurant on site.

$$ **Mimpi Resorts**, Tulamben and Menjangen, www.mimpi.com. The Tulamben location was the original divers' resort and sits right on the beach near the *Liberty* wreck. A little cramped but a great location. The newer **Menjangen Resort** is on Banyuwedang Bay opposite the national park. Both resorts have on-site dive centres and good restaurants.

Lush green paddy fields in Bali

Surface interval

24 hours in Singapore

Southeast Asia's Lion City is an amazing place to acclimatize to the heat and lifestyle of this tropical continent. Changi Airport is without doubt one of the best, calmest and most efficient airports in the world, while the city itself is a fabulous amalgamation of cultures and colours. Start with a trip to Chinatown and investigate this historic part of the city with its temples, gardens and a great street market. Stop here for lunch before walking up to Clarke Quay on the Singapore River. Old 'bumboats' ply the river so hop on for a short cruise, ending at the mouth of the river where you can view the Merlion statue, Singapore's mascot. Next, head to Orchard Road for some retail therapy – but beware – this is an enormous area. Start at the western end and finish in the east as this is close to Singapore's most famous landmark, Raffles Hotel. Step into the bar and billiard room for a Singapore Sling and, if late, stay for dinner too. The evening buffet is incredible. Or if you're raring to go, head back to the river where there is lively nightlife at Boat Quay.

If you do have a second day there's also Sentosa Island, a 'theme' park of sorts but with an aquarium that's worth seeing: you can even dive the shark tank if you like! Plus there's a great zoo and night safari, a bird park and the botanical gardens, Little India, museums and so much more. And if you only have a few hours stopover at the airport, there are free city tours that will get you back in time for your flight.

Sleeping

$$ **Albert Court**, 180 Albert St, Singapore 189971, T+65 6339 3939. Converted from pre-war shops near Little India, this small traditional-looking hotel is very comfortable.
$$ **Carlton Hotel Singapore**, 76 Bras Basah Rd, Singapore 189558, T+65 6338 8333. Right beside **Raffles**, a modern hotel with good access to Orchard Road and the museums.
$$ **Novotel**, 177 A River Valley Rd, Singapore 179031, T+65 6338 3333. Classy rooms in a great location, on the Singapore River at Clarke Quay.

Eating

The world's cuisines are at your fingertips. See it and try it! Divers might like to avoid restaurants that advertise shark fin soup, but these are getting rarer. **Brewerks Microbrewery** on Clarke Quay is great for drinks and people-watching and the **House of Thai** on Purvis St, near Raffles, is superb.

Transport

Singapore's entire transport system is clean, quick and cheap. There are buses, the MRT (metro) and metred taxis. Pick up a map as you arrive at Changi: this will show you all highlights as well as how to get around.

$$$ **Alila Manggis**, Buitan, Manggis, Karangasem, T+62 (0)3 6341011, www.alilahotels.com. Upmarket hotel near Candidasa with easy access to the dive areas on Bali's east coast.
$$ **The Watergarden**, Jl Raya, Candidasa, T+62 (0)363 41540, www.watergardenhotel.com. Incredibly peaceful and charming Balinese hotel where each room has a private tropical garden with a deck sitting over a magnificent koi carp pond.

Eating

Indonesian food, Balinese, Chinese, seafood, Mexican, Thai – you fancy it, you'll get it right across the island. There is more fast food in the Kuta area, and better chances of Balinese in Candidasa. However, it's unlikely that you'll find anything other than delicious food wherever you stay.
Jimbaran Seafood Café, there are many seafood cafés along Jimbaran Beach but this has to be the best. It's only 15 mins from the Kuta area but a little hard to find. Many taxi drivers head for the north end where prices are higher, so ask yours to head south to the Italian consulate and turn there. When you reach the beach, near Jl Kenanga Jati and Jl Raya Uluwatu, between **Hotel Puri Bamboo** and **Villa Hanani**, there is a row of eight

Temple at Ulun Danau

open-air cafés with plastic chairs. The **Jimbaran Seafood Café** is in the middle, the seafood is exquisite and unbelievably cheap, around US$5 a head.

Ku De Ta, Jl Laksmana No 9, Seminyak, T+62 (0)361 736 969. Fabulously trendy, horribly expensive but fantastic fusion food with the best views of posers and breathtaking Balinese sunsets.

Festivals

They say there is a festival somewhere on Bali every day of the year. They are the very essence of Balinese life, the balance between order and disorder. If you hear of one, go and observe: etiquette requires you stand politely back, but tourists are not resented. There are festivals dedicated to the arts, the birth of a goddess, retreat ceremonies, parades to the sea to cleanse villages, special prayer days for the dead and harvest festivals. The Balinese calendar is only 210 days long, so actual dates vary. **Galungan** is the most important Balinese holiday and symbolises the victory of virtue over evil. **Nyepi**, Balinese New Year, is a day of total silence. No activity whatsoever is allowed, even electricity is banned except in hotels. On New Year's Eve, purification and sacrificial rites are followed by dancing through the villages. Men carry *ogoh-ogoh (demon images) and make as much noise as possible. This wakes up all the evil spirits then, on Nyepi, Bali is so quiet the spirits can't find anyone and leave the island for good. A* **Balinese cremation** is regarded as a sacred duty as it liberates the deceased soul, allowing it to enter a higher world and be free for reincarnation. If you're invited to a ceremony, don't miss it – this is a joyous celebration.

Ceram Sea island

Sights

There is more to do and discover in Bali than you can imagine. The island is world-famous for its arts, crafts, dance and music. Bali virgins should take a day tour to get a feel for the incredibly beautiful landscape and distinctive culture. Prices for land tours that include 3 or 4 of the sights below can cost as much as US$100 per person and you may find yourself squashed into a minibus with a group of strangers. Alternatively, book through a full-service dive centre like **AquaMarine Diving** (above) as they will be able to arrange for you to go with a staff member or to recommend a reliable guide with a private minibus. This way the rate will be more like US$40-50 per day for the whole minibus.

Ubud The artistic and cultural heartland of the island – full of art galleries, dance, music and retail therapy to die for. Surrounding villages specialize in handicraft production.

A Balinese parade

Barong and Kris dances These impressive dance dramas represent the everlasting struggle between good and evil. They are performed in Ubud or Batubulan and are accompanied by traditional gamelan music.

Kintamani A cool mountain region of volcanoes and crater lakes surrounded by deep green rice paddies.

Bedugul Mystical Pura Ulun Danau Bratan on the shore of Lake Bratan is one of Bali's most beautiful temples. Note that to enter any temple, a sash should be worn around your waist. These can be hired or bought for very little.

Tanah Lot Bali's most important temple is built on a rocky outcrop overlooking the sea. It is just half an hour from Kuta and is breathtaking – if busy – at sunset.

Bali Aga Village, Tenganen Bali Aga were the island's inhabitants before the arrival of Hindu Javanese. The village retains its ancient customs by allowing only minimal contact with outsiders.

Bali Barat National Park Extensive area of woodlands and coastal areas that house some of Bali's usual wildlife including rare birds, monkeys and iguanas.

Komodo and Nusa Tenggara

Liveaboards

Although there is plenty of accommodation right across this chain of beautiful islands, there is really only one practical way to enjoy the diving – get a liveaboard. There are many, many operators to suit all budgets.

Adventure H2O, PO Box 3824, Denpasar, T+62 (0)361 283381, www.adventureh2o.com. A modern catamaran that divides its year between diving and surfing. Dive tours are hosted by the renowned divemaster, Larry Smith. Routes include Komodo and Irian Jaya.

Baruna Adventurer, Jl By Pass I Gusti Ngurah Rai 300B Tuban, T+62 (0)361 753820, www.komodo-divencruise.com. Good quality, value for money liveaboard. Routes include Bali and Komodo.

Kararu Dive Voyages, Jl Danau Poso 65 B/C Blanjong, Sanur 80238, T+62 (0)361 282931, www.kararu.com. Two well run, luxury liveaboards that ply the Komodo route and also some exciting outlying destinations like Irian Jaya, Alor and the Banda Sea. *Sea Safari III* is a traditional phinisi schooner and *Voyager* is a new, steel-hulled vessel.

Manado and Lembeh

Sleeping and diving

In this area there are dive centres based inside nearly every hotel.

$$$-$$ **Kungkungan Bay Resort**, Kungkungan Bay, 95500 Bitung, T+62 (0)438 30300, www.kungkungan.com. The American owned resort that 'discovered' diving in the Lembeh Straits. Now larger and busier but still charming. Dive operations run by Eco-divers.

$$ **Lembeh Resort**, Box 117, Bitung 95500, T+62 (0)5500139, www.lembehresort.com. Sitting on the slopes of Lembeh Island, this relaxed and friendly 13-room resort is beautifully landscaped, with cool breezes and fantastic views of the strait. Dive operations are run by Murex.

$$ **Hotel Santika & Dive Centre Thalassa**, PO Box 1682, 95016 Manado, T+62 (0)431 850230, www.thalassa.net. Located on the beach at Tanjung Pisok, directly opposite the Bunaken Marine Park, this is the only 4 star hotel in Manado. Modern rooms with views over the marine park. Excellent Dutch-run dive centre – this is a great place to do a course.

$ **Murex Dive Resort**, Jl Raya Trans Sulawesi Desa Kalasey I, Manado 95361, T+62 (0)431 826091, murexdive.com. Founded by Dr and Mrs Batuna, pioneers of diving in this area, and still run by their family. Charming Indonesian bungalows in a water-garden setting. Packages are good value, including diving and all meals.

Sights

Not as cultural as Bali, there is still plenty to explore in this area. Day trips are available from any of the resorts and usually include several features of the Minahasa Highlands. This extremely mountainous area is covered with clove trees, vanilla and rice fields. Tours also visit villages that specialize in pottery making or traditional house building.

Lokon and Mahawu Volcanoes These volcanoes have smoking crater lakes. Lokon, the prettier, requires a 45-mins climb but can be done by the reasonably fit.

Lake Linow A beautiful but strange lake, which changes colour from red to green and sometimes blue.

Japanese Caves Built during WWII and mainly used as storage for supplies. You can visit the caves while driving along the road between Kiawa and Kawangkoan, two scenic countryside villages.

Watu Pinawetengan A carved, table-shaped stone around which the ancient chieftains of Minahasan tribes discussed unification, peace and war against enemies.

Sawangan Ancient Park A collection of ancient *Waruga* stone sarcophagi of from the megalithic age. There is also a small museum on site.

Tangkoko Rainforest Tour The tip of north Sulawesi is covered in tropical rainforest. Tangkoko National Park and Dua Saudara cover 9000 ha from sea level up to 1000 m. This spectacular area is home to several unique animals including monkeys, birds, butterflies and tropical plants. The main attraction is the Tarsius – the smallest primate in the world. Walking tours are best at dusk when you are more likely to see one. Beware of the mosquitoes.

Irian Jaya

Sleeping and diving

Papua Diving, Kri Island, Sorong, T+62 (0)411 401660, www.papua-diving.com. The lone dive resorts in this region are Kri Eco Resort and Sorido Bay Resort. Both are run by Papua Diving. The Eco Resort is extremely simple and for budget-minded divers only while Sorido Bay is more upmarket.

Liveaboards

The two main liveaboard operators are Kararu and Adventure H2O. See listings under Komodo and Nusa Tenggara.

Local agents

Dive The World – Indonesia, www.divetheworldindonesia.com. A useful website and booking service for Indonesian boats, dive centres and liveaboards.

SongLine Cruises of Indonesia, Jl Nemon Raya No 32 C, Ponkok Pinang, Jakarta, T+62 (0)217 294684, www.songlinecruises.com. Website for the Traditional Fleet of Indonesia. Excellent source of information on, and bookings for, a wide variety of liveaboards from high end to absolute backpacker. Nationwide routes.

International agents

Dive Discovery, 7 Mark Dr, Suite 18, San Rafael, California, 94903, T+1 (1)800 886 7321/415 444 5100, www.divediscovery.com. Dive travel specialists based in San Francisco, have close links with all Indonesia operators and can issue and send air tickets to anywhere in the world. They will also tailor-make an itinerary.

Tank lady at Tulamben

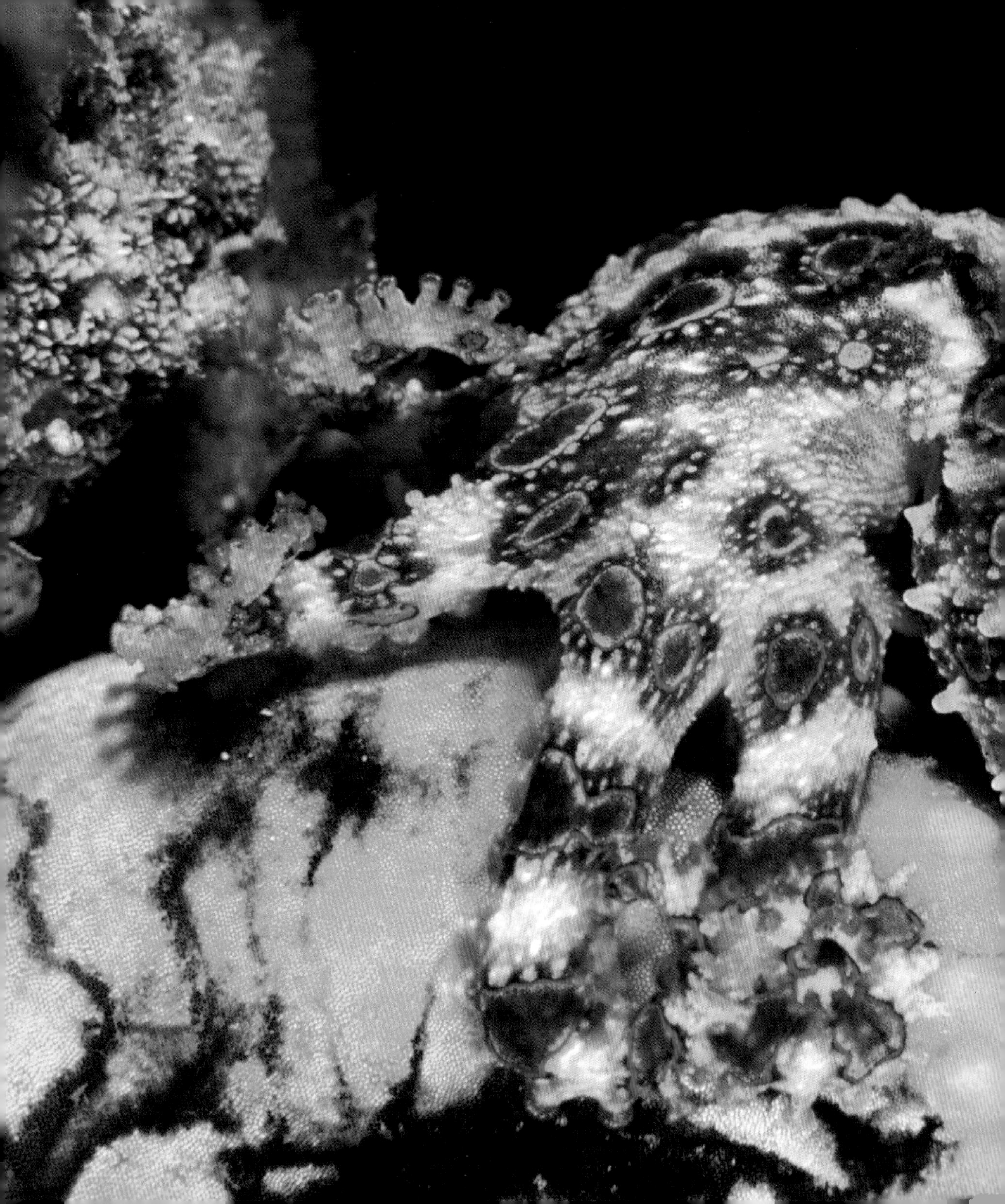

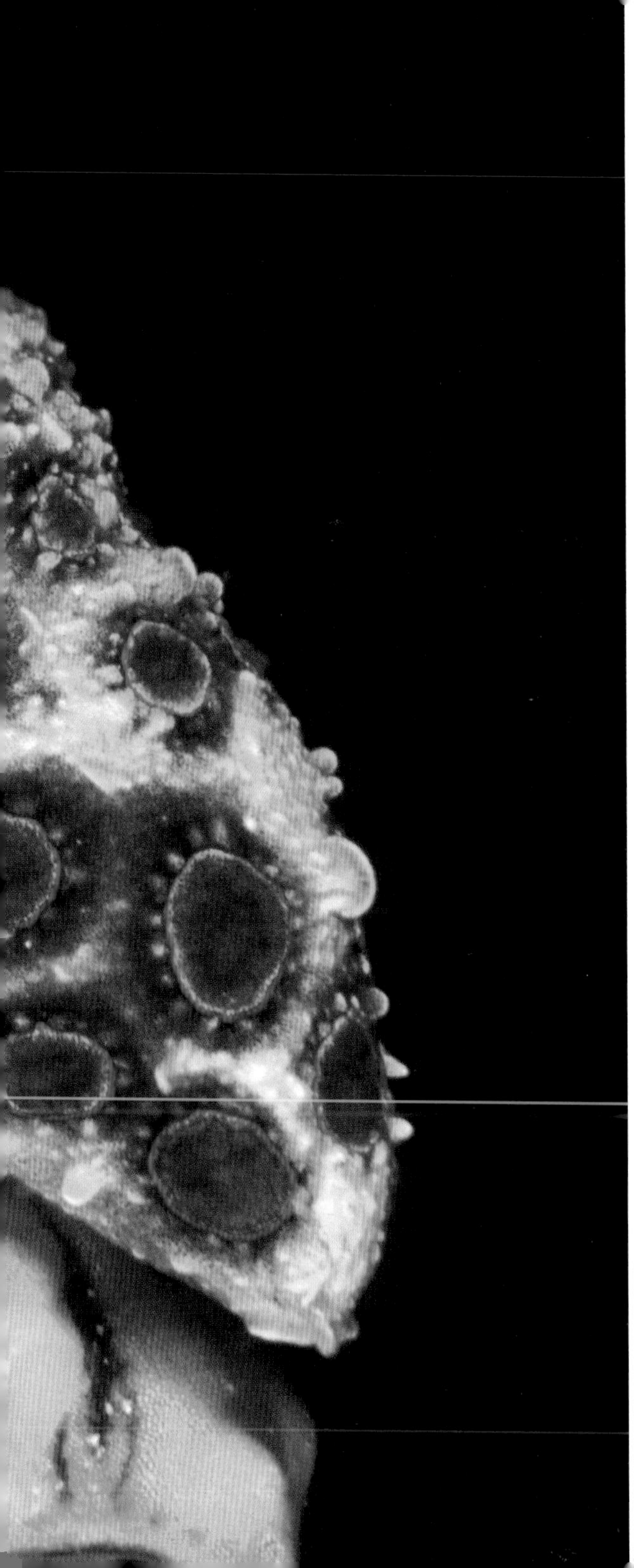

Malaysia

Warning signals: always anti-social and potentially deadly, the blue ringed octopus, *Hapalochlaena lunulata*

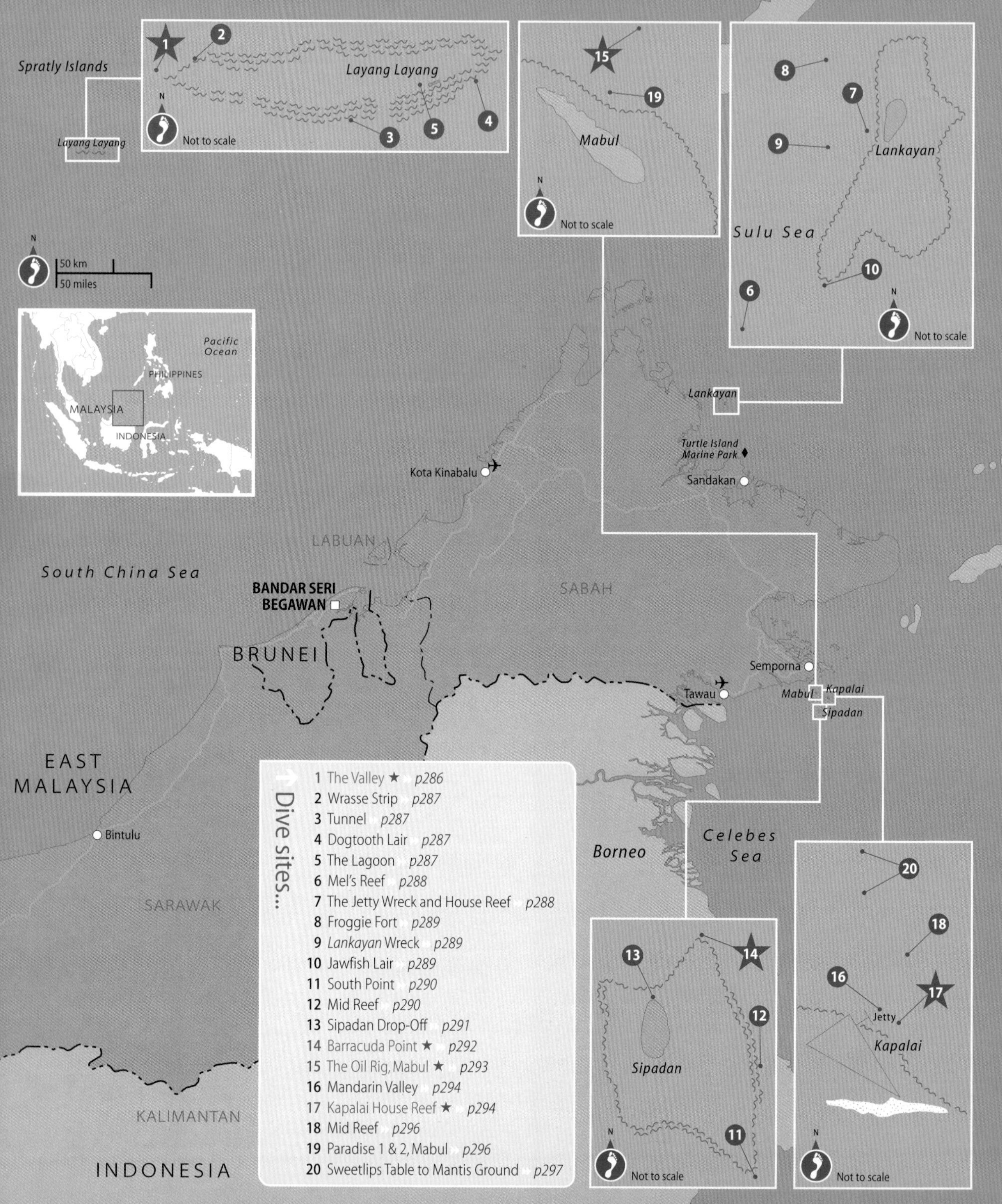
Spratly Islands
Layang Layang
Not to scale
Mabul
Lankayan
Sulu Sea
50 km
50 miles
Pacific Ocean
PHILIPPINES
MALAYSIA
INDONESIA
Lankayan
Turtle Island Marine Park
Kota Kinabalu
Sandakan
LABUAN
South China Sea
SABAH
BANDAR SERI BEGAWAN
BRUNEI
Semporna
Tawau
Mabul
Kapalai
Sipadan
EAST MALAYSIA
Bintulu
Borneo
Celebes Sea
SARAWAK
KALIMANTAN
INDONESIA
Sipadan
Jetty
Kapalai
Dive sites...
1 The Valley ★ p286
2 Wrasse Strip p287
3 Tunnel p287
4 Dogtooth Lair p287
5 The Lagoon p287
6 Mel's Reef p288
7 The Jetty Wreck and House Reef p288
8 Froggie Fort p289
9 Lankayan Wreck p289
10 Jawfish Lair p289
11 South Point p290
12 Mid Reef p290
13 Sipadan Drop-Off p291
14 Barracuda Point ★ p292
15 The Oil Rig, Mabul ★ p293
16 Mandarin Valley p294
17 Kapalai House Reef ★ p294
18 Mid Reef p296
19 Paradise 1 & 2, Mabul p296
20 Sweetlips Table to Mantis Ground p297

Introduction

The sea is perfectly flat, an everlasting sheet of blue glass. The only disturbance is the wake your boat leaves behind. Ahead, the horizon appears flawless, then in a flash, it transforms into an island, so lovely you can't quite believe your eyes. You've just stepped inside a picture postcard.

Descend below the water line and the idyllic charm gives way to high drama and polished theatrics as the sea's predators arrive en masse. They are so close you could touch them; not just one species but several take part in the show. Species that you never imagined would share the same stage. Later, you dive again and the picture has changed completely. Now everything is smaller in scale – no bigger than your hand – but, like some childhood easter egg hunt, you are rewarded with prize after prize.

This is diving in Malaysia: a fascinating mix of the large and the small. You'll find the most impressive marine realm off the magical, mystical island of Borneo, where you can also discover how life used to be and perhaps wonder if that's how it should be now. This is no Eden, but you could be forgiven for believing that it comes pretty close.

There's a golden triangle marked out by the Litigan Reefs. Step from Kapalai to Mabul to Sipadan and discover incredible treasures.

Malaysia rating

Diving
★★★★★

Dive facilities
★★★★

Accommodation
★★★★

Down time
★★★

Value for money
★★★★★

Essentials

Malaysia

Location	2°30′ N, 112°30′ E
Neighbours	Brunei, Indonesia, Philippines, Singapore, Thailand
Population	23,953,136
Land area in km²	328,550
Marine area in km²	1,200
Coastline in km	4,675

Getting there and around

Finding your way to Malaysia is not difficult, although reaching the island of Borneo, where the best diving is found, involves a little extra effort. First of all, target getting to Kuala Lumpur. **Malaysia Airlines** (www.malaysiaairlines.com) have many flights from across the world to the capital. From there you will need to transfer to Kota Kinabalu on Borneo and onwards again to reach your final dive destination using the Malaysian domestic airline network. Flights are frequent with good connections and although you may do a few hops, you can usually get where you need to fairly quickly.

There are many other carriers flying to KL – **Singapore Airlines**, **Qantas**, **Qatar** and **Delta** are just a few options. You could then connect to a new low-cost carrier called **Air Asia** (www.airasia.com) who fly to both Kota Kinabalu and Tawau on the east coast. Alternatively if you travel via Hong Kong, **Dragon Air** (www.dragonair.com) also have flights to Kota Kinabalu.

Once you are on Borneo, your dive centre will advise on transfers. For Layang Layang, the resort charters a small aircraft every couple of days. For Lankayan, you will be collected from Sandakan airport for a scenic speedboat transfer. The resorts that are clustered in the Sipadan area collect their clients from Tawau airport and transfer by road to Semporna then by boat to the relevant hotel.

As all these resorts are on offshore islands, heading out to explore the countryside would involve a transfer back to the coast. In which case, it would make more sense to arrange a tour. See page 299 for ideas.

Finally, should you decide to stay on Peninsular Malaysia, to head to Tioman or Redang perhaps, it's likely that you will need to transfer from KL's international airport to Subang Airport on the other side of the city. The mainland is not highly recommended as a dive destination but has beautiful holiday islands. Take advice from your resort on the best way to get there.

The lagoon at Kapalai

Language

The national language of Malaysia is Bahasa which is used by the 50% of the country's inhabitants. However, with large groups of other language speakers, English is used widely. Despite the similarity in name, Bahasa Indonesia and Bahasa Malaysia are not exactly the same.

good morning (till 1200)	*selamat pagi*
good afternoon (1200-1400)	*selamat tengah hari*
good afternoon (1400-1900)	*selamat petang*
good evening	*selamat malam*
welcome	*selamat datang*
goodbye (if you are leaving)	*selamat jalan*
and if you are staying	*selamat tinggal*
yes	*ya*
no	*tidak*
please	*sila*
thank you	*terima kasih*
sorry!	*ma'af*
how much is ...	*berapa harga ini ...*
you're welcome	*sama-sama*
good	*bagus*
great dive!	*menyelam yang bagus!*
one beer/water	*satu bir/air*

Local laws and customs

Malaysia is Asia's melting pot. About half the country consists of indigenous Malay people, a third are Chinese,10% are Indian and the rest are a curious melange of backgrounds. As such, cultural norms are an interesting and occasionally odd mix. On the mainland, some areas are strongly Muslim, so be sure to dress conservatively. Women should take note of what locals are wearing. The Borneo states are far more Chinese influenced, though, with quite a large population of Filipinos working in dive related areas. These people are so friendly that the usual levels of courtesy and politeness will go a long way.

Safety

Generally, crimes against tourists are rare in Malaysia. Like anywhere, be sensible in big cities, leaving valuables like cash and passports in your hotel safe. Don't leave flashy dive or camera bags unattended and no one should accept drinks from strangers. Of course, once you reach your dive resort, these concerns become almost irrelevant as there's nowhere to go. Be aware that Malaysia probably has the strictest Asian laws on drug possession, which carries a mandatory death sentence.

It's been a few years since terrorism hit Malaysia's shores. After the Sipadan kidnappings back in 2000, the government stationed Armed Forces on all offshore islands. These places are now about as safe as you can get and the soldiers who watch over you are all utterly charming. However, many governmental advisories still recommend caution. Before planning a trip, take advice from those on the ground (your travel agent, dive centre or hotel) and bear in mind that government websites naturally err on the side of caution.

Health

Apart from the usual hot sun and stinging bug warnings, Malaysia has few health issues for visitors, though note that you need to be careful with drinking water. All the offshore islands are reliant on watermakers (often reverse osmosis) or importing water by tanker and you will probably be supplied with drinking water in your room. Should anything out of the ordinary occur, it is good to know that both doctors and chemists are well trained, many in the UK, as there are close links between UK and Malay universities.

Costs

When it comes to costs, standards and value, there is little to worry about with Malaysia. All the island resorts tend to be charming but simple, with just enough creature comforts to keep most happy. The only downside is that there is little choice. The only island with more than one accommodation option is Mabul. Meals and diving are generally included in accommodation rates so your only extras will be souvenirs and drinks, which are not too heavily marked up – a beer is about US$1.50. Should you choose to stop over in Kuala Lumpur or Kota Kinabalu, there are plenty of hotels in all categories. Tipping is not expected – bigger hotels and restaurants will include a service charge on their bills. On the islands, most resorts have a staff fund box in reception or will leave you an envelope with your final bill. What you leave is entirely up to you and should reflect the level of service you were given.

Airlines, all in KK → Malaysia T+60 (0)88 239310, Air Asia KK T+60 (0)88 316826, Singapore T+60 (0)88 219940, Dragon T+60 (0)88 254733. **Embassies**, all in KL → UK T+60 (0)3 2170 2200, USA T+60 (0)3 2168 5000, Australia T+60 (0)3 2146 5555, Canada T+60 (0)3 2718 3333. **Malaysia country code** → +60. **IDD code** → 00. **Police** → 999.

Fact file

International flights	Malaysia, Singapore, Qantas, Qatar, Delta
Departure tax	If not included in your ticket, International M$40, Domestic M$5
Entry	Visas not required for EU, US or Commonwealth citizens
Internal flights	Malaysia Airlines, Air Asia
Ground transport	Plenty but use private rather than public
Money	US$1 = M$3.8 (ringgit)
Language	Bahasa Malaysia, English widely spoken
Electricity	240v
Time zone	GMT +8
Religion	Muslim, Buddhist, Hindu, Christian

The frogfish strike takes 6 milliseconds

Mantis shrimp peering from his burrow

Dive brief

Diving

Malaysia is a geographically widespread country. She has 11 'mainland' states which sit between Thailand and Singapore plus another two states, and a federal territory, on the island of Borneo.

When it comes to diving, **Borneo** is the place to head. Her two states, Sabah and Sarawak, and the Territory of Labuan, are washed by the South China, Sulu and Celebes Seas. Being surrounded by open ocean currents makes for an incredibly diverse set of marine environments. Sabah – which translates as the 'Land below the Wind' – is ringed by a mass of marine reserves, idyllic islands and 75% of the country's reefs. The diving here is superlative and your only problem will be choosing between resorts. Sarawak, surprisingly, has little or no organized diving and although Labuan has some interesting wrecks, the unreliable conditions mean the territory is mostly bypassed.

Peninsular Malaysia – which sits between the South China Sea and the Straits of Malacca – has plenty of diving but suffers in comparison to spectacular Sabah. The west coast is not regarded as much of a dive destination to those in the know. A history of heavy shipping, trade and industry has taken its toll on the marine environment. Over on the east coast, a string of picturesque islands are favoured by Asian divers who live close by. Diving here is regarded somewhat as a 'stopover' or weekend destination for training but if you have a few days to spare it may be worth a detour.

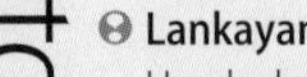

Bottom time

Layang Layang
Open water diving with the potential for outstanding visibility and hordes of pelagics » p286

Lankayan
Heads down for a marine treasure hunt but remember to look up occasionally » p288

Sipadan
A legend amongst legends, this tiny island has a huge reputation » p290

Kapalai
Ranking right up near the very top of the 'best muck diving in the world' list » p293

Mabul
Another marine treasure hunt with a few surprises to keep you on your toes » p293

Diversity reef area 3,600 km^2

CORAL SPECIES	FISH SPECIES	FISH SPECIES UNDER THREAT	PROTECTED REEFS/MARINE PARKS
350	368	20	44

The leafy filefish acting like weed

Malaysia is an interesting country no matter what part you are in but for us, there is only one dive option and that's Borneo. While we found diving on the mainland disappointing, every single resort off the state of Sabah knocks pretty much anywhere else for six. There's big stuff, little stuff, more little stuff, lovely locations and the people are friendly. But perhaps the one thing that links them all is that the resorts still have that feel that you know you are somewhere a long way from home.

Snorkelling

Location, location, location – it's all down to where you are. The diverse environments around Borneo mean that some places you can and some places you can't. If you are travelling with a non-diver who loves to snorkel, Kapalai's beautiful lagoon is probably the best option. Elsewhere will be limited by weather conditions. Likewise, on the peninsula, conditions vary with the seasons. The many shallow reefs can be seen easily from the surface when the visibility is right.

The big decision

If you are travelling a long way to dive Malaysia it's a good idea to see more than one area. The islands off the peninsula's east coast are lovely but experienced divers may find them lacking. Sabah, however, has several first-class options. Each island resort has its unique features so choosing where to go should be based on what you want to see. Do you want to swim with pelagics or spend your time with your nose down a hole hunting for weird and wonderful species? Do you want a variety of diving or to be able to chill out on a beach? Travelling between the resorts isn't difficult so it's possible to do a multi-centre trip. The only other thing to consider is the time of year. A couple of these resorts are seasonal so choose your time carefully.

Buddy line

Hands off – don't touch!

There are things you can and things you can't touch and the clever bit is to know which is which. It's drummed into all training divers not to touch the reef as it's so easy to do damage. It's said that one finger's touch can kill up to 200 years of hard coral growth as the pressure damages the coral's delicate coating allowing both marine and human bacterias to attack. No matter how hard we try, at some time we may be forced to put a hand down. Many people aim for rock or what they think is dead coral but it's amazing how something you thought was rock, or dead, will suddenly turn into a mass of gently waving polyps at the first sign of a current. And you may have just killed it! Many resorts now ask divers to leave gloves off, hoping to encourage a hands-off policy but many ignore the request. You should always respect rules like this. They are made to ensure the reefs get to live for another generation – or more.

Dive data

Seasons	May-September, mostly good countrywide, October-April, restricted in some areas
Visibility	5 metres inshore to 40 metres and over in open water
Temperatures	Air 22-32°C; water 26-31°C
Wet suit	3 mm full body suit
Training	Courses are not common – ask in advance
Nitrox	At some resorts on Mabul
Deco chambers	Labuan, Singapore

The depths of a Sipadan wall

Dive log

Layang Layang

Fly an hour northwest from Kota Kinabalu into the South China Sea and you will find yourself hovering over a series of land masses known as the Spratly Islands. Sitting at the southern end is Layang Layang, just one of many islands whose ownership has long been fought over.

For decades, China, the Philippines, Vietnam and Taiwan have laid claim to the isolated and mostly uninhabited islands nearest their territorial waters. As Layang Layang sits closest to Borneo, a Malaysian Navy outpost was built there to ensure Malaysia's interest over the Spratlys was not lost in the melee. And as it's surrounded by incredible coral reefs, creating a dive resort as well seemed an obvious choice.

Layang Layang, or Swallow's Reef, is a submerged oval with just one tiny, barren island. This was expanded to create an airstrip which hangs above the outer edge of the reef. Beside that runs a strip of land bordering a delightful, turquoise lagoon. Steep walls, constructed of pristine hard corals, drop away from the outer edge of the lagoon and these offer a haven to masses of pelagic life. While the corals and reef life alone are worth a visit, most come for the curious hammerhead phenomena. Every Easter, large schools swarm into Layang then head off again a few weeks later. At other times turtles, reef sharks and schooling pelagic fish are common. The resort is also a bird sanctuary where rare brown boobies nest.

Conditions here are variable. The atoll is so exposed: winds can whip the sea into a frenzy and the dive boats struggle to exit the channel to the outer reef. Currents can be strong and surface conditions rough. Late in the year, when the winds really pick up, the resort closes for a few months. However, in season, when conditions are good, they are very, very good – and visibility can seem limitless.

1 The Valley

- **Depth**: 35 m
- **Visibility**: fair to stunning
- **Currents**: medium to strong
- **Dive type**: day boat
- **Snorkelling**: no

At first glance, this site looks like nothing much, just a flat slope with small crusting corals, sponges and some fish. But descend to 30 metres and the action starts: lots of small whitetip sharks and handfuls of large grey reefs appear out in the blue; there are dogtooth tuna and several giant trevally. These swoop to and fro in the current that pushes against the western tip of the lagoon. A cluster of blackfin barracuda joins the throng then as you start ascending, another huge ball of barracuda appear overhead. In shallower waters there is a 'valley' scooped out of the the reef where you find large turtles resting, juvenile whitetips under some bommies and a gigantic ball of schooling jacks. Napoleon wrasse, batfish and more turtles arrive and if you focus your attention on the reef you can also see smaller animals like pufferfish and razorfish.

The arc-eye hawkfish waiting for dinner

The cubist Picasso triggerfish

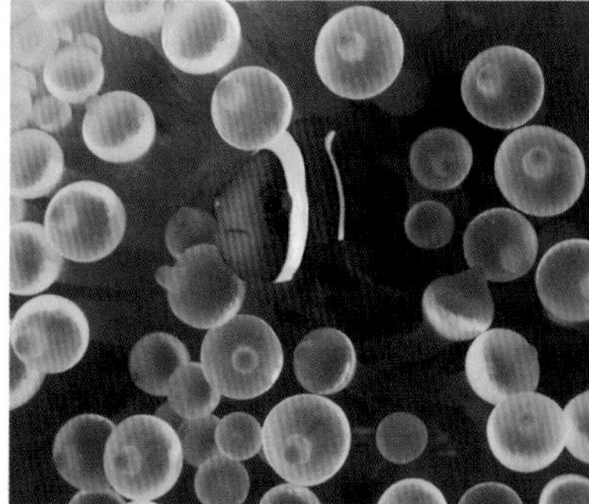

Juvenile tomato clownfish

2 Wrasse Strip

- **Depth**: 35 m
- **Visibility**: fair to stunning
- **Currents**: medium to strong
- **Dive type**: day boat
- **Snorkelling**: no

This is the next site along from the Valley and, on a 'good' day, the currents will carry you along so you get to do two sites at once. However, the dive is better when it's not so strong and you have time to admire the shallower part of the reef. This gentle slope is covered in a variety of hard corals and crusting sponges. It's fairly pretty terrain inhabited by soldier and triggerfish and all sorts of wrasse. Many cluster under table corals where you can also spot reef fish such as boxfish, angels and butterflies. Just past 20 metres the slope drops into a wall and there is a colourful bed of waving gorgonians, whip corals and some lush soft coral growth. Both whitetips and blacktips swim amongst the rocky hard corals.

3 Tunnel

- **Depth**: 27 m
- **Visibility**: fair to great
- **Currents**: mild to strong
- **Dive type**: day boat
- **Snorkelling**: no

Sitting just outside the exit channel from the lagoon, this dive has interesting, multi-level terrain covered in lots of healthy hard corals. The best part of the dive is in the shallower sections before the reef drops to a wall. There are several gullies in the reef, one of which is a distinct tunnel shape. Along its sides are masses of reef fish including several kinds of butterflies, arc-eyed hawkfish, coral trout, wrasse and fusiliers. On the sloping parts of the reef large turtles lumber past, stopping briefly to gnaw at a sponge and smile for the camera. This site is equally good at night – if the current is low – when morays emerge from their hidey-holes and crustaceans come out to feed.

4 Dogtooth Lair

- **Depth**: 25 m
- **Visibility**: low to medium
- **Currents**: mild to strong
- **Dive type**: day boat
- **Snorkelling**: no

Lying behind the resort, this site gets mixed currents. From the surface you can admire a racing pod of dolphins playing in the waves while, below, your dive profile becomes a zigzag pattern along the wall and slope. The dive is named after the pack of enormous tuna that often lurk here but is equally likely to have turtles and schools of jacks. Rumour has it that this is also a prime site for hammerheads. These appear in enormous gangs around Easter when the resort is at its busiest. At other times whitetips park at the cleaner stations for a spruce up as do large honeycomb groupers. There are also lots of nudibranchs along with robust ghost pipefish and coral banded shrimp hiding under small corals.

5 The Lagoon

- **Depth**: 30 m
- **Visibility**: poor
- **Currents**: none to slight
- **Dive type**: shore
- **Snorkelling**: yes

If you are interested in fish nurseries, then it's worth diving right in front of the resort. You can start from the boat jetty or walk a little way past the swimming pool and slowly fin back. The visibility is never outstanding but there are loads of critters. On the sandy sea bed are masses of dragonets, upside-down jellyfish, gobies with their commensal shrimp partners, twintail and headshield slugs and pipefish. Holes in the sand reveal the spearchucker mantis shrimp surrounded by sail fin gobies. Small corals are ringed by tiny white triggerfish, baby lionfish, juvenile butterflies, damsels and sweetlips plus the outrageously coloured Picasso triggerfish. Look out for the unusual anemone with pink tips that protects tiny tomato clownfish.

Tales from the deep

A diving recipe

Dive, eat, sleep in hammock under trees. Dive, eat, chat, dive, eat, sleep. Repeat until your time and money has expired. Layang Layang is a relaxed and friendly place, the staff are easy to deal with and know their sites and the critters well. The diving is superb and although it was the end of the season there was still the odd hammerhead cruising about. It was unusual NOT to see turtles on each dive and I was starting to feel a little blasé about seeing whitetips (if that's possible...). Each dive bought a feeling of awe. The water clarity and colour, the size, abundance and variety of fish life or even the scale of the reef walls and drop-offs were all difficult to comprehend. "Wow!" is about the most adequate way to sum up the whole experience.

Estelle Zauner, Dive Instructor, Newcastle, UK

Jack soup

Lankayan

Due east from Kota Kinabalu is the town of Sandakan and, just an hour or so by boat into the Sulu Sea, is Lankayan. This small island is ringed by a shining white beach and covered in a labyrinth of unruly green jungle. It's so lovely it's almost a cliché of itself, too cute for words or even a postcard but not too pretty for a dive resort, the only habitation on the island.

Lankayan is surrounded by a set of flat plateaux that gradually shelve and drop off into a healthy reef system. There are no great walls but gentle slopes covered, primarily, in hard corals. The island was declared a Marine Conservation Area in 2000 shortly after a survey confirmed very high bio-diversity and little coral bleaching.

Conditions are easy, strong currents are rare and the water's surface is usually smooth, though, visibility is variable and can be quite poor. This is due to the very shallow reef structures, proximity to the mainland and high plankton concentration. Consequently, diving here is about looking for the animals that thrive in these nutrient rich conditions. And there are plenty, including rare rhinopias and occasional whalesharks that come to feed. There are even some good wrecks to explore and the very special treat of walking with blacktip sharks. The shallows here are a nursery for them. You can stand in ankle deep water and have 50-centimetre long babies swim around your toes!

As access to this year-round diving is via Sandakan it's worth stopping there to see the outstanding Sepilok orang-utan Sanctuary, a not-to-be-missed experience (see page 299).

6 Mel's Reef

- **Depth**: 21 m
- **Visibility**: low to good
- **Currents**: none to mild
- **Dive type**: day boat
- **Snorkelling**: possibly

Mel's is a roundish sea mound characterised by several large bommies sitting on its top. These are decorated with schooling fish but if the visibility is low they appear as ghostly shadows in the blue. The main attraction then becomes searching for the small critters that live amongst the soft corals and algaes. There are several different types of flabellina nudibranch and the highly decorated chromodoris kunei nudi. Orang-utan crabs reside in soft corals plus there are lionfish, juvenile sweetlips and blennies. Bigger creatures include cuttlefish, that blend in perfectly with the background, and bluespotted stingrays under small table corals. There are even translucent shrimps hanging on the black coral bushes.

7 The Jetty Wreck and House Reef

- **Depth**: 20 m
- **Visibility**: fair to good
- **Currents**: mild
- **Dive type**: shore
- **Snorkelling**: yes

This shore dive can be done whenever you want, day or night. Entry is right under the pier where a rope on the seabed leads down to the wreck of a small fishing boat. There is lots of activity on the way: a discarded tyre is full of catfish that come racing out if you shine a torch on them; and a bit further on clusters of trunkfish and cardinalfish shelter inside a group of tyres, their treads smothered with hingebeak and cleaner shrimps. When you reach the wreck there are puffers and a lot of lionfish. Decorator crabs and spider crabs shroud the slowly rotting

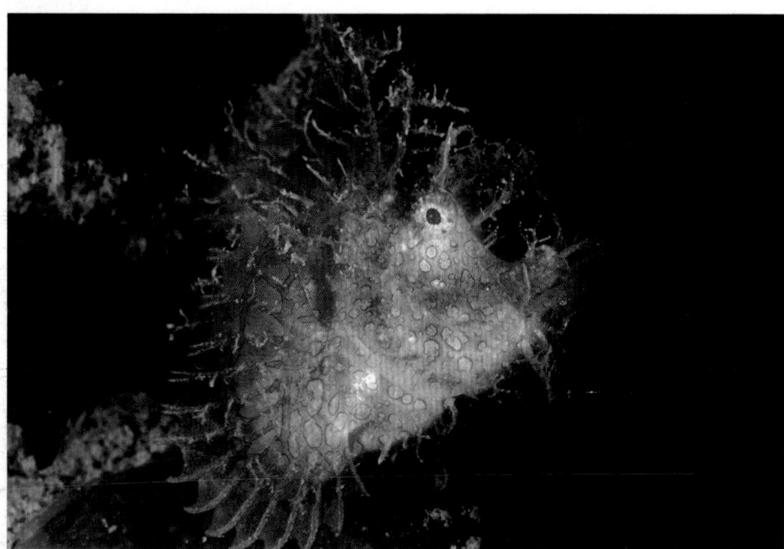

The weedy scorpionfish, *rhinopias frondosa*

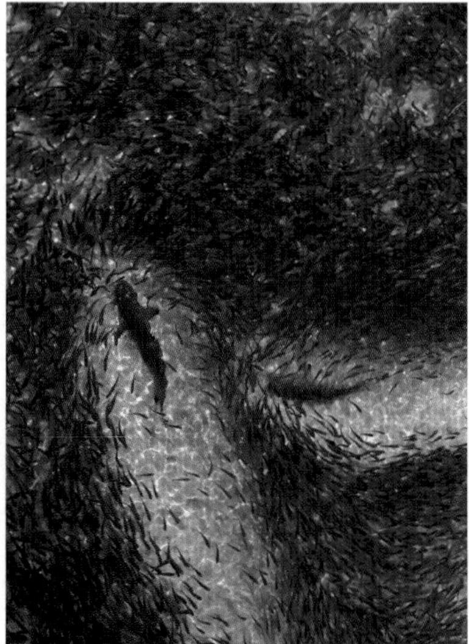

Baby blacktip sharks in ankle deep water

timbers which are covered in small corals, sponges and little shells, including some minute cowries. A school of jacks hovers over the mast. On the way back up, another rope diverts divers back via two pyramids made of timber. These artificial reefs attract many nudibranchs and batfish amongst others. On the sand are an incredible number of cowries, bluespotted rays and the odd decorator crab with an upside-down jellyfish attached to its back. Needlefish hover over the many anemones occupied by skunk or Clarke's clownfish and there is one very unusual saddleback anemonefish family.

8 Froggie Fort

- **Depth**: 22 m
- **Visibility**: poor to good
- **Currents**: mild to strong
- **Dive type**: day boat
- **Snorkelling**: possibly

Consisting of a sloping reef in an oval shape, this dive proves to be something of a surprise. Around its base, emerging from the sand, are rows of pastel toned gorgonians. Beneath which you can often find the star of the dive – a rare *Rhinopias frondosa* or weedy scorpionfish. This outrageously patterned and decorated fish, only about the size of a hand, is also flat like its relative, the leaf scorpionfish, but distinguished by really beautiful markings and fronds on his skin. Up at the top of the mound, where the hard corals are in good condition, is a bed of staghorn coral. White leaffish reside amongst the branches and you can see adults sitting beside their young.

9 *Lankayan* Wreck

- **Depth**: 25 m
- **Visibility**: poor to good
- **Currents**: mild
- **Dive type**: day boat
- **Snorkelling**: unlikely

Lying upright in 30 metres are the remains of this illegal fishing trawler. It was sunk on purpose after being caught poaching in the Sulu Sea in 1998. The boat is only about 30 metres long and in reasonable condition, though the timbers are starting to rot down while it is being colonised. The exterior is coated in enormous oyster clams. As you check out the compartments in the hold where the fishermen used to hide their catch lionfish, groupers and coral trout patrol the hull while schools of ever-present jacks hang above her. The macro life is unusual – there

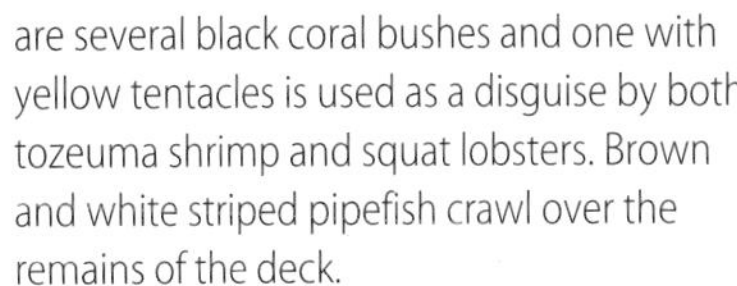

are several black coral bushes and one with yellow tentacles is used as a disguise by both tozeuma shrimp and squat lobsters. Brown and white striped pipefish crawl over the remains of the deck.

10 Jawfish Lair

- **Depth**: 22 m
- **Visibility**: poor to fair
- **Currents**: mild
- **Dive type**: day boat
- **Snorkelling**: possibly

True to its name, this site is renowned for its resident giant jawfish. The divemasters delight in showing off their pets and tempt them out with scraps of fish. The jawfish will come right out of their holes and, despite having a huge head, are actually much smaller than that smiling, tennis ball-sized face would have you think. These chaps grow to about 25 centimetres or so long, unlike a standard jawfish which rarely tops 10 centimetres. The remainder of the dive involves investigating the extensive variety of corals looking for pipefish, frogfish and orang-utan crabs, all of which are regularly found here. You may even spot a baby nurse shark under a table coral.

The bluestriped fang blenny

Swarming under the jetty

The beautiful porcelain crab

Sipadan

A legend for divers the world over, Sipadan is one of those dive destinations that everyone knows and everyone wants to see. This deep green, circular island, rimmed by bleached white sand and encapsulated by a perfect blue sea, is now shut, but, fortunately, only in terms of accommodation.

In 2004 a move was made to turn the island into a World Heritage Site. However, concerns were voiced by environmentalists that the effects of continually increasing diver numbers would irreparably damage the reefs. It was also felt that people staying on the island were affecting the already fragile ecosystem. Sipadan is a small island with just a handful of dive sites and the damage was obvious. After much to-do, including a court case in Kuala Lumpur, all resort operators were asked to leave and a programme to rehabilitate the island has commenced. This includes the removal of all buildings except those used by the Parks Service and a beach clean up which, it is hoped, will aid turtle nesting. Divers now stay at the nearby resorts on Mabul and Kapalai which all schedule daily dives to Sipadan but numbers are, at least, restricted. Time will tell how much this helps with the regeneration of the reef system and whether World Heritage status will be granted.

If you are looking for big stuff, then the year-round Sipadan diving is for you. Turtles are everywhere, so prolific and inquisitive that they will follow you around. Sharks are easy to spot and there are phenomenal numbers of barracudas at Barracuda Point. There are also plenty of smaller animals to hunt for in the shallows when conditions allow.

Currents here are variable and most dives are done as drifts. Athough they are not always that strong, the currents can quickly turn fierce resulting in a complete about face halfway through a dive.

Masked puffer at home

Sipadan reef and sweepers

11 South Point

- **Depth**: 25 m
- **Visibility**: fair to stunning
- **Currents**: mild to strong
- **Dive type**: day boat
- **Snorkelling**: unlikely

The furthest site from the island's jetty, South Point is not dissimilar to her neighbouring dives. In fact all the sites here have a similar profile. The island is rimmed by a steep wall that is said to eventually drop to over 600 metres. It is topped by a sloping plateau where the corals can be colourful depending on whether the currents have encouraged them out to feed. Where this site stands out is that it seems to be a haven for all the island's turtles. Although some report diving here and not seeing a single one, mostly there are so many that you can hardly move past them. They are incredibly inquisitive and not at all afraid of divers. One can be feeding on a coral outcrop (attracting majestic and imperial angels or butterflyfish who scavenge for their scraps), then see a diver, decide that is far more interesting and swim over to join them. The top of the reef is a little scrappy but you may spot a shark or school of bumphead parrots.

12 Mid Reef

- **Depth**: 16 m
- **Visibility**: fair to good
- **Currents**: light to strong
- **Dive type**: day boat
- **Snorkelling**: unlikely

On the wall that runs between Barracuda and South Points is a dive that can be difficult at times. You can enter while the water is dead calm then, within a few moments, run into currents moving at an unimaginable speed. Thermoclines, down- and up-draughts can all turn the site into a roller coaster ride and be a lot of fun for that but watch your buoyancy! Then again, it can also be completely still. There are masses of turtles here as well, some resting on little ledges on the wall, others heading off to investigate other sections of reef. The wall itself has many fans and black corals decorating the steeper surfaces while, up on the plateau, the hard corals harbour lots of interesting small animals that you can hunt around for when the currents are being cooperative.

13 Sipadan Drop-Off

- **Depth**: 35 m
- **Visibility**: poor to fair
- **Currents**: slight to strong
- **Dive type**: day boat
- **Snorkelling**: no

What made Sipadan famous a long time ago was the jetty drop-off. You could simply slide into your kit and wander off the beach and onto the amazing wall. It was known as the best house reef in the world for many a year. Within a 10 metre or so fin you could slip over the lip of the reef and find schools of batfish or jacks right there to greet you. Then you descend past small crevices and overhangs painted with brightly coloured coral and every tropical fish imaginable. It is likely that you will see at least a shark or two, and a dozen or so turtles. At night, the shallows are alive with crabs and shrimp, the sandy beach area has shells and gobies and beneath the jetty are urchins, starfish and schools of catfish. To the east of the jetty, at about 18 metres, is the entrance to Turtle Cave. This series of interconnecting caverns is a fairly dangerous place, full of the remains of drowned turtles. It is thought that they go in at night and get lost as there is no daylight to guide them back out. Beware – the same could happen to divers who enter without both a torch and a divemaster.

Blenny on a sponge

One turtle was very nosy... he deserted his meal on the reef to check out Shaun's camera, then promptly bit the flash! Perhaps the bright orange strobe looked like a sponge.

> **To find a world of beauty, separated from the ordinary, that is the siren song of diving. Occasionally, the experience far exceeds the dream. This was one of those moments. Floating in the middle of the universe, never wanting to leave.**
>
> *Bruce Brownstein, Venice, California*

14 Barracuda Point

- **Depth**: 28 m+
- **Visibility**: fair to stunning
- **Currents**: mild to ripping
- **Dive type**: day boat
- **Snorkelling**: unlikely

Perhaps Sipadan's most famous dive, this submerged point sits to the east of the boat jetty. The wall is sheer and the crusting corals and sponges make it incredibly colourful. As you descend to 30 metres there is a full quota of schooling small fish – butterflies, tangs and surgeons – but most outstanding is the enormous amount and sizes of black coral bushes. Every one seems to have a longnose hawkfish in it, or be swarmed by lionfish, and interspersed with gigantic fans in many colours. Turtles swim along with divers to keep them company, sometimes one will have a batfish hovering beneath his belly. At the top of the reef the corals are less impressive but whitetips rest peacefully on the sand. Grey reef sharks approach from behind, heading for the school of jacks that are just around the bend. Large turtles visit cleaning stations while Napoleon wrasse and giant tuna pass by in the blue. Although the dive starts along the wall and drifts towards them, the infamous barracuda school is usually spotted from the surface. There are hundreds in the ball, sitting right on the top of the reef. They move apart for a few moments then reconfigure into a perfect spiral – breathtaking.

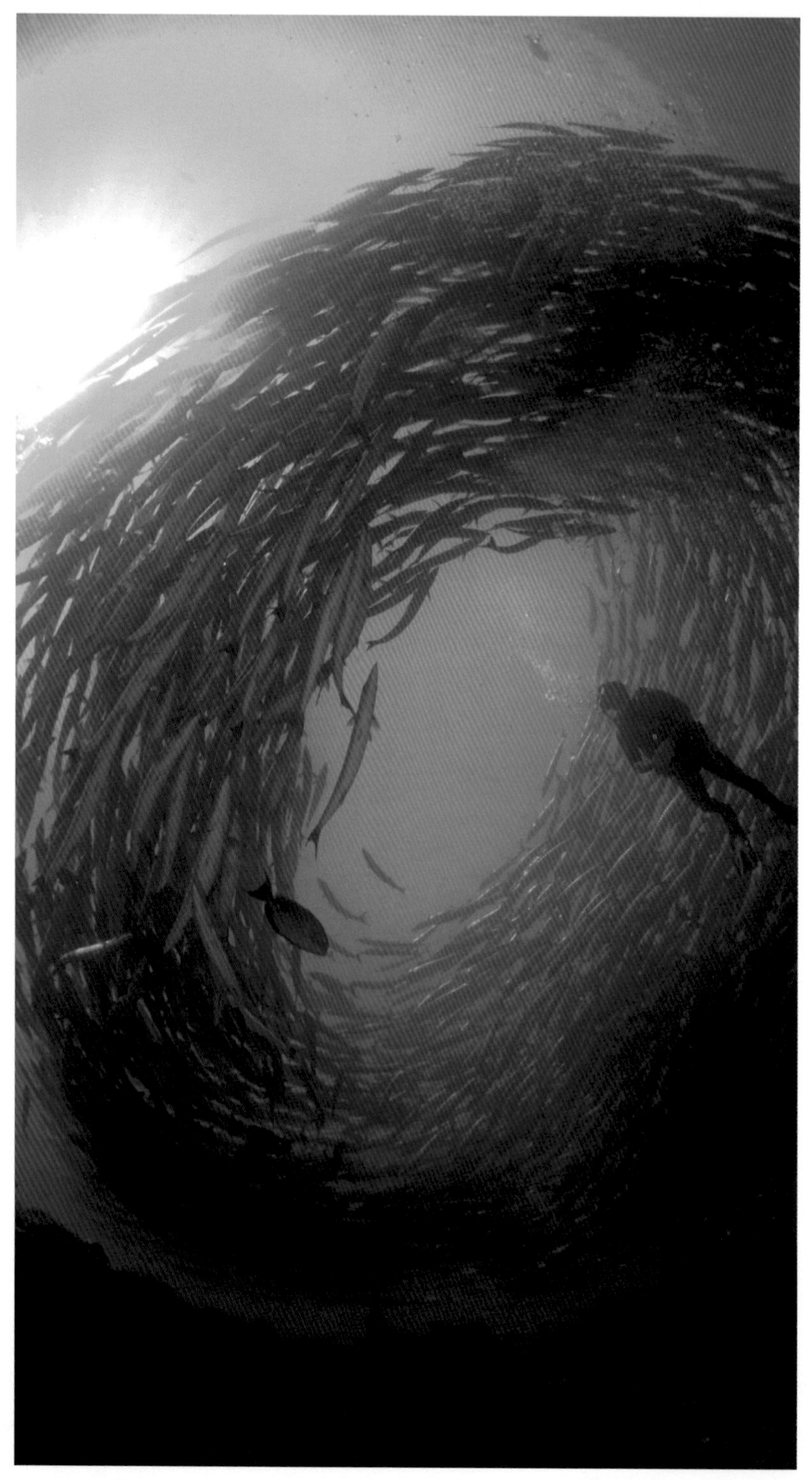

Kapalai and Mabul

Just a short motor from Sipadan, these two islands were long overshadowed by their more famous big brother. All three sit on the Litigan Reefs and are excellent dive areas in their own right. However, now the younger siblings are getting the attention they deserve as divers are forced to relocate to one of them.

Mabul

Well known as a macro destination to die for, Mabul does not disappoint. Comparatively large, this island sits on the edge of a continental shelf with a small village and several resorts of varying standards. Offshore, there is even a hotel housed in a converted oil rig. It is frankly one of the ugliest things you will ever see, until you get beneath it and discover it's also one of the best muck dives you will ever do. Shore dives are equally impressive and the conditions are easy enough. Occasional currents may divert a chosen dive but you can always go another day.

Kapalai

Although charted on older maps, there is only a sand bar remaining from what was once a small island. At low tide you can walk along the beach that emerges, spotting shells and tiny critters caught in puddles. This flat topography is similar underwater, yet visibility here is reasonable as the reef mounds are washed daily by the tides. Corals tend to be low lying to the contours of the landscape but they're all pretty healthy and a haven for masses of weird and wacky critters. The resort itself is a water village – eco-friendly wooden bungalows perch on stilts over an aquarium-like lagoon. It is a delightful place, perfect for romantics. Diving here, and in Mabul, is year-round and suitable for everyone as currents are easily avoided.

15 The Oil Rig, Mabul

- **Depth**: 18 m
- **Visibility**: poor to good
- **Currents**: mild, occasional surface currents
- **Dive type**: day boat
- **Snorkelling**: no

The massive and incredibly ugly oil derrick that has been parked just off Mabul's shores is, surprisingly, an exercise in nature's power over man. Humanity does its best to mess up the landscape but nature has its own cunning ways of turning that around. The pylons supporting the rig are eerie, reminiscent of a wreck dive, and swarmed by jacks and snappers. The seabed beneath is studded with man-made detritus, though the creatures don't seem so bothered and have started a recycling programme: ropes have been colonized by iridescent sponges that shelter tiny gobies; piles of building detritus have stonefish squatters; and a giant moray called Elvis lives under an old cage. There are crocodilefish and flying gurnards carpeting the sand, ornate ghost pipefish in fans and lime green frogfish hang out in old car tyres. A pile of metal sheets and pipes has yet more frogfish in varying colours, scorpionfish and morays are everywhere; and there are mantis shrimp and jawfish, cardinals and nesting sergeant majors. The list could go on – and extend to the areas outside the pylons where you can investigate the small patches of reef that are equally well colonized.

Hermit crab in hiding

Frogfish camouflage gone awry

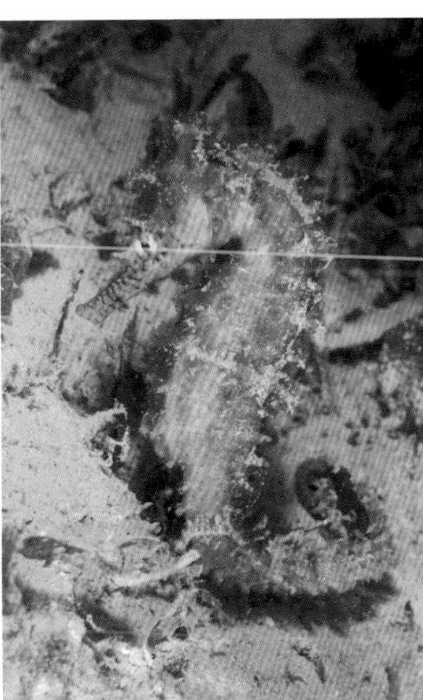
Seahorse disguised as seagrass – almost

16 Mandarin Valley

- **Depth**: 7 m
- **Visibility**: good
- **Currents**: mild
- **Dive type**: shore
- **Snorkelling**: yes

Dusk is not the moment to pull up a chair and watch a stunning sunset at Kapalai, not when you could be under the jetty in just seven metres watching one of the most fascinating events in the marine world. Every evening, minute mandarinfish emerge from the rubble to perform the most elegant of mating rituals. Just before sunset, tiny shadows appear as the larger males approach diminutive females. But the girls are picky. Sometimes one will swim up and kiss her suitor before dashing back to safety. Then the man of her dreams will appear and she will ascend far up into the water column sitting on her partner's pelvic fin. At the moment of climax, a cloud of white eggs and sperm materialises in a puff of white then the fish disappear at the speed of light. Should a little voyeurism not be your thing, you could drop to nine metres and search for the resident ghost pipefish, the flamboyant cuttlefish (they mate at dusk, too) or the myriad frogfish that are found here frequently.

Sometimes we rank a site by the amount of film that gets used. It used to be good if all 36 frames went. Then it was a splendid dive if we finished two films. But on occasion, it's more about how quickly a film goes. One night on Mandarin Valley it took less than 20 minutes!

Mandarinfish pair on a baby-making session

17 Kapalai House Reef

- **Depth**: 23 m
- **Visibility**: good
- **Currents**: mild
- **Dive type**: day boat/shore
- **Snorkelling**: yes

Day or night, bright sun or setting sun, you just can't beat it. This is a superlative dive, or set of dives. The front of the resort, where the lagoon drops away, is edged by a small wall. Dropping in from the boat about 300 metres from the jetty, you can slowly work your way back at about 14 metres. The shallow reef isn't all that pretty but there is masses of life: turtles, cuttlefish, crocodilefish and lots of crabeye gobies. Frogfish are unbelievably common with beautiful red adults and their young, just an inch big. Razorfish dance on the sand near banded pipefish, lots of jawfish, marbled dragonets and really friendly batfish! As an alternative, you can start at the jetty and go down to about 23 metres where a small wooden fishing boat sits on the sandy seabed. It has been colonised quite extensively, with morays underneath and lionfish inside but the most impressive resident is a football-sized grey and pink frogfish. Back up in the shallows you can spot almost any critter you heart desires: ghost pipefish, blue ringed octopus, stonefish, flat worms and nudibranchs. At night, the lights from above attract more life into the lagoon: snowflake morays wiggle around pylons; squat lobsters sit in fans; mantis shrimp peer out from their burrows; and parrotfish retreat to their bubbles. Juvenile nursesharks and batfish swing past and more bluerings appear to hunt.

Up close and personal

There is a resident pink frogfish that has been living in the same finger sponges for well over a year and has been known to the divemasters since he was just an inch long!

18 Mid Reef

- **Depth**: 20 m
- **Visibility**: good
- **Currents**: mild to medium
- **Dive type**: day boat
- **Snorkelling**: possibly

A flat reef on the outer edge of the Kapalai plateau is covered in small crusting corals and sponges. Occasional outcrops lift the terrain up and down. The current can be a little strong so the fish shelter in small caverns but it's never so bad as to spoil a dive. This dive, like most here, is all about spotting the smaller reef building creatures. There are a large variety of nudibranchs including the outrageous solar powered nudibranch, several ornate ghost pipefish and leaffish. Jawfish are tempted from their lairs by scraps of squid, as are blue or black ribbon eels. Bluespotted rays and turtles swim past. Primitive looking xenocarcinus tuberculatus crabs nestle on whip corals, competing with tiny gobies for space. In fact, the whips here are a hive of activity with several bumble bee shrimp on another and dasycaris shrimp on the next. Spearchucker mantis shrimps are stationed all over the sand and octopus lurk in amongst the rubble. Longnose and pixie hawkfish perch on small corals. There is a resident pink frogfish that has been living in the same finger sponges for well over a year and has been known to the divemasters since he was just an inch long!

Tales from the deep

Where memories are made

Ah Kapalai... what can I say?! My exclamation has become a bit of a joke amongst our friends, but if your idea of heaven is listening to gentle waters lapping beneath you as you sleep and being awoken by the sounds of trumpetfish chasing glassy sweepers out of the water, then this is for you.

It's the ideal place if you are into small critters, gentle currents and beautiful sunsets. There were things here I had never seen before like: mating mandarinfish, blue ringed octopus and flamboyant cuttlefish – and all resident on probably the best house reef I have dived. It was so good, I even managed to give up some of those sunsets and go night diving! Kapalai is the most idyllic, fascinating and not to mention romantic place that I have spent time in, a place where memories are made.

Jill Keen, Polegate, East Sussex

19 Paradise 1 & 2, Mabul

- **Depth**: 25 m
- **Visibility**: good
- **Currents**: mild, strong patches
- **Dive type**: day boat/shore
- **Snorkelling**: for confident swimmers

Just out the front of the Sipadan Water Village the beach leads away to a flat bottom of sand and seagrasses. This is Paradise 1, a cracking dive for critters with divemasters leading you from one weird animal to the next before you've had a moment to admire each. There are flying gurnards, fingered dragonets, tiny scorpions and dwarf lionfish, inimicus (or devilfish), longsnout pipefish, snake eels and filefish.

As you grow accustomed to what you are seeing, you start to notice some even weirder fish variations such as a hairy, decorated filefish, a wacky long-legged crab and juvenile fish just a few millimetres long. Tiny mantis shrimp peek out of their burrows while stonefish and flounder try to disguise themselves. Small octopus hide beneath coconut shells and even smaller blue ringed octopus sneak into old beer bottles. The palm fronds that get caught hanging on buoy lines are used by squid to lay their eggs and you can sometimes see upwards of twenty females laying – males try to protect their females and often end up in a fight with an interloper. If you then swim a little further along, you reach Paradise 2 which has a small patch of fringing reef. You see slightly fewer 'muck' critters here and a few more free swimmers like batfish and young wrasse, clowns in their anemones and, at dusk, you may spot mandarinfish when they come out to feed.

The male flamboyant cuttlefish trying to evade the camera

20 Sweetlips Table to Mantis Ground

- **Depth**: 32 m
- **Visibility**: good
- **Currents**: mild
- **Dive type**: day boat
- **Snorkelling**: no

The topography here is similar to the other open reefs near Kapalai but these two sites are close together so you can visit both on one dive. Starting on Sweetlips Table, it's an extremely unusual occurrence but you might spot a free swimming blue ribbon eel, though they duck back into their holes pretty quickly. There are tiny cockatoo waspfish, the thumbcracker mantis shrimp and plenty of nudibranchs. Juvenile sweetlips flit around doing their manic dance. Travelling over the gully that heads to Mantis Ground there are octopus in the rocks and jawfish in the sand. You can spot the male incubating eggs in his mouth at certain times of year. Mantis Ground lives up to its name with several different coloured spearchuckers popping out from their burrows and dendronephthya crabs sitting near their soft coral hosts.

Coral bommie, Borneo style

Temperatures rising

But only for some...
Malaysia's mainland is a hot destination for Asian residents. Both qualified and trainee divers head to the islands off the east coast in the summer months to relax, do a little diving or continue with courses they have started at home. The conditions here are perfect for that, with shallow reefs and warm waters just an hour or two away making the perfect long weekend. But for the long haul diver this area is less appropriate. The northeast winds bring rain from November to February so the water is cool and visibility is minimal. Diving is said to be available from April to October but in reality, if it's stormy and few people are about, the dive centres cancel their trips. Even when the weather is lovely, visibility can still be limited. However, many of these island groups are so picturesque that if you're in the region and you're just as happy to absorb the atmosphere, you may enjoy what diving there is. Many good creatures are sighted - whalesharks cruise the coast and turtles are frequent visitors – but the main focus is on smaller creatures as spotting them isn't dependent on clear water. Some of the better destinations include:

Perhentian Islands Inside the Terengganu Marine Park, these tiny, pretty and very 'Robinson Crusoe' islands are ringed by potential dive sites. Mostly, these tend to be rocky outcrops with cracks and crevices to investigate.

Redang Island Just below Perhentian and also part of Malaysia's first marine park, Redang consists of a main island surrounded by a cluster of smaller ones. It can get reasonable visibility at times as there are deeper drop-offs.

Lang Tengah Regarded as one of the nation's best-kept secrets, this undeveloped little island has pristine beaches and unspoiled tropical jungle interior. Diving is, like its neighbours, gentle and easy going.

Tenggol Island Regarded as having some of the best diving on the peninsula as it's a bit further from the coast. The west of the island is a steep-sided wall while on the east you may find some intriguing critters lurking in the sand.

Tioman Island As lovely as you might remember it from *South Pacific*. The island is a marine park but surrounding waters are shallow and best suited to beginners There is more challenging diving way offshore and a couple of small wrecks. The island is equally known for its jungle walks, bird life and flora.

Lankayan Island

Drying out

Kapalai resort

Borneo is a nature lover's delight with incredible, indigenous flora and fauna as well as some captivating landscapes.

Kota Kinabulu

Sleeping

$$$-$$ **Sutera Harbour Resort**, 1 Sutera Harbour Bld, 88100 Kota Kinabalu, T+60 (0)88 318 888. A convenient and pleasant complex with several hotels, a spa, golf course, sports facilities, many restaurants and free airport transfers. The resort also owns the North Borneo Railway and can arrange a variety of day trips.

Liveaboards

MV Celebes Explorer, PO Box 12248, Kota Kinabalu, T+60 (0)88 221586, www.borneo.org. The only liveaboard operating in this region, with either 3 or 4 day itineraries.

Ocean Rover, 3/20 Moo 5, Viset Rd, Tambon Rawai, Ampur Muang, Phuket, 83100, Thailand, T+66 (0)76 281387, www.ocean-rover.com. This high-class vessel cruises the peninsula's east coast in summer visiting Tioman, Redang, Tenggol and Perhentian. Emphasis is on a mix of dive and land activities.

Local agent

Dive The World – Malaysia, 225 The Peak, Tanjung Lipat, Kota Kinabalu, T+60 (0)88 232042, www.DiveTheWorldMalaysia.com. A helpful and knowledgeable agent for all Borneo dive centres.

Layang Layang

There's just the one resort on this isolated island in the Spratly Group. Transfers from KK take 1 hr 15 mins on a private charter.

Sleeping and diving

$$ **Layang Layang Island Resort**, office in Kuala Lumpur, T+60 (0)3 2162 2877, www.layanglayang.com. Rooms are built in 'longhouses' and feel rather like a comfy American motel. Good views towards the sea. Weekly packs for roughly US$1200 include all meals and diving.

Lankayan

Again just one resort on this isolated island in the Sulu Sea. Transfers from KK take 40

What happens when you eat too well!

Layang Layang's location

mins on **Malaysian** to Sandakan, then another 1 hr by speedboat to the resort.

Sleeping and diving

$$ **Lankayan Island Resort**, 484 Bandar Sabindo, 91021 Tawau, Sabah, T+60 (0)89 765200, www.lankayan-island.com. Picture-postcard perfect with a laid-back atmosphere. Weekly packages from US$1000 including all meals, transfers and diving.

$$ **Sepilok Nature Resort**, 484 Bandar Sabindo, 91021 Tawau, Sabah, T+60 (0)89 765200, www.sepilok.com. Delightful wooden chalets overlooking a tropical garden rimmed lake. The resort has a collection of 150 different Asian orchid species and a fabulous restaurant.

Sights

Not far from Lankayan is the **Turtle Island Marine Park**, a set of three islands where turtles come to nest. There is no established diving here and facilities are very limited. However, Lankayan also operates a small turtle hatchery so you won't miss out. Far more interesting and actually an unmissable experience is the **Sepilok Nature Resort** in Sandakan. From here you can walk to the nearby Kabili-Sepilok Forest Reserve and the Orang-utan Rehabilitation Centre. Captive or abandoned orang-utans are helped to readjust to life in the wild but can be seen at feeding times. There is also a Sumatran rhino breeding programme in progress.

Surface interval

24 hours in Kota Kinabalu

Because getting to Borneo means going through Sabah's capital, you may as well take a day to see this pleasant, small city and her surrounds. The KK Heritage Walk is a guided two hour walk around the city's landmarks including Australia Place, one of the oldest parts of town, then on to various museums, monuments and memorials. Contact the Tourism Board; about RM100 per person.

Those who have the inclination to climb mountains will be sorely tempted to take a slightly longer break and scale Mt Kinabalu (trips take two days). If time is short you can visit Malaysia's first World Heritage Site, Kinabalu Park and experience just a little of the incredible range of plant, animal, insect and bird life. The Poring Hot Springs are nearby and day trips that cover both will be around US$60.

A slightly more relaxed day can be had by taking the North Borneo Railway journey through the countryside to the agricultural region of Papar. The restored 100 year-old train chugs past mangrove swamps, traditional villages and markets. Return trip about US$70.

Kapalai and Mabul

Reaching both destinations is done by flying to Tawau, 50 mins on **Malaysia Airlines** or **Air Asia** from KK or 40 mins on **Malaysian** from Sandakan. Once you are in Tawau, your resort will collect you by minibus for the drive to Semporna, up to 1½ hrs. From there, it's a speedboat ride to Kapalai or Mabul, another 40 mins.

Sleeping and diving

$$$-$$ **Sipadan-Mabul Resort** & **Mabul Water Bungalows**, PO Box 15571, Kota Kinabalu, T+60 (0)88 230006, www.sipadan-mabul.com.my & www.mabulwaterbungalows.com. Long-established operator with 2 resorts, the original with basic accommodation and a second, better, set of water bungalows. Weekly packages, depending on resort, around US$1000-1400 including all meals, transfers and diving.

$$$-$$ **Sipadan Water Village Resort**, PO Box 62156, 91031 Tawau, T+60 (0)89 752996, www.sipadan-village.com.my. More upmarket bungalows built over the water. Weekly packages range from US$1500-1800 including all meals, transfers and diving.

$$ **Sipadan Kapalai Resort**, 484 Bandar Sabindo, 91021 Tawau, T+60 (0)89 765200, www.sipadan-kapalai.com. Almost perfect in every way – romantic, spacious, bug free. No air-con, just sea-breeze cooled. Weekly packs for around US$1000 including all meals, transfers and unlimited diving.

International agents

Reef & Rainforest, 400 Harbor Dr, Sausilito, California 94965, T+1 (1)415 2891760, www.reefrainforest.com. Full service, dive and adventure agency near San Francisco, for tailor-made tours.

Sepilok orang-utan sanctuary

Native orchid

Philippines

Pots of gold: the end of a coral rainbow in the Filipino World Heritage site at Tubbataha

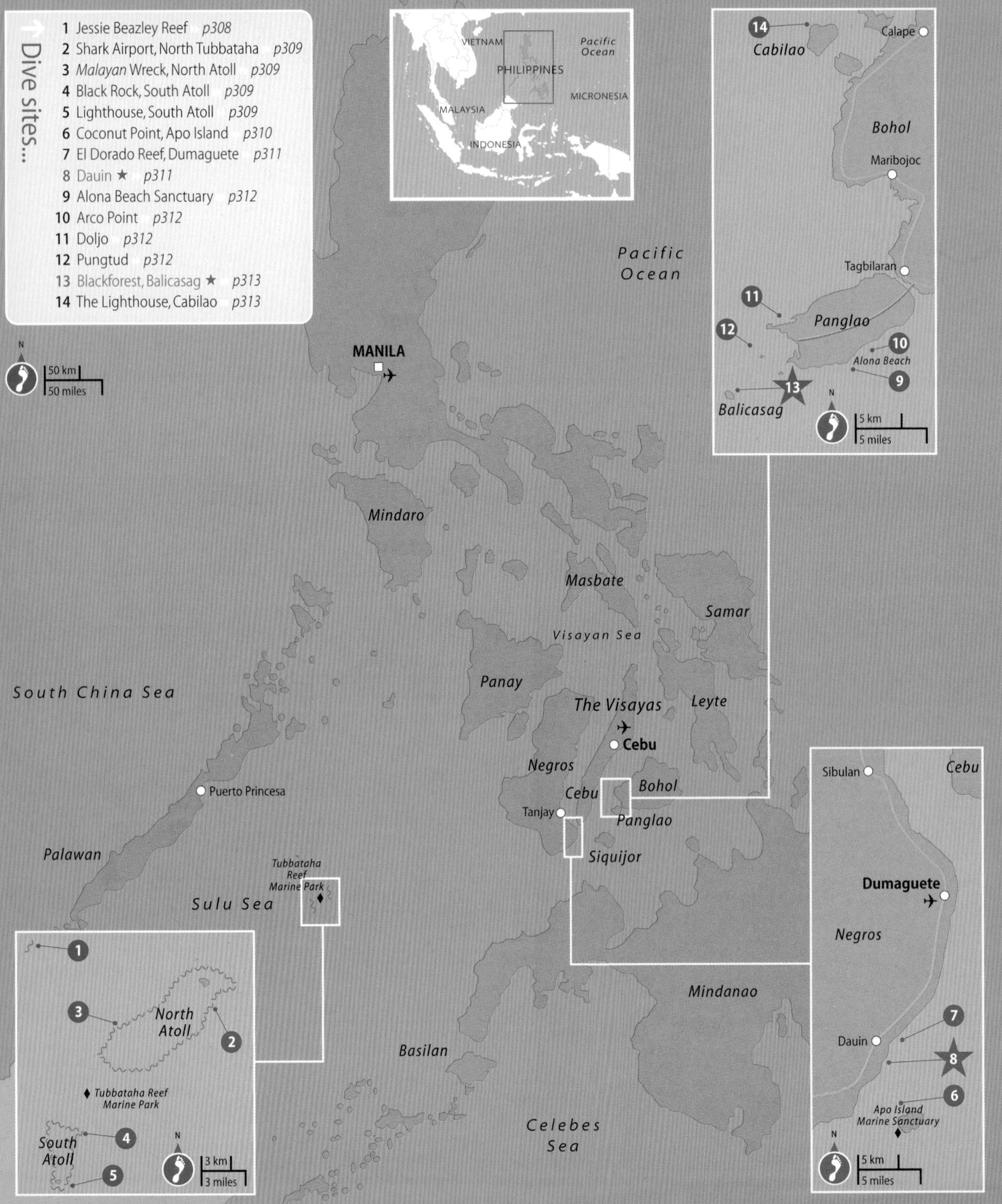

Dive sites...
1 Jessie Beazley Reef p308
2 Shark Airport, North Tubbataha p309
3 Malayan Wreck, North Atoll p309
4 Black Rock, South Atoll p309
5 Lighthouse, South Atoll p309
6 Coconut Point, Apo Island p310
7 El Dorado Reef, Dumaguete p311
8 Dauin ★ p311
9 Alona Beach Sanctuary p312
10 Arco Point p312
11 Doljo p312
12 Pungtud p312
13 Blackforest, Balicasag ★ p313
14 The Lighthouse, Cabilao p313
50 km
50 miles
VIETNAM
PHILIPPINES
Pacific Ocean
MICRONESIA
MALAYSIA
INDONESIA
Cabilao
Calape
Bohol
Maribojoc
Tagbilaran
Panglao
Alona Beach
Balicasag
5 km
5 miles
MANILA
Pacific Ocean
Mindaro
Masbate
Samar
Visayan Sea
Panay
The Visayas
Leyte
Cebu
South China Sea
Negros
Bohol
Cebu
Tanjay
Panglao
Siquijor
Puerto Princesa
Palawan
Tubbataha Reef Marine Park
Sulu Sea
Sibulan
Cebu
Dumaguete
Negros
Mindanao
Dauin
Apo Island Marine Sanctuary
North Atoll
Tubbataha Reef Marine Park
South Atoll
3 km
3 miles
Basilan
Celebes Sea

Introduction

When it comes to romantic locations it would be hard to beat sitting at night under a coconut palm, on a snow-white Filipino beach, cool sand between your toes, icy glass in your hand and balmy night breeze in your hair.

The view out to sea is interrupted by rows of *bancas* – traditional timber and bamboo outriggers – that are lined up, awaiting the next day's quota of divers. They make great dive boats, perfect for hovering over a dive site, and the bamboo poles are amazingly effective stabilisers for kitting up. Below lies the colourful reef, tantalizing and thick with tropical fish and colourful gardens of coral. You wonder what is hiding amongst it all as you drop through the water. In some regions it's a wealth of unusual, small marine animals, in others there's the chance to spend time with plentiful pelagics.

Above the waves, the islands also have the ability to surprise. Just a short hop away from more popular routes for well-heeled divers, this is a destination that retains a sense of the past. It may seem a little dated for some tastes but others will find it refreshing to be in a country that's not rushing headlong into the future.

“” *The Filipinos are welcoming and open, their biggest wish to ensure you love their islands as much as they do.*

Philippines rating

Diving
★★★★

Dive facilities
★★★★

Accommodation
★★★

Down time
★★

Value for money
★★★★

Essentials

Getting there and around

Travel to the Philippines is by no means difficult despite **Philippine Airlines** not having as extensive a network as it once did. If you live anywhere in Europe, you will be routed via a major Middle East or Asian hub. One of the most convenient routes is with **Singapore Airlines** to Manila via Changi or the connection to their subsidiary, **Silk Air**, which takes you to 'second' city Cebu. **Qatar** (www.qatarairways.com) fly via Doha direct to Manila or to Cebu via Singapore. For those flying from Japan, Australia or the US, **Philippine Airlines** can link their internal flights to the long hauls.

There are several other internal airlines in the country including **Air Philippines** (www.airphils.com), **South East Asian Air** (www.flyseair.com), **Cebu Pacific** (www.cebupacificair.com) and **Asian Spirit** (www.asianspirit.com). Between them they can get you almost anywhere although some internal trips can be just as easily achieved by ferry or **fast catamarans** (www.oceanjet.net). Note that their schedules change frequently.

One of the peculiarities of Filipino dive trips is that hotels and operators do not always supply transfers from the airport. This is because they usually involve a small hop on a ferry to another island. However, you will be given full instructions and an outline for each of the dive resorts featured is provided on pages 314-315. Local taxis are cheap and the drivers very helpful. They are especially good at ensuring you reach the first available ferry as sometimes an extra one will have been added or, in low season, stopped. In the cities there are ultra-colourful, but crowded, jeepney buses – you will probably find taxis a better option.

Lettuce coral on Apo Reef

A beach in the Visayas

Language

Despite the centuries of Spanish domination, English is actually the language of the Philippines and is spoken by pretty much the entire nation. The national language, Filipino is a derivative of Tagalog, the most widely spoken indigenous language. If you ask any divemaster or hotel staff what they speak, they look at you quizzically then usually come up with Tagalog. Here are a few words you are likely to hear:

hello	*kumusta*
goodbye	*paalam*
welcome	*mabuhay*
yes	*o-o*
no	*hindi*
I don't know	*di ko alam*
please	*paki*
thank you	*salamat po*
sorry!	*paumanhin po!*
how much is...	*magkano...*
good	*mabait*
great dive!	*tamang sisid!*
one beer/water	*isa pa pong beer/tubig*

Philippines

Location	13°00′ N, 122°00′ E
Neighbours	Indonesia, Borneo Hong Kong, Palau, Vietnam
Population	87,857,473
Land area in km²	298,170
Marine area in km²	1,830
Coastline in km	36,289

Local laws and customs

This is a deeply religious land though it's easy to forget that as you stand beneath a city skyline obliterated by posters depicting American movies, pop stars and mobile phone companies. Move your eyes just a little to see that the rest of the horizon is lined with churches. The Philippines were a Spanish colony for 350 years and 85% of the country is Catholic. The country was sold to America in 1898 for US$20 million and it remained a US possession for 50 years. The American influence seems dominant on the surface but deep down the Filipino nature is still devout. Outside Manila or Cebu, life is more relaxed with fewer Western influences. Remember that you need to be respectful but otherwise there are no specific dress codes or courtesies to be observed.

Safety

When it comes to safety, geography is all important. All government advisories warn against travel to Mindanao and the Sulu Archipelago (Basilan, Tawi-Tawi and Jolo). These very southern islands are the base for the extremist Muslim Abu Sayyaf group, so should be avoided. The good news is that the dive regions of the central Visayas and the Tubbataha Marine Park are over an hour's flight from southern Mindanao and have been unaffected by political problems. Palawan, the most westerly island and departure point for Tubbataha, was targeted in 2000 but has seen nothing since. There have been isolated terrorist actions throughout the country, including Manila, so before wandering off from your hotel get some local advice. Having said that, the risk is probably no worse than in any major city: don't carry valuables around especially after dark, don't leave a bag unattended and don't move away from well lit and well populated areas. Once you are on the islands, it is extremely unlikely that you will find anything to trouble you, even petty crime is minimal as it really doesn't sit well with the people's religious nature. What also doesn't sit well is any form of drug use and the penalties are severe.

Health

Healthcare facilities depend on where you are. Manila has plenty and the islands have fewer and of varying standards. However, health risks are generally low. AIDs is spreading, as is the sex trade, so be wary. There are insect borne diseases but these tend to be in remote, hilly regions rather than on the coast. Malaria is almost unheard of in the Visayas but is a problem in Palawan. Water can be an issue. Some hotels will have purified tap water but check before drinking on the islands. Some still have only brackish water so you will know straight away not to drink that.

Airlines → Asian Spirit T+63 (0)2 8403811, British Airways T+63 (0)2 8170361, Cebu Pacific T+63 (0)2 5285171, Philippine Airlines T+63 (0)2 8166691, Qantas T+63 (0)2 8120607, Singapore Airlines T+63 (0)2 8104951, United T+63 (0)2 8187321. **Embassies** → UK T+63 (0)2 8167116, USA T+63 (0)2 528,6300, Australia T+63 (0)2 7578100. **Philippines country code** → +63. **IDD code** → 00. **Police** → 166.

→ Fact file

International flights	Singapore Airlines, Silk Air, Qatar, Qantas, United
Departure tax	US$10 if not included in your ticket
Entry	EU, USA and Commonwealth – valid passport for stays up to 21 days
Internal flights	South East Asian Air, Air Philippines, Cebu Pacific and Asian Spirit
Ground transport	Jeepney buses, ferries and taxis
Money	US$1 = 55 pesos
Language	English and Tagalog plus regional dialects
Electricity	220v
Time zone	GMT +8
Religion	Roman Catholic

Costs

Of all Southeast Asia's dive destinations and possibly of any other continent, the Philippines could easily be said to be the cheapest. That doesn't mean that standards are low. Accommodation options vary but most are in the 2-3 star range. On the islands you will get far more than you expected for the price – room rates are so low it's hard to believe it. As time goes on, many older guesthouses are rebuilt to a higher standard but the smaller ones can still be charming. Large complexes are rare as land is at a premium on the small islands, plus there simply isn't enough passing tourism to justify that type of resort. Meals costs a few dollars and drinks are unbelievably cheap. At a beach bar, a local beer can be under 50 cents and a gin and tonic easily under US$1. More sophisticated establishments will add a service charge of 10% and some also show a government tax of 12%. If no service charge is on your bill, tipping is the norm, at around 5-10% . For drivers, guides and divemasters, see page 14.

Named after the bird, the equally impressive cockatoo waspfish

Dive brief

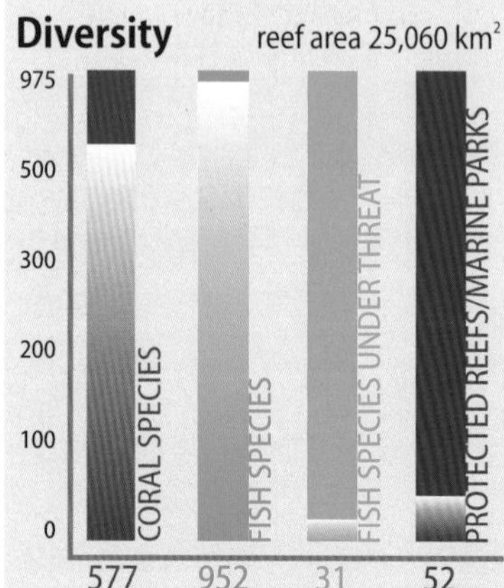

Diving

Can you imagine a country with 7107 (or so) individual islands all ringed with coral reefs? That must be something like 70,000 dive sites to choose from. What a concept.

The Philippines are located within the Pacific's Ring of Fire and, just as significantly, make up a segment of the Coral Triangle. This imaginary boundary is bordered by nearby Indonesia, Papua New Guinea, Malaysia and the Philippines. Within this small space there are more marine species than elsewhere on the planet – more varieties of coral, more fish and more critters. The Filipino islands have their fair share of this wealth. There are luxurious coral reefs, awesome walls, mysterious wrecks, critters by the bucketload and countless marine reserves.

This is also a dive destination that once suffered from a reputation for serious fish bombing and environmental damage to the reefs. However, you will be surprised at the number of small exclusion bays that are patrolled by local villagers. These people have learnt the value of creating protected nursery grounds, if only to be able to fish beyond the no-go zones. There's a huge number of marine reserves across the country including two UNESCO Biosphere Reserves and two World Heritage Sites.

Conditions are fairly easy going. The islands are naturally tidal and currents can be strong but dive centres sensibly divert to protected sites when necessary. Visibility is usually good; murkier in the shallows and crystal clear in oceanic open waters like those around Tubbataha.

Bottom time

Tubbataha
Accolades abound, endorsing the only atolls in the country, now a World Heritage Site » *p308*

The Visayas
Island after island, reef after reef, there are masses of outstanding dives in the central Visayas » *p310*

The spear chucker mantis shrimp

Oriental wrasse in a crinoid

Each night we would head to the beach, bury our toes in the cool sand, and watch our G&Ts sweat quietly on the table. We were completely chilled out, so thoroughly relaxed we'd go into pause mode. Content with the day's diving we would wonder why we had never considered visiting this country before. It was just wonderful. So much so that by the end of two weeks we really didn't want to leave. In fact, we went back within a year just to see if it really was as good as we thought. And it was.

Snorkelling

For the non-diver who likes to join in the fun, the Philippines is a feast. Small reefs run right up to the beach, shallow drop offs are protected and currents are fairly predictable. The water is warm and usually clear enough for surface huggers to still get a good peak below the water line. Options are plenty and the only thing to watch out for is kicking the coral or putting your feet on something sharp or stinging.

The big decision

The Philippines has not fared well with the world's press. Computer viruses and political troubles in the far south have given the impression that this is one tropical idyll that could well be avoided. And genuinely this a great shame as this is a friendly, welcoming country with plenty to offer the travelling diver – not least a well established dive industry with a wide a range of destinations. There are few liveaboards to give you a broader view of the country so choose two slightly different destinations or simply kick back and relax.

A startled, anemone-clad decorator crab

Dive data

Seasons	June-October is rainy; November-February is cool and dry; March-May is hot and dry
Visibility	10-40 metres
Temperatures	Air 23°-32°C; water 25°-30°C
Wet suit	3 mm shorty or full body suit
Training	Courses available in most hotels, standards vary
Nitrox	Not easily available
Deco chambers	Manila, Batangas and Cebu

Conservation

Seahorse trade and conservation

Famous for living in monogamous pairs, and even more so for the fact that the male gets pregnant, you would think that seahorse numbers would be self-sustaining. However, seahorses are one of the most endangered species on the planet. Their environments are continually under threat: seagrass beds are dredged for landfill, mangroves are cut, corals are dynamited and estuaries are polluted. Live seahorses are captured in their hundreds of thousands, destined for aquariums in North America, Europe, Japan or Taiwan. However, the majority of landed seahorses go to traditional Chinese medicine and its derivatives. It's a shock to learn that these are recognized by the World Health Organisation as providing a viable healthcare option, with treatments believed to benefit conditions ranging from respiratory disorders to sexual dysfunction.

The good news is that small-scale seahorse conservation initiatives have been established to recognize the needs of communities that depend on seahorses for income and medicines. Projects in the Philippines and Vietnam are experiencing initial success. So the next time you go diving, should you be lucky enough to find one of these exceptional sea creatures, then count yourself lucky and savour the memory. Who knows how long they will be with us?

Dive log

Tubbataha

There's nothing but blue as far as you can see in any direction. Bright blue sky and deep blue sea. It feels like you are in the middle of nowhere but it's actually the middle of the Sulu Sea in the far west of the Philippine archipelago, en route to the Tubbataha Reef Marine Park.

An hour or so by plane from either Manila or Cebu is the island of Palawan, a beautiful place and a dive destination of some note. However, most divers travel through just to reach the unique Tubbataha Marine Reserve. Designated a World Heritage Site in 1993, the reserve encapsulates the only two atolls in the Philippines. North and South Reef are separated by an 8-km-wide channel. North Reef is a rectangular, continuous platform about 16 km long and 4.5 km wide. The inner, sandy lagoon is just 24 metres deep. South Reef is smaller, triangular shaped, less than 2 km wide and also encloses a sandy lagoon. Both atolls are landless, except for one tiny sand cay each. These are used by birds and turtles as nesting sites.

Tubbataha can only be dived in the late spring due to rough sea crossings at other times. Currents are variable and most dives are drifts. Tenders follow diver bubbles in case of a change of direction but, arriving early on a spring morning, you are greeted with a glassy surface and nothing but sunshine. Underwater, steep-sided walls rim oval reefs with visibility to die for. Peer down enormous drops coated in gorgonians and impressive sponges. In the open water you will see pelagics: reef sharks, barracuda and tuna all cruise by at a lazy pace. Turtles are all over the reef tops and rays flit by frequently. Whilst not the prettiest of reef systems – reef tops have been damaged by illegal fishing and coral growth is inhibited by natural weather conditions – this is definitely the place for big guys.

Blue water flight

1 Jessie Beazley Reef

- **Depth**: 32 m
- **Visibility**: good to great
- **Currents**: can be strong
- **Dive type**: liveaboard
- **Snorkelling**: current dependent

Just north of Tubbataha's reef system, Jessie Beazley is a regular stopover for liveaboards. The reef here is in good condition with a shallow top level rising to 5 metres and the deepest vertical wall dropping to a sandy bed at about 60 metres. The walls are covered in fans and branching corals that house lots of small colourful fish. However, the main action is off the wall with plenty of pelagic species. There are barracuda and tuna, several shark species (but only the whitetips come in close) and quite a lot of schooling fish. At night on the shallower sections there are saron shrimp peeking out from the coral, decorator crabs, squat lobsters and seahares.

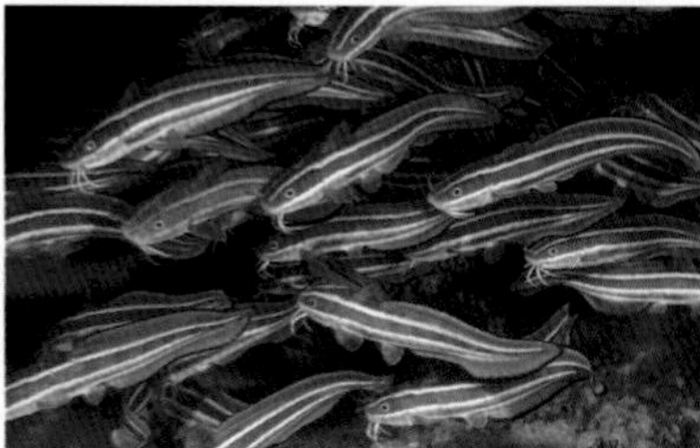

Catfish swim huddled in a ball

2 Shark Airport, North Tubbataha

- **Depth**: 35 m
- **Visibility**: stunning
- **Currents**: can be strong
- **Dive type**: liveaboard
- **Snorkelling**: current dependent

One of the north's shallower dives, a gentle slope drops away from the reef rim before turning into the wall. There are some overhangs, caves and crevices that head deep into no man's land but as the visibility is so amazing you can see a long way down. The wall is decorated with bright seafans and some soft corals while pelagic fish pass by. There are jacks and rainbow runners and the ever-present whitetips that hover on the tails of snappers. Heading back up, the sloping section pans out into a long strip of sand – the airport – surrounded by coral bommies. For some reason, this sandy ledge is covered in sharks – whitetips rest there in neat squadrons. They don't even move off when divers approach, unless they get too close. This is a great site for a night dive too, although the sharks will have taken off by dusk.

3 *Malayan* Wreck, North Atoll

- **Depth**: 32 m
- **Visibility**: stunning
- **Currents**: none to strong
- **Dive type**: liveaboard
- **Snorkelling**: yes

Inside the lagoon on the southwestern edge of the atoll is an exposed rusting wreck, the *Malayan*, while outside a gentle slope drops way down into the sea. As the topography is comparatively gentle there are many ledges worth exploring. Lobsters are easy to spot and you might even encounter a nurse shark lurking in one. You will definitely see loads of reef sharks swimming past the wall and there are also plenty of turtles, though there are sharks and turtles everywhere in Tubbataha. It becomes a standing joke back on board as divers compete on the numbers seen. They are always there but always wary and rarely swim close. The top level of the reef is a patchy garden of mixed corals with a few giant clams, sea cucumbers and pufferfish.

4 Black Rock, South Atoll

- **Depth**: 38 m
- **Visibility**: stunning
- **Currents**: mild to strong
- **Dive type**: liveaboard
- **Snorkelling**: yes but current dependent

The geography of the south atoll is somewhat gentler than the sharp walls of the north but this sloping reef eventually goes well beyond where you should be – it's hard to remember when the visibility is so clear. The wall has substantial gorgonians and some impressive barrel sponges swarmed by schools of reef fish. Rainbow runners are interspersed with an occasional tuna or barracuda while on the wall there are squirrel and soldierfish, lionfish and morays. Eaglerays have been seen here but most exciting, on the right day, are the mantas. They are not a regular attraction but when they do arrive there are often several of them and they hang around for hours at a time, lazily flapping about.

5 Lighthouse, South Atoll

- **Depth**: 29 m
- **Visibility**: stunning
- **Currents**: mild to strong
- **Dive type**: liveaboard
- **Snorkelling**: yes but current dependent

There are several dives within sight of the Lighthouse. They all spread away from the southern point on a sloping gradient. The reef's surface is covered in small leather corals, whips and sponges which attract many smaller creatures such as starfish, anemones and clownfish, damsels and anthias. Closer in to shore are some seagrass beds that attract rays to feed – you can see grey rays and bluespotted rays hovering about and also more turtles, many of which are quite young and only the size of dinner plates.

Tales from the deep

Turtle overload

I was looking for a liveaboard in Southeast Asia and wanted it to go to a little dived area. When I found this trip to Tubbataha it seemed perfect so I booked it. Looking back it was a funny trip - the only thing that stands out in my memory was the turtles. The reefs were fine and the water was incredibly clear, but my overwhelming impression is turtles, turtles and more turtles. I always rate a destination by whether I would go back.

I really like the Philippines and I enjoyed this trip but I don't think I would repeat it as there are so many other parts of the country I *do* want to try.

Keith Gretton, Nottingham, UK

Turtle on retreat

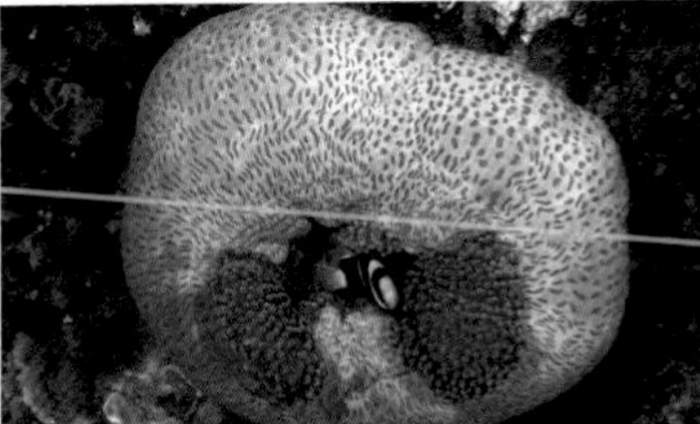
Anemone with its commensal clownfish

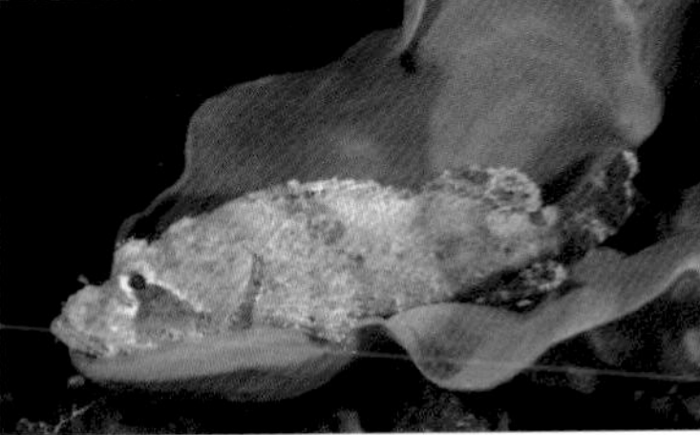
Scorpionfish resting

The Visayas

Half way down the Philippine map is the Visayas, the central region of tiny islands, deservedly famous for their powdery white beaches and relaxed lifestyle. Once the preserve of long-term travellers who tried to keep it quiet, the islands' reputation finally leaked out.

There's an international airport at Cebu which provides access to dive resorts just a short ferry ride away. And some of these possess sub-aqua splendour that really must be seen. There are so many wonderful dive areas in the Visayas it's amazing that there's no liveaboard. Some appear but then just as quickly disappear again. Perhaps that's because life on the islands is simply too appealing. Diving is supported by lots of high-quality, often European-run, dive centres and conditions are fairly easy going.

Panglao Island Just a quick hop from Cebu to Bohol and you'll find a destination loved by anyone who has ever been out this way. Alona Beach on Panglao may not be sophisticated but it's definitely one of the best 'no news-no shoes' destinations. There are several dive centres, many small charming hotels and masses of stunning dive sites, all within minutes of shore. Just off the perfect white beach are caves to swim through, deep walls smothered in coral and enormous elephant ear sponges that hide matching football-sized frogfish. Sail a little north to Cabilao to find deep drifts that host hammerheads or west to immerse yourself in the black coral forests of Balicasag.

Negros The coastal reefs of eastern Negros were once regarded as damaged due to overfishing. Then someone got the idea to teach local fishing communities about the value of the dive dollar and the coast around Dumaguete is now riddled with tiny marine sanctuaries and projects for sustainable fishing. This is probably one of the best macro locations you will ever find. Think of a critter, mention it to the divemaster and off you go to see it. And just in case you might (unbelievably) get bored with all that, a short sail away is the country's most successful marine sanctuary, Apo Island. An experiment in marine rejuvenation, this splendid island is home to turtles, schooling pelagics and pristine hard corals.

6 Coconut Point, Apo Island

- **Depth**: 28 m
- **Visibility**: stunning
- **Currents**: slight to ripping
- **Dive type**: day boat
- **Snorkelling**: possibly

Apo sits in the channel between Negros and Siquijor islands and as such is an open water dive that contrasts sharply with the shallow waters on the nearby coast. This is big blue territory with all sorts of pelagic species. The island's highly successful marine sanctuary is run by local people with great enthusiasm. There are several dives but Coconut Point is the big-thrill experience. It catches some very strong currents, especially as you head out to the point, and as ever it's the currents that attract the fish. The dive commences over a flat reef that has a good cover of hard corals. It then slopes out to a tongue with steep walls where jacks, snapper and rainbow runners patrol. There is a sandy cut that provides some shelter if the current is really ripping and from here you can watch turtles, enormous groupers, Napoleon wrasse and whitetip sharks.

Pufferfish in a tin

Sea snake at Apo Island

7 El Dorado Reef, Dumaguete

- **Depth**: 16 m
- **Visibility**: medium to good
- **Currents**: slight to strong
- **Dive type**: shore
- **Snorkelling**: yes

Just out the front of El Dorado, one of the original dive resorts in the region, is this amazing beach dive. Wander out from the restaurant then fin down over the dark sand slope. This descends to about 20 metres and around a circular bed of staghorn corals, past some coral bommies and back up to the seagrass bed near the start. There are some items of rubbish about: a few tyres and logs that encourage animals to hide out. It's a bit like a treasure hunt especially at night – in a single dive you can see five or six different types of frogfish, crinoid shrimp, nudibranchs and a few leaffish. Shining your torch around may suddenly spotlight a barracuda, which is a bit of a shock in the dark! Then there are plenty of shells, flatworms, crabs, shrimps and bluespotted rays moving around the sandy areas.

8 Dauin

- **Depth**: 30 m
- **Visibility**: medium to good
- **Currents**: slight to medium
- **Dive type**: shore/day boat
- **Snorkelling**: yes

For anyone interested in small cryptic marine dwellers, this is simply heaven. The dive starts at a bamboo pyramid, a man-made structure of roped up bamboo poles. You can spend a lot of time here inspecting it for creatures. There are white clown frogfish, brown painted ones, pipefish and shrimp hidden in cracks and crevices, and a barred blenny living in a carved hole. As you head south across the crest of the slope, there are logs surrounded by balling catfish, old tyres with dwarf lionfish and flying gurnards on the sand. A little further along you see snake eel noses poking from the sand then it's down to a hollow where a black crinoid houses tiny ornate ghost pipefish. At the base of the slope, a rubbish pile is the known homepatch of several seahorses. These are permanent residents and you can often see a male one with a tummy full of eggs. The spot is also good for morays, flamboyant cuttlefish and stonefish encounters. If you were to fin a little north of here, you would come across the wrecks of some old cars, then a wooden *bangka*, all of which are smothered in life – lionfish, scorpions and batfish. There is even a rare, juvenile zebra batfish on occasion. Or you could turn south and uphill to spin along the edge of the coral sanctuary with its baby sharks and butterflyfish then back along the crest until – if you are really lucky – you spot the mimic octopus. He resides very close to a snake eel and, in fact, usually appears as one. The giveaway is when he extends a lone tentacle pretending to be a seasnake then suddenly transforms into a mantis shrimp! Quite a spectacle. Finally, heading past the pyramid, there is a broad patch of seagrass in shallow water that makes a perfect, extended safety stop. In fact, you can spend a very long time here hunting for critters in amongst the green blades. There are more frogfish and seahorses, juvenile razorfish, fingered dragonets, devilfish and a spectacular find for patient spotters is the Pegasus seamoth.

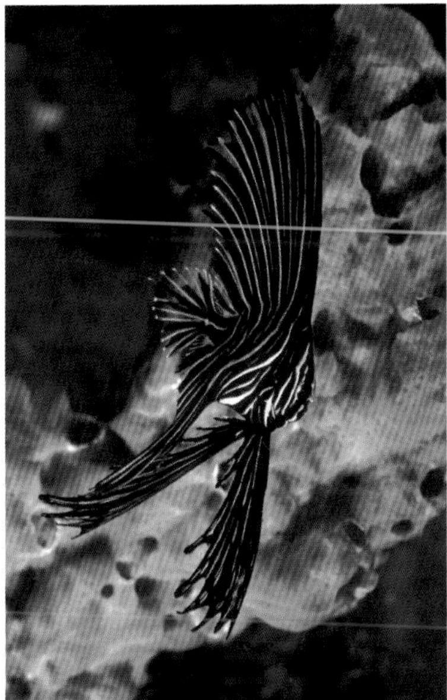

A very rare juvenile zebra batfish

Ornate ghost pipefish trying to blend in

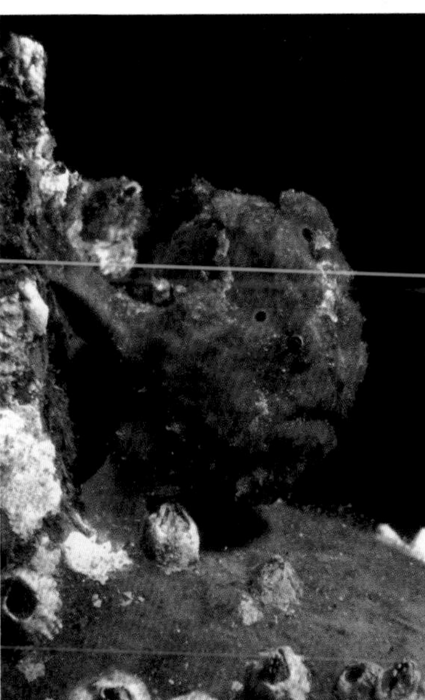

This frogfish lives on Dauin's bamboo pyramid

9 Alona Beach Sanctuary

- **Depth**: 20 m
- **Visibility**: good to great
- **Currents**: slight to medium
- **Dive type**: shore/day boat
- **Snorkelling**: yes

The pristine beach at Alona is very shallow, so much so that at low tide boats struggle to cross it. To protect the reef from damage a section is buoyed off and the area below is now a sanctuary. At high tide the reef is at 10 metres and at its edge, the drop off descends to about 20 metres. The wall is cut with vertical crevices and there is a broad array of hard corals and fans, tunicates and small sponges. It's colourful with plenty of fish to admire both day and night. In fact, the reef top is one of the best night dives in the area and slow inspection of the many small outcrops will reveal a myriad of weird critters. There are parrot and cardinalfish, flatworms, nudibranchs, shells, frogfish, tiny cuttlefish, tiny cuttlefish nabbing cardinalfish and lionfish preying on whatever they can.

10 Arco Point

- **Depth**: 28 m
- **Visibility**: good to great
- **Currents**: slight to medium
- **Dive type**: day boat
- **Snorkelling**: yes

Heading east from the section of beach where the village is, you come across this small, submerged point. In the top of the reef, sitting right on the beautiful white sand, is a blue hole about 2 metres wide. This descends through the reef and emerges on the wall at about 20 metres and is lined with soft corals and whips, lots of small morays and plenty of fish. After exiting you swim to the base of a completely vertical wall where there is one of the largest purple fan corals you will ever see. A patch of tubastrea is a known haunt for frogfish. The wall winds in and out, lined with plenty of corals, then it's back up on the sandy flat reef for a safety stop. You can go critter hunting over the sand where there are motionless pipefish and inimicus, ribbon eels, pufferfish and many sand dwellers.

11 Doljo

- **Depth**: 32 m
- **Visibility**: good to great
- **Currents**: slight to strong
- **Dive type**: day boat
- **Snorkelling**: yes

Just around the northwestern point of Panglao the topography changes to sloping wall formations. This drop off is coated in fans interspersed with enormous elephant's ear sponges. As the current here can be strong at times these are used by several types of fish as a perch. They sit inside and watch the passing show, and if that show includes lunch, so much the better. You can hop from a pink sponge with a pink scorpionfish to a grey sponge with a matching frogfish. The divemasters like to play games with divers, waving vaguely at an area to see if you can spot well camouflaged creatures. There are also long, trailing finger sponges that are equally good hiding spots for black frogfish and schools of young batfish, which are often just the size of your hand.

The menacing grimace of a snake eel

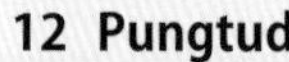

12 Pungtud

- **Depth**: 24 m
- **Visibility**: good
- **Currents**: slight to medium
- **Dive type**: day boat
- **Snorkelling**: yes

Bordering the submerged wall on the western tip of Panglao, this dive can be swept by currents. As you descend over the first section of wall, it blazes with brightly coloured feeding soft corals. There are snapper and mackerel off in the blue and large puffers sit closer in. As you round the bend, the current drops away and you have more time to investigate the wall's residents. You can find interesting small creatures like orang-utan crabs and bright nudibranchs. Up on the reef flat are even more curious critters: snake eels, twintailed slugs and balls of catfish. Banded seasnakes are surprisingly common; you can see as many as five on a single dive.

13 Blackforest, Balicasag

- **Depth**: 33 m
- **Visibility**: good to stunning
- **Currents**: slight to strong
- **Dive type**: shore/day boat
- **Snorkelling**: yes

Just 40 minutes southwest of Bohol is one of the country's best known marine sanctuaries. Balicasag Island is under the jurisdiction of the Philippine Navy and there is a small resort. The beaches are ringed by sudden drop-offs which, combined with strong currents, attract pelagic species. One of the best dives is Blackforest, a swathe of incredibly prolific black corals that shimmer in gold and silver whenever the current is running. Although black corals tend to be found mostly in deep water, there is a patch here that comes right up to 30 metres and many animals hide in amongst them – giant frogfish are regular finds. Meanwhile, out in the blue are balls of jacks, batfish and moorish idols. A school of barracuda pass by then, as you ascend, you find ledges and patches of sloping sand. Looking down you will spot nudibranchs, pipefish and tiny scorpionfish.

The wings of the flying gurnard

Reticulated moray looking at the lens

14 The Lighthouse, Cabilao

- **Depth**: 20 m
- **Visibility**: good to stunning
- **Currents**: slight to strong
- **Dive type**: shore/day boat
- **Snorkelling**: yes

It takes about two hours to sail from Panglao to Cabilao but as a day trip, it's worth it. You can also stay here; the triangular island is as lovely as any in the area. Each side is lined with dive site after dive site. Like Alona, these tend to have shallow, flat reef tops with steep walls. One of Cabilao's features though are extensive areas of good hard corals. Another is that, in the cooler months (December-April), there is the possibility of seeing large, migrating schools of hammerheads near the lighthouse. The rest of the year it's more likely that you'll spot a passing whitetip or two. The walls are painted with corals and sponges and plenty of tropical fish. Up in the shallows there is a seagrass bed that has plenty of small finds. There are catfish, tiny caverns full of banded pipefish, stone, scorpion and leaffish. If you were staying here, obviously it would be a great night dive.

The wall at Pungtud

Tales from the deep

One-two-three: count the firsts

Blackforest, as its name suggests, is an enchanting site where I experienced three firsts! On this one dive, there were gentle currents. At the beginning, we stumbled on a playful baby whaleshark that took pleasure out of diver's bubbles bursting and tickling its 'undercarriage'. Then as we descended to the sea bottom, the divemaster proudly unveiled my first harlequin ghost pipefish – what more could one ask for! (Score: 1 pelagic, 1 macro). The special finale came when we were greeted with the biggest school of spiralling jacks I've ever seen – what a treat! This was certainly one of my best dives ever.

Carol Lim, Editor, Asian Diver

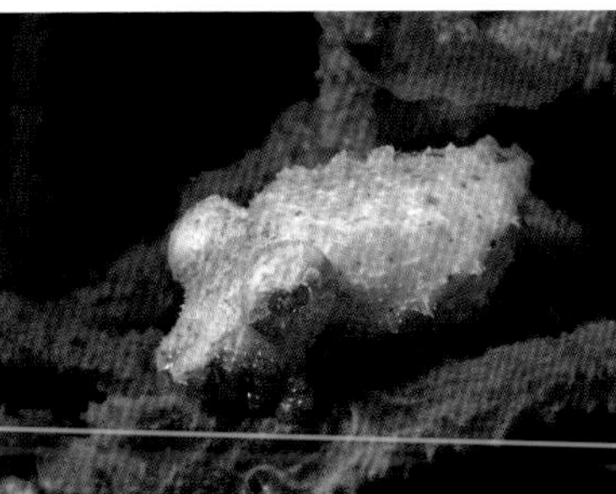

This stumpy-spined cuttlefish is just 50 mm long

The *cymbiola vespertilio* shell has no common name

Drying out

The Philippine islands don't rage with cultural sites but there are a few good attractions for drying out days.

Tubbataha

Although a web search will reveal several liveaboard boats that trek out to Tubbataha it can be difficult to get accurate, up-to-date information. One reliable operator is The Explorer Fleet, a division of Cruise Island Adventures. Itineraries work to flight schedules so you are unlikely to need to stop in Puerto Princesa, the capital of Palawan, unless you choose to. PP is 1 hr and 10 mins from Manila.

Liveaboards

MY Stella Maris Explorer, Cruise Island Adventures, 4/F Metrostar Building Metropolitan Av, Makati City, T+63 (0)35 8906778, www.explorerfleet.com. Stella Maris is just one of the vessels in this fleet that has schedules through Tubbataha. Another part of the company is Scuba World which has several resorts throughout the country and can arrange multi-centre trips. www.scubaworld.com.ph

The Visayas – Panglao Island

Sitting on the south coast of Panglao is Alona Beach. To get there means catching a fast ferry from Cebu to Tagbilaran, the capital of Bhol, then taking a short drive over the even shorter bridge that connects the two islands. Transfer time from Cebu airport should be under 2 hrs.

Dive centres

Philippine Islands Divers – Bohol, Alona Beach, Danao, Panglao, T+63 (0)38 5029048, www.phildivers.com. Dive company with a very informative website and German, Swiss, French, Japanese and Filipino divemasters. Also on Malapascua Island, T+63 (0)32 4371088.

Sea Explorers, 36 Archbishop Reyes Av, Knights of Columbus Square, Cebu City, T+63 (0)32 2340248, www.sea-explorers .com. One of the region's most professional dive groups with 6 centres across the Visayas. Swiss-owned with multilingual guides.

Sleeping and diving

$ **Alona Kew White Beach Resort**, Tawala, Panglao Island, Bohol, T+63 (0)38 5029027,

Traditional fishing fleet near Dumaguete

Boat boy on Alona Beach

www.alonakew.com. Charming beachfront resort in the Filipino style.
$ **Alona Palm Beach Resort**, T+63 (0)38 5029141, www.alonapalmbeach.com. More modern accommodation and working with Philippine Islands Divers, as above.
$ **Alona Tropical Beach Resort**, Alona Tropical Resort, Alona Beach, Panglao, T+63 (0)38 5029024. Nice older style property at the end of the beach and working with Sea Explorers, www.sea-explorers.com.

Eating

All the resorts on Alona have restaurants attached plus there are several small beach-front cafés where you will be amazed at how they can turn out such delicious meals from a kitchen the size of a handkerchief.

Sights

Bohol was a Spanish settlement and you can spend a lazy day touring some of her features. Any dive centre will organize a driver and car for you. There are a few 17th and 18th century churches and Tagbilaran has some attractive tree-lined plazas, colonial houses and a small museum. If you prefer something more natural take a cruise along the **Loboc River** in a pumpboat, passing local villages, or you could go hiking in the hills. The most famous attraction is the **Chocolate Hills**, a landscape of 1200 grassy mounds that look like someone tipped up bags of sugar in rows. In the summer, the domes turn brown, transforming the area into rows of 'chocolate' mounds. This is regarded as a national monument. The province is also home to the world's smallest primate, the tarsier. This diminutive creature is endangered and you can see them at several reserves.

Jeepney in Cebu City

The Visayas – Negros

The small city of Dumaguete sits on Negros Oriental. The city is a 1 hr 15 mins' flight from Manila or about 3 hrs by fast ferry from Cebu City. The resorts are then just 20-30 mins' drive.

Sleeping and diving

$$ **Pura Vida Beach and Dive Resort**, Washington St, Dauin, Negros Oriental, T+63 (0)35 4252284, www.pura-vida.ph and www.sea-explorers.com. A newer resort built on eco-lines and with well-known Sea Explorers on site.
$$-$ **Bahura Resort and Spa**, Dauin, Negros Oriental, T+63 (0)35 8906778, www.bahura.com. This new and modern resort is right on Dauin Beach. It has a range of accommodation options and an in-house dive centre.
$ **El Dorado Beach Resort**, Lipayo, Dauin, Negros Oriental, T+ 63 (0)35 4252274. An older resort but rather nice. Good restaurant right on the beach and a Swiss-run dive operator called Dive Society on site.

Eating

All resorts have onsite restaurants and it would be unusual to stray far. There are plenty of eating places in Dumaguete City if you fancy a day out with food styles ranging from Filipino and Chinese to fast-food joints.

Sights

Negros has less of an historical nature to divert you away from the marine realm but if you like hiking there are two good walks that can be done in a day. The **twin crater lakes** are surrounded by a forest canopy and are several hours' hike from the town of Sibulan. The **Casaroro Falls** are hidden amidst thick forest trees and can only be reached by hiking through steep, narrow trails from Valencia. There's plenty of retail therapy in **Dumaguete City** and **Tanjay** is known as the Christmas Village as the town remains decorated for 365 days a year.

The Chocolate Hills

Manila

Hustling, bustling, messy, noisy. Manila is safe enough but has no real appeal for divers. However, if you have to pass through on your way to the islands, book into a hotel near the airport and catch up on some sleep before flying out again. These 4-star hotels are remarkably good value and less than 15 mins transfer. If you go further afield note that Manila's notorious traffic can turn a 20 min transfer into well over an hour.

Sleeping

$$$ **Heritage Hotel Manila**, Roxas Blvd, Pasay City, Metro Manila, T+63 (0)2 8548888, www.heritagehotelmanila.com. A block from the Hyatt with similar facilities but a bit more expensive.
$$ **Hyatt Regency**, 2702 Roxas Blvd, Pasay City, Metro Manila, T+63 (0)2 8331234, www.manila.regency.hyatt.com. Four-star luxury at reasonable rates if you book online. Packages include a scrumptious breakfast and airport transfers.

The diminutive tarsier

Micronesia

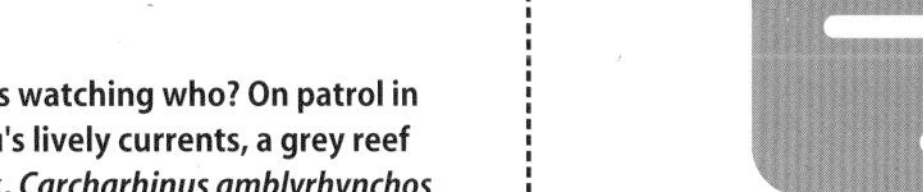

Who's watching who? On patrol in Palau's lively currents, a grey reef shark, *Carcharhinus amblyrhynchos*

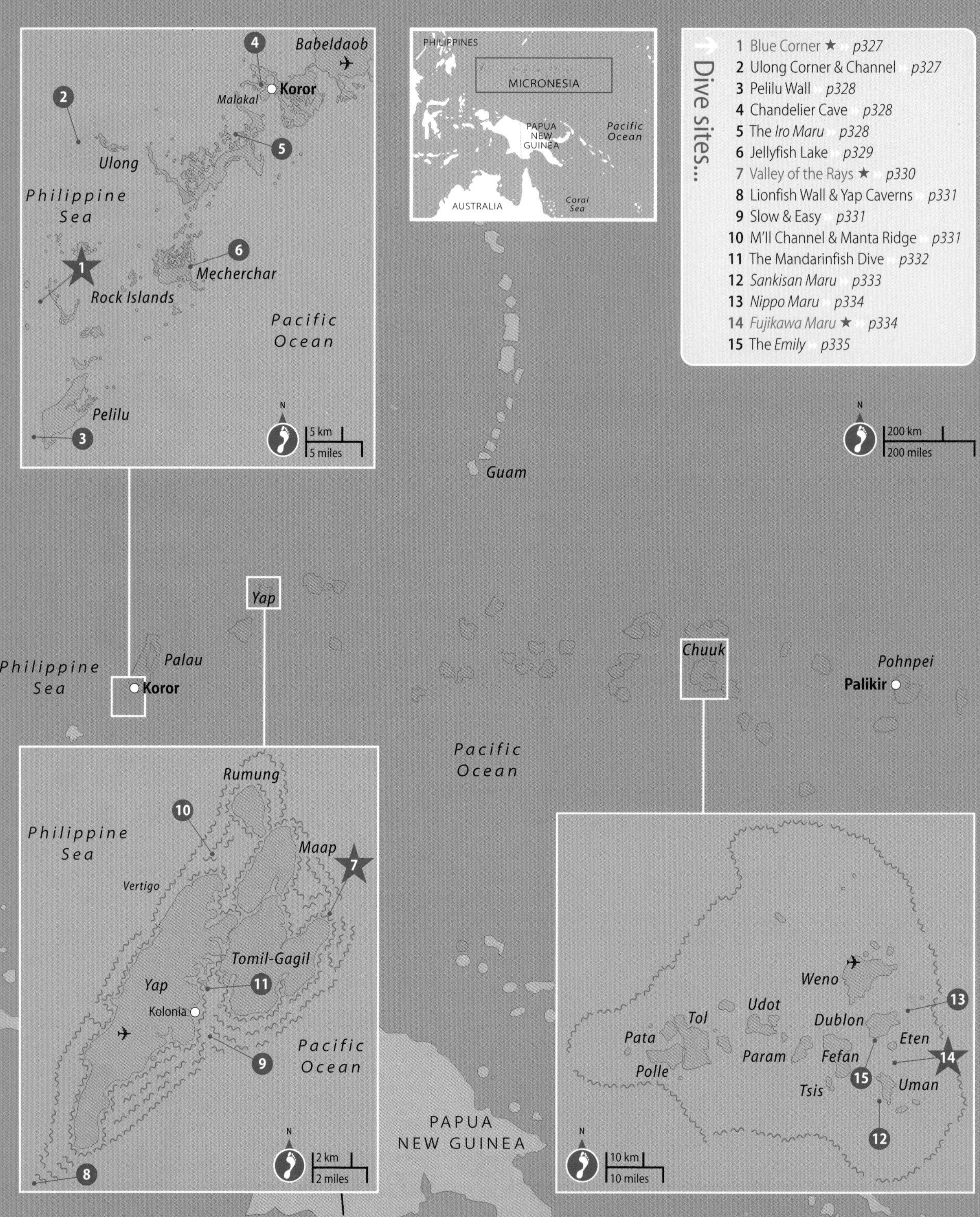

Dive sites...
1 Blue Corner ★ p327
2 Ulong Corner & Channel p327
3 Pelilu Wall p328
4 Chandelier Cave p328
5 The Iro Maru p328
6 Jellyfish Lake p329
7 Valley of the Rays ★ p330
8 Lionfish Wall & Yap Caverns p331
9 Slow & Easy p331
10 M'll Channel & Manta Ridge p331
11 The Mandarinfish Dive p332
12 Sankisan Maru p333
13 Nippo Maru p334
14 Fujikawa Maru ★ p334
15 The Emily p335
Babeldaob
Koror
Malakal
Ulong
Philippine Sea
Mecherchar
Rock Islands
Pacific Ocean
Pelilu
5 km
5 miles
PHILIPPINES
MICRONESIA
PAPUA NEW GUINEA
Pacific Ocean
AUSTRALIA
Coral Sea
200 km
200 miles
Guam
Yap
Palau
Koror
Chuuk
Pohnpei
Palikir
Pacific Ocean
Rumung
Maap
Vertigo
Tomil-Gagil
Yap
Kolonia
2 km
2 miles
PAPUA NEW GUINEA
Weno
Udot
Tol
Dublon
Pata
Eten
Param
Fefan
Polle
Uman
Tsis
10 km
10 miles

Introduction

Flying in to Micronesia is an unforgettable experience. The aerial views are of awe-inspiring beauty: handfuls of green islands are sprinkled over deep blue seas. There is no development here, no high rise, no motorways. Micronesia sits quietly apart from the 'real' world.

The island groups of Palau, Yap and Chuuk are like a set of triplets, each beautiful, each charming but, for divers, each one with its own personality. Palau is the precocious one, leaping to the fore to display her many talents; she has a bit of everything and something for every visitor. Yap stands shyly to the side, modest about her own charms, yet quietly proud of her year-round populations of manta rays. Nearby lurks Chuuk, moody and mysterious but admired for her Second World War wrecks. But though each of them have their own specific features to sell, they are all set against a backdrop of a prolific marine realm.

On land, it's a little contradictory, too. Each of them has developed at a different pace: one rushing headlong towards a western future; one shying away from outside influences; and one that's just not sure which way to jump.

“” The challenge was in being somewhere completely new, where you think you know what to expect, then realizing you didn't have a clue.

Micronesia rating

Diving
★★★★★

Dive facilities
★★★★

Accommodation
★★★★

Down time
★★★

Value for money
★★★

Essentials

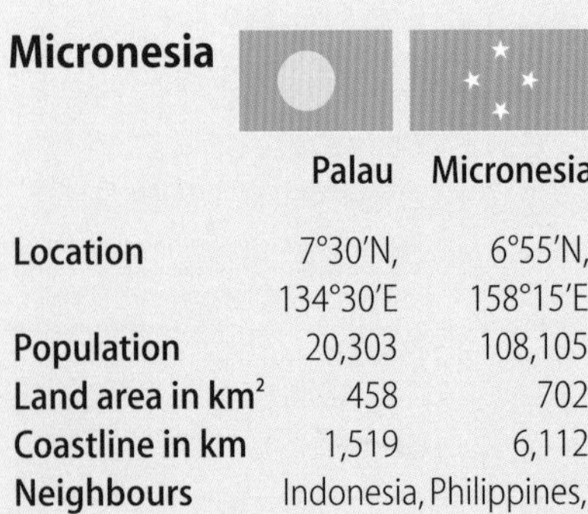

Micronesia

	Palau	Micronesia
Location	7°30'N, 134°30'E	6°55'N, 158°15'E
Population	20,303	108,105
Land area in km²	458	702
Coastline in km	1,519	6,112
Neighbours	Indonesia, Philippines, Japan, Hawaii	

Getting there and around

There's hard to get to, there's expensive to get to, and then there's Micronesia. But before you give up, do bear in mind that there are potentially huge rewards for those who make the effort to go. The only airline that runs any sort of consistent service to the Republic of Palau and the Federated States of Micronesia (FSM) is **Continental Airlines** (www.continental.com). Previously known as **Air Micronesia**, this service has been through many incarnations but remains one with no competition that can charge what it likes – and does.

Continental's Micronesia flights depart from Manila, Hong Kong, Taipei, Tokyo, Los Angeles, Honolulu, Cairns or Bali to Guam, where you transfer to another flight for your final destination. Guam is a US Territory so this means clearing American immigration and hanging about in the airport before departing again. A better option is to fly from Manila direct to Palau. There are twice weekly flights and the Saturday flight then travels onwards to Yap. On any other day of the week, or to get to Chuuk (Truk), you have to go via Guam.

Many airlines have flights to the hub cities listed above but it's worth investigating if a particular airline has links with Continental so you can make a through booking. It also appears that US travel agents have access to cheaper fares than those in other countries so you could enquire through them.

The Rock Islands

Transfers on all the islands will be handled by your dive operation or hotel. For a bit of sightseeing in Palau, taxis are the best way to get about and reasonably economical (so long as you don't catch too many). In Yap, many sights are within walking distance but you can also take a taxi. On Chuuk, you are unlikely to go very far – see safety below for advice.

Dive boats off Ulong Island

Language

The lingua franca is English. Those wishing to try some of the local languages may well find themselves up against it. In Palau many dive crews are Filipino, in Yap they all seem to come from Chuuk while in Chuuk they might be from an outlying island and look at you blankly when you try using a word or two. All the same, it can never hurt to try:

Palauan

hello	*alii*	thank you	*ulang*
goodbye	*mechik'ung*	sorry!	*komeng!*
yes	*choch'oi*	no problem	*diak a mondai*
no	*diak*	cool or ok	*keblois*
please	*adang*		

Yapese

hello	*mogethin*	thank you	*kammegar*
goodbye	*kefel*	sorry!	*sirow!*
yes	*arrogon*	no problem	*dari fan*
no	*danga*	good	*mangil*
please	*wenig*		

Chuukese

hello	*ras annim*	please	*kose mochen*
goodbye (if staying)	*kenne no*	thank you	*kinisou*
goodbye (if leaving)	*kenne nom*	sorry!	*tirow* or *omusalo*
yes	*uu (wu)*	no problem	*lese wor* (or)
no	*apw*	ok	*mi och*

Barracudas avoiding a grey reef shark

Airlines → Continental on Palau T+680 (1)488 2448, on Yap T+691 (1)350 2702, on Chuuk T+691 (1)330 2424. **Embassies** → The closest UK Embassy is in Fiji T+679 3229100. The US Embassy is in the FSM capital, Pohnpei T+691 (1)320 2187 as is the Australian Embassy T+691 (1)320 5448. **Palau country code** → +680. **FSM country code** → +691. **IDD code** → 011. **Police** → 911.

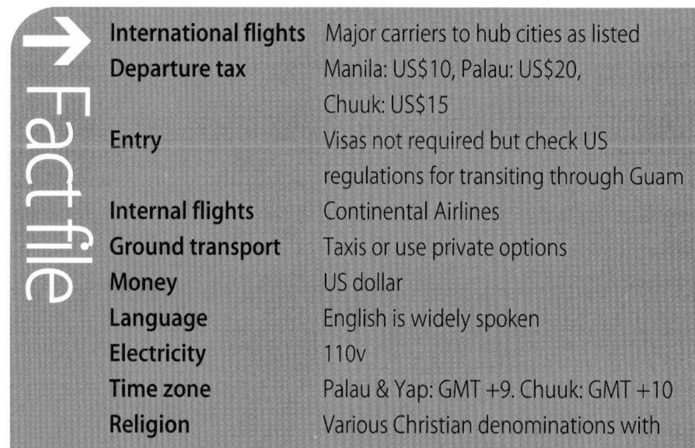

Fact file

International flights	Major carriers to hub cities as listed
Departure tax	Manila: US$10, Palau: US$20, Chuuk: US$15
Entry	Visas not required but check US regulations for transiting through Guam
Internal flights	Continental Airlines
Ground transport	Taxis or use private options
Money	US dollar
Language	English is widely spoken
Electricity	110v
Time zone	Palau & Yap: GMT +9. Chuuk: GMT +10
Religion	Various Christian denominations with many fringe and evangelical forms

Terry's dive brief for the *Iro*

Health

There are no specific inoculations or warnings for either Palau or Micronesia. There is malaria but reported incidences are extremely rare. Take the usual precautions to protect against insect bites. Drinking water is either bottled or is filtered and food standards are generally high. Koror on Palau has an excellent hospital with a double lock decompression chamber. There is also one in the small but well equipped hospital on Yap and there are unconfirmed reports of a new chamber on Chuuk.

Costs

All three islands covered in this chapter can be said to be expensive. There is little agriculture or industry so much has to be imported. Costs aren't so high as to be prohibitive. In general most things are just a little bit more expensive than in the US. The US dollar is also the official currency. A beer will be US$3-4, a glass of wine, US$4-5. Meals tend to be international style and around US$10 for a main course. Accommodation is limited everywhere except in Palau which has the most options in all prices ranges. Yap has just a handful and the lower end places are not really worth investigating. Chuuk has only two land options and these are similarly priced (see page 336). There are substantial marine park fees in Palau (US$35) and Chuuk (US$30).

Local laws and customs

Each of the islands that are loosely grouped together as Micronesia were first inhabited by seafarers from the countries we now know as Indonesia and the Philippines. Their ancient cultures were quite sophisticated with highly structured social groups but as each island developed in isolation from each other so their cultures differ.

Palau's history reaches back to the Stone Age when it was a highly family orientated and matrilineal society. Women were in charge of finances and men had to ask permission to spend! After several centuries of European colonialism, the islands were subsequently influenced by the Japanese during the Second World War and the Americans after the war. Independence was granted in 1994. The net result is a melting pot of cultures with a cosmopolitan atmosphere. The biggest influence now is probably Chinese but with workers from the Philippines, Japan, America and Europe. You are unlikely to see much in the way of tradition, except perhaps some money beads in a souvenir shop. One thing you will also see is a substantial use of turtle shell and corals for making nicknacks. Don't buy these items as the trade should be discouraged and import of turtle shell to many countries is illegal. As ever, dress neatly, be respectful of the elderly and should you be invited into someone's home, take off your shoes.

Yap's traditional stone money

On entry to Palau, a customs gent pulled our small group over. "See what they do," he said, nodding at a young Chinese girl, "they think they can fool us." And he opened a toothpaste box. The tube inside was packed to bursting with drugs. He waved us through without so much as a glance at our dive bags, and yes, we left suitably impressed by his subtle warning.

Yap is far more traditional. The islands were only opened for tourism in 1989 and her culture remains fairly true to the past. The powerful Yapese empire was pretty much ignored until the whaling industry arrived in the 1800s bringing with it European, Japanese and American influences. The village remains the social hub and each chief still holds sway over his clan. The sexes live fairly separate lives and although this is changing, there is a determination to keep traditions alive. Rumang has closed its doors to all but locals. They even took away the bridge to the island! People are friendly but come across as being rather shy. Always say hello to anyone you pass, ask permission to walk across someone's land, even if it appears to be public, and never photograph a person without asking first. Women must cover their thighs and covered knees are a good idea, too. Never step across someone who is sitting and carry something if you go for a walk. Being empty handed is said to show signs of being a troublemaker.

Chuuk's contemporary history seems to have eroded much of her past. There are few traditions, at least none that are obvious to a travelling diver. There was no substantial European contact until the Spanish came in the 1800's to collect beche de mer (sea cucumbers). The Germans briefly took hold at the end of the century until the Japanese were given control in a League of Nations treaty around the end of the First World War. Part of the Federated States of Micronesia, Chuuk is the most populous state and as such has the highest quota of senators in government. Yet it also appears the most rundown and is struggling to cope with the modern world. Island life is based on a clan system though this is not as influential as it once was. The elderly are greatly respected by younger people and women bow to men. Women also dress conservatively in long loose dresses that were introduced by missionaries and it is regarded as tasteless to bare your thighs. A little difficult for divers! Technically, Chuuk is dry – alcohol is prohibited in an attempt to control crime (see safety below).

One thing that is consistent across all the islands are heavy penalties for drug offences and possession of a firearm. Homosexuality is technically illegal and laws are occasionally enforced.

Safety

It may be hard to believe that a tiny Pacific paradise can be troubled but then, nowhere is immune these days. **Palau** is considered safe to visit but there is a curfew in force from 0230-0500 in an attempt to control local drinking. There is a also a high incidence of road accidents so it's a good idea to use a taxi rather than hire a car.

Yap is more laid-back with few alcohol related issues, probably because most people spend their whole day chewing betelnut. It is peeled and chewed with lime (the stuff they put in mortar) and a green leaf. It is said to have a mild narcotic effect and also disintegrates teeth. How does this rank as a danger? Well, you have to be wary of the constant jets of bright red saliva produced by users.

Chuuk is deeply troubled by a lack of employment. Young men move to Weno, the main island, hoping to make their fortune but there simply is no work. This leads to the usual social problems and specifically to alcohol abuse. The island is supposedly dry but there is little evidence that it is. You should stick to your hotel and take advice before heading out on your own. There are tales of people being attacked, even in a hire car, so if you want to sightsee talk to reception who can pair you off with a local guide.

The wreck of the *Iro* in Palau

Buddy line

The Nitrox versus air argument

It seems that everywhere you go these days you get pushed to do a Nitrox course. But you have to wonder why that is – is it really such a good thing? Some claim you get longer at depth, that it's safer and you feel better after a dive. But ask yourself: do I need longer, is it really safer? Is it a good idea to be limited to a particular depth by a potentially lethal gas?

Well, here are some answers. Firstly, there is no evidence that Nitrox is safer than air nor that it reduces the risk of a DCS. Check out the figures with DAN. You will get a few extra minutes at depth (which means the range between 20 and 35 metres), but that will be dependant on how much oxygen is in your mix: the more oxygen, the shallower you need to stay. With Nitrox there are also concerns with gas blending, analysing errors, the CNS clock and so on.

However, the biggest issue is not the technology; it's human error. What happens if you go past your depth limit? Most say they won't but what if you drop that US$5000 camera outfit and it's just out of reach at 40 metres? Or you see a rare fish at 42 metres? Worse still, you see your buddy sinking inexplicably into the blue and you can't go down to help them?

So what is it that creates the myth that Nitrox is safer? Nitrox diving almost always requires use of a computer, and this along with depth limitations makes for an extra element of planning and caution. This is, without doubt, a very good thing. Many people also say that they feel less fatigued and are less prone to headaches.

As ever you pay your money and you take your choice, but one more thought on the safety angle – find out if your divemaster is using Nitrox. If so, is he going to risk his own life to help a person in trouble?

Dive brief

Bottom time

Palau
An incredibly impressive variety of dive types with pelagics, critters, wrecks, caves and reefs » p326

Yap
Mantas, mantas and more mantas. All year. As guaranteed as any event in the marine world can be » p330

Chuuk
The legendary war graveyard. A whole fleet of Japanese planes, cargo and warships sitting on the bottom of a lagoon » p333

Diving

Micronesia is a very loose, geographic description and, depending what atlas you look in, her resident nations can vary. The only reason some are grouped together is that after the Second World War, the UN and US chose to form federations of certain Pacific island groups. Some of these lasted and some didn't. Each island has its own distinct history that has been influenced by colonialism, wars, missionary infiltration and geopolitical interests right up until today. For divers, the three most visited destinations are the Republic of Palau and, in the Federated States of Micronesia, Yap and Truk Lagoon – more properly know as Chuuk.

These three island groups may well be linked by airline routes and political alliances but there the similarities end. In all other ways, especially diving, they couldn't be more different and each has a unique feature or two.

As you fly in to **Palau** you get your first view of just how breathtaking her landscape is. Sell your grandmother for a window seat or you'll find yourself sitting on a stranger's lap. Once you hit the water, you won't be disappointed with the outstanding variety of diving. Here, the most popular attractions have to be sharks and pelagic fish. **Yap** is less than an hour's flight north and is famous for just one thing, her large resident manta populations. There is much more to discover than these incredibly graceful beasts, however, with large populations of diminutive mandarinfish as well as some very good reefs. **Chuuk** and her famous lagoon is only a couple of hours away but it requires stopping in American Guam to get there. If you are into wrecks and war history, this is an unrivalled destination, but there is little else as the outer reefs have been battered by both man and nature.

Diversity* reef area 5,500 km^2

Coral species	Fish species	Fish species under threat	Protected reefs/marine parks
388	534	1	9 (Palau) 0 (FSM)

*Palau and FSM figures combined

Male mandarinfish posing for the camera, or a waiting lady

We were lucky enough to be able to take an extended trip out to these islands and it still wasn't long enough. A week in Palau gave us a week's great diving but not enough time to enjoy her many cosmopolitan land attractions. Five dive days in Yap gave us manta after manta encounter but barely time to see her charming southern reefs, and six dive days on Chuuk – on land – was enough. But, oh to have been floating over that amazing lagoon on a boat. The question is, would we go back? Yes, to Palau and Yap in a heartbeat but to Chuuk, only if we could get on a liveaboard.

Dive data

Seasons	Year round diving but with the most rain between July and October
Visibility	10 metres inshore to 40 metres further offshore
Temperatures	Air 26-32°C; water 28-30°C
Wet suit	3 mm shorty or full body suit
Training	Courses in Palau or Yap
Nitrox	Check with your resort or liveaboard
Deco chambers	Palau, Yap, Guam

Dive conditions also vary considerably from one island group to the next and are completely influenced by local geography. The only similarities are water temperature and tropical marine life. Biodiversity is highest in Palau and decreases the further east you head.

Snorkelling

This is another of those location, location, location moments. The majority of wrecks in Chuuk are beyond 20 metres – snorkelling will be limited – but there are some wonderful aeroplane wrecks in shallow waters near Eten Island. Over in Yap, the mangrove-rimmed channels can be murky with strong currents on tidal changes. Some of the outer walls come up to 10 metres but currents can be strong there too so you will need to be advised by your dive team. In Palau, there are plenty of beautiful white sand beaches with offshore reefs where a snorkel can be rewarding but these sites are not likely to be where the dives are. Parts of the Rock Islands are closed to protect nesting species such as turtles but Palau does have one of the planet's ultimate snorkelling destinations, the Jellyfish Lake.

The big decision

This is probably the longest, least convenient dive trip you will ever do so there is no question that you should do all three islands at once. However, that will mean taking the best part of three weeks, or four if you really want to do it properly. The transport issues mean you may lose up to two days getting there and a day each time you transit between islands. If you have less time then Palau and Yap work well together providing you can commence your trip from Manila. It would be hard to see Palau in less than a week. Yap needs five days, any less in low season and you would risk missing the mantas. Chuuk? Well, a week if you are on a liveaboard, four or five dive days from land though you may still not see as much as you should.

Japanese insignia on porcelain

Jacks heading towards the sun

Palau

The legend goes that these islands were formed after the birth of a boy named Chuab. He grew into a giant and consumed all the village's food, and even some of the other children. The villagers were so worried they decided the only solution was to kill him. They built a bonfire and tricked him into standing in the middle of it by saying it was for a special feast. The fire engulfed him and he fell into the sea. The parts of his body that protruded from the sea became the many islands of Palau.

Geographically, these islands are either limestone or volcanic in origin (not human, obviously) and nearly all are ringed by reefs. These drop to extreme walls perforated by caves and tunnels that have been flooded by the sea. The largest island is Babeldaob but most diving is centred around the islands to her south. Koror, the capital, and Malakal, the harbour, are linked by road bridges. The lagoon near Malakal has enough wrecks to give Chuuk a run for its money plus there are plenty of macro-specific sites and some rather unusual shallow cave dives.

A little further south are the picturesque limestone Rock Islands which have dramatic undercuts and look almost like they are hovering above the sea. This is also where you will find the stunning Jellyfish Lake, one of several marine lakes and an unmissable experience. At the bottom of the chain is Pelilu Island which was the scene of a horrendous land battle in the Second World War.

Palau sits between the North Pacific and the Philippine Sea so her marine life is influenced by two environments. This creates an incredible amount of dive diversity with reefs, walls, wrecks, lakes, caves – you name it you can probably do it here. Conditions tend to be fairly easy; when there are currents it's usually at sites that attract pelagics. Although the diving here is year round, there are a few seasonal features although nothing is ever guaranteed. Shark mating season is February to April, moorish idol migration is March, groupers spawn in May and June, and manta rays, though expected December to February are seen all year.

Red whips and blue waters

Paguritta crabs are just 10 millimetres long

1 Blue Corner

- **Depth**: 32 m
- **Visibility**: fair to stunning
- **Currents**: ripping
- **Dive type**: day boat/liveaboard
- **Snorkelling**: no

Palau's most famous dive is quite a spectacle. Entry is over the edge of a wall that curves outwards to a promontory. Divers often drop straight into a school of chevron barracuda that thicken the water then swim along the wall to a deep crevice lined with fan corals. Just beyond this is where divers ascend to the plateau above and hook on to a rock, to wait for the show. Near the crevice there are a few grey reefs patrolling and, on the other side of the plateau, is a jumbo school of jacks. Then, as the current lifts to rip-your-mask-off levels, the action starts. Lots of sharks – greys, a few blacktips and a few whitetips – swoop across the vista. They are surrounded by schooling fish such as fusiliers and redmouth triggers. Napoleon wrasse swim in and out and you notice a few turtles sitting on the plateau behind, calmly chomping on sponges. The sharks circle closer and closer while jacks hang close to their tails. More greys and whitetips patrol below the front of the wall surrounded by blue trevally and another school of barracuda. Eventually, you have to lift off and can either drift along the reef rim over beds of lettuce leaf coral and more sharks or head back over the plateau spotting morays and turtles.

2 Ulong Corner & Channel

- **Depth**: 33 m
- **Visibility**: good
- **Currents**: medium to ripping
- **Dive type**: day boat/liveaboard
- **Snorkelling**: no

Ulong Island is where the US version of TV's *Survivor* was filmed. The island is a pretty stop but more significantly leads to an exposed dive area. Ulong Corner and Channel are swept by currents which attract sharks – and divers. Entry is over a small wall which leads to a natural amphitheatre where divers hook on and wait for the show to commence. There are small whitetip sharks waiting in the wings but they keep away while several larger and more inquisitive greys approach those sitting in the front rows. They swoop so close you feel the need to pull back. After a while at this spot, it's time to move the show down the channel and, unhooking from your rock, you are swept away, accompanied by schools of snappers and trevally. The current is quite frisky and it's off for a rollercoaster ride through steep walls and schooling big-eyes. Part way along the channel you reach an extensive patch of lettuce leaf corals. The delicate folds are a deep brown with many rabbitfish tucked in between them. A few sharks and a turtle keep you company towards the end of the ride but they disperse as soon as the current spits you out over a patch of bright white sand.

Hanging on at Blue Corner

Tales from the deep

Lost in the Blue

Palau, to me, 18 years ago was a delightfully 'local' Pacific paradise. It offered little for flower-shirted tourists seeking 5-star Western luxury and everything for the traveller savouring unspoiled culture and nature combined. Little had changed in 2005 although some 5-star resorts are now dotted around. The pace is still as slow and the people just as relaxed and friendly.

Snorkelling was my passion all those years ago and my vivid memories are of the fish nursery beds – natural, protected aggregations of millions of juveniles sheltering between the Rock Islands for which Palau is famed. This trip revealed where all those fish end up as adults. Several previous remote diving expeditions in this prolific Pacific region hadn't prepared me for the sensual feast that is on offer at the southern end of Babeldaop.

Blue Corner is the fish dive to end all fish dives. Hooked onto the reef edge, hovering slightly buoyant above hundreds of metres of blue, I lost myself in the fish festival frolicking around me. Huge schools of snapper and jacks heaved through the blue, patrolled by whitetips and grey reef sharks, dwarfed by the odd lone Napoleon wrasse and the occasional tuna. The finale was a squadron of chevron barracuda, gliding slowly in over the reef top and then moving into formation, turning in unison into the current once settled into position. What an incredible sight – one we went back for a second and third time.

Sue Laing, Sydney, Australia

3 Pelilu Wall

- **Depth**: 28 m
- **Visibility**: excellent
- **Currents**: medium to ripping
- **Dive type**: day boat/liveaboard
- **Snorkelling**: no

Both sides of the southern tip of Peliliu are swept by currents where the Pacific and the Philippine Sea meet. This dive commences by swimming into a circular hole in the reef about 3 metres across with small soft corals lining its walls. Dropping another few metres, you exit through another hole in the wall and directly below, reaching to about 35-40 metres, is the most spectacular and colourful garden of soft corals in masses of different hues. It's so colourful, it's almost gaudy. There are black coral bushes and rows of fans that have grown in horizontal tiers to catch the sunlight from above. Amongst them are large puffers and queen triggerfish feeding on the wall, banded angels and many variations of anthias multiply the rainbow effect. Schools of pyramid butterflies and redmouth triggers hover in the blue with a couple of passing sharks, Napoleon wrasse and mackerel.

Corals on Pelilu Wall

4 Chandelier Cave

- **Depth**: 10 m
- **Visibility**: excellent at the top
- **Currents**: none
- **Dive type**: day boat/liveaboard
- **Snorkelling**: no

In a lovely cove just across from the port at Malakal is this small, hidden cave system. Entry is just before a buoyed off area which stops boats mooring too close. The cave mouth is perhaps 5 metres wide but as soon as you go inside it opens to a gaping space. The stalactites at the beginning are quite rounded, perhaps reshaped by seawater movement. There are four chambers inside the caves and you can ascend inside each in turn. The top of each has an air gap where freshwater percolates through from the land above, creating spectacular sculptures. The formations are breathtaking, glittering with absorbed minerals and appearing as pleats of fabric or pencil-thin icicles. It's incredibly pretty but can get crowded with divers. Ensure you stay well above the bottom to avoid stirring up the silt and take a good torch (or two).

The limestone formations of Chandelier Cave

5 The *Iro Maru*

- **Depth**: 33 m
- **Visibility**: good
- **Currents**: medium to ripping
- **Dive type**: day boat/liveaboard
- **Snorkelling**: no

The *Iro* was a fleet oiler built by the Japanese between 1919 and 1921. Used specifically to haul stores, munitions and 8,000 tons of oil to war fleet units, her movements during the war are reasonably well documented. On 31 March, 1944, she was attacked by Yorktown VB-5 bombers and hit twice: once on the port side forward of midships, the other on the aft starboard quarter.

The view of this wreck as you descend falls somewhere between awe-inspiring and intimidating. This is one very big ship at 145 metres long. Dropping past the bowmast, the first thing you see is the large bandstand gun platform. On top of this 'spoked wheel' is a 5.5 inch bow gun that measures nearly 9 metres long, with the barrel about 5 metres. Travelling along the deck you come to a small cabin where two very curious batfish lurk. A little further is the entry to an open hold which contains oil drums and machinery but it's murky inside so best not to go in. The whole wreck is covered in masses of corals, the hard corals are in great condition, surprising on such a well dived wreck. There are also hundreds and hundreds of living shells – clams, mussels, barnacles, oysters and razor clams – and many dead ones littering the decks. There are alternating masts and kingposts which rise up to 8 metres and the forward one is a great place to offgas as you can hunt for small fish and nudibranchs at the same time.

Grey reef shark at Blue Corner

The sensation of swimming with these velvet skinned, pulsating animals is both bizarre and beautiful, a very calming experience.

6 Jellyfish Lake

- **Depth**: 33 m
- **Visibility**: good
- **Currents**: none
- **Dive type**: shore
- **Snorkelling**: yes

The marine lake on Mecherchar Island is just one of many found in Palau. Their depths are seawater and fed by hidden channels to the sea, while the top layer of water is fresh, diluted by rain. The animals that live inside these lakes have grown and adapted to exploit the unusual environment. Reaching this particular lake requires a trek through the jungle, up a steep and very slippery track. It's quite hard going but it only takes 10 minutes to descend again to a pontoon overlooked by emerald hills and surrounded by mangroves. The water is murky as you enter, with just an occasional polka-dot cardinal hovering around, but as you swim across the lake you see one, then another and then suddenly there are hundreds of mastigias jellies in pale apricot plus an occasional moon jelly. The mastigias species lost their capacity to sting as their only predator is a small anemone that lives under the mangroves. They spend their days circumnavigating the lake, following the movement of the sun's rays. As you snorkel, be aware of what you are doing with your fins – a hefty kick will destroy any jelly you make contact with. Under the mangroves, you find more cardinals, anemones, tube worms and tiny puntang gobies.

Yap

From the air Yap appears as a single triangular island but, on closer inspection, her gently rolling landscape is divided by three channels into four tightly-knit land masses: Yap,Tomil-Gagil, Maap and Rumung. There are also 134 outlying islands and atolls.

The marine world here is something of a surprise. Each of the channels that separate the islands are rather shallow, lined by mangrove swamps and with thick areas of seagrass. The water is nothing if not murky but head seawards, over the surrounding lagoon and it's all change. Where the surf breaks against the submerged reef edges the visibility clears and the marine landscape is transformed into a lively series of coral-clad hills and valleys.

Fifteen miles further east is the **Yap Trench**, one of the deep water trenches that form part of the Pacific Ring of Fire. The water plummets to a depth of over 8000 metres which explains its deep shade of blue. Of course, you won't get down that far but you will see plenty of pelagics as they are attracted to this environment. The manta populations are world famous and sharks flock here as well.

However, Yap is becoming equally well known for its macro life. There is a good selection of the small and often wacky reef-building animals to look for if you can just drag yourself away from the mantas. The southern reefs are impressive and, despite some typhoon damage a couple of years ago, there is plenty of coral. Conditions vary from the east, or windward, side to the west of the island, so there is always somewhere to go, even when the weather is less than perfect.

7 Valley of the Rays

- **Depth**: 16 m
- **Visibility**: medium to great
- **Currents**: mild to strong
- **Dive type**: day boat
- **Snorkelling**: possibly

Yap's resident mantas are known to like the plankton rich waters that flow out from her shallow channels. At this site on the east coast the channel descends to a deep valley with a sandy bottom. There are three cleaning stations that are known to attract the mantas – Merry-go-round, Carwash and Manta Rock. The dive plan involves swimming from one to another until you find something. At first this may seem hopeless, until you suddenly notice the grey wing flap of an approaching manta. Effortless in the current, it glides towards your dive group, while a gang of four or five settles right over the nearest cleaning station. You've only been in Yap a few hours, in the water a few minutes, and it's hard to believe this is happening. The mantas are so close you could touch them, in fact, you know that as you sit on the sand in absolute awe that they are watching you too, and with barely disguised amusement. More mantas arrive in small groups, take turns at the cleaning station, then move off again. At the same time, those waiting their turn will pull into the channel behind so you need to have eyes in the back of your head. The currents can be strong, but this does not deter these magnificent animals from scooping plankton and bits of floating weed into their mouths.

8 Lionfish Wall & Yap Caverns

- **Depth**: 26 m
- **Visibility**: good to great
- **Currents**: mild to strong
- **Dive type**: day boat
- **Snorkelling**: possibly

There are dives all the way to the south of the island where the reef veers further away from land. The water can be a bit rough as well because the surf pushes in from two different directions. As you round the southern tip of the submerged reef, the walls become much steeper than those on the east and much prettier. The vertical surface of Lionfish Wall drops to about 45 metres and is covered in pastel tree-fern corals. There are moray noses sticking out and even a lionfish or two. More prominent though are the incredible number of big-eyes, coral trout and groupers. Looking into small cracks and crevices you can spot leaffish, carpet anemones with 'popcorn shrimp' crawling over them and nudibranchs. Off in the blue are bumphead parrots and Napoleon wrasse. The terrain becomes more rocky as you move along the wall to the Yap Caverns. These cuts and tunnels in the reef wall are just big enough to swim in and out of. You are likely to meet a young whitetip en route and one cavern harbours a substantial school of copper sweepers. Above the caverns for a safety stop, you find carpets of cup corals, marbled dragonets and lots of anthias flitting about.

Lionfish on the move

9 Slow & Easy

- **Depth**: 19 m
- **Visibility**: poor to good
- **Currents**: mild
- **Dive type**: day boat
- **Snorkelling**: possibly

Heading away from town through the channel there are several dives just before the break in the reef. On the left, against a mini-wall, is this critter hunter's favourite. Although the site can be murky, depending on the tides, there are lots of interesting creatures to see. The edge of the reef slopes down from about 3 metres to 18 metres where the sandy seabed is peppered with coral bommies. In amongst the varying bits of terrain are lionfish, anemones with their clowns, crabs and nudibranchs. Huge pufferfish are stationary on the sand with shrimp and goby partnerships beside them. There are clusters of pipefish, crocodilefish and lizardfish. Hiding under a rock is the juvenile six-lined soapfish while the legs of a lonely stand of staghorn are hidden by yellow cardinalfish and blue anthias dance above.

Solitary triplefin on a coral

10 M'll Channel & Manta Ridge

- **Depth**: 27 m
- **Visibility**: medium to great
- **Currents**: mild
- **Dive type**: day boat
- **Snorkelling**: possibly

The ride from Kolonia north through the channel that divides Yap from Tomil-Gagil and Maap is a mysterious tour through mangroves and past silent villages. At the mouth of the channel the boat moors over one of Yap's most famous sites. In the middle of M'll Channel is a manta station. Divers wait on the rubbly bottom but if the rays haven't arrived within about 10 minutes the divemasters head off down to Manta Ridge. Along the channel are outcrops of coral, anemones and clownfish but you'll be keeping your eyes on the blue to catch a glimpse of what's out there. It could be a manta speeding past, a flock of eagle rays or a small shark. At the ridge there is another cleaning station and here the mantas arrive silently to sit over everyone's heads. This is the area where, between December and April, the mantas come to mate, doing belly rolls and acrobatics to impress each other.

Another manta!

11 The Mandarinfish Dive

- **Depth**: 7 m
- **Visibility**: poor
- **Currents**: no
- **Dive type**: day boat
- **Snorkelling**: possibly

A few minutes from Manta Ray Bay but inside the channel are some small, uninhabited islands. The divemasters know several spots which are residential areas for mandarinfish. In just about 3 metres of murky water are some stands of "organ-pipe" coral surrounded by rubble and patches of staghorn. Descending seconds before dark, you spot the male mandarins skittering about on the seabed but they are still wary in the fading sunlight. As it gets darker they become far more active, the males chasing the ladies up and down. Eventually, a pair begin mating, rising slowly up into the air until they are disturbed, inevitably, by the equally numerous but very aggressive – and hungry – pyjama cardinals who are out to make war, not love. The mandarinfish keep at it though, climbing up through the water column, the male displaying all the while.

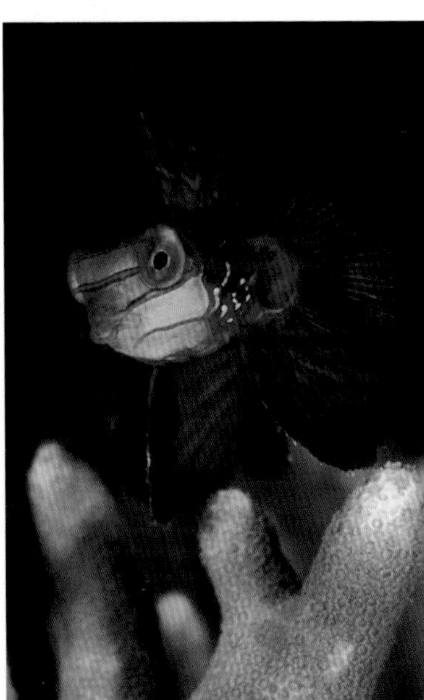
The male mandarinfish on the prowl

Tales from the deep

A lifelong dream

For all my diving life, 30 plus years, I had been dreaming of diving with the famous and magnificent mantas of Yap. Then in 2002, I finally had the good fortune to go there, to meet Bill Acker and his crew and experience Yap diving for myself.

Over time, Bill and I became good friends and we soon cooked up the idea for me to go to Yap on an annual basis to search for increasingly popular 'exotic critters' as an addition to the mantas. 'Critters' are the marine animals that survive by being invisible or by looking like something that they are not, masterfully using the art of camouflage to survive.

We would go and dive a variety of new areas looking for these unusual forms of marine life. And what we discovered was that Yap does, indeed, produce a multitude of these critters; more than enough to keep serious hunters satisfied and bragging about their discoveries back at the dive shop. Rainbow Reef on O'Keefe's Island is one of the best mandarinfish dives on the planet! Plus, the normally evasive saron shrimp is common here. And at the dive site known as Macro, ghost pipefish, nudibranchs, mantis shrimp and halimeda crabs are all found by the Yap divemasters. The host sea fans for pygmy seahorses are also in Yap, but these little rascals have so far evaded detection. We know that they have to be there and we'll keep looking until we find them.

In addition to the mantas and the exotic critters, Yap has one of the healthiest shark populations I've ever seen. At the dive site known as 'Vertigo', grey reef sharks, black and whitetips and an occasional hammerhead are seen. All that is necessary to 'call' them is to circle around the mooring in the dive boat and they come.

There is tremendous satisfaction in diligently searching the dramatic drop-offs and channels in Yap for small marine life while the shadows of giant manta rays overhead distract and amaze you. Happy Diving!

Larry Smith, legendary Divemaster and critter 'guru', was born in Texas but is based in Bali when he's not off pioneering another dive region.

Pipefish are found at many of Yap's sites

Chuuk

It's 0530 on 17 February 1944 and Japanese radar detect the approach of an aircraft squadron. The attack begins within the hour. An estimated 100 American planes in the first wave (out of a total of 450), blitz what was thought to be an impenetrable fortress. Operation Hailstone continues for two days and annihilates the Japanese fleet stationed in Truk Lagoon.

Standing on a flawless beach, under a rustling coconut palm looking at a perfectly calm sea, it's hard to imagine the devastation of those two days. The islands of modern Chuuk seem so far removed you could almost convince yourself it had never happened until, of course, you get below the water.

The Japanese Imperial Fleet had long recognized the value of Chuuk's completely enclosed lagoon. They felt that having a few entry and exit channels would make the lagoon easy to defend against a naval attack – but it also made it a trap. There are forty or so shipwrecks lying on the lagoon floor and each and every one is a sumptuous artificial reef. These are an incredible tour through a moment in history. Each of the wrecks is a testimonial to her purpose: you will discover the remains of tanks and jeeps, anti-aircraft guns and torpedo tubes and much more ammunition than you care to think about. There are broken aircraft and abandoned submarines but you won't find any human remains: as many as could be recovered were returned to their homeland, regarded as vital to Japanese religious beliefs. You also won't see as many artefacts as you may have thought. Sadly, many small items have been systematically plundered – by tourists desperate for a souvenir, by locals who try to profit from selling artefacts to other tourists and by local fishermen who have salvaged explosives for their own use.

The dives here tend to be deep – not so deep as to be dangerous but most are well beyond 20 metres. There are some wrecks which sit at 50 metres plus, which is well beyond Nitrox limitations. For air divers, these should be approached carefully and planned thoroughly. Take safety stops at several levels. Operators ensure that emergency tanks are always hung at 5 metres. Water temperatures are consistent year round with an average of 28°C. Currents are rare, with just occasional surface movement, and visibility can be said to be good year round although less clear in the rainy season when there are also plankton and jellyfish blooms.

There are also dives on the outer reefs, some known for their shark populations, but a combination of natural and man-made damage means that these reefs are not really worth the diversion away from the wrecks.

12 *Sankisan Maru*

- **Depth**: 48 m
- **Visibility**: fair to excellent
- **Currents**: no
- **Dive type**: day boat/liveaboard
- **Snorkelling**: unlikely

The *Sankisan* is regarded as the prettiest wreck but her history is unknown. She appears to have been either a Japanese vessel launched in 1942 or an American one, launched as the *Red Hook* in Washington and later captured by the Japanese. Whatever the truth, the ship was around 4700 tons, 112-115 metres long and nearly 16 metres wide. Sitting off Uman

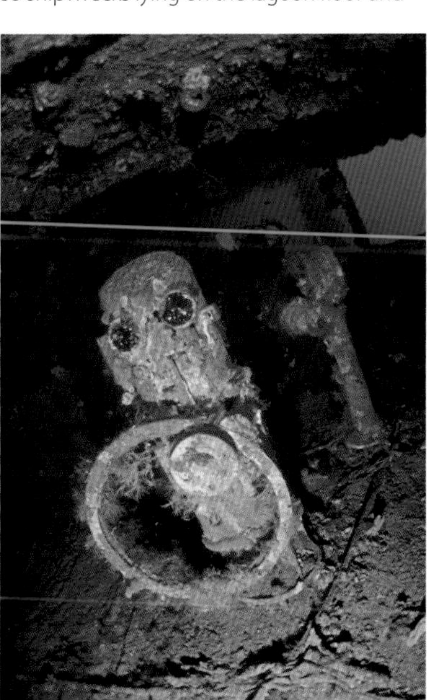

The bridge on the *Nippo Maru*

Coral growth is lush on the *Sankisan Maru*

 Island, her destruction was caused by strafing from American aircraft but there are no accurate records confirming this.

As a dive site, the *Sankisan's* reputation is for coral gardens, which makes it a strange introduction to the wrecks in the lagoon. As you descend over the broken hull, the view is one of rainbow-hued reefs rather than disintegrating metal. Dive plans involve visiting the first hold, which is carpeted in bullets and shells, then back up to deck level, past the remains of some vehicles, then down onto the next hold. This one has a truck and a flat bed lorry, a porthole and boxes full of medicine bottles, their contents an ominous, chalky white. The divemasters then swim through a warren of corridors and out through the third hold, past spare parts for engines. Back up on the deck the midships section is quite broken up but covered in coral growth. Metal joists and beams drip with colour and you see the sort of fish that you normally only see on a reef – longnose hawkfish, moorish idols and mimic filefish. You can plan your dive to first visit the ruined stern (48 metres) where the remains of the propeller and rudder are said to be or spend time circumnavigating and investigating the incredible growth on the foremast.

13 *Nippo Maru*

- **Depth**: 38 m
- **Visibility**: fair to excellent
- **Currents**: no
- **Dive type**: day boat/liveaboard
- **Snorkelling**: no

The *Nippo* was built in 1936 in Kobe as a cargo-passenger vessel but she was requisitioned in 1941 and refitted to carry water tanks, ordnance and munitions. She arrived in Chuuk in a convoy transporting troops, one week before being hit three times in the midships area by 500lb bombs. The *Nippo* was first discovered in 1969 by the Cousteau expedition near Eten Island but her location was 'lost' until the late '80s when the ship's bell was discovered, engraved with both English and Japanese characters.

At 107 metres long the remains of the *Nippo* could easily take three dives to fully investigate and, as she is sitting at over 50 metres, dives should be carefully planned. The stern is most impressive. As the light fades, and the hull takes on that ghostly quality, a series of three Howitzers emerge. To their side are a series of gun mounts and a barrel gun platform. Inside the deepest hold is more artillery while the next one heading upwards has medical supplies, bowls, wheels and tyres. Another has water tanks, shells and beer bottles. To the port side of the deck is a well preserved armoured tank, although its turret gun is missing. A final entry is made into the shallowest hold – and perhaps the most harrowing – where you are reminded what went on here. Surrounded by a swathe of bullets are several gas masks.

14 *Fujikawa Maru*

- **Depth**: 34 m
- **Visibility**: fair to excellent
- **Currents**: no
- **Dive type**: day boat/liveaboard
- **Snorkelling**: unlikely

The most popular wreck in the lagoon must be the *Fujikawa*, a passenger ship built for the New York run. She was requisitioned in 1940 for naval use as an armed transport ship for the delivery of aircraft and spares, amongst other things. She was damaged while at anchor in Kwajalein and towed to Chuuk for repairs arriving on 31 January 1943.

Coral clad mast, *Sankisan Maru*

Fish swarming around a deep water propeller

Medicine bottles on the *Nippo Maru*

The *Fujikawa* is an excellent wreck but showing obvious signs of wear. This is probably because she is upright and one of the shallower dives with plenty of interest on the deck at just 17 metres. Descent is usually straight down to the very impressive, coral encrusted bow gun. This enormous weapon rests at only about 12 metres, bathing in the suns rays. Her coating of leather, crusting soft corals and sponges is incredibly lush, although you can hardly see them for the amount of fish that swarm around. Dropping below the gun mount and onto the deck there are two memorial plaques, one for the ship itself and another for well respected local diver and explorer, Kimiuo Aisek. The two front holds are full of aircraft paraphernalia – spares, propellors, wings, engines and the fuselages of four aircraft. The divemasters say they are Japanese Zero fighters. Heading out of the second hold you can swim through the engine room, a fascinating maze of walkways and engines lit by sunshine from above. A cabin still has a bathroom area and you can see wash basins and urinals. All the holds heading to the stern can be investigated but the most curious is the last, full of sake bottles, china and mess kits.

15 The *Emily*

- **Depth**: 17 m
- **Visibility**: fair to good
- **Currents**: no
- **Dive type**: day boat/liveaboard
- **Snorkelling**: possibly

Japanese flying boats were manufactured by the Kawanishi Company. Prior to the war they had been associated with the Short Brothers of Belfast, makers of Sunderland and Sandringham flying boats. However, the Japanese Navy wanted faster and stronger boats, so after several modifications, Kawanishi developed the *H8K*, later known as *Emily* and regarded as the finest flying boat of the war. She was also nicknamed the *Flying Porcupine* due to her heavy armaments. Designed as a transporter she was more often used for bombing and reconnaissance.

The Emily lies just to the south of Dublon Island in around 16 metres of water. Like many other wrecks, her history is a little blurred and no doubt embellished over the decades. One legend is that she was shot down while returning some Japanese dignitaries to base after a trip to Palau but this theory has been questioned as there are no signs of bullet damage. She is badly broken up and upside down on the seabed. More recent thinking suggests that she may have been low on fuel and resorted to flying on her inner engines. She seems to have landed heavily and flipped over; the propeller blades of her outer engines are not bent while the inner engine props are bent forward, indicating that she was moving backwards as she went under.

You can muse on all this as you swim around her and under her wings. The cockpit is rather crushed but segments of the fuselage are intact. You can poke your nose inside and see glassy sweepers sheltering or small colonies of coral and sponges starting to form. Like all the wrecks, some artefacts have been moved around and part of the cockpit dashboard and some telecommunication equipment sits in the sand. Not far from here is the wreck of a Zero fighter that is almost completely intact. She sits just off Eten Island in about 10 metres. Although you can't do them both on one dive, the divemasters tend to bring you to snorkel over the Zero while gassing off between dives.

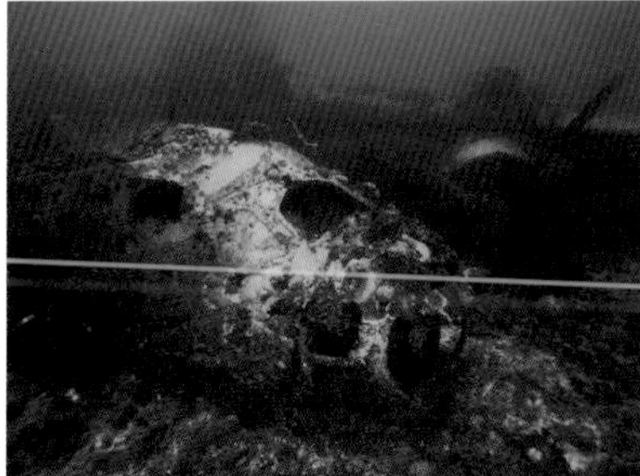
The *Emily* flying boat

The bow gun on the *Fujikawa*

A ghostly Zero fighter

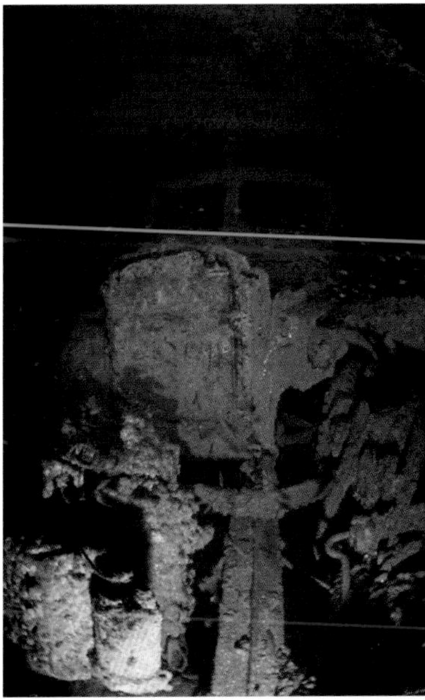
A supply truck on the *Hoki Maru*

Drying out

Yap main street

Micronesia's land side attractions tend to take a back seat when compared with other countries but there is just enough to do to give you a flavour of life on each of these Pacific islands.

Manila

As the best flight for Palau and Yap leaves Manila early on a Saturday morning, chances are you will end up spending the night there. Book into a hotel overnight (such as the **Hyatt**) and catch up on some sleep before flying out again. See Philippines chapter, pages 314-315 for hotel details.

Palau

There are many resorts and hotels on Palau at all sorts of levels. Pick your hotel in conjunction with your dive centre unless you only need a night or two on land.

Dive centres

Fish 'n Fins, PO Box 142, Koror, Palau 96940, T+680 (1)488 2637, www.fishnfins.com. One of Palau's most diverse dive operations with a full daily dive programme, courses, great photo facilities, a shop and they will collect divers from any hotel.

Sam's Tours, PO Box 7076, Koror, Palau 96940, T+680 (1)488 1062, www.samstours.com. Full service operation with many courses.

Chuuk beach looking over the lagoon

Sleeping

$$ **The Carolines Resort**, Box 399, Koror, Palau 96940, T+680 (1)488 3754, www.carolinesresort.com. Small boutique hotel with traditional Palauan bungalows. Great views and free transfers from the airport and to town.

$$ **West Plaza Malakal**, PO Box 280, Koror, Palau 96940, T+680 (1)488 5291, email west.plaza@palaumet.com. One of a series of good quality, locally owned hotels. Huge rooms just a hop from the harbour so good for pre- or post- liveaboard trips.

Liveaboards

Big Blue Explorer, **Cruise Island Adventures**, 4/F Metrostar Building, Metropolitan Ave, Makati City, Philippines, T+63 (0)890 6778, www.explorerfleet.com. Large vessel with plenty of space but small, budget style cabins. Great dive set up and camera room.

Ocean Hunter I & II, PO Box 964, Koror, Palau 96940, T+680 (1)488 2637, www.oceanhunter.com. Two luxury vessels, one for just 6 divers, the other takes 12. All cabins are en suite and very smart. Also affiliated to **Fish 'n Fins**.

Eating

There are good quality restaurants right across the island. The excellent **Ba-ra-cu-da Restaurant** is part of the **Fish 'n Fins** clan, catch a taxi to M dock for their superb Mediterranean food. In the harbour area try the **Palm Bay Bistro and Brewing Company** opposite the **West Plaza Malakal** which was winner of the 2004 Rock Island Chef Competition.

Sights

Much of what there is to do and see around the islands is water based – kayaking, canoeing, snorkelling tours around the Rock Islands and so on. You could take a land tour to a traditional village with ancient meeting houses, carvings and paintings or take a rainforest hike to a waterfall. If you are on Pelilu, there are many Second World War sites and memorials. Koror town has a

National Museum, US$5, and the **Etpison Museum** with a collection of art and ancient artefacts. The **Palau International Coral Reef Centre** (aka aquarium) is at M dock and costs $7.

Yap

Diving is the principal tourism activity on Yap so there are just a handful of accommodation and dive options.

Sleeping and diving

$$ **Manta Ray Bay Hotel** and **Yap Divers**, PO Box MR, Yap 96943, T+691 (1)350 2300, www.mantaray.com. What can you say – the original, the best, setting the standards. Lovely rooms, morning coffee delivery, good restaurant on site, great dive set up, camera facilities and even a unique PADI Speciality Manta Ray Awareness course.

$$ **O'Keefe's Waterfront Inn**, 2 Waterfront Rd, Yap 96943, T+691 (1)350 6500, www.okeefesyap.com. Delicious New England style inn right beside **Yap Divers**. Small but perfectly formed rooms with well thought out features like kit drying cabinets on the balcony.

Eating

The **Mnuw** is a schooner-turned-restaurant moored at Manta Ray Bay and serves a mix of American and oriental food. Opposite there is a small café called the **Oasis** which makes a nice change for lunch, or head uphill to the swanky **Traders Ridge Resort**. Their American chef creates some impressive 'fusion' style meals.

Sights

Yap is regarded as retaining the most traditional lifestyle in the Federated States of Micronesia but you may not see much more than around compact Kolonia, the capital. A morning can be whiled away by stopping at the **Yap Art Studio and Gallery** to admire the work of local artists. Then head back towards town and wander up the traditional stone pathway that starts by the defunct Ocean View Hotel and has a large stone money disc marking the entrance. The path is cool and shady, lined with plants and flowers. At the top you come to a paved road where you can either turn left and past St Mary's church and school, head right all the way up Medeqdeq Hill or go straight across and down a slippery stone path to Chamoor Bay. In the bay is the **Ethnic Art Institute** where you might find women weaving traditional cloth or men carving. Another walk heads from here to **Balabat**, known as the stone money bank as the road is lined with a large collection of *rai*, the enormous stone discs that were traditionally used to display the wealth of a village.

Chuuk

Despite this island's amazing dive potential, there are few facilities for divers or for tourism generally for that matter – with just 2 resorts and 2 liveaboards.

Sleeping and diving

$$ **Blue Lagoon Resort and Dive centre**, PO Box 340, Weno, Chuuk State, 96942, T+691 (1)330 2727, www.bluelagoonresort.com. By far the better located of the 2 resorts, beautiful grounds, decent restaurant and lovely rooms. Perfect for stopping for a few nights before a liveaboard but let down by a neglected dive operation that is in serious need of upgrading.

$$ **Truk Stop Hotel and Dive Centre**, PO Box 546, Chuuk 96942, T+691 (1)330 4232, www.trukstop.com. This modern hotel suffers from being in the centre of town. However, the dive operation is said to have good kit facilities, nitrox and professional guides. Rumour has it that it is possible to stay at **Blue Lagoon** and dive with **Truk Stop**.

Liveaboards

Odyssey Adventures, 4417 Beach Blvd, Ste. 200 Jacksonville, FL 32207, T+1 (1)904 346 3766, www.trukodyssey.com. The principal liveaboard for Chuuk which leaves from the **Blue Lagoon Hotel's** dock. It can take up to 2 years to get a booking on this boat but it would be worth waiting for.

SS Thorfinn, Seaward Holidays Micronesia, PO Box 1086, Weno, Chuuk State, 96942, T+691 (1)330 3040. Large ex-research vessel that has recently undergone a refit. The boat appears to cater for budget divers and acts more like a floating hotel.

Sights

The airport on Chuuk is, by island standards, quite sophisticated so your first view of the town as you drive towards your hotel may come as a shock. It's dusty, rundown and really not appealing. Considering the safety issues, be careful about wandering around. You could take a day trip that covers the Japanese War Memorial, Nefo Cave and Japanese Gun and on to the Japanese Lighthouse, though you may feel that you have seen enough Japanese artefacts underwater. The tiny museum is closed and, currently, there are no plans to reopen it.

International agencies

Reef & Rainforest, 400 Harbour Drive, Sausalito, California 94965, T+1 415 289 1760, www.reefrainforest.com. Full service, dive and adventure travel agency near San Francisco, with good resort and liveaboard contacts and access to cheaper **Continental Airlines** rates.

Big Blue Explorer in Palau

Spam, spam, spam, spam …

Australia

Galápagos

GALAPAGOS CLASSIC CRUISES

The diving specialists to the Galapagos Islands ...

Dive with the hammerheads, mantas, penguins, sea lions, marine iguanas, eagle rays and whale sharks!
Excellent choice of liveaboards from 7-15 days to suit both groups and individuals.
Shore based diving also available.
Special offers throughout the year!

Amazon . Cotopaxi . Andes . Machu Picchu

Also: Cocos Islands . Honduras . Mexico
Easter Island . Venezuela . Fiji .
Tonga . Tahiti . Papua New Guinea
South Africa . Arctic . Antarctica

GALAPAGOS CLASSIC CRUISES AND WORLD ADVENTURES
6 Keyes Road,
London NW2 3XA
Tel: +44 020 8933 0613
Fax: +44 020 8452 5248

E mail: galapagoscruises@compuserve.com
or Info@galapagoscruises.co.uk
www. galapagoscruises.co.uk

Photography Martin Sutton

East Africa

Egypt

Maldives

Thailand

Thailand

Indonesia

Index

All dive sites listed in this book are indexed here and highlighted as follows:

Alice in Wonderland (Fij) 102

Country/region abbreviations: Australia = (Aus), Papua New Guinea = (PNG), Solomon Islands = (Solm), Fiji = (Fij), Galápagos = (Glpgs), Belize = (Blz), Mexico = (Mex), Honduras = (Hon), Egypt = (Egy), East Africa = (EAF), Maldives = (Mald), Thailand = (Thai) Indonesia = (Ind), Malaysia = (Mas), Philippines = (Phi), Micronesia (Mic)

A

B

C

Marine species index

The marine species listed on this page are photographed throughout the book and the relevant page numbers for each picture are given below.

Footprint credits
Text editor: Alan Murphy
Map editor: Sarah Sorensen
Proof reader: Sarah Sorensen
Picture editor and layouts: Patrick Dawson

Publisher: Patrick Dawson
Editorial: Sophie Blacksell, Felicity Laughton, Nicola Jones
Cartography: Robert Lunn, Claire Benison
Design: Mytton Williams
Sales and marketing: Andy Riddle
Advertising: Debbie Wylde
Finance and administration: Elizabeth Taylor

Photography credits
Front and back cover images, inside covers and flaps: Shaun Tierney/SeaFocus
Inside images: SeaFocus (www.seafocus.com).

Print
Manufactured in India by Nutech Print Services, Delhi.

Footprint feedback
We try as hard as we can to make each Footprint guide as up to date as possible but, of course, things always change. If you want to let us know about your experiences – good, bad or ugly – then don't delay, go to **www.footprintbooks.com** and send in your comments.

Every effort has been made to ensure that the facts in this guidebook are accurate. However, travellers should still obtain advice from consulates, airlines etc about travel and visa requirements before travelling. The authors and publishers cannot accept responsibility for any loss, injury or inconvenience however caused.

Publishing information
Footprint Diving the World
1st edition

April 2006

ISBN 1 904777 59 7
CIP DATA: A catalogue record for this book is available from the British Library

Published by Footprint
6 Riverside Court
Lower Bristol Road
Bath BA2 3DZ, UK
T +44 (0)1225 469141
F +44 (0)1225 469461
discover@footprintbooks.com
www.footprintbooks.com

Distributed in the USA by
Publishers Group West

The colour maps are not intended to have any political significance.

Credit where it's due . . .

When you embark on a project like this, you think it's going to be just like relating all your favourite dive tales over a glass or two. Then you suddenly realize just how much effort it will take! Much of that effort was aided and abetted by our support network of friends and colleagues.

So without further ado, and not meaning to sound like a slushy Oscar winner, our thanks to:

Cindi La Raia (**1**) for teaching us all about the vagaries of dive travel; Larry Smith (**2**) for handing us the understanding, and instilling our deep love, of what makes a reef work; Gerry Stevens for sharing his extensive knowledge of the airline industry and Doctor Joann Gren (**3**) who ensured we didn't make any serious medical clangers.

Bruce Brownstein (**4**), Jill and Sean Keen (**5**), Andrew and Sue Perkins (**6**), Sue Laing (**7**) and Annabel Thomas went above and beyond the call of duty by contributing their thoughts, being sounding boards and the best of dive buddies.

Many more people took part in the research, contributed their favourite dive tales, kept us focussed on what divers really want and most importantly, listened to us carrying on about little else for over a year.

Thanks isn't enough, but goes to: David Barr (**3**), Carole Bellars, Dave Black, Roy Calverley and Diana Standen (**8**), Charlotte Carlsen, Marcus Cathrein (**9**), Sophie de Lagarde-Durante, Michelle Gaut (**10** middle), Keith Gretton (**11** middle), Sheldon Hey, Alex Khachadourian, Anne-Marie Kitchen-Wheeler and Matt Kitchen, Gavin Macaulay, Phillip Martyn (**12** right), Monty Sheppard (**13**), Vladimir Soto (**14**), Stephen Soule, Sue Starkie, Zerine Tata, Hans Tibboel (**15**), Phil and Patricia Tobin (**16**), Suzanne and Steve Turek (**17**) Inés and Antonio Yturbe (**18**) and Estelle Zauner (**19**). And our apologies if we have missed anyone!

We have worked for many magazines over the years and many editors have supported, coaxed and encouraged us. They include: Carol Lim, Dave Moran, Gavin Parsons, Mark Evans, Peter Rowlands and Heneage Mitchell. But especially big thanks to the gorgeous David Espinosa (**20**), the incorrigible Frank Raines and the ever lovely Maria Hayward.

Many dive operations across the world have been supportive and happy to ensure our memories weren't muddied and details were up to date, even when our queries had nothing to do with them. In **Australia**: John (**21**) and Linda Rumney, Trina Baker, Dieter and Karen Gerhard; Linda Cash and Katrina Bird. **Belize**: Alan Cull, Sue Hamilton and Elvis Leslie. **Galápagos**: Dolores Diez.

Honduras: Terry Evans. **Indonesia**: Tony Rhodes (**22**) and Lisa Crosby, Simone Gerritsen, Max Ammer and Danny Charlton. Malaysia: Veronica and Peter Lee, Lawrence Lee. **Maldives**: Charlie and Ali Sabree. **Mexico**: Franco Spina. **Micronesia**: Navot Bornovski, Bill Acker and Gardenia Walter. **Papua New Guinea**: Max Benjamin and Alan Raabe, Linda and Tony Honey, Dik Knight. **Solomons**: Rick Belmare. **Thailand**: Gregory Carlysle-Slater, Jeroen Deknatel, Holger Schwab.

The following people helped ensure we got to the right places at the right time: Jenny Collister at Reef and Rainforest; Rob Bryning of Maldives Scuba Tours; Ania Mudrewicz of Galápagos Classic Cruises; Michelle Dee at Singapore Airlines; Ruth Skipsey at Journey Latin America and Cindi La Raia at Dive Discovery.

Bali's (**23**) life would have gone into meltdown without the TLC supplied by Fiona Kinnear and Jane Matthews. Special thanks to Kirk Rumney and Steve Thomson who helped run our lives, and hers, when we weren't there to do so ourselves.

Finally, thanks to Chris Nelson and Demi Taylor (for kicking the series off); Debbie Wylde, Patrick Dawson, Andy Riddle and the entire team at Footprint who would have worked their dive booties off if they had them, but especially to Alan Murphy, to whom we would like to award an honorary "c" card as he now knows more about diving than most qualified divers.

Bibliography

The following resources were our principal forms of reference, although there were many more:

Research and reference:
Reefbase (www.reefbase.org), Fishbase (www.fishbase.org). Earthtrends (earthtrends.wri.org), The CIA World Factbook (www.cia.com), Starfish (www.starfish.ch), Coral Realm (www.coralrealm.com).

Marine identification:
The World Atlas of Coral Reefs (Spalding, Ravilious and Green); Reef Fish Identification (Allen, Steene, Humann & DeLoach); World of Water Marine Publications (Neville Coleman); IKAN Reef & Fish Guides (Debelius, Kuiter, Norman, Halstead)

Historical information on the wrecks in Chuuk:
Hailstorm over Truk Lagoon by Klaus Lindemann: WWII Wrecks of the Kwajalein and Truk Lagoon by Dan E. Bailey: Michael McFadyen, www.michaelmcfadyenscuba.info

Photography

Cameras: Nikon F90 SLRs in Sea and Sea housings; Nikonos V; Nikon 5200 digital in WP-CP2
Flashes: Ikelite Substrobe 50's and Sea and Sea YS90 duos
Lenses: Nikon 105mm micro, 60mm micro, 20mm, 17-35 zoom and 16mm
Film: Fujichrome Velvia 50, Fujichrome Velvia 100 and Fujichrome Provia 100F, www.fuji.co.uk
And thanks to Jon Cohen and Jerry Deeney at Fuji Professional Film for their support.
Suppliers: Kevin Reed at Aquaphot (www.aquaphot.net), Cameras Underwater, Steve Warren at Ocean Optics
Processing: Dan Tierney at the Dairy Studio in London (www.thedairystudio.com); FotoHub for film processing in Singapore (www.fotohub.com).

Thanks again to Sean Keen, John Rumney and any of you who ever clicked a camera and then sent us one of the shots on this page!

14
15

16
17
18

19
20

21
22
23